THE DECALOGUE AND ITS CULTURAL INFLUENCE

Hebrew Bible Monographs, 58

Series Editors
David J.A. Clines, J. Cheryl Exum, Keith W. Whitelam

Editorial Board
A. Graeme Auld, Marc Brettler, David M. Carr, Paul M. Joyce,
Francis Landy, Lena-Sofia Tiemeyer, Stuart D.E. Weeks

THE DECALOGUE
AND ITS CULTURAL INFLUENCE

Edited by
Dominik Markl

SHEFFIELD PHOENIX PRESS

2017

Copyright © 2013, 2017 Sheffield Phoenix Press
First published in hardback, 2013
First published in paperback, 2017

Published by Sheffield Phoenix Press
Department of Biblical Studies, University of Sheffield
Sheffield S3 7QB

www.sheffieldphoenix.com

All rights reserved.
No part of this publication may be reproduced or transmitted in any form or by any means, electronic or mechanical, including photocopying, recording or any information storage or retrieval system, without the publisher's permission in writing.

A CIP catalogue record for this book
is available from the British Library

Typeset by CA Typesetting Ltd
Printed on acid-free paper by Lightning Source UK Ltd, Milton Keynes

ISBN-13 978-1-909697-06-5 (hardback)
ISBN-13 978-1-910928-30-1 (paperback)
ISSN 1747-9614

CONTENTS

Preface — ix
Acknowledgments — xii
Abbreviations — xiv
List of Contributors — xvii

INTERDISCIPLINARY PERSPECTIVES
ON THE DECALOGUE'S CULTURAL RADIANCE
   Dominik Markl — 1

Part I
ANTIQUITY—BIBLICAL FOUNDATIONS AND EARLY DEVELOPMENTS

THE TEN WORDS REVEALED AND REVISED:
THE ORIGINS OF LAW AND LEGAL HERMENEUTICS IN THE PENTATEUCH
   Dominik Markl — 13

THE RECEPTION HISTORY OF THE DECALOGUE THROUGH EARLY
TRANSLATIONS: THE CASE OF THE SEPTUAGINT, PESHITTA AND TARGUMS
   Innocent Himbaza — 28

THE DECALOGUE IN PSEUDO-PHOCYLIDES AND SYRIAC MENANDER:
'UNWRITTEN LAWS' OR DECALOGUE RECEPTION?
   J. Cornelis de Vos — 41

THE DECALOGUE IN THE NEW TESTAMENT APOCRYPHA:
A PRELIMINARY OVERVIEW AND SOME EXAMPLES
   Hermut Löhr — 57

Part II
Middle Ages—Liturgy, Homily and Theology

The Decalogue in Western Theology from the
Church Fathers to the Thirteenth Century
  Miguel Lluch Baixauli   75

The Decalogue in Jewish Liturgy
  Ruth Langer   85

Vernacular Treatments of the Ten
Commandments in Anglo-Saxon England
  Aaron J Kleist   102

The Ten Commandments in the Ethiopic Tradition
  Ralph Lee   141

Thomas Aquinas on the Ten Commandments
and the Natural Law
  Randall B. Smith   148

Part III
Worldwide Dissemination in Early Modern Catechisms and Catechesis

The Dissemination of the Decalogue in English and
Lay Responses to its Promotion in Early Modern
English Protestantism
  Ian Green   171

Repurposing the Decalogue in Reformation England
  Jonathan Willis   190

The Reception of the Decalogue in Protestant Catechisms
  Hans-Jürgen Fraas   205

The Decalogue and the Moral Manual Tradition:
From Trent to Vatican II
  James F. Keenan   216

The Decalogue in American Catechisms
of the Sixteenth Century
  Luis Resines   232

The Decalogue in Late Medieval and Early Modern Imagery:
Catechetical Purpose and Theological Implications
  Veronika Thum   258

Part IV
INTERPRETATIONS AND TRANSFORMATIONS IN THE EIGHTEENTH TO TWENTY-FIRST CENTURIES

'THE LAW OF TEN COMMANDMENTS':
WILLIAM BLAKE AND THE DECALOGUE
Christopher Rowland — 281

JOSEPH HAYDN'S *DIE HEILIGEN ZEHN GEBOTE ALS CANONS* AND
SIGISMUND NEUKOMM'S *DAS GESETZ DES ALTEN BUNDES, ODER DIE GESETZGEBUNG AUF SINAÏ*:
EXEMPLIFICATION OF CHANGES IN MUSICAL SETTINGS OF THE TEN COMMANDMENTS DURING THE EIGHTEENTH AND NINETEENTH CENTURIES
Luciane Beduschi — 296

THE LAW AND THE ARTIST IN THE AGE OF EXTREMES:
ON THOMAS MANN'S *DAS GESETZ*
Gerhard Lauer — 318

THE DECALOGUE: THE SCHOLARLY TRADITION CRITIQUED
David J.A. Clines — 333

THE RECEPTION OF THE DECALOGUE IN FILM:
KRZYSZTOF KIEŚLOWSKI'S *DECALOGUE*
Lloyd Baugh — 343

THE TEN COMMANDMENTS AND THE PROBLEM OF
LEGAL TRANSPLANTS IN CONTEMPORARY AMERICA
Steven Wilf — 354

Index of References — 371
Index of Personal Names — 376

Preface

John Barton

Reception history is one of the most inviting, yet also one of the most difficult, fields in the study of the Bible today. It is difficult because it involves so many layers of expertise. The reception-historian does not only need a comprehensive knowledge and understanding of the biblical text itself, but also familiarity with the cultures and intellectual background of the many diverse ages in which it has been read and appropriated; and in addition needs to be versed in media other than writing, including the visual and performing arts. But it is inviting because it carries its practitioners so far beyond the confines of ordinary textual study, with its concern for language and text, and out into an ocean of interdisciplinary engagement with writings that have, after all, stimulated the imaginations as well as the intellects of generations of religious (and non-religious) readers. The Decalogue is an obvious candidate for a reception-historical treatment. It has acquired over the centuries an enormous weight of commentary, and has been assimilated into the most varied cultures. Though a text, it has often also been an icon, appearing on walls in churches and now even in American courthouses. The subject was ripe for study, and the conference at which the papers in this book were delivered marked a significant milestone in biblical reception history.

There is however a certain ambiguity in the ultimate aim of reception history, which we can focus by asking: How does reception history differ from the history of interpretation? Many of the papers published here clearly belong to the latter. History of interpretation is a much longer-established aspect of biblical study. It is conventional for commentaries to begin with a survey of existing critical literature—usually that of 'modern times', but sometimes going back to rabbinic and patristic sources. But the aim is usually to provide some historical depth and background for the commentator's own interpretation. It is assumed that the text has a determinate meaning, but that this can be illuminated by understanding how it has been read in the past; or else that past interpretations have been erroneous, and need to be studied in order to be ruled out. Reception history as currently practised can look, superficially, like the history of interpretation, but for most practitioners it inhabits a different mental universe. Within that universe it is generally taken as a given that texts do *not* have determinate meanings, but their meaning is a kind of sum of, or selection from, what they have been taken to mean. A text means what serious commentators (or artists, or composers, or writers) have found in it, and we learn not simply from the text itself, but from the layers of meaning it has acquired down the ages. A biblical text such as the Decalogue is what H.-G. Gadamer called a 'classic' text, whose meaning cannot possibly be exhausted by a 'historical-critical' analysis in abstraction from its history of reading, use, and reflection. For reception history, films such as the Decalogue series by Kieślowski are not mere 'artistic' embroidery on a fixed text; rather, in watching them we learn what the Decalogue is capable of meaning, at a profound level.

The border between reception history and history of interpretation is in practice porous, and students of the Bible are not required to declare their membership of one or the other movement. Nevertheless, the conceptual difference is important, since the aim of the two tasks is differently conceived, and one is not simply a subset of the other. In my own view, each could learn from the other: histories of interpretation need to be alert to interpretations that are expressed not only in commentaries but also in works of art; while reception history needs to accept that even historical-critical commentary is a kind of reception. But they do represent two different ways of understanding what the study of the Bible is ultimately about. In principle, the history of interpretation is a traditional humanistic discipline, continuous with critical reading of the text itself: it owes much to the Renaissance and the Enlightenment, even though its roots go back further than either. In principle, reception history is a child of postmodernism, opposed to 'objectivity' in interpretation, and anxious to respect readings by non-traditional interpreters. There are the makings of a serious disagreement here. Yet in practice, they rub along well enough in the world of biblical studies, and many interpreters take a little from both. In the present volume it would be hard to sort the papers into two tidy and distinct piles, even though some clearly veer more in one direction than the other.

Even a relatively unreconstructed historical critic (such as myself) would be stupid to ignore the insights that reception history is bringing into the study of the Bible, or indeed to deny its inherent fascination. Whatever the theoretical underpinnings of the discipline, in practice it uncovers insights that conventional biblical criticism has been unaware of. Cecil B. DeMille's *The Ten Commandments*, which I saw when it was first released, was sometimes wooden in its literal attachment to the biblical text; yet even it conveyed some sense of grandeur and momentous importance in the giving of the Commandments (carefully written in Palaeo-Hebrew characters) that can be lost in the minutiae of traditional textual study. At the very least it reminds us of why we bother to study this text at all. Historical criticism, and its adjunct, the history of interpretation, can sometimes leave this question not just unanswered but actually unasked, almost as though it is not quite polite to raise it.

The manuscripts from the Dead Sea contain a number of examples of what has come to be called 'Rewritten Bible'—updated versions of biblical books. Indeed, even before the Dead Sea discoveries such rewrites were known—works as the longer Greek version(s) of Esther, and the book of Jubilees. Traditional criticism has had difficulty in knowing quite how to read such works. But for reception history they are simply earlier examples of the (literary) reception of the base texts, on a par with modern reworkings such as Thomas Mann's *Das Gesetz* or his great *Joseph* tetralogy. And if we can learn about the Bible from the former, then surely also from the latter? Textual history and reception history here blend into each other.

I hope this volume will stimulate not only further practical work on both the history of interpretation and of reception history, but also theoretical reflection on their relationship to each other and their place within current biblical study. It provides a wonderful spectrum of possibilities for theoretically minded biblical scholars to work on, as well as many highly illuminating examples of practical criticism and reception.

ACKNOWLEDGMENTS

Dominik Markl

Heythrop College celebrated the 400th anniversary of its foundation in 2014. What began as a small Jesuit College in Louvain and then in Liège (Belgium) became part of University of London and was located in the heart of Kensington. I am delighted to express my gratitude for all their generous collegial and financial support, without which the conference 'The Influence of the Decalogue' (15-17 April 2012) and the publication of this volume would not have been possible. I would like to say special thanks to my Principals John McDade and Michael Holman, SJ, Vice Principal-Academic Gwen Griffith-Dickson, Head of Department Michael Kirwan, SJ, Director of Research Michael Lacewing, and my colleague in Old Testament Studies Ann Jeffers. I hope that this volume expresses my appreciation for the atmosphere of diversity and creativity that I greatly enjoyed at Heythrop.

John Barton and Christopher Rowland were spontaneously supportive of my idea of an interdisciplinary conference on the Decalogue and suggested that it be organized in cooperation with Christine Joynes, Director of the Centre for Reception History of the Bible at the University of Oxford. This was the starting point of a most delightful cooperation. The conference would not have been possible without Christine's commitment, latterly while she was on maternity leave. Participants in the conference were delighted to congratulate her on the recent birth of her fourth child, Catherine. Since John Barton first opened the door to the conference, I am delighted that his thoughtful preface introduces this volume.

I wish to express special gratitude to Paul Joyce and Sarah Foot, the previous and current Chairs of the Faculty of Theology of the University of Oxford for their personal support and the sponsorship of the conference by the Faculty. Participants in the conference enjoyed the great hospitality of Campion Hall, for which we owe special gratitude to Brendan Callaghan, SJ, Master of the Hall. Sessions were held in the wonderful atmosphere of Trinity College and we appreciated the kindness of all members of staff. Many thanks to Katie Plumb for her practical support for the organization of the conference.

David Clines kindly suggested the inclusion of this volume in the Hebrew Bible Monographs series. The book owes a lot to his great experience as an editor. I would like to express my special appreciation to Liz and Julian Lock for their professional copy-editing. Joseph Munitiz, SJ, spontaneously agreed to help with special issues of translation.

I am especially delighted to thank all participants of the conference for their great commitment and cooperation, but also for sharing their fascinating insights and for the spirit of friendship, beyond the amiability of politeness, that human efforts can create. My gratitude includes all authors of the volume who were not able to participate in the conference. When I met James Keenan in Nairobi and Ralph Lee at his house in Addis Ababa, it felt like a continuation of the spirit that we had enjoyed at the conference in Oxford.

The conference was concluded by a concert from the Heythrop College Consort, conducted by Joey Draycott, at Jesus College Chapel. Their fine interpretation of musical settings of the Ten Commandments by Thomas Tallis, Johann Michael Bach, Johann Sebastian Bach, Joseph Haydn and Sigismond Neukomm brought to life everything around which our reflections revolved, and which hopefully comes to light in this book: the beauty of creative engagement with the seriousness of the religious ethics that has come down to us in the biblical writings.

ABBREVIATIONS

AB	Anchor Bible
AnBib	Analecta biblica
ARG	*Archiv für Reformationsgeschichte*
BHT	Beiträge zur historischen Theologie
BibOr	*Biblica et orientalia*
BWANT	Beiträge zur Wissenschaft vom Alten und Neuen Testament
BZNW	Beihefte zur *ZNW*
CBQ	*Catholic Biblical Quarterly*
CChr	Corpus christianorum
CChrSA	Corpus christianorum. Series apocryphorum
CH	Ælfric of Eynsham, *Catholic Homilies*
CSEL	Corpus scriptorum ecclesiasticorum latinorum
DJD	Discoveries in the Judaean Desert
FRLANT	Forschungen zur Religion und Literatur des Alten und Neuen Testaments
GCS	Griechische christliche Schriftsteller
HTKAT	Herders theologischer Kommentar zum Alten Testament
HTR	*Harvard Theological Review*
IDB	George Arthur Buttrick (ed.), *The Interpreter's Dictionary of the Bible* (4 vols.; Nashville: Abingdon Press, 1962).
JETS	*Journal of the Evangelical Theological Society*
JQR	*Jewish Quarterly Review*
JPS	Jewish Publication Society
JSOTSup	*Journal for the Study of the Old Testament*, Supplement Series
KJV	King James Version
LAB	Liber antiquitatum biblicarum
LCL	Loeb Classical Library
MT	Masoretic text
NAB	New American Bible
NASB	New American Standard Bible
NEB	New English Bible
NETS	*New English Translation of the Septuagint* (ed. A. Pietersma and B.G. Wright; Oxford: Oxford University Press, 2007).
NHC	Nag Hammadi Codices
NHS	Nag Hammadi Studies
NICOT	New International Commentary on the Old Testament
NIV	New International Version
NKJV	New King James Version
NRSV	New Revised Standard Version
NTOA	Novum Testamentum et orbis antiquus
OBO	Orbis biblicus et orientalis
OTL	Old Testament Library

OTP	James Charlesworth (ed.), *The Old Testament Pseudepigrapha* (Garden City, NY: Doubleday, 1963–1965).
PG	J.-P. Migne (ed.), *Patrologia cursus completa… Series graeca* (166 vols.; Paris: Petit-Montrouge, 1857–83).
PL	J.-P. Migne (ed.), *Patrologia cursus completus… Series prima [latina]* (221 vols.; Paris: J.-P. Migne, 1844–65).
PVTG	Pseudepigrapha Veteris Testamenti graece
RB	*Revue biblique*
RevQ	*Revue de Qumran*
RevThom	*Revue thomiste*
RHE	*Revue d'histoire ecclésiastique*
RSV	Revised Standard Version
SBLSCS	SBL Septuagint and Cognate Studies
SBS	Stuttgarter Bibelstudien
SEJ	Studies in European Judaism
SNTU	Studien zum Neuen Testament und seiner Umwelt
STC²	A.W. Pollard and G.R. Redgrave, *A Short-Title Catalogue of Books Printed in England … 1475–1640* (3 vols.; London: Bibliographical Society, 2nd edn, revised and enlarged by W.A. Jackson, F.S. Ferguson and K.F. Pantzer, 1976–91).
SVTP	Studia in Veteris Testamenti pseudepigrapha
TLZ	*Theologische Literaturzeitung*
TS	*Theological Studies*
TU	Texte und Untersuchungen
TZ	*Theologische Zeitschrift*
VC	*Vigiliae christianae*
VTSup	*Vetus Testamentum*, Supplements
WA	M. Luther, *Kritische Gesamtausgabe* (= 'Weimar' edition)
WMANT	Wissenschaftliche Monographien zum Alten und Neuen Testament
WUNT	Wissenschaftliche Untersuchungen zum Neuen Testament
ZAW	*Zeitschrift für die alttestamentliche Wissenschaft*
ZNW	*Zeitschrift für die neutestamentliche Wissenschaft*

LIST OF CONTRIBUTORS

John Barton is Emeritus Oriel and Laing Professor of the Interpretation of Holy Scripture at the University of Oxford. He is a Fellow of the British Academy. His books include *The Bible: The Basics* (Routledge, 2010); *Religious Diversity in Ancient Israel* (ed. with Francesca Stavrakopoulou; T & T Clark International, 2010); *The Nature of Biblical Criticism* (Westminster John Knox, 2007).

Lloyd Baugh is a Canadian Jesuit priest and retired professor of the Pontifical Gregorian University in Rome, where he also served as Dean of the Faculty of Social Sciences. Author of three books and eighty articles, his teaching and research interests include: the Jesus- and Christ-Figure films; the films of Krzysztof Kieslowski; and the use of film texts for theological (fundamental, moral, spiritual) reflection, and for interreligious dialogue, prayer experience, spiritual exercises and video divina. He has taught in England, Europe, Canada, the USA, Madagascar and the Philippines, and is presently completing a book-length study of Kieslowski's *Decalogue* films.

Luciane Beduschi After having taught Music History and Music Theory at the Sorbonne University (Paris), Paul-Valéry University (Montpellier), and Skidmore College (Saratoga Springs, NY), Luciane Beduschi is now an independent scholar. Her works on music theory and analysis have been published in the US, France, Belgium, England, Germany, Portugal, and Brazil.

David J.A. Clines is Emeritus Professor of Biblical Studies at the University of Sheffield, England. He is the editor of the eight-volume *Dictionary of Classical Hebrew*, and the author of the three-volume commentary on Job in the Word Biblical Commentary series. He is currently working on a book to be called *Play the Man! The Masculine Imperative in the Bible*. He is a director and publisher of Sheffield Phoenix Press.

Hans-Jürgen Fraas was Professor of Religious Education at the University of Augsburg (1969–1980) and is Emeritus Professor at the University of Munich. His books include *Katechismustradition: Luthers kleiner Katechismus in Kirche und Schule* (Vandenhoeck & Ruprecht, 1971); *Die*

Religiosität des Menschen (Vandenhoeck & Ruprecht, 1990); *Bildung und Menschenbild in theologischer Perspektive* (Vandenhoeck & Ruprecht, 2000). He is an ordained minister of the Bavarian Lutheran Church.

Ian Green taught history for over thirty years at The Queen's University of Belfast, and is currently an Honorary Professorial Fellow in the School of History, Classics and Archaeology of the University of Edinburgh. His books include *'The Christian's ABC': Catechisms and Catechizing in England c.1530–1740* (Clarendon Press, 1996); *Print and Protestantism in Early Modern England* (Oxford University Press, 2000); *Humanism and Protestantism in Early Modern English Education* (Ashgate, 2009); and he is currently preparing *Word, Ritual and Image in Early Modern English Protestantism* (for Oxford University Press).

Innocent Himbaza is Senior Lecturer in the Faculty of Theology, University of Fribourg, Switzerland. He is a specialist in the textual criticism and textual history of the Hebrew Bible. He is the editor of the book of Leviticus in the Biblia Hebraica Quinta Project. His books include *Le Décalogue et l'histoire du texte* (Fribourg Academic Press and Vandenhoeck & Ruprecht, 2004); *Un carrefour dans l'histoire de la Bible: Du texte à la théologie au IIe siècle avant J.-C.* (ed. with Adrian Schenker; Fribourg Academic Press and Vandenhoeck & Ruprecht, 2007). Currently he is preparing a commentary on the book of Malachi.

James F. Keenan, SJ, is Canisius Professor and director of the Jesuit Institute at Boston College. A Jesuit priest since 1982, he received a licentiate (1984) and a doctorate (1988) from the Pontifical Gregorian University in Rome. He is the founder of Catholic Theological Ethics in the World Church. Among his recent books are: *A History of Catholic Moral Theology in the Twentieth Century: From Confessing Sins to Liberating Consciences* (Continuum, 2010); with Dan Harrington, *Paul and Virtue Ethics* (Rowman and Littlefield, 2010) and *Ethics of the Word: Voices in the Catholic Church Today* (Rowman and Littlefield, 2010). He also edited *Catholic Theological Ethics, Past, Present, and Future: The Trento Conference* (Orbis, 2011). He is presently working on two manuscripts, on ethics and the university and a history of moral theology.

Aaron J Kleist currently teaches at Biola University, near Los Angeles, where he specializes in Anglo-Saxon homiletics and digital manuscript editing. His research on reconstructing medieval texts through digital editions brought him to serve as a Fulbright Senior Specialist at the University of Fribourg, Switzerland in 2008, and at the University of Munich in 2011. His publications include *Striving with Grace: Views of Free Will in Anglo-Saxon*

England (University of Toronto Press, 2008), an edited collection on *The Old English Homily* (Brepols, 2007), and *The Digital Ælfric* (www.biola. edu/aelfric), funded by a National Endowment for the Humanities' Collaborative Research Grant, 2006–2011.

Ruth Langer is Professor of Jewish Studies in the Theology Department at Boston College, Associate Director of its Center for Christian–Jewish Learning and an ordained rabbi. She writes and speaks in two major areas: the development of Jewish liturgy and ritual, and Christian-Jewish relations. Her books include *Cursing the Christians? A History of the Birkat HaMinim* (Oxford University Press, 2012), *To Worship God Properly: Tensions between Liturgical Custom and Halakhah in Judaism* (Hebrew Union College Press, 1998), *Liturgy in the Life of the Synagogue: Studies in the History of Jewish Prayer* (ed. with Steven Fine; Eisenbrauns, 2005).

Gerhard Lauer is Chair of Digital Humanities at the University of Basel. Previously, he was Chair for German studies at University of Göttingen (2002–2017). His major research interests include (German) literary history, digital humanities and cognitive literary studies. He is co-founder of the *Journal of Literary Theory*. His books include *Kunst und Empfindung: Zur Genealogie einer kunsttheoretischen Fragestellung in Deutschland und Frankreich im 18. Jahrhundert* (ed. with Elisabeth Décultot; Winter, 2012); *Die Erfindung des Schriftstellers Thomas Mann* (ed. with Michael Ansel; de Gruyter, 2009); *Die Rückseite der Haskala: Geschichte einer kleinen Aufklärung* (1650–1770) (Wallstein, 2008).

Ralph Lee is researcher at Ludwig Maximilian University of Munich for the project 'Textkritische Ausgabe und Übersetzung des 1 Henoch', funded by Deutsche Forschungsgemeinschaft. His research concentrates on Syriac and Ethiopic Christianity. His PhD thesis, *Symbolic Interpretations in Ethiopic and Ephremic Literature* at the School of Oriental and African Studies (University of London) was published under the title *Symbolic Interpretations in Ethiopic and Early Syriac Literature* (Peeters, 2017).

Miguel Lluch Baixauli († 2015) was Professor of the History of Theology and the Church at the Faculty of Theology of the University of Navarra, and a Roman Catholic priest. He had earned a doctorate in Theology at the University of Navarra (1988) as well as a doctorate in History at the University of Louvain-la-Neuve (1994). He was director of the Institute of Anthropology and Ethics of the University of Navarra from 2001 to 2010. His books include *La teología de Boecio* (Eunsa, 1990), *Boezio: La ragione teologica* (Jaca Book, 1997), *Formación y evolución del tratado escolástico sobre el Decálogo (1115–1230)* (Peeters, 1997).

Hermut Löhr is Professor of New Testament and Ancient Judaism at the University of Bonn. He is co-editor of *Forschungen zur Religion und Literatur des Alten und Neuen Testaments* (Vandenhoeck & Ruprecht) and *Themen der Theologie* (Mohr Siebeck). He has been on the editorial Board of *New Testament Studies* (2010 to 2013). His books include *Umkehr und Sünde im Hebräerbrief* (de Gruyter, 1994) and *Studien zum frühchristlichen und frühjüdischen Gebet: Eine Untersuchung von 1 Clem 59 bis 61* (Mohr Siebeck, 2003); and he is the editor of *Abendmahl* (Mohr Siebeck, 2012). Together with J.C. de Vos, he directed the project 'Der jüdische Nomos zwischen Normativität und Identität am Beispiel Alexandrias im 1.-3. Jh. n.Chr.' at the University of Münster.

Dominik Markl is Associate Professor of Hebrew Bible at the Pontifical Biblical Institute in Rome. Previously he taught at Heythrop College (University of London), Hekima College in Nairobi (Catholic University of Eastern Africa) and the Jesuit School of Theology in Berkeley, CA (Santa Clara University). His books include *Der Dekalog als Verfassung des Gottesvolkes* (Herder, 2007), *Gottes Volk im Deuteronomium* (Harrassowitz, 2012) and *The Fall of Jerusalem and the Rise of the Torah* (ed. with Peter Dubovský and Jean-Pierre Sonnet; Mohr Siebeck, 2016).

Luis Resines is a Roman Catholic priest and teaches pastoral theology and pastoral catechesis in the Augustinian Theological Centre in Valladolid. He has worked and published on the history of catechesis, particularly catechesis in America in the sixteenth century. His books include *Catecismos americanos del siglo XVI* (2 vols.; Junta de Castilla y León, Consejería de Cultura y Turismo, 1992), *La catequesis en España: Historia y textos* (Biblioteca de Autores Cristianos, 1997), *Diccionario de los catecismos pictográficos* (Diputación de Valladolid, 2007) and *Catecismos Pictográficos de Pedro de Gante, incompleto y mucagua* (Fundación Universitaria Española, 2007).

Christopher Rowland is Emeritus Dean Ireland's Professor of the Exegesis of Holy Scripture at the University of Oxford. He has written on the history of apocalypticism and its importance for the interpretation of the New Testament. He has continued to explore this theme in his *Blake and the Bible* (Yale University Press, 2010). His other books include *Christian Origins: The Setting and Character of the Most Important Messianic Sect of Judaism* (SPCK, rev. edn, 2002), *The Revelation of Jesus Christ* (with Judith Kovacs; Blackwell Bible Commentaries, 2004), *The Cambridge Companion to Liberation Theology* (Cambridge University Press, rev. edn, 2007) and *The Mystery of God: Early Jewish Mysticism and the New Testament* (with Christopher Morray-Jones; Brill, 2009).

Randall Smith is Professor of Moral Theology and holds the Scanlan Chair of Theology at the University of St. Thomas in Houston, Texas. He is grateful to the University of Notre Dame's Center for Ethics and Culture and the Notre Dame Jacques Maritain Center for providing the time and resources to complete the chapter in this volume. Prof. Smith's most recent book is *Reading the Sermons of Thomas Aquinas: A Beginner's Guide* (Emmaus, 2016). He has another book under review entitled *Principia: Aquinas, Bonaventure, and the Culture of Preaching and Prologues at Paris*.

Veronika Thum was a journalist with the *Süddeutsche Zeitung*. In 2006, she published her PhD dissertation, *Die Zehn Gebote für die ungelehrten Leut': Der Dekalog in der Graphik des späten Mittelalters und der frühen Neuzeit* (Deutscher Kunstverlag), and in 2011, the book *Weltgeschichte in Bildern. Die Historische Galerie König Maximilians II. im Maximilianeum* (Scaneg). Currently, she is working on *Zwei Tympana an St. Martin in Landshut – eine Dekalogdarstellung?*

J. Cornelis de Vos is currently interim Professor of New Testament Studies at the University of Münster. Together with Hermut Löhr, he was head of the project 'Der jüdische Nomos zwischen Normativität und Identität am Beispiel Alexandrias im 1.–3. Jh. n.Chr.' His books include *Das Los Judas: Über Entstehung und Ziele der Landbeschreibung in Josua 15* (Brill, 2003); *Heiliges Land und Nähe Gottes: Wandlungen alttestamentlicher Landvorstellungen in frühjüdischen und neutestamentlichen Schriften* (Vandenhoeck & Ruprecht, 2012); *Rezeption und Wirkung des Dekalogs in jüdischen und christlichen Schriften bis 200 n.Chr.* (Brill, 2016).

Steven Wilf is the Anthony J. Smits chair in Global Commerce and Associate Dean for Research and Faculty Development at the Law School of the University of Connecticut, where he founded the Intellectual Property Program. A scholar whose research focuses upon intellectual property law, historical jurisprudence and legal history, he seeks to address the fundamental ways that the origins of legal processes effect normative outcomes. Numerous essays and a recent book, *The Law Before the Law* (Rowman & Littlefield, 2008), explore imaginative, often extra-official understandings of legalism. His latest book is *Law's Imagined Republic: Popular Politics and Criminal Justice in Revolutionary America* (Cambridge University Press, 2010).

Jonathan Willis is Senior Lecturer in Early Modern History and Director of the Centre for Reformation and Early Modern Studies (CREMS) at the University of Birmingham. His research focuses on questions of religious belief, culture and identity in the English reformation. He is the author of *Church Music and Protestantism in Post-Reformation England: Discourses,*

Sites and Identities (Ashgate, 2010), editor of *Sin and Salvation in Reformation England* (Ashgate, 2015), and has written numerous essays and articles on music and the Decalogue reformation in England. His most recent book is *The Reformation of the Decalogue: Religious Identity and the Ten Commandments in England, c.1485–1625* (Cambridge 2017).

INTERDISCIPLINARY PERSPECTIVES
ON THE DECALOGUE'S CULTURAL RADIANCE

Dominik Markl

This volume unites authors from various disciplines within the humanities, who approach a broad spectrum of ways in which the Ten Commandments have been received through history, applying their own respective methods. While biblical studies continues to integrate reception history and to develop an understanding of its hermeneutical aims—as John Barton shows in his preface—this collection of articles is not primarily an endeavour within biblical studies, but an interdisciplinary effort.[1] It is to be hoped that this approach will enrich both biblical scholars and researchers from any other discipline touched by the cultural radiance of the Decalogue.

This brief introduction aims first to outline the scope of the present volume within the development of scholarship on the topic. Secondly, it will reflect on three specific aspects of the Decalogue's cultural influence.

1. *The Scope of the Present Volume in the Context of Related Scholarship*

The Decalogue is one of the most intensely studied texts in history.[2] Not surprisingly, therefore, a great number of publications has been dedicated to specific aspects of its appropriation. Only three previous collections of articles will be specifically mentioned here.[3] First, there is the volume *The Ten Commandments in History and Tradition*,[4] which offers a wide range of

---

1. Probably not more than a quarter of the contributors would consider themselves biblical scholars.
2. For a survey of respective research see D. Markl, 'The Decalogue in History: A Preliminary Survey of the Fields and Genres of its Reception', *Zeitschrift für altorientalische und biblische Rechtsgeschichte* 18 (2012), pp. 279-93.
3. The only systematic monograph on the reception of the Decalogue is P.G. Kuntz, *The Ten Commandments in History: Mosaic Paradigms for a Well-Ordered Society* (Grand Rapids: Eerdmans, 2004). This book concentrates on the Decalogue's treatment in selected authors from Philo to Nietzsche.
4. This volume originally appeared in Hebrew, edited by B.-Z. Segal (Jerusalem: Magnes, 1985); English version, G. Levi (ed.), *The Ten Commandments in History and Tradition* (Publications of the Perry Foundation for Biblical Research; Jerusalem: Magnes, 1990).

articles, especially on Jewish reception. Secondly, *The Decalogue in Jewish and Christian Tradition* contains some significant contributions, especially three articles on the New Testament and two on the early Jewish and Christian reception.[5] And thirdly, there is the recent collection *The Decalogue through the Centuries*.[6]

While the present volume does not claim to offer a comprehensive history of the reception of the Ten Commandments, it is devoted to providing a more comprehensive perspective by widening the range of genres and concentrating on themes that have been treated less thoroughly or not at all in previous anthologies. The sequence of topics roughly follows the historical development of Decalogue reception. Accordingly, the volume is divided into four parts, proceeding from the beginnings of Decalogue reception in antiquity to an intensification of interest especially in late mediaeval times, the climax in the early modern period and a gradual transformation in the eighteenth to twenty-first centuries.

The first part of the book moves from the first literary construction of the Decalogue's reception within the Pentateuch (Dominik Markl, pp. 13-27) to Innocent Himbaza's analysis of its early reception through translations (pp. 28-40) and examples from early Jewish wisdom literature and the New Testament Apocrypha, investigated by J. Cornelis de Vos (pp. 41-56) and Hermut Löhr respectively (pp. 57-71).[7] Other prominent topics from this period, such as the Decalogue in early Jewish literature, especially Philo, and in the New Testament, have been analysed in earlier publications.[8]

The second part starts with two articles that draw lines from antiquity to the Middle Ages. Miguel Lluch Baixauli shows the continuity and development of the treatment of the Decalogue in Western theology from the Church Fathers to the thirteenth century (pp. 75-84). Ruth Langer discusses

---

5. Y. Hoffman and H.G. Reventlow (eds.), *The Decalogue in Jewish and Christian Tradition* (Library of Biblical Studies, 509; New York: T. & T. Clark, 2011).

6. J.P. Greenman and T. Larsen (eds.), *The Decalogue through the Centuries: From the Hebrew Scriptures to Benedict XVI* (Louisville: Westminster John Knox, 2012). After three articles on Old Testament, New Testament and early Christian reception (pp. 1-66), this volume presents treatments of the Decalogue by a selection of theological writers: Thomas Aquinas, Moses Maimonides, Martin Luther, John Calvin, John Owen, Lancelot Andrewes, John Wesley, Christina Rossetti, Karl Barth, John Paul II and Benedict XVI (pp. 67-227).

7. The latter two authors work together within the Cluster of Excellence 'Religion and Politics' of the University of Münster (Germany) on 'The Decalogue as a Religious, Ethical and Political Base Text'. Each of the first two authors had previously published a doctoral dissertation on the Decalogue.

8. Cf. especially several contributions in Hoffman and Reventlow (eds.), *The Decalogue in Jewish and Christian Tradition* (pp. 50-116); S.J. Pearce, 'On the Decalogue', in: L.H. Feldman *et al.* (eds.), *Outside the Bible: Ancient Jewish Writings Related to Scripture* 1 (Philadelphia: Jewish Publication Society, 2013), pp. 989-1032.

the role of the Ten Commandments in Jewish liturgy from the second temple period to mediaeval tradition, anticipating its use up to the present day (pp. 85-101). The following three papers concentrate on subjects which are diverse in both genre and cultural context. Aaron J Kleist analyses the Decalogue in Anglo-Saxon England, especially in the works of Ælfric of Eynsham (pp. 102-40).[9] The contribution of Ralph Lee brings Africa into the geographical scope of this volume; mediaeval texts from Ethiopia developed their specific tradition of ancient Christian Decalogue reception (pp. 141-47). Randall Smith discusses the philosophical treatment of the Decalogue as related to the Natural Law in the works of Thomas Aquinas and other mediaeval writers (pp. 148-68).

Part three presents analyses of the dissemination of the Ten Commandments in early modern catechisms and catechesis. The first two articles concern early modern England. While Ian Green treats the dissemination of the Decalogue and lay responses to it (pp. 171-89), Jonathan Willis discusses its repurposing in Reformation England (pp. 190-204). H.-J. Fraas then summarizes the role of the Ten Commandments in Protestant catechisms and catechesis from the Reformation to the present day (pp. 205-15), while the following two contributions relate to the Roman Catholic tradition: James Keenan presents reflections on the Moral Manual tradition from the Council of Trent to Vatican II (pp. 216-31); and Luis Resines introduces his work on the Commandments in early missionary catechesis among native Americans, including his study of pictographic catechisms (pp. 232-57).[10] The third part is concluded by Veronika Thum's analysis of the Decalogue in late mediaeval and early modern European imagery (pp. 258-77), which reveals not only differences, but also parallel developments among the emerging denominations.

The fourth part of the book, moving on to the role of the Decalogue in more recent times, is marked by a great interdisciplinary variety. In another study of images, Christopher Rowlands analyses William Blake's critical engagement with the Ten Commandments in his art (pp. 281-95).[11] Luciane

---

9. By mentioning the law code of King Alfred the Great, A. Kleist's article touches the field of Decalogue reception in mediaeval law; see J. Mielke, *Der Dekalog in den Rechtstexten des abendländischen Mittelalters* (Untersuchungen zur deutschen Staats- und Rechtsgeschichte, 29; Aalen: Scientia, 1992).

10. This contribution is exemplary of the Christian missionary attempts in early modern times. Whereever missionaries arrived, the Ten Commandments were among the very first texts translated into indigenous languages and eventually printed. For examples see D. Markl, *Der Dekalog als Verfassung des Gottesvolkes: Die Brennpunkte einer Rechtshermeneutik des Pentateuch in Exodus 19–24 und Deuteronomium 5* (Herders biblische Studien, 49; Freiburg: Herder, 2007), p. 280.

11. On the Decalogue in art see espescially T.C. Aliprantis, *Moses auf dem Berge Sinai: Die Ikonographie der Berufung des Moses und des Empfangs der Gesetzestafeln*

Beduschi contributes a first systematic analysis of the musical reception of the Decalogue, especially in works of Joseph Haydn and Sigismund von Neukomm (pp. 296-317).[12] Gerhard Lauer reflects on the role of the Ten Commandments in Thomas Mann's novella *Das Gesetz* as an example of how morality is to be continually reinvented by artists (pp. 318-32). David Clines takes a critical look at the treatment of the Decalogue by Biblical scholars (pp. 333-42). Krzysztof Kieślowski's Decalogue films and the morality reflected within them are the subject of Lloyd Baugh's paper (pp. 343-53). Steven Wilf concludes the book with his article on the 'Ten Commandments and the Problem of Legal Transplants in Contemporary America' (pp. 354-70).

Despite the diversity and the wide scope of the contributions presented here, readers will become aware that this is no more than an attempt to outline the horizon of a comprehensive approach to the reception history of the Decalogue. Some themes, such as the Samaritan Decalogue inscriptions,[13] mediaeval *exempla* or the 'stories' based on the Ten Commandments (from the eighteenth to the early twentieth centuries)[14] and others are not represented at all in this volume. It also lacks any consideration of the Decalogue in Orthodox Christianity.[15]

On a geographical level, this volume does not offer any exploration of the Decalogue's history in Asia. It would be fascinating to take a closer look

(Reihe Kunstgeschichte, 20; Munich: Tuduv, 1986); V. Thum, *Die Zehn Gebote für die ungelehrten Leut': Der Dekalog in der Graphik des späten Mittelalters und der frühen Neuzeit* (Munich: Deutscher Kunstverlag, 2006); Olivier Christin, *Les yeux pour le croire: Les dix commandements en images XVe–XVIIe siècle* (Paris: Éditions du Seuil, 2003); J. Ribner, *Broken Tablets: The Cult of the Law in French Art from David to Delacroix* (Berkeley: University of California Press, 1993); M. Lechner, 'Zehn Gebote', in E. Kirschbaum (ed.), *Lexikon der christlichen Ikonographie*, IV (Freiburg: Herder, 1972), pp. 564-69; M.M. Mochizuki, *The Netherlandish Image after Iconoclasm, 1566–1672: Material Religion in the Dutch Golden Age* (Burlington: Ashgate, 2008), pp. 251-67.

12. To my knowledge, the only previous contribution on the musical reception was P.G. Kuntz, 'Luther und Bach: Ihre Vertonung der Zehn Gebote', in E. Donnert (ed.), *Europa in der frühen Neuzeit* (Festschrift Günter Mühlpfordt; Göttingen: Vandenhoeck & Ruprecht, 2005), pp. 99-106.

13. O. Keel, 'Zeichen der Verbundenheit: Zur Vorgeschichte und Neudeutung der Forderung von Deuteronomium 6,8f und Par,' in P. Casetti, O. Keel and A. Schenker (eds.), *Mélanges Dominique Barthélemy* (OBO, 38; Fribourg: Fribourg University Press, 1981), pp. 159-240, 175-78, lists fourteen inscriptions, which date from the third century CE to early medieval times.

14. Cf. Markl, 'The Decalogue in History', p. 283, on 'literary transformations'.

15. On Gregory of Palamas's fourteenth-century interpretation see Kuntz, *The Ten Commandments*, pp. 27-34; for a translation of the text see S. Mouselimas, 'Saint Gregory Palamas' The Decalogue of the Law according to Christ, That Is, the New Covenant,' *The Greek Orthodox Theological Review* 25 (1980), pp. 297-305.

at its inculturation on the Asian continent, from a Nestorian explanation of the Ten Commandments (Chinese, possibly seventh century CE)[16] to early modern missionary expositions.[17] The themes chosen in relation to other continents are also eclectic and singular rather than representative. Moreover, this volume does not venture to reconstruct the enormous historical influence of single Commandments, in phenomena such as iconoclasms[18] or the observance of the Sabbath and Sunday rest.[19]

Moreover, the following themes that would deserve more attention should not remain unmentioned here:

- Gnostic treatments of the Decalogue such as Ptolemy's *Letter to Flora* (second century CE)[20]
- Manichaean adaptations of the Decalogue;[21]

---

16. See Y. Saeki, *Nestorian Documents and Relics in China* (Tokyo: Toho Bunkwa Gakuin 1951), pp. 114-36; for a new translation see L. Tang, *A Study of the History of Nestorian Christianity in China and its Literature in Chinese: Together with a New English Translation of the Dunhuang Nestorian Documents* (European University Studies, 27/87; Frankfurt: Peter Lang, 2004), esp. pp. 145-51. Saeki, *Nestorian Documents*, pp. 113-24, suggests a dating in the earliest possible period (between 635 and 641 CE). However, the text still awaits detailed analysis.

17. See P. Braido, *Lineamenti di storia della catechesi e dei catechismi: dal 'tempo delle riforme' all'età degli imperialismi (1450-1870)* (Studi e ricerche di catechetica, 14; Turin: Elle di Ci, 1991), pp. 123-33; P.C. Phan, *Mission and Catechesis: Alexandre de Rhodes and Inculturation in Seventeenth-Century Vietnam* (New York: Orbis Books, 1998), esp. pp. 111-21. For an example from the Philippines see A.-M. Rosales, *A Study of a 16th Century Tagalog Manuscript on the Ten Commandments: Its Significance and Implications: Juan de Oliver's 'Declaracion de los mandamientos de la ley de Dios'* (Quezon City: University of the Philippines, 1984).

18. The prohibition of images is closely related to iconoclasm; see M. Aston, *England's Iconoclasts*. I. *Laws against Images* (Oxford: Clarendon, 1988), pp. 220-342.

19. K.A. Strand (ed.), *The Sabbath in Scripture and History* (Washington: Review and Herald, 1982), contains a rich collection of contributions on the historical development of the reception of the Sabbath Commandment (despite the unconcealed tendency of this book to promote Seventh-Day Adventist views). On the political implications of the interpretation of the Fourth Commandment in early modernity see R. Bast, *Honor your Fathers: Catechisms and the Emergence of a Patriarchal Ideology in Germany, 1400–1600* (Studies in Medieval and Reformation Thought, 63; Leiden: Brill, 1997).

20. See G. Quispel (ed.), *Ptolémée: Lettre à Flora: Texte, traduction et introduction* (Sources chrétiennes, 24; Paris: Cerf, 1949); B. Layton, *The Gnostic Scriptures* (New York: Doubleday, 1987), pp. 306-15, esp. 311; and the rich analysis by A. von Harnack, 'Der Brief des Ptolemäus an die Flora: Eine religiöse Kritik am Pentateuch im 2. Jahrhundert', in his *Kleine Schriften zur alten Kirche*. I. *Berliner Akademieschriften 1890–1907* (Opuscula, 9/1; Leipzig: Zentralantiquariat der DDR, 1980), pp. 591-629.

21. M. Tardieu, *Manichaeism* (transl. M.B. DeBevoise; Urbana, IL: University of

- the allegorical interpretation of David's ten-stringed harp as an allusion to the Ten Commandments, which was introduced at the latest by Athanasius (fourth century CE) and remained a standard motif through Medieval interpretations of the Psalms;[22]
- kabbalistic interpretations of the Decalogue, e.g. in the *Bahir* (1176 CE) or the *Zohar* (thirteenth century CE);[23]
- the astrological correlation between the Ten Commandments and the planets, which seems to have been introduced by Abraham Ibn Esra in his commentary on Exodus (1153 CE) and to which Jean Bodin referred in his *Colloquium* (early 1590s).[24]

Notwithstanding the limits of the present volume, we shall try to offer a few more general reflections on the Decalogue's influence.

Illinois Press, 2008), pp. 68-69; N. Tajadod, *Mani le Bouddha de lumière: Catéchisme manichéen chinois* (Sources Gnostiques et Manichéennes; Paris: Le Cerf, 1990), p. 218; for German translations of relevant sources see A. Böhlig, *Die Gnosis*. III. *Der Manichäismus* (Bibliothek der alten Welt; Zürich and München: Artemis, 1980), pp. 40-41, 189-90, 203, 206, 208.

22. See H. Giesel, *Studien zur Symbolik der Musikinstrumente im Schrifttum der alten und mittelalterlichen Kirche (von den Anfängen bis zum 13. Jahrhundert)* (Kölner Beiträge zur Musikforschung, 94; Regensburg: Gustav Bosse, 1978), pp. 146-49; M. van Schaik, *The Harp in the Middle Ages: The Symbolism of a Musical Instrument* (Amsterdam: Rodopi, 1992), pp. 81, 156. The background of this motif is the instrument mentioned in Ps. 33.2; 92.4; 144.9. The Hebrew expression נבל עשור) was rendered ψαλτήριον δεκάχορος in LXX and 'psalterium decem chordarum' in the Vulgate. There is archaeological evidence of a Phoenician ten-stringed instrument from the eighth century BC: C. Sachs, *The History of Musical Instruments* (New York: W.W. Norton & Company, 1940), p. 118.

23. See A. Kaplan (ed.), *The Bahir: An Ancient Kabbalistic Text Attributed to Rabbi Nehuniah ben HaHakna* (New York: Samuel Weiser, 1979), p. 47, no. 124; D.C. Matt (ed.), *The Zohar*, ספר הזהר, IV (Pritzker Edition; Stanford: University Press, 2007), pp. 476-534. An intriguing example of the reception of kabbalistic elements in a Decalogue painting of Russian Orthodox dissenters was analysed by I. Rodov, 'Kabbalistic Traces in a Russian Old-Believer Painting', in W. Moskovich, R. Mnich and R. Tarasiuk (eds.), *Galicia, Bukovina and Other Borderlands in Eastern and Central Europe: Essays on Interethnic Contacts and Multiculturalism* (Jews and Slavs, 23; Jerusalem and Siedlce, 2013), pp. 13-34.

24. D.U. Rottzoll (ed.), *Abraham Ibn Esras langer Kommentar zum Buch Exodus.* II. *Parascha Jitro bis Pekudej (Ex 18–40)* (Studia judaica, 17/2; Berlin: W. de Gruyter, 2000), pp. 615-21; J. Bodin, *Colloquium of the Seven about Secrets of the Sublime: Colloquium heptaplomeres de rerum sublimium arcanis abditis* (trans. M. Leathers and D. Kuntz; Princeton, NJ: Princeton University Press, 1975), p. 190; G. Miletto, 'Die Bibel zwischen Tradition und Innovation', in G. Veltri and G. Necker (eds.), *Gottes Sprache in der philologischen Werkstatt: Hebraistik vom 15. bis zum 19. Jahrhundert* (SEJ, 11; Leiden: Brill, 2004), pp. 97-110, esp. 101.

2. The Decalogue's Cultural Radiance through Two and a Half Millennia

The abundant traces of the Decalogue's influence may seem overwhelming to anybody who begins to study it in greater depth, but it is the more important to try to isolate issues of particular interest and relevance. The following reflection will concentrate on just three topics: the double nature of the Decalogue as religious law; its common inheritance by different religions and denominations; and a critical look at its reception history.

Within the Pentateuch, the Decalogue is presented as the programmatic starting point of Israel's law, given immediately by God at Sinai (Exod. 20) and interpreted by Moses in Moab (Deut. 5). Being of divine origin, Israel's law does not depend on any political authority such as a king,[25] but is to be studied and kept by the people as a whole (Deut. 31.9-13). This concept of divine law is unique to Israel in the Ancient Orient. How has this idea played out in the Decalogue's reception history?

While the Decalogue has predominantly been studied, taught and interpreted in religious contexts—such as Torah study, preaching and catechesis—it has at some points in history entered, or at least touched, the sphere of secular law: for example in the early mediaeval Bavarian Laws, which refer directly to the Sabbath Commandment;[26] in Philipp Melanchthon's idea of the Christian magistrate as the 'guardian of both tables of the law' (*custodia utriusque tabulae*);[27] and in contemporary discussions in the US (see Steven Wilf's article). If one considers the use of the Mosaic tablets as a symbol of law even in the context of the French Revolution,[28] it seems that the idea of the divine origin of law symbolized by the tablets of the Decalogue has been adopted in secular contexts, particularly during crises when political identities were and are to be redefined. As a matter of course, the promotion of the Decalogue into the sphere of secular law has sparked conflict and discussion regarding the relationship between politics and religion since early modern times.

Through the ethical amplification of the Ten Commandments (as far as we can reconstruct them) in the teaching of Jesus, the Decalogue became the critical element in the diverging hermeneutical approaches to the Torah which were to separate the religious practices of emergent Christianity and Rabbinic Judaism. Since the Decalogue became the pre-eminent centre of divine law for Christians, who increasingly neglected the practical relevance

---

25. The law is strictly seen above the highest political authority, since the king is instructed to study the Torah daily and act according to it: Deut. 17.18-20.

26. D. Augsburger, 'The Sabbath and Lord's Day during the Middle Ages', in Strand (ed.), *The Sabbath in Scripture and History*, pp. 190-214 (199).

27. R. Bast, 'From the Two Kingdoms to Two Tables: The Ten Commandments and the Christian Magistrate,' *ARG* 89 (1998), pp. 79-85.

28. Ribner, *Broken Tablets*.

of the rest of the Torah, Rabbinic Judaism sought to avoid any hermeneutical elevation of the Ten Commandments in order to emphasize the validity of the Torah in its entirety.

However, their common heritage and the symbolical power of the tablets of the divine law has brought the two religions at times surprisingly close to each other. We could experience this, for example, by taking a walk from London's Temple Church to the Bevis Marks Synagogue: in the Temple Church we may contemplate the Ten Commandments in English on Sir Christopher Wren's altar screen (1682), while the Torah shrine in the synagogue (1701) presents the Ten Commandments in Hebrew. In both cases they appear in golden letters on two black, round-topped tablets.[29]

The Decalogue brought the Christian denominations even tragically close when they were fighting each other most fiercely.

> As the Ten Commandments rose to new prominence in the systems of indoctrination devised by all major confessions, Catholic theologians… employed the same images as Protestants in powerful petitions, urging their princes as Christian magistrates to enforce the Decalogue for the sake of moral betterment and religious orthodoxy. In one of the more bitter ironies of the age, both sides regularly promised that God would reward such zeal with peace and prosperity.[30]

From a Christian perspective, these observations prompt us to see the Decalogue as a reminder of a core religious ethics, which would have spared much bloodshed had it been taken seriously simply as such, and to remain aware of this ethics' rootedness in the Hebrew Bible, which Christians respectfully share with their Jewish 'elder brothers and sisters'.

Like many other biblical texts, the Decalogue has lost its innocence through history. Some forms of abuse by Christian zealots have proved particularly destructive. Painting with a broad brush, yet not entirely wrongly, one could say that in the name of the Decalogue witches were burnt and the ancient religions of the Americas were ruthlessly exterminated. Historical facts such as these cannot be piously overlooked.

Does the Decalogue—despite its historical constraints and despite its historical abuse—have any value as a source of serious and creative ethical engagement today? It seems clear that the Ten Commandments, which

---

29. It would be interesting to explore if this design of the Torah shrine was imposed by the architect Joseph Avis, who was a Quaker, or if it was approved of or wished by the community; or, moreover, how the depiction of the tablets in synagogues and churches influenced each other and what they signified for the relationship between Jewish and Christian communities in early modern times.

30. Bast, 'From the Two Kingdoms to Two Tables,' pp. 94-95. In one of the less bitter ironies of the age, the image of Martin Luther as a preacher found its way into the *Catechismus romanus* (see the article of Veronika Thum, p. 275).

played such prominent role in catechetical teaching from the Reformation to the twentieth century, have lost their dominant centrality in Christian ethics during the last decades.[31] To some contemporary readers, the Ten Commandments may seem to be a symbol of the dull and antiquated ethics of religious institutions, which are out of touch with new developments.

However, during the same period, the Ten Commandments have received renewed creative attention from authors and artists who are not committed to institutional religious teachings. The First and Second World Wars gave rise to Hollywood's blunt moral propaganda in Cecil DeMille's *The Ten Commandments* (1923 and 1956), but also to Thomas Mann's reflection on Moses' commandments with its fine ethical implications (see Gerhard Lauer's article). When the grand narrative of Soviet Communism was breaking down, Krzysztof Kieślowski released his subtle films based on the Decalogue (1989). The French author Christophe Donner, who had left his atheist family and was inspired by Paul Ricœur's approach to the Bible, has written ten stories entitled *Le décalogue* (Paris: Stock, 2000), in which the main characters are children and adolescents.[32] The creativity of artists, arising from unexpected directions, gives the Decalogue the chance of being perceived in a new and inspiring light.[33]

---

31. The remarkable continuity of the Decalogue's role from the sixteenth to the twentieth century in both the Protestant and the Roman Catholic tradition, but also its decline in the twentieth century, become clearly visible in the articles by Hans-Jürgen Fraas and James Keenan in this volume.

32. A comparable book is A. Longo, *Dieci* (Milan: Adelphi, 2007). These short stories are set in the context of the Neapolitan mafia. Ironically, Kieślowski's, Donner's and Longo's works are shaped in structural analogy to the pious stories or tales about the Ten Commandments of earlier centuries, while their subtle treatment of the moral questions concerned are, of course, in stark contrast to the simple and often naive doctrine of their predecessors.

33. Since the first edition of this collection, six books on the reception of the Decalogue have come to my attention: J.C. de Vos, *Rezeption und Wirkung des Dekalogs in jüdischen und christlichen Schriften bis 200 n.Chr.* (AJEC, 95; Leiden: Brill, 2016); U. Peter-Spörndli, *Die Zehn Worte vom Sinai: Die Rezeption des Dekalogs in der rabbinischen Literatur* (Berlin: Pro Business, 2012); L. Smith, *The Ten Commandments: Interpreting the Bible in the Medieval World* (Leiden: Brill, 2014); Y. Desplenter, J. Pieters and W. Melion (eds.), The *Ten Commandments in Medieval and Early Modern Culture* (Intersections, 52; Leiden: Brill, 2017); J. Willis, *The Reformation of the Decalogue: Religious Identity and the Ten Commandments in England, c.1485–1625* (Cambridge: Cambridge University Press, 2017); Y.S.L. Chan, *The Ten Commandments and the Beatitudes: Biblical Studies and Ethics for Real Life* (Lanham: Rowman & Littlefield, 2012). For the discussion on the reception of the Decalogue in the Qur'an see A. Neuwirth, 'A Discovery of Evil in the Qur'an? Revisiting Qur'anic Versions of the Decalogue in the Context of Pagan Arab Late Antiquity' (trans. W.S. Chahanovich), in her *Scripture, Poetry, and the Making of a Community: Reading the Qur'an as a Literary Text* (Oxford: Oxford University Press, 2014), pp. 253-76.

Part I

ANTIQUITY—BIBLICAL FOUNDATIONS AND EARLY DEVELOPMENTS

THE TEN WORDS REVEALED AND REVISED: THE ORIGINS OF LAW AND LEGAL HERMENEUTICS IN THE PENTATEUCH

Dominik Markl

The Ten Commandments' reception history begins within the literary context in which they have come down to us—the Pentateuch. God reveals them at Mount Sinai according to Exodus 20, and Moses renders them in a modified form 40 years later in Moab according to Deuteronomy 5. Although the historical question as to which version is the (more) original has been intensely discussed,[1] the hermeneutical problem as to what sense

---

1. On the history of this research see E. Otto, 'Alte und neue Perspektiven in der Dekalogforschung', in his *Kontinuum und Proprium: Studien zur Sozial- und Rechtsgeschichte des Alten Orients und des Alten Testaments* (Orientalia biblica et christiana, 8; Wiesbaden: Harrassowitz, 1996), pp. 285-92; F.-L. Hossfeld, 'Der Stand der Dekalogforschung', in B.M. Levinson and E. Otto (eds.), *Recht und Ethik im Alten Testament: Beiträge des Symposiums 'Das Alte Testament und die Kultur der Moderne' anlässlich des 100. Geburtstags Gerhard von Rads (1901–1971) Heidelberg, 18.–21. Oktober 2001* (Altes Testament und Moderne, 13; Münster: Lit-Verlag, 2004), pp. 57-65. Today, most scholars no longer think that the Decalogue represents ancient Israelite tribal law or even that it may originate in Mosaic legislation, but rather that the Ten Commandments are a rather late composition, deliberately placed at the beginning of biblical legislation and preceding the law codes in Exodus as well as in Deuteronomy as a summary of significant rules. The origin of the Decalogue, therefore, is not to be sought outside the Bible, but within the formation of biblical legislation. The controversy as to which of the two versions is older and which of the contexts is the original setting was fought through in a paradigmatic way by Frank Lothar Hossfeld and Axel Graupner in Bonn over two decades. Hossfeld had argued in his monograph from 1982 that Deuteronomy represents the original setting and context of the Decalogue, whereas Graupner argued for Exodus as the original context. See, for example F.-L. Hossfeld, *Der Dekalog: Seine späten Fassungen, die originale Komposition und seine Vorstufen* (OBO, 45; Freiburg: Universitätsverlag, 1982); 'Zum synoptischen Vergleich der Dekalogfassungen. Eine Fortführung des begonnenen Gesprächs', in his edited *Vom Sinai zum Horeb: Stationen alttestamentlicher Glaubensgeschichte* (Festschrift E. Zenger; Würzburg: Echter, 1989), pp. 73-117; A. Graupner, 'Zum Verhältnis der beiden Dekalogfassungen Ex 20 und Dtn 5: Ein Gespräch mit Frank-Lothar Hossfeld', *ZAW* 99 (1987), pp. 308-29; 'Die zehn Gebote im Rahmen alttestamentlicher Ethik. Anmerkungen zum gegenwärtigen Stand der Forschung', in H.G. Reventlow (ed.), *Weisheit, Ethos und Gebot: Weisheits- und Dekalogtraditionen in der Bibel und im frühen Judentum* (Biblisch-theologische

the two versions make together within the final form of the Pentateuch has not been addressed until recently.[2]

This paper will argue that the two versions of the Decalogue play a key role for the legal hermeneutics of the Pentateuch in its final form which initiates and foreshadows the Ten Commandments' rich reception history. The argument will be unfolded in five stages. After discussing the two literary contexts of the Ten Commandments within the books of Exodus and Deuteronomy and their differences, their function for the legal hermeneutics of the Pentateuch will be evaluated. A hermeneutical overview of their earliest reception history concludes the article.

1. *The Decalogue within the Book of Exodus*

The Ten Commandments solemnly introduce the divine revelation of law at Sinai. They are placed at the centre of an awe-inspiring theophany and they are presented as the only words that God speaks directly to the whole people of Israel.

The Decalogue occupies a structurally prominent position at the beginning of the second half, and therefore in a central passage, of the book of Exodus.[3] While the first half of the book tells how Yhwh rescues Israel from oppression in Egypt and leads them to Sinai (Exod. 1–18), the second half is staged entirely at Sinai and revolves around the themes of God's covenant

---

Studien, 43; Neukirchen–Vluyn: Neukirchener Verlag, 2001), pp. 61-95. For the latest suggestion see E. Blum, 'The Decalogue and the Composition History of the Pentateuch', in T.B. Dozeman *et al.* (eds.), *The Pentateuch: International Perspectives on Current Research* (Forschungen zum Alten Testament, 78; Tübingen: Mohr Siebeck, 2011), pp. 289-301. On the relationship between the Decalogue and ancient Near Eastern legal texts see E. Otto, 'Der Dekalog im Horizont des Alten Orients', in his *Altorientalische und biblische Rechtsgeschichte: Gesammelte Studien* (Beihefte zur Zeitschrift für altorientalische und biblische Rechtsgeschichte, 8; Wiesbaden: Harrassowitz, 2008), pp. 531-38.

2. See, for example, P.D. Miller, 'The Place of the Decalogue in the Old Testament Law: The Book of Exodus', in his *The Way of the Lord: Essays in Old Testament Theology* (Forschungen zum Alten Testament, 39; Tübingen: Mohr Siebeck, 2004), pp. 3-17 [= *Interpretation* 43 (1989), pp. 229-42]; 'The Good Neighborhood: Identity and Community through the Commandments', in his *Way of the Lord*, pp. 51-67 [= W.P. Brown (ed.), *The Character of Scripture: Moral Formation, Community, and Biblical Interpretation* (Grand Rapids: Eerdmans, 2002), pp. 55-72]; D. Markl, *Der Dekalog als Verfassung des Gottesvolkes: Die Brennpunkte einer Rechtshermeneutik des Pentateuch in Exodus 19–24 und Deuteronomium 5* (Herders biblische Studien, 49; Freiburg i.Br.: Herder, 2007).

3. This concerns the literary structure of the book of Exodus. In quantitative terms, the Decalogue is located just before the middle of the book. Exodus 1–19 contains 7,540 words, while Exod. 20.18–40.38 contains 8,845 words.

with Israel (Exod. 19–24; 32–34) and his presence in the midst of his people in the sanctuary (Exod. 25–31; 35–40). God reveals the Decalogue at the climax of the theophany that takes place on the third day of Israel's stay at Sinai (Exod. 19.16–20.18). While the Decalogue seems to interrupt the narrative of the theophany and to intrude into the narrated world from another sphere,[4] the Ten Commandments are closely linked to their narrative setting within the book of Exodus. This section unfolds some aspects of these narrative links, which are of hermeneutical significance.

The Prologue, Exod. 20.2, forms the most prominent and fundamental link between the Commandments and the narrative of Israel's Exodus from Egypt: 'I am Yhwh your God, who brought you out from the land of Egypt, from the house of slaves'. Yhwh's introduction to the first text of divine 'legislation'[5] at Sinai lays the hermeneutical foundation for all further divine law. Since God rescued Israel from Egypt, all further divine law is meant to preserve their freedom.[6] Moreover, the first nominal clause 'I (am) Yhwh your God', which can also be translated 'I, Yhwh, (am) your God', grounds Israel's law in its relationship with God, which is reinforced through the making of the covenant.

The making of the Sinai covenant develops over an extensive narrative arc within Exodus 19–24.[7] As soon as Israel arrives at Sinai (Exod. 19.1), Moses ascends the mountain and Yhwh offers Israel a covenant: 'Now

---

4. The loose connection between the Decalogue and its immediate narrative context (Exod. 19.25; 20.18) has often been interpreted as a sign of the Decalogue's secondary insertion into its narrative context. On a synchronic level, Christoph Dohmen suggested that the people, within the world of the narrative, did not understand the content of God's speech but only heard God's voice: C. Dohmen, *Exodus 19–40* (HTKAT; Freiburg i.Br.: Herder, 2004), pp. 76f; '"Es gilt das gesprochene Wort". Zur normativen Logik der Verschriftung des Dekalogs', in C. Frevel *et al.* (eds.), *Die Zehn Worte: Der Dekalog als Testfall der Pentateuchkritik* (Quaestiones disputatae, 212; Freiburg i.Br.: Herder, 2005), pp. 43-56. For arguments against this view see Markl, *Dekalog*, pp. 129-31.

5. For a discussion of which texts can be classified as 'legal' within the Pentateuch see D. Markl, 'Narrative Rechtshermeneutik als methodische Herausforderung des Pentateuch', *Zeitschrift für altorientalische und biblische Rechtsgeschichte* 11 (2005), pp. 107-21 (110-15).

6. See P.D. Miller, 'The Story of the First Commandment: The Book of Exodus', in his *Way of the Lord*, pp. 3-17 [= *American Baptist Quarterly* 21 (2002), pp. 234-46]; F. Crüsemann, *Bewahrung der Freiheit: Das Thema des Dekalogs in sozialgeschichtlicher Perpektive* (Kaiser Traktate, 128; Munich: Kaiser, 1983).

7. For an elaborate explanation of my understanding of the making of the Sinai covenant see Markl, *Dekalog*, pp. 33-173; for a brief summary G. Fischer and D. Markl, *Das Buch Exodus* (Neuer Stuttgarter Kommentar. Altes Testament, 2; Stuttgart: Katholisches Bibelwerk, 2009), pp. 214-16; on the relationship between narrative and law in Exodus 19–24 compare J.M. Sprinkle, 'Law and Narrative in Exodus 19–24', *JETS* 47 (2004), pp. 235-52.

then, if you obey my voice and keep my covenant you shall be my jewel out of all the peoples' (Exod. 19.5). The people answer this offer positively in Exod. 19.8: 'All that Yhwh has spoken we will do'. After three days of preparations (Exod. 19.10-15), God appears on Mount Sinai (Exod. 19.16-25) and proclaims the Decalogue as the first text containing the covenant stipulations (Exod. 20.1-17). Overwhelmed by this awesome theophany (Exod. 20.18), the people ask Moses to mediate for them, confirming their obedience to Moses' words: 'You speak to us and we will listen' (Exod. 20.19).

Moses relates the content of the 'Book of the Covenant' (Exod. 20.22–23.33) both orally (Exod. 24.3) and, on the next day, in written form (Exod. 24.4, 7). After each proclamation the people renew their commitment to the Commandments and thus ratify the covenant: 'All the words that Yhwh has spoken we will do' (Exod. 24.3) and 'All that Yhwh has spoken we will do, and we will listen' (Exod. 24.7). All these speech acts are decisive for Yhwh's and Israel's mutual commitment to the covenant relationship, while Moses' speech in Exod. 24.8 just confirms the contract that has already been made: 'See the blood of the covenant that Yhwh has made with you in accordance with all these words'.

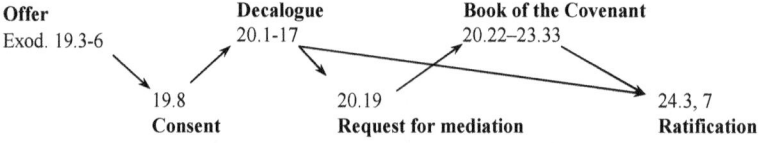

Thus, the Decalogue forms part of a dialogue between God and Israel (mediated by Moses) which unfolds over four days within the world of the narrative. The narrative context shows that Israel's repeatedly expressed free consent forms the basis for both the validity of the covenant and the binding force of the stipulations expressed in the Decalogue and the Book of the Covenant respectively.[8] Moreover, the Decalogue can be seen as a hermeneutical prelude to the Book of the Covenant, which can be read as expanding on several Commandments.[9]

The Prologue (Exod. 20.2) connects the Decalogue not only with the first half of the book and the making of the covenant, but also with Israel's breaking of the covenant. The way they express their worship of the golden

---

8. This feature of the Sinai covenant remarkably resembles the modern idea of 'constitutional consensus' as the basis of the validity of the legal systems of modern democratic states; see Markl, *Dekalog*, p. 166.

9. See R.G. Kratz, 'Der Dekalog im Exodusbuch', *Vetus Testamentum* 44 (1994), pp. 205-38; L. Schwienhorst-Schönberger, 'Das Verhältnis von Dekalog und Bundesbuch', in Frevel *et al.* (eds.), *Die Zehn Worte*, pp. 57-75.

calf (Exod. 32.4) ironically perverts Yhwh's solemn proclamation from the beginning of the Decalogue:[10]

Exod. 20.2: I am Yhwh your God (אלהיך), who brought you out from the land of Egypt...!
Exod. 32.4: These are your gods (אלהיך), O Israel, who brought you up out of the land of Egypt!

Similarly, Yhwh's reconciliation with Israel in Exod. 34.6f. contrasts with his self-characterization within the Ten Commandments (Exod. 20.5f.). While God emphasizes his zeal for justice and for 'steadfast love' (חסד) within the Decalogue, he emphasizes his mercy and inverts the sequence of his propositions in Exod. 34.6f.[11]

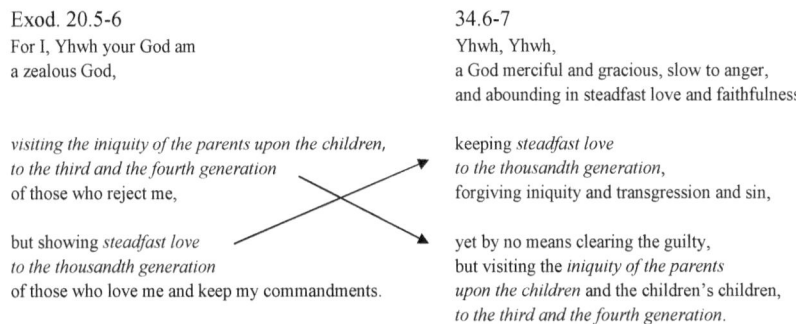

Exod. 20.5-6
For I, Yhwh your God am
a zealous God,

visiting the iniquity of the parents upon the children,
to the third and the fourth generation
of those who reject me,

but showing *steadfast love*
to the thousandth generation
of those who love me and keep my commandments.

34.6-7
Yhwh, Yhwh,
a God merciful and gracious, slow to anger,
and abounding in steadfast love and faithfulness,

keeping *steadfast love*
to the thousandth generation,
forgiving iniquity and transgression and sin,

yet by no means clearing the guilty,
but visiting the *iniquity of the parents*
upon the children and the children's children,
to the third and the fourth generation.

Thus, the first section of the Decalogue provides the core elements from which the climaxes of the golden calf episode in Ex 32–34 are formed.[12] Whereas Israel breaks the prohibition of idolatry (Exod. 20.4f.) by making the golden calf (Exod. 32.1-6) and perverts Yhwh's Prologue to the Decalogue (Exod. 20.2) by worshipping it (Exod. 32.4), God heals the relationship by rewording his self-characterization, which had provided the reason for the prohibition of images (Exod. 20.5-6; 34.6-7).

---

10. Thus, D. Patrick, 'The First Commandment in the Structure of the Pentateuch', *Vetus Testamentum* 45 (1995), pp. 107-18 (117), fittingly calls the worship of the golden calf 'a parody of Yahwism'.

11. On the formula of grace in Exod. 34.6f. see R. Scoralick, *Gottes Güte und Gottes Zorn: Die Gottesprädikationen in Exod. 34,6f und ihre intertextuellen Beziehungen zum Zwölfprophetenbuch* (Herders biblische Studien, 33; Freiburg i.Br.: Herder, 2002); M. Franz, *Der barmherzige und gnädige Gott: Die Gnadenrede vom Sinai (Exod. 34, 6-7) und ihre Parallelen im Alten Testament und seiner Umwelt* (BWANT, 160; Stuttgart: Kohlhammer, 2003).

12. The related vocabulary was carefully analysed by M. Mark, *'Mein Angesicht geht' (Exod. 33.14): Gottes Zusage personaler Führung* (Herders biblische Studien, 66; Freiburg i.Br.: Herder, 2011), pp. 381-417. For an analysis of the structure of Exod. 20.2-7 see R. Meynet, 'I due decaloghi, legge di libertà (Es 20.2-17 & Deut. 5.6-21)', *Gregorianum* 81 (2000), pp. 659-92 (660-62).

Exod. 20.2-5a	Prologue and prohibition of images	→ perverted and broken	in 32.1-6
Exod. 20.5b-6	reason for the prohibition of images	→ transformed and deepened	in 34.6-7

This leads to the motif of the tablets, which symbolically underlines the breaking and the re-establishment of the covenant. Seeing the golden calf with his own eyes, Moses is infuriated and breaks the tablets (Exod. 32.19), which he had received just a short time before as a final symbol of the covenant (compare Exod. 24.12; 31.18). Only after Moses' intense intercessions on behalf of the people (Exod. 32.31–33.6, 12-23) does God command Moses to renew the tablets (Exod. 34.1), which initiates God's mercy and reconciliation. Although Exod. 34.28 does not make entirely clear which 'ten words' (עשרת הדברים) are written on the tablets, Moses' accounts of the events at Horeb in Deuteronomy clarify that the Decalogue of Exod. 20 is supposed to be written there (Deut. 4.12f.; 5.22; 10.4).

Beyond their symbolic function within the making, breaking and renewal of the covenant, the tablets also form the centre of the sanctuary, which God describes to Moses in Exodus 25–31 and which can finally be constructed and erected after the renewal of the covenant (Exod. 35–40). Moses is to place the 'testimony, which I shall give you' (Exod. 25.16, 21) in the Ark of the Covenant. Although this could be identified as an allusion to the previously announced presentation of the tablets (compare נתן in Exod. 24.12; 25.16, 21; 31.18), readers are assured only by Moses' account in Deuteronomy that the 'testimony' is identical with the tablets (Deut. 5.22; 10.1-5).

Thus, the 'tablets' and the 'testimony' both appear in several structurally vital passages in the second half of Exodus. The 'tablets' form a narrative frame around the instructions for the sanctuary in Exod. 24.12–31.18; they mark the breaking and renewal of the covenant in Exod. 32.19; 34.1, 4, 28 as well as Moses' contrasting descents from the mountain in Exod. 32.15f. and 34.29. Moreover, God commands Moses to place the 'testimony' in the Ark of the Covenant at the beginning of the covenant instructions (Exod. 25.16, 21), which is done only in the final text concerning the erection of the sanctuary (Exod. 40.20).

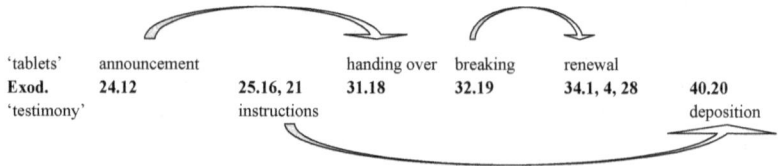

'tablets'	announcement		handing over	breaking	renewal	
Exod.	**24.12**	**25.16, 21**	**31.18**	**32.19**	**34.1, 4, 28**	**40.20**
'testimony'		instructions				deposition

The tablets are not only a structurally vital motif, but also a symbol at the centre of God's further revelations: 'There I will meet with you, and from above the mercy seat, from between the two cherubim that are on the ark of the covenant, I will deliver to you all my commands for the Israelites' (Exod.

25.22; compare also 30.6, 36). Thus, the tablets and the text written on them can be seen as a hermeneutical centre from which all further commands of God originate. The tablets are placed at the centre of the holy of holies and they characterize the central meaning of the tabernacle, since the Ark can be called 'ark of the testimony' (e.g. Exod. 39.35) and even the sanctuary as a whole can be referred to as the 'dwelling of the testimony' (e.g. Num. 1.50).[13]

Thus the Decalogue is a crucial text within the narrative structure of the book of Exodus. The story of Israel's rescue from Egypt in the first half of the book forms the origin of all divine law at Sinai according to the Prologue of Exod. 20.2. The First Commandment (Exod. 20.2-6) provides the starting point from which the golden calf episode unfolds (Exod. 32–34). Moreover, the Decalogue is systematically connected to the Book of the Covenant by the making of the Sinai covenant in Exodus 19–24. And the motifs of the 'tablets' and the 'testimony' systematically connect the Decalogue with the narrative development of Exodus 24–34 and the centre of the sanctuary (in the narrative arc of Exod. 25.16–40.20). Although the Ten Commandments seem to have been developed at a rather late stage, they form a focal point of the narrative of Exodus in its canonical form.

2. *The Decalogue within the Book of Deuteronomy*

The reason why Moses renders the Decalogue for Israel in Deuteronomy 5 is given by the plot of the book of Numbers. Israel stays at Sinai until 'the cloud lifted from over the tabernacle of the covenant' (Num. 10.11). On their way towards the Promised Land, the people continue to revolt so that Yhwh's anger is kindled and he decides: 'In this wilderness they shall come to a full end, and there they shall die' (Num. 14.35). This happens within 40 years (Num 26.63-65; 32.10-13). Therefore Moses addresses the second generation of Israel in Moab in the fortieth year of the Exodus (Deut. 1.3), expounds his teaching (Deut. 1–30) and hands it over in written form (Deut. 31.9-13, 24-29) before his death (Deut. 34.5).[14]

As in the book of Exodus, the Decalogue occupies a structurally highly significant position within the book of Deuteronomy. Moses quotes the Ten

---

13. As a consequence, the tablets also form the centre of the Temple in Jerusalem. A last reference to them is made at the dedication of Solomon's temple in 1 Kgs 8.9: 'There was nothing in the ark except the two tablets of stone that Moses had placed there at Horeb, where Yhwh made a covenant with the Israelites, when they came out of the land of Egypt'.

14. T.A. Fretheim, 'The Ark in Deuteronomy', *CBQ* 30 (1968), pp. 1-14 (5): 'The necessity for Deuteronomy is much the same as that for the second set of tablets, the stubbornness and rebellion of the people'. On the 'book' of the written Torah within Deuteronomy, see J.-P. Sonnet, *The Book within the Book: Writing in Deuteronomy* (Biblical Interpretation Series, 14; Leiden: E.J. Brill, 1997).

Commandments at the beginning of his longest and central speech within the book. Deuteronomy 5–26 contains Moses' recollection of the theophany at Horeb (Deuteronomy's name for Sinai), including his presentation of the Decalogue (Deut. 5) and teaching of Yhwh's further commandments (Deut. 6–26).[15]

The transition between Moses' repetition of the Ten Commandments in Deut. 5.6-21 and the introduction of further commandments in Deut 6.1-3 is decisive for the legal hermeneutics of Deuteronomy within the Pentateuch.[16] Moses recalls Israel's request at Horeb that he should speak to them instead of Yhwh (Deut. 5.24-27, compare Exod. 20.19) and relates Yhwh's positive answer (5.28-31; no equivalent in Exod.). Since Moses' introduction of his teaching in Deuteronomy 6–26 precisely refers to God's speech from Horeb (5.31), it is clear that the Torah of Deuteronomy 6–26 is meant to substitute for the Book of the Covenant (Exod. 20.22–23.33).[17]

Deut. 5.31	6.1
But you, stand here by me, and I will tell you all the *commandment, the statutes and the ordinances, that you shall teach them,* so that they may *do* them *in the land* that I am giving them *to possess it.*	Now this is the *commandment, the statutes and the ordinances that Yhwh your God charged me to teach you* to *do* (them) *in the land* that you are about to cross into *to possess it.*

With the claim that the speeches following Deut. 6.1 contain the teaching conveyed by God to Moses at Horeb, the authority of the Book of the Covenant is transferred to the Deuteronomic law. Although Deuteronomy 6–26 is implicitly presented as an exposition of the Book of the Covenant,[18] the existence of the latter is neglected in Deuteronomy, probably to avoid a conflict of authority.

---

15. For a detailed explication of my understanding of the literary structure of Deuteronomy, see D. Markl, *Gottes Volk im Deuteronomium* (Beihefte zur Zeitschrift für altorientalische und biblische Rechtsgeschichte, 18; Wiesbaden: Harrassowitz, 2012), pp. 18-46; idem, 'Deuteronomy's Frameworks in Service of the Law (Deut. 1–11; 26–34)', in G. Fischer, D. Markl and S. Paganini (eds.), *Deuteronomium—Tora für eine neue Generation* (Beihefte zur Zeitschrift für altorientalische und biblische Rechtsgeschichte, 17; Wiesbaden: Harrassowitz, 2011), pp. 271-83.

16. For the narrative function of Deuteronomy 5 within Deuteronomy, see N. Lohfink, 'Reading Deuteronomy 5 as Narrative', in B.A. Strawn and N.R. Bowen (eds.), *A God So Near: Essays on Old Testament Theology* (Festschrift P.D. Miller; Winona Lake: Eisenbrauns, 2003), pp. 261-81: 'Deuteronomy 5 recounts the beginning of the book's story. This fact underscores the importance of its content' (p. 265).

17. Compare the more elaborate argument in D. Markl, 'Moses Prophetenrolle in Dtn 5; 18; 34. Strukturelle Wendepunkte von rechtshermeneutischem Gewicht', in Fischer *et al.* (eds.), *Deuteronomium*, pp. 51-68 (55f.).

18. In fact, many laws of Deuteronomy are seen as *Fortschreibungen* of laws of the

Just as the Book of the Covenant could be read as an elaboration of the Commandments of the Decalogue (see above), the Torah of Deuteronomy 6–26 is also systematically connected with the Decalogue. Moses' parenetical teachings in Deuteronomy 6–11 revolve around the First Commandment.[19] The composition of the legal corpus that follows, Deuteronomy 12–25 seems to be systematically influenced by the sequence of the Ten Commandments.[20] In addition, the programmatic homily of Deut. 4.1-40 exposes Israel's experience of the theophany at Horeb and the prohibition of images as a theological centre (esp. 4.9-31).[21] The motif of the tablets of the Commandments is introduced in 4.13; 5.22 and reappears in Moses' account of the episode of the golden calf in 9.9-11, 15, 17; 10.1-5.

Both the structural position of the Decalogue within Deuteronomy and its thematic and systematic connections with Moses' theological preaching and the central law code leave no doubt that the Ten Commandments play a decisive role in the conception and the legal hermeneutics of Deuteronomy. However, only a more detailed look at the differences between the versions of Exod. 20 and Deut. 5 will reveal the Decalogue's significance within the Pentateuch as a whole.

3. The Differences between the Two Versions (Exod. 20.2-17; Deut. 5.6-21)

The most obvious difference between the two versions of the Decalogue in Exod. 20.2-17 and Deut. 5.5-21 is that Moses' rendering in Deut. 5 is significantly longer (see appendix below, pp. 26-27). While the version of Exodus 20 has only two little additions,[22] the version of Deuteronomy 5 contains several additional words, and even phrases. Three times Moses'

Book of the Covenant: B.M. Levinson, *Deuteronomy and the Hermeneutics of Legal Innovation* (New York: Oxford University Press, 1997); E. Otto, 'Biblische Rechtsgeschichte als Fortschreibungsgeschichte. Eine kritische Diskussion mit B.M. Levinson', in his *Altorientalische und biblische Rechtsgeschichte: Gesammelte Studien* (Beihefte zur Zeitschrift für altorientalische und biblische Rechtsgeschichte, 8; Wiesbaden: Harrassowitz, 2008), pp. 496-506 [= *BibOr* 56 (1999), pp. 5-14].

19. Compare N. Lohfink, *Das Hauptgebot: Eine Untersuchung literarischer Einleitungsfragen zu Dtn 5–11* (AnBib, 20; Rome: Pontifical Biblical Institute, 1963).

20. See G. Braulik, *Die deuteronomischen Gesetze und der Dekalog: Studien zum Aufbau von Deuteronomium 12–26* (SBS, 145; Stuttgart: Katholisches Bibelwerk, 1991); an alternative suggestion was made by K. Finsterbusch, 'Die Dekalog-Ausrichtung des deuteronomischen Gesetzes. Ein neuer Ansatz', in Fischer *et al.* (eds.), *Deuteronomium*, pp. 123-46.

21. G. Braulik, *Die Mittel deuteronomischer Rhetorik* (AnBib, 68; Rome: Pontifical Biblical Institute, 1978); K. Holter, *Deuteronomy 4 and the Second Commandment* (Studies in Biblical Literature, 60; New York: Peter Lang, 2003).

22. Both additions concern the Hebrew conjunction ו, in my translation rendered 'nor' (Exod. 20.4) and 'or' (20.17).

voice seems to interrupt the quotation of God's voice: 'as Yhwh your God commanded you' in Deut. 5.12 and 16, and 'therefore Yhwh your God commanded you to keep the Sabbath day' (5.15).[23]

Most differences between the two versions do not affect the Commandments' substance, but only details of their wording.[24] However, there are changes of exegetical significance. An obvious example is seen in the last Commandment in Deut. 5.21. Here, the order of 'wife' and 'house' is switched, and 'coveting' (חמד) the neighbour's wife is distinguished from 'desiring' (אוה) any other property of the neighbour. These changes seem to raise the dignity of the wife from being just part of the neighbour's property to a significant individual to be 'coveted' rather than 'desired' like anything else.

The most substantial differences occur in the rewording of the Sabbath Commandment (Deut. 5.12-15). While the Exodus version grounds Sabbath observance in the sequence of six days of work and a seventh day of rest (Exod. 20.8-11) structuring the events of creation according to Gen. 1.1–2.3, Moses' rendering in Deut. 5 underlines the social dimension of the Sabbath. First, an emphatic repetition is added in Deut. 5.14: 'so that your male and female slave may rest as well as you'. Secondly, Moses refers to the Exodus experience as the foundation of Sabbath keeping: 'Remember that you were a slave in the land of Egypt, and Yhwh your God brought you out from there with a mighty hand and an outstretched arm' (5.15).

We can, therefore, conclude that even if Moses preserves the substance of the Commandments, he deals with the text with considerable freedom—significantly rephrasing some of the social commandments. Given the unique authority that is attributed to the Decalogue within the contexts of both Exodus 20 and Deuteronomy 5, the most important question remains as to why 'Moses' (and, behind this figure, the authors or redactors of Deuteronomy) dares to make any changes in these special and directly revealed words of God at all.

---

23. On the interruptions in Deut. 5.12, 16 see, most elaborately, G. Braulik, 'Der unterbrochene Dekalog. Zu Deuteronomium 5,12 und 16 und ihrer Bedeutung für den deuteronomistischen Gesetzeskodex', *ZAW* 120 (2008), pp. 169-83. While it seems to me still most plausible to understand these phrases as referring back to God's revelation of the Decalogue at Horeb, Braulik suggests to understand them as cataphoric allusions to elaborations of the respective commandments within the Deuteronomic Code. Unlike Braulik ('Der unterbrochene Dekalog', p. 173) I think the interruptions are not to be perceived as the voice of the narrator, because the direct address ('you') clearly hints at the voice of Moses. The interruptions by the narrator in Deut. 2.10-12, 20-23 are marked by references to Israel in third person (2.12) or no reference to Israel at all.

24. For a list and analysis of the differences see Markl, *Dekalog*, pp. 209-17.

4. The Decalogue as the Origin of Law and Legal Hermeneutics in the Pentateuch

The foregoing observations have consequences for the literary structure and the legal hermeneutics of the Pentateuch as a whole. First, the most significant observations regarding the literary function of the Decalogue need to be seen together.

Whereas in Exodus 20 the Decalogue is spoken by God himself within the making of the Sinai Covenant, it is Moses who quotes the Decalogue in Deuteronomy 5 for the second generation in Moab, as part of his attempt to explain God's teachings from Sinai for them at the border of the Promised Land. In both contexts the Decalogue forms the beginning of major corpuses of legislation. Within Exodus, the Decalogue is followed by the Book of the Covenant. Within Deuteronomy, it is followed by the Deuteronomic law code, which implicitly replaces the Book of the Covenant. The Decalogues, therefore, serve a systematic purpose for the legislation of the Pentateuch, summarizing basic aspects of the biblical legislation that is unfolded in the legal corpuses.

Moreover, both versions of the Decalogue are interwoven into wider literary contexts, especially through the Sabbath Commandments. The two versions of the Decalogue together ground the Sabbath in both creation (Gen. 1f.) and the redemption of Exodus 1–15—two crucial theological narratives of the Pentateuch.[25] In this way, the two Decalogues bind the narratives, theology and law of the Pentateuch together through wide-ranging intertextual links.[26]

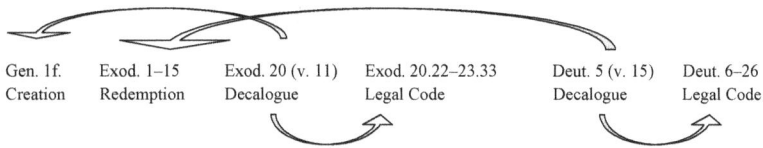

| Gen. 1f. | Exod. 1–15 | Exod. 20 (v. 11) | Exod. 20.22–23.33 | Deut. 5 (v. 15) | Deut. 6–26 |
| Creation | Redemption | Decalogue | Legal Code | Decalogue | Legal Code |

The prominent role of the Decalogue within the literary structure of the Pentateuch raises the question as to what its hermeneutical function is. Proclaimed by God himself in a great theophany to the whole people of Israel, written on the two stone tablets with the finger of God and deposited in the very heart of the sanctuary, the Ten Commandments possess the highest

---

25. G.A. Klingbeil, 'The Sabbath Law in the Decalogue(s): Creation and Liberation as a Paradigm for Community', *Revue biblique* 117 (2010), pp. 491-509, argues that 'contextualization' within the Pentateuch is a key reason for the difference between the two versions of the Sabbath Commandment.

26. These observations seem to suggest that the Decalogues in their final form are strongly influenced by authors or redactors who conceived wide-ranging ideas about the theology and legislation of the Pentateuch.

authority. Sinai/Horeb is the geographical symbol of the origin of the law, and the Decalogue on its two stone tablets is the symbol of the original divine law itself, which is meant to be moved from Sinai to Yhwh's chosen place (Deut. 12.5), that is, Jerusalem (2 Sam. 6).

It is most surprising, therefore, that Moses is portrayed as making changes to the very wording of the Ten Commandments. Moses' relative freedom in rewording the Decalogue, and especially the Sabbath Commandment, is of the highest significance for the legal hermeneutics of the Pentateuch.[27] Since these profoundly special words can be altered and revised by a religious authority such as Moses, legal revision is introduced as a hermeneutical principle at the very core of the divine law. This principle is enacted in the arrangement of the two legal corpora following the two versions of the Decalogue. The Book of the Covenant is reworded and de facto replaced by Moses' explanation of the Torah in Deuteronomy 6–26. The two versions of the Decalogue therefore represent both the most original divine law from Sinai and the paradigmatic case for legal revision and development in the Bible.

5. *A Hermeneutical Overview of the Earliest Reception History*

Although the Decalogue is given the highest authority within the Pentateuch, there is little evidence of its reception in the rest of the Old Testament. There seem to be allusions to social commandments in Jer. 7.9 and Hos. 4.2, and the prologue of Exod. 20.2/Deut. 5.6 may be alluded to in Hos. 12.10 and 13.4 and in Ps. 81.11. However, these passages do not provide any clear evidence of the external recognition of the Decalogue's central role, as it is constructed within the Pentateuch.

There is clear evidence of the Decalogue's use in early Jewish prayer, and the Ten Commandments are quite frequently discussed in early Jewish literature.[28] Philo of Alexandria's work *De decalogo* brought the interpretation

---

27. The question of the legal hermeneutics of the Pentateuch was introduced by N. Lohfink, *Prolegomena zu einer Rechtshermeneutik des Pentateuch*, in his *Studien zum Deuteronomium und zur deuteronomistischen Literatur*, V (Stuttgarter biblische Aufsatzbände, 38; Stuttgart: Katholisches Bibelwerk, 2005), pp. 181-231 [= G. Braulik (ed.), *Das Deuteronomium* (Österreichische biblische Studien, 23; Frankfurt a.M.: Lang, 2003), pp. 11-55]. See also Markl, *Rechtshermeneutik*; *Dekalog*, pp. 172f., 252f.; *Volk im Deuteronomium*, pp. 297-300; E. Otto, *Deuteronomium 1–11* (HTKAT; Freiburg i.Br.: Herder, 2012), pp. 258-82.

28. On the role of the Decalogue in early Jewish literature see Ruth Langer's article in this volume (pp. 85-101); on its role in Early Jewish literature compare U. Kellermann, 'Der Dekalog in den Schriften des Frühjudentums. Ein Überblick', in H.G. Reventlow (ed.), *Weisheit, Ethos und Gebot*, pp. 147-226; G. Stemberger, 'Der Dekalog im frühen

of the Commandments to a first climax.[29] However, the influence of Philo's work remained limited within Jewish reception, since Rabbinic Judaism was hesitant to emphasize the Decalogue's importance.

For the history of Christian reception of the Ten Commandments, Jesus' explanation of the Commandments at the Sermon on the Mount seems to be decisive.[30] Jesus refers to the prohibitions of murder and adultery to generalize their ethical meaning: even anger against a brother and looking lustfully at a woman amount to the gravity of murder and adultery (Mt. 5.21f., 27f.). This treatment of the Commandments opens the way to the ethical generalization that guides the hermeneutics of countless catechetical explanations of the Commandments in the history of Christianity.

Both Philo and Jesus are prominent disciples of Moses, who adopted the interpretative freedom encouraged by Moses' own hermeneutical freedom as portrayed in Deuteronomy 5. The reception history of the Decalogue, therefore, begins in the literary contexts where it originates. The prominence that the Pentateuch accords to this text laid the foundation for its vast reception history: its perception as central to the divine law that in turn became central to Christian ethical teaching; and its documentation on tablets of stone that became iconic in the history of art.

Judentum', *Jahrbuch für biblische Theologie* 4 (1989), pp. 91-103; on the Fourth Commandment esp. H. Jungbauer, *'Ehre Vater und Mutter': Der Weg des Elterngebots in der biblischen Tradition* (WUNT, 146; Tübingen: Mohr Siebeck, 2002).

29. Cf. the study of Y. Amir, 'The Decalogue according to Philo', in B.-Z. Segal and G. Levi (eds.), *The Ten Commandments in History and Tradition* (Publications of the Perry Foundation for Biblical Research; Jerusalem: Magnes Press, 1990), pp. 121-60; S.J. Pearce, 'On the Decalogue', in L.H. Feldman, J.L. Kugel and L.H. Schiffman (eds.), *Outside the Bible: Ancient Jewish Writings Related to Scripture* 1 (Philadelphia: Jewish Publication Society, 2013), pp. 989-1032; H. Svebakken, *Philo of Alexandria's Exposition on the Tenth Commandment* (Brown Judaic Studies, Studia Philonica Monographs, 6; Atlanta: Society of Biblical Literature, 2012).

30. Jesus seems to have presupposed the validity of the Ten Commandments, as esp. Mk 10.19/Mt. 19.18f/Lk. 18.20 suggest; compare H. Löhr, 'Jesus and Ten Words', in T. Holmén and E. Porter (eds.), *Handbook for the Study of the Historical Jesus*, IV, *Individual Studies* (Leiden: E.J. Brill, 2011), pp. 3135-54. For a study of the Ten Commandments' reception within the New Testament see D. Sänger, 'Tora für die Völker—Weisungen der Liebe. Zur Rezeption des Dekalogs im frühen Judentum und Neuen Testament', in Reventlow (ed.), *Weisheit, Ethos und Gebot*, pp. 97-146.

Exodus 20.2-17

² I am Yhwh your God, who brought you out of the land of Egypt,
out of the house of slavery. ³ You shall have no other gods before me.
⁴ You shall not make for yourself an idol +NOR+ any image, whether from anything in heaven above, or on the earth beneath, or in the water under the earth.
⁵ You shall not bow down to them or worship them; for I, Yhwh, your God am a jealous God, punishing children for the iniquity of parents, to the third and the fourth generation of those who reject me, ⁶ but showing steadfast love to the thousandth generation of those who love me and keep my commandments.
⁷ You shall not make wrongful use of the name of Yhwh your God,
for Yhwh will not acquit anyone who misuses his name.

⁸ Remember the sabbath day, and keep it holy.

⁹ Six days you shall labor and do all your work.
¹⁰ But the seventh day is a sabbath to Yhwh your God; you shall not do any work,
you, or your son or your daughter, your male or female slave,
or your livestock,
or the alien resident in your towns.

¹¹ For in six days Yhwh made heaven and earth, the sea, and all that is in them, but rested the seventh day.
Therefore Yhwh blessed the sabbath day and consecrated it.
¹² Honour your father and your mother,

so that your days may be long
in the land that Yhwh your God is giving you.

¹³ You shall not murder.
¹⁴ You shall not commit adultery.
¹⁵ You shall not steal.
¹⁶ You shall not bear false witness against your neighbor.
¹⁷ You shall not covet your neighbour's house;
you shall not covet your neighbour's wife, or male or female slave,
+OR+ his ox, or donkey, or anything that belongs to your neighbour.

Deuteronomy 5.6-21

⁶ I am Yhwh your God, who brought you out of the land of Egypt,
out of the house of slavery. ⁷ You shall have no other gods before me.
⁸ You shall not make for yourself an idol, whether from anything
in heaven above, or on the earth beneath, or in the water under the earth.
⁹ You shall not bow down to them or worship them; for I, Yhwh, your God am a
jealous God, punishing children for the iniquity of parents, +BOTH+ to the third and
the fourth generation of those who reject me, ¹⁰ but showing steadfast love to the
thousandth generation of those who love me and keep my commandments.
¹¹ You shall not make wrongful use of the name of Yhwh your God,
for Yhwh will not acquit anyone who misuses his name.

¹² **Observe** the sabbath day and keep it holy,
+AS YHWH YOUR GOD COMMANDED YOU.+
¹³ Six days you shall labor and do all your work.
¹⁴ But the seventh day is a sabbath to Yhwh your God; you shall not do any work,
you, or your son or your daughter, +OR+ your male or female slave,
+OR YOUR OX OR YOUR DONKEY+, or +ANY OF+ your livestock,
or the resident alien in your towns,
+SO THAT YOUR MALE AND FEMALE SLAVE MAY REST AS WELL AS YOU.+
¹⁵ **Remember that you were a slave in the land of Egypt, and Yhwh your God brought you out from there with a mighty hand and an outstretched arm.**
Therefore Yhwh **your God commanded you to keep the sabbath day.**
¹⁶ Honour your father and your mother,
+AS YHWH YOUR GOD COMMANDED YOU,+
so that your days may be long +AND THAT IT MAY GO WELL WITH YOU+
in the land that Yhwh your God is giving you.

¹⁷ You shall not murder.
¹⁸ +NEITHER+ shall you commit adultery.
¹⁹ +NEITHER+ shall you steal.
²⁰ +NEITHER+ shall you bear witness **of vanity** against your neighbor.
²¹ +NEITHER+ shall you covet your neighbour's **wife**.
+NEITHER+ shall you **desire** your neighbour's **house**, +HIS FIELD+, or male or
female slave, his ox, or donkey, or anything that belongs to your neighbour.

CAPITALS FRAMED BY "+" INDICATE PLUSES.
Bold print indicates other differences.

The Reception History of the Decalogue through Early Translations: The Case of the Septuagint, Peshitta and Targums

Innocent Himbaza

1. *Reception History and Interpretations in Early Translations*

Early translations such as the Septuagint, Peshitta and Targums are considered to be good witnesses to the biblical text. However, since *traduttore, traditore* (to translate is to betray), we need first to establish the fidelity with which these textual witnesses render the Decalogue. Second, some textual differences between the Hebrew Masoretic text (MT) and the translations raise the question of their *Vorlage*. Did the translators read the same text as the one we have in MT? Third, the two versions of the Decalogue (Exod. 20 and Deut. 5) contain textual differences, and translations don't always reflect these differences in the same way. Thus, when one studies the reception history of the Decalogue through early translations, one must simultaneously keep in mind these several aspects of the topic.

Reading the Decalogue in the Septuagint, Peshitta and Targums leads to the following question: do these translations reflect interpretations of the Decalogue? The answer is in the affirmative, even though not all of the particular readings should be considered as reflecting an interpretation by the translators. It should also be recalled that each of the translations studied here has its own history and characteristics. The Septuagint is the most ancient and contains significant particular readings. In some cases it may contain earlier material than MT,[1] while the Targums often reflect the same text as MT but include additions.[2] The Peshitta, 'simple translation', reflects MT but it has some connections with the Septuagint and the Targums.

---

1. Adrian Schenker (ed.), *The Earliest Text of the Hebrew Bible. The Relationship between the Masoretic Text and the Hebrew Base of the Septuagint Reconsidered* (SBLSCS, 52; Atlanta: Society of Biblical Literature, 2003).

2. Joseph Ribera-Florit characterizes the Targum as 'une version commentée en araméen du Texte Massorétique': Joseph Ribera-Florit, 'Le Targum', in Adrian Schenker and Philippe Hugo (eds.), *L'enfance de la Bible hébraïque: Histoire du texte de l'Ancien Testament* (Le monde de la Bible, 52; Geneva: Labor & Fides, 2005), pp. 220-37 (220).

Thus, the title of this study, 'The Reception History of the Decalogue through Early Translations', should not automatically suggest that there was one fixed Hebrew text of the Decalogue which may have been interpreted or altered in the translations. The history of the Hebrew text is not to be read as music *all'unisono*. Let us recall two remarks of Emanuel Tov about MT.[3]

> However, one thing is clear, it should not be postulated that MT better or more frequently reflects the original text of the biblical books than any other text. Furthermore, even were we to surmise that MT reflects the 'original' form of Scripture, we would still have to decide *which* form of MT reflects this 'original text', since MT itself is represented by many witnesses that differ in small details.

When comparing the Decalogue text of MT with that of early translations, such as the Septuagint, Peshitta and Targums, one observes four types of differences.

First, early translations contain readings unknown in MT but attested in other Hebrew textual witnesses such as the Samaritan Pentateuch or Qumran manuscripts. These types of readings, found in the Septuagint and the Peshitta, indicate that the translators may have used a Hebrew *Vorlage* which contained differences from the text of MT.

Second, early translations contain readings lacking in one version of MT but attested in another. It is often observed that readings of Deuteronomy 5 are integrated in the version of Exodus 20 in the translations. This type of difference indicates that there was a harmonization between the two versions of the Decalogue. This phenomenon is also attested in some Hebrew witnesses, such as the Samaritan Pentateuch, the Nash Papyrus and Qumran texts such as 4QDeut[n], 4QPhyl G, 4QPhyl J, and 4QMez A.

Third, early translations at times contain words or phrases from MT but in a different order. It should be recalled, however, that the same phenomenon is also attested amongst the two versions of MT itself, especially for the order of the Commandments against murder, theft and adultery, and for the order of the house and the wife in Exod. 20.17 and Deut. 5.21. Scholars have proposed literary reasons to explain this case.[4]

---

3. Emanuel Tov, *Textual Criticism of the Hebrew Bible* (Minneapolis: Fortress Press, 3rd edn, 2012), pp. 11-12. For more details on the Decalogue see Moshe Greenberg, 'The Decalogue Tradition Critically Examined', in Ben-Zion Segal and Gershon Levi (eds.), *The Ten Commandments in History and Tradition* (Jerusalem: Magnes Press, 1990), pp. 83-119.

4. For the Sixth to the Eighth Commandments, see Adrian Schenker, 'Die Reihenfolge der Gebote der zweiten Tafel. Zur Systematik des Dekalogs', in Adrian Schenker, *Recht und Kult im Alten Testament: Achtzehn Studien* (OBO, 172; Freiburg / Göttingen: Universitätsverlag / Vandenhoeck & Ruprecht, 2000), pp. 52-66. For the Tenth Commandment, see Alexander Rofé, 'The Tenth Commandment in the Light of Four Deuteronomic Laws', in Segal and Levi (eds.), *The Ten Commandments*, pp. 45-65, esp. pp. 48-52.

30   *The Decalogue and its Cultural Influence*

Fourth, early translations contain particular readings found neither in MT nor attested in any other textual witness. This type can be divided into two categories: textual cases and texts which are clearly intentional interpretations. The last category is particular to the Targums.

In what follows I shall restrict myself to some particular readings in each of the three witnesses: the Septuagint, the Peshitta and the Targums. The main question is whether these particular readings have something to say about the reception history of the Decalogue.

2. *Particular Readings in the Septuagint*

The Septuagint contains many textual differences from MT. All of these differences cannot be explained by the fact that the Septuagint is a translation. Indeed, many of them are known in other Hebrew witnesses such as the Samaritan Pentateuch, the Qumran manuscripts and the Nash Papyrus.[5] What are the particular readings in the Septuagint?

(1) The Septuagint version of Exod. 20.12 qualifies the land given by the Lord as τῆς ἀγαθῆς, 'good'.

MT:
Honour your father and your mother, so that your days may be long in the land that the LORD your God is giving you (NRSV).

Septuagint:
Honor your father and mother so that it may be well with you and tso that you may be longlived on the **good** land that the Lord your God is giving you. (NETS).

First of all, let us observe that the reading ἵνα εὖ σοι γένηται ('so that it may be well with you') is not attested in MT of Exod. 20, while it is known in the parallel passage of Deut. 5.16. This reading resulted from harmonization between the two versions. The same reading is well known in the Nash Papyrus, which is in Hebrew.

The particular reading on which we focus is τῆς ἀγαθῆς ('good'). The qualification of the land as 'good' is lacking in the whole Hebrew tradition (MT, Samaritan Pentateuch, Nash Papyrus, Dead Sea Scrolls: 4QDeut[n], 4Qphyl G, XQphyl 3), where it would be read הטובה. It is also lacking in

---

    5. For the textual comparison see Innocent Himbaza, *Le Décalogue et l'histoire du texte: Etudes des formes textuelles du Décalogue et leurs implications dans l'histoire du texte de l'Ancien Testament* (OBO, 207; Fribourg / Göttingen: Academic Press / Vandenhoeck & Ruprecht, 2004), pp. 117-66.

the Targums and in the Vulgate. The only textual witness which contains this reading is the Syriac version (Peshitta) of Deuteronomy. The reading of the Peshitta in Deut. 5.16 is *ṭbt'*.

One observes that this reading is found neither in the Septuagint version of Deut. 5.16 nor in the Peshitta version of Exod. 20.12. Thus such a reading must be considered as reflecting an evolution of the text in its reception history. Indeed, it is difficult to imagine that the word 'good' was the original reading and was felt to be erroneous, or was omitted in all the witnesses where it is lacking. It is rather preferable to think that a scribe may have added it. The addition may have been made directly in the Septuagint or, more probably, in its *Vorlage*.[6]

The Septuagint actually renders the two Hebrew words ארץ and אדמה with the same Greek word, γῆ. It should be recalled that the expression האדמה הטובה does not occur in the Pentateuch of MT. One possibility is that the Greek translator of Exodus 20 assimilated this passage to the occurrences of the expression 'good land' (הארץ הטובה), as at Exod. 3.8. However, since this expression occurs many times in Deuteronomy, one would expect an assimilation in the same book. That is why the second possibility, that the word was added in a Hebrew text, is preferable.

Thus the assimilation and harmonization of different texts reflects one of the ways of reading the Bible in its reception history during the Hellenistic and Roman periods.

(2) Another particular reading in the Septuagint is found at Exod. 20.17/ Deut. 5.21. Here we read οὔτε παντὸς κτήνους αὐτοῦ ('or any animal of his').

MT: Exod. 20.17
You shall not covet your neighbour's house; you shall not covet your neighbour's wife, or male or female slave, or ox, or donkey, or anything that belongs to your neighbour (NRSV).

MT: Deut. 5.21
Neither shall you covet your neighbour's wife. Neither shall you desire your neighbour's house, or field, or male or female slave, or ox, or donkey, or anything that belongs to your neighbour (NRSV).

Septuagint: Exod. 20.17/Deut. 5.21
You shall not covet your neighbor's wife; you shall not covet your neighbor's house or his field or his male slave or his female slave or his ox or

---

6. Carmel McCarthy suggests that the Hebrew text underlying the Septuagint already contained the varying forms: Carmel McCarthy, *Deuteronomy* (Biblia hebraica quinta, 5; Stuttgart: Deutsche Bibelgesellschaft, 2007), pp. 53*-54*.

his draft animal **or any animal of his** or whatever belongs to your neighbor (NETS).

The two versions of the MT are slightly different whereas those of the Septuagint are well harmonized. Once again, this observation illustrates the phenomenon of harmonization in the reception history of the Decalogue. Different elements and different orders are harmonized in the translation.

The equivalent Hebrew text of the Greek οὔτε παντὸς κτήνους αὐτοῦ ('or any animal of his') would read וכל בהמתו. This reading, which is not found in any other textual witness, may have been added in order to complete the list of what one should not covet. Contrary to the case studied before, the reading we are studying here is known in both versions of the Decalogue in the Septuagint.

When comparing the text of this verse in the Septuagint with that of Exod. 20.10/Deut. 5.14, we find a significant similarity with Deut. 5.14. Here the Hebrew reading וכל בהמתך or the Greek καὶ πᾶν κτῆνός σου ('or any animal of yours') is put at the end of the list of animals that should rest on the Sabbath day. It is then possible that the Septuagint reading at Exod. 20.17/Deut. 5.21 resulted from an assimilation to Deut. 5.14. The Greek translator or the scribe of his Hebrew *Vorlage* intended to complete the list of the animals according to what he had read some verses before.

These cases reflect an internal interpretation of the text within its reception history. However, we cannot assert that these additions were either put in by the translator or 'found' in the *Vorlage* he used.[7]

(3) The third case is specific to a single manuscript of the Septuagint. The famous Vaticanus manuscript (MS B), dated to the fourth century and one of the oldest and most important manuscripts of the Septuagint, contains a long addition in Deut. 5.12-15.

Septuagint: Deut. 5.12-15
Keep the day of the sabbaths to consecrate it, as the Lord your God commanded you. 13 Six days you shall labor and do all your labor, 14 but on the seventh day there is Sabbata to the Lord your God; you shall not do in it any labor—you and your son and your daughter, your male slave and your female slave, your ox and your draft animal and any animal of yours and the guest within your gates so that your male slave and your female slave may rest as well as you. 15 And you shall remember that you were a domestic in the land of Egypt, and the Lord your God brought you out from there with

---

7. For the history of the Septuagint text of the Decalogue, see Innocent Himbaza, 'Le texte du Décalogue de la Septante raconte sa propre histoire', in Rémi Gounelle and Jean-Marc Prieur (eds.), *Le Décalogue au miroir des Pères* (Cahiers de la Biblia Patristica, 9, Strasbourg: Université Marc-Bloch, 2008), pp. 7-27.

a strong hand and with a high arm; therefore, the Lord your God instructed you to keep the day of the sabbaths and to consecrate it (NETS).

MS B: Deut. 5.12-15
Keep the day of the sabbaths to consecrate it, as the Lord your God commanded you. 13 Six days you shall labor and do all your labor, 14 but on the seventh day there is Sabbata to the Lord your God; you shall not do in it any labor – you and your son and your daughter, your male slave and your female slave, your ox and your draft animal and any animal of yours and the guest ~~within your gates~~ **who resides among you. For in six days the Lord made the heaven and the earth and the sea and all things in them**, so that your male slave and your female slave **and your ox** may rest as well as you. 15 And you shall remember that you were a domestic in the land of Egypt, and the Lord your God brought you out from there with a strong hand and with a high arm; therefore, the Lord your God instructed you to keep the day of the sabbaths and to consecrate it.

This is one of many examples of internal textual differences amongst Greek manuscripts. Thus, when one talks about the 'interpretation' of the Septuagint one should take note of the actual text of the Septuagint in question, since it is represented by manuscripts with some textual differences.

In this case, the first addition, 'who resides ... in them' comes from Exod. 20.11. However, its reading in Deuteronomy would not be considered as an intentional harmonization with the parallel passage of Exodus because it is misplaced.[8] The second addition, 'and your ox', is placed in the margin of the manuscript. It may result from a comparison with other Greek sources. However, since ancient recensions of Aquila and Symmachus contain the same plus in the form of ἄνον instead of ὑποζύγιον, it is possible that this plus comes from a different Hebrew source.

To summarize, assimilation to another version of the Decalogue or comparison with different manuscripts of the same passage may have influenced some actual readings in the Septuagint and especially in the Decalogue. Liturgical reasons have probably favored harmonization even though this phenomenon is found in non-liturgical manuscripts.[9] The reception history

---

8. An intentional harmonization of the two reasons given for keeping the Sabbath day is found in 4QDeut^n. See Eugene Ulrich *et al.* (eds.), *Qumran Cave 4. IX. Deuteronomy, Joshua, Judges, Kings* (DJD, 14; Oxford: Clarendon Press, 1995), p. 125. The reason given in Exod. 20.11 is added to that of Deut. 5.15. Contrary to what we read in MS B of the Septuagint, here the passage from Exodus is well placed.

9. This kind of harmonization is more visible in some Qumran Phylacteries and Mezuzot. It has been observed that those harmonizing manuscripts were probably copied by memory. Innocent Himbaza, 'Le Décalogue du Papyrus Nash, Philon, 4Qphyl G, 8Qphyl 3 et 4Qmez A', *RevQ* 79 (2002), pp. 411-28.

of the Septuagint demonstrates that in ancient Judaism the Decalogue was read and could be interpreted in different ways. Interpretations found in the Decalogue are not therefore necessarily to be described as 'Christian'.

3. *Particular Readings in the Peshitta*

As we observed in the previous section, the Peshitta—the Syriac translation of the Bible—also contains minor textual differences from the Hebrew MT.

(1) The first case concerns an interpretive translation found in Exod. 20.2/ Deut. 5.6.

MT:
I am the Lord your God, who brought you out of the land of Egypt, out of the house of slavery (NRSV).

Here the Peshitta doubles the pronoun, *'n' 'n'* to render the Hebrew אנוכי ('I am'). The double pronoun is actually used in the Peshitta to emphasize the identity of God. Indeed, many occurrences of 'I am the Lord' are rendered with the same double pronoun in the Peshitta. The manuscript G of the *Fragmentary Targum* (*Frag. Targ.* G) also contains a double pronoun in Exod. 20.2.

In the same verse, the word הוצאתיך, 'who brought you out', is rendered with *d'sqtk* 'who brought you up'. The use of 'bring up' (עלה hiphil) instead of 'bring out' (יצא hiphil) may be understood as an interpretation of the translator.[10]

(2) The particular reading with which we are dealing is found in Deut. 5.21. Here we read the plus *wl' krmh* 'nor his vineyard'. This plus is inserted after the word 'field', before the 'male slave'. The Hebrew text would read וכרמו.

MT:
Neither shall you covet your neighbor's wife. Neither shall you desire your neighbor's house, of field, or male or female slave, or ox, or donkey, or anything that belongs to your neighbor (NRSV).

Peshitta:
You shall not covet your neighbor's wife, neither shall you covet your neighbor's house, nor his field, **nor his vineyard**, nor his manservant, nor his maidservant, nor his ox, nor his ass, nor anything that is your neighbor's (trans. George M. Lamsa).

---

10. Lamsa's English translation of the Peshitta does not reflect these observations.

First of all, one observes that the Peshitta (as it is the case in the Septuagint) uses the same verb twice, *l'trṭ*, while the MT uses two different verbs: 'you shall not covet' (לא תחמוד) and 'you shall not desire' (לא תתאוה). In that case, it is possible that the reading of Deuteronomy in MT resulted from literary motives. The wife is isolated from other elements one should not covet. According to many scholars, the reading of Deuteronomy reflects the humanism of the Deuteronomist.[11] The Septuagint (οὐκ ἐπιθυμήσεις) and the Peshitta would have kept the oldest reading of the Decalogue, which is also found in the Exodus version of MT. This is a question of the internal history of the text of the Decalogue, since it exists in two different versions.

The Peshitta reading 'nor his vineyard' is not found in any other textual witness. It probably reflects an interpretation raised in the reception history of the Decalogue in order to complete the list of important elements that one should not covet. Here we observe the same phenomenon as in the Septuagint, even though elements added are not the same.

To summarize, in both Septuagint and Peshitta, the reading 'or anything that belongs to your neighbor' (Deut. 5.21) was not judged to be sufficient. So their scribes, or the scribes of their *Vorlagen*, decided to add 'nor his vineyard' (Peshitta) and 'or any animal of his' (Septuagint). In the reception history of the Decalogue, some scribes felt the need to complete the text. Examples taken from the Septuagint and the Peshitta constitute the evidence of this need.

4. *Particular Readings in the Targums*

It is well known that targumic literature often functions as biblical commentary. Therefore, interpretations are easily identifiable from textual expansions. However, some interpretations are also reflected in the terms chosen by translators to render the Hebrew text.

(1) To begin with this last type of interpretation, I restrict myself to Exod. 20.7/Deut. 5.11. Here 'to take the name in vain' is rendered with 'to swear'. This reading, לא תימי, 'you shall not swear', is found in many targumic witnesses such as *Targum Onqelos* and *Fragmentary Targum* (MS 110). The *Targum Pseudo-Jonathan* uses לא ישתבע with the same meaning, while the *Targum Neofiti* (לא יסב) is in agreement with MT.

MT:
You shall not make wrongful use of the name of the Lord your God, for the Lord will not acquit anyone who misuses his name (NRSV).

---

11. Moshe Weinfeld, *Deuteronomy 1–11: A New Translation with Introduction and Commentary* (AB, 5; New York: Doubleday, 1991), pp. 317-18.

Targum Onqelos:
Do not swear in vain with the name of the Lord your God, for the Lord will not acquit the one who swears falsely with his name (Aramaic Bible).

It has been observed that the *Fragmentary Targum* (MS 110) keeps the idea of 'to swear' alongside that of 'to take a false oath'. It renders the Commandment as follows: '…you shall not swear by the name of the Lord in vain, nor shall you take a false oath in my name…'.[12]

The reading of the targumic tradition may have been influenced by Lev. 19.12. In general the rabbinic tradition explains the expression נשא את שם יהוה, 'to take the name of the Lord', as meaning 'to swear'.[13] It should be noted, however, as scholars have understood it, that the prohibition in this Commandment may be applied to any abuse or profanation of the name of God such as magic, adjurations, cursing, manipulation, etc.[14]

(2) The second case concerns the numbering of the Commandments. Long targumic expansions of the Decalogue are well known in *Targum Neofiti*, *Targum Pseudo-Jonathan* and the *Fragmentary Targum*. Besides the textual content, targumic traditions seem to reflect a discussion on the numbering of the Commandments. They especially focus on which must be considered as the 'first' Commandment. That is why many targumic texts add דבירא קדמיא, 'first word', and sometimes דבירא תניא, 'second word', while the number of other Commandments is not explicitly given.

In the Targums, the first Commandment always corresponds to 'I am the Lord your God, who brought you out of the land of Egypt…' (Exod. 20.2/Deut. 5.6). The second is 'you shall not have other gods before me' (Exod. 20.3/Deut. 5.7). This numbering of the first and second Commandments reflects the more widespread opinion in rabbinic tradition (*y. Ber.* 3c).

In *Targum Neofiti* and *Targum Pseudo-Jonathan* each Commandment is introduced by a liturgical phrase 'My people, Israelites'. According to this indication, the Decalogue is divided as follows:

---

12. Michael L. Klein, *The Fragment-Targums of the Pentateuch. According to their Extant Sources*. II. *Translation* (AnBib, 76; Rome: Biblical Institute Press), 1980, p. 53; Bernard Grossfeld, *The Targum Onqelos of Exodus. Translated with Apparatus and Notes* (The Aramaic Bible, 7; Wilmington, DE: Michael Glazier, 1988), pp. 55-56.

13. See Benno Jacob, *The Second Book of the Bible: Exodus* (Hoboken, NJ: Ktav, 1992), pp. 556-59; Jeffery H. Tigay, *Deuteronomy* דברים (The JPS Torah Commentary; Philadelphia: The Jewish Publication Society, 1996), p. 67.

14. Weinfeld, *Deuteronomy 1–11*, pp. 278-79; Cornelius Houtman, *Exodus*. III. *Chapters 20–40* (Historical Commentary on the Old Testament; Leuven: Peeters, 2000), pp. 34-35.

1. My people, Israelites, I am the Lord...
2. My people, Israelites, You shall not have any other god...
3. My people, Israelites, None of you do swear in vain...
4. My people, Israelites, Keep the Sabbath day...
5. My people, Israelites, Every man be careful with the honor of his father...
6. My people, Israelites, Do not be murderers...
7. My people, Israelites, Do not be adulterers...
8. My people, Israelites, Do not be thieves...
9. My people, Israelites, Do not carry yourselves as false witnesses...
10. My people Israelites, Do not be covetous...[15]

Hebrew manuscripts of the MT reflect the discussions on the numbering of the Commandments as well. This is clear from two different cantillations, as Mordechai Breuer showed.[16] One of them considers 'I am the Lord your God...' as the first Commandment, while the second considers 'I am the Lord your God...' and 'You shall not have other Gods...' together as the first Commandment.

It is interesting to recall that Philo of Alexandria (*Dec.* 51) and Flavius Josephus (*Ant.* 3.90-92) considered the interdiction of making any idol (Exod. 20.4/Deut. 5.8) as the Second Commandment. Through their paraphrase, the Decalogue is divided as follows:

Philo:
1. The monarchical principle by which the world is governed.
2. Idols of stone and wood and images in general made by human hands

Josephus:
1. The first word teaches us that God is one and that he only must be worshiped.
2. The second commands us to make no image of any living creature for adoration.[17]

---

15. For an English translation, see Ernest G. Clarke, *Targum Pseudo-Jonathan: Deuteronomy* (The Aramaic Bible, 5B; Collegeville, MN: Liturgical Press, 1998), pp. 21-23.

16. Mordechai Breuer, 'Dividing the Decalogue into Verses and Commandments', in Segal and Levi (eds.), *The Ten Commandments*, pp. 291-330, esp. pp. 304-306.

17. For the Greek text and the translation, see F.H. Colson, *Philo in Ten Volumes with an English Translation. VII. De Decalogo, De specialibus legibus* (Cambridge, MA: Harvard University Press; London: Heinemann, 1984), pp. 30-31; H.StJ. Thackeray, *Josephus with an English Translation. VI. Jewish Antiquities, Books I–IV* (Cambridge, MA: Harvard University Press; London: Heinemann, 1957), pp. 360-61.

Philo and Josephus divide the second Commandment of the Targum into two parts and the first part ('you shall not have any other gods...': Exod. 20.3/Deut. 5.7) is included in the first Commandment.

Later in the Middle Ages, Abraham Ibn Ezra said that אנכי, 'I am the Lord your God...' (Exod. 20.2/Deut. 5.6), does not belong to the Decalogue. According to him, the first Commandment is לא יהיה לך, 'you shall not have any other gods...' (Exod. 20.3/Deut. 5.7).[18]

Thus there were differing opinions about the numbering of the Commandments of the Decalogue, and the targumic tradition reflects one of them. This is one of the aspects of the reception history of the Decalogue. The numbering of the Commandments still divides scholars and Churches.[19]

(3) Amongst targumic expansions of the Decalogue, one should mention the consequences of the violation of Commandments Six to Ten, the so-called second table. Such commentaries are lacking in *Targum Onqelos*. *Targum Neofiti* and *Targum Pseudo-Jonathan* explain those consequences as follows:

6. My people, Israelites, Do not be murderers...for it is because of murderers that the sword emerges upon the world.
7. My people Israelites, Do not be adulterers...for it is because of the sin of adulterers that death (pestilence: *Targ. Neof.* Deut.) emerges upon the world.
8. My people Israelites, Do not be thieves...for it is because of their sins that famine emerges upon the world.
9. My people Israelites, Do not carry yourselves as false witnesses...for it is because of the sins of false witnesses that clouds come forth but rain does not fall and that drought emerges upon the world (...that wild beasts attack the sons of men: *Targ. Neof.* Deut).
10. My people Israelites, Do not be covetous...for it is because of the sins of the covetous that kingdoms attack sons of men and covet their property to take them (and exile comes upon the world: some MSS).

It is interesting to observe that natural disasters such as lack of rain are amongst the direct consequences of violation of one of the Commandments of the Decalogue. The link between false witnesses and the lack of rain is to be understood as resulting from divine intervention, while sword, famine, death, war and exile result from human misbehavior.

Comparing the first and the second table in *Targum Neofiti* and *Targum Pseudo-Jonathan*, one observes that targumic expansions of the second

---

18. Ibn Ezra considers לא תחמוד (Exod. 20.17/Deut. 5.21) as containing two different Commandments. See Himbaza, *Le Décalogue et l'histoire du texte*, pp. 104-105.

19. Himbaza, *Le Décalogue et l'histoire du texte*, pp. 93-116.

table show a more parenetic character than those of the first table. To summarize, the reception history of the Decalogue in the targumic literature is characterized by discussion on many topics, such as the understanding of the Hebrew text, division in the Commandments and the varying consequences of their violation.

5. *Conclusion*

The sheer importance of the Decalogue has probably influenced its textual evolution and the proliferation of its interpretations. The textual evolution of the Decalogue is perceptible within Hebrew tradition,[20] but early translations extended the phenomenon. I summarize the effects of the reception history of the Decalogue through early translations in four points:

Understanding of the Hebrew Text
In 1984, Emanuel Tov wrote an article with the title: 'Did the Septuagint Translators Always Understand their Hebrew Text?'[21] If we were to ask this question about the Decalogue we would respond positively. The study of the Decalogue actually shows no ignorance amongst the translators and there are no conjectural translations. This observation is valid for translators of the Septuagint, Peshitta and Targums. The textual differences are not a result of misunderstanding by the translators.

The Hebrew Text Underlying the Translations
As far as the Hebrew text underlying the translations is concerned, one should not exclude the possibility that early translators could have received the Decalogue in different textual forms. In some cases, this is the best way of explaining textual differences. This applies particularly to the Greek Septuagint, since the Targums and Peshitta are closer to the MT. The reception history of the Decalogue may reflect an evolution of the Hebrew text before its translation.

Division
The numbering of the Commandments is one of the aspects of the Decalogue that has been discussed for a long time. This discussion is more frequent in targumic literature than in the Septuagint, while ancient manuscripts of the

---

20. The discovery of the Dead Sea Scrolls demonstrated that interpretations are also known within the ancient Hebrew textual tradition.
21. Emanuel Tov, 'Did the Septuagint Translators Always Understand their Hebrew Text?', in A. Pietersma and C.E. Cox (eds.), *De Septuaginta* (Festschrift J.W. Wevers; Mississuaga, Ontario: Benben Publications, 1984), pp. 53-70 (reprinted in Emanuel Tov, *The Greek and Hebrew Bible. Collected Essays on the Septuagint* [VTSup, 72; Leiden: E.J. Brill, 1999], pp. 203-18).

Peshitta do not exhibit a division of the Decalogue in the same manner. The layout and marginal notes of the Greek Vaticanus manuscript in Exodus 20 clearly reflect the discussion on the division of the Decalogue since here the Commandments are numbered. The climax of the discussion amongst different traditions is the identification of the First and Second Commandments. Interestingly, manuscripts of the Targums and the Septuagint are altogether in agreement with the division that became predominant in Judaism.[22]

Interpretations

The Septuagint, Peshitta and Targums are examples of textual witnesses in which early interpretations of the Decalogue are found. These interpretations may reflect discussions on the content of the Decalogue, how it should be understood as one code of laws in two versions and how the Commandments should be numbered. It has also been observed that, especially in targumic literature, other interpretations of the Decalogue deal with the consequences of violation of its Commandments. This kind of interpretation gives some Commandments of the Decalogue a parenetic character.

---

22. The case of MS B (Vaticanus) is astonishing since the ancient Christian tradition (Origen, *Homilies on Exodus VIII*, 2, and Augustine, *Sermons* VIII on the Old Testament and CCL on the Liturgical Seasons) adopted different divisions. For an English translation, see Origen, *Homilies on Genesis and Exodus* (trans. Ronald E. Heine; Washington, DC: Catholic University of America Press, 1982), p. 318; Augustine, *Sermons I* (The Works of Saint Augustine; trans. Edmund Hill, Brooklyn, NY: New City Press, 1990), p. 253, and *Sermons III* (The Works of Saint Augustine; trans. Edmund Hill; New Rochelle, NY: New City Press, 1993), p. 123.

The Decalogue in Pseudo-Phocylides and Syriac Menander: 'Unwritten Laws' or Decalogue Reception?

J. Cornelis de Vos

1. Introduction

1.1. The Issue at Stake

What we know as the second table of the Decalogue and what we know as wisdom literature both deal with universal wisdom. A formula such as 'you shall not kill' can emerge in either corpus without interdependence—and we have numerous examples.[1] Human life is a universal value, and the simplest means of expressing the defence of life is this apodictic prohibition on killing.[2] The other Commandments of the second table may be viewed similarly.

Many of the Commandments in the second table also occur in what are known as unwritten laws in classical Greek writings. When we read early Jewish wisdom literature and surmise that the Decalogue is quoted or alluded to, we must always ask whether this is really the case. The allusion may well be to a Greek unwritten law. Or possibly the author wants to refer to both corpuses, thus satisfying Jews and non-Jews or Hellenized Jews.

For the first table of the Decalogue, with its more particularistic commandments, distinguishing echoes in other texts is not so problematic. However, the first table is hardly referred to in early Jewish literature—or, incidentally, in the New Testament, which has more echoes of the second table. However, compared to the bulk of Jewish Second Temple literature, echoes of the Decalogue in early Jewish literature are rather marginal.[3]

---

1. See, for example, Aristotle, *Rhet.* 1.13.1373b2, where he deals with general or unwritten law and refers to Empedocles (*Aristotle, On Rhetoric: A Theory of Civic Discourse* [trans. George Alexander Kennedy; New York: Oxford University Press, 2nd edn, 2007]): 'And, as Empedocles says about not killing a living thing,

 'Tis not just for some and unjust for others,
 but the law for all, it extends without a break
 Through the wide-ruling ether and the boundless light.'

2. See, on the prohibition against killing, J. Cornelis de Vos and Hermut Löhr (eds.), *'You Shall Not Kill': The Prohibition of Killing in Ancient Religions and Cultures* (Supplements to the Journal of Ancient Judaism, 27; Göttingen: Vandenhoeck & Ruprecht 2018).

3. Ulrich Kellermann invented the term 'Dekalogschweigen' (Decalogue silence)

Before considering the principal question of what criteria we have for isolating Decalogue quotations and allusions, we have to deal with the unwritten laws.[4] What are unwritten laws? Unwritten laws are, simply put, laws that are not written. This statement is, however, misleadingly straightforward. First of all, we know that there was a concept of unwritten laws because they are referred to in Greek classical literature, and some have since been written down. Secondly, there are opposing concepts of unwritten laws. Thirdly, what does 'unwritten' mean? Does it mean that there is some sort of canon with laws that are deliberately not written down? Or do the unwritten laws simply comprise all the laws that do not happen to have been recorded?[5]

To begin with the second point: Aristotle had two concepts of unwritten laws—although, it must be said, he did not acknowledge this discrepancy.[6] In chap. 10 of the first book of *Rhetorica* he distinguishes specific law (ἴδιος νόμος) and common law (κοινὸς νόμος), and equates the unwritten law with the latter. The unwritten or general law consists of 'whatever...seems to be agreed to among all'.[7] In chap. 13 Aristotle again divides the law into specific and common law. He designates specific law as 'being what has been defined by each people in reference to themselves'.[8] However, he then subdivides the

---

for this; see his 'Der Dekalog in den Schriften des Frühjudentums: Ein Überblick', in Henning Graf Reventlow (ed.), *Weisheit, Ethos und Gebot: Weisheits- und Dekalogtraditionen in der Bibel und im frühen Judentum* (Biblisch-theologische Studien, 43; Neukirchen–Vluyn: Neukirchener Verlag, 2001), pp. 147-226 (169); cf. Frank-Lothar Hossfeld and Klaus Berger, 'Dekalog', in *Neues Bibel-Lexikon* (Zürich: Benziger Verlag, 1991), I, pp. 400-405 (402). This evaluation, however, is too radical—as Kellermann's very exposition of Decalogue echoes in early Jewish literature shows. There are plenty of Decalogue echoes in the Jewish literature of the Second Temple period—even more than those dealt with by Kellermann. The most obvious one can be found in 4 Macc. 2.5-6: 'The Law says: "You shall not covet the wife of your neighbour, nor that which belongs to your neighbour...".' Other references can be found in the works of, among others, Philo of Alexandria, Josephus, Pseudo-Philo, Jesus Sirach, Aristobulus, Pseudo-Aristeas, Pseudo-Phocylides, Pseudo-Orpheus (recension C), Pseudo-Menander or Syriac Menander, and Pseudo-Menander in the Dramatist Gnomologion. See my monograph *Rezeption und Wirkung des Dekalogs in jüdischen und christlichen Schriften bis 200 n.Chr.* (AJEC 95; Leiden: Brill, 2016).

4. For a detailed analysis of the concept of 'unwritten law' in antiquity, see Martin Ostwald, 'Was There a Concept of ἄγραφος νόμος in Classical Greece?', in Edward N. Lee, Alexander P.D. Mourelatos and Richard Porty (eds.), *Exegesis and Argument: Studies in Greek Philosophy* (Festschrift Gregory Vlastos; Assen: Van Gorcum, 1973), pp. 70-104.

5. Cf. also the discussion in Aristotle, *Rhet.* 1.13.1374a11-14.

6. See Ostwald, ἄγραφος νόμος, pp. 77-78. Kennedy (*Aristotle, On Rhetoric*, p. 102 n. 227) makes a conjecture in the text of *Rhet.* 1.13.1373b2 in order to avoid the contradiction of 1.10.1368b3.

7. Aristotle, *Rhet.* 1.10.1368b3.

8. Aristotle, *Rhet.* 1.13.1373b2.

specific laws into written and unwritten. Thus he restricts the unwritten laws to a fraction of the customs and traditions of a state, to that part that is not written down. The common law, in contrast, pertains to 'that which is based on nature; for there is in nature a common principle of the just and unjust'.[9]

This dichotomy demonstrates that Aristotle had both a more specific and a more universal concept of the unwritten laws;[10] something which can, similarly, be found in early Jewish writings, as I shall show.

1.2. Criteria for Distinguishing Decalogue Echoes

The principal question addressed here is whether criteria for distinguishing Decalogue reception in wisdom literature exist. The commonly accepted works on distinguishing scriptural echoes are those by Dietrich-Alex Koch and Richard B. Hays.[11] They both deal with the use of Scripture in the writings of Paul, but we can apply their criteria to other scriptural echoes as well.

In *Die Schrift als Zeuge* ('The Gospel as Testimony'), Koch differentiates four basic forms of scriptural intertextuality:[12] (1) quotation; (2) paraphrase; (3) allusion; and (4) use of biblical language. A quotation is, according to Koch, 'a conscious transfer of a foreign written (or, more rarely, oral) formulation...that an author has reproduced in his own work, that can be recognized as such'.[13]

Koch helpfully details the various forms of quotation. However, for our topic of Decalogue reception his analysis is less helpful. Where we encounter, for example, the phrase 'you shall not kill', it is clear that this is the same wording as in the Decalogue; it is, however, not at all clear that this is a *conscious* adoption of the Decalogue. For the other categories—paraphrase, allusion and biblical language—it is even more difficult to determine if a passage echoes the Decalogue or not. It is also possible for conscious adoption of the Decalogue not to be easily recognizable. The turn of phrase itself does not suffice to associate the passage with the Decalogue.

---

9. Aristotle, *Rhet.* 1.13.1373b2. Further references at Ostwald, ἄγραφος νόμος, p. 72 n. 7.

10. As Ostwald has demonstrated, there were various concepts of unwritten law in Classical Greece (ἄγραφος νόμος, esp. pp. 99-104).

11. Dietrich-Alex Koch, *Die Schrift als Zeuge des Evangeliums: Untersuchungen zur Verwendung und zum Verständnis der Schrift bei Paulus* (BHT, 69; Tübingen: J.C.B. Mohr [Paul Siebeck], 1986); Richard B. Hays, *Echoes of Scripture in the Letters of Paul* (New Haven: Yale University Press, 1989).

12. Koch, *Die Schrift als Zeuge*, pp. 10-24.

13. '[Eine] bewußte Übernahme einer fremden schriftlichen (seltener: mündlichen) Formulierung...die von einem Verfasser in seiner eigenen Schrift reproduziert wird und als solche erkennbar ist' (Koch, *Die Schrift als Zeuge*, p. 11).

More useful for the discussion at hand are the seven criteria developed by Hays.[14] They are: (1) *Availability*: 'Was the proposed source of the echo available to the author and/or original readers?'[15] (2) *Volume*: Hays does not clearly define this concept. He generally uses it to refer to the degree of reception of the pre-text, on the one hand, and to the importance and distinctiveness of the pre-text and its echo in this individual context, on the other. (3) *Recurrence*: how often do words, verses, or longer units from a pre-text recur in the receiving text? (4) *Thematic coherence*: 'How well does the alleged echo fit into the line of argument…?'[16] (5) *Historical plausibility*: is the intended effect of the echo historically plausible for the one who employs the echo, and could the readers or hearers have understood it? (6) *History of interpretation*: 'Have other readers, both critical and pre-critical, heard the same echoes?'[17] This requires further discussion, into which I shall not enter here. The last criterion, (7) *Satisfaction*, poses the question: is the intertextual relation satisfactory for the modern reader? This is a rather subjective category, but of no less importance than the others, owing to the difficulty in determining and quantifying intertextual relationships.

2. *The Decalogue in Two Early Jewish Writings*

Everything I have written so far appears to be more or less self-evident. Therefore I would like to give two examples from early Jewish wisdom literature, the sentences of Pseudo-Phocylides and the sentences of Pseudo- or Syriac Menander. In the case of Pseudo-Phocylides it seems to be quite clear that he[18] is alluding to the Decalogue, although the fact that we must go beyond Koch and Hays to prove it makes this a good test case. Isolating echoes of the Decalogue in the sentences of Pseudo-Menander is far more complicated—if it is possible at all. Judging whether or not the Decalogue is rendered can only be done using circumstantial evidence, as if in a court of law. Hays's criteria help us in that. But, in addition to using his criteria, we have to work through the thoughts and methods of an author of Jewish wisdom whom we suspect may have used the Decalogue. If the circumstances speak more for non-dependence than for dependence on the Decalogue, then 'the accused is discharged'.

---

14. Hays, *Echoes of Scripture*, pp. 29-32.
15. Hays, *Echoes of Scripture*, p. 29.
16. Hays, *Echoes of Scripture*, p. 30.
17. Hays, *Echoes of Scripture*, p. 31.
18. Pseudo-Phocylides was a male; see, for example, *Ps.-Phoc.* 2: Φωκυλίδης ἀνδρῶν ὁ σοφώτατος (although ἀνδρῶν instead of ἀνθρώπων could be due to the poetic form of the sentences); besides, teaching wisdom in (early) Judaism was most often reserved to men. Also the Syriac Menander was male; see, for example, v. 246.

2.1. Pseudo-Phocylides: A Clear Example of Decalogue Reception

An unknown author has bequeathed to us a compilation of gnomic sentences in hexameters. He pretends to be the famous poet Phocylides of Miletus from the sixth century BCE. In reality, according to the *communis opinio*, the author was a Jew who lived between 50 BCE and 50 CE. The sentences of this Pseudo-Phocylides resemble the traditional biblical wisdom found in Proverbs, Sirach and the Wisdom of Solomon.[19]

Immediately after the prologue of his compilation (vv. 1-2), a subsequent section of text reminds us strongly of the Decalogue:

Pseudo-Phocylides 3-8[20]	Exod. 20.2-17; Deut. 5.6-21	
3	Μήτε γαμοκλοπέειν, μήτ' ἄρσενα Κύπριν ὀρίνειν,	οὐ μοιχεύσεις.	20.13 5.17
	Commit not adultery nor rouse homosexual passion,	You shall not commit adultery.	
4	μήτε δόλους ῥάπτειν, μήθ' αἵματι χεῖρα μιαίνειν.	οὐ φονεύσεις.	20.15 5.18
	stitch not wiles together nor stain your hands with blood.	You shall not murder.	
5	Μὴ πλουτεῖν ἀδίκως, ἀλλ' ἐξ ὁσίων βιοτεύειν.	οὐ κλέψεις.	20.14 5.19
	Do not become unjustly rich, but live from honourable means.	You shall not steal.	
6	Ἀρκεῖσθαι παρ' ἑοῖσι καὶ ἀλλοτρίων ἀπέχεσθαι.	οὐκ ἐπιθυμήσεις τὴν γυναῖκα τοῦ πλησίον σου ...	20.17 5.21
	Be content with what you have and abstain from what is another's.	You shall not covet your neighbour's wife ...	

---

19. See, for introductory questions, Pascale Derron (ed.), *Les Sentences du Pseudo-Phocylide: Texte, traduction, commentaire* (Collection des universités de France; Paris: Les Belles Lettres, 1986), pp. vii-cxvi; Pieter Willem van der Horst, *The Sentences of Pseudo-Phocylides: With Introduction and Commentary* (SVTP, 4; Leiden: E.J. Brill, 1978), pp. 55-83; idem, 'Pseudo-Phocylides', in *OTP*, II, pp. 565-82; Max Küchler, *Frühjüdische Weisheitstraditionen: Zum Fortgang weisheitlichen Denkens im Bereich des frühjüdischen Jahweglaubens* (OBO, 26; Freiburg: Universitätsverlag, 1979), pp. 301-18; Johannes Thomas, *Der jüdische Phokylides: Formgeschichtliche Zugänge zu Pseudo-Phokylides und Vergleich mit der neutestamentlichen Paränese* (NTOA, 23; Freiburg: Universitätsverlag, 1992), pp. 1-22; Nikolaus Walter, 'Poetische Schriften: Pseudepigraphische jüdisch-griechische Dichtung: Pseudo-Phokylides, Pseudo-Orpheus, Gefälschte Verse auf Namen griechischer Dichter', in Hermann Lichtenberger (ed.), *Jüdische Schriften aus hellenistisch-römischer Zeit*, IV/3 (Gütersloh: Gütersloher Verlagshaus, 1983), pp. 182-96; Walter T. Wilson, *The Sentences of Pseudo-Phocylides* (Commentaries on Early Jewish Literature; Berlin: W. de Gruyter, 2005), pp. 3-41.

20. Text: Derron (ed.), *Les Sentences du Pseudo-Phocylide*; trans: van der Horst, *The Sentences of Pseudo-Phocylides*.

7	ψεύδεα μὴ βάειν, τὰ δ' ἐτήτυμα πάντ' ἀγορεύειν.	οὐ ψευδομαρτυρήσεις κατὰ τοῦ πλησίον σου μαρτυρίαν ψευδῆ.	20.16 5.20
	Tell not lies, but speak always the truth.	You shall not bear false witness against your neighbour.	
8	Πρῶτα θεὸν τιμᾶν, μετέπειτα δὲ σεῖο γονῆας.	[20.2-11; 5.6–15] [20.12; 5.16]	
	Honour God first and foremost, and thereafter your parents.		

The thematic similarity to the Decalogue in these verses of Pseudo-Phocylides is clear. It is also obvious that there are a few dissimilarities as well. I begin with the dissimilarities:

- No single word in these verses, apart from conjunctions and prepositions, matches a word from the Decalogue.
- Pseudo-Phocylides uses the stylistic device of the *parallellismus membrorum* for the Decalogue Commandments of the second table.
- The order in Pseudo-Phocylides is different from that in the Decalogue in three cases:
    o The first three verses (3-5) have the order adultery–murder–theft, deviating from the order in the Hebrew versions of the Decalogue.
    o The prohibition on coveting appears before the prohibition on lying, which differs from the Decalogue.[21]
    o The first table comes after the second. In other words, to honour God appears after the ethical Commandments, and the same applies to the Commandment to honour one's parents.
- In v. 8 the first part of the Decalogue is summarized, whereas in the preceding verses, except for v. 6, every Commandment is dealt with in more detail.
- A closer look at both texts reveals that the themes do not match exactly, or even slightly, and that there are additional items to those found in the Decalogue (prohibitions on homosexuality and on unjust wealth).

Despite the dissimilarities, I consider this text to be a clear allusion to the Decalogue; in Hays's terms, the volume of the echo is very high. All the differences can be explained by the form of the compilation and by its intention. Putting myself in the position of the author of the verses: how would I process the Decalogue?

---

21. In fact, the Decalogue Commandment is not about lying, but about false witness. On the theme of lying in the Jewish tradition see David Gregory Monaco, *The Sentences of the Syriac Menander: Introduction, Text and Translation, and Commentary* (Gorgias Studies in Classical and Late Antiquity; Piscataway, NJ: Gorgias Press, 2013), pp. 140-41.

To begin with the *form*: the sentences of Pseudo-Phocylides are written in hexameters. This explains many deviations from the wording of the Decalogue. How could the author express 'you shall not commit adultery' in his own poetic style? Οὐ μοιχεύσεις did not suffice for a hexameter.[22] Therefore he used μῆτε γᾰ|μο̄κλο̄πε̆|ε̄ιν, literally 'do not steal matrimony', to fill half of his hexameter. This is a satisfactory and suitable equivalent to 'you shall not commit adultery'. Then he added the phrase μῆτ' | ᾱρσε̆νᾰ | Κῡπρῐν ο̆|ρτῠνε̆ῑν in order to complete his hexameter. Considering this, the shape of the remaining verses becomes clear. The author had to expand the short commandments and, conversely, shorten the rather long prohibition on coveting the neighbour's wife, house and so on.

Now to the *themes*: although there is no correspondence between the individual words used, the question is whether there is a thematic correspondence between the sentences of Pseudo-Phocylides and the Decalogue. As already pointed out, γαμοκλοπέειν in the first half of v. 3 is a satisfying equivalent for μοιχεύειν. However, the parallel in the second half of the verse, with its prohibition on arousing homosexual passion, expresses a completely different idea: an idea that does not occur in the Decalogue. Why did the author add this? First of all, more content was needed for his hexameter; it is worth noting that each Commandment of the second table has its own hexameter. Secondly—and now I come to the point of transculturation—there is an obvious intention of placing the arousing of homosexual passion in the same category as adultery for the audience. This audience probably consisted of non-Jews from the Hellenistic–Roman world. In this world homosexuality was more accepted than among Jews, although definitely not by all.[23] For Pseudo-Phocylides, as a Jew, it was a serious problem. He tried to convince his audience by means of transculturation, first by using the name Phocylides and secondly by using the metonym Κύπρις from Hellenistic imagery to denounce 'love'. For Pseudo-Phocylides the only permissible sexual relationship was that between husband and wife and—as becomes clear later in his compilation—the only legitimization of sex was procreation (vv. 175-206, esp. 175). Moreover in other early Jewish writings adultery is linked with homosexuality or, in general, with sexual behaviour considered to be abnormal.[24] For us it is very

---

22. It is too short and has four long syllables. As Pseudo-Phocylides liked the infinitive in order to express a commandment, he could have written μήτε μοιχεύειν or μήτε μοιχευέειν. For the so-called imperatival infinitive, which occurs throughout in vv. 3-8 and also elsewhere in *Pseudo-Phocylides*, see Küchler, *Frühjüdische Weisheitstraditionen*, pp. 266-70, esp. 270. However, this did not yield enough syllables either and also has too many long syllables.

23. See the literature in Wilson, *The Sentences*, pp. 79-80 n. 25.

24. See the references in Wilson, *The Sentences*, 79. See below for the role of Lev. 18–20 in this tradition.

interesting that Pseudo-Phocylides—as well as Philo and Josephus[25]—used the Decalogue to inculcate this additional prohibition.

The syntactical relationship between the two stances, and therefore between the prohibition of adultery and that of homosexual relations, is not directly clear. Is it synonymous, synthetic, antithetic or climactic? In the first two instances we actually have one prohibition; in the two last instances we have two prohibitions. The other hexameters do not help us to determine a scheme in the relationship between the two halves of each verse. Verse 4 seems to consist of synonymic parallels, v. 5 of antithetic parallels and v. 6 of synthetic parallels, while v. 7 returns to antithetic parallels. Another possibility is the relationship of general to specific. It is possible that Pseudo-Phocylides worked just like Philo of Alexandria, who used the Commandments of the Decalogue as general headings and subsumed all the other prescriptions of the Bible as specific laws.[26] Pseudo-Phocylides would, then, start with the general prohibition of adultery and add the specific prohibition of homosexuality. This only applies for v. 3a compared to 3b with its additional prohibition. However, all the items in this summary of the Decalogue return in the remaining parts of the compilation.[27] *Pseudo-Phocylides* 3-8 functions as a *propositio* that presents the themes of the consecutive text, functioning as a *probatio*.[28] In terms of the status of the Decalogue, and irrespective of the relationship of the parallels in the *parallellismus membrorum*, this means that it is some sort of constitution for all the moral advice that follows.

What about the deviation in order in *Ps.-Phoc.* 3-8? The sequence adultery–murder–theft in the first three verses (3-5) is different from the Masoretic versions of, respectively, Exod. 20.13-15 and Deut. 5.17-19; they both read murder–adultery–theft. However, *Ps.-Phoc.* 3-5 is in alignment with the Septuagint version of Deut. 5.17-19.[29] Moreover, it could even be inappropriate to speak about a deviating order, for the sequence of the short commandments seems to be rather fluid in antiquity. Four of the six possible sequences occur in the testimonies.[30]

---

25. Wilson (*The Sentences*, p. 79, n. 23) refers to Philo, *Hypothetica* 7.1; cf. *Abr.* 135-36; *Spec. leg.* 2.50; and Josephus, *Apion* 2.199, 215; cf. 201.

26. See Yehoshua Amir, 'The Decalogue according to Philo', in Ben-Zion Segal and Gershon Levi (eds.), *The Ten Commandments in History and Tradition* (Publications of the Perry Foundation for Biblical Research; Jerusalem: Magnes Press, 1990), pp. 121-60.

27. See the list in Wilson, *The Sentences*, p. 77: *Ps.-Phoc.* 3: cf. 67, 177-82, 190-91, 213-14; 4: cf. 32-34, 57-58; 5: cf. 42-47, 61-62; 6: cf. 18, 70-74, 135-36, 154; 7: cf. 12, 16-17, 48-50, 8: cf. 53-54, 106, 111, 179-80, 220-22.

28. For the designations *propositio* and *probatio* see Wilson, *The Sentences*, pp. 76-77.

29. The corresponding text in Exod. 20.13-15 has the order adultery–theft–murder; see n. 30 below.

30. (1) *Murder–adultery–theft*: Exod. Masoretic Text (MT), Vetus Latina (VL); Deut. MT, VL; Josephus, *Ant.* 3.92; *Apoc. Abr.* 24.4-6; Mt. 19.18; Mk 10.19; (2) *murder–theft–adultery*:

That the author should alter the order between the prohibition of lying and of coveting has an inner logic. He connected the Commandment not to steal with the Commandment not to covet, which he altered to make it a Commandment to be self-sufficient 'and to abstain from what is another's'. Such a disposition safeguards against the temptation to steal and to covet.[31] By connecting not lying with honouring God and parents, Pseudo-Phocylides stressed the veracity of this honour.

How to explain the reversal of the tables? To honour God and to honour one's parents summarizes the first table and appears after the ethical commandments.[32] It is likely that in the early Jewish period the Commandment to honour one's parents was thought to belong to the first table. Philo of Alexandria amply explains that parents recreate God's creation by procreating children (*Dec.* 106-20). In his view, parents are God-like and that is why they belong to the first table.[33] The outline of the summary of the Decalogue in *Pseudo-Phocylides* would also sustain this hypothesis—although it must be noted that this is a circular argument.

The whole compilation begins with the words 'These counsels of God by His holy judgments Phocylides the wisest of men sets forth, gifts of blessing' (*Ps-Phoc.* 1-2). Pseudo-Phocylides aims to give βουλεύματα, 'counsels'. These counsels are as moral in nature as the content of the compilation.[34] This is the reason why Pseudo-Phocylides begins immediately—after the prologue—with the counsels.

---

no testimony; (3) *adultery–murder–theft*: Nash Papyrus; Deut. LXX; Philo, *Rer. div. her.* 173; *Dec.* 36, 51; *Ps.-Phoc.* 3-5; Lk. 18.20; Rom. 13.9; cf. *LAB* 11.10-13 and Jas 2.11 which have the order adultery–murder; (4) *adultery–theft–murder*: Exod. LXX; *Ps.-Men.* 9-10; (5) *theft–murder–adultery*: *LAB* 44.6, 7; (6) *theft–adultery–murder*: no testimony.

31. See Wilson, *The Sentences*, pp. 80-81 (81).

32. See, for the Commandment to honour one's parents in the sentences of Pseudo-Phocylides, Harry Jungbauer, '*Ehre Vater und Mutter*': *Der Weg des Elterngebots in der biblischen Tradition* (WUNT 2/146; Tübingen: Mohr Siebeck, 2002), pp. 212-16.

33. However, as I said, this is likely, but not certain. Philo of Alexandria liked symmetry, and that could have been the reason for his dividing the tables of the Decalogue into two sets of five (*Dec.* 50–51). Whether or not the Commandment to honour one's parents belonged to the first table, the fact remains that the first part of the Decalogue appears after the second part in *Pseudo-Phocylides*; see further Jungbauer, '*Ehre Vater und Mutter*', pp. 217-30.

34. Also the last two verses show that the compilation deals with moral issues. They say: 'These are the mysteries of righteousness (δικαιοσύνης μυστήρια); living thus may you live out a good life, right up to the threshold of old age' (*Ps.-Phoc.* 229-30). Verses 1-2 together with 229-30 form the so-called σφραγίς of the composition; see van der Horst, *The Sentences of Pseudo-Phocylides*, pp. 107, 109-10, 260; Walter T. Wilson, *The Mysteries of Righteousness: The Literary Composition and Genre of the Sentences of Pseudo-Phocylides* (Texts and Studies in Ancient Judaism, 40; Tübingen: J.C.B. Mohr [Paul Siebeck], 1994), pp. 146-77, and his *The Sentences*, pp. 68-69.

The author summarized the commandments in relation to God because they are the most specific. Doing otherwise would have betrayed his Jewishness and hindered his intended persuasive effect on non-Jews.[35] Incidentally, this could also be the reason that Pseudo-Phocylides did not immediately begin his compilation with a sentence about God. The combination of reverence for God and for parents does not only occur in Jewish wisdom literature but also in the so-called unwritten laws.[36] Additionally, it is one of the most frequently occurring formulations.[37] Thus, the Jew Pseudo-Phocylides manages also here to connect with Greek-Hellenistic traditional items.

To turn to the criteria of Hays:

- *Availability*: for Pseudo-Phocylides, as a Jew, the Decalogue was surely available. Whether the same applies to his addressees cannot be confirmed, although it is not likely.
- *Volume*: there is a high degree of volume in the allusions of *Ps.-Phoc.* 3-8. Each verse refers to a Commandment from the Decalogue and the verses appear in a series. This volume, however, is not apparent for people who are not acquainted with the Decalogue.
- *Recurrence*: all the themes from the summary of the Decalogue recur in the compilation. This is not directly a recurrence of echoes; it is rather an unfolding of the themes addressed in and implied by the Decalogue Commandments.
- *Thematic coherence*: there is, certainly, thematic coherence. All the themes of vv. 3-8 that function as *propositio* recur in the remaining work.
- *Historical plausibility*: it is historically plausible that the author tried to inculcate Jewish morality into non-Jewish addressees—we have enough examples of that in the early Jewish literature.[38] It was important, however, that the addressees should not (and in all probability they would not) notice that this was a summary of the Jewish Decalogue.
- *Satisfaction*: yes.

---

35. See, among others, Wilson, *The Sentences*, p. 75.

36. See, for the connection between the two Commandments, Klaus Berger, *Die Gesetzesauslegung Jesu: Ihr historischer Hintergrund im Judentum und im Alten Testament*. I. *Markus und Parallelen* (WMANT, 40; Neukirchen–Vluyn: Neukirchener Verlag, 1972), pp. 284-87; Jungbauer, '*Ehre Vater und Mutter*', pp. 143-51; and Wilson, *The Sentences*, pp. 82-83.

37. See the examples in Küchler, *Frühjüdische Weisheitstraditionen*, pp. 244-45; Wilson, *The Sentences*, 75-76.

38. Examples would be Josephus, Philo of Alexandria, Aristobulus, Pseudo-Aristeas, *Joseph and Aseneth*. This does not exclude the possibility that the works could also be meant as an internal corroboration for Jews.

Nevertheless, we have to add two further specifications, both relating to the volume criterion. Looking first at the matter of form, we must consider that poetic form introduces its own complications into the question of scriptural echoes. Secondly, we must consider the matter of pseudonymity. How do we appraise the disguising of scriptural references and an extensive degree of transculturation?

2.2. *Syriac Menander: A Questionable Example of Decalogue Reception*

Now, I come to my second example. Some verses in the sentences of the Syriac or Pseudo-Menander could be taken as echoes of the Decalogue.[39] Before we consider these verses, I would like to say something about the Syriac Menander himself. Just like Pseudo-Phocylides, Syriac Menander offers a compilation of wisdom sentences. Effectively, all we know for sure is that a person under the name of Menander wrote poetic wisdom sentences, and that we have a text in Syriac.[40] The remaining introductory questions are very hard to answer.

- *Author*: who was Menander? It is agreed that this was not the famous poet Menander from the fourth/third century BCE.[41] About this Pseudo-Menander we know hardly anything. We only know him through his sentences.
- *Date*: wisdom is hard to date, but there are some hints that point to the period between 150 and 400 CE. This is not a very precise dating. Most scholars are in favour of a dating in the third century CE.[42]
- *Provenance*: actually, we do not know. Egypt or, more specifically, Alexandria could have been the place where the florilegium was composed. If the sentences were originally written in Greek, then a misunderstanding of νομός, '[Egyptian] district', as νόμος, 'law', could have led to the Syriac translation *pwsqnk* in *Syr. Men.* 365.[43]

---

39. There is another Pseudo-Menander; see H. Attridge, 'Fragments of Pseudo-Greek Poets', in *OTP*, II, pp. 821-30 (829-30).

40. Syriac text in Jan P.N. Land (ed.), *Anecdota syriaca*, I (Leiden: E.J. Brill, 1862), pp. 64-73; additions and corrections in William Wright, 'Anecdota syriaca', *Journal of Sacred Literature and Biblical Record* 3 (1863), pp. 115-30; and Jan P.N. Land (ed.), *Anecdota syriaca*, II (Leiden: E.J. Brill, 1868), pp. 17-19, 25-26. See, on the edition of Land, Küchler, *Frühjüdische Weisheitstraditionen*, pp. 304-305 (cf. 303-18). See also the recent work of Monaco (*The Sentences of the Syriac Menander*). Further introduction to *Syriac Menander* at T. Baarda, 'The Sentences of the Syriac Menander', in *OTP*, II, pp. 583-90 (584-85).

41. See, for the sentences of the 'classical' Menander, the edition and translation of Carlo Pernigotti (*Menandri Sententiae* [Studi e testi per il Corpus dei papiri filosofici greci e latini, 15; Florence: Olschki, 2008]).

42. Küchler, *Frühjüdische Weisheitstraditionen*, p. 316; Baarda, 'The Sentences of the Syriac Menander', pp. 584-85.

43. Thus Jean-Paul Audet, 'La sagesse de Ménandre l'Egyptien', *RB* 59 (1952), pp.

— *Original language*: this is also unknown. Was it Syriac, Aramaic, Greek or Hebrew?[44] The argument above about a possible mistranslation from Greek into Syriac suggests that Greek must have been the original language—this, however, is no more than a possibility, and the argument is obviously circular.

Having said this, there is a relative consensus that the text stems from the third century CE, possibly from Egypt or Alexandria, and that it was originally written in Greek.[45]

One important question remains: was Pseudo-Menander Jewish or non-Jewish?[46] The answer depends on our judgment of the content of the sentences. And, of course, with respect to a possible allusion to the Decalogue in his work we have—again—a circular argument. If we suppose him to be Jewish, it is more probable that he alluded to the Decalogue than if we think he was not. There are many parallels in the Jewish wisdom books, Proverbs, Sirach and the sentences of Pseudo-Phocylides which make it likely that the Syriac Menander was Jewish as well.[47] But the parallels could equally refer to pagan wisdom and not to 'genuine' Jewish wisdom.[48] And there are also parallels with the sentences of the authentic Menander.[49]

It holds true that wisdom is, in general, a universal phenomenon. That is why it is hard to attribute wisdom to specific groups or denominations. Throughout his work Pseudo-Menander displays a monotheistic attitude which speaks in favour of his being Jewish. He also often writes about the reverence that humans owe to the one God. However, he could equally have been Christian, a God-fearer, or even a Hellenist who was sympathetic to

---

55-81 (73 n. 1). Audet's argument (p. 77) that 'water' in *Syr. Men.* 3 also points to Egypt is rather unconvincing, as Küchler (*Frühjüdische Weisheitstraditionen*, p. 316) and Baarda ('The Sentences of the Syriac Menander', p. 585) rightly comment. For critique on the νομός–νόμος argument see Monaco, *The Sentences of the Syriac Menander*, pp. 26-28, especially p. 28.

44. Baarda, 'The Sentences of the Syriac Menander', p. 584. Audet ('La sagesse de Ménandre', p. 73 n. 1) and Küchler (*Frühjüdische Weisheitstraditionen*, p. 316) opt for Greek as the original language.

45. See, however, Monaco (*The Sentences of the Syriac Menander*, pp. 26-42), who defends Edessa as provenance and Syriac as the original language.

46. Arguments in Küchler, *Frühjüdische Weisheitstraditionen*, pp. 313-14, 317-18; and Baarda, 'The Sentences of the Syriac Menander', pp. 587-89.

47. Thus, Monaco, *The Sentences of the Syriac Menander*, pp. 49-57.

48. Baarda, 'The Sentences of the Syriac Menander', pp. 586-87.

49. See the lists with parallels to biblical and so-called pagan literature at Yury Arzhanov, 'Quellen und Gesamtkonzeption der syrischen Menander-Sentenzen', *Simvol* 56 (2010), 340-62 [Russian; German translation: http://rub.academia.edu/YuryArzhanov/Papers/1210776/Beobachtungen_zu_den_Menander-Sentenzen_in_syrischen_Spruchsammlungen (accessed 17 September 2012)].

monotheism. In contrast, *Syr. Men.* 263-64 speaks about gods in the plural, but this could merely be a reference to a local cult. Nevertheless, taking all the clues provided in the text together, it is more likely that the author was Jewish than that he was not.[50]

In vv. 9 and 10 we encounter the combination 'Fear God, and honour [your] father and mother'.[51] This combination resembles the one in *Pseudo-Phocylides* 8.[52] Just as in Pseudo-Phocylides, this could be a summary of the first table. However, in the lines preceding vv. 9-10, Pseudo-Menander praises productivity and procreation (*Syr. Men.* 2-8). In the lines following our verses, Pseudo-Menander exhorts his addressees to honour those who are before them, that is, people who are older than them (*Syr. Men.* 11-14). Within this context, 'fear God, and honour [your] father and mother' means in paraphrase: fear God, who is the cause and at the beginning of all; honour your parents, who are the cause and at the beginning of yourself. *Syr. Men.* 9-10 is concerned with the acknowledgment of all who are prior. In line 13, indeed, Pseudo-Menander says it explicitly: 'Honour him who is older than you'.[53] This is of no concern for the Decalogue in its original meaning. The Commandment to honour one's parents (Exod. 20.12; Deut. 5.16) related in its initial setting to securing the livelihood of elderly parents by their children.[54] But, of course, the interpretation of Pseudo-Menander could reflect a contemporaneous understanding of this Commandment. Both references to that which is earlier or those who are older[55] as well as the combination of reverence for God and parents frequently occur in the unwritten laws, as already stated.

Nevertheless, Pseudo-Menander could be alluding to the Decalogue, or could be *also* alluding to the Decalogue. After the verses about parents, the admonition 'you shall not murder' appears (*Syr. Men.* 15), following

---

50. With Baarda, 'The Sentences of the Syriac Menander', p. 589.

51. The verse numbering is from Baarda ('The Sentences of the Syriac Menander'), who lists divergent numberings in the margin. The translation leans on Baarda and on Friederich Schulthess, 'Die Sprüche des Menanders', *ZNW* 32 (1912), pp. 199-224. Schulthess translates *Syr. Men.* 9-10 with 'Vor allem sollst du Gott fürchten…' (p. 202). However, Baarda ('The Sentences of the Syriac Menander', p. 592) judges 'vor allem' ('especially') to belong to the preceding saying.

52. The difference from Pseudo-Phocylides is that the latter has the wording 'honour God' (θεὸν τιμᾶν; for this combination see Jungbauer, '*Ehre Vater und Mutter'*, pp. 143-51), whereas Pseudo-Menander has 'fear God' (*mn 'lw' lmdḥl*). The verb *dḥl* has, in collocation with 'God', in general the meaning 'to worship'; see Jessie Payne Smith (ed.), *A Compendious Syriac Dictionary: Founded upon the Thesaurus Syriacus of R. Payne Smith* (Eugene, OR: Wipf & Stock, 1999), pp. 88-89.

53. Cf. also the so-called epitome of Syriac Menander, 2-4.

54. Jungbauer, '*Ehre Vater und Mutter'*, pp. 80-87.

55. See the parallels at Baarda, 'The Sentences of the Syriac Menander', p. 592.

the same order as the Decalogue.⁵⁶ However, after 'you shall not murder' there are admonitions to honour one's parents again (*Syr. Men.* 20-24), which disrupt the order of the Decalogue. There are more reminiscences of Decalogue themes in *Syriac Menander*. To honour God recurs in *Syr. Men.* 123 and 361; to honour one's parents, in addition to vv. 20-24, in vv. 82-98, 211-12, 359 and 364-67 (cf. 345-46); the theme of adultery in vv. 45-46, 240-47 and 347-51; theft in vv. 51, 145-47, 154-56, 158, 248-49, 295-96; and false witness in v. 144. *Syr. Men.* 145-47, dealing with possessions and theft, could also be an allusion to the last Commandment of the Decalogue.⁵⁷ The theme of murder does not recur after vv. 15-19; however there is a warning against killing in v. 159. It is, thus, likely that all, or almost all, the Commandments of the Decalogue recur in *Syriac Menander*. Just as in the sentences of Pseudo-Phocylides, the first table is summarized by the double Commandment to fear or honour God and one's parents—the Commandment to honour one's parents probably belonged to the first table in the Second Temple period, as previously stated. However, it is obvious that there is no clear Decalogue structure.⁵⁸ In contrast with Pseudo-Phocylides, alleged allusions to the Decalogue are scattered all over the work of Pseudo-Menander. Additionally, the themes of adultery and theft reappear more than once.

Let us apply Hays's criteria to the sentences of the Syriac Menander in relation to Decalogue echoes:

— *Availability*: if Pseudo-Menander was a Jew, he was surely acquainted with the Decalogue; if he was not, he could have been acquainted with it.
— *Volume*: there are a couple of possible echoes of the Decalogue; however, there is no *series* of Decalogue echoes, and there is no clear Decalogue structure.
— *Recurrence*: all the themes of the Decalogue echoes recur in the compilation.
— *Thematic coherence*: Syriac Menander deals with moral sentences which are more or less clustered. The thematic coherence lies in the morality that connects the second table of the Decalogue with his work.

---

56. Thus Berger, *Die Gesetzesauslegung Jesu*, p. 306. He points to a traditional connection with Gen. 9.6. This means that the punishment for bloodshed is the death penalty (*Syr. Men.* 18-19).

57. See especially the list of themes in Pseudo-Menander in Küchler, *Frühjüdische Weisheitstraditionen*, pp. 307-308.

58. Berger, *Die Gesetzesauslegung Jesu*, pp. 265-66, simply postulates, without further discussion, that *Syriac Menander* does not allude to the Decalogue.

- *Historical plausibility*: we do not know. As with respect to Pseudo-Phocylides, the hearers/readers would probably not identify Pseudo-Menander as a Jew—if he was a Jew.
- *Satisfaction*: Barely.

We may now change our assumptions and suppose that Pseudo-Menander was a Jew and wanted to capture the Decalogue in his wisdom compilation for non-Jews. As with Pseudo-Phocylides he would not want to betray his Jewishness. If we take the wording 'fear God and honour [your] father and mother' as a summary of the first table, then, as already said, all or almost all the Commandments of the Decalogue appear, spread broadly over the whole compilation. Is this likely? No, not really. The echoes of the Decalogue are too faint, and there are too many sections dealing with customary wisdom items such as eating and drinking; behaviour towards spouses, children, neighbours, rich and poor people; and coping with death.

Therefore, my guess is—and it is no more than a guess—that the Decalogue belonged to the cultural memory of Pseudo-Menander and of Jews in general in antiquity. It is very possible that Pseudo-Menander quoted from this tradition without directly pointing to the Decalogue. For him the prescriptions of the Decalogue were just as universal as the prescriptions of the unwritten laws, which is why he was able to merge them.

We know from other sources that the prescriptions of the Decalogue and other texts were conflated in antiquity. I shall go back a little before I return to the work of Pseudo-Menander. Already in the work of Pseudo-Phocylides we can observe a merging of the Decalogue with other traditions. Karl-Willem Niebuhr has shown that almost every verse of *Ps.-Phoc.* 3-8, the text we looked at, has counterparts in Leviticus 19; the only exception is v. 3b, which has parallels in Leviticus 18 and 20.[59] It is very possible that the two Decalogue versions coalesced with the Decalogue-like chapter of Lev. 19.[60] In turn, this amalgamated Decalogue (Exod. 20/Deut. 5/Lev. 19) was, via Lev. 19, connected with Leviticus 18 and 20. Both these latter chapters deal with sexual prescriptions, a theme that is very present in early Jewish writings, especially in wisdom literature. In many writings, every form of (what was seen as) abnormal sexual behaviour is condemned. Philo of Alexandria uses the Decalogue prohibitions on adultery and coveting one's neighbour's wife as a summary or heading under which to describe such behaviour in detail.[61] If we assume that Pseudo-Phocylides did the

---

59. Karl-Wilhelm Niebuhr, *Gesetz und Paränese: Katechismusartige Weisungsreihen in der frühjüdischen Literatur* (WUNT, 2/28; Tübingen: J.C.B. Mohr [Paul Siebeck], 1987), pp. 15-20.

60. Niebuhr, *Gesetz und Paränese*, 20. For Lev. 19 and 18 as a background to various verses in Pseudo-Phocylides, see Thomas, *Der jüdische Phokylides*, pp. 57-102, 161-70.

61. See, for example, Philo, *Dec.* 121-31, 168-69, and *Spec. leg.* 3.7-82.

same, we can understand why he connected the prohibition on adultery with the prohibition on homosexuality (*Ps.-Phoc.* 3) that can be found in Lev. 18.22 and 20.13. A further prominent theme in Leviticus 18–20 is respectful behaviour towards the parents (Lev. 19.3; 20.9), including many rules pertaining to sexual behaviour towards relatives of the father and / or the mother.

Did Pseudo-Menander also depend on this amalgamated Decalogue tradition? This is very possible. If he really was a Jew, the Decalogue belonged to his cultural memory and was at the same time the receptacle for prescriptions judged to be equally normative. That many of these sentences can also be found in the so-called unwritten laws presented a challenge to Jewish writers. They could either show that they, in fact, belonged to the Decalogue tradition (Pseudo-Phocylides, Philo of Alexandria)[62] or, in the case of Pseudo-Menander, merge the extended Decalogue with the Greek-Hellenistic unwritten laws. Pseudo-Menander used this amalgamated tradition without exactly knowing what came from where. The common denominator is that all the prescriptions were regarded as universal and apprehensible for all humans. Of course, this hypothesis must remain speculative as it cannot be proved, only surmised.

3. *Conclusions*

For Pseudo-Phocylides, and probably also for Pseudo-Menander, the Decalogue was so important that it was used to present Jewish wisdom in a Hellenistic disguise. In the work of Pseudo-Phocylides this is more or less explicit, and he clearly uses the wording of the Decalogue for his transculturation. In the work of Pseudo-Menander, the Decalogue seems to have gained the same status as universally apprehensible unwritten law and seems to belong to the author's cultural memory. In both works the 'written laws' are, in a somewhat Aristotelian way, the law of God for Jews of which the Decalogue is the summary and, at the same time, the unwritten universal law (κοινὸς νόμος) that they wanted to instil into their non-Jewish neighbours.

---

62. Philo of Alexandria even consciously begins his work *De decalogo* with a reference to the unwritten laws of which the Decalogue is only the written version (*Dec.* 1).

THE DECALOGUE IN THE NEW TESTAMENT APOCRYPHA: A PRELIMINARY OVERVIEW AND SOME EXAMPLES

Hermut Löhr

1. *The Importance of Asking about the Role of the Decalogue in Early Christianity*

The bibliography on the history of the Ten Words' reception in early Christianity is astonishingly small. While for the canon of the New Testament, at least, some overviews and detailed investigations can be mentioned,[1] the

---

1. Cf. Christoph Burchard, 'Nächstenliebegebot, Dekalog und Gesetz in Jak 2,8-11', in E. Blum *et al.* (eds.), *Die hebräische Bibel und ihre zweifache Nachgeschichte* (Festschrift R. Rendtorff; Neukirchen–Vluyn: Neukirchener Verlag, 1990), pp. 517-33; David Flusser, 'The Ten Commandments and the New Testament', in B.-Z. Segal and G. Levi (eds.), *The Ten Commandments in History and Tradition* (Jerusalem: Magnes Press, 1990), pp. 219-46; Reginald H. Fuller, 'The Decalogue in the New Testament', *Interpretation* 43 (1989), pp. 243-55; Jey J. Kanagaraj, 'The Implied Ethics of the Fourth Gospel', *TynBul* 52 (2001), pp. 33-60; Dan Lioy, *The Decalogue in the Sermon on the Mount* (Studies in Biblical Literature, 66; New York: Peter Lang, 2004); Hermut Löhr, 'Jesus and the Ten Words', in T. Holmén and S.E. Porter (eds.), *Handbook for the Study of the Historical Jesus*, IV (Leiden: E.J. Brill, 2011), pp. 3135-54; Lioy, 'Der Dekalog im frühesten Christentum und in seiner Umwelt', in W. Kinzig and C. Kück (eds.), *Judentum und Christentum zwischen Konfrontation und Faszination* (Judentum und Christentum, 11; Stuttgart: Kohlhammer, 2002), pp. 29-43; Gotthold Müller, 'Der Dekalog im Neuen Testament: Vor-Erwägungen zu einer unerledigten Aufgabe', *TZ* 38 (1982), pp. 79-97; Lidija Novakovic, 'The Decalogue in the New Testament', *Perspectives in Religious Studies* 35 (2008), pp. 373-86; Wilhelm Pratscher, 'Die Bedeutung des Dekalogs im Neuen Testament', *SNTU* 26 (2001), pp. 189-204; Dieter Sänger, 'Tora für die Völker—Weisungen der Liebe. Zur Rezeption des Dekalogs im frühen Judentum und Neuen Testament', in Henning Graf Reventlow (ed.), *Weisheit, Ethos und Gebot. Weisheits- und Dekalogtraditionen in der Bibel und im frühen Judentum* (Biblisch-theologische Studien, 43; Neukirchen–Vluyn: Neukirchener Verlag, 2001), pp. 97-146; Jan G. van der Watt, 'Radical Social Redefinition and Radical Love: Ethics and Ethos in the Gospel according to John', in his edited *Identity, Ethics, and Ethos in the New Testament* (BZNW, 141; Berlin: W. de Gruyter, 2006), pp. 107-34; van der Watt, 'Ethics and Ethos in the Gospel According to John', *ZNW* 97 (2006), pp. 147-76; Frederick E. Vokes, 'The Ten Commandments in the New Testament and in First Century Judaism', in F.L. Cross (ed.), *Studia evangelica V. Papers Presented to the Third International*

state of research is less satisfying with regard to early Christian literature outside the canon, especially aside from the texts of the early Church Fathers.[2] As far as I can see, there has been no thorough investigation of the history of the reception of the Decalogue in these texts until now.

But why should we ask about the reception of the Ten Words in early Christian literature? What insights do we expect to gain?

First, the quest for the role of the Decalogue in early Christianity is part of a broader investigation into the moral norms and standards of an emerging new religious group and confession. The fact that, according to common opinion, the Ten Words are of major importance in the history of Christian moral reflection and exhortation through the centuries encourages us to ask about their position at the *beginnings* of Christianity. Is early Christian moral thought generally structured by the Ten Words? How did early Christianity perceive the relation between the Decalogue and, for example, the Sermon on the Mount? What did the Christians of the first centuries think about the importance of the Decalogue for Jewish and Gentile followers of the new faith respectively?

These questions already suggest a further aspect of the subject chosen: the use of the Decalogue, while basically a proof of the close relation between emerging Christianity and Judaism, could in fact signal sharp differences with regard to the importance of the Torah in its entirety for religious and moral orientation among Jews and Christians. In this respect, the selection and relevance of single commandments (or series of commandments) from the Decalogue may point to underlying religious beliefs and theological ideas.

In fact, a textual detail such as how the author or enunciator of the Decalogue is indicated (for example in the context of quotations from the text itself) can be revealing with regard to the implied theology or Christology

---

Congress on New Testament Studies Held at Christ Church, Oxford, 1965. II. *The New Testament Message* (TU, 103; Berlin: Akademie Verlag, 1968), pp. 146-54. Parts of this bibliography and that provided in n. 2 below were prepared in a project on the reception history of the Decalogue in Judaism and early Christianity (first and second century CE) at the University of Münster.

2. Cf. Guy Bourgeault, *Décalogue et morale chrétienne. Enquête patristique sur l'utilisation et l'interprétation chrétienne du décalogue de c. 60 à c. 220* (Recherches publiées par les Facultés de la Compagnie de Jésus à Montréal, 2; Paris: Desclée, 1971); Rémi Gounelle (ed.), *Le décalogue au miroir des Pères* (Cahiers de Biblia Patristica, 9; Strasbourg: Centre d'analyse et de documentation patristiques, 2008); Robert M. Grant, 'The Decalogue in Early Christianity', *HTR* 40 (1947), pp. 1-17; Miguel Lluch-Baixauli, 'La interpretación de Orígenes al decálogo', *Scripta theologica* 30 (1998), pp. 87-109; Willy Rordorf, 'Beobachtungen zum Gebrauch des Dekalogs in der vorkonstantinischen Kirche', in W.C. Weinrich (ed.), *The New Testament Age: Essays in Honor of Bo Reicke*, II (Macon, GA: Mercer University Press, 1984), pp. 431-42.

of the text. Via the Decalogue, early Christian documents tried to express the new faith within a traditional Jewish frame: one God of the Old and the New Testament; one God incarnate in Jesus Christ.

Going further, some of the texts not only associate God or Jesus Christ with the proclamation of the Decalogue, but also present human beings from the recent past—that is, Christians or, more precisely, Jews who had converted to Christianity—proclaiming the Ten Words or parts of them. It would be more to the point to speak in the singular: the extant witnesses attribute the task of proclaiming the Ten Words in Christian mission almost exclusively to Peter. The importance of Peter is evident already from the New Testament writings.[3] He was probably one of the first followers of Jesus, perhaps the spokesman of the disciples and, almost certainly, one of the leaders of the first community in Jerusalem. However, the motif of Peter proclaiming a Christianized Torah is a later development and may have contributed to the literary and iconographic type of *traditio legis*, the presentation of a written law by Jesus to Peter.[4]

2. *Some Remarks on the 'New Testament Apocrypha'*

The so-called 'New Testament Apocrypha' do not form a historically defined corpus or canon of texts. While the notion of Christian apocryphal writings goes back well into the patristic period,[5] even today no consensus exists on the exact delimitation of the category and its contents. And, indeed, the texts categorized as New Testament Apocrypha stem from different times and regions; it is currently a matter of debate whether the designation *New Testament* Apocrypha, with its explicit reference to and distinction from the canonical texts, is justified in historical (to be distinguished from *theological*) terms. Some propose to change the designation to 'early Christian', 'altkirchliche' or 'antike christliche'[6] Apocrypha, thus loosening the connection to the New Testament canon (which, however, still persists in

---

3. Cf. Martin Hengel, *Der unterschätzte Petrus. Zwei Studien* (Tübingen: Mohr Siebeck, 2nd edn, 2007).

4. Cf. Klaus Berger, 'Der traditionsgeschichtliche Ursprung der "Traditio Legis"', *VC* 27 (1973), pp. 104-22, for the literary tradition. For the iconography, cf. Mikael Bøgh Rasmussen, '*Traditio Legis*—Bedeutung und Kontext', *Acta hyperborea* 8 (2001), pp. 21-52; Walter N. Schumacher, 'Traditio legis', in *Lexikon der christlichen Ikonographie*, IV (repr., Freiburg: Herder, 1994), cols. 347-51.

5. Cf. Wilhelm Schneemelcher, 'Die Begriffe: Kanon, Testament, Apokryph', in W. Schneemelcher (ed.), *Neutestamentliche Apokryphen in deutscher Übersetzung*, I (Tübingen: J.C.B. Mohr [Paul Siebeck], 6th edn, 1990), pp. 1-7.

6. For this label, see Christoph Markschies, 'Haupteinleitung', in C. Markschies and J. Schröter (eds.), *Antike christliche Apokryphen in deutscher Übersetzung. I. Evangelien und Verwandtes*, I (Tübingen: Mohr Siebeck, 7th edn, 2012), pp. 1-180 (2-9).

the word 'Apocrypha' itself…). As a detailed analysis of modern research would illustrate, different texts were labelled as 'New Testament Apocrypha' at different times. Incidentally, the US theologian and scholar Edgar J. Goodspeed published a small book on 'Modern Apocrypha' in 1931,[7] in which he digs out such fine examples as the 'Aquarian Gospel', the 'Twenty-ninth Chapter of Acts' and the 'Gospel of Josephus'—as the subtitle of Goodspeed's monograph puts it, (once) famous biblical hoaxes.

Any treatment of the early Christian writings labelled as 'New Testament Apocrypha' should be aware of the fact that the existing scholarly collections contain quite diverse writings which do not necessarily belong to the same historical context. Despite the fact that the extant forms of these different texts seem, more often than not, to take New Testament genres as their literary model, a closer look reveals an astonishing creativity and variety of literary structures. We should be wary of generalizing even about the social and cultural position of their authors and implied readers: the perception of the New Testament Apocrypha as popular literature of the lower classes is not warranted.

Nevertheless, these texts have one important feature in common: self-evidently, in different ways, they focus on the beginnings of Christianity in the times of Jesus and the Apostles.[8] This common ground is understood as an important and perhaps normative past; it provides a reason to develop new narratives, visionary experiences, and reports or letters forming parts of fictional dialogues. The historical value of these texts for the time they concern is minimal. What we can study, however, with the help of these texts and their outlook on the primitive times of Christian faith, is the emergence, development and differentiation of a notion of the past—or, to borrow a key word from cultural studies, the 'collective memory'[9] of the beginnings. The New Testament Apocrypha provide us with pictures of their own beginnings that early Christians developed, wrote, read or listened to, and probably enjoyed.

All this is to say that the result of this investigation cannot and will not be representative of *one* specific epoch or region of the history of early Christian thought. The systematization developed here does not insinuate coherence or dependence. In fact, direct links between texts attributed to the New Testament Apocrypha do exist, so in some cases it is justified to speak of influence or reception. But this seems to be rather the exception than the rule. And, while this article tries to give an overview and some prominent

---

7. Cf. Edgar Johnson Goodspeed, *Modern Apocrypha* (repr., Boston: Beacon Press, 1956).

8. This does not mean that they necessarily refer to the earliest Christian *texts*!

9. For this category, cf. the seminal monograph by Maurice Halbwachs, *La mémoire collective* (Paris: Presses universitaires de France, 1950), which was published only after the author's death in Buchenwald in 1945.

examples, it does not aspire to be exhaustive. So any further hint, any new evidence brought forward by scholarship is welcome and will help to complete the picture.

3. *A Short Overview of the Use of the Decalogue in the New Testament Apocrypha—and Some Examples*

At first glance, the role and importance of the Decalogue in the New Testament Apocrypha appear to be marginal. In this vast and not exactly fixed corpus of texts (which, in an extended form, is represented, for example, by the two volumes of the French edition of the Pseudepigrapha in the Bibliothèque de la Pléiade,[10] or by the Italian edition in three volumes edited by Mario Erbetta),[11] I recognize some thirty examples of evident allusion to or quotation from the Decalogue. As far as I can see, quotations of the Decalogue in its entirety do not occur, but single commandments or clusters of two or three appear repeatedly in the texts. A preference for one of the two biblical versions of the Decalogue (Exod. 20.2-17 or Deut. 5.6-21) cannot be observed in these examples. Interestingly, the motif of the stone tablets, directly linked to the Ten Words in Exod. 32.28 and Deut. 4.13, 5.22 and 10.4,[12] which acquired considerable importance for the iconography of the Decalogue both Jewish and Christian, is alluded to only rarely in the texts.[13]

It would be premature, however, to deduce from these first impressions that the Ten Words are of no importance for the different pictures of Christianity's beginnings that are represented in the Apocrypha, and hence that the collective memory of Christianity in the first centuries did not recall the Ten Commandments very well.

The picture changes when we take into account the primarily narrative character of the texts in question, which rarely make use of direct quotations from the Bible or other authoritative writings, and also when we compare the use of the Decalogue here with that of other texts from the Old

---

10. François Bovon, Pierre Geoltrain and Jean-Daniel Kaestli (eds.), *Ecrits apocryphes chrétiens* (2 vols.; Paris: Editions Gallimard, 1997–2005).

11. Mario Erbetta (ed.), *Gli apocrifi del Nuovo Testamento*, I.1–II (repr., Genoa: Marietti, 1983–2003).

12. According to Exod. 24.12; 31.18, the contents of the stone tablets are not limited to the Ten Words. For the motif in Jewish and Christian texts of antiquity, see Hermut Löhr, 'Steintafeln. Tora-Traditionen in 2Kor 3', in D. Sänger (ed.), *Der zweite Korintherbrief. Literarische Gestalt—historische Situation—theologische Argumentation* (Festschrift D.-A. Koch; FRLANT, 250; Göttingen: Vandenhoeck & Ruprecht, 2012), pp. 175-87.

13. I found it only in the late (fifth-century?) *Act. Andr. Matt.* 29.4. For the date of the text cf. Jean-Marc Prieur, 'Actes d'André et Matthias', in Bovon, Geoltrain and Kaestli (eds.), *Ecrits apocryphes chrétiens*, II, pp. 485-519 (489ff.).

Testament. At the present state of research it is not possible to give exact figures: detailed analyses of the reception of the Bible in several of these early Christian texts are still lacking. It appears, however, that the Decalogue is in fact one of the few Old Testament texts that is cited repeatedly *verbatim* or almost *verbatim*, and which, together with sections of the Matthaean Sermon on the Mount, is appealed to directly in passages containing models of Christian moral instruction.

3.1. *The First Commandment and Christology*
An explicit account of the proclamation of the Decalogue at Mount Sinai is given in a predication of Peter narrated in a Christian text[14] from the middle of the fourth century CE[15] called the 'Recognitions' (*Recognitiones*) of Pseudo-Clement. The *Recognitiones* are the Latin version (by Rufin), while a quite different Greek version is called *Homiliae* ('Predications'). Both versions probably go back to a basic text (*Grundschrift*) from the middle of the third century CE, which might have been called περίοδοι Πέτρου. The *Grundschrift* possibly uses other sources, but no scholarly consensus on this subject exists.[16]

The romance gives an autobiographical account of a character called Clement (known from other early Christian texts and probably a historical person from the Christian community in Rome in the later first century)[17] and narrates his conversion (and its extensive prehistory) to Christian faith, which was brought about by Peter. This narrative frame is used to stage a plurality of public discourses and private dialogues which contain Christian

---

14. Whether the Pseudo-Clementines can justly be labelled a 'novel' or 'family romance' is a matter of dispute; cf. István Czachesz, 'The Clement Romance: Is It a Novel?', in J.N. Bremmer (ed.), *The Pseudo-Clementines* (Studies on Early Christian Apocrypha, 10; Leuven: Peeters, 2010), pp. 24-35.

15. For the date of *Ps.-Clem. Rec.* cf. Pierre Geoltrain, 'Roman Pseudo-Clementin, Introduction', in Bovon, Geoltrain and Kaestli (eds.), *Ecrits apocryphes chrétiens*, II, pp. 175-87.

16. For a short overview cf. Hans-Josef Klauck, *Apokryphe Apostelakten. Eine Einführung* (Stuttgart: Katholisches Bibelwerk, 2005), pp. 206-208. For a highly hypothetical reconstruction of the history of the text, cf. Jürgen Wehnert, *Pseudoklementinische Homilien. Einführung und Übersetzung* (Kommentare zur apokryphen Literatur, 1/1; Göttingen: Vandenhoeck & Ruprecht 2010), pp. 31-33. For the history and state of research, see also Frédéric Amsler, 'Etat de recherche récente sur le roman pseudo-clémentin', in Amsler *et al.* (eds.), *Nouvelles intrigues pseudo-clémentines. Plots in the Pseudo-Clementine Romance* (Publications de l'Institut romand des sciences bibliques, 6; Prahins: Editions du Zèbre, 2008), pp. 25-45; F. Stanley Jones, 'The Pseudo-Clementines: A History of Research', *The Second Century* 2 (1982), pp. 1-33; 3 (1983), pp. 63-96.

17. For the figure in early Christian literature and beyond, cf. Klauck, *Apokryphe Apostelakten*, pp. 204-205.

teachings and theology; this, it appears, is the major point of interest of the romance. One of the main characters is Peter. Like his opponent, Simon Magus, the figure of Peter is taken from earlier Christian texts, but developed considerably further. Thus, in the Pseudo-Clementines, Peter has become the apostle to the nations instead of Paul, who only plays a minor and negative role in the narrative.[18] Peter is the leader and teacher of his co-disciples, an orator both rhetorically gifted and philosophically trained and, at the same time, a miracle-worker who can confront the mighty deeds of Simon.

The passage *Ps.-Clem. Rec.* I 27-71 is part of a longer instruction given to Clement by Peter regarding the basics of the new faith. The passage can be characterized as an overview of the history of salvation from its beginnings, that is, from the creation of heaven and earth by God. The passage has no parallel in the *Homiliae*. It belongs, according to scholarly consensus, to the *Grundschrift* mentioned above, and probably goes back to an even older Jewish–Christian source.[19] In *Rec.* I 35, Peter gives an account of the proclamation of the Decalogue:

> After this, Moses, by the command of God, whose providence is over all, led out the people of the Hebrews into the wilderness; and, leaving the shortest road which leads from Egypt to Judaea, he led the people through long windings of the wilderness, that, by the discipline of forty years, the novelty of a changed manner of life might root out the evils which had clung to them by a long-continued familiarity with the customs of the Egyptians. Meantime they came to Mount Sinai, and thence the law was given to them with voices and sights from heaven, written in ten precepts [*decem conscripta praeceptis*], of which the first and greatest was that they should worship God Himself alone, and not make to themselves any other appearance or form to worship [*aliam speciem vel formam*] (*Ps.-Clem. Rec.* I 35.1-2).[20]

In this short passage nothing more is given of the contents of the Decalogue. While the proclamation of the law (and the way into the wilderness) are presented as means to cleanse the people of the bad habits of Egyptian paganism, the passage focuses on the First Commandment, stressing the exclusivity of the worship of God and the prohibition on worshipping idols

---

18. It is not warranted to interpret Simon Magus as Paul in disguise throughout the Pseudo-Clementines, although in some passages anti-Pauline polemics seem to have been linked to the figure of Simon.

19. Cf. F. Stanley Jones, *An Ancient Jewish Christian Source on the History of Christianity. Pseudo-Clementine Recognitions 1.27-71* (Texts and Translations, 37; Christian Apocrypha Series, 2; Atlanta: Scholars Press, 1995).

20. Translation: Thomas Smith, in A. Roberts and J. Donaldson (eds.), *The Ante-Nicene Fathers*, VIII (repr., Grand Rapids: Eerdmans, 1970), p. 87, slightly adapted. Latin text: B. Rehm (ed.), *Die Pseudoklementinen. II. Rekognitionen in Rufins Übersetzung* (GCS, Berlin: Akademie Verlag, 1965), p. 28.

of him (other Gods and their representations are seemingly not in question). The ban on images pronounced in Exod. 20.4-6/Deut. 5.8-10 is not seen as a separate commandment, but as a part and a specification of the First and primary Commandment.

Other passages focusing on the First Commandment can be found in our literature: *Ps.-Clem. Hom.* XVI 12.1-2 is part of a confrontation between Peter and Simon Magus in Laodicea; the passage was probably created by the redactor of the *Homiliae*.[21] In this theological discussion, Simon refers to the Holy Scriptures in support of his thesis of a plurality of gods. More specifically, he links Gen. 1.26, which describes the creation of humanity, both male and female, by God and quotes God as saying 'Let us create human beings', to Gen. 2.7, which gives a more down-to-earth report of this event. The plural subject ('let us...') in the former passage proves, according to Simon, that at least two gods were involved in the act of creation. Peter refutes this argument and explains the somewhat problematic plural by referring to divine Wisdom, also presented as a partner in dialogue with God in other passages from the Scriptures (cf. Prov. 8.30 LXX):

> And Peter answered: 'One is He who said to His Wisdom, "Let us make a man". But His Wisdom was that with which He Himself always rejoiced as with His own spirit. It is united as soul to God, but it is extended by Him, as hand, fashioning the universe. On this account, also, one man was made, and from him went forth also the female. And being a unity generically, it is yet a duality, for by expansion and contraction the unity is thought to be a duality. So that I act rightly in offering up all the honour to one God as to parents' (*Ps.-Clem. Hom.* XVI 12.1-2).[22]

The conclusion alludes to the Decalogue and draws parallels between the First Commandment and the Fifth (or Fourth), which obliges one to honour one's parents. This parallelism, which is only mentioned *en passant*, is reminiscent of Philo's interpretation of the importance and position of the Commandment, which does not focus, however, on reverence for God, but on the generative power of both God and human parents:

> After dealing with the seventh day, He gives the fifth commandment on the honour due to the parents. This commandment He placed on the border-line between the two sets of five; it is the last of the first set in which the most sacred injunctions are given, and it adjoins the second set which contains the just with regard to human beings. The reason I consider is this: we see that parents by their nature stand on the border line between the mortal and the

---

21. For the theological background of this passage, cf. Marie-Ange Calvet, in her translation of *Ps.-Clem. Hom.*, in Bovon, Geoltrain and Kaestli (eds.), *Ecrits apocryphes chrétiens*, II, p. 1505, note *ad loc.*

22. Translation: Thomas Smith, in Roberts and Donaldson (eds.), *The Ante-Nicene Fathers*, VIII, p. 315. Greek text: B. Rehm (ed.), *Die Pseudoklementinen. I. Homilien* (GCS, Berlin: Akademie Verlag, 1953), pp. 223-24.

immortal side of existence, the mortal because of their kinship with human beings and other living beings through the perishableness of the body; the immortal because the act of generation assimilates them to God, the generator of the All (Philo, *De decalogo* 106-107).[23]

A third example of the use of the First Commandment is to be found in a much older Christian text of a different kind. The so-called *Ascensio Isaiae* focuses, in two major sections, on acts and visions of the prophet Isaiah. The text, which is widely known for its description of the martyrdom of the prophet, was originally written in Greek, but is nowadays preserved in its entirety only in Ethiopic. Other translations (into Latin, Coptic and Old Slavonic) have survived in fragments. It is a matter of dispute whether the first part (chaps. 1–5) goes back to a Jewish Martyrdom of Isaiah, a thesis brought forward for the first time by Friedrich Lücke in 1832 and still favoured today by many. Be that as it may, the *Ascensio* in its present form is a Christian writing, probably from the beginning of the second century.[24] A passage in 4-6 is relevant here. The context is an extended eschatological prophecy delivered by Isaiah to King Hezekiah and the prophet's own son, Yashuv. It predicts the descent of Beliar, 'the great ruler', from heaven to earth at the end of days. Beliar will appear on earth in form of an unjust king, a murderer of his own mother. He will persecute 'the twelve apostles of the Beloved One', that is, of Jesus Christ. The prophecy continues:

> This ruler, Beliar, will come in the form of that king, and with him will come all the powers of this world, and they will obey him in every wish. By his word, he will cause the sun to rise by night, and the moon also he will make to appear at the sixth hour. And he will do everything he wishes in the world; he will act and speak like the Beloved One, and will say: 'I am the Lord, and before me there was no one' (*Asc. Isa.* 4.2-6).[25]

The first part of the passage might very well remind us of the self-presentation of God in the opening lines of the Decalogue, in Exod. 20.2-3 and Deut. 5.6-7, while its second part has no analogue in these passages. A closer parallel to the complete phrase can be found in Isa. 43.10-11, a passage, which, however, gives the two phrases in reverse order:

---

23. Translation: Francis Henry Colson, *Philo, with an English Translation*, VII (LCL, 1958), p. 61 (adapted); Greek text on p. 60.

24. For an introduction to the text, cf. Enrico Norelli, 'Ascension d'Isaïe. Introduction', in Bovon, Geoltrain and Kaestli (eds.), *Ecrits apocryphes chrétiens*, I, pp. 501-505.

25. Translation: Michael A. Knibb, in James H. Charlesworth (ed.), *The Old Testament Pseudepigrapha. II. Expansions of the 'Old Testament' and Legends, Wisdom and Philosophical Literature, Prayers, Psalms, and Odes, Fragments of Lost Judeo-Hellenistic Works* (London: Darton, Longman & Todd, 1985), p. 161 (slightly adapted). An extended commentary on the passage is provided by Enrico Norelli, *Ascensio Isaiae. Commentarius* (CChrSA, 8; Turnhout: Brepols, 1995), pp. 241-53.

> You are my witnesses, says the Lord, and my servant whom I have chosen, so that you may know and believe me and understand that I am he. Before me no god was formed, nor shall there be any after me. I, I am the Lord, and besides me there is no saviour (NRSV).

It is interesting to note that the Septuagint version of v. 10 adds 'other' before 'god', a detail *not* transferred to Beliar's speech in the *Ascensio*. So, while the passage cannot be identified with certainty as a quotation from the Decalogue, it is interesting for its presentation of God's opponent referring to the central idea expressed in the First Commandment, but also in other biblical (especially prophetic) texts.

This motif is used again later, in the context of the heavenly journey of the prophet and his vision of the seventh heaven and of God. Isaiah reports what he heard of God addressing his Son:

> And I heard the voice of the Most High, the Father of my Lord, as he said to my Lord Christ, who will be called Jesus: 'Go out and descend through all the heavens. You shall descend through the firmament and through that world as far as the angel who is in Sheol, but you shall not go as far as Perdition... And none of the angels of that world shall know that you are Lord with me of the seven heavens and of their angels. And they shall not know that you are with me when with the voice of the heavens I summon you, and their angels and their lights, and when I lift up my voice to the sixth heaven, that you may judge and destroy the princes and the angels and the gods of that world, and the world which is ruled by them, for they have denied me and said: "We alone are, and there is no one besides us"' (*Asc. Isa.* 10.7-13).[26]

This interest in God's unity and uniqueness, which is in opposition to the idea of a plurality of gods, has to be reconciled with a Christology which puts Jesus Christ, the Son of God, on a level that is second or equal to God.

The subject is developed further in other texts by attributing the Ten Words to Jesus Christ. So the *Acts of Andrew and Matthew*, an apocryphon narrating the story of those apostles in the land of the cannibals, and probably to be dated to the fifth century,[27] gives, in chaps. 8–10, an account of a dialogue between Jesus (disguised as a helmsman) and Andrew. In reaction to a question asked by Jesus, Andrew professes that Jesus is the creator of heaven and earth, vaguely recalling Exod. 20.11, but not focusing on the Sabbath Commandment as such.

The connection is made more explicit in another late New Testament apocryphon, according to Michel van Esbroeck dating to the fifth century, but possibly of later origin, the so-called 'Letter of Jesus Christ Concerning Sunday', preserved in Greek in a fifteenth-century manuscript, but also in

---

26. Translation: Michael A. Knibb, in Charlesworth (ed.), *The Old Testament Pseudepigrapha*, II, p. 173.

27. Cf. n. 13.

a Latin manuscript going back to the twelfth century.[28] According to 2.16, the fictionalized Jesus confirms that he created heaven and earth in six days, and that he rested on the seventh day. While this clearly refers back to the first story of creation in Gen. 1, at the same time it alludes to the Decalogue, especially to the Sabbath Commandment in the Exodus version, by admonishing its readers to respect the Sabbath rest. In these exemplary texts, Jesus has clearly taken the position of God as the creator of the world and author of the Ten Words.[29]

3.2. *Moral Instruction via the Ten Words*
The moral importance of the Decalogue for the Christian faith is announced in the Apocrypha in different ways. I have already mentioned the important role that Peter plays in some of our writings for the moral orientation of Christian faith. This motif is also linked from time to time to the Ten Commandments, thus preparing for the notion of Peter as the main recipient and preacher of the *nova lex* delivered by Christ.[30]

Various passages, again from the Pseudo-Clementine *Homiliae*, can illustrate this: In *Ps.-Clem. Hom.* V 26.3, in the context of a love-letter to a certain Apion faked by Clement, allusion is made to the Seventh (Sixth) Commandment warning against adultery. *Ps.-Clem. Hom.* XII 14.1 (cf. also *Ps.-Clem. Hom.* IX 13.1) forbids suicide, possibly relying on the Sixth (Fifth) Commandment.

According to *Ps.-Clem. Hom.* IX 23.1s., Peter concludes a predication in Phoenician Tripolis with a moral exhortation in which he refers to the

---

28. Cf. Irena Backus, 'Lettre de Jésus Christ sur le dimanche. Introduction', in Bovon, Geoltrain and Kaestli (eds.), *Ecrits apocryphes chrétiens*, II, pp. 1101-1106.

29. For the motif of Jesus Christ as creator in the New Testament Apocrypha, see also *Mart. Luc.* 62. In *Act. Paul.* 3.17, allusion to the first two commandments is made in a speech delivered by Paul in front of the proconsul Cestillius. In the immediate context reference is made to the mission of the Son of God. Additionally, one should mention a passage from the Gnostic Gospel of the Egyptians (III and IV), in which the great angel Sakla seems to allude to the Second Commandment: 'And after the founding [of the world] Sakla said to his [angels], "I, I am a [jealous] god, and apart from me nothing has [come into being]"' (IV 58.23-26)—Coptic text: Alexander Böhlig and Frederik Wisse (eds.), *Nag Hammadi Codices III,2 and IV,2. The Gospel of the Egyptians (The Holy Book of the Great Invisible Spirit)* (NHS, IV; Leiden: E.J. Brill, 1975), p. 126; translation: Alexander Böhlig and Frederik Wisse, 'The Gospel of the Egyptians [III,2 and IV,2]', in J.M. Robinson (ed.), *The Nag Hammadi Library in English* (Leiden: E.J. Brill, 1977), pp. 195-206 (201). Reference is made to the Second Commandment in another text from Nag Hammadi, the Second Treatise of the Great Seth, in NHC, VII 51.30. The prohibition against bearing false witness is mentioned in the same text, in 52.35. The First Commandment is referred to by the Cosmocrator in 53.30, and the Second Commandment is uttered by the Archon in 64.18-25.

30. See above pp. 59, 62-63.

Decalogue (especially to the First and Seventh Commandments, but possibly also to the 'second tablet' in general) in an abbreviated form:

> This then we would have you know, that unless any one of his own accord give himself over as a slave to demons, as I said before, the demon has no power against him. Choosing, therefore, to worship one God, and refraining from the table of demons, and undertaking chastity with philanthropy and righteousness, and being baptized with the thrice-blessed invocation for the remission of sins, and devoting yourselves as much as you can to the perfection of purity, you can escape everlasting punishment, and be constituted heirs of eternal blessings (*Ps.-Clem. Hom.* IX 23.1-2).[31]

This passage should not be interpreted only in relation to the Ten Words, but may also have been influenced by the so-called Apostolic Decree, whose earliest attestation in Christian literature can be found in Acts 15.20, 29.[32]

A direct quotation from the series of prohibitions of the Decalogue can be found in *Ps.-Clem. Hom.* X 6.2-4, again in a predication delivered in Tripolis by Peter:

> Since, then, by acting like irrational animals, you have lost the soul of man from your soul, becoming like swine, you are the prey of demons. If, therefore, you receive the law of God, you become men. For it cannot be said to irrational animals, 'Thou shalt not kill, thou shalt not commit adultery, thou shalt not steal', and so forth. Therefore do not refuse, when invited, to return to your first nobility; for it is possible, if you be conformed to God by good works (*Ps.-Clem. Hom.* X 6.2-4).[33]

The text makes use of a cluster of three commandments forbidding murder, adultery and stealing. The sequence of the three commandments is that of Exod. 20.13-15/Deut. 5.17-19 MT (cf. also Mk 10.19 and Mt. 19.18), while the Septuagint of both texts, but also Philo (*Dec.* 29), the Nash Papyrus,[34] Paul in Rom. 13.9, Lk. 18.20, and Jas 2.11 follow a different order.[35] A variant of this grouping of the commandments is used in *Ps.-Clem. Hom.* VII 4.4, again in a discourse by Peter. Here the same series of

---

31. Translation: Thomas Smith, in Roberts and Donaldson (eds.), *The Ante-Nicene Fathers*, VIII, p. 279. Greek text: Rehm (ed.), *Die Pseudoklementinen*, I, p. 141.

32. Cf. also *Ps.-Clem. Hom.* VII 4.2; XIII 4.2; cf. Jürgen Wehnert, *Die Reinheit des 'christlichen Gottesvolkes' aus Juden und Heiden. Studien zum historischen und theologischen Hintergrund des sogenannten Aposteldekrets* (FRLANT, 173, Göttingen: Vandenhoeck & Ruprecht, 1997).

33. Translation: Thomas Smith, in: Roberts and Donaldson (eds.), *The Ante-Nicene Fathers*, VIII, p. 281. Greek text: Rehm (ed.), *Die Pseudoklementinen*, I, p. 144.

34. Francis Crawford Burkitt, 'The Hebrew Papyrus of the Ten Commandments', *JQR* 15 (1903), 392-408.

35. Cf. Klaus Berger, *Die Gesetzesauslegung Jesu. Ihr historischer Hintergrund im Judentum und im Alten Testament. I. Markus und Parallelen* (WMANT, 40; Neukirchen–Vluyn: Neukirchener Verlag, 1972), pp. 261-62, 362-95.

three commandments (in the same order) is combined with the basic idea of the Golden Rule:

> And you may all find out what is good, by holding some such conversation as the following with yourselves: You would not like to be murdered; do not murder another man; you would not like your wife to be seduced by another; do not you commit adultery: you would not like any of your things to be stolen from you; steal nothing from another (*Ps.-Clem. Hom.* VII 4.4).[36]

According to *Ps.-Clem. Hom.* XI 5.1-3, Peter alludes to the Decalogue in another predication addressed to the masses in Tripolis. This allusion is cast into the form of a rhetorical question:

> Can it therefore be said that, for the sake of piety towards God, you worship every form, while in all things you injure man who is really the image of God, committing murder, adultery, stealing, and dishonouring him in many other respects? But you ought not to do even one evil thing on account of which man is grieved. But now you do all things on account of which man is disheartened. Injustice and grief emerge when you murder and spoil his goods and whatever else you know which you would not receive from another. But you, being seduced by some malignant reptile to malice, by the suggestion of polytheistic doctrine, are impious towards the real image, which is man, and think that you are pious towards senseless things (*Ps.-Clem. Hom.* XI 5.1-3).[37]

The passage alludes freely to different commandments of the Decalogue, going well beyond the initial question and referring to veneration of foreign gods, idolatry and murder. In addition, the phrase 'and whatever else you know which you would not receive from another', introduces the Golden Rule in its negative version as a summary.

According to the so-called *Visio Esdrae* (recension B), during his visit to the underworld, Ezra perceives human beings ripped by beasts. The accompanying angel explains, 'These are the ones who moved the landmarks and spoke false testimony',[38] thus alluding to the Ninth (Eighth) Commandment, but also to the prohibition against moving landmarks in Deut. 19.14 and 27.17.[39] The eschatological outlook provides moral orientation and implicit exhortation.

---

36. Translation: Thomas Smith, in: Roberts and Donaldson (eds.), *The Ante-Nicene Fathers*, VIII, p. 268. Greek text: Rehm (ed.), *Die Pseudoklementinen*, I, p. 118.

37. Translation: Thomas Smith, in Roberts and Donaldson (eds.), *The Ante-Nicene Fathers*, VIII, p. 285. Greek text: *Die Pseudoklementinen*, I, pp. 155-56.

38. My translation. Latin text: Otto Wohl (ed.), *Apocalypsis Esdrae. Apocalypsis Sedrach. Visio Beati Esdrae* (PVTG, 4; Leiden: E.J. Brill, 1977), p. 58. The translation of the Latin word *terminus* by 'last things', proposed by Michael Edward Stone, 'Questions of Ezra', in James H. Charlesworth (ed.), *The Old Testament Pseudepigapha*, I (Garden City, NY: Doubleday, 1983), p. 590, note *ad loc.*, is unwarranted in my opinion.

39. Job 24.2 suggests that the moving of a landmark was considered as a specific kind of theft.

The Ethiopic Text of the (Greek) Apocalypse of Peter, Chapter 11, which may go back to the first half of the second century CE,[40] is part of a visionary description of the place of final judgment. It presents human beings punished for specific sins. Again, the eschatological outlook serves to transmit a moral message. The text mentions, *inter alia*, those who did not honour father and mother, thus alluding to the Fourth (Fifth) Commandment. But other sins mentioned in the context do not appear to be directly related to the commandments of the Decalogue.

These and other passages from the New Testament Apocrypha demonstrate convincingly that the collective memory of Christianity that expresses itself in these texts is very well aware of the importance of the Ten Commandments for moral instruction and orientation at the beginnings of Christianity, in continuity with Jewish morality and in contrast to pagan mores. By using free adaptation and paraphrase, and by combining Decalogue Commandments with other rules and principles, it follows older paths both Jewish and Christian in the reception history of the Decalogue. I cite one more example, chosen from the fifth-century *Acts of Peter and Andrew* (5.3). Again Peter speaks—this time preaching to a workman after performing a miracle:

> Peter says to him: 'Rise, O man. We are not gods, but apostles of the Good God. He has elected us, and we are twelve. He has given us good instructions, so that we can instruct the people and they will be saved from death and inherit eternal life.' Peter installs himself in front of the other, and says: 'You shall love the Lord your God from all your soul and from all your heart. You shall not commit adultery. You shall not steal. You shall not bear false witness. Raise your children in the fear of the Lord. And you will have a good life [καλὴν ζωήν] and will enter into His glory' (*Act. Petr. Andr.* 5.3).[41]

Apart from being reminiscent of New Testament texts (Mk 12.30 par. Mt. 22.37; Lk. 10.27; Acts 14.15), the passage clearly alludes to Deut. 6.4-5, along with a cluster of prohibitions from the Decalogue (against adultery, stealing and false witness). The reference to the 'good life'[42] links this group of precise commandments to a more general standard of morality and its aims which could be accepted by Christians and non-Christians alike. At the same time, a strong soteriological and eschatological overtone can be heard: the end of morality is the entry into the glory of God.

---

40. Cf. C. Detlef G. Müller, 'Offenbarung des Petrus', in W. Schneemelcher (ed.), *Neutestamentliche Apokryphen. II. Apostolisches. Apokalypsen und Verwandtes* (Tübingen: Mohr Siebeck, 6th edn, 1997), pp. 562-78 (563-64).

41. My translation. Greek text: Maximilian Bonnet (ed.), *Acta Apostolorum Apocrypha*, II/1 (repr., Darmstadt: Wissenschaftliche Buchgesellschaft, 1959), p. 120.

42. The rendering of the phrase as 'vie parfaite' by Jean-Marc Prieur, which would refer to Mt. 5.48, is not warranted; cf. Jean-Marc Prieur, in Bovon, Geoltrain and Kaestli (eds.), *Ecrits apocryphes chrétiens*, II, p. 530.

4. Summary

This article asked about the role of the Ten Commandments in the so-called New Testament Apocrypha. The designation 'New Testament Apocrypha' does not refer to a historically fixed corpus or canon of texts, but to a variety of Christian documents, representing different genres, times, regions and theological positions. The common denominator of these texts is an orientation towards Jesus and the apostles, but also towards the genres of New Testament literature, while allowing for a variety of forms. However, with regard to plots and stories, the texts go far beyond the material contained in the canonical literature. The New Testament Apocrypha can be understood as expressions of the collective memory of Christianity in antiquity regarding its beginnings.

The role of the Decalogue in the New Testament Apocrypha is a limited but important one. Most significant for our concerns here are the Pseudo-Clementine *Recognitiones* and *Homiliae*, but examples from other, earlier texts (including some of the Gnostic apocrypha) could also be presented. The First Commandment (or the *Shema*) is adduced to discuss the fundamental understanding of God as the creator of heaven and earth and as the father of Jesus Christ. In addition to this theological and Christological concern, the Ten Words are used to express basic moral convictions in early Christianity. Peter is presented repeatedly as referring to the Decalogue, thus confirming his outstanding importance for the collective memory of early Christianity.

Part II

MIDDLE AGES—LITURGY, HOMILY AND THEOLOGY

THE DECALOGUE IN WESTERN THEOLOGY FROM THE CHURCH FATHERS TO THE THIRTEENTH CENTURY

Miguel Lluch Baixauli

The first moral and theological treatise on the Decalogue is *On the Decalogue* by Philo of Alexandria.[1] In this work, Philo develops the meaning of the law and each of the Commandments in a speculative moral sense. Although he belongs not to the Christian tradition but to the Jewish one, and his work was to have no continuity as a literary genre, his treatise was to prove extremely influential from a doctrinal point of view.[2]

In early Christian literature, the example of Philo was lost, and we have no treatise on the Decalogue from the first three centuries. Frequent reference is made to the precepts of Sinai in sermons and other moral and theological works by the Fathers and by ecclesiastical writers, but the commandments are not set out in systematic fashion.[3] One exceptional example from the patristic period is Origen's Eighth Homily on *Exodus*, which has the title 'On the Beginnings of the Decalogue'.[4] In this work, Origen renewed and enriched the previous tradition, and his Homily was to be a point of reference for later Christian tradition.[5]

The most important writer for the development of mediaeval and later thinking on the Decalogue was St Augustine of Hippo (354–430).[6] In his

---

1. Valentin Nikiprowetky (ed.), *De Decalogo. Introduction, traduction et notes* (Les oeuvres de Philon d'Alexandrie, 23; Paris: Cerf, 1965).

2. Miguel Lluch Baixauli, 'El tratado de Filón sobre el Decálogo', *Scripta theologica* 29 (1997), pp. 415-41.

3. Cf. Guy Bourgeault, *Décalogue et morale chrétienne. Enquête patristique sur l'utilisation et l'interprétation chrétiennes du décalogue de c. 60 à 220* (Recherches publiées par les Facultés S.J. de Montréal, Théologie, 2; Paris: Desclée de Brouwer; Montreal: Bellarmin, 1971).

4. Origen, *Homélies sur l'Exode* (ed. Marcel Borret; Sources chrétiennes, 321: Paris: Cerf, 1985), no. VIII ('De initio Decalogi'), pp. 240-77.

5. Miguel Lluch Baixauli, 'La interpretación de Orígenes al Decálogo', *Scripta theologica* 30 (1998), pp. 87-109.

6. Augustine, *Quaestionum in Heptateuchum*, 2, CChr, Series Latina, XXXIII, pp. 70-174; *Sermones* 8 ('De decem plagis Aegyptiorum et decem praeceptis legis'), 9 ('De decem chordis sermo habitus Chusa'), CChr, Series latina, XLI, pp. 79-99, 105-51.

work, we find an original handling of the subject which breaks with patristic tradition on some points. His writings on the Decalogue attain a new depth and order in their explanations and interpretation of each of the Commandments. St Augustine would leave his mark on the later Latin tradition in various literary genres, but his writings on the Decalogue are not yet systematic treatises. In fact, they are sermons (*tractatus*) and commentaries on the Bible.[7]

The immediate successor of St Augustine, St Caesarius of Arles, devoted some sermons to the Decalogue in which his dependence on St Augustine is evident.[8] However, in another sermon he also introduced significant elements from the tradition that goes back to Origen's homily.[9]

After this, St Isidore of Seville[10] and then the Venerable Bede[11] opened a new era in the history of thinking on the Decalogue. In their extensive compilations of biblical commentaries, they discussed the Decalogue within the texts on the book of Exodus. They received the tradition from St Augustine and handed it down to future generations. Bede also inherited and passed on the tradition from Origen, which is completely absent from Isidore's text. The only exception might be the small treatise by Alcuin of York (c. 731–804) entitled *On the Ten Words of the Law or a Brief Explanation of the Decalogue*.[12] The contents are dependent on Augustine, Isidore and Bede, but this work has the distinction of being the first free-standing commentary on the Decalogue in the western Latin tradition.[13]

The genre of biblical commentary was to prove extremely important for the history of mediaeval teaching on the Decalogue, because a large number of writers contributed to the development of this genre from its origin in the late tenth century to its definitive consolidation as the *Glossa ordinaria* in the early thirteenth century. These texts are commentaries on the Scripture, and contain discussions of the Commandments. The *Glossa* came to

---

7. Miguel Lluch Baixauli, 'El Decálogo en los escritos de San Agustín', *Anuario de historia de la iglesia* 8 (1999), pp. 125-44.

8. Caesarius, *Sermo sancti Augustini episcopi de decem verbis legis et decem plagis* and *De convenientia decem plagarum Aegypti et decem praeceptorum legis*, CChr, Series latina, CIII, pp. 407-13, 413-16.

9. Caesarius, *Sermones* 99 ('De decem plagis'), CChr, Series latina, CIII, pp. 403-406.

10. Isidore, *Mysticorum expositiones sacramentorum seu Quaestiones in Vetus Testamentum. In Exodum*, 29–31, *PL*, LXXXIII, cols. 301A-304A.

11. Bede, *In Pentateuchum commentarii. Exodus. Explanatio in secundum librum Mosis*, *PL*, XCI, 285-332; *Quaestionum super Exodum Dialogus*, *PL*, XCIII, cols. 366-88.

12. Alcuin, *De decem verbis legis seu brevis expositio decalogi*, *PL*, C, cols. 567-70.

13. Miguel Lluch Baixauli, 'La interpretación del Decálogo en los siglos VII al IX. San Isidoro de Sevilla, Beda el Venerable y los escritores carolingios', *Scripta theologica* 33 (2001), pp. 71-102.

have great authority, and was a means for the transmission of interpretations that came to be discussed in later theological treatises. In the most accessible of the texts that have been handed down to us, we at once notice the presence of the two great textual traditions: that of Origen, and that of St Augustine. The latter was probably passed on through the commentary by St Isidore which was known to the Carolingians. Regarding the Decalogue, the *Glossa* on Exodus can be attributed with a fair degree of certainty to Gilbert the Universal. In reality it is an almost uninterrupted sequence of quotations and adaptations from Origen, which the author does not attempt to disguise.

If we look at the bibliography on the Ten Commandments in the Western Christian tradition, we can draw the following conclusion: there are no treatises on the Ten Commandments understood as writings other than commentaries or glosses on the biblical text until the twelfth century. Such works appear for the first time in the *sententiae* of Anselm of Laon, and in the first systematic theological works written by the members of his school, in concrete, in the collection known as *Sententie Anselmi*.

Continuity of theme can be observed in the subsequent treatises, but such works did not become widespread until the thirteenth century. Analysis of the Decalogue was only present in some writings that were concerned with the Bible and the history of salvation, while other systematic works of the time organized according to a logical or thematic structure did not make a specific place for the Decalogue, and did not discuss each Commandment in detail. The authors who included the Decalogue in their theological explanations were, after the School of Laon, Hugh of St Victor, Otto of Lucca in the *Summa sententiarum*, the unidentified authors of *Ysagoge in theologiam* and Peter Lombard. It appears in their systematic theology structured around the sacred Scripture and organized in terms of the history of salvation. However, the Decalogue is absent from other theological systematizations of the twelfth century, such as those of Peter Abelard, Robert Pullen, Roland Bandinelli, Master Herman and Robert of Melun.

From the early thirteenth century onwards, new literary genres would be added to those mentioned above, such as the *Commentaries on the Sentences of Peter Lombard*, which all Masters of Theology had to write, and the great *Summae theologiae*, which would include discussion of the Ten Commandments. The so-called *University Sermon* would also come into being, in which the literature on the Decalogue would undergo further developments. However, we can say that all of this new literature was to be founded on the teachings concerning the Ten Commandments developed by the schools of the early twelfth century, and in particular, those which based their theological explanations on a historical and biblical scheme.

Let us consider three examples of treatises that post-date Lombard. First, there is that of his disciple, Peter of Poitiers, who was the first to use the method of questions on Lombard's text, which was later to evolve into the school commentary that became widespread after the Fourth Lateran Council and which would give rise to hundreds of scholastic commentaries within the framework of university education.

Secondly, we have the treatise by William of Auxerre that forms part of his *Summa aurea*. This work sets a precedent for the genre of the great *summa* which would follow in the course of the thirteenth century. In William of Auxerre's treatise, this form is already mature, and from then on, its development can be said to be complete.

We must also mention Robert Grosseteste's *De decem mandatis*. Although this was composed after the period when the genre could be said to be developing, since it has been dated to around 1230, it is of great interest because it is a monograph. Grosseteste handled the Ten Commandments on their own, outside the framework of the theological *Summa*. This example is unprecedented in terms of its literary form, and is a perfect representative of how the patristic and mediaeval doctrinal tradition was received at that time. It was to be the forerunner of the works focusing entirely on the Ten Commandments that were soon to appear all over Europe.[14]

Later Developments in the Treatise on the Decalogue in Thirteenth-Century Theology

The theology of the Decalogue was to find abundant expression in different literary genres from the thirteenth century onwards. Regarding the theological treatise itself, which originated in the twelfth century, there was expansion on a large scale. Here I shall confine myself to mentioning a few of the most outstanding examples.

William of Auvergne's treatise *De legibus* cannot properly speaking be regarded as a study of the Decalogue, but is rather a comparison between the Old and New Law. There are some isolated references to the Ten Commandments, but its main theme is the issue of 'De cessatione legalium', which was of particular interest to the writers of the day.

The *Summa de bono* by Philip the Chancellor, which attained great importance among the theological writings of the mid thirteenth century, does not discuss the Decalogue.

The *Summa* by Roland of Cremona, known as the *Liber quaestionum*, explains the teaching on the Decalogue at great length, but although the

---

14. Miguel Lluch Baixauli, 'Formación y evolución del tratado escolástico sobre el Decálogo (1115–1230)', *Bibliothèque de la RHE* 80 (1997).

ideas in this work originate from the period when its author was teaching in Paris, that is, from the beginnings of University scholasticism, it was actually composed in Italy towards the end of his life, and should therefore be treated as dating from much later than the early period on which we are focusing.

Another extremely interesting example, but which belongs to a different literary genre, is that of the references to the Decalogue in the *Summa confessorum* by Thomas of Chobham, subdean of Salisbury. This Summa for confessors became widely known after 1216.

There are abundant theological writings on the Decalogue in the work of Alexander of Hales and his school. His *Gloss on the Sentences of Peter Lombard* is of particular interest, since, as we know, it was Alexander who introduced Lombard's work into the university as the basis for teaching theology. We also find references to the Ten Commandments in his *Quaestiones disputatae*,[15] and above all, in the great systematic theological study, the *Summa halensis*, which was composed by his School, and which constitutes the longest mediaeval treatise on the Decalogue.[16]

St Bonaventure also discussed the Decalogue in his Commentary on Lombard's Sentences, written when he was a young university teacher.[17] Later, in some lectures at the university when he was General of the Franciscan Order, he was to unleash the critical movement against the radical Aristotelianism of the University of Paris.[18]

St Thomas Aquinas discussed the Decalogue at different periods in his life. There are some references to the Ten Commandments in his 'quodlibet' writings,[19] but there are basically three main texts that are important to understand his theology on the Decalogue: in chronological order, his Commentary on Lombard's Sentences, Question 100 of I–II of the *Summa theologiae*, and his Collations on the Ten Commandments, which are likely to have been preached in Naples in Lent 1273, that is, near the

---

15. *Magistri Alexandri de hales Glossa in quatuor librum sententiarum Petri Lombardi* (Bibliotheca franciscana scholastica Medii Aevi, 12–15, 4 vols; Florence: Quaracchi, 1951–57); *Quaestiones disputatae 'antequam esse frater'* (Bibliotheca franciscana scholastica Medii Aevi, 19–21, 3 vols.; Florence: Quaracchi, 1960).

16. Miguel Lluch Baixauli, 'La Trinidad y el Decálogo. Los preceptos de la primera tabla en la Escuela de Alejandro de Hales', *Scripta theologica* 37 (2005), pp. 99-140.

17. Bonaventure, 'In tertium librum sententiarum', in *Opera omnia*, III (Florence: Quaracchi, 1887).

18. Bonaventure, 'Collationes de decem praeceptis', in *Opera omnia*, V (Florence: Quaracchi, 1891), pp. 507-32.

19. Palémon Glorieux, 'La littérature quodlibetique de 1260 à 1320', *Bibliothèque thomiste* 5 (1925), pp. 276-90.

end of his life, and which have been passed down to us in the 'reportatio' by Peter of Andria.[20]

John Duns Scotus ushered in a new era in the doctrinal history of the Decalogue in his 'Commentary on the Sentences'.[21] When he suggested that the Commandments on the second tablet were not part of natural law because they had sometimes been the object of divine dispensations, Duns Scotus broke with the tradition that had been unanimous in its response to the old question concerning dispensations. In his view, these Commandments do not have the same force of obligation as natural law, and their authority only rests on the fact that they adhere to the invariable, necessary principles of natural law. Once this breach had been opened, the theological treatise on the Decalogue entered the modern age.

Some Doctrinal Issues[22]

Obviously, each of the Commandments and the law of the Decalogue as a whole raise a large number of issues of theological, moral, ethical, anthropological and cultural interest. In what follows, I shall mention some of the questions that arise most frequently.

Of great importance is the explanation as to how the Ten Commandments can be reduced to the single, twofold Commandment of Love, along with the inseparable unity of the two sections, the first referring to God and the second to our neighbour. Another subject of interest is the immutable nature of natural law, and the interpretation of some moral cases supplied by the Old Testament in which the natural law seems to be broken at God's command. Other issues include explanations concerning the adoration due to God and the distinctions in the degrees of adoration owed to the Holy Trinity, the humanity of Christ, the Blessed Virgin, angels, human beings

---

20. Maria Fabianus Moos (ed.), *Sancti Thomae Aquinatis. Scriptum super sententiis magistri Petri Lombardi. Scriptum super libro tertio sententiarum*, Distinctiones 37-40 (4 vols.; Paris: Lethielleux, 1929–47), III, pp. 1230-1313; *Summa theologiae I–II, Tractatus VIII, Quaestio 100*; Jean-Pierre Torrell (ed.), 'Les *Collationes in decem preceptis* de saint Thomas d'Aquin: édition critique avec introduction et notes', *Revue des sciences philosophiques et théologiques* 69 (1985), pp. 5-40, 227-63.

21. Duns Scotus, Distinctiones 37-40, in *Opera omnia*, XV (repr. Farnborough: Gregg International, 1969), pp. 738-1099.

22. All these examples are to be found in the course of the literary tradition that has formed the subject of this study. Some of the authors develop certain aspects more than others, but we can safely say that everything constitutes a body of doctrinal literature that was known and accepted by all concerned. For a detailed analysis of the aspects mentioned here, the reader may consult the 'Index of names' and 'Subject index' of my monograph cited above: 'Formación y evolución del tratado escolástico', pp. 245-53. On these pages, I indicated where each author discussed each of these topics in his works.

and sacred objects; the affirmative meaning of the commandments taken together and the explanation of their expression in the form of prohibitions; the developing understanding of the sense of freedom with which the law of God endows Christians; references to the angels and demons.

Another recurring issue is the reference to animals as examples or symbols of human morality, both virtues and vices, and as objects of certain precepts, such as 'thou shalt not kill'.

Some authors discuss the contrasting views on philosophers, pagan authors, Jews, heretics and poets that appear in the literature on the Decalogue. All these figures appear frequently, sometimes considered in themselves, at other times referred to in allegorical interpretations, or as quoted or contested authorities.

Speculative developments also appear, which are increasingly rich in their comprehension of the human character. Thus we find writers who bear witness to the growing understanding and terminological clarification of the meaning of concupiscence, which is the legacy of original sin but is not sin in itself, being rather the occasion of both sin and virtue. We also find explanations of the different passions of the human soul and will—appetite, desire, intention, consent and delectation—using the terminology proper to each period.

We also encounter references to work and contemplation in the context of the Commandment to rest on the seventh day, as well as reflections on the dignity of the human person, the explicit consideration of women within the framework of the Ten Commandments, and interesting theological reflections, albeit sometimes of a tangential nature, on topics such as the creation, Christology, the Holy Spirit, the Church and eschatology.

The reception and explanation of the Ten Commandments, as far as their number, contents and internal division are concerned, are generally the same throughout mediaeval tradition, although there are some variants and exceptions. There are some grammatical variations in their wording which do not affect their meaning. As for their order, in some cases the Commandment not to commit adultery appears before the Commandment not to kill. Regarding their division, there are always ten Commandments, but sometimes the Commandment to worship God and not worship idols is understood as two different Commandments while covetousness is grouped together without distinguishing between coveting one's neighbour's wife and his possessions. This variant can be understood by a literal reading of the text of Exodus which, as we know, in the Vulgate does not distinguish the neighbour's wife from the rest of his goods. The inseparable unity of the two tablets is a constant in mediaeval Christian tradition. Although two groups of Commandments are distinguished, all ten are understood as natural law, and all ten can be reduced to the one, double Commandment to love God and one's neighbour.

The Decalogue is understood as divine law that can be located between natural law and the law of grace. These authors all believe that the 'ten words' needed to be revealed because of the degradation of humankind: the law written upon human hearts was no longer enough. They all consider that the Ten Commandments still hold in the era of grace, but they also all believe that the Commandments have been brought to their fullness by Christ. The Decalogue is different from the rest of the Old Covenant, because it is still valid, and it has not been superseded. With the exception of the literal obligation to observe the Sabbath, the Ten Commandments of Sinai are valid for Christians, because they are also Commandments of Christ: the New Testament and the Church teach us how to read and understand them. The law is the same, but now we receive it in hearts that have been renewed by grace.

The different meanings of sacred Scripture (literal and spiritual in the broad sense) are used to interpret some of the Commandments. We find increasingly technical developments of the different meanings encompassed by the text of the Commandments. This is the case with the Commandment to sanctify the seventh day, which gives rise to lengthy speculation in Christian tradition. This is a precept which is still valid in its moral sense, but not in the literal one, because Christians do not celebrate Saturday, like the Jews, but Sunday, and they do so in a different way. This leads to increasingly wide-ranging speculations. As far as the other Commandments go, their literal meaning always holds true for Christians, although there is a growing volume of spiritual and moral explanations that enrich our literal understanding.

The literal sense of the rejection of idolatry is upheld by all the authors, but their moral interpretation of what rejecting idols means varies somewhat. Idols are everything that is opposed to God, or which is liable to replace him. This is an interesting issue that sheds light on the views of the period, because of the variation in the type of thing that is regarded as an obstacle to the relationship between humankind and God in each era, and the differences in each author's interpretations.

In the context of rejecting idols, we find discussion of the good or bad nature of artificial works in comparison with natural ones. God made what is natural. These authors ask whether it is legitimate for people to transform God's work. Here, the distinction is made between the work of art, or human work in general, and idols. It is clearly stated that not all works of humankind are idols. There are works of God, of nature and of art. Not all artificial human constructions are bad. Only those works which humans turn into idols to replace God can be said to be wrong.

We also find references to the different ways in which Jews and Christians understand the law and the Commandments. This question is particularly frequent when the Sabbath is discussed, but also arises in the context of the prohibition on the adoration of images, the divinity of Christ, the Eucharist, the prohibition of wrongful desires rather than just external acts, and the point that it is dangerous for Christians to understand the Decalogue in the spirit of the Old Covenant. In addition to the points of controversy, we also find a series of areas where Judaism and Christianity appear to have common ground: the perfect continuity between the two alliances, the statement that in Israel there were already 'children of the new alliance' when they understood the law in its fullness, and so on. The literature on the Decalogue can thus be used to trace the development of how Christian intellectuals saw the Jewish religion and people over the course of the Middle Ages.

A set of images was passed down from one generation to another. This was the case with the comparison between the Ten Commandments and the ten Plagues of Egypt, and with the comparison between the Decalogue and the ten-stringed psaltery. As far as places are concerned, we find Mount Sinai as the image of the Sermon on the Mount in the New Testament. In terms of time, the moment when Israel received the tablets (*digitus Dei*) is compared to Pentecost, when the Church received the Holy Spirit (*spiritus Dei*).

In general, despite the mediaeval taste for number symbolism, few applications of this type of symbolism are to be found in the literature on the Decalogue, except for a very few instances referring only to the perfection of the number ten and, occasionally, the number seven. However, we do find many parallels, such as those involving the six days of creation, or the six ages or millennia of the history of the world, which are mentioned in the context of resting on the seventh day.

There is also Trinitarian significance in the first three Commandments of the first tablet. Since these three refer to God, this inspires a development whereby each of these precepts is related to one of the persons of the Holy Trinity. The first is related to the Father, the second to the Son, and the third to the Holy Spirit. In the earliest treatises this is a simple reference, but the theme is later developed with increasing depth and richness. These explanations also contain observations about the relationship between the Holy Trinity and the moral life of the Christian. For example, we find discussion of the parallels between the Ten Commandments, the cardinal virtues, the capital sins and the gifts of the Holy Spirit.

Another frequently used parallel is that between the human father and our heavenly Father. The Fourth Commandment is the first that belongs to the second tablet, because human fatherhood is the image of divine fatherhood. In this context, the authors also gradually developed ideas about the duty to obey and respect one's parents, and the notion of spiritual fatherhood.

Yet another constant feature of this tradition is the discussion of certain episodes in the sacred Scripture in which one of the Ten Commandments seems not to have been obeyed. The most frequent instances are: the episode in which the Jews stole from the Egyptians when they left Egypt, Rahab's lie to protect the spies sent by Joshua to Jericho, Jacob's impersonation of Esau, Abraham's intention to kill his son Isaac, the Hebrew midwives' lies to the Pharaoh to save the Hebrew boys, and so on. The explanations on these points are almost unanimous, and the answers always fit with tradition, although a slight development in the explanations can be perceived. In all these examples, the writers maintain the balance between confirming that these natural moral precepts are immutable, and emphasizing God's authority as Lawmaker, since in each case, God knows what is right and wrong.

To conclude, I would like to point to one important issue that runs through this study: the idea of progress and tradition. The authors depend on each other, doctrine is preserved in its fundamental form, and yet there is constant development. The arguments are presented in a new style, answers are perfected, greater depth is achieved, new issues are raised, but there is always a common thread, which everyone accepts. All the authors take this common ground as their basis when they are trying to move forward.

The Decalogue in Jewish Liturgy

Ruth Langer

The Decalogue is surprisingly absent from today's Jewish liturgical experience. Of course, it appears in due course twice in the annual lectionary cycle, in which traditional Jews read every word of the Torah (Pentateuch). The rabbinic understanding is that the late-spring biblical harvest festival, Shavuot (the Feast of Weeks, Pentecost), was also the day on which God revealed the Torah on Mount Sinai. This led to the Decalogue, and Torah more generally, being the liturgical focus of the day. Nevertheless, the absence of the Decalogue from daily prayers has frequently seemed strange, generating a source of ritual and theological tension in the Jewish world percolating even into those times when it is present. There is evidence for ritual use of the Decalogue among Jews before the destruction of the Temple, making its subsequent absence only more peculiar. This essay will first survey this early evidence and the tension it created; it will then discuss the ways that the Shavuot liturgy exhibits this tension between a focus on the Decalogue and on Torah as a whole, as well as ways that Jews of various times and places have sought to reintegrate the Decalogue into their daily prayers.

Had there been a biblical text commanding the regular recitation of the Decalogue or recording some precedent that might function as a source of imitation, the rabbis would almost certainly have incorporated the text into their liturgy. We see such a case with the *shema'*, whose first paragraph (Deut. 6.4-9) commands, 'these words shall be on your heart. You shall speak of them…when you lie down and when you rise up…' This generated a twice-daily recitation of precisely this text, with the times for proper recitation loosely tied to customary times (and postures) for sleeping and getting up.[1]

There are scholars who suggest that at least an annual recitation of the Decalogue can be traced to the pre-rabbinic period. Moshe Weinfeld[2] writes that, based on the accepted ancient Near Eastern custom of renewing

---

1. Mishnah Berakhot chap. 1 does not invoke this language directly, but the Talmudic discussions of it do.
2. Moshe Weinfeld, 'The Uniqueness of the Decalogue and its Place in Jewish Tradition', in Ben-Zion Segal (ed.), *The Ten Commandments in History and Tradition* (trans. Gershon Levi; Jerusalem: Magnes, 1990), pp. 21-44.

covenants annually, one would expect precisely such a ceremony in Israelite temples, in which the Decalogue was declared. Evidence for such ceremonies comes from echoes of the final Commandments of the Decalogue in Psalms 50 and 81, which he understands as composed for recitation on the festival of Shavuot (Pentecost). However, he here retrojects an a priori assumption about the linkage between Shavuot and Sinai themes, something that he fails to demonstrate for the biblical period.

Weinfeld cites voluminous sources to establish this linkage, but none actually names both the celebratory gathering for the pilgrimage festival and a ritual focus on the Decalogue or the giving of Torah. For example, he cites a line from the Qumran Damascus Document that he connects with the ceremony for those entering the community's covenant in the Rule of the Community (1QS I.16).[3] However, the second text provides no date for the ritual, and the Damascus Document's evidence fails on a number of other levels. It tells us, 'All those who dwell in the camps shall gather in the third month and curse the one who deviates right or left from the *Torah*' (4QD^a 1.17; 4QD^e 7.ii.11). Current understanding interprets this segment of the Damascus Document as a ritual that preceded and prepared for the celebration of Shavuot, not one that took place on the festival itself; it punished transgressors of Torah in general by their expulsion from the community.[4] Thus, Weinfeld's claim that 'this ceremony was conducted on the Festival of Shavuot' and included specific reference to Sinai and the Decalogue[5] cannot be sustained. His argument that Sinai themes inform Acts 2's description of Pentecost is more, much more, plausible,[6] but this text's date places us already in the late first century, after the destruction of the Temple.

Rabbinic tradition records that before the destruction of the Jerusalem Temple, the Decalogue was indeed part of the priests' daily morning liturgy, recited in conjunction with and before the *shema'* (Deut. 6.4-9, 11.13-21, and Num. 15.37-41) during a hiatus in their sacrificial functions.[7] Other evidence suggests the strong possibility that this concatenation of the Decalogue with the *shema'* represents a custom not confined to the priestly

---

3. Which he calls the 'Manual of Discipline'. The full references appear in a later Hebrew version of this in his *The Decalogue and the Recitation of 'Shema': The Development of the Confessions* (Tel Aviv: Hakibbutz Hameuchad, 2001), p. 113.

4. Yonder Moynihan Gillihan, *Civic Ideology, Organization, and Law in the Rule Scrolls: A Comparative Study of the Covenanters' Sect and Contemporary Voluntary Associations in Political Context* (Leiden: E.J. Brill, 2012), pp. 270-75. My thanks to Professor Gillihan for his help with this point.

5. Weinfeld, 'Uniqueness of the Decalogue', p. 39. His 2001 Hebrew publication nuances this point and expresses a shade less certainty.

6. Weinfeld, 'Uniqueness of the Decalogue', pp. 40-43.

7. *Tam.* 5.1.

cult of Jerusalem. First published in 1903 and today dated to c.150 BCE,[8] the so-called Nash Papyrus is a Hebrew liturgical text from Egypt containing the Decalogue followed by the *shema'*. The version of the Decalogue found there most closely resembles that of Exodus 20 (with references to Egypt as a 'house of slavery' removed!), meaning that its choice of passages may not derive from the biblical juxtaposition of these passages in Deuteronomy 5 and 6.[9] The papyrus's Hebrew text closely parallels that which apparently underlies the Septuagint's translation. This includes the appearance of a liturgical bridge between the two passages reading, ואלה החוק[י]ם והמשפטים אשר צוה משה את [בני] [ישרא]ל במדבר בצאתם מארץ [מצרים שמ]ע]' ('and these are the statutes and the ordinances that Moses commanded the children of Israel in the wilderness when they left Egypt. Hear… ').[10] This language appears in the Septuagint as an expansion of Deut. 6.4, preceding its literal translation. This suggests that these words reflect a liturgical reality in both witnesses. Worthy of mention in this context are also the *tefillin* (phylacteries) found at Qumran that include the Decalogue from Deuteronomy along with the *shema'*. Note, however, that these texts were enclosed in a leather capsule and would not have been read.[11]

However, these witnesses are insufficient to establish that Jews everywhere were participating in a liturgical recitation of the Decalogue at this time or that it had any place in their synagogues which were, as yet, primarily a place for the reading and teaching of Scripture rather than of prayer.[12] In addition, there is no evidence that the Decalogue remained part of daily rabbinic liturgy as it emerged after the 70 CE destruction of the Jerusalem

---

8. Moshe Greenberg, 'Nash Papyrus', in Michael Berenbaum and Fred Skolnik (eds.), *Encyclopaedia judaica* (Detroit: Macmillan Reference USA, 2nd edn, 2007), XIV, pp. 783-84. The manuscript itself is in the holdings of the Cambridge University Library (Or. 233). The original publication was by F.C. Burkitt, 'The Hebrew Papyrus of the Ten Commandments', *JQR* 15 (1903), pp. 392-408.

9. See Reuven Kimelman's detailed discussion of the relationship between the Decalogue and the *shema'* in his 'The *Shema'* and its Rhetoric: The Case for the *Shema'* Being More than Creation, Revelation, and Redemption', *Journal of Jewish Thought and Philosophy* 2 (1992), pp. 135-43. He is clearly correct that the *shema'* 'usurp[ed] the role of' the Decalogue in Jewish liturgical practice, but he may give too much historical credence to the later midrashic attempt to explain its received reality.

10. Ephraim E. Urbach, 'The Role of the Ten Commandments in Jewish Worship', in Segal (ed.), *The Ten Commandments in History and Tradition*, p. 163. Urbach discusses the rabbinic sources in much more detail than I do here.

11. Yigael Yadin, *Tefillin from Qumran (X Q Phyl 1-4)* (Jerusalem: Israel Exploration Society, Shrine of the Book, 1969), pp. 27-29.

12. Stefan C. Reif, *Judaism and Hebrew Prayer: New Perspectives on Jewish Liturgical History* (Cambridge: Cambridge University Press, 1993), p. 83. When rabbinic prayer became the dominant liturgy of the popular synagogue is a matter of significant scholarly dispute. I believe it likely took many centuries after the destruction of the Temple, particularly in the areas away from direct rabbinic leadership.

Temple by the Romans. The earliest rabbinic discussions of this liturgical context, from the early third century CE, speak of 'reciting the *shema*'' as the technical name for the ritual and know only the recitation of three biblical passages, not four; the first, the Decalogue, has disappeared.[13] The Talmud, redacted a few centuries later, does discuss this omission. In the name of two mid to late third-century sages, Rav Matna and Rabbi Samuel bar Naḥman, the Jerusalem Talmud records, 'It would have been proper to recite the Decalogue daily. Why do we not recite it? Because of the claim of the *minim* (sectarians) that only these were given to Moses at Sinai.'[14] The parallel passage in the Babylonian Talmud records instances from the third to the fifth centuries, when a series of Babylonian communities sought to reinstate the daily Decalogue, but their requests were denied 'because of the seditious talk of the *minim*'.[15] As Ezra Fleischer notes, 'There is no custom in the realm of [Jewish] liturgy whose *absence* is documented and explained in the Talmudic sources in such a clear manner'.[16]

Attention to this reality continues in contemporary scholarship. Who these *minim* are has been the subject of much debate. The word itself simply means 'kinds' or 'sorts', and the early rabbis simply apply it as a term of opprobrium to Jews who do not accept their leadership or whom they considered heretical. Among others, this did include Jewish-Christians and eventually extended to include Gentile Christians.[17] However, even where Christians have given precedence to the Decalogue over the rest of the Pentateuch's contents in actual practice, there is no evidence that they claimed that 'only the Ten Commandments were given at Sinai'.[18] It is also not cer-

---

13. The first three chapters of Mishnah Berakhot present the various laws about the ritual but presuppose significant familiarity with it. *Ber.* 2.2 in passing provides a delineation of the segments of this liturgy: it discusses the subsections between which one might, if necessary, interrupt this liturgical element; and then it presents the logic underlying the ordering of the biblical selections. In neither list does it mention the Decalogue.

14. *y. Ber.* 1.5 (4 in the Leiden MS), 3c.

15. *b. Ber.* 12a, there without the explicit explanation of what trouble the sectarians were causing. My translation of *tar'omet* as 'seditious talk' is according to Marcus Jastrow, *A Dictionary of the Targumim, the Talmud Babli and Yerushalmi, and the Midrashic Literature* (New York: G.P. Putnam, 1903), p. 1701.

16. *Eretz-Israel Prayer and Prayer Rituals as Portrayed in the Geniza Documents* (Jerusalem: Magnes, 1988), p. 259 [Hebrew].

17. See my *Cursing the Christians? A History of the Birkat HaMinim* (New York: Oxford University Press, 2012), pp. 59-60, 78-81, and Chapter 1 *passim*, and its notes (which discuss some of the voluminous literature on the subject).

18. See Urbach, 'The Role of the Ten Commandments', pp. 170-71. A letter of Pliny the Younger dated 112 CE does suggests that the Christians of Bithynia were reciting the Ten Commandments daily. This may, however, be more a continuation of Temple practice. See the discussion of Casper J. Kraemer, Jr, 'Pliny and the Early Church Service: Fresh Light from an Old Source', *Classical Philology* 29 (1934), pp. 293-300.

tain that the troublemakers who made such a claim continued to have a real presence among the Jewish community.

Ephraim Urbach hypothesizes that the fact that people continually sought to reinstate the Decalogue suggests that the reason for its abolition was no longer current.[19] In making this claim, though, he presupposes that the populace understood that the historical situation had changed, but that the rabbis insisted on maintaining what had become their ingrained tradition. However, rabbinic texts record only the perceptions of these elite leaders. If we read between the lines, we can suggest the possibility that the general populace was simply not particularly interested in the rabbinic investment in this bit of history. Drawing on a general knowledge of Scripture and simple logic, they regularly sought greater liturgical prominence for this central text of Torah. In their eyes, that it had been abolished once need not determine later practice. In this, we may have a first glimpse of a tug of war between this rabbinic tradition that resists privileging the Decalogue over other parts of the Pentateuch and popular demand to do exactly that. This tension breaks through intermittently and finds expression in various corners of Jewish liturgical life.

Indeed, the Decalogue does seem to have had an ongoing role in the Sabbath and holiday liturgy of the Jews following the Rite of the Land of Israel. This rite was fortuitously preserved for us because the Jews of the Ben Ezra Synagogue in Cairo, who followed it long after it had met its demise in the Land of Israel itself, tossed worn Hebrew manuscripts into an attic storeroom, known as a *geniza*. Discovered and purchased by westerners in the mid 1890s, it has provided scholars with a treasure trove of information.[20] Among the manuscripts was a document dated to the spring of 1211 which provided a list of customs that this community promised to preserve, including a 'procession with the Torah scroll that is known as "the book of the song" from the ark to the reading desk and the reading of the Ten Commandments and returning it to the ark'.[21] This pledge to uphold the customs of the community was a response to the pressure placed upon these Jews by Abraham Maimonides, who sought to bring their rite into conformity with Babylonian custom, which he succeeded in doing soon thereafter in spite of this pledge.[22] Based on some liturgical fragments from the *geniza*, Jacob

---

19. Urbach, 'The Role of the Ten Commandments', p. 169.

20. For a history of the *geniza*, see Adina Hoffman and Peter Cole, *Sacred Trash: The Lost and Found World of the Cairo Geniza* (New York: Schocken, 2011).

21. Fleischer, *Eretz-Israel Prayer*, pp. 219-20. The original publication of this material was by Jacob Mann, *The Jews in Egypt and in Palestine, under the Fatimid Caliphs*, I (Oxford: Oxford University Press, 1920), pp. 222-23. Fleischer, *Eretz-Israel Prayer*, pp. 264-65, establishes that this was the custom of the leading rabbinic academy of the Land of Israel, and not only of the Jews of Fustat.

22. Elisha Russ-Fishbane, 'The Maimonidean Legacy in the East: A Study of Father and Son', *JQR* 102 (Spring 2012), pp. 204-11.

Mann was able to locate this reading of the Decalogue within the larger liturgy. It followed the early morning recitation of Psalms and preceded the Song at the Sea (Exod. 15); this in turn was followed by the statutory blessings that precede the *shemaʻ*.[23] On the basis of a wider selection of manuscripts, Ezra Fleischer surmises that this was never a weekday liturgy.[24]

The Decalogue in these manuscripts includes introductory verses from the beginning of Deuteronomy 5, with their emphasis on the eternality of the Sinai covenant, and continues through the summary verse at the end, 5.19. Ezra Fleischer suggests that this indicates that the recitation here was not merely to remind the worshippers of the text.

> If that were the intention—they certainly would have chosen the Exodus language. The intention of those formulating the rite was to emphasize the authority of the commandments at all times, not only through their content, but also on the basis of the covenant that was enacted through them between God and Israel through the generations.

Fleischer also notes that the introductory language's reference to 'statutes and ordinances' might function as a counter to the claims of the *minim* and to emphasize that the revelation at Sinai was of the entire Torah.[25] Other manuscripts continue with additional verses, such as Deut. 30.11-15, 33.4 and 4.44 (in that order) that construct an even more obvious liturgical statement to this effect.[26] In addition, some manuscripts indicate that the recitation was communal, preceded by the standard Torah blessing and other key scriptural passages, like those about that day's sacrifices.[27] However, other manuscripts lack this liturgical element altogether, suggesting that it was not universally preserved in this rite.[28]

Do these *geniza* fragments represent an effort to restore the Decalogue or do they represent the continuation of the earlier situation, before the daily recitation was ended? Fleischer suggests that it is unlikely that Jews in the post-Talmudic period would have deliberately acted against the Talmudic injunctions, particularly because one of the most elaborate witnesses seems to come from the seat of rabbinic leadership itself. He suggests instead that

---

23. 'Genizah Fragments of the Palestinian Order of Service', *Hebrew Union College Annual* 2 (1925), pp. 281-85. Mann's discussion here lacks the richer data that inform Fleischer's discussion. Fleischer published the relevant part of the manuscript, Cambridge T-S K27/57, p. 2, in *Eretz-Israel Prayer*, p. 261.

24. Fleischer, *Eretz-Israel Prayer*, p. 271. Weekday prayers would be shortened because of work demands.

25. Fleischer, *Eretz-Israel Payer*, p. 262 and n. 17; pp. 262-63 also reproduce Mann's second text.

26. Fleischer, *Eretz-Israel Prayer*, p. 268.

27. Fleischer, *Eretz-Israel Prayer*, pp. 269-70.

28. Fleischer, *Eretz-Israel Prayer*, p. 271.

what the Talmudic texts record was not the abolition of all recitation of the Decalogue but rather just its recitation in conjunction with the *shema'*. While the *shema'* was early formalized as a key component of the daily prayers, the same cannot be said about the early morning prayers and songs preceding it in the morning. Its greater flexibility allowed those Jews who so wished to continue to recite the Decalogue, but in a new context.[29] However, we should note that there is no evidence to prove or disprove Fleischer's assumption of continuity. He may well be granting the rabbinic academy and Talmudic tradition more authority than it actually had over lived liturgical practice. What is evident is that in spite of rabbinic objections, even some rabbis following the customs of the Land of Israel included a formal recitation of the Decalogue in their Sabbath and festival services at least until the thirteenth century.[30]

The place where the Decalogue does take over in most dramatic form, albeit with clear rabbinic consent, is in the redefinition of the Shavuot pilgrimage festival. Other Temple-focused holidays had themes and rituals that (relatively) easily translated to an ongoing observance outside Jerusalem before the Temple's destruction and hence after it fell as well. However, the Bible defines Shavuot as the completion of the counting of seven weeks from a day during Passover, during which a sheaf of barley was offered each day in the Temple (Lev. 23.15ff.). Which day precisely began this counting was a matter of significant dispute in the late Second Temple period. The specific ritual marking the fiftieth day was the offering of the first fruits of the wheat harvest (Exod. 34.22). *Meg.* 3.5 lists Deut. 16.9-12 as the Torah reading for Shavuot. This rather bare-bones text (from the deuteronomic festival calendar) mentions only the counting of weeks, the agricultural nature of the holiday, and that its rejoicing needs to take place 'in the place where the Eternal your God will choose to establish his name', that is, Jerusalem. Based on all this, and as an extension of the biblical name for the day that comes immediately after the fall festival of Sukkot (Booths/Tabernacles),[31] the early rabbis called the holiday '*Aṣeret*, meaning that it was the gathering that concluded the Passover season, not a fully free-standing festival. Unlike other holidays, they gave it no dedicated tractate or extended discussion in the Mishnah.

However, *t. Meg.* 3.5, a more or less contemporaneous text with the Mishnah,[32] adds, 'and there are those who say [that the Torah reading is],

---

29. Fleischer, *Eretz-Israel Prayer*, p. 272.
30. Fleischer, *Eretz-Israel Prayer*, pp. 273-74.
31. See the descriptions of this eighth day in the same passages listed above, following the description of Sukkot.
32. The relative dating of Mishnah and Tosefta is currently a matter of significant scholarly discussion. It had previously been assumed that the Tosefta collected

"In the third month"'. In other words, the Tosefta records an acceptable, but presumably less common, alternative tradition that the Shavuot reading begins with Exodus 19. People advocating this custom presumably counted beginning on the second day of Passover, making the fiftieth day coincide with the dates of the Sinai narrative. Thus, it was appropriate for them to read the Sinai narrative and give Shavuot a more specific meaning. The Jerusalem Talmud alludes to this tradition in its comment on the Mishnah but presents no resolution.[33] Is it possible that this innovation came into Judaism as a response to the Christian Pentecost? Just as the nascent Christian community celebrated their having received the Spirit on that day (Acts 2), so too now Jews would celebrate their receiving God's Word, the Torah.[34]

In contrast to the Jerusalem Talmud, the Babylonian Talmud cites the Tosefta and adds 'Here where we observe two days, we read them both, but in reverse order'—the Sinai narrative on the first day, and the deuteronomic prescription on the second.[35] This custom eventually became universal outside the Land of Israel. Curiously, the reading of the festival calendar remained the reading for the second day instead of displacing it with a reading of the deuteronomic version of the Sinai narrative, perhaps relegating the festival description to the *maftir*, the additional reading. This may be because a festival *maftir* generally describes the sacrifices that would have been offered on that day, making Num. 28.26-31 (today's text) more appropriate.

However, even inside the land, where the norm remained to observe a single day of the holiday, the reading became Exodus 19–20. The sermon for Shavuot in the fifth-century midrashic compilation, the *Pesiqta d'Rav*

---

materials that had been excluded from the Mishnah and presented them as a commentary on the slightly earlier text. Today, some scholars suggest that a form of the Tosefta may have predated the Mishnah, although it received another later editorial layer. See, for example, Judith Hauptman, *Rereading the Mishnah: A New Approach to Ancient Jewish Texts* (Tübingen: Mohr Siebeck, 2005).

33. *y. Meg.* 3.5, 74b.

34. Israel Jacob Yuval raises this possibility in his *Two Nations in your Womb: Perceptions of Jews and Christians in Late Antiquity and the Middle Ages* (trans. Barbara Harshav and Jonathan Chipman; Berkeley: University of California Press, 2006), p. 24.

35. *b. Meg.* 31a. Rabbinic practice is that all holidays (but not fast days) are observed for two days outside the Land of Israel. The original reasoning given is that when calendation was based on actual sighting of the new moon, those living too far from Jerusalem (or the later rabbinic court) would not hear the news in time to be sure whether the month started one day or the next (the lunar month is 29¼ days, creating the uncertainty). This system continued even when the calendar began to be set by calculation in the fourth century. Today, when communication is not the issue and Jewish life is vibrant in the Land of Israel, this second day has the additional theological function of reinforcing the centrality of life in Israel for diaspora Jews.

Kahana, is on the Exodus reading.³⁶ The slightly later but also holiday-centered midrashic collection, *Pesiqta Rabbati*, focuses entirely on the Decalogue, although it introduces its discussion with a meditation on Moses' experience in encountering God and receiving revelation.³⁷ Thus, a revolution took place in the meaning of the holiday, one enabled by at least two factors: a recognition that the interval between the Exodus and Sinai matched the calendar decreed for the agricultural holiday; and a precedent, at least for Passover, of reading from Torah the chapter that reflected directly on the historical events of the day (Exod. 12) and not just the dictates for its ongoing observance.

This focus on the moment of revelation and the Decalogue itself shaped the liturgical poetry for the holiday. *Piyyut*, Hebrew liturgical poetry, designed originally to substitute for statutory texts of the prayers, emerged in the Land of Israel in the Byzantine period. The first poets known by name date to the fifth century CE, and the most enduring poetry for Shavuot, written by the great master Elazar b'Rabbi Kalir, apparently precedes the Arab conquest in the early seventh century. Kalir's poetry was adopted by the Jews of Byzantine Italy, and from there was carried north into the Rhineland by the end of the first millennium. There it set the pattern for new Ashkenazi (northern/central European) poetry, including, particularly, poetry written there for the second day of the holiday that was observed only in the diaspora.³⁸ It is this aggregate of liturgical poetry that made the Decalogue and the experience of Sinai into the dominant theme, not only in the Torah reading and sermon, but also in the central prayers.

This complex poetry is written in deliberately difficult Hebrew, full of allusions to Bible and its midrashic interpretations by the rabbis. Its beauty lies in its ability to communicate content while adhering to formal structural patterns of acrostics, complex rhymes, line length³⁹ and incorporation

---

36. Translated into English by William G. Braude and Israel J. Kapstein, *Pesiqta de-Rab Kahana: R. Kahana's Compilation of Discourses for Sabbaths and Festal Days* (Philadelphia: Jewish Publication Society of America, 1975), *Pisqa* 12. Of course, it is possible that this compilation emerges from a community following this custom. We cannot argue from it to a universal change.

37. Translated into English by William G. Braude, *Pesikta Rabbati: Discourses for Feasts, Fasts, and Special Sabbaths* (New Haven, London: Yale University Press, 1968), I, Piska'ot 20-24.

38. Presumably other diaspora Jews also had composed *piyyut* for the second day, but the Ashkenazi communities preferred these new compositions while preserving those of Kalir, whom they revered and considered a source of liturgical authority (see my 'Kalir Was a Tanna: Rabbenu Tam's Invocation of Antiquity in Defense of the Ashkenazi Payyetanic Tradition', *Hebrew Union College Annual* 67 [1996], pp. 95-106). The thematic focus of *piyyut* for the second day remains Sinai and the Decalogue even when the lectionary is the festival sacrifices.

39. True meter is added to this list only in medieval Spain in a body of poetry that

of biblical verses or snippets thereof. Any translation is therefore necessarily inadequate. Medieval Jews themselves recognized that full appreciation of the poetry required study of it before the holiday and critiqued situations where lack of understanding undermined synagogue decorum.[40] Consequently, beginning in the nineteenth century, most Ashkenazi Jews ceased reciting this poetry except on the most solemn days of the year, Rosh Hashanah and Yom Kippur (the New Year and Day of Atonement, in the early fall).[41] Printers of modern prayer books mostly omit it or consign it, untranslated, to the back of the book, where synagogues ignore it. Of contemporary prayer books with English translations, only the five-volume *Complete ArtScroll Machzor*[42] presents the poetry, translates it and accompanies it with substantial commentary. This prayer book follows the Eastern Ashkenazi (Polish) rite and will, of necessity, form the point of reference for our discussion here.[43]

Full discussion of the poetry for Shavuot would require a book of its own, so I will present here only a summary and analysis of its reflections on the Decalogue.[44] The oldest layer, the Kalirian,[45] is an elaborate series of poems known as a *qedushta'*[46] inserted into first three blessings of the

does not enter into our discussion here. These poems do adhere to a standard number of beats per stich.

40. See my *To Worship God Properly: Tensions Between Liturgical Custom and Halakhah in Judaism* (Cincinnati: Hebrew Union College Press, 1998), p. 132.

41. Langer, *To Worship God Properly*, pp. 182-85.

42. *Machzor Ateres Zvi, The Complete ArtScroll Machzor, Shavuos* (ed. Meir Zlotowitz and Avie Gold; trans. and commentary Nosson Scherman; New York: Mesorah Publications, 1995).

43. Most western Ashkenazi congregations (those represented in the highly respected Heidenheim *maḥzor*) recited Kalir's poetry on the second day and that of Simon bar Isaac (see below) on the first. The Sephardi (Spanish and Portuguese) rites ceased reciting an analogous corpus of prayers in the medieval period because of both an aesthetic shift that led them to jettison received compositions and concerns about the legitimacy of interrupting statutory prayers. See Langer, *To Worship God Properly*, pp. 147-82.

44. Any full discussion must consult Jonah Fraenkel, *Maḥzor Shavuot according to All the Branches of the Ashkenazi Rite* (Jerusalem: Koren, 2000) [Hebrew], which aggregates all the available evidence from manuscript and printed editions.

45. For a partial English analysis of segments of Kalir's poem for Shavuot, focused narrowly only on the Decalogue, see Aharon Mirsky, 'The Ten Commandments in the Liturgical Poetry of Eleazar Kallir', in Segal (ed.), *The Ten Commandments in History and Tradition*, pp. 343-54. Note that this English version does not present the entirety of the original Hebrew article because of translation difficulties. Also of interest are the two following essays in this volume, on a Judeo-Arabic poem wrongly attributed to Saadia Gaon, and on poetry in Spain and Yemen.

46. Sometimes called a *qeroveṣ*, particularly in Ashkenaz. *Qedushta'* is the term preferred in contemporary scholarly discourse.

'*amidah*,[47] leading up to the recitation of the first verse of the *qedushah*, the angelic liturgy (Isa. 6.3) in the third blessing. In his introductory triad of poems, Kalir first evokes the thunder and lightning that accompanied revelation when the Israelites arrived at Sinai, then turns to Moses' experience in receiving revelation and then to God's coming down on the mountain to present the Torah to Israel after other nations had rejected it.[48] The fourth poem, which begins the elaborations less tied to the statutory liturgical stations, quickly summarizes the Decalogue itself, giving a few words of comment on each Commandment.[49] Kalir embedded his name as the acrostic of the fifth poem. He begins with a discussion, replete with multiple echoes in midrash, of the significance of God's beginning the Decalogue with the first (silent) letter of the Hebrew alphabet; he then reflects on the people's inability to receive direct revelation. In the sixth poem,[50] Torah speaks in the first person at great length, describing its own history from God's creating it two thousand years before the rest of creation, through the entire narrative history of Genesis and Exodus up to the moment that God gave it to Israel at Sinai. In the seventh poem, Kalir presents a lengthy twelve-stanza composition, the last ten of whose stanzas discourse on each of the Ten Commandments in turn, giving this poem its distinctive name '*dibrin*', that is, the Aramaic for 'words', as the Bible itself names the Decalogue's Commandments (Exod. 34.28; Deut. 4.13; 10.4). Finally, the *qedushta'* concludes with another lengthy poem, the eighth element, that begins with a meditation on the complexity of the commandments revealed in the entirety of Torah, then turns to a number of midrashim about the experience of revelation, and concludes, as one would expect, in a literary transition to the angelic liturgy, here with a particular focus on the angels' response to Sinai.[51]

---

47. The '*amidah* (literally, 'standing' for its posture) is also known in early rabbinic texts simply as *hatefillah* (the prayer) or colloquially as *shemoneh 'esreh* (eighteen, for its original structure of eighteen benedictions on weekdays). This is the central element of every rabbinic prayer service, three times a day on weekdays and four on Sabbaths and festivals. On Sabbaths and festivals, it consists of a series of seven benedictions. The *qedushta'* originally substituted for the body of the first two benedictions and introduced the third. Outside the rite of the Land of Israel, it came to be recited in addition to the statutory texts of these prayers.

48. A well-known midrashic motif that Kalir's audience probably would have recognized.

49. Mirsky's English article comments only on this fourth poem, where the Hebrew original discusses the seventh as well. Note that the translator has run together the fourth poem and the first two stanzas of the seventh poem.

50. The *ArtScroll* footnote (p. 230) indicating that this poem is not by Kalir but by Shimon bar Yitzchak (Simon bar Isaac, see below) is almost certainly wrong. The poem is unsigned, but is consistent with the norms of Kalir's poetry. See Fraenkel, *Mahzor Shavuot*, p. xxiv.

51. Printed in the back of the *ArtScroll Machzor*, pp. 656-58, with no translation and with the note that 'some congregations recite' it.

This sequence sets the pattern for a set of poems for the same stations, very similar in their general content, on the second day of the holiday, written by the early and influential Ashkenazi rabbi and cantor, Simon bar Rabbi Isaac (c. 950, Mainz–c. 1020).[52] He wrote prolifically for many of the poetic stations for which Kalir either did not write or for which his poetry was not preserved.[53] Simon's poetry also dominates Ashkenazi traditions for the morning *shema'* blessings (the *yoṣerot*) on the first day, perhaps because what little Kalir wrote was not transmitted.[54] Here, the initial poem, the *yoṣer*, is the most elaborate, and in Simon's composition for the first day which he built around citations from Proverbs 8's hymn to wisdom, Torah again speaks in the first person about its own experience of revelation. Only in the last poem in the blessing following *shema'*, the *zulat*, leading up to the words 'there is no God like you', does Simon specifically structure his poem around the Ten Commandments. The first word(s) of each Commandment open each stanza, which itself consists of three short rhymed lines on the theme of the blessing. The first letters of the stanzas themselves embed the poet's name. His name requires an eleventh stanza, introduced by 'and all' from Exod. 20.15. The first composition (*guf hayoṣer*) found in the *ArtScroll Machzor* for the second day is by an unknown Simon,[55] and it is less sophisticated, with the *yoṣer* recapping the content of revelation and summarizing the Ten Commandments. The rest of the poems for this section of the liturgy all duplicate those recited on the first day, including the final one with its emphasis on the Decalogue directly. There was some local variation in the traditions of poetry.[56]

---

52. According to Avraham Grossman, *The Early Sages of Ashkenaz: Their Lives, Leadership and Works (900–1096)* (Jerusalem: Magnes, 1988), pp. 88, 92 [Hebrew].

53. More poetry by Kalir has been discovered among the documents from the Cairo *geniza*. Studies of his poetry have been published almost entirely in Hebrew, most notably by Shalom Spiegel, Ezra Fleischer (including in the context of his larger studies of liturgical poetry) and Shulamit Elizur.

54. Fleischer publishes a Kalir *yoṣer* for Shavuot from the *geniza* in his *The Yoṣer: Its Emergence and Development* (Jerusalem: Magnes, 1984), pp. 102-106 [Hebrew]. The individual stanzas of the first poem conclude with citations of the opening words of each of the Ten Commandments, and the second poem (from another manuscript), which would conclude a series, does not focus on the Decalogue directly. This suggests that Simon did not know these poems, as Kalir's poetry generally sets the model that Ashkenazi poets imitate.

55. See Fraenkel, *Maḥzor Shavuot*, p. xix n. 97, who points out that it has been mistakenly attributed to Simon bar Isaac.

56. The Heidenheim *maḥzor* provides three texts: this, as the text of most Polish and Bohemian Jews; an anonymous second text of similar structure as the text of most German communities; and a third, by Joseph Tov Elem, as the text of 'some communities'. W. Heidenheim, *Gebete für das Wochenfest mit deutscher Uebersetzung* (repr., Rödelheim: I. Lehrberger & Co., 1870), p. 268. Fraenkel, *Maḥzor Shavuot*, xxii,

For the evening services, all Ashkenazi rites incorporated the poetry of the leading French sage Rabbi Joseph bar Samuel Tov Elem (c. 980–c. 1050),[57] usually for the first day,[58] and of Rabbi Isaac ben Moses (d. 1096, Mainz) for the second.[59] The Western rite used instead the poetry of Rabbi Eliezer ben Natan (c. 1090–1170, Mainz) for the second night. The poetry for the evening service is always brief on evenings when a festive meal follows. However, this poetry too is structured by the opening words of the Decalogue (plus some additional surrounding verses) along with an alphabetical acrostic concluding with the poet's name, here spread out over the four blessings surrounding the recitation of *shema'*.

Several additional poetic traditions became part of the Shavuot experience. In the additional (*musaf*) service that follows the Torah reading, many communities, including those of the Sephardi rites, recited on the first day an ancient genre known as *'azharot*, 'warnings', which summarize the entirety of the Torah's commandments.[60] Two poems also reflect a medieval custom of translating Scripture, often in expansive ways, into the vernacular. In late antiquity, this vernacular was Aramaic and, even in medieval Europe, this remained the language for these poems. One, about Moses' experience in receiving the Decalogue, was inserted just before the reading of that text.[61] The other—and the only one of any of these poems still regularly recited today—precedes the first day's reading of Exodus 19–20 and reflects mostly on the angels' response to revelation.[62] Thus, the traditions

---

identifies the third as originating in the French rite which died out with the expulsions of Jews from France in the fourteenth century.

57. According to Avraham Grossman, *The Early Sages of France: Their Lives, Leadership and Works* (Jerusalem: Magnes, 1995), p. 48 [Hebrew].

58. Fraenkel, *Maḥzor Shavuot*, p. xv.

59. There is some dispute over his identity and whether he is the rabbi martyred by the Crusaders. See Fraenkel, *Maḥzor Shavuot*, p. xv n. 63, and Grossman, *The Early Sages of Ashkenaz*, pp. 393-94.

60. *ArtScroll Machzor*, pp. 659-66 (untranslated). The origin of this genre of *piyyut* is unknown, but it is already found in the earliest preserved Jewish prayer book, from the ninth century CE, the *Seder Rav Amram Gaon* (ed. D. Goldschmidt; Jerusalem: Mosad ha-Rav Ḳuḳ, 1971), II.97, p. 131. This early version has no discernible organizing principle and does not follow the Talmudic understanding that these commandments number 613. The author of this text knew Babylonian rabbinic teachings. The poem that comes at this point on the second day is apparently an ancient fragment of an introduction to the *'azharot* which have themselves dropped out, perhaps because of their length (Fraenkel, *Maḥzor Shavuot*, pp. xi-xiv, xxxvi-xxxix).

61. *ArtScroll Machzor*, pp. 658-59 (untranslated). Some medieval communities also inserted Aramaic poetic translations after the reading of each of the commandments (Fraenkel, *Maḥzor Shavuot*, pp. xxix-xxxiv).

62. *ArtScroll Machzor*, pp. 266-73. Its original location was after the reading of Exod. 19.1. Whether this genre goes back to roots in the Land of Israel is unknown (Fraenkel, *Maḥzor Shavuot*, p. xxviii and n. 165).

of liturgical poetry transformed the Shavuot liturgy into one that focused intensely on the experience of the Sinai revelation from the perspectives of God, the angels, Torah itself and Israel. While the Decalogue takes precedence, this poetic corpus adamantly presents Sinai as the place and time of the revelation of the entirety of the Pentateuch. The poetry does not allow one to say 'only these were given at Sinai'.

The demise of this poetry is part of the demise of liturgical poetry in general that accompanied a modern demand for shorter, more comprehensible services according to new aesthetics.[63] On Shavuot, in particular, this may have been hastened by the rise in popularity of the *Tiqqun Leil Shavuot*, a Shavuot vigil where participants study Torah all night in preparation for a morning service at which the lectionary (if no longer the poetry) is the Decalogue. The *Tiqqun* originated in the mystical kabbalistic teachings of Rabbi Isaac Luria in the sixteenth century. Luria's text involves reading in order the beginning and end of: each of the weekly lectionary portions of the entirety of Torah, the books of the rest of the Bible, the Mishnah, the *Sefer Yeṣirah* and the *Zohar*. In the midst of the *Zohar* readings one finds Maimonides' list of all 613 commandments. The only texts read in more expansive fashion are all the biblical passages having to do directly with the Decalogue or the narratives surrounding it, as well as the commandments about Shavuot itself[64] and special functions of the priests. This ritual then also combines an emphasis on Sinai as the point of revelation of the entirety of Torah, written and oral,[65] with special emphasis on the themes of the day—including the Decalogue. It functions, through ritualized study, as a personal 'standing at Sinai' while also embodying the tension between giving special emphasis to the Decalogue and celebration of the entirety of revelation.[66]

Just as the formal morning recitation of the Decalogue bowed to rabbinic disapproval and largely disappeared, so too did most of the *piyyut*. However,

---

63. On this dynamic, see my *To Worship God Properly*, pp. 182-85.

64. This is also the topic of the *Zohar* passage.

65. 'Written Torah' refers to the canon of the entire Hebrew Bible. 'Oral Torah' refers to the traditions of its interpretation in rabbinic Judaism, a tradition that the rabbis also trace back to Sinai. Its redaction begins with the Mishnah in the early third century CE, and it remains an open category, with key texts achieving written form by around the end of the first millennium. The 'textualization' of these materials is a matter of much scholarly discussion today. See most recently, Talya Fishman, *Becoming the People of the Talmud: Oral Torah as Written Tradition in Medieval Jewish Culture* (Philadelphia: University of Pennsylvania Press, 2011).

66. Today, many communities study, but in less ritualized fashion, with opportunities to learn from a broader range of texts and approaches to them. Congregations toward the liberal end of the Jewish spectrum may offer late-night study sessions but rarely go all night.

the popular desire to elevate the Decalogue never really disappeared. The strongest performative statement of this is the custom of standing when the Decalogue is read from the Torah scroll, a custom that mimics the posture of the Israelites at Sinai and which persists in spite of occasional but significant rabbinic disapproval. Elevating one part of Torah over the rest is simply problematic. This disapproval, though, seems mostly to emerge where the ruling rabbis are applying theoretical legal norms and are not invested in the customs of the community concerned, a phenomenon that often accompanied mass migrations.[67] The general consensus over the centuries has been to allow this custom to persist, perhaps because protest is futile.[68]

Two final customs that do persist today require mention. The first needs only brief comment: by the medieval period, it had become customary to differentiate the four services of the Sabbath by varying the introductions to the central blessing of its *'amidah*, the sanctification of the day. In the morning, the theme is the revelation of the Sabbath Commandment at Sinai. The liturgy utilizes a fragment of a *piyyut* which, although today followed by Exod. 31.16-17, initially probably introduced the text of the Sabbath Commandment from the Decalogue in its deuteronomic form. In his detailed discussion of this text, Naphtali Wieder suggests that this fragment comes from a *piyyut* that incorporated poetry into each of the seven blessings of the Sabbath (or festival *'amidah*), with the poem now used here treating what in Jewish counting is the fourth Commandment.[69]

Finally, when one turns to the end of the weekday morning service in a contemporary orthodox prayer book, one will often find that there are additional passages of various sorts printed there, with the recommendation that

---

67. On this phenomenon, see my *To Worship God Properly*, especially the conclusion.

68. See Urbach's discussion and citation of the Maimonidean sources, 'The Role of the Ten Commandments', pp. 186-89. The issue emerges periodically even today. See, for example, the 1985 responsum of Rabbi Eliezer Yehuda Waldenberg (1916–2006, Jerusalem), *Ṣiṣ Eliezer* 17.26 [Hebrew] (Bar-Ilan Responsa database, v. 20), where he rules that one should follow the established custom of a congregation. He also rejects relying on the Maimonidean sources that Urbach cites, saying that anything that has emerged recently from manuscript obviously did not form part of the ongoing legal tradition of Jewish life. Note that the custom to stand and feel a sense of participation extends also to hearing the Song at the Sea (Exod. 15), both in its daily recitation and in its ritual lectionary reading in the normal cycle and on the seventh day of Passover. Thus, this gesture is not confined to the three readings of the Decalogue during the liturgical year (twice from the lectionary cycle and once on Shavuot).

69. Naphtali Wieder, '"*Yismaḥ Moshe*"—Opposition and Defense', in *The Formation of Jewish Liturgy in the East and the West: A Collection of Essays* (Jerusalem: Ben-Zvi Institute, 1998), I, pp. 295-322 [Hebrew]. Other themes are: Sabbath rest in the evening, with a citation of Gen. 2.1-3; the Sabbath sacrifice in the additional service, with a citation of Num. 28.9-10; and the eschatological Sabbath (without citing verses directly) in the afternoon service.

these ought to be recited daily, although outside the context of public liturgy. Exactly which passages appear varies, but they frequently include the Decalogue.[70] This ritual seems to derive from a discussion by the *Tur* ('*Oraḥ Ḥayyim* 1, Rabbi Jacob ben Asher, c. 1269, Cologne–c. 1343, Toledo) in which he suggests that the person who awakens too early to begin the morning prayers immediately (while it is still dark) should express and reinforce his piety by reciting various petitionary prayers and biblical passages, including the Decalogue. This directive was by no means self-evident, especially in Spain, for Rabbi Solomon ben Adret (the Rashba, 1235–1310, Barcelona) had ruled recently and explicitly in two separate *responsa* that the Decalogue may not be recited.[71] However, these sources together suggest that Spanish Jews really wanted to find a way to recite the Decalogue daily.

In his comment on the *Tur*, the *Beit Yosef* (Joseph Karo, 1488, Toledo–1575, Safed) mentions and dismisses the Talmudic prohibition on reciting the Decalogue, concluding that that prohibition only applies to public recitations. He writes, 'In private, where there can be no claims of the *minim*, it is good to recite it, for by means of this, one will daily recall standing at Sinai and by this strengthen one's faith'. The sixteenth-century Polish Rabbi Moses Isserles (Cracow, 1525 [1530?]–1572), in his objection to the *Tur*'s proposal, simply cites the Rashba's responsa.[72] In his more influential commentary on Karo's *Shulḥan 'Arukh* ('*Oraḥ ḥayyim* 1.5), where Karo had omitted the public / private distinction, Isserles omits the Rashba's absolute objection and instead makes certain to reinsert Karo's public/private distinction. This indeed becomes the practice. More modern commentators on this passage, like the *Mishnah Berurah* (Israel Meir Ha-Kohen, 1839–1933, Poland/Belarus), emphasize that the Decalogue may not even be printed in a prayer book designed for public use, and that it should not be incorporated even into the introductory prayers (which now have a more or less fixed and public format). Recitation as an act of ritualized Torah study after public prayer has ended completely is accepted, as is established in the comment of the *Sha'arei Teshuva* (Chaim Mordechai Margulies, c. 1780–1820, Dubno) on the *Shulḥan 'Arukh*.

Thus, the Decalogue, though it no longer has the prominent role in Jewish liturgy that Mishnah Tamid 5.1 suggests it once had, continues to play a large role in the Jewish liturgical imagination. This is evident in the

---

70. As well as Maimonides 'Thirteen Principles of Faith' and a kabbalistic collection of six (or in eastern Sephardi tradition, ten) biblical events that one should remember daily that includes standing at Sinai (through a citation of Deut. 4.9-10) and the Sabbath (through a citation of Exod. 20.8).

71. *Responsa*, I.184 and III.289.

72. According to the version on the Bar-Ilan Responsa Database (v. 20), which includes the fuller version of the comments of Isserles here.

transformation of Shavuot and the development of a rich poetic heritage for it that drew heavily on the Decalogue. It is even more evident in the constant tug of war between those seeking a means to incorporate the text more fully into the daily or weekly liturgy and those seeking to honor the rabbinic abolition of exactly such a recitation. In the end, the recitation (and the visual representation of the Decalogue in synagogues)[73] wins rabbinic accommodation, albeit not through a reintegration of the text into the center of the prayers.

---

73. On this, see Gad B. Sarfatti, 'The Tablets of the Law as a Symbol of Judaism', in Segal (ed.), *The Ten Commandments in History and Tradition*, pp. 383-418.

VERNACULAR TREATMENTS OF THE TEN COMMANDMENTS IN ANGLO-SAXON ENGLAND

Aaron J Kleist

Vernacular Sources of the Decalogue

A hunt for the Ten Commandments in Anglo-Saxon England must naturally encompass two categories of texts: vernacular translations of Scripture on the one hand, and quotations from Scripture—whether taken directly or through intermediate sources—on the other. The first category may likewise be broken into two parts: translations of Exod. 20.2-17 and Deut. 5.6-21, the primary law-giving passages from the Old Testament, and quotations from these passages elsewhere in the Bible.[1] If extant witnesses to the Latin Old Testament in Anglo-Saxon England are limited in number[2] to begin with, scanter still are biblical books translated into Old English. The Anglo-Saxons appear never to have had a full Bible in their own language; rather, at various points, they translated the Psalms, the Gospels, and the first seven books of the Bible.[3] The last only appears

---

1. As intra-biblical quotations from and allusions to the Decalogue abound, most are beyond the scope of this study; one exception, however, is the episode of Jesus and the Rich Man (e.g., Mt. 19.16-22), which, as it quotes half of the Commandments together, will be included in the editions below.

2. Richard Marsden's seminal work on *The Text of the Old Testament in Anglo-Saxon England* (Cambridge: Cambridge University Press, 1995) studies 17 manuscripts from the second half of the sixth century to the middle of the eleventh century that circulated in early England; these likely constitute the remnants of six complete Latin Bibles and at least eight volumes of Old Testament material—part-Bibles that, along with gospelbooks, epistles, and psalters, Marsden argues, were far more common than full pandects in the Anglo-Saxon period (pp. 2-3). (By way of contrast, some 82 witnesses survive of the Old English Gospels: Helmut Gneuss, *Handlist of Anglo-Saxon Manuscripts* [Tempe: Arizona Center for Medieval and Renaissance Studies, 2001], p. 166). Of the 17, however, only three preserve the Ten Commandments as set forth in Exodus or Deuteronomy (Marsden, *The Text of the Old Testament*, pp. 40-41).

3. For the partial or complete Old English glosses to Latin psalters, see, for example, M.J. Toswell, 'The Relationship of the Metrical Psalter to the Old English Glossed Psalters', *English Studies* 78 (1997), pp. 297-315, and (for the text), *Liber*

in a smattering of manuscripts: a nearly complete copy of the full text, known as the *Heptateuch*, appears in Oxford, Bodleian Library, Laud Misc. 509 [MS L2], while a lavishly illustrated, complete copy of the first six books (the *Hexateuch*) is found in Oxford, Bodleian Library, Hatton 113 [E2].[4] Portions of individual books survive in seven other manuscripts, but none of these contain in the text of Deuteronomy, and only one—New York, Pierpont Morgan Library, G. 63 [P]—preserves the account from Exodus. Ælfric of Eynsham (of whom more anon) was responsible for part of the translation,[5] which he produced between 992

Psalmorum: The West-Saxon Psalms (ed. James Wilson Bright and Robert Lee Ramsay; Boston and London: D.C. Heath, 1907). Speaking of vernacular 'translations' more broadly, one might consider poetic renderings of biblical books such as *Genesis [A* and *B], Exodus,* and *Daniel* in Oxford, Bodleian Library, Junius 11 (5123) (tenth or eleventh century, S. England [perhaps Christ Church, Canterbury]). *Exodus,* however, the most likely to speak of the law-giving at Sinai, in fact only treats episodes from Gen. 22 and Exod. 11–14 (Marsden, *The Text of the Old Testament,* p. 442), and thus falls outside the scope of this inquiry.

4. The only portion missing from L2 is Gen. 3.20–5.12. For full details of all Heptateuch manuscripts, see *The Old English Heptateuch and Ælfric's Libellus de veteri testamento et novo,* I (ed. Richard Marsden; Early English Text Society, OS 330; London: Oxford University Press, 2008), p. xxxvii. For a delineation of manuscript sigla used in this study, see Appendix I.

5. Peter Clemoes identified Ælfric's sections as Gen. 1.1–3.24, 5.32–9.29, 11.32b ('Her swutelað...', originally 12.0 in *The Old English Version of the Heptateuch* [ed. S.J. Crawford; Early English Text Society, OS 160; London: Oxford University Press, rev. edn, 1969], p. 114)—22.24 (with 23.1–24.10 originally by Ælfric but revised by the anonymous compilers); Num. 13.1–13.3, 13.4 excluding 'ðe is genemned', and 13.18 to the end of the book (26.65, preceded by an interpolation from 31.5-18); Josh. 1.11 ('hig gearcian...')–11.23, 14.2 (interposed between 21.43 and 23.1), and 21.41–24.33; and the whole of Judges; with Deut. 32.48–34.12 and Josh. 1.1-10 'being influenced by a pre-existing summary by Ælfric' (Peter Clemoes, 'The Composition of the Old English Text', in *The Old English Illustrated Hexateuch: British Museum Cotton Claudius B. IV* [ed. C.R. Dodwell and Peter Clemoes; Early English Manuscripts in Facsimile, 18; Copenhagen: Rosenkilde & Bagger, 1974], pp. 48, 44; Clemoes, 'The Chronology of Ælfric's Works', in *Old English Prose: Basic Readings* [ed. Paul E. Szarmach; London: Garland, 2000], pp. 29-72 [reprinted from Peter Clemoes (ed.), *The Anglo-Saxons: Studies in Aspects of their History and Culture Presented to Bruce Dickins* (London: Bowes & Bowes, 1959), pp. 212-47], p. 56; and Marsden, *The Text of the Old Testament,* p. 404). More recently, however, Marsden has affirmed (perhaps speaking more generally) that 'To Ælfric we now assign Genesis 1–24.26, Numbers 13–end and all of Joshua; to Anonymous, the rest': 'Ælfric's Errors: The Evidence', in *Essays for Joyce Hill on her Sixtieth Birthday* (ed. Mary Swan; Leeds Studies in English, NS 37; Leeds: University of Leeds, School of English, 2006), pp. 135-60 (136).

and 1005,[6] while at least two anonymous translators completed the rest during the first half of the eleventh century.[7] However many copies may once have existed, therefore,[8] our evidence for Old English versions of the primary Old Testament passages comes from three copies of one text from the late tenth and eleventh century. Aside from Old English biblical quotations from these passages—Christ's quotations in the Gospels, for example, included under the respective Commandments below—the *Heptateuch* thus constitutes our main source for the original Decalogue in Old English.

As for non-biblical sources in which the Commandments appear, one might expect these to be far more extensive and disparate in nature. In fact, however, direct quotations of this material are not only surprisingly rare, but in most cases reflective of the work of one man. Two outliers are the earliest and (perhaps) latest witnesses to extra-biblical quotations of the Commandments: the law-code of King Alfred the Great[9] and the lengthier version of the prose *Solomon and Saturn*.[10] The prologue to Alfred's

---

6. Here and hereafter dates for Ælfrician material are taken from Clemoes, 'The Chronology of Ælfric's Works'; for Ælfric's portion of the Heptateuch, see p. 56.

7. Richard Marsden, 'Translation by Committee? The "Anonymous" Old English Heptateuch', in R. Barnhouse and B.C. Withers (eds.), *The Old English Hexateuch: Aspects and Approaches* (Kalamazoo: Medieval Institute Publications, Western Michigan University, 2000), pp. 41-89.

8. Clemoes describes the first six books (not Judges) as having been 'quite widely disseminated in the eleventh century' ('The Composition of the Old English Text', p. 42).

9. On whom see, for example, David Pratt, *The Political Thought of King Alfred the Great* (Cambridge: Cambridge University Press, 2007), the collection of studies in Timothy Reuter (ed.), *Alfred the Great: Papers from the Eleventh Centenary Conferences* (Aldershot and Burlington: Ashgate, 2003), or, more generally, Justin Pollard, *Alfred the Great: The Man Who Made England* (London: John Murray, 2005). For the role of the king himself in the composition of the Alfredian canon, see, for example, Janet Bately, 'The Alfredian Canon Revisited: One Hundred Years On', in Reuter (ed.), *Alfred the Great*, pp. 107-20; Malcolm R. Godden, 'Did King Alfred Write Anything?', *Medium ævum* 76 (2007), pp. 1-23; and Bately, 'Did King Alfred Actually Translate Anything? The Integrity of the Alfredian Canon Revisited', *Medium ævum* 78 (2009), pp. 189-215.

10. The lengthier prose text here should be distinguished from three works of the same name that appear in Cambridge, Corpus Christi College 422, pp. 1-26 (first half of the tenth century): two poetic works, *Solomon and Saturn I* and *II*, and the shorter prose text that appears between them. While *Solomon and Saturn I* and the shorter prose work deal largely with issues surrounding the Pater Noster, and *Solomon and Saturn II* presents a widely ranging riddle-based contest, the lengthier prose text in MS SS is 'simply a congeries of unattributed questions and answers' (Katherine O'Brien O'Keeffe, 'Solomon and Saturn, Prose', in Michael Lapidge *et al.* [eds.],

law-code, likely issued in the 880s or early 890s,[11] seeks to set English jurisprudence in the context of biblical history, and to this end translates, paraphrases or summarizes laws both from the Old Testament (portions of Exod. 20–23) and the New (the apostolic edict on the Mosaic code found in Acts 15.23-29).[12] A translation of the Decalogue from Exodus is here set out in full. The prose *Solomon and Saturn*, on the other hand, while of unknown date, appears in a manuscript of the mid-twelfth century (SS). The text consists of a series of questions and answers on biblical and extra-biblical matters that often reflect popular culture or apocryphal tradition rather than orthodox doctrine. At one point, for example, Saturn asks Solomon why the sea became salty. The latter replies that the salt came from the tears of Moses, who wept to see the idolatry of the Israelites, and threw the two tablets of the Ten Commandments into the sea.[13] The association of Moses's response to Israelite idolatry—their worship of the golden calf during Moses's prolonged stay on Mount Sinai, one assumes (Exod. 32.1-20)—with the sea does not come not from the biblical text, and no source for the exchange has been found elsewhere.[14] Nevertheless, this context too prompts a full listing of the Commandments.

Other than the exceptions of Alfred's law-code and the prose *Solomon and Saturn*, the main texts in which the vernacular Decalogue appears are directly related to a single individual: Ælfric of Eynsham, the prolific tenth-century monk who devoted himself to making fundamental Christian doctrine accessible to Anglo-Saxon believers.[15] Between 989 and 995,[16]

The Blackwell Encyclopaedia of Anglo-Saxon England [Oxford: Blackwell, 2001], p. 425; see also Patrick P. O'Neill, 'On the Date, Provenance and Relationship of the "Solomon and Saturn" Dialogues', *Anglo-Saxon England* 26 [1997], pp. 139-68).

11. Simon Keyes and Michael Lapidge, *Alfred the Great: Asser's 'Life of King Alfred' and Other Contemporary Sources* (Harmondsworth: Penguin, 1983), p. 304.

12. On the Prologue, see, for example, Marsden, *The Text of the Old Testament*, pp. 401-402.

13. *Solomon and Saturn* §42 (*The 'Prose Solomon and Saturn' and 'Adrian and Ritheus'* [ed. James E. Cross and Thomas D. Hill; Toronto: University of Toronto Press, 1982], p. 31); see also the analogous exchange in *Adrian and Ritheus* §25 (Cross and Hill [eds.], *The Prose Solomon and Saturn*, p. 38).

14. Cross and Hill (eds.), *The Prose Solomon and Saturn*, p. 108.

15. For an introduction to Ælfric, see Joyce Hill, 'Ælfric: His Life and Works', in Hugh Magennis and Mary Swan (eds.), *A Companion to Ælfric* (Leiden and Boston: Brill, 2009), pp. 35-65.

16. For the debate over the dating of the *Catholic Homilies*, see Clemoes, 'The Chronology of Ælfric's Works', p. 56, and *Ælfric's Catholic Homilies: The First Series, Text* (ed. Peter Clemoes; Early English Text Society, SS 17; Oxford: Oxford University Press, 1997), p. 161; *Ælfric's Catholic Homilies: The Second Series, Text* (ed. Malcolm Godden; Early English Text Society, SS 5; London: Oxford University Press, 1979), pp. xci-xciii; *Ælfric's Catholic Homilies: Introduction, Commentary, and*

Ælfric compiled the *Catholic Homilies* (*CH*), two volumes of sermons for various points in the liturgical year. During Lent, in particular, Ælfric expected laity to be in his audience and wrote with them in mind.[17] Among the basic doctrines that Ælfric sought to impart during this time were the Ten Commandments, and discussions of them form part of both of his homilies for Mid-Lent Sunday (*CH* 1.12 and 2.12). The occasion suggested itself nicely for the topic, as the Gospel reading for the day was Jn 6.1-14, Christ's feeding of the five thousand. Augustine had explained the five loaves that Christ distributed to the people as the five books of Moses, and Bede adopted this interpretation in his homily on this passage.[18] These homilies by Augustine and Bede comprise the only treatments of the feeding of the five thousand in the homiliary of Paul the Deacon, one of Ælfric's key sources for the *Catholic Homilies*,[19] and Ælfric draws on them both for his first Mid-Lent address.[20] While Ælfric later excised his delineation of the Decalogue from *CH* 1.12, saving it for a more extended treatment in *CH* 2.12, both the nature of his Lenten audience and the exegesis of his sources for the pericope of the day led Ælfric to meditate on the Commandments in these sermons.

It would not be the last time Ælfric found the Decalogue worthy of discussion. Around 1006[21] he produced three works that all treat the subject: *De sex etatibus huius seculi*, the *Decalogus Moysi*, and his *Second Old English Letter for Wulfstan*. The first is a treatment of world history and doctrine that survives, along with its companion-piece, *De creatore et creatura*, solely in one manuscript, the battered and fire-scathed London,

---

Glossary (ed. Malcolm Godden; Early English Text Society, SS 18; Oxford: Oxford University Press, 2000), pp. xxxii, xxxv.

17. See Robert K. Upchurch, 'Catechetic Homiletics: Ælfric's Preaching and Teaching during Lent', in Magennis and Swan (eds.), *Companion to Ælfric*, pp. 217-46 (219).

18. *In euangelium Ioannis tractatus*, 24.5 (CChr, Series Latina, XXXVI, p. 246, lines 16-17) and *Homiliae euangelii*, II.2 (CChr, Series Latina, CXXII, p. 196, lines 112-15), respectively.

19. See, for example, Cyril L. Smetana, 'Ælfric and the Early Medieval Homiliary', *Traditio* 15 (1959), pp. 163-204, and his 'Paul the Deacon's Patristic Anthology', in Paul E. Szarmach and Bernard F. Huppé (eds.), *The Old English Homily and its Backgrounds* (Albany, NY: State University of New York Press, 1978), pp. 75-97; and *Ælfric's Catholic Homilies* (ed. Godden), pp. xli, lviii.

20. Godden (ed.), *Ælfric's Catholic Homilies*, p. 95.

21. Clemoes, 'The Chronology of Ælfric's Works', p. 57, and (for the *Decalogus Moysi*) his 'The Old English Benedictine Office, Corpus Christi College, Cambridge, MS 190, and the Relationship between Ælfric and Wulfstan: A Reconsideration', *Anglia* 78 (1960), pp. 265-83 (281).

British Library, Cotton Otho C. i, vol. 2 [SE].[22] *De creatore* begins acephalously with teaching on the Trinity and moves through Adam's expulsion from Eden; *De sex etatibus* then continues the account of humankind, placing it in the framework of the Six Ages and providing, in passing, some commentary on the Commandments.[23] These two texts, along with a partial copy of a third piece by Ælfric,[24] constitute folios 149^r-155^v of SE; originally part of a separate manuscript, now lost,[25] they could conceivably bear witness to another copy of Ælfric's 'Commonplace Book' or Scrapbooks—raw material for his writings such as extracts, abridgments, epitomes of patristic and continental works and (as here) short compositions of his own.[26] John Pope, for example, suggests that *De creatore* and *De sex etatibus* 'may have formed the body of an instructive letter of the sort that Ælfric wrote for Wulfgeat and for Sigeweard'—possibly members of the local gentry who wrote to Ælfric about theological matters.[27]

Our second work, the *Decalogus Moysi*, appears in a similar context: a unique copy in what may be an Ælfrician Scrapbook[28] which influenced

---

22. On which manuscript, see, for example, Theodore H. Leinbaugh, 'A Damaged Passage in Ælfric's *De Creatore et Creatura*: Methods of Recovery', *Anglia* 104 (1986), pp. 104-14, and *Homilies of Ælfric: A Supplementary Collection* (ed. John C. Pope; Early English Text Society, OS 259–260; 2 vols.; London: Oxford University Press, 1967–68), I, p. 86.

23. On the Six Ages, see, for example, Aaron J Kleist, 'The Influence of Bede's *De temporum ratione* on Ælfric's Understanding of Time', in Gerhard Jaritz and Gerson Moreno-Riano (eds.), *Time and Eternity: The Medieval Discourse* (Turnhout: Brepols, 2003), pp. 81-97.

24. *De populo Israhel*, now printed as *Supplementary Homilies*, 2.20 (*Homilies of Ælfric* [ed. Pope], II, pp. 641-60).

25. See Leinbaugh, 'A Damaged Passage', and *Homilies of Ælfric* (ed. Pope), I, p. 86.

26. On possible witnesses to Ælfric's Scrapbooks, see Aaron J Kleist, 'Assembling Ælfric: Reconstructing the Rationale behind Eleventh- and Twelfth-Century Compilations', in Magennis and Swan (eds.), *A Companion to Ælfric*, pp. 369-98 (381-85).

27. *Homilies of Ælfric* (ed. Pope), I, p. 87. For a discussion of Wulfgeat and Sigeweard, see Catherine Cubitt, 'Ælfric's Lay Patrons', in Magennis and Swan (eds.), *A Companion to Ælfric*, pp. 165-92 (186-87).

28. MS B2, the first 34 folios of which preserve, as Joyce Hill notes, 'what is apparently a florilegium compiled by Ælfric'—though she goes on to warn firmly that 'there are problems in straightforwardly attributing [this collection] to Ælfric' ('Life and Works', pp. 39-40). Ælfric's authorship of the *Decalogus*, in any case, proposed tentatively by Fehr (Bernhard Fehr, *Die Hirtenbriefe Ælfrics in altenglischer in lateinischer Fassung* [reprinted with a supplement by Peter Clemoes, Darmstadt: Wissenschaftliche Buchgesellschaft, 1966], p. 190), was confirmed by Clemoes ('Supplement to the Introduction', in Fehr, *Die Hirtenbriefe Ælfrics*, pp. cxxvii-cxlviii [cxlvii-cxlviii], and 'Old English Benedictine Office', pp. 277-80) and

those around him—in this case, Wulfstan the Homilist, Archbishop of York (1002–1023).[29] The *Decalogus* is in Latin, and thus would not bear mentioning in this context, save for its influence on at least four vernacular works associated with the Archbishop:

1. his Her ongynð be cristendome (Homily Xc),
2. the related De preceptis Domini,
3. his Institutes of Polity, and
4. his treatise on *Grið* ('Sanctuary').

The process of transmission is somewhat complex, as Wulfstan used the *Decalogus* in various ways. The text appears, in an abbreviated but otherwise faithful form, first of all in Wulfstan's Latin *De cristianitate* (Homily Xb), the rough model for (1) his vernacular Xc, and scholars have argued that Ælfric's work was the source for the relevant parts of these sermons.[30] Portions of the *Decalogus* also appear, however, in two Latin works in Cambridge, Corpus Christi College 190 [O], Part I, a version of Wulfstan's Handbook.[31] On the one hand, Xb's abbreviation occurs in *De initio creature* (O, pp. 1-2 [2]), including an introductory sentence in Xb that is not found in the *Decalogus*.[32] On the other, a sentence from the *Decalogus*

Christopher Jones, 'Meatim Sed et Rustica: Ælfric of Eynsham as a Medieval Latin Author', *Journal of Medieval Latin* 8 (1998), pp. 1-57 (11-12). The *Decalogus Moysi* is found in MS Bl, fols 31^r-32^r.

29. On whom see, for example, Patrick Wormald, 'Archbishop Wulfstan: Eleventh-Century State-Builder', in Matthew Townend (ed.), *Wulfstan, Archbishop of York* (Turnhout: Brepols, 2004), pp. 9-27, and Dorothy Bethurum, 'Wulfstan', in Eric Gerald Stanley (ed.), *Continuations and Beginnings: Studies in Old English Literature* (London: Nelson, 1966), pp. 210-46.

30. Karl Jost, *Wulfstanstudien* (Bern: A. Francke, 1950), p. 49, and 'Einige Wulfstantexte und ihre Quellen', *Anglia* 56 (1932), pp. 265-315 (278); *The Homilies of Wulfstan* (ed. Dorothy Bethurum; Oxford: Clarendon Press, 1957), p. 323.

31. Mildred Budny describes this material in O as 'works by [Wulfstan], addressed to him, of interest to him, and used by him in his own texts' (*Insular, Anglo-Saxon and Early Anglo-Norman Manuscript Art at Corpus Christi College, Cambridge: An Illustrated Catalogue* [2 vols.; Kalamazoo: Medieval Institute Publications, 1997], I, p. 535). On other witnesses to Wulfstan's Handbook (formerly known as his 'Commonplace Book'), see Hans Sauer, 'Zur Überlieferung und Anlage von Erzbischof Wulfstans "Handbuch"', *Deutsches Archiv für Erforschung des Mittelalters* 36 (1980), 341-84 (trans. as 'The Transmission and Structure of Archbishop Wulfstan's Commonplace Book', in Paul E. Szarmach [ed.], *Old English Prose*, pp. 339-93).

32. Xb, lines 10-11, read: 'Mandata igitur legalia Dominus Moysi et Israhelitico populo de Monte Sinai ostendit, ita dicens...' (Dorothy Bethurum [ed.], *The Homilies of Wulfstan*, p. 194), while the sentence in *De initio* opens with the slight variation of 'Mandata quoque legalia moysi'.

that Wulfstan uses later in Xb, calling believers to honour God as their Father and the Church as their Mother, appears in *In nomine Domini* (O, pp. 94-96, at 94)—but without the initial two words found in both the *Decalogus* and Xb.[33] Material thus seems to have been transmitted from a copy of Ælfric's *Decalogus* to Xb and thence both to O and to Xc. The last, however, is also related to another vernacular version of the *Decalogus*: (2) *De preceptis Domini* in Cambridge, Corpus Christi College 201 [C1]. The text is one of three on p. 52 of C1 that reproduce material from Xc: *De preceptis* corresponds to Xc, lines 20-38 (*Homilies of Wulfstan* [ed. Bethurum], p. 201), save for an altered introduction; its successor, *De uitis principalibus*, corresponds to Xc, lines 62-66 (p. 203); and the final entry, *De uirtutibus*, corresponds to Xc, lines 67-71, save for its adapted conclusion (p. 203).[34] Wulfstan is known for adapting and reusing his own work, and it is possible that these short pieces in C1 may be by Wulfstan himself.[35] At the same time, while it is possible that these pieces antedate Wulfstan's sermons, and that Xc draws on both Xb and *De preceptis*,[36] Andy Orchard also notes that 'as a powerful and evidently widely respected figure, Wulfstan's works were often imitated by contemporary and

33. Namely, 'nam spiritaliter' before 'Deus pater noster est et aecclesia mater nostra, quos debemus semper honorare' (Bethurum [ed.], *The Homilies of Wulfstan*, p. 195, and Fehr, *Die Hirtenbriefe Ælfrics*, p. 198, apparatus). The image of God as the Father of believers and the Church as their Mother might seem a commonplace, and similar statements do occur, e.g. in Augustine, *Sermones* 12.10.10 (CChr, Series Latina, XLI, p. 300, lines 267-68) and Bede, *In Pentateuchum commentarii* 2.20 (*PL*, XCI, col. 319C); nonetheless, the precise language of this sentence is not found elsewhere, and thus makes the parallel here striking. Ælfric's comment in the *Decalogus* occurs in his commentary on the Fourth Commandment (regarding parents), and derives from his vernacular exegesis found earliest in *CH* 2.12.316-17 (Godden [ed.], *Second Series*, p. 119), which appears to be original to him (Godden [ed.], *Ælfric's Catholic Homilies*, p. 459).

34. Bethurum does not appear to collate this material, as she draws on C1, pp. 56-60, for her edition of Xc (Bethurum [ed.], *The Homilies of Wulfstan*, p. 200, apparatus).

35. On Wulfstan's compositional methodology, see, for example, Andy Orchard, 'Wulfstan as Reader, Writer, and Rewriter', in Aaron J Kleist (ed.), *The Old English Homily: Precedent, Practice, and Appropriation* (Turnholt: Brepols, 2007), pp. 311-41, and Jonathan Wilcox, 'The Dissemination of Wulfstan's Homilies: The Wulfstan Tradition in Eleventh-Century Vernacular Preaching', in Carola Hicks (ed.), *England in the Eleventh Century: Proceedings of the 1990 Harlaxton Symposium* (Stamford: Paul Watkins, 1992), pp. 199-217. Jost views *De preceptis* as a work by Wulfstan; see 'Einige Wulfstantexte', pp. 278-79, and Enid Raynes, 'MS. Boulogne-sur-Mer 63 and Ælfric', *Medium ævum* 26 (1957), pp. 65-73 (71).

36. Clemoes, 'Supplement to the Introduction', p. cxlviii, and Dorothy Bethurum, 'Archbishop Wulfstan's Commonplace Book', *Publications of the Modern Language Association* 57 (1942), pp. 916-29 (992-93).

later writers, in ways often difficult to distinguish from his own revisions'.[37] One could thus envision a compiler mining Xc for material that ultimately appeared in C1, rather than *De preceptis* and its companions representing early drafts of Xc. Either way, however, behind both vernacular pieces Ælfric's *Decalogus Moysi* is arguably to be found. Lastly, the text had a small but noteworthy impact on two other works by Wulfstan: (3) his *Institutes of Polity*, a detailed consideration of the roles of ecclesiastical and secular authorities, and (4) *Grið*, a treatise 'on the security of churches and clergy'.[38] In both, quoting his own translation of the sentence in Xc, Wulfstan reproduced that Ælfrician exhortation that had apparently caught his eye: the call to honour God as one's Father and the Church as one's Mother.[39] Altogether, then, the textual influence of the *Decalogus* may be traced as follows:

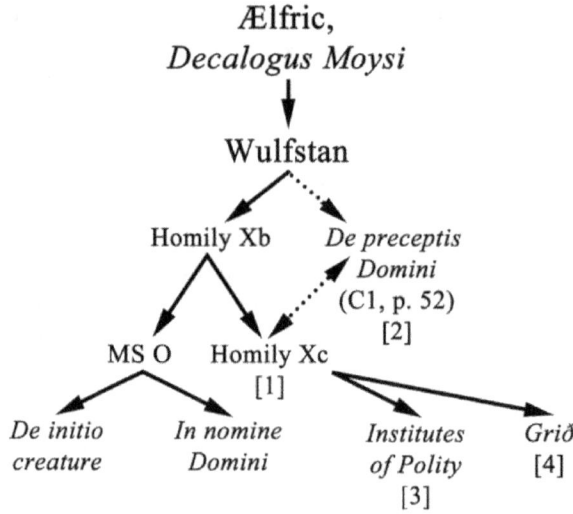

37. Orchard, 'Wulfstan as Reader', p. 316.
38. Patrick Wormald, *Legal Culture in the Early Medieval West: Law as Text, Image and Experience* (London: Hambledon Press, 1999), p. 244.
39. The text from Xc, 'Ealle we habbað ænne heofonlicne fæder ond ane gastlice modor, seo is ecclesia genamod, þæt is Godes cyrice, ond ða we sculan æfre lufian ond weorðian' ('We all have one heavenly father and one spiritual mother, who is called *ecclesia*, that is, God's Church, and those we must love and honour forever'), appears as *I Polity* §99 and *II Polity* §204 (Karl Jost, *Die 'Institutes of Polity, Civil and Ecclesiastical': Ein Werk Erzbischof Wulfstans von York* [Schweizer anglistische Arbeiten, 47; Bern: Francke, 1959], p. 138); while a slightly shorter version, 'Ealle... cyrice', appears in *Grið*; see Jost, 'Einige Wulfstantexte', pp. 265-315 (279-80); and Clemoes, 'Supplement to the Introduction', p. cxlviii.

The third treatment of the Decalogue by Ælfric is yet another work associated with the Archbishop: Ælfric's *Second Old English Letter for Wulfstan*.[40] Having learnt that Ælfric had previously ghostwritten for Wulfsige III, bishop of Sherborne (c. 993–1002), to clergymen in Wulfsige's diocese, Wulfstan likewise commissioned Ælfric to write pastoral letters on his behalf. After Ælfric composed his *First* and *Second Latin Letter for Wulfstan* in 1005, the Archbishop, seeking to maximize their impact on the unlearned, requested him to make versions of these works available in the vernacular. By the following year Ælfric had complied, noting, however, that in these works he rearranged material and translated not word for word but *sensum ex sensu* ('according to the sense').[41] In the *Second Old English Letter*, however, he also made two significant additions: a section not found in the Latin letter regarding the rites for Maundy Thursday, Good Friday and Easter eve (§§23–63), and a conclusion which discusses the Ten Commandments and eight deadly sins rather than the priestly responsibilities treated in the Latin (§§120–98). As it happens, however, the extant conclusion to the *Second Latin Letter* (§§73–90) may not be Ælfric's original: interpolating material from passages in Ælfric's earlier *Latin Letter to Wulfstan*, a response to certain theological questions from the Archbishop, the conclusion may be a later addition made by Wulfstan or his circle.[42] Consequently, the discussion of the Commandments in the *Second Old English Letter* may reflect Ælfric's original Latin text. Either way, this vernacular letter provides not simply a straightforward list of commands, as in Alfred's law-code, *Solomon and Saturn*, the *Decalogus Moysi* and *CH* 1.12; but commentary on them as well, as in *CH* 2.12 and *De sex etatibus huius*. While constraints of space do not permit us to examine and contrast such exegeses here, we can at least show in brief how these vernacular versions of the Decalogue differ.[43]

---

40. On Wulfstan's use of this and other Ælfrician material, see Malcolm Godden, 'The Relations of Wulfstan and Ælfric: A Reassessment', in Townend (ed.), *Wulfstan*, pp. 353-74.

41. *First Old English Letter for Wulfstan*, §1 (Fehr, *Die Hirtenbriefe Ælfrics*, p. 68).

42. Clemoes, 'Supplement to the Introduction', pp. cxxxv-cxxxvii, and *Councils and Synods, with Other Documents Relating to the English Church. I. AD 871–1204. Part I. 871–1066* (ed. Dorothy Whitelock, Martin Brett and Christopher N.L. Brooke; Oxford: Clarendon Press, 1981), p. 257.

43. The editions below reflect only part of the surviving evidence; variants from both vernacular and Anglo-Latin versions of the Commandments, however, as well as discussions of Anglo-Saxon commentaries on the Decalogue, will be included in my forthcoming edition of Ælfric's *Decalogus Moysi*.

First Commandment: Vernacular Versions

Biblical Passages (Primary Sources)

OEHept[44]	[Exod. 20.1][45] God spræc þus: [20.2] Ic eom Drihten þin God. [20.4] Ne wirc þu þe agrafene godas, [20.5] ne ne wurða. Ic wrece fædera unrihtwisnysse on bearnum, [20.6] and ic do mildheortnysse þam þe me lufiað and mine bebodu healdað. [Deut. 5.6][46] Ic eom Drihten eowre God þe eow ut alædde of Egipta lande of þeowette. [5.7] I. Nafa þu fremde Godas beforan me. [5.8] II.[47] Ne wirce þu græftgeweorc, ne nanes cynnes anlicnyssa, ne þa ne wurða. [5.9] Ic eom Drihten eower God þe wrece fædera unrihtwisnissa on hira bearnum, [5.10] and miltsie þam þe me lufiað and mine bebodu healdað.

Quoted Passages (Secondary Sources)

Alf LC[48]	Ic eom dryhten ðin God. Ic ðe utgelædde of Egipta londe ond of hiora ðeowdome. Ne lufa ðu oþre fremde godas ofer me.
Æ CH 1.12[49]	[Moyses] awrat eac on ðære gesetnysse þæt] nan man ne scolde bugan to nanum deofulgilde, ac scolde gehwa hine gebidddan to gode anum, se ðe ana is soð god;
Æ CH 2.12[50]	Þæt forme bebod is: Drihten ðin god is an god.

44. In order to facilitate comparison of Decalogue versions and provide accessible texts primarily for literary study, the following quotations from manuscripts and printed sources offer semi-diplomatic editions using modern punctuation, silently expanded abbreviations, capitalization of proper nouns, 'v' printed as 'u', e-caudata ('ę') printed as 'ae', '7' printed as 'ond', and standardized word division based on normal dictionary practice.

45. Quotations from Exodus in the *Heptateuch* are taken from *The Old English Heptateuch* (ed. Marsden), pp. 115-16. Marsden prints the text from L2, fol. 56[v].

46. Quotations from Deuteronomy in the *Heptateuch* are taken from Marsden (ed.), *The Old English Heptateuch*, p. 158. Marsden prints the text from L2, fol. 85[v].

47. Here and below, I place text from the Old English version of Deuteronomy next to its analogous passages, even though it differs in its enumeration of the Decalogue; what Deuteronomy labels the Second Commandment is thus here printed with the First, and so on.

48. Quotations from the prologue to Alfred's law-code are taken from *Die Gesetze der Angelsachsen* (3 vols.; ed. Felix Liebermann; Halle: Max Niemeyer, 1903–16), I (1903), pp. 26-47 (26-29). Liebermann prints the text in parallel columns from E1, fol. 36[r]; G, fols 51[r-v]; and H3, fol. 11[r]. I print the text here from E1.

49. Quotations from Ælfric's first mid-Lent homily, *Dominica in media quadragessima* (*CH* 1.12)—or rather, from the passage excised by Ælfric himself from the early copy of *CH* 1.12 in A2, fols 64[r-v]—are taken from *First Series* (ed. Clemoes), p. 531, lines 12-19.

50. Quotations from Ælfric's second mid-Lent homily, *Dominica in media quadragesime* (*CH* 2.12), are taken from *Second Series* (ed. Godden), pp. 110-26 (114, lines 138-47). Godden prints the text from K, fols 171[r]-178[r] (173[r]).

Æ SE[51]	Eg[o sum Dominus Deus tuus. Ic eom][52] Drihten þin God. Ne wyrc þu nateshwon þe sylfum oþre godas.
Æ 2OEL[53]	Ego[54] sum Dominus Deus tuus, qui eduxi te de terra Egypti; non habebis deos alienos coram me. Þæt is on englisc: Ic eom drihten, ðin God; ic, þe þe alædde of Egypta lande; ne hafa þu ællfremde godas ætforan me nateshwon. [Ðis is ðæt forme bebod...]
W Xc[55]	Ego sum Dominus Deus tuus, et reliqua. Ic eom ðin Drihten, he cwæð, þe gelædde þe ut of Egypt. Ne weorða þu fremde godas.
W DpD[56]	Ego Dominus Deus tuus, et reliqua. Ic eom þin drihten, he cwæð, ðe gelædde þe ut of Egypt. I. Ne weorða ðu fre[m]de godas.
SS[57]	[Ic þe secge,] þæt forme word wæs, Non habeos deos alienos, þæt ys, Ne lufa þu oðerne god ofer me.

First Commandment: Textual Notes

While space at present prohibits detailed comparison of vernacular versions of the Commandments, one question almost silently present in the passages above is precisely where the First Commandment begins. In many modern English translations of the Bible, the issue is obscured by

51. Readings from Ælfric's *De sex etatibus huius seculi* are taken from SE, fols. 151ᵛ-152ᵛ and 154ʳ⁻ᵛ, with reference to Hildegard L.C. Tristram, *Sex aetates mundi: Die Weltzeitalter bei den Angelsachsen und den Iren. Untersuchungen und Text* (Heidelberg: Carl Winter, 1985), pp. 195-201 (199-200).

52. Text lost to the damaged right-hand edge of MS, which (to judge from the longest surviving line, plus any additional space in the margin) may here have had room for 20–25 characters, using abbreviations for *Dominus Deus tuus*. Tristram has the overly truncated, macaronic reading 'Eg[o sum] Drihten þin God' (p. 199). Likewise, the *Dictionary of Old English*'s transcription, usually an invaluable reference, should in this case be taken with caution, as it prints what is clearly legible without indicating what partial readings remain: here, for example, it reads 'Drihten þin God' without reference to 'Eg[o]' or any missing text (see, http://www.doe.utoronto.ca/pages/pub/web-corpus.html [accessed 12 February 2013]).

53. Quotations from Ælfric's *Second Old English Letter for Wulfstan* are taken from Fehr, *Die Hirtenbriefe Ælfrics*, pp. 146-221 (190-203, §§122-44). Fehr prints the text in parallel columns from O, pp. 336-49 (344-46); X, fols 111ʳ-124ʳ (118ᵛ-121ʳ); B/Oz, fols 137ʳ-140ᵛ (139r-139ᵛ); and V, fols 13ᵛ-15ʳ; along with N2, fols 106ʳ-107ᵛ, at other points in the Letter. I print the text here from O.

54. An interlinear gloss ('.I.'), not in the main hand, appears over *Ego* in X, fol. 119ʳ, suggesting that the First Commandment begins here.

55. Quotations from Wulfstan's Homily Xc, *Her ongynð be cristendome*, are taken from Bethurum (ed.), *The Homilies of Wulfstan*, pp. 200-10 (201). Bethurum edits the text from E2, fols 38ʳ-44ʳ (39ʳ).

56. Quotations from *De preceptis Domini* are taken from C1, p. 52.

57. Quotations from *Solomon and Saturn I* §43, found only in SS, fols. 86ᵛ-93ᵛ (91ᵛ-92ʳ), are from Cross and Hill (eds.), *The Prose Solomon and Saturn*, pp. 31-32.

editors' tendency to indent blocks of text to make ten individual verses stand out.[58] Historically, however, theologians have differed as to whether the Decalogue begins with Exod. 20.3 ('You shall have no other gods before me') or the opening address in 20.2 ('I am the Lord your God'). Judaism largely took the latter position, viewing 20.3-6 as the Second Commandment.[59] In the first century CE, however, the Jewish philosopher and historian Philo and Josephus identified 20.3 as the First Commandment and 20.4 ('You shall not make for yourself an image') as the Second.[60] Origen, who quotes Philo and Josephus by name in his works some two centuries later, seems to be responsible for introducing the system into the patristic tradition,[61] and Reformed and Orthodox Christians have followed it thereafter.[62] This approach had further enumerative implications: as the Commandments must total ten, those who viewed these initial verses as multiple precepts by necessity had to interpret the final verse ('You shall not covet your neighbour's house, nor his wife' [20.17]) as a single injunction. Augustine of Hippo (AD 354–430) rejected this approach, arguing that Moses' two tablets contained three and seven commands respectively, with the admonition to honour one's parents

58. See Exod. 20.1-17 and Deut. 5.6-21 in, for example, RSV (London: Nelson, 1965 [Roman Catholic edition]), NEB (Cambridge: Cambridge University Press, 1970), NASB (with paragraph marks rather than indentation) (Cambridge: Cambridge University Press, 1977), NKJV (London: Nelson, 1982), NIV (London: Hodder & Stoughton, 1984), Living Bible (Eastbourne: Kingsway, 1987), NRSV (London: Nelson, 1989), and NAB (Oxford: Oxford University Press, 1995). For a detailed discussion of the following, see Aaron J Kleist, 'The Division of the Ten Commandments in Anglo-Saxon England', *Neuphilologische Mitteilungen* 103 (2002), pp. 227-40; certain data and conclusions, however, are revised here.

59. For more information on different Jewish systems of cantillation, or ways of marking the text for public recitation, see Kleist, 'The Division of the Ten Commandments', and Mordechai Breuer, 'Dividing the Decalogue into Verses and Commandments', in Ben-Zion Segal and Gershon Levi (eds.), *The Ten Commandments in History and Tradition* (Jerusalem: Eisenbrauns, 1990), pp. 291-330 (291 and 309-11).

60. See *Dec.* 14.65 (in *Philo* [trans. F.H. Colson, G.H. Whitaker and Ralph Marcus; 10 vols.; Cambridge, MA: Harvard University Press, 1929–62], VII [1958], p. 38) and *Ant.* 3.91 (in *Josephus* [trans. H.StJ. Thackeray and Ralph Marcus; 8 vols.; London: Heinemann, 1913–67], IV [1930], p. 360). For Philo's and Josephus's division of the Commandments, see Moshe Greenberg, 'The Decalogue Tradition Critically Examined', and Yehoshua Amir, 'The Decalogue according to Philo', in Segal and Levi (eds.), *Ten Commandments in History and Tradition*, pp. 83-120 (98) and 121-60.

61. N.R.M. de Lange, *Origen and the Jews* (Cambridge: Cambridge University Press 1976), pp. 16-17; see Origen, *In Exodum homilia* 8.2 (*PG* XII, col. 351C).

62. Information on Reformed, Orthodox, Lutheran and Roman Catholic traditions is taken from W. Harrelson's convenient chart in *The Ten Commandments and Human Rights* (Philadelphia: Fortress, 1980), p. 47.

(20.12) forming the first entry on the second tablet, and the final verse offering dual injunctions against greed and lust (on which more anon). On the precise identity of the First Commandment, however, he is not always clear: sometimes in this regard he speaks generally of the command to worship one God,[63] or (paraphrasing 20.3) describes the need to worship one God and have no others beside him.[64] Formative to his thought, however, appears to have been Christ's statement that 'primum omnium mandatum est audi Israhel Dominus Deus noster Deus unus est' ('The first of all commandments is: "Hear, O Israel: the Lord your God, the Lord is one"'),[65] for at least thrice it is the verse to which Jesus refers, Deut. 6.4, that Augustine cites as the First Commandment of the Decalogue.[66] For Augustine, the verse is an apt distillation of the opening verses of Exod. 20—the statement of the Lord's identity, the admonition to have no other gods before him and the injunction against making images and worshipping them. As he says, 'in primo praecepto...prohibetur coli aliqua in figmentis hominum Dei similitudo' ('in this Commandment [Deut. 6.4, and Exod. 20.3-6 by extension], we are prohibited from worshiping any images made by humans in the likeness of God').[67] What is more, he views the verse as pertaining not just to God as a whole but to the Father in particular, just as the Second Commandment pertains to the Son and the Third pertains to the Spirit. Since Jesus attests that the whole law is summed up in the imperatives to love God with all one's heart and to love one's neighbour as oneself,[68] Augustine maintains, we should understand the contents of the first tablet, aptly Trinitarian in number, to pertain to our love for God.[69]

Augustine's association of the first tablet with a triune set of God-centered directives was readily adopted by other early Church writers, but

---

63. 'Unum Deum colere...nobis praecipitur' ('We are commanded...to worship one God') (*In Ioannis euangelium tractatus* 3.19 [CChr, Series Latina, XXXVI, p. 28, lines 5-6]).

64. 'Primum praeceptum in Lege de colendo uno Deo, Non erunt, inquit, tibi dii alii praeter me' ('The First Commandment in the Law about worshipping one God says: "You shall not have other gods besides me"') (*Sermones* 8.4 (*De decem plagis Ægyptiorum et decem praeceptis legis*) [CChr, Series Latina, XLI, p. 82, lines 88-89]).

65. Mk. 12.29, quoted by Augustine for example in *Speculum de scriptura sacra, De Euangelio secundum Marcum* 12 (*PL*, XXXIV, col. 983).

66. *Contra Faustum Manichaeum* 15.5 (CSEL, 25, p. 425, lines 1-2), *Breviarum in Psalmos* 32 (*PL*, XXVI, col. 915A), and *Enarrationes in Psalmos* 32.6 (CChr, Series Latina, XXXVIII, p. 251, lines 9-11).

67. *Epistula* 55.11.20 (CSEL, 34.1, p. 190, lines 23-24).

68. Mk. 12.30-31, quoting Deut. 6.5 and Lev. 19.18.

69. *Quaestionum in Heptateuchum* 2.71.2 (CChr, Series Latina, XXXIII, p. 103, lines 1154-55) and *Sermones* 9.7 (CChr, Series Latina, XLI, p. 120, lines 258-67).

they differed as to which verse constituted the First Commandment. Cassiodorus (c. 485–585) affirmed that the first tablet related to the Trinity, but identified its initial precept as 20.3 ('You shall have no other gods before me').[70] Isidore of Seville (c. 560–636), quoting from Augustine, embraced the latter's connection of the Commandment with Deut. 6.4 and the first person of the Trinity.[71] In Anglo-Saxon Northumbria, quoting from Isidore, Bede (c. 672–735) also linked the opening Commandments to the love of the Trinity, and the First Commandment with the Father, but then defined the First explicitly as encompassing Exod. 20.2-6, straight from 'I am the Lord your God'.[72] Back on the Continent, another Northumbrian, Alcuin (c. 735–804), quoted straightforwardly from Isidore, affirming Isidore's teaching on Deut. 6.4 and the first person of the Trinity.[73] Alcuin's student, Rabanus Maurus (c. 776/84?–856), quoting Alcuin, did the same.[74] To varying degrees, all these authorities were known and influential in Anglo-Saxon England.[75]

Later Anglo-Saxon writers responded and contributed to the debate in a variety of ways. The *Old English Heptateuch*, first of all, complicates matters by not dividing the commands in Exodus and not translating 20.3 at all. Its version of Deuteronomy, on the other hand, does delineate the

---

70. *Expositio Psalmorum* 32.2 (CChr, Series Latina, XCVII, p. 285, line 64), associating David's ten-stringed harp with the Decalogue—as did Augustine before him, e.g. in *Enarrationes in Psalmos* 32.6.

71. *Quaestiones in Vetus Testamentum. In Exodum* 29.2 (*PL*, LXXXIII, col. 301B).

72. *In Pentateuchum commentarii* 2.20 (*PL*, XCI, col. 318BC). A few sentences later, however, he refers in shorthand to the 'primum mandatum, "Non habebis deos alienos [Exod. 20.3]"', suggesting that he might view Exod. 20.2 ('I am the Lord your God') as prefatory and 20.3 as the First Commandment proper (*In Pentateuchum commentarii* 2.20 [*PL*, XCI, col. 318D]).

73. *De decem uerbis legis seu breuis expositio Decalogi* (*PL*, C, col. 567D).

74. *Commentarius in Matthaeum* 6.22 (*PL*, CVII, col. 1062BC) begins with an extract from Augustine, *Sermones* 9.7 (CChr, Series Latina, XLI, p. 120, lines 263-65) before paralleling content from Bede, *In Pentateuchum commentarii* 2.20 (*PL*, XCI, col. 318BC).

75. Four copies of Cassiodorus's *Expositio Psalmorum*, five to Isidore's *Quaestiones in Vetus Testamentum*, and one of Rabanus Maurus's *Commentarius in Matthaeum* survive in manuscripts written or owned in Anglo-Saxon England (Gneuss, *Handlist of Anglo-Saxon Manuscripts*, pp. 35, 42, 51, 83, 111, 124; 44, 79, 110, 111, 146; and 52, respectively). Works by Bede and Alcuin circulated widely in Anglo-Saxon England, but to my knowledge, no evidence survives of witnesses to or use of Bede's *In Pentateuchum commentarii* or Alcuin's *De decem uerbis legis*; see Gneuss, *Handlist of Anglo-Saxon Manuscripts*, pp. 155-56 and 150-51; and 'Titles by Source Author Bede' and 'Titles by Source Author Alcuin', *Fontes anglo-saxonici*, http://fontes.english.ox.ac.uk/ (accessed September 2012).

Commandments, using Roman numerals in both extant witnesses to identify Deut. 5.7 ('You shall have no other gods', the equivalent of Exod. 20.3) as the First and 5.8-10 ('You shall not make an image', the equivalent of Exod. 20.4-6) as the Second.[76] While they may not have known it,[77] the anonymous translators were thus following in the footsteps of Philo, Josephus, Origen and Cassiodorus before them. Next, we come to Ælfric, who over his career enumerates the Commandments in various ways. In *CH* 2.12, drawing on Isidore,[78] he cites Deut. 6.4 as the initial command. In the *Second Old English Letter for Wulfstan*, perhaps reflecting Bede or Rabanus Maurus, he quotes Exod. 20.2-3, describing those verses as the 'forme bebod' ('First Commandment').[79] In the *Decalogus Moysi*, though he quotes Exod. 20.2-3—omitting 20.4-6 altogether—either he or the scribe of MS B1 inserts a Roman numeral 'I.' before 20.3 ('You shall have no other gods'). As a result, descendants of the *Decalogus*, Wulfstan's Homily Xb and *De preceptis Domini*, reflect the same division. *Solomon and Saturn*, though likely independent of Ælfric's influence, preserves it as well, placing them within a tradition dating at least from Ælfric to that followed by Lutherans and Roman Catholics today.[80]

First Commandment: Contemporary Commentary

Of our texts, only three provide sustained (if somewhat brief) exegetical treatments of the Decalogue, and all of these, unsurprisingly, are by Ælfric:[81] his second Mid-Lent homily (*CH* 2.12), *De sex etatibus huius*

---

76. See MSS L2, fol. 56ᵛ, and B2, fol. 97ᵛ.

77. No works by Philo survive from Anglo-Saxon England, though one copy of Josephus's *Antiquitates judaicae* and two copies of Origen's *In Exodum homilia* survive that were written or owned in Anglo-Saxon England (Gneuss, *Handlist of Anglo-Saxon Manuscripts*, pp. 83, 51, 111). As noted above, greater evidence remains for the Anglo-Saxons' knowledge of Cassiodorus.

78. Godden (ed.), *Ælfric's Catholic Homilies*, p. lvi.

79. Fehr, *Die Hirtenbriefe Ælfrics*, p. 192, §123. Bede was a major source for Ælfric, but the latter may not have known Bede's *In Pentateuchum commentarii* (Godden [ed.], *Ælfric's Catholic Homilies*, pp. l-li). It is possible that he knew Rabanus Maurus, but it has been difficult to prove concretely; as Godden states, '[Rabanus's] *Commentarius in Matthaeum*...draw[s] on the same exegetical traditions as Ælfric and often shows parallels, but there are no similarities of phrasing or distinctive details which might suggest that he knew these works' (Godden [ed.], *Ælfric's Catholic Homilies*, p. lix).

80. Here and below, for a visual guide to traditions of enumerating the Commandments, see Appendix II.

81. On Ælfric's exegetical practice and its near-uniqueness among Anglo-Saxon homilists, see for example, Aaron J Kleist, *Striving with Grace: Views of Free Will in Anglo-Saxon England* (Toronto: University of Toronto Press, 2008), p. 169.

seculi and *Second Old English Letter for Wulfstan*. He nearly provided a fourth: in his first Mid-Lent sermon (*CH* 1.12), discussing Christ's feeding of the five thousand (Jn 6.1-14), he had identified the five loaves with which the crowd was fed as the Pentateuch; the youth to whom the loaves originally belonged, he explained as 'þæt iudeisce folc, þe ða fif bec rædde, and ne cuðe þæron nan gastlic andgit ær ðan þe crist com and þa bec geopenade and hyra gastlice andgit onwreah' ('the Jewish people, who read the five books, but did not know of any spiritual meaning in them before Christ came, opened the books, and revealed their spiritual sense').[82] Feeling the need to give his audience both some background to the Pentateuch—readings of which formed part of the liturgy for Lent[83]—and insight into the spiritual (*gastlice*) significance thereof, Ælfric initially attempted to give a quick introduction to Moses, the Exodus and the Ten Commandments. Soon, however, he decided that the subject warranted more than an excursus. In the earliest extant revision of the homily, he deleted the passage, noting in his own hand that 'Ðeos racu [is] fullicor on ð[ære] oðre bec, ond w[e hi] forbudon on [ðys]ere þy læs þe h[it æ]þryt þince gif [heo] on ægðre bec b[eo]' ('This explanation is given more completely in the other volume; we have cancelled it in this one lest it seem tedious that it appears in both volumes').[84] This 'other volume' is the *Second Series*, and the text in question is *CH* 2.12. Earlier in the homily, Ælfric had discussed the Ten Plagues that fell on Egypt (Exod. 7.14–12.32) and noted the numerological parallel with the Commandments.[85] While Augustine had made detailed comparisons of the two—the Nile's water is changed to blood just as those who worship idols exchange God's purity for corruption, and so on[86]—Ælfric instead takes the opportunity to

---

82. *CH* 1.12.75-78 (Clemoes [ed.], *First Series*, pp. 277-78).

83. Exodus being read in particular; see Godden (ed.), *Ælfric's Catholic Homilies*, pp. 95, 449, and *CH* 2.12.1-2 (Godden [ed.], *Second Series*, p. 110).

84. Clemoes (ed.), *First Series*, p. 65, discussing (and reconstructing text lost to leaf-trimming during the binding of) MS A2, fol. 64; Clemoes prints the cancelled passage in *First Series*, p. 531 (App. A.1).

85. 'Is eac to understandenne þæt þæt egyptisce folc wearð mid tyn wítum geslagen, and tyn bedboda wæron awritene on ðam twam tabelum Godes folce to rihtinge' ('It should also be understood that the Egyptians were struck with ten plagues, and ten commandments were written on the two tablets as instruction for God's people' [*CH* 2.12.334-36 (Godden [ed.], *Second Series*, p. 119)]).

86. *Sermones* 8.4, 12-13, and *Sermones X* 1.3, 12-13 (CChr, Series Latina, XLI, pp. 82-83, 89-91, and *PL*, XLVI, col. 948 and cols. 952-54). While this association of the Plagues and the Commandments may have its roots in Augustine, however, and while Ælfric seems to have read 'a good range of Augustine's sermons' outside patristic compendia such as that of Paul the Deacon, Godden notes that Ælfric's immediate source for this comment is Isidore's *Quaestiones in Vetus Testamentum* (Godden [ed.], *Ælfric's Catholic Homilies*, pp. 460 and xlviii).

discuss one of his favorite subjects: the Trinity. Using Deut. 6.4 ('The Lord your God is one God') as his starting point, he describes the triune nature and unity of the divine persons before tying the point explicitly to the verses in Exodus: 'Þisne ænne God we sceolon […] wurðian, for ðan ðe […] nis nan oðer god buton him anum' ('This one God we must […] worship, because […] there is no other god save him alone').[87] Ælfric's comments in his *Second Old English Letter* likewise focus on the Trinity, as well as the need to avoid their counterpart, 'dwolican godas [þe sind] gramlice deoflu' ('false gods, [which are] cruel devils'); as with *De sex etatibus*, however, which here offers no commentary beyond Scripture itself, the *Letter* draws not on Deuteronomy 6, but solely on the accounts of the Decalogue in Exodus.[88]

Second Commandment: Vernacular Versions

OEHept	[Exod. 20.7] Ne nem þu Drihtnes naman on ydel; ne byð unscyldig, se ðe his naman on ydel nemð. [Deut. 5.11] III. Ne nemne ge Drihtnes naman on idel, for þam þe ne bið he unscildig se þe for idelum þinge his naman nemð.

Alf LC	Ne minne noman ne cig ðu on idelnesse; forðon þe ðu ne bist unscyldig wið me, gif ðu on idelnesse cigst minne noman.
Æ CH 1.12	[…] ne nan man ne sceolde nemnian godes naman to nanre ydelnysse;
Æ CH 2.12	Þæt oðer word is: Ne underfoh ðu ðines drihtnes naman on ydelnysse.
Æ SE	Ne un[derfoh ðu on ydelnysse][89] þines drihtnes naman.
Æ 2OEL	Ðæt oþer bebod is þus: *Non*[90] *adsumas nomen domini dei tui in uanum*; Ne underfoh ðu on idelnisse þines drihtines naman.
W Xc	Ne þu þines Drihtnes naman ne namie on idel.
W DpD	II. Ne þu þines drihtenes naman. ne namige on idel.
SS	Þæt oðer word wæs: *Non adsumes nomen domini in uanum*; Ne cig [þ]u[91] godes naman on ydel.

---

87. *CH* 2.12.265-67 (Godden [ed.], *Second Series*, p. 117).

88. 'Sum' in *Ego sum Dominus Deus tuus* links the text to Exod. 20.2 rather than Deut. 5.6, as does 'coram me' in *non habebis deos alienos coram me* (which the *Letter* quotes) in the following verse.

89. Text lost to damaged right-hand edge of MS, which may here have had room for 15-20 characters. Tristram has 'Ne un[derfo ðu on idel]' (p. 199).

90. An interlinear gloss ('.II.'), not in the main hand, appears over *Non adsumes* in X, fol. 119ʳ.

91. Text lost to damaged top left-hand corner of MS.

120   *The Decalogue and its Cultural Influence*

Second Commandment: Textual Notes

Of the authors and texts under consideration, only Cassiodorus and the *Old English Heptateuch* identify Exod. 20.7 ('You shall not take God's name in vain') as the Third Commandment; Augustine, Isidore, Bede, Rabanus Maurus and the remaining Anglo-Saxon authors all see it as the Second.

Second Commandment: Contemporary Commentary

If, in treating the First Commandment in *CH* 2.12, Ælfric departs from his Isidorean source in order to discuss the Trinity,[92] for the Second he returns to Isidore for commentary that he will reproduce in the *Second Old English Letter* and *De sex etatibus* as well. Contemplating the injunction against taking the Lord's name in vain, Isidore recalls Paul's statement that 'uanitati creatura subiecta est' ('the created order was subjected to futility [vanity]' [Rom. 8.20]). Since a creature in this sense is 'vain' (*uana*), and, moreover, changeable (*mutabilis*), treating God's name as *uanum* is equivalent to calling the unchanging, eternal Son, through whom all things were created, a mere creature.[93] In effect, therefore, by denying Christ's divinity, taking God's name in vain espouses Arian Christology. Such exegesis was not original to Isidore, but to Augustine,[94] who was quoted (directly or indirectly) by Isidore, Bede, Alcuin and Rabanus Maurus in turn.[95] Ælfric, however, reproduces not simply the warning against believing 'þæt he wære witodlice anfeald mann' ('that [Christ] in truth was simply a man'),[96] or the association of the Second Command with Rom. 8.20, but the idea of mutability found only in Isidore and Augustine before him: 'ælc gesceaft is ydelnysse underðeod, þæt is awendedlicnesse' ('every creature is subjected to vanity, that is, change').[97] In one copy of the analogous passage in the *Second Old English Letter*, the

---

92. Godden (ed.), *Ælfric's Catholic Homilies*, p. 456.

93. See Mal. 3.6 and Col. 1.16, and Isidore, *Quaestiones in Vetus Testamentum, In Exodum* 29.3 (*PL*, LXXXIII, col. 301BC).

94. *Epistula* 55.11.20 (CSEL, 34.1, p. 191, lines 3-8).

95. Bede, *In Pentateuchum commentarii* 2.20 (*PL*, XCI, col. 318C); Alcuin, *De decem uerbis legis* (*PL*, C, col. 567D); and Rabanus Maurus, *Commentaria in Exodum* 2.12 (*PL*, CVIII, col. 99AB). As noted above, Cassiodorus does reflect Augustine's view that 'referamus tria ad Deum, qui trinitas est' ('we should associate [the first] three with God, who is the Trinity' [*Expositio Psalmorum* 32.2 (CChr, Series Latina, XCVII, p. 284, line 63)]), but does not identify individual verses with specific persons therein.

96. *De sex etatibus*, MS SE, fol. 154ʳ.

97. *CH* 2.12.271-72 (Godden [ed.], *Second Series*, p. 117).

Tremulous Hand of Worcester makes explicit the connection of the Old English to the Vulgate, glossing *underþeod*, *idelnysse*, and *awendedlicnysse* as *subiecta*, *uanitati*, and *mutabilitas*, respectively.[98]

Third Commandment: Vernacular Versions

OEHept	[Exod. 20.8] Gehalga þone restedæg. [20.9] Wirc six dagas ealle þine weorc. [20.10] Se seofoða ys Drihtnes restedæg þines Godes. Ne wirc þu nan weorc on þam dæge, ne nan þara þe mid þe beo. [20.11] On six dagon God geworhte heofenan and eorðan and sæ and ealle þa þing þe on him synd, and reste þy seofoðan dæge and gehalgode hyne. [Deut. 5.12] IIII. Heald þone restedæg, þæt þu hine halgige swa Drihten þe bebead and þus cwæð: [5.13] Wirc six dagas [5.14] and freolsa þone seofoðan; [5.15] gemunað þæt ge silfe wæron þeowe on Egipta lande and ic eow alisde.
Alf LC	Gemyne þæt ðu gehalgige þone ræstedæg; wyrceað eow VI dagas ond on þam siofoðan restað eow; forðam on VI dagum Crist geworhte heofonas ond eorðan, sæs ond ealle gesceafta þe on him sint, ond hine gereste on þone siofoðon dæg, ond forðon Dryhten hine gehalgode.
Æ CH 1.12	[...] ond scolde gehwa freolsian þone sunnandæg mid arwyrðnysse;
Æ CH 2.12	Þæt ðridde word is: Beo ðu gemyndig þæt ðu ðone restendæg freolsige.
Æ SE	Heald þone restedæg mid rihtum biggengum.
Æ 2OEL	Ðæt þridde bebod is: Memento[99] ut diem sabbati sanctifices; þæt is on urum gereorde: Beo ðu gemindig þæt þu gehalige restendæg.
W Xc	Wite þæt ðu þæne restedæg freolsige georne.
W DpD	III. Wite þæt þu þone restedæg freolsige georne.
SS	Þæt ðridd[e word wæs]:[100] Healdað þone halgian restendæg;

Third Commandment: Textual Notes

Almost without exception, our Western patristic and Anglo-Saxon authors view the admonition to honour the Sabbath (Exod. 20.8-11) as the Third Commandment. Cassiodorus does identify the previous verse regarding the Lord's name as the Third, but groups Exod. 20.8-11 along with it, understanding the Sabbath rest to honour God's name as well.[101] Only

---

98. MS X, fol. 119ᵛ.
99. An interlinear gloss ('.III.'), not in the main hand, appears over *Memento* in X, fol. 119ᵛ.
100. Text lost to damaged top right-hand corner of MS.
101. 'Tertium, Non assumes tibi nomen Dei tui in uacuum, in quo iungit et de sabbato' ('Third: "You shall not take the name of your God in vain", to which [the

Deuteronomy in the *Heptateuch* designates the Sabbath as the Fourth Commandment ('IIII').

Third Commandment: Contemporary Commentary

Continuing his Trinitarian interpretation of the first tablet, Augustine had explained Scripture's teaching about the Sabbath in terms of the work of the Spirit. The rest enjoined to believers, he said, is the tranquillity and freedom that comes from a clean conscience—the product, in other words, of the Spirit's sanctification.[102] Isidore, while preserving Augustine's Trinitarian focus, offered a more eschatological perspective. Alluding to the final day of rest for believers that Hebrews links back to God's seventh-day rest (4.9-10), Isidore spoke not only of the sanctifying work of the Spirit needed to enter that final rest, but of the Seventh Age of the world in whch that rest would be found.[103] Bede, quoting Isidore, unsurprisingly affirmed these millennial overtones,[104] and Alcuin and Rabanus Maurus drew verbatim from Isidore as well.[105] Ælfric, strikingly, does nothing of the sort. In the *Catholic Homilies*, in an extended passage of his own,[106] he proactively addresses various issues that may or may not have troubled his audience. First, he says, God 'rested', not because he was weary, but in the sense that he stopped arranging (*dihtian*) or initially setting things up; thereafter, he multiplied his creatures, but created no more kinds of them. It is this ongoing renewal of the Earth, Ælfric explains, of which Jesus speaks when one Sabbath he says, 'Pater meus usque modo operatur, et ego operor' ('My Father is at work to this day, and I am working').[107] Second, Ælfric specifies what 'kinds' God initially created: males and females, bodies and souls, new specimens of which he creates every day. Third, he acknowledges that the Sabbath originally fell on Saturday;

---

verses] about the Sabbath also connect' [*Expositio Psalmorum* 1.32.2 (CChr, Series Latina, XCVII, p. 285, lines 65-66)]).

102. *Sermones* 8.6 (CChr, Series Latina, XLI, pp. 84-85, lines 155-58).

103. *Quaestiones in Vetus Testamentum, In Exodum* 29.4-6 (*PL*, LXXXIII, cols 301C-302A).

104. *In Pentateuchum commentarii* 2.20 (*PL*, XCI, col. 318C); see also Kleist, 'The Influence of Bede's *De temporum ratione*', pp. 81-97.

105. *De decem uerbis legis* (*PL*, C, col. 568BC) and *Commentaria in Exodum* 2.12 (*PL*, CVIII, col. 99A), respectively.

106. Godden (ed.), *Ælfric's Catholic Homilies*, p. 457; and Malcolm Godden, 'Anglo-Saxons on the Mind', in Michael Lapidge and Helmut Gneuss (eds.), *Learning and Literature in Anglo-Saxon England* (Cambridge: Cambridge University Press, 1985), pp. 271-98 (283).

107. Jn 5.17.

it was Christ's resurrection, he notes, that made us shift our veneration to Sunday. Finally, returning somewhat to the spirit of his Isidorean source, Ælfric points his audience to the hope of everlasting life, a final day of rest without any night—if they rid their lives of the corresponding darkness of sin.[108] It is the last two points on which Ælfric focuses in his *Second Old English Letter*. Even as the Mosaic law required the Jews to abstain from 'ðeowetlicum weorcum' ('servile labors'—possibly alluding to the command for servants to rest [Exod. 20.10b], but generally descriptive of quotidian duties), so Christians spiritually honour the Sabbath by abstaining from sinfulness, even as Christ said: 'Omnis qui facit peccatum seruus est peccati' ('Everyone who sins is a slave of sin').[109] Cutting to the chase in *De sex etatibus*, Ælfric defines the one who honours the Sabbath thus: 'se ðe his lif leofað on rihtum geleafan, ond [to his Drihtne ge]byhð swa swa he selost mæg, ond his Drihten gegladað mid godum weorcum' ('he who lives his life in right belief, and bows to his Lord as best he may, and gladdens his Lord with good works').[110]

Fourth Commandment: Vernacular Versions

OEHept	[Exod. 20.12] Arwurða fæder and modor.
	[Deut. 5.16] V. Arwurða þinum fæder and þine modur, þæt þu si langlife and þæt þu si welig on þam lande þe God þe sillan wile.
OEGosp[111]	[Mt. 19.19] Wurþa þinne[112] fæder and modor.
	[Mk 10.19] Wurða þinne fæder ond þine modor.
	[Lk. 18.20] Wurþa þinne fæder ond þine modor.

108. *CH* 2.12.273-311 (Godden [ed.], *Second Series*, pp. 118-19).
109. Jn 8.34; Fehr, *Die Hirtenbriefe Ælfrics*, p. 196, §127.
110. MS SE, fol. 154^r.
111. Quotations from the Old English Gospels are from *The Old English Versions of the Gospels*. I. *Text and Introduction* (ed. R.M. Liuzza; Early English Text Society, OS 303; Oxford: Oxford University Press, 1994), pp. 39, 82, 140. Liuzza edits these texts from Cambridge, Corpus Christi College 140 (first half of the eleventh century, Bath), fols 2^r-45^v (Matthew), 46^r-71^r (Mark), and 73^r-114^r (Luke).
112. While Robert Weber for this verse simply prints *honora patrem* (*Biblia sacra iuxta Vulgata uersionem* [Stuttgart: Deutsche Bibelgesellschaft, 4th edn, 1994], p. 1555), Liuzza notes that *honora patrem tuum* is a 'ubiquitous' variant in Anglo-Saxon Latin Gospels that underlies the vernacular possessive pronoun here; see *The Old English Versions of the Gospels*. II. *Notes and Glossary* (ed. R.M. Liuzza; Early English Text Society, OS 314; Oxford: Oxford University Press, 2000), pp. 27-29.

Alf LC	Are ðinum fæder ond þinre medder, ða þe Dryhten sealde, þæt ðu sie þy leng libbende on eorþan.
Æ CH 1.12	[...] and scolde arwyrðian his fæder ond his moder, ond se ðe wyrigð oððe gremað fæder ond moder he bið deaðes scyldig.
Æ CH 2.12	On ðære oðre tabelan wæs þæt forme bebod: Arwurða ðinne fæder and þine moder.
Æ CH 2.25[113]	[...] arwurða þinne fæder and ðine modor.
Æ SE	[Arwurða] þinne fæder ond þine moder symle, þæt þu lange lybbe on þam behatenum la[ndum].[114]
Æ 2OEL	Ðæt feorðe bebod is: *Honora*[115] *patrem tuum et matrem tuam*; ðæt is engliscre spræce: Arwyrða þinne fæder and eac þinre meder.
W Xc	Weorða geornlice fæder ond modor.
W DpD	IIII. Wurða geornlice fæder ond modor.
SS	Ðæt [feorðe word][116] wæs: Ara þinon fæder and þinre meder;

Fourth Commandment: Textual Notes

Two points bear mentioning here regarding enumeration and intertextuality. As regards the former, aside from Deuteronomy in the *Heptateuch*, all our Western patristic and Anglo-Saxon authors view honouring parents (Exod. 20.12) as the Fourth Commandment. Key to this interpretation is the division of the Decalogue between the two tablets. Augustine acknowledges, for example, that some had viewed Exod. 20.3-11 (through the Sabbath) as containing four commands related to God, and Exod. 20.12-17 (dividing the last verse into two) as containing six commands related to human beings: traditional Judaism, Philo, Josephus and Origen would ostensibly fall into that camp.[117] For Augustine and his followers, however, the decisive factor is Paul's statement in Ephesians that honouring

---

113. Quotations from Ælfric's homily for *Dominica viii post Pentecosten* (*CH* 2.25) are taken from Godden (ed.), *Second Series*, pp. 230-34 (233, lines 87-90). Godden prints the text from K, fols 213ʳ-214ᵛ (214ʳ).

114. In both cases, text lost to damaged right-hand edge of MS, which may here have had room for 5-10 characters.

115. An interlinear gloss ('.IIII.'), not in the main hand, appears over *Honora* in X, fol. 120ʳ; '.I.' likewise appears over *Arwyrða*, reflecting Ælfric's assertion that this is the first commandment on the second of Moses's tablets (Fehr, *Die Hirtenbriefe Ælfrics*, p. 196, §128).

116. Text lost to damaged top right-hand corner of MS.

117. Augustine, *Quaestionum in Heptateuchum* 61.1 (CChr, Series Latina, XXXIII, p. 102, lines 1137-41). In fact, Philo had suggested that there might have been five on each tablet (*Dec.* 12.50), but the practical idea sems to have gained little historical traction.

one's father and mother 'est mandatum primum' ('is the First Commandment'): the precept regarding parents is 'first', they said, inasmuch as it headed up the second tablet.[118] Combined with the potent Trinitarian imagery made possible by viewing the first three commands as a unit, such exegesis solidified the connection of Exod. 20.12 with the Fourth Commandment.

In terms of intertextuality, while quotations from or allusions to individual verses from the Decalogue abound within Scripture, far beyond the scope of this study to trace, one occasion in the New Testament is worthy of note inasmuch as it reproduces five of the Commandments in a cluster: the Rich Man and Jesus. In this episode from the Synoptics, a rich man asks Jesus what he must do to have eternal life. Jesus responds by listing certain of the Commandments, and the man affirms that he has kept them; Jesus, viewing him with compassion, tells the man to sell all he has and follow him. The rich man goes away sad, whereupon Jesus delivers the famous pronouncement that it is harder for the rich to enter heaven than a camel to go through the eye of a needle—an impossibility save for the grace of God. The precise commandments mentioned differ slightly in the Gospel accounts: Matthew lists the injunctions against murder[119] (V), adultery (VI), theft (VII), and false witness (VIII) before the need to honour parents (IV) and love one's neighbour as oneself—a charge from Lev. 19.18 which Jesus elsewhere (Mt. 22.37-40) cites along with loving the Lord God (Deut. 6.5) as the greatest of commandments (Mt. 19.16-26). Mark omits the levitical charge and varies the order slightly, speaking of adultery (VI), murder (V), theft (VII), and false witness (VIII), as well as defrauding others (*ne fraudem feceris* [Mk 10.19]) and honouring one's parents (IV). Luke parallels the list in Matthew, save for the charge to love one's neighbour (Lk. 18.20). In each case, the order of the Commandments

---

118. Eph. 6.2-3; *Sermones* 9.7, 33.4 (CChr, Series Latina, XLI, p. 121, lines 274-84; and p. 415, lines 82-83, 89-94). The Apostle's immediate point is that this 'est mandatum primum in promissione, ut bene sit tibi et sis longeuus super terram' ('is the first commandment with a promise: "that it may go well with you, and that you may live long on the earth"')—a point Augustine does acknowledge elsewhere (*Quaestiones Veteris et Novi Testamenti* 1.7 [*PL*, XXXV, col. 2222] and *Contra Faustum Manichaeum* 15.7 [CSEL, XXV, p. 429, lines 16-18]). While Weber does not list 'Honora patrem tuum et matrem tuam, quod est mandatum primum' as a variant for Mt. 15.4, where Jesus castigates the Pharisees for hindering others from aiding their parents (see below), it appears to have been prevalent enough for Isidore (*Quaestiones in Vetus Testamentum, In Exodum* 29.8 [*PL*, LXXXIII, col. 302BC]), Bede (*In Pentateuchum commentarii* 2.20 [*PL*, XCI, col. 318D]), Alcuin, *De decem uerbis legis* [*PL*, C, col. 567A] and Rabanus Maurus (*Commentaria in Exodum* 2.12 [*PL*, CVIII, col. 99C]) to attribute the sentence to the Gospel ('Euangelium') or Christ in the Gospel ('Dominus in Euangelio').

119. A term here used loosely to encompass unlawful killing, however defined.

may seem unusual, but serves a shrewd rhetorical purpose: Jesus appears to move inexorably towards the command not to covet—ostensibly the rich man's weakness—before veering away at the final moment, returning to the safer ground of honouring one's parents (IV). The device opens the way for the man's joyful claim of righteousness, only to reveal the more poignantly how far he—and every sinner by extension—yet has to go.

Fourth Commandment: Contemporary Commentary

Ælfric's rendition of the story of Rich Man and Jesus in *CH* 2.25 is somewhat of an amalgamation. In the main, Ælfric follows the account in Matthew 19, moving from murder to loving one's neighbour and speaking of the desire to be perfect, details found only in the first Gospel.[120] A couple elements, however, he draws from elsewhere: the rich man comes and falls down at Jesus' feet, as in Mk 10.17,[121] and Jesus responds by saying 'Anes ðinges ðe is wana' ('One thing yet you lack'), as in Lk. 18.22.[122] When it comes to the Fourth Commandment, however, the text is straightforward: 'arwurða þinne fæder and ðine modor' ('Honor your father and your mother'), he says. Ælfric adds more when commenting on the command in *CH* 2.12, the *Second Old English Letter* and *De sex etatibus*. First, he affirms that this instruction to honour parents was the first Commandment on the second tablet, the contents of which pertained to the love of one's fellow humans.[123] Second, he keeps in mind the connection between Exod. 20.12 and 21.17 that Christ makes when condemning pharisaical practices regarding parents: 'Deus dixit, "honora patrem et matrem" et "qui maledixerit patri uel matri morte moriatur"' ('God said, "Honor [your] father and mother", and "Let him who curses [his] father or mother be put to death"'). He who curses, or even exasperates (*tyrigð*), his parents, Ælfric says, is *deaðes scyldig* ('worthy of death').[124] Third, he

---

120. The clause 'si uis perfectus esse, uade...' ('if you wish to be perfect, go...') appears in Mt. 19.21; Ælfric likewise acknowledges that it is an act of perfect men (*fulfremedra* [*manna*]) to give up all they have to follow Jesus (*CH* 2.25.93-95; see also 2.25.77-78 [Godden (ed.), *Second Series*, pp. 233 and 232]).

121. Perhaps it is this detail that leads Godden to say that 'Ælfric's version...is not from Matthew, from which Haymo and Bede [Ælfric's sources for *CH* 2.25] quote, but from the parallel version in Mc 10.17-22' (Godden [ed.], *Ælfric's Catholic Homilies*, p. 568).

122. *CH* 2.25.92 (Godden [ed.], *Second Series*, p. 233).

123. *CH* 2.12.141-43, 255-60 (Godden [ed.], *Second Series*, pp. 115, 117); Fehr, *Die Hirtenbriefe Ælfrics*, p. 196, §128.

124. *CH* 2.12.313-14 (Godden [ed.], *Second Series*, p. 119); see also the *Second Old English Letter* §129 (Fehr, *Die Hirtenbriefe Ælfrics*, p. 196) and *De sex etatibus*, MS SE, fol. 154ʳ, neither of which mentions *tirgan* along with the memorably rhyming *wiergan* ('to curse').

sets forth an allegorical interpretation of the verse, calling believers to honour God as Father and the Church as their Mother, that later appears in his *Decalogue* and thence in Wulfstan's Homily Xb and in *In nomine Domini*. Finally, echoing on an allegorical level Exodus's encouragement to honour one's parents 'þæt þu lange lybbe on þam behatenum la[ndum]' ('that you may live long in the promised land'),[125] in *De sex etatibus* Ælfric enjoins his audience to honour God and the Church that they might live forever 'on þam heof[onum þe] God us eallum behet' ('in heaven, which God promised to all of us').[126]

Fifth to Eighth Commandments: Vernacular Versions

OEHept	[Exod. 20.13] Ne sleh þu. [20.14] Ne synga þu. [20.15] Ne stel þu. [20.16] Ne beo þu on liesre gewitnysse ongen þinne nehstan. [Deut. 5.17] VI. Ne beo þu manslaga. [5.18] VII. Ne unrihthæme þu. [5.19] VIII. Ne stel þu. [5.20] IX. Ne sege þu lease gewitnyssa.
OEGosp	[Mt. 19.18] Ne do þu mannslyht. Ne do þu unrihthæmed. Ne stel þu. Ne sege þu lease gewittnysse. [Mk 10.19] Ne unrihthæm þu. Ne slyh þu. Ne stel þu. Ne sege þu lease gewitnesse. [Lk. 18.20] Ne ofslyh ðu. Ne fyrena þu. Ne stel þu. Ne leoh þu.

Alf LC	Ne sleah ðu. Ne lige ðu dearnenga. Ne stala ðu. Ne sage ðu lease gewitnesse.
Æ CH 1.12	[He cwæð eac] ne hæm ðu unrihtlice. Ne ofslyh ðu mann. Ne stala ðu. Ne beo ðu leasgewita.
Æ CH 2.12	Þæt oðer bebod: Ne hæm ðu unrihtlice. Þæt ðridde: Ne ofslih ðu mannan. Þæt feorðe: Ne stala ðu. Þæt fifte: Ne beo ðu leas gewita.
Æ CH 2.25	Ne ofslih ðu mann. Ne unrihthæm ðu. Ne stala ðu. Ne beo ðu leas gewita.
Æ SE	Ne ofsleh þu man. [...] Ne unrihthæm þ[u.][127] [...] Ne stala þu nateshwon. [...] [Ne beo ðu leas][128] gewita.

125. MS SE, fol. 154ʳ (with text lost to damaged right-hand edge of MS, which may here have had room for 5-10 characters), with 'promised land' slightly altering 'terram quam Dominus Deus tuus dabit tibi' ('the land which the Lord your God will give to you' [Exod. 20.12]).
126. MS SE, fol. 154ʳ (with text lost to damaged right-hand edge of MS, which may here have had room for 5-10 characters).
127. Text lost to damaged right-hand edge of MS, which may here have had room for 5-10 characters.
128. Text lost to damaged right-hand edge of MS, which may here have had room for 15-20 characters. Tristan prints 'N[e...]', but in fact only the first minim of 'Ne' is visible.

Æ 2OEL	Þæt[129] fifte bebod is: *Non occides*; Ne ofsleh ðu nænne mann. [...]
	Þæt sixte bebod is: *Non[130] mechaberis*; Ne unriht hæm ðu. [...]
	Þæt seofoðe bebod is: *Non[131] furtum facies*; ðæt is: Ne stala þu. [...]
	Þæt eahtoðe bebod is: *Non loqueris[132] contra proximum tuum falsum testimonium*; Ne beo ðu leas gewyta.
W Xc	Ne beo ðu ænig manslaga. Ne afyl þe mid forligere. Ne sceaþa ðu. Ne leoh þu.
W DpD	V. Ne beo ðu ænig manslaga. VI. Ne afil þe mid forlegere. VII. Ne scaða þu. VIII. Ne leoh ðu.
SS	[Þæt fifte][133] word wæs: *Non occides*, Ne sleh þu man u[nscil]dine.[134] Þæt VI word wæs: *Non mechaberis*, on unriht ne hæm þu. Þæt VII word wæs: Ne stala þu. Þæt VIII word wæs: Ne sæge lease gewitnysse.

Fifth to Eighth Commandments: Textual Notes

In the case of the injunctions against murder and adultery, it was not just enumeration that proved an issue for Church writers, but the order of precepts as well. While Cassiodorus consistently viewed the former as the Fifth Commandment and the latter as the Sixth,[135] Augustine, Isidore, Bede, Alcuin and Rabanus Maurus were wont on occasion to speak of adultery first and murder afterwards.[136] Among our Anglo-Saxon writers

129. An interlinear gloss ('.V.'), not in the main hand, appears over *Ðæt fifte* in X, fol. 120ʳ; '.II.' likewise appears over *Ne ofsleh*, indicating the commandment's position on the second of Moses' tablets.

130. '.VI.' appears over *Non mechaberis* in text supplied by a later glossator in the left-hand margin of X, fol. 120ᵛ, to replace the Sixth Commandment omitted by the original scribe, likely through eyeskip; both the numbering of commandments and marginal addition may be in the same hand.

131. An interlinear gloss ('.VII.'), not in the main hand, appears over *Non* in X, fol. 120ᵛ; '.III.' likewise appears over *ne stala*, indicating the commandment's position on the second of Moses's tablets—erroneously, since *ne stala* should be fourth according to Ælfric's calculations, but likely reflecting confusion resulting from the omission of the Sixth Commandment by the original scribe.

132. An interlinear gloss ('.VIII.'), not in the main hand, appears over *Non* in X, fol. 120ᵛ; '.V.' likewise appears over *Ne beo*, indicating the commandment's position on the second of Moses' tablets.

133. Text lost to damaged top right-hand corner of MS.

134. Text lost to damaged top right-hand corner of MS.

135. Or at least listed *Non occides* before *Non moechaberis* on the two occasions he mentioned the matter: see *Expositio Psalmorum* 32.2 and 75.12 (CChr, Series Latina, XCVII, p. 285, lines 68-69; and CChr, Series Latina, XCVIII, p. 696, line 214).

136. On some eight occasions, Augustine places *Non moechaberis* before *Non occides*; but on at least twenty he does the opposite—in one case, reversing the order just a few lines after having stated it the first way (*Quaestionum in Heptateuchum* 71.4 and 6 [CChr, Series Latina, XXXIII, p. 104, lines 1204-1206; and p. 105, line

(not counting the *Heptateuch* with its idiosyncratic numbering), only Ælfric reflects this vaccilating tendency, placing 'ne hæm ðu unrihtlice' ('Do not have intercourse unlawfully') before 'Ne ofslyh ðu mann' ('Do not kill humans') in the *Catholic Homilies*, but not in his writings thereafter. In *CH* 2.12, Ælfric actually reverses the order in his Isidorean source, which clearly identifies *Non occides* ('You shall not murder') as the Fifth Commandment.[137] His goal may have been internal consistency, as the result corresponds to the order of Commandments that Ælfric originally included in *CH* 1.12, marked for excision, and then treated at greater length in *CH* 2.12. That list, however, seems itself to have been an original Ælfrician addition that goes strikingly counter to his sources for the rest of the homily, all of which place *Non occides* before *Non moechaberis* ('You shall not commit adultery').[138] It is uncertain, therefore, what interpretive

1247]). Isidore lists *Non moechaberis* first in *Quaestiones in Vetus Testamentum, In Genesin* 25.8 (*PL*, LXXXIII, col. 260B) and *De ordine creaturarum* 13.4 (*PL*, LXXXIII, col. 945C), but *Non occides* first in *Quaestiones in Vetus Testamentum, In Exodum* 29.10-11 (*PL*, LXXXIII, col. 302CD) and *Quaestiones in Vetus Testamentum, In Josue* 9.3 (*PL*, LXXXIII, col. 375C). Thrice Bede speaks first of *Non moechaberis*, and six times refers first to *Non occides*—again, at one point, within but a few lines of each other (*In Pentateuchum commentarii* 2.20 [*PL*, XC, cols 318C, 319D]). Alcuin puts *Non moechaberis* first in *De decem uerbis legis* (*PL*, C, col. 569AB), but reverses the order thrice in *Expositio in Psalmum* Praef. (*PL*, C, col. 597A) and *Commentaria in S. Iohannis Euangelium* 3.12.3-4 and 5.27.16-17 (*PL*, C, cols 820B, 899C). Rabanus Maurus almost always mentions *Non moechaberis* first (on five occasions all told), but once does the opposite—just a few lines before reverting to his usual pattern (*Enarratio super Deuteronomium* 1.11 [*PL*, CVIII, cols. 862C, 863C]).

137. *CH* 2.12.317-25 (Godden [ed.], *Second Series*, p. 119) and Isidore, *Quaestiones in Vetus Testamentum, In Exodum* 29.10-11 (*PL*, LXXXIII, cols. 302C-303A); see also Godden (ed.), *Ælfric's Catholic Homilies*, p. 459.

138. *CH* 1.12.74-84, the passage where Ælfric initially delivered his excursus on Moses and the Commandments, draws on Augustine, *In Iohannis Euangelium tractatus* 24.5 (CChr, Series Latina, XXXVI, p. 246, lines 1-12; Godden [ed.], *Ælfric's Catholic Homilies*, p. 98). Godden describes the *Tractatus* as a work Ælfric knew and consulted as a matter of course (Godden [ed.], *Ælfric's Catholic Homilies*, p. xlviii), and murder appears before adultery twice therein, at *Tractatus* 3.19 and 49.12 (CChr, Series Latina, XXXVI, p. 29, lines 18-19, and p. 426, lines 25-26). Other works that Godden lists as possible ultimate or immediate sources for *CH* 2.1 include Alcuin's *Commentaria in S. Iohannis Euangelium* (which puts *Non occides* first at 3.12.3-4 and 5.27.16-17, noted above), Bede's *Homiliae* (which does the same in 2.2 [CChr, Series Latina, CXXII, p. 195, lines 68-70], a sermon Ælfric knew [Godden (ed.), *Ælfric's Catholic Homilies*, p. li]), Haymo of Auxerre's *Homiliae de tempore* (which follows suit at Homily 49 [*PL*, CXVIII, col. 285D], the possible source for *CH* 1.12), and Smaragdus's *Collectiones in Euangelia et Epistolas* (which likewise speaks first of murder at *PL*, CII, col. 163D).

Fifth to Eighth Commandments: Contemporary Commentary

Ælfric defines a *manslaga* ('murderer'), to begin with, in broad terms. In *CH* 2.12, first of all, he says that anyone who kills another person,[139] brings about someone's death through false accusation, perverts (*forpærð*) another's soul by enticing it to sin,[140] or fails to save lives by providing for the hungry and naked is a *manslaga* who will be judged for his cruelty.[141] Isidore, Ælfric's immediate source for the passage,[142] draws the connection between disregarding the needy and homicide, but mentions neither false accusation nor enticement to evil. Ælfric could have been informed, however, by any number of biblical passages relating to the subject— Christ's treatment of anger and censorious words as murder (Mt. 5.21), James's admonition not to ignore others' physical needs (2.16), the parable of the Rich Man and Lazarus (Lk. 16.19-25), God's injunction to warn the wicked or be held accountable for their blood (Ezek. 3.18, quoted both by Ælfric and Wulfstan after him),[143] to name but a few. Ælfric underscores the need to care for the poor in his *Second Old English Letter*, but adds a couple of details as well: it is the greatest sin (*seo mæste sinn*), he says, to kill an innocent man (*unscyldigne mann*) or to slay his soul by leading him into sin.[144] In *De sex etatibus*, Ælfric similarly affirms that killing is *seo mæste synn*, but tweaks his definition somewhat: the greatest sin is for someone to kill an *unscyldigne mann* in anger—or for him to renounce or oppose (*wiðsace*) God; these two sins are the greatest that people can commit.[145] This understanding of the gravity of murder may be unique to Ælfric: while the Church Fathers described various malefactions as the

---

139. On the extent to which Anglo-Saxons viewed certain kinds of killing as permissible, see for example James E. Cross, 'The Ethic of War in Old English', in Peter Clemoes and Kathleen Hughes (eds.), *England before the Conquest* (Cambridge: Cambridge University Press, 1971), pp. 269-82.

140. A point Ælfric clarifies in *CH* 2.13.63-65 (Godden [ed.], *Second Series*, p. 129; a reference noted by Godden [ed.], *Ælfric's Catholic Homilies*, p. 459).

141. *CH* 2.12.320-25 (Godden [ed.], *Second Series*, p. 119).

142. *Quaestiones in Vetus Testamentum, In Exodum* 29.10 (*PL*, LXXXIII, col. 302CD); Godden (ed.), *Ælfric's Catholic Homilies*, p. 459.

143. Ælfric, *CH* 2.20.146-51 (Godden [ed.], *Second Series*, p. 194), and Wulfstan, Homily 6.10-14 and 17.38-56 (Bethurum [ed.], *The Homilies of Wulfstan*, pp. 142, 243-44); see 'Records for Source Title Ez', *Fontes anglo-saxonici*, http://fontes.english.ox.ac.uk/ (accessed September 2012).

144. *Second Old English Letter* §§132–33 (Fehr, *Die Hirtenbriefe Ælfrics*, p. 198).

145. *De sex etatibus*, MS SE, fol. 154[r].

preeminent vice—pride, for example[146]—the phraseology Ælfric uses in his *Decalogus Moysi*, 'Maximum peccatum est occidere innocentem' ('The greatest sin is to slay the innocent'), does not appear among their works.[147] Nor, despite the influence of the *Decalogus* on works related to Wulfstan, does innocence form part of their articulations of this Commandment. The word does occur, however, in one surprising place: the prose *Solomon and Saturn*. Of all the Anglo-Saxon treatments of the Decalogue, *Solomon and Saturn* is one work that Ælfric seemingly does not influence. In their edition of the text, James Cross and Thomas Hill note that there are no parallels to its treatment of the Decalogue in extant Latin dialog texts, and that it seems to be based simply on the Exodus account in the Vulgate.[148] When it comes to the Fifth Commandment, however, they note that the prohibition against killing a *man unscildine* is reminiscent of Ælfric's version in the *Second Old English Letter* and *Decalogus Moysi*.[149] While it is by no means certain that *Solomon and Saturn* on this point reflects an Ælfrician perspective, the parallel is noteworthy, for these appear to be the only texts in Old English that discuss this Commandment in terms of shedding innocent blood.

Regarding adultery, theft and false witness, less perhaps may be said— in part because Isidore, Ælfric's source for this material in *CH* 2.12, is less than voluble in his comments.[150] Speaking of adultery, first of all, Ælfric may distinguish between non-marital and extra-marital sexual relations in *CH* 2.12, his point in *De sex etatibus* and the *Second Old English Letter* (respectively) is that sex outside of marriage is not only wrong, but defiling to those who commit it.[151] Turning to theft, while in the *Letter* he likens a robber to a wolf and condemns rich persons who oppress the poor—stealing openly, as it were—in his other works he simply states that the subject 'is gehwilcum men full cuð' ('is fully known to everyone').[152]

---

146. See for instance Ambrose, *Expositio de Psalmo cxviii* 7.8 (CSEL, LXII, p. 131, lines 17-18).

147. Fehr, *Die Hirtenbriefe Ælfrics*, p. 198, apparatus. Ælfric goes on in the *Decalogus* to make a further intriguing distinction, stating that while withholding aid from the needy is bad, killing someone's soul by leading it into evil is even worse than ending an innocent person's life (Fehr, *Die Hirtenbriefe Ælfrics*, p. 198, apparatus).

148. Cross and Hill (eds.), *The Prose Solomon and Saturn*, p. 109.

149. Cross and Hill (eds.), *The Prose Solomon and Saturn*, p. 32.

150. Isidore, *Quaestiones in Vetus Testamentum, In Exodum* 29.11-13 (*PL*, LXXXIII, cols. 302D–303A); Godden (ed.), *Ælfric's Catholic Homilies*, p. 459.

151. *CH* 2.12.317-20 (Godden [ed.], *Second Series*, p. 119), *Second Old English Letter* §§134–35 (Fehr, *Die Hirtenbriefe Ælfrics*, p. 200), and *De sex etatibus*, MS SE, fol. 154^r.

152. *Second Old English Letter* §§136–37 (Fehr, *Die Hirtenbriefe Ælfrics*, p. 200), *CH* 2.12.325-26 (Godden [ed.], *Second Series*, p. 119), and *De sex etatibus*, MS SE, fol. 154^r.

As for false witness, in *CH* 2.12 Ælfric is content to affirm abruptly that 'Þis bebod wiðcweð leasung' ('this command forbids lying'); in *De sex etatibus* and the *Letter*, however, he paraphrases Proverbs to emphasize not only that false witnesses will surely be punished, but that liars will lose their lives.[153] In the *Letter*, furthermore, he presses the point home: woe to those, he says, who twist the truth for bribes, for in taking that money they sell their very selves.[154]

Ninth and Tenth Commandments: Vernacular Versions

OEHept	[Exod. 20.17] Ne wilna þu þines nehstan huses, ne þu his wifes, ne his wyeles, ne his wylne, ne his oxan, ne his assan, ne nan þara þinga þe his synd. [Deut. 5.21] X. Ne girn þu þines nehstan wifes, ne his huses, ne his landes, ne nan þæra þinga þe his beoð.

Alf LC	Ne wilna ðu þines nehstan ierfes mid unryhte.
Æ CH 1.12	Ne gewilna ðu oðres mannes wifes, ne ðu ne ge oðres mannes æhta.
Æ CH 2.12	Þæt sixte: Ne gewilna ðu oðres mannes wifes. Þæt seofoðe: Ne gewilna ðu oðres mannes æhta.
Æ SE	Ne gewilna þu nateshwon oðres man[nes wifes;][155] ne gewilna þu eac oðres mannes æhta.
Æ 2OEL	Ðæt nigoðe bebod is: Non[156] concupisces uxorem proximi tui; Ne gewylna ðu oðres mannes wifes. Ðæt teoðe bebod is: Non[157] concupisces ullam rem proximi tui; Ne gewilna ðu oðres mannes æhta.

153. 'Testis falsus non erit inpunitus, et qui loquitur mendacia peribit' (Prov. 19.9). See *CH* 2.12.327-28 (Godden [ed.], *Second Series*, p. 119), *Second Old English Letter* §§138–41 (Fehr, *Die Hirtenbriefe Ælfrics*, pp. 201-202), and *De sex etatibus*, MS SE, fol. 154ʳ.

154. The *Decalogus Moysi* echoes and amplifies these sentiments from the *Letter*: 'Nam scriptum est: "Testis falsus non erit inpunitus, et qui loquitur mendacia peribit." Multi homines emunt sibi falsos testes, sed ue illis qui mutant ueritatem in mendacium, et ue illi qui accepit pecuniam et perdit se ipsum mentiendo' ('For it is written: "A false witness will not go unpunished, and he who speaks lies will perish." Many men buy false witnesses for themselves, but woe to those who change truth into a lie, and woe to the one who receives money and loses himself by lying' [Fehr, *Die Hirtenbriefe Ælfrics*, p. 202, apparatus]).

155. Text lost to damaged right-hand edge of MS, which may here have had room for 10-15 characters.

156. An interlinear gloss ('.IX.'), not in the main hand, appears over *Non concupisces* in X, fol. 120ᵛ.

157. An interlinear gloss ('.X.'), not in the main hand, appears over *Non concupisces* in X, fol. 121ʳ.

W Xc	Ne gyrn ðu oðres mannes wifes, ne æniges þinges þe oðer man age ne gyrn þu on unriht
W DpD	IX. Ne girn ðu oðres mannes wifes, X. ne æniges þincges þe oðer man age. Ne girn ðu on unriht.
SS	Þæt IX word wæs: Non concupiscens rem et omnia proximi tui, Ne gewilna ðu oðres mannes æhta myd unrihte. Þæt X word wæs: Non concupiscens uxorem proximi tui, Ne gewilna ðu oðres mannes wyfes on unriht.

Ninth and Tenth Commandments: Textual Notes

In many ways, how theologians approached the final Commandments depended directly on their understanding of the First. For traditional Judaism, Philo, Josephus and others, distinguishing between Exod. 20.2 or 20.3 ('I am the Lord your God' or 'You shall have no other gods before me') and 20.4 ('You shall not make for yourself an image') meant that the last verse had to be a single precept if the Commandments were to total ten: 'Non concupisces domum proximi tui, nec desiderabis uxorem eius, non seruum, non ancillam, non bouem, non asinum, nec omnia quae illius sunt' ('You shall not covet your neighbour's house; nor shall you desire his wife, nor his servant, nor his maidservant, nor his ox, nor his donkey, nor anything that belongs to him' [20.17]).[158] For most of our Western and Anglo-Saxon writers, however, their treatment of Exodus's opening verses as a unit (or the substitution of Deut. 6.4 ['The Lord your God is one God"] for them) had as its corollary a view of coveting as two commandments, one dealing with lust and the other with avarice. In support of this approach, authorities from Augustine onwards relied not on Exod. 20.17, but on its counterpart from Deuteronomy: 'Non concupisces uxorem proximi tui, non domum, non agrum, non seruum, non ancillam, non bouem, non asinum, et uniuersa quae illius sunt' ('You shall not covet your neighbour's wife, nor his house, nor his field, nor his servant, nor his maidservant, nor his ox, nor his donkey, nor anything that belongs to him' [5.21]). The change in language is slight but significant, as material goods and servants are listed after (and thus associated with) another's house as opposed to his wife. Indeed, Augustine and others were wont to summarize the cumbersome list of possessions by quoting the Tenth Commandment as 'Non concupisces ullam rem proximi tui' ('You shall not desire anything belonging to your neighbour')[159]—a tradition followed in

---

158. Cassiodorus, who had conflated the verses regarding taking God's name in vain (Exod. 20.7) and the Sabbath (20.8-11), viewing the whole as the Third Commandment, likewise spoke of Exod. 20.17 as the Tenth (*Expositio Psalmorum* 32.2 [CChr, Series Latina, XCVII, p. 285, lines 70-71]).

159. Augustine may in fact only quote the whole of Deut. 5.21b once, as part of

the Latin of Ælfric's *Second Old English Letter* and *Decalogus Moysi*, as well as in *Solomon and Saturn*, and nearly all our authors' vernacular equivalents.[160] The *Heptateuch*, of course, is an exception as ever, translating Deut. 5.21 in full and calling both parts of it (regarding wives and possessions) the Tenth Commandment. Alfred's law-code is also unusual, however, for while its final entry, 'Ne wilna ðu þines nehstan ierfes mid unryhte' ('You shall not sinfully desire your neighbour's possessions'), reflects the abbreviated *Non concupisces ullam rem*, it makes no mention of coveting wives, leaving the number of commandments effectively at nine. Finally, *Solomon and Saturn* throws a curve ball that may go back to Augustine, as it specifies *Non concupiscens rem* as the Ninth Commandment and *Non concupiscens uxorem* as the Tenth.[161] For all such variations, however, the Anglo-Saxon tradition in the main seems to have been a unified one, drawing on Augustinian language and a Western tradition of enumeration to bring to a close their delineation of the Decalogue.

---

selected verbatim extracts from the book (*Speculum de Scriptura sacra, De Deuteronomio* 5 [*PL*, XXXIV, col. 896]); on ten occasions, however, he renders the verse as 'Non concupisces rem proximi tui' (e.g., *In Ioannis euangelium tractatus* 3.19 [CChr, Series Latina, XXXVI, p. 29, lines 20-21]), including once without the accompanying 'Non concupisces uxorem' (*Sermones* 251.8 [*PL*, XXXVIII, col. 1171]). Other authors who quote the abbreviated version include Cassiodorus, *Expositio Psalmorum* 118.20 (CChr, Series Latina, XCVIII, p. 1068, line 415); Isidore, *Quaestiones in Vetus Testamentum, In Genesin* 25.8 and *In Exodum* 29.15 (*PL*, LXXXIII, cols. 260C and 303B)]); Bede, *In Pentateuchum commentarii* 2.20 (*PL*, CI, col. 318D [in which a slightly expanded form ('Non concupisces rem proximi tui, domum et omnia illius') appears later at *PL*, CI, col. 319D]) and *In S. Ioannis euangelium expositio* 11 (*PL*, XCII, col. 778A); Alcuin, *De decem uerbis legis* (*PL*, C, col. 570A) and *Commentaria in S. Iohannis Euangelium* 5.27.16-17 (*PL*, C, col. 899C); and Rabanus Maurus on four occasions, including *Commentaria in Exodum* 2.12 (*PL*, CVIII, col. 100A) and *Commentarium in Matthaeum* 6.22 (*PL*, CVII, col. 1063A).

160. For which see the table above. Wulfstan's Latin Homily Xb and the Wulfstan-derived *De initio creature* are exceptions to this trend, for, though they draw on Ælfric's *Decalogus Moysi*, they nonetheless quote Deut. 5.21 from the Vulgate in full.

161. Half the time, Augustine reverses the order of the final commandments, placing 'Non concupisces rem proximi tui' before 'Non concupisces uxorem proximi tui' on five occasions (e.g., *Enarrationes in Psalmos* 73.2 [CChr, Series Latina, XXXIX, p. 1005, lines 8-9]), while keeping *uxorem* before *rem* at four other points (including *Sermones* 9.7 and 33.4 [CChr, Series Latina, XLI, p. 121, lines 286-87, and p. 415, lines 86-87], where he explicitly designates the injunctions against lust and avarice as the Ninth and Tenth Commandments, respectively). Others appear to have been more consistent about interpreting 'Non concupisces rem' as the last Commandment—until *Solomon and Saturn*.

Ninth and Tenth Commandments: Contemporary Commentary

Ælfric's comments on the final Commandments are once again brief. Indeed, in terms of coveting another man's wife, his *Second Old English Letter* and *De sex etatibus* simply let the biblical injunction stand on its own.[162] In *CH* 2.12, however, he follows Isidore in distinguishing between lustful desire (the Ninth Commandment) and adulterous action (the Sixth [or, as Ælfric would have it here, the Fifth] Commandment): if men guard their minds, he says, they will stay far from sinful deeds.[163] The opposite balance is true for coveting another's possessions: *CH* 2.12 states merely that the verse prohibits worldly avarice, while the *Letter* and *De sex etatibus* draw additional conclusions for their audience. The former affirms that individuals should only have possessions that they rightfully acquired; they may give to others voluntarily, but must acquire goods from others only in a godly manner, lest they lose them.[164] The result, states the latter, tying aptly back to the Seventh Commandment, is that theft and wickedness (*reaflac ond unriht*—both action and attitude, perhaps) will be extinguished.[165] With such words, the three sustained commentaries on the Commandments come to an end.

Conclusion

In the broader picture, Old English accounts of the Decalogue manifest a remarkable degree of homogeneity. In their understanding of the division and language of the Commandments, they reflect largely Augustinian traditions that directly and indirectly informed Ælfric of Eynsham, whose Latin and vernacular writings shaped most Anglo-Saxon treatments of the subject that now survive. At the same time, the number of such accounts is few: while numerous allusions to individual commands may lie scattered through the Old English corpus, full lists of the Decalogue—to say nothing of sustained exegesis thereon—are limited to the scant selection we have surveyed in this study. Broad homogeneity, moreover, is scarcely

---

162. Fehr, *Die Hirtenbriefe Ælfrics*, p. 202, §142; MS SE, fol. 154ʳ.
163. Isidore, *Quaestiones in Vetus Testamentum, In Exodum* 29.14 (*PL*, LXXXIII, col. 303A); and *CH* 2.12.238-32 (Godden [ed.], *Second Series*, p. 119). As Ælfric stresses fidelity to marriage vows in the injunction against adultery, and speaks of defiling another's wife when warning against lust, Godden suggests (intriguingly if not completely compellingly) that 'Ælfric's language perhaps implies that the distinction is not so much between act and desire but between the fornication of a married man with another woman...and the fornication of a man with a married woman' (Godden [ed.], *Ælfric's Catholic Homilies*, pp. 459-60).
164. Fehr, *Die Hirtenbriefe Ælfrics*, p. 202, §143-44.
165. MS SE, fol. 154ʳ.

monolithic uniformity: authors might be influenced in their choice of words, verses, and interpretation by a host of competing strands of textual tradition—and Ælfric, for one, was sophisticated enough in his use of sources to weigh the authority of one over another and insert teaching of his own tailored for his audience as well. If systematic examination of these accounts has hitherto been lacking, the absence of a critical edition assembling the evidence for comparison may well have been to blame. While the above represents but a small step in that direction, one hopes that giants standing hereafter on these paltry shoulders may bring about discoveries hitherto unimagined.

Appendix I: Manuscript Sigla

The Decalogue appears in a range of Anglo-Saxon texts, versions of which appear in some three dozen manuscripts. To facilate reference to editions of these texts, I have retained the sigla employed therein. Where editors employ the same siglum for different manuscripts, I have alphabetized them and distinguished them numerically: Cambridge, University Library Ii. 2. 11—MS A in Liuzza's edition of the Old English Gospels—is thus here designated A1, while London, British Library, Royal 7 C. xii—MS A in Clemoes's edition of Ælfric's First Series of *Catholic Homilies*—appears as A2. Where editors assign different sigla to the same manuscript, I have printed both: Oxford, Bodleian Library, Bodley 343 (B for Godden and Oz for Fehr) thus becomes B/Oz.[166] Information regarding manuscript dates, origin and provenance is taken from Helmut Gneuss, *Handlist of Anglo-Saxon Manuscripts* (Tempe: Arizona Center for Medieval and Renaissance Studies, 2001) and N.R. Ker, *Catalogue of Manuscripts Containing Anglo-Saxon* (Oxford: Clarendon Press, rev. edn, 1990).

EDITIONS
Homilies of Wulfstan, ed. Bethurum: B1, C1, E2, and I
First Series, ed. Clemoes: A2
Solomon and Saturn, ed. Cross and Hill: SS
Fehr, *Die Hirtenbriefe Ælfrics*: Bl, N2, O, B/Oz, V, and X
Second Series, ed. Godden: B/Oz, C2, D, F, K, H1, M, N1, and U
Liebermann, *Die Gesetze der Angelsachsen*: E1, G, and H3
Old English Versions of the Gospels, ed. Liuzza: A1, B3, C3, Cp, H2, L1, R, and Y
Old English Heptateuch, ed. Marsden: B2, L2, and P

MANUSCRIPTS

A1 Cambridge, University Library Ii. 2. 11 (third quarter of the eleventh century, Exeter) [Liuzza]

A2 London, British Library, Royal 7 C. xii (end of the tenth century, SW England, prob. Cerne) [Clemoes]

B1 Cambridge, Corpus Christi College 419 and 421, pp. 1-2 (first half of the eleventh century, SE England?; provenance Exeter), pp. 204-29, at p. 207 [Bethurum]

---

166. London, British Library, Cotton Nero A. i, fols. 3-57 (Liebermann's G) and fols. 70-177 (Bethurum's I) were originally separate manuscripts that were bound together by 1580 (N.R. Ker, *Catalogue of Manuscripts Containing Anglo-Saxon* [Oxford: Clarendon Press, rev. edn, 1990], p. 215); they are now designated as Ker §163/Gneuss §340 and Ker §164/Gneuss §341, respectively.

B2	London, British Library, Cotton Claudius B. iv (first half of the eleventh century) [Marsden]
B3	Oxford, Bodleian Library, Bodley 441 (2382) (first half of the eleventh century, SE England?) [Liuzza]
B/Oz	Oxford, Bodleian Library, Bodley 343 (2406) (second half of the twelfth century)
Bl	Boulogne-sur-Mer, Bibliothèque Municipale 63, Part 1 [fols. 1-34] (first half of the eleventh century, England [provenance Saint-Bertin])
C1	Cambridge, Corpus Christi College 201, Part I, Section B (middle of the eleventh century, New Minster, Winchester?) [Bethurum]
C2	Cambridge, Corpus Christi College 303 (Rochester, first half of the twelfth century) [Godden]
C3	London, British Library, Cotton Otho C. i, vol. 1 (first half of the eleventh century) + London, British Library, Otho B. x, fol. 51^r [Liuzza]
Cp	Cambridge, Corpus Christi College 140 (first half of the eleventh century, Bath)
D	Oxford, Bodleian Library, Bodley 342 (2405) (beginning of the eleventh century, Canterbury or Rochester; prov. Rochester)
E1	Cambridge, Corpus Christi College 173 (laws copied second quarter of the tenth century; Wessex, perhaps Winchester) [Bethurum]
E2	Oxford, Bodleian Library, Hatton 113 (5210) (second half of the eleventh century [1064x83], Worcester) [Bethurum]
F	Cambridge, Corpus Christi College 162, Part I (beginning of the eleventh century, SE England)
G	London, British Library, Cotton Nero A. i, fols. 3-57 (third quarter of the eleventh century)
H1	London, British Library, Cotton Vitellius C. v (tenth or eleventh century, SW England) [Godden]
H2	Oxford, Bodleian Library, Hatton 38 (4090) (twelfth or thirteenth century) [Liuzza]
H3	Rochester Cathedral Library, A. 3. 5 [Textus Roffensis] (first half of the twelfth century, Rochester) [Liebermann]
I	London, British Library, Cotton Nero A. i, fols. 70-177 (first quarter of the eleventh century [1003x23], Worcester or York)
K	Cambridge, University Library, Gg. 3. 28 (end of the tenth or beginning of the eleventh century)
L1	Oxford, Bodleian Library, English Bib. C. 2 (31345) (first half of the eleventh century) [Liuzza]
L2	Oxford, Bodleian Library, Laud Misc. 509 (942) (second half of the eleventh century) [Marsden]

M	Cambridge, University Library, Ii. 4. 6 (middle of the eleventh century, New Minster, Winchester)
N1	London, British Library, Cotton Faustina A. ix (first half of the twelfth century) [Godden]
N2	London, British Library, Cotton Tiberius A. iii, fols. 2-173 (middle of the eleventh century, Canterbury CC) [Fehr]
O	Cambridge, Corpus Christi College 190 (Part I [pp. iii-xii and 1-294], first half of the eleventh century, Worcester?, provenance Exeter by the second half of the eleventh century; Part II, middle and third quarter of the eleventh century, Exeter)
P	New York, Pierpont Morgan Library, G. 63 (second half of the eleventh century)
R	London, British Library, Royal 1. A. xiv (second half of the twelfth century)
SE[167]	London, British Library, Cotton Otho C. i, vol. 2 (fols. 1^r-61^v: beginning of the eleventh century, SW England?; fols. 62^r-155^v: middle of the eleventh century, probably Worcester; provenance whole MS Worcester)
SS[168]	London, British Library, Cotton Vitellius A. xv, fols. 4-93 (middle of the twelfth century)
U	Cambridge, Trinity College, B. 15. 34 (middle of the eleventh century, prob. Canterbury CC)
V	London, British Library, Cotton Vespasian D. xiv, fols. 4-169 (middle of the twelfth century)
X	Oxford, Bodleian Library, Junius 121 (5232) (third quarter of the eleventh century, Worcester)
Y	New Haven, Beinecke Library 578 (late tenth or first half of the eleventh century, SE England?)

---

167. *De sex etatibus huius seculi* is not yet in print (ed. forthcoming by Kleist), but is here edited from Cotton Otho C. i, vol. 2, and designated SE.

168. As *Solomon and Saturn I* is found only in Cotton Vitellius A. xv, its editors do not assign it a siglum; for our purposes, however, SS seems appropriate. At some point, SS was bound with another collection from the tenth or eleventh century: Cotton Vitellius A. xv, fols. 94-209, the Beowulf manuscript.

Appendix II: Traditions of Enumerating the Commandments

		Traditional Judaism	Philo	Josephus	Origen	Reformed and Orthodox Christian	Augustine	Cassiodorus	Isidore	Bede	Alcuin	Rabanus Maurus	OE Heptateuch [Deut.]	Ælfric: CH II.12	Ælfric: 2nd OE Letter	Ælfric: Decalogus Moysi	Wulfstan Xb	De preceptis Domini	Solomon and Saturn	Lutheran and Roman Catholic
Exod. 20.2/ Deut. 5.6	'I am the Lord your God'	1	—	—	—	—	—	—	—	[1]	—	1	—	—	1	—	—	—	—	—
Exod. 20.3/ Deut. 5.7	'You shall have no other gods'	2	1	1	1	1	1	1	—	1	1	1	1	—	1	1	1	1	1	1
Exod. 20.4-6/ Deut. 5.8-10	'You shall not make an image'	2	2	2	2	2	1	2	—	1	1	1	2	—	—	1	1	1	1	1
Deut. 6.4	'The Lord your God is one God'	—	—	—	—	—	1	—	1	—	1	—	—	1	—	—	—	—	—	—
Exod. 20.7/ Deut. 5.11	'You shall not take God's name in vain'	3	3	3	3	3	2	3	2	2	2	2	3	2	2	2	2	2	2	2
Exod. 20.8-11/ Deut. 5.12-15	'Remember to keep the Sabbath holy'	4	4	4	4	4	3	3	3	3	3	3	4	3	3	3	3	3	3	3
Exod. 20.12/ Deut. 5.16	'Honor your father and your mother'	5	5	5	5	5	4	4	4	4	4	4	5	4	4	4	4	4	4	4
Exod. 20.13/ Deut. 5.17	'You shall not kill'	6	6	6	6	6	5/6	5	5/6	5/6	5/6	5/6	6	6	5	5	5	5	5	5
Exod. 20.14/ Deut. 5.18	'You shall not commit adultery'	7	7	7	7	7	6/5	6	6/5	6/5	6/5	6/5	7	5	6	6	6	6	6	6
Exod. 20.15/ Deut. 5.19	'You shall not steal'	8	8	8	8	8	7	7	7	7	7	7	8	7	7	7	7	7	7	7
Exod. 20.16/ Deut. 5.20	'You shall not bear false witness'	9	9	9	9	9	8	8	8	8	8	8	9	8	8	8	8	8	8	8
Exod. 20.17a/ Deut. 5.21	'You shall not covet your neighbour's house'	10	10	10	10	10	—	9	—	—	—	—	—	—	—	—	—	—	—	—
Exod. 20.17b/ Deut. 5.21	'Nor shall you desire his wife [...]'	10	10	10	10	10	—	10	—	—	—	—	—	—	—	—	—	—	—	—
Deut. 5.21a	'You shall not covet your neighbour's wife'	—	—	—	—	—	9/10	—	9	9	9	9	—	9	9	9	9	9	10	9
Deut. 5.21b	'You shall not covet your neighbour's goods'	—	—	—	—	—	10/9	—	10	10	10	10	9	10	10	10	10	10	9	10

The Ten Commandments in the Ethiopic Tradition

Ralph Lee

The Ethiopian Orthodox *Tewahədo*[1,2,3] Church has as one of its central images the Ark of the Covenant. Edward Ullendorff, in his seminal Schweich Lectures,[4] described the significant veneration accorded to the Ark in the Ethiopian Christian tradition: the Ark, known as the *tabot*, during festivals is 'carried in solemn procession accompanied by singing, dancing, beatings of staffs or praying sticks, rattling of sistra, and sounding of other musical instruments';[5] and during the liturgy it takes the place of the altar and 'symbolizes the tablets of the Covenant and the scrolls of the law'.[6] The enduring significance of the Ark and its contents is understood in part through the symbolism of the *tabot* or ark enshrined in the holiest place of each contemporary Ethiopian Orthodox church: 'the tabot takes the form of a large tablet of wood carved with a cruciform design, the text of the Ten Commandments, and the dedication to the saint in whose name the church

---

1. Ethiopic characters, both in Amharic and Ge'ez are transcribed according to the rules used in the *Encyclopaedia aethiopica*, see http://www1.uni-hamburg.de/EAE/transf.html (accessed 4/2/2013).
2. This is the proper title of the Ethiopian Church. The word *tawaḥədo* means 'fusion' or 'unity'; see Wolf Leslau, *Comparative Dictionary of Ge'ez (Classical Ethiopic)* (Wiesbaden: Harrassowitz Verlag, 2006), p. 609. Here *tawaḥədo* refers to the fusing of humanity and divinity in the person of Christ and is a reflection of the non-Chalcedonian miaphysite Christology of the Ethiopian Orthodox Church. For a detailed discussion of Ethiopian Christology see A. Grillmeier, *Christ in Christian Tradition*. II. *From the Council of Chalcedon (451) to Gregory the Great (590–604), Part Four: The Church of Alexandria with Nubia and Ethiopia after 451* (trans. O.C. Dean; London: Mowbray, 1996).
3. The abbreviation 'EC' after some dates refers to the 'Ethiopian Calendar', which starts on the 11th of September in the Gregorian Calendar, and on the 12th of September in the year before a Gregorian leap year. It has 12 lunar months, and one of 5 or 6 epagomenal days. The year 2005 started on the 11th of September, 2012.
4. The Schweich Lectures of the British Academy, 1967, published as Edward Ullendorff, *Ethiopia and the Bible* (repr., London: Oxford University Press, 2006).
5. Ullendorff, *Ethiopia and the Bible*, p. 85.
6. Ullendorff, *Ethiopia and the Bible*, p. 85.

is consecrated...the tabot sits on a stand, known as the manbara tabot or "Seat of the Tabot", within the Sanctuary'.[7]

The Ethiopian Church makes a strong claim to possess the original Ark and its contents. Whatever is now housed in a small chapel in the holy city of Aksum, devout Christians vigorously assert it to be the genuine Ark. Contemporary legends tell of how the first priests who sought to move the Ark to its current location in 1965 died when they touched it, evoking 2 Sam. 6.6-7, and a second cohort of priests were successful only after an extended period of prayer and fasting. The earliest independent account of Ethiopia's strong claim to possess the Ark is found in the *History of the Churches and Monasteries of Egypt* by *Abu Ṣāliḥ,* the twelfth-century CE Armenian traveller.[8] This account evokes an image of the Ark similar to Ullendorff's contemporary view, and connects it with 'Israeli' heritage in Ethiopia. While some of the historicity of this account could be challenged, it is an interesting and evocative early account of the Ethiopian tradition:

> The Abyssinians possess also the Ark of the Covenant, in which are the two tables of stone, inscribed by the finger of God with the commandments which he ordained for the children of Israel. The Ark of the Covenant is placed upon the altar, but is not so wide as the altar; it is as high as the knee of a man, and is overlaid with gold; and upon its lid there are crosses of gold; and there are five precious stones upon it, one at each of the four corners, and one in the middle. The liturgy is celebrated upon the Ark four times in the year, within the palace of the king; and a canopy is spread over it when it is taken out from [its own] church to the church which is in the palace of the king: namely of the feast of the great Nativity, on the feast of the glorious Baptism, on the feast of the holy Resurrection, and on the feast of the illuminating Cross. And the Ark is attended and carried by a large number of Israelites descended from the family of the prophet David, who are white and red in complexion, with red hair. In every town of Abyssinia there is one church, as spacious as it can possibly be.[9]

---

7. David Appleyard, 'Ethiopian Christianity', in Ken Perry (ed.), *The Blackwell Companion to Eastern Christianity* (Oxford: Blackwell, 2007), p. 134. See also Richard Pankhurst, 'Some Brief Notes on the Ethiopian Tabot and Mänbärä Tabot', *Quaderni di studi etiopici* 8–9 (1987–88). For a discussion of the possible origins of the *tābot* and how it featured early in other Christian traditions see Alphonse Raes, 'Antimension, Tablit, Tabot', *Proche-Orient chrétien* 1 (1951).

8. This work has been attributed to *Abu Ṣāliḥ,* the twelfth-century CE Armenian traveller, and the text was translated by Evetts and Butler. It appears, however, that he was only the owner of one of four manuscripts that comprise the work, and that the work was composed between the mid-twelfth and the mid-fourteenth centuries. See Witold Witakowski, 'Coptic and Ethiopic Historical Writing', in Sarah Foot and Chase F. Robinson (eds.), *The Oxford History of Historical Writing.* II. *400–1400* (Oxford: Oxford University Press, 2012).

9. B.T.A. Evetts and A.J. Butler, *The Churches and Monasteries of Egypt and Some*

With the Ark as a strong focus of Ethiopian Christianity, symbolic interpretations of the Ark and the tablets of stone on which the Ten Commandments were written are important. This brief article will outline the imagery surrounding the Ten Commandments using three primary sources. First, there is the late thirteenth- or early fourteenth-century CE compilation[10] *Kəbrä Nägäśt*,[11] or 'The Glory of the Kings', the Ethiopian national epic, which contains a symbolic theological background to the understanding of the Ark in the Ethiopian Orthodox Church. It relates the legend of the Ark of the Covenant coming to Ethiopia and the conversion of the Ethiopians to Judaism, and asserts the Solomonic lineage of the Ethiopian kings. Secondly, there are the *andəmta*[12] Bible commentaries, a comprehensive corpus of literature written down in the late seventeenth century CE, but whose origins probably date from the advent of Christianity in Ethiopia in the fourth century CE.[13] Thirdly we have the *Dəggʷa*, a hymn book composed in Ge'ez whose origins are with the sixth century CE writings of the Ethiopian St Yared.[14]

Neighbouring Countries, Attributed to Abu Salih, the Armenian (Anecdota oxoniensia; Oxford: Clarendon Press, 1895), pp. 287-88.

10. Paolo Marrassini, 'Kebra Nagast', in Siegbert Uhlig (ed.), *Encylopaedia aethiopica*. III. *He–N* (Wiesbaden: Harrassowitz Verlag, 2007).

11. There is a critical edition of this text with a German translation in C. Bezold, *Kebra Nagast: Die Herrlichkeit der Könige nach den Handschriften in Berlin, London, Oxford und Paris zum ersten Mal im äthiopischen Urtext herausgegeben und mit deutsche Übersetzung versehen* (Abhandlung der philosophisch-philologischen Klasse der Königlich Bayerischen Akademie der Wissenschaften, 23; Munich: Akademie der Wissenschaften, 1909). There is also a slightly wanting English translation, E.A. Wallis Budge, *The Kebra Nagast* (New York: Cosmio Books, 2004). An excellent discussion of its contents can be found in Ullendorff, *Ethiopia and the Bible*, pp. 74-79, and a thorough analysis of its sources is found in a PhD thesis supervised by Ullendorff, D.A. Hubbard, *The Literary Sources of the Kebra Nagast* (St Andrews University, 1956). A PDF copy of this thesis is available at http://research-repository.st-andrews.ac.uk/handle/10023/544 (accessed 14 January 2013).

12. This name derives from the use of *andəm*, shorthand for 'and one also says' to introduce successive interpretations.

13. For a detailed study of this commentary tradition see Roger W. Cowley, *The Traditional Interpretation of the Apocalypse of John in the Ethiopian Orthodox Church* (University of Cambridge Oriental Publications, 33; Cambridge: Cambridge University Press, 1983); and his *Ethiopian Biblical Interpretation: A Study in Exegetical Tradition and Hermeneutics* (University of Cambridge Oriental Publications, 38; Cambridge: Cambridge University Press, 1988).

14. See Sergew Habteselassie, 'Yared (Saint), 6th Century, Orthodox, Ethiopia', in L.H. Ofosu-Appiah (ed.), *The Encyclopaedia africana: Dictionary of African Biography*. I. *Ethiopia–Ghana* (New York: Reference Publications, 1997); Habtemichael Kidane, '*Dəggʷa*', in Siegbert Uhlig (ed.), *Encyclopaedia aethiopica*. II. *D–Ha* (Wiesbaden: Harrassowitz Verlag, 2005).

Possibly one of the earliest indigenous references to the place of the Ark and the Ten Commandments in Ethiopian Christianity is found in the *Kəbrä Nägäśt*. Chapter 42 of this work recounts the restatement of the Ten Commandments by Zadok the priest to Menilik—the son, according to legend, of the Queen of Sheba and King Solomon[15]—shortly before Menilik left for Ethiopia with the Ark. This section of the text is, according to Hubbard,[16] part of the original Sheba Cycle, which is of unknown date and may be pre-Christian, and reflects the early embodiment of the importance of the Ten Commandments within the Ethiopian psyche.

The *Kəbrä Nägäśt* also contains symbolic references to the Ten Commandments, or to the tablets of stone. For instance in the following, from chap. 11, suggested by Hubbard to be part of the final additions to the work from the late thirteenth or early fourteenth century CE,[17] Christ is implicitly symbolized as the Ten Commandments:

> And if the heavenly Zion had not descended and if he had not put on the flesh of Adam then the Word of God would not have appeared and our salvation would not have been; the evidence is in the symbol, the heavenly Zion is likened to the Mother of the Redeemer, Mary, for the constructed Zion also contains in her the Ten Commandments of the Law which were written by His hand, and He himself, the Creator, dwelt in the womb of Mary, through whom all things came into being.[18]

Later, in chap. 98 of the *Kəbrä Nägäśt*, we find an elaborate symbolic interpretation of the Ark and its contents, where Christ again is symbolized by the Ten Commandments written on the tablets of stone:

> The gold is the purity of the Godhead which came down from heaven, because the Godhead understands the whole of heaven and earth, and likewise the Ark, the dwelling place of the Heavenly Zion, is plated with gold. And the Ark is to be interpreted as Mary, and the wood which will not rot is to be interpreted as Christ Our Saviour, and the Gomor which is the gold container which is inside the Ark is to be interpreted as Mary, and the Manna which is in the container is interpreted as the flesh of Christ which came down from heaven, and the Word of God which is written on the Two Tablets is to be interpreted as Christ the Son of God, and the spiritual Zion[19] is to be interpreted as the light of the Godhead.[20]

---

15. Bezold, *Kebra Nagast*, pp. 41-44. The same can be found in Budge's English translation, *The Kebra Nagast*, pp. 50-52.

16. Hubbard, 'The Literary Sources of the Kebra Nagast', p. 409.

17. Hubbard, 'The Literary Sources of the Kebra Nagast', p. 410.

18. Bezold, *Kebra Nagast*, p. 6, col. a, lines 5-14; also in Budge, *The Kebra Nagast*, p. 8.

19. In the *Kəbrä Nägäśt*, 'Zion' is synonymous with both the Ark and St Mary.

20. Bezold, *Kebra Nagast*, 137b 9-24; also in Budge, *The Kebra Nagast*, p. 90.

The Ethiopian commentary tradition, known as *andəmta*, also makes brief but important references to the Ten Commandments and the stone tablets, which clearly reflect a similar symbolic approach to the *Kəbrä Nägäśt* and the *andəmta*.

Two passages in the commentary tradition make specific reference to the Ten Commandments and how they might be classified.[21] At Exod. 20.26 the commentary reflects on the classification of the Ten Commandments, with the suggestion that the injunction against coveting is the most important, and sees the Ten as intrinsically linked to further commands in Leviticus and Apostolic literature:

> ...the Ten Commandments are classified in this way: do not worship idols, do not swear an oath [falsely], honour the Sabbath, honour your father and mother, do not murder, do not commit adultery, do not steal, do not bear false witness, do not covet, nine commandments, and the tenth is love your neighbour. Leviticus also adds [further] writing, but not only this, for the Apostles said, in the Sinodos,[22] that 'do not covet' is the more fitting than all. They also counted [do not worship idols] as two, [do not worship] the sun, moon and stars, and [also] do not worship their images. These are what are called the Ten Commandments.[23]

The Exod. 24.12 commentary makes a slightly different classification, with 'do not worship idols' being separate, suggesting its heightened importance:

> You will lay the foundation for Israel, I will give you the two precious[24] tablets the nine commands and the 'do not worship idols' that I have written; one says 'I will give you the two precious tablets which have on them the nine commandments and the "do not worship idols" that I wrote by divine nature'.[25]

The commentary on Exod. 34.28 introduces several symbolic interpretations of the stone tablets and explains why there were two of them, more in the style of the interpretations found in the *Kəbrä Nägäśt*:

---

21. Summary thoughts are often given at the end of groups of verses in the Ethiopic commentaries, so that commentary does not always refer to the verse number given.

22. The *Sinodos* is a book of Church Orders, attributed to the Apostles, with somewhat varying contents; see Roger W. Cowley, 'The Biblical Canon of the Ethiopian Orthodox Church Today', *Ostkirchliche Studien* 23 (1974), pp. 318-23.

23. Anonymous, *mäṣäḥaftä bəluyat: orit zäfəṭrät (zälədät), orit zäḍä'at* (Addis Ababa: *tənśa'e masatämya därəğət*, 1999 EC), p. 127.

24. The word here is *'ənqʷu* which generally means 'pearl' or 'precious stone'. It is not absolutely clear why the word is used here, but it is also associated with an Ethiopian legend that a pearl was placed in the belly of Adam, which was passed down through the generations to St Mary and then Christ. The pearl seems to be symbolic of the pure human nature of Christ and St Mary in the Orthodox Tradition.

25. Anonymous, *mäṣäḥaftä bəluyat: orit zäfəṭrät (zälədät), orit zäḍä'at*, p. 149.

Moses remained on Mount Sinai for forty days and forty nights without eating a morsel, or drinking any water. God wrote the Ten Commandments on the two tablets and gave them to him. This is a symbol: the first set of tablets of Adam, since they came from nothing, they are a symbol that Adam came into being without seed; the two groups [of commandments] [are a symbol] of the soul and the flesh; that they were broken because of idolatry is a symbol of Adam's being injured by sin; the later tablets [are a symbol] of Our Lady: 'cut [them] like the former ones' means that she did not come into being by seed or by intercourse; the writing [is a symbol] of the flesh that he took from her; the word is the divine word, this is a symbol of how the Lord appeared by divine action, and that he was born without seed. One [interpreter] says, the first tablets [are a symbol] of the Law, the later tablets of the Gospel, the first tablets were broken as the Law of the Old Testament has passed, the later tablets will remain, since the Law of the Gospel will remain.[26]

The hymn book, the *Dəggʷa*, makes frequent symbolic allusions relating to the incarnation. The Ark is seen primarily as a symbol of St Mary and of divine indwelling, so the objects found inside the Ark are symbolic of Christ. In the following hymn for the feast of the assumption, on the Ethiopian date of *Nähase 16*, St Mary is described with language from the Song of Songs, and then is compared with the new chariot of Abinadab (Aminadab), which bore the Ark, here symbolizing Christ, to Jerusalem.[27] The symbolism immediately shifts to Mary being the Ark containing the tablets of the law:

> My sister, bride of Paradise
> Your ways, my dove, [are] beautiful
> The fragrance of your perfume is more than all mouths
> The fragrance of her mouth
> is like apple,
> The fragrance of her mouth
> is like apple,
> Like the skin of a pomegranate.
> I compared her to the
> Chariot of Ami[na]dab
> Her neck is like the tower of David
> Her tablets [are] of the Law,
> Glory surrounds her.[28]

26. *Mäṣäḥaftä bəluyat: orit zäfəṭrät (zälədät), orit zäḍä'at*, p. 221.
27. See 2 Sam. 6.
28. Fifteenth-century MS EMML 2542, p. 113, col. c. So far no critical study of the text of the *Dəggʷa* has been conducted, meaning that ancient sources and contemporary editions used in the Church are not always consistent. The distinguished Ethiopian scholar Kidanawald Kifle states that, 'the work is attributed to Yared in the time of King GabraMesqel, but later people added to it...the *Dəggʷa is not just Yared's*' (Kidanawald Kifle, *mäṣäḥafä səwasəw wägəs wämäzgäbä qalat* [Addis Ababa: Artistic

Furthermore, the same passage describes Christ as the 'new commandment' carried in the womb of Mary, the symbolism is of the New Testament superseding the Old, with the tablets symbolizing the 'Word of the Father' as divine presence:

> The beauty of her face, completely pleasing,
> The opening of her mouth from fragrant paradise
> The new commandment was carried in her womb
> For our lame heart he is a staff.
> The dwelling place of the Word of the Father,
> For the Holy Tabernacle, which the hand of man did not make,
> Whom Ezra saw, the heavenly hosts looking on her [saying],
> Let us bow down to her, and let us give thanks for her honour.[29]

The imagery is developed further not only by making a symbolic connection with the Arks, including Noah's Ark, but by addressing Mary as 'Perfect Tabernacle', another symbol of divine immanence. The later printed edition of this passage expands the symbol to include the construction of the Ark: the gold that adorned the Ark is a symbol of purity and so of virginity; the clothes in one piece refer to the cover of the Ark, comprising the mercy seat and the cherubim, being of one piece of wood, indicating unbroken signs of virginity. Here Mary is also portrayed as the bearer of the stone tablets, which symbolize Christ:

> Mary is the Ark of Noah, Broad Tabernacle, sealed in virginity.
> Who is like you who was chosen from among women,
> Holy Mary luxuriously adorned,
> wrapped with clothes of gold in one piece
> whom they will not humble, Tabernacle of the Testament,
> Ark which has the Ten Commandments in her.
> Daughter of light, servant of our salvation,
> in our bridal chamber your Son surrounded with glory.[30]

This brief survey of Ethiopian themes related to the Ten Commandments gives an outline of the ancient imagery and symbolism that are a common feature of contemporary Ethiopian Orthodox Christianity.

Printing House, 1948 EC), p. 338). Notwithstanding this, all of the versions reflect indigenous Ethiopic thought.

29. This passage is only found in the contemporary printed version of the hymn book: Yared, *mäṣäḥafa dəggʷa zäqədus yared (bäməśraq goğam hagärä säbkät ṣə/bet asatamit*, 1999 EC), p. 520 col. a, line 25–col. b, line 2.

30. Yared, *mäṣäḥafa dəggʷa zäqədus yared*, 520 b 17-26.

Thomas Aquinas on the Ten Commandments and the Natural Law

Randall B. Smith

To begin with, let me suggest that Thomas Aquinas's famous discussion in qq. 90-97 of the *prima secundae* of the *Summa of Theology*—a selection often published separately under the title 'The Treatise on Law'[1]—should be seen in terms of a larger theological project in the second part of the *Summa*, one which involved integrating the new Aristotelian 'virtue-ethics' approach to morality that was becoming popular in the mid-thirteenth century on the one hand with the 'law-based' approach that Thomas had inherited from the Old Testament Scriptures on the other. In what follows, I want to sketch out Thomas's approach to the Decalogue, along with a bit of the historical context that helped make that approach possible.

---

1. I still have my trusty 1963 Gateway edition of the so-called *Treatise on Law*, which I used as a freshman in college, with the introduction by Stanley Parry, reprinted from the 1948 Benziger Brothers edition of the Fathers of the English Dominican Province translation of the *Summa of Theology*: Thomas Aquinas, *Treatise on Law* (Chicago: Henry Regnery, 1963). In 1996, Gateway replaced this translation with the translation of R.J. Henle, SJ, and gave the text a new introduction by Ralph McInerny. Henle's translation had originally appeared with facing Latin text in a 1993 volume published by the University of Notre Dame Press. Regnery Press had also published a volume in 1948 under the title *The Treatise on Law*, as part of their 'The Great Books Foundation' series. All of these volumes share the title 'Treatise on Law', and all contain only qq. 90-97 of the *prima secundae* of the *Summa*. Things may be changing, though. In 2000, Hackett published the *Treatise on Law* translated by Richard Regan and although it contained only qq. 90–97 in their entirety, it also included a 'note' on qq. 98–108, several articles from q. 100 on 'the moral precepts of the Old Law' and one article from q. 105 dealing with the Old Law. And finally, 2009 saw the publication by St Augustine's Press of Alfred J. Freddoso's translation of 'the complete text' of the 'Treatise on Law'. The front cover of the volume proclaims itself proudly (and accurately) as 'the *only* free-standing English translation of the entire *Treatise*, which includes both a general account of law (Questions 90–92) and also specific treatments of what St Thomas identifies as the five kinds of law: the eternal law (Question 93), the natural law (Question 94), human law (Questions 95–97), the Old Law (Questions 98–105), and the New Law (Questions 106–108)'.

The Importance of the Old Law in the Thirteenth Century

The noted French Dominican scholar Marie-Dominique Chenu once suggested that it should give us pause when we realize that most of the subjects in Thomas's *Summa* that *we* in the modern world consider absolutely essential, such as the proofs for the existence of God or the nature of the theological *scientia*, often occupy no more than one column in the Leonine edition and include generally no more than three or four objections and responses, whereas the Questions on the Old Law, by contrast, are by far the longest in the whole *Summa*, many of them extending to over 30 Leonine columns and employing as many as 15 objections and 15 responses.[2] What might seem to us to a rather odd disproportion is brought into a somewhat different perspective, however, when we discover that nearly every major theologian in and around Paris in the thirteenth century wrote similarly long and extremely detailed commentaries on the Mosaic Law of the Old Testament, most of them containing what we find in Thomas's *Summa*: namely, a short introductory section laying out the various definitions and distinctions among the different types of law (in Thomas's *Summa*, that would be qq. 90 through 97), which serves as a preface to a much longer—indeed, in most cases, a *very* long—treatise on the Old Law.[3] A broad study of these *summae* suggests, thus, that the really burning question on the minds of Thomas and his contemporaries was precisely the status of the literal meaning of the Mosaic Law of the Old Testament, which all agreed was based on a fundamental structure provided by the Decalogue.

Why this renewed interest in the Old Testament Mosaic Law? In brief, let me suggest it had to do with a convergence of factors: renewed interest in the literal sense of the Old Testament, on the one hand, along with the cultural challenges presented by the rediscovered and newly translated Aristotelian corpus, on the other. As Beryl Smalley and others have shown, the thirteenth century saw a flowering of interest in the *literal* or *plain* meaning of the Old Testament.[4] At roughly the same time, the newly translated texts

---

2. Cf. M.-D. Chenu, OP, 'La théologie de la loi ancienne selon saint Thomas', *RevThom* 61 (1961), pp. 485-97 (486). 'C'est d'ailleurs donner une suite, et une suite raisonnable, à la surprise que les lecteurs de la *Somme*, professionnels ou non, éprouvent en voyant les trois articles concernant les dispositifs cultuels de la Loi [q. 102, a. 4, 5, 6] s'étendre sur quarante-neuf colonnes, alors que les articles touchant la plus exigeante métaphysique théologique dépassent rarement une colonne. Il faut, même si on n'est pas d'accord, donner un sens à ce *fait*.'

3. For a good overview, see Beryl Smalley, 'William of Auvergne, John of La Rochelle and St Thomas Aquinas on the Old Law', in *St Thomas Aquinas (1274-1974): Commemorative Studies* (Toronto: Pontifical Institute of Mediaeval Studies, 1974), II, pp. 1-71.

4. See Beryl Smalley, *The Study of the Bible in the Middle Ages* (Oxford: Oxford University Press, 1941); reprinted most recently by University of Notre Dame Press, 1989.

of Aristotle were flooding into the medieval Christian universities, opening up exciting new intellectual vistas for some, while seeming to present dangerous new threats to others.[5] With Aristotle's *Ethics*, scholars were uncovering, it seemed, a total science of ethics whose foundations and formulations were completely independent of biblical revelation. In this new cultural context, dominated as it was by reverence for logical categories and the arts of dialectic, the old modes of moral teaching by means of biblical moral allegory of the sort showcased by Gregory the Great in his famous *Moralia in Job* were in serious intellectual circles no longer considered adequate foundations for a serious ethical *scientia*. It was within the context of these challenges that Christian theologians of the thirteenth century such as Thomas Aquinas had to give a convincing account of how the Bible, with all its various odd and seemingly disconnected laws, could still be considered a reliable source of ethical knowledge.

Another contributing factor, falling somewhere between these other two, was the influence of the work of the Jewish philosopher Maimonides, who had argued, on good Aristotelian principles in the *Guide for the Perplexed*, that if laws are ordinances of reason, then God, since he is the most reasonable Lawgiver, must have given the Jewish people the most reasonable laws.[6] Reading Maimonides inspired medieval Christian theologians to believe that they too could discover sensible 'reasons' for each of the precepts of the Old Testament law, which they promptly set about to try to do in these long treatises on the Old Law.[7]

The concern to establish a rational foundation for a theologically meaningful biblical ethics led these scholars to undertake a critical reappropriation of the classical natural law tradition. It was St Paul who was understood to have opened the door to this sort of approach when he wrote in his Letter

---

5. The story of the 'Aristotelian invasion' and its various influences on medieval Christian thought is well told in David Knowles, *The Evolution of Medieval Thought* (New York: Vintage Books, 1964); see esp. Chapter 15 ('The Rediscovery of Aristotle') and Chapter 18 ('The Philosophical Revolution of the Thirteenth Century'). For another good treatment, see the essay on 'The Reception and Interpretation of Aristotle's *Ethics*' by Georg Wieland in Norman Kretzmann *et al.* (eds.), *The Cambridge History of Later Medieval Philosophy: From the Rediscovery of Aristotle to the Disintegration of Scholasticism, 1100–1600* (Cambridge: Cambridge University Press, 1982); and for additional background information, see also in the same volume the earlier essays on 'Aristoteles Latinus' by Bernard Dod and on 'The Medieval Interpretation of Aristotle' by C.H. Lohr. For a good account of the ecclesiastical reaction to Aristotle especially in and around Paris, see John F. Wippel, 'The Parisian Condemnations of 1270 and 1277', in Jorge Gracia and T. Noone (eds.), *A Companion to Philosophy in the Middle Ages* (Oxford: Blackwell Publications, 2003).

6. See Moses Maimonides, *Guide for the Perplexed*, part III, chaps. 31-54.

7. For Maimondes' influence on these early thirteenth-century treatises on the law, see Smalley, 'William of Auvergne', esp. pp. 30-31, 33-34, 36, 43, 52, 60, and 62.

to the Romans that, 'when Gentiles that have not the law do by nature the things of the law, these, though they have not the law, are yet a law unto themselves, in that they show the work of the law written on their hearts' (Rom. 2.14). The context here, of course, is the question of how the Gentiles, who did not have the written Jewish law, could be held accountable by God for not following the written laws, precepts and prohibitions, for which Paul's answer was to reply that the Gentiles *did* have the law, at least in a certain sense, because they had another law—the unwritten law, or what came to be called the natural law—*written*, as it were, *on their hearts*.

Reading this passage from Paul's Letter to the Romans in terms of the natural law had become standard practice by Thomas's time. Contemporary studies on the *Ordinary Gloss* show that when a thirteenth-century reader of Paul's letter would get to this passage in Rom. 2.14 in his or her Bible, he or she would find the following gloss: '[Paul] had said that a Gentile is condemned if he has acted wickedly and saved if he has acted well. But since he does not have the law and does not know, as it were, what is good or what is evil, it would seem that neither should be imputed to him. On the contrary, the apostle says that even if he does not have the written law, he has the natural law…'[8] Indeed, in q. 91, art. 2 of the *prima secundae*, Thomas Aquinas answers the question 'Whether there is in us a natural law' by citing in his *sed contra* the authority of this very gloss, saying: 'A gloss on Romans 2.14: "When the Gentiles, who have not the law, do by nature those things that are of the law", comments as follows: "Although they have no written law, yet they have the natural law…"'.

The Decalogue as a Revealed Articulation of the Natural Law

So what does any of this have to do with the Decalogue? Well, if we read the *whole* of the final section from the *prima secundae* of Thomas's *Summa of Theology* on law and grace—not stopping, as so often happens, after Question 97—what we will find is that, according to Thomas, the content of the natural law is revealed authoritatively in the moral precepts of the Old Law, especially those of the Decalogue. But to understand the relationship

---

8. There is fortunately now a convenient English translation of the entire *Glossa ordinaria on Romans* (trans. with an introduction and notes by Michael S. Woodward; Kalamazoo: Medieval Institute Publications, 2011); see esp. pp. 39-41 for the glosses on Rom. 2.14 and following. The references to the natural law are frequent throughout this entire section. On p. 41, for example, in reference to the verse in Rom. 2.17 that reads in part 'But if you are called a Jew and rely on the law…', the gloss comments: 'The Gentile has only the natural law, but you, a Jew, have more…you do not wander into errors as those who are without the law'. The glosses on Rom. 6–8 are also a good section in which to find frequent references to the natural law. See *Glossa ordinaria*, pp. 88-137.

between the Old Law and the natural law as Thomas does, we must begin with an important distinction.

In *Summa theol.* 1–2, q. 98, art. 5, Thomas announces to his reader that: 'the Old Law showed forth (*manifestabat*) the precepts of the natural law'.[9] And yet, in saying this, we must be careful to distinguish, as Thomas does, between the moral precepts (*moralia*), the ceremonial precepts (*cæremonialia*), and the judicial precepts (*judicialia*) of the Old Law.[10] It is only the first of these, says Thomas, the moral precepts, that relate directly to the natural law. The latter two, the ceremonial and judicial precepts, are essentially positive law precepts given by God to the Jewish people to deal with their particular needs during the historical circumstances of the Old Testament period. Though related to the natural law, they represent more specific 'determinations' of the natural law. These precepts, says Thomas, were explicitly binding only on the Jewish people and only until the coming of Christ.[11]

When it comes to the moral precepts, on the other hand, they are said to be binding on all people at all times because, according to Thomas, they are *de lege naturae*.[12] Indeed, the identity between the moral precepts of the Old Law and the natural law is expressed in particularly strong terms. In q. 99, art. 4 of the *prima secundae*, for example, Thomas says that the moral precepts refer to the *dictamen* of the natural law. He uses the same term when he distinguishes the moral precepts from the judicial and ceremonial precepts in q. 104, art. 1, declaring there that the moral precepts 'derive their binding force (*vim obligandi*) from the *dictamen* of reason itself (*ex ipso dictamine rationis*)'.[13]

Now this term, *dictamen*, carries strong connotations in Latin which we have trouble capturing with any single English term. Often, the English words 'utterance', 'statement', or 'dictum' are forced into service.[14] In

---

9. Cf. *Summa theologiae* (hereafter *Summa theol.*) 1–2, q. 98, art. 5.
10. See *Summa theol.* 1–2, q. 99, arts. 2-4.
11. On this, see esp. *Summa theol.* 1–2, q. 99, art. 4: 'We must therefore distinguish three kinds of precept in the Old Law, viz., *moral* precepts, which are dictated by (*dictamen* of) the natural law; *ceremonial* precepts, which are determinations of [the general principles of the natural law that apply to] the divine worship; and *judicial* precepts, which are determinations of [the general principles of the natural law that apply to] the justice to be maintained among men'. It is worth noting, in this regard, that in the *Glossa ordinaria on Romans*, to which Thomas referred frequently as we know from numerous citations throughout the *Summa theol.* (see, for example, n. 8 above), we find next to the text of Rom. 3.31 ('Do we therefore destroy the law through faith? By no means! Rather we establish the law') a gloss that reads: 'i.e., the moral precepts of the law'.
12. See *Summa theol.* 1–2, q. 98., art. 5 and *Summa theol.* 1–2, q. 100, art. 1.
13. *Summa theol.* 1–2, q. 104, art. 1.
14. On this, cf. for example the definitions of *dictamen* given by R.J. Deferrari in his

the Latin Middle Ages, however, the term *dictamen* referred primarily to a written dictation, taken down by a scribe, which represented in writing an authoritative statement, usually from a superior to his subordinates.[15] The scribal art of taking dictation was, in fact, called the *ars dictaminis*. In Lewis and Short's Oxford Latin Dictionary, we find under the entry for *dictamen* the following: 'late Latin for *dictum, praescriptum*', and most tellingly, '*praeceptum*'. Now why would a *dictamen*, a dictation, come to be understood as a 'prescript' or, more tellingly, a 'precept'? Because a *dictamen*, in addition to being a precise written account of someone's words (their *dicta*, as it were), carried with it a clear authority of command— the authority of the one whose words had been so scrupulously recorded— and thus constituted for those under that person's authority a 'precept' or a 'command'. What Thomas is implying, then, I suggest, when he uses the word *dictamen* here, is that the moral precepts of the Old Law should be understood to serve a written articulation of what the natural law expresses in an unwritten way, just as a medieval *dictamen* was a written dictation of a royal command that was expressed originally in an unwritten way.

Why Do We Need a Revealed Articulation of the Natural Law?

But why do we need a divinely revealed *dictamen* of the natural law if the natural law is in us 'naturally'? Thomas's answer and the answer of his Christian contemporaries is that the moral precepts of the Old Law are

Latin–English Dictionary of St Thomas Aquinas (St Paul: Daughters of St Paul, 1960, 1986).

15. The *ars dictaminis*, the art of letter writing, became a very precise and valued one during the Middle Ages. Scribes trained in letter writing were invaluable at court. The treatises on the 'art' applied Ciceronian rhetorical principles to the actual mechanics of writing a letter. As a result, a five-part letter format was developed and systematized. The art became so systematized, in fact, that collections of formularies and model letters (*dictamina*) began to circulate for verbatim copying by those unable or unwilling to compose letters of their own. The association of *dictamina* with form letters need not concern us at present, although I believe it strengthens my case that the word *dictamen* was frequently associated with the notion of verbatim copying. The literature on the *ars dictaminis* is vast, but there is a useful introduction to the development of the practice in James J. Murphy, '*Ars dictaminis*: The Art of Letter-Writing', in *Rhetoric in the Middle Ages: A History of Rhetorical Theory from Saint Augustine to the Renaissance* (Berkeley: University of California Press, 1974, 1981). For annotated guides to the bibliography, see Murphy, 'Letter Writing: *Ars dictaminis*', Chapter 4, in *Medieval Rhetoric: A Select Bibliography* (Toronto: University of Toronto Press, 2nd edn, 1989), pp. 76-103; and Luke Reinsma, 'The Middle Ages', in Winifred Bryan Horner (ed.), *Historical Rhetoric: An Annotated Bibliography of Selected Sources in English* (Boston: G.K. Hall, 1980), pp. 43-108. An account of more recent scholarship can be found in Martin Camargo, *Ars dictaminis, ars dictandi* (Turnhout: Brepols, 1991). Camargo has a bibliography of current scholarship, but only works not listed in either Murphy or Reinsma.

needed as a remedy for sin: in particular, as an instruction to remedy the ignorance that resulted from sin. Dom Odon Lottin has accurately described this theology of history as follows:

> The school of Anselm of Laon spread, on the subject of the natural law, a conception which exercised a profound influence. Before the epoch of the Mosaic Law, humanity was subject to the reign of the natural law, which *naturalis ratio* dictated to them. It was condensed into this principle: Do not do to another that which you would not want for him to do to you. But this natural reason was soon obfuscated by sin, to the point that few men remained faithful to the true God. The Mosaic Law, thus, became necessary to revive the natural law in the heart of man.[16]

And indeed, we find this same theology of history at work in Aquinas. In *Summa theol.* 1–2, q. 98, art. 6, for example, Thomas argues that humanity's chief defect since the Fall has been pride, and thus 'it was fitting that the Law should be given at such a time a would be appropriate for the overcoming of man's pride'. Now humanity is proud of two things in particular, says Thomas: knowledge and power.

> He was proud of his knowledge, as though his natural reason could suffice him for salvation: and accordingly, in order that his pride might be overcome in this matter, man was left to the guidance of his reason without the help of a written law: and man was able to learn from experience that his reason was deficient, since about the time of Abraham man had fallen headlong into idolatry and the most shameful vices. Wherefore, after those times, it was necessary for a written law to be given as a remedy for human ignorance: because 'by the Law is the knowledge of sin' (Rom. 3.20).[17]

In this regard we must remember that, for Thomas and his contemporaries, the operations of human nature since the Fall are not at all the workings of a well-oiled and efficient machine. Human nature has been so corrupted by the effects of sin that what was characteristic or 'natural' for human beings in that time when their nature was healthy and uncorrupted is no longer so. Humanity's acts and dispositions are the result of severely weakened capacities. Certainly one of the most often ignored categories of law within the Treatise on Law is what Thomas calls in the *Summa theol.* 'the law of the *fomes* [i.e., fuel] of sin' and what he calls elsewhere, more

---

16. Cf. O. Lottin, *Le droit naturel chez Saint Thomas d'Aquin et ses prédécesseurs* (Bruges: Beyaert, 2nd edn, 1931), p. 27: 'L'école d'Anselme de Laon a répandu, au sujet de la loi naturelle, une conception qui a exercé une profonde influence. Avant l'époque de la Loi mosaïque, l'humanité était soumise au règne de la loi naturelle que lui dictait la *ratio naturalis*. Elle se condensait en ce principe: Ne fais pas à autrui ce que tu ne voudrais pas qu'on te fît. Mais cette raison naturelle fut bientôt obnubilée par le péché, au point que peu d'hommes restèrent fidèles au vrai Dieu. La Loi mosaïque devenait ainsi nécessaire pour faire revivre la loi naturelle au coeur de l'homme.'

17. *Summa theol.* 1–2, q. 98, art. 6.

simply, 'the law of concupiscence'.[18] In either case, what Thomas is actually referring to is what St Paul describes when he says in Rom. 7.23 that 'I see another law at work in my members, fighting against the law of my mind, and bringing me under captivity under the law of sin which is in my members'. As Paul makes clear, he *knows* the law; indeed, he even 'delights' in it. And yet he finds that he *still* cannot *do* it, stating famously: 'For the good which I would do, I do not; but the evil which I would not, that I do' (Rom. 7.19).

So too on Thomas's understanding, our 'natural' powers—and in particular, the power of the natural law; that is, the light of natural reason by which we come to know what ought to be done and what ought to be avoided—has been corrupted by sin, especially original sin. Thus, according to Thomas, we must consider human nature in two ways: first, in its full integrity or wholeness (*in sui integritate*), as it was in the first man before he sinned, and second, as it exists in us now, corrupted owing to original sin (*corrupta in nobis post peccatum primi parentis*).[19] At their creation, before the Fall, human beings were able to act in accord with the natural law. It was at that point, says Thomas, 'according to his proper natural condition that [man] should act in accordance with reason'; indeed, 'this law was so effective in man's first state', says Thomas, 'that nothing either outside or against reason could take man unawares'. After man turned away from God, however, 'he fell under the influence of his sensual impulses', which began to rule him as though they themselves were a kind of law. This law, the law of the *fomes*, is, says Thomas, 'a deviation from the law of reason'. The more human beings fell under its sway, the more they 'departed from the path of reason'—so much so that Thomas proclaims rather dramatically in his *Collationes de decem praeceptis* that 'the law of nature was *destroyed* by the law of concupiscence'.[20]

The result, according to Thomas, is that, in their present fallen state, humans are largely *not* able—that is, no longer able—to do the good proportioned to their nature.

> In the state of integrity of nature (*in statu naturae integrae*) man by his natural endowments could will and do the good proportioned to his nature (*homo per sua naturalia velle et operari bonum suae naturae proportionatum*),

---

18. On the 'fomes' of sin, see esp. *Summa theol.* 1–2, q. 91, art. 6; and for the term *lex concupiscentiae*, see for example the proemium of his *Collationes de decem praeceptis* where he speaks of a 'fourfold law' (*quadruplex lex*) found in humans: *et prima quidem lex naturae, quam Deus in creatione infudit; secunda lex concupiscentiae; tertia lex Scripturae; quarta est lex caritatis et gratiae, quae est lex Christi.*

19. On this cf., for example, *Summa theol.* 1–2, q. 109, art. 2.

20. Thomas Aquinas, *The Commandments of God: Conferences on the Two Precepts of Charity and the Ten Commandments* (trans. L. Shapcote, OP; London: Burns Oates & Washbourne, 1937), Prologue, p. 2.

which is the good of acquired virtue... But in the state of corrupted nature (*sed in statu naturae corruptae*), man falls short even of what he can do by his nature (*etiam deficit homo ab hoc quod secundum suam naturam potest*), so that he is unable to fulfill all of it by his own natural powers.[21]

On Thomas's account therefore, our understanding has been obscured because of sin, and we need a sort of divinely given 'brush-up course' on the fundamental principles of the moral life, principles that we could and should know by reason alone, but too often lose sight of because our intellect has been blinded by sin. Given this account, since the moral precepts of the Old Law represent a divinely authorized revelation of the fundamental precepts of the natural law, then we can (and indeed *should*) use the moral precepts of the Old Law to help reacquaint us with the natural law.

The Three Grades of Moral Precept in Aquinas

And what would such a revealed picture of the natural law look like? Well, if we turn to Question 100 of the *prima secundae* of the *Summa of Theology*, we find Thomas describing in several places the sort of hierarchy he believes obtains among the moral precepts of the law.[22] There he identifies three 'levels' or 'grades' (the word is *gradus* in the original Latin) of moral precept in the law, which he distinguishes according to their degree of universality or particularity and thus according to their accessibility to human reason. Thus, according to Thomas, just as every judgment of speculative reason proceeds from the natural knowledge of first principles, so every judgment of practical reason proceeds from 'certain naturally known principles'.[23] First in order among these naturally known principles are what Thomas calls 'the first and common precepts of the natural law, which are *per se nota* to human reason'.[24] It is generally known that there have been virtually endless debates among scholars in the twentieth century about what the primary precepts of the natural law might be.[25] Indeed, this is often

---

21. *Summa theol.* 1–2, q. 109, art. 2.
22. For a more developed treatment of Thomas's treatment of the relationship between the natural law and the Mosaic Law, see my article 'What the Old Law Reveals about the Natural Law according to Thomas Aquinas', *The Thomist* 75 (January 2011), pp. 95-139.
23. *Summa theol.* 1–2, q. 100, art. 1.
24. See, for example, *Summa theol.* 1–2, q. 100, art. 3, ad 1.
25. In this regard, R.J. Armstrong's book entitled *The Primary and Secondary Precepts in Thomistic Natural Law Teaching* (The Hague: Martinus Nijhoff, 1966) is very instructive. Examples of what might constitute the primary, invariable precepts of the natural law range from Viktor Cathrein's 'You should observe the order which is fitting for you as a rational being, in your relations with God, your fellow men and yourself', to Louis Le Fur's 'one ought to pay compensation for damage unjustly inflicted on another

taken to be one of the most debated issues in contemporary natural law theory. And yet, for all that, if we read beyond the confines of q. 97 into qq. 98 and following on the Old Law, we will soon discover without much difficulty what Thomas considers the primary precepts of the natural law to be. In q. 100, art. 3, for example, he says very explicitly of the two great commandments to 'love the Lord your God with all your heart, soul, and mind', and to 'love your neighbor as yourself', that 'these two precepts are the first and common precepts of the natural law, which are self-evident to human reason'.[26] Thomas makes clear elsewhere that there are also other, alternative forms of the commandment 'Love your neighbor as yourself', such as 'Do unto others as you would have them do unto you', or the negative form of the same, 'Don't do to others what you wouldn't want them to do to you'. These function for Thomas as the primary precepts of the natural law.

The precepts of the second 'grade', then, are said to be derived from those of the first and are related to them as 'conclusions to common principles'. They still concern matters so evident (*adeo explicita*), says Thomas, that 'at once, after very little consideration (*statim, cum modica consideratione*), one is able to approve or disapprove of them by means of these common first principles'.[27] This is a relatively simple moral judgment, insists Thomas, of which everyone, even the untrained, is capable.[28] As examples of the second 'grade' of precept—those which 'the natural reason of every man of its own accord and at once, judges ought to be done or not done'—Thomas lists the following: 'Honor your father and mother', 'Thou shalt not kill', and 'Thou shalt not steal'[29]—in other words, the basic Commandments of the Decalogue.

The third 'grade' of precept, finally, are those that require a more complex moral judgment. These, says Thomas, require not a 'slight consideration' (*modica consideratione*) as do the precepts of the second grade, but 'much consideration' (*multa consideratio*) of the various circumstances. Not all are able to do this carefully, says Thomas, 'but only those who are wise; just as it is not possible for all to consider the particular conclusions of the

---

person', to Armstrong's own suggestion: 'the sexual relationship requires some form of regulation'. Another favorite of scholars is the principle that 'good is to be done and evil avoided', which Thomas mentions in passing in *Summa theol.* 1–2, q. 94, art. 2. On the relationship between the principle that 'good is to be done and evil avoided' and the 'first and common precepts of the law', see the discussion in my dissertation, '*Regula caritatis*: The Natural Law and its Relationship to the Old Law, the New Law, and the Virtues in Thomas Aquinas's Moral Theology' (Dissertation, University of Notre Dame, 1998), pp. 109-64.

26. *Summa theol.* 1–2, q. 100, art. 3, ad 1.
27. *Summa theol.* 1–2, q. 100, art. 1.
28. Cf. *Summa theol.* 1–2, q. 100, art. 11.
29. *Summa theol.* 1–2, q. 100, art. 1.

sciences, but only for those who are philosophers'.[30] As an example of this third 'grade' of precept—those, he says, 'which are judged by the wise to be done after a more subtle (*subtiliori*) consideration of reason'—Thomas lists: 'Rise up before the hoary head, and honor the person of the aged man'.[31] Thomas insists that even the precepts of this third 'grade' belong to the law of nature (*de lege naturae*), and yet they are such that 'they need to be taught, the wiser giving instruction to the less wise'.[32]

Thomas helpfully summarizes the essential elements of this threefold hierarchy in *Summa of Theology* 1–2, q. 100 (art. 11), declaring that: 'The moral precepts derive their efficacy from the very dictate of natural reason... And of these there are three grades (*triplex est gradus*).'[33]

> [First] For some are <u>most certain</u> (*certissima*), and <u>so evident as to need no promulgation</u> (*ideo manifesta quod editione non indigent*). **Such are the commandments of the love of God and our neighbor**, and others like these [such as 'Do unto others as you would have them do unto you'] ... which are, as it were, the ends of the commandments (*fines praeceptorum*); and so no man can have an erroneous judgment about them (*unde in eis nullus potest errare secundum iudicium rationis*).
>
> [Second] Some precepts are <u>more particular</u> (*magis determinata*), the reason of which any person, even an uneducated one, can at once easily grasp (*quorum rationem statim quilibet, etiam popularis, potest de facili videre*); and yet they need to be promulgated, because human judgment, in a few instances, happens to be led astray concerning them. **These are the precepts of the decalogue**.
>
> [And third] Again, there are some precepts the reason for which is not so evident to everyone, but only to the wise (*quorum ratio non est adeo cuilibet manifesta, sed solum sapientibus*); and **these are the moral precepts added to the decalogue**...[34]

This, in a nutshell, is Thomas's outline of the Decalogue and its relationship to the natural law. Although Thomas has added his usual precision to the discussion, I suggest he is not being particularly unique or original here. One can find nearly identical comments throughout the Christian intellectual tradition about the relationship between the natural law and the two commandments to 'love God' and 'love your neighbor as yourself', as well as about the relationship between the two love commandments and the two tablets of the Decalogue.

30. *Summa theol.* 1–2, q. 100, art. 1.
31. *Summa theol.* 1–2, q. 100, art. 1.
32. *Summa theol.* 1–2, q. 100, art. 1.
33. The division of the text and the textual emphases in the following paragraph are my own; they were done to make the structure and substance of the text easier for the reader to grasp.
34. *Summa theol.* 1–2, q. 100, art. 11.

A Look at Aquinas's Medieval Predecessors

It is beyond the scope of the present work to go into the patristic sources of this tradition, largely because they are so vast and go back to the earliest Church,[35] but I hope the reader will bear with me if I provide a smattering of examples from some of Thomas's immediate predecessors in attempt to give a sense of the sort of historical and intellectual context within which Thomas was working.

There is, first of all, the great Anselm of Laon (d. 1117), founder of one of the most important and widely influential theological schools of the early twelfth century, who declared in his *Sentences on the Divine Page*, for example, that: 'The natural law is this: what you do not wish to be done to you, you do not do to others'.[36] Later in the twelfth century, we find Hugh of St Victor (d. 1141),writing in Book I of the *De sacramentis* that

> [God] wrote one precept in man's heart: 'See you never do to another what you would hate to have him do to you' (Tob. 4.16). Concerning those which are to be ordered, similarly one precept: 'Whatsoever you would that men should do to you, do you also to them' (Mt. 7.12), so that clearly man might learn from consideration of himself of what nature he should maintain himself toward his neighbor.[37]

Then shortly thereafter, in the same section, he adds: 'But those which under the natural law had been included in two precepts, afterwards through the written law were set forth and distinguished in these seven which were published in the second table [of the Decalogue]'.[38] Thus for Hugh, as later also for Thomas Aquinas, the Decalogue is understood to be divided according to the two 'tables' or tablets: the first relating to the love of God, the second relating to the love of neighbor. In the text above, however, Hugh is speaking of the two precepts customarily related to the 'second tablet': 'Do

---

35. For an interesting overview of the role of the Golden Rule among the Fathers, see Albrecht Dihle, *Die goldene Regel: Eine Einführung in die Geschichte der antiken und frühchristlichen Vulgärethik* (Göttingen: Vandenhoeck & Ruprecht, 1962). On p. 27, for example, Dihle lists some 27 references to the Golden Rule in patristic literature, with references including the *Didache*, Justin, Tertullian, Irenaeus, Clement of Alexandria, Lactantius, John Chrysostom, Jerome, Augustine and others.

36. Anselm of Laon, *Sententie diuine pagine*; see F. Bliemitzrieder, *Anselms von Laon Systematische Sentenzen* (Beiträge zur Geschichte der Philosophie des Mittelalters, 18; Münster: Aschendorff, 1919), p. 79: *Lex naturalis hec est: quod tibi non uis fieri, alii ne feceris.*

37. Hugh of St Victor, *De sacramentis* 1.11.9 (*PL*, CLXXVI, col. 347B); cf. *On the Sacraments of the Christian Faith* (trans. Roy J. Deferrari; Cambridge, MA: The Medieval Academy of America, 1951), p. 186.

38. Hugh of St Victor, *De sacramentis* 1.11.9 (*PL*, CLXXVI, col. 348A); *On the Sacraments of the Christian Faith*, p. 187.

unto others as you would have them do unto you', and the negative form of the same, from the book of Tobit (4.16): 'Don't do to others what you don't want done to you'. This is why he speaks only of the 'seven' Commandments written on the second table, and not the three on the first, which refer to the love of God. In the context, however, Hugh makes clear that both, when understood properly, must be related to the love of God.

Both Anselm and Hugh had a profound effect on the work of the mid-twelfth century canon lawyer Gratian, whose *Decretum*, like Peter Lombard's *Sentences*, quickly gained prominence after its publication and became a standard textbook among university students. It was Gratian who famously described the natural law as 'that which is contained in the Law and the Gospel'. 'By it', says Gratian (that is, by the natural law), 'each person is commanded to do to others what he wants done to himself and is prohibited from inflicting on others what he does not want done to himself.'[39] Once Gratian had picked up this tradition, we find it repeated over and over by the legion of medieval commentators on the *Decretum* called the 'decretists'. Sicard of Cremona (d. 1215), for example, to name just one, tells his readers that, 'the natural law consists in precepts such as to love the Lord your God'.[40] So, too, the *Summa lipsiensis* (c. 1186–87) quotes as an authority St Hilary as saying: 'the natural law is to do injury to no one, carry off nothing of anyone's and, to speak more generally: not to do something to someone that one does not wish done to oneself'.[41]

As we move to the early thirteenth century, we find William of Auxerre, master of theology at Paris (d. 1231), claiming in his *Summa aurea* that

> These are two rules of the natural law, in which are contained all the precepts of the natural law—those which pertain to neighbors, namely: 'Don't do to others what you do not wish done to you'; and 'All things that you would wish that men do to you, do also to them'; and those which pertain to God are contained in this: 'Love the Lord your God', etc. For this is a precept of the natural law because natural reason dictates this, even though one is unable to fulfill this on one's own.[42]

William distinguishes among the various precepts of the natural law not, as Thomas does, in terms of three 'grades' of universality and comprehensibility,

---

39. Gratian, *The Harmony of Discordant Canons*, D. 1, pt 1; see *Gratian: The Treatise on Laws (Decretum DD. 1–20) with the Ordinary Gloss* (trans. James Gordley; Washington, DC: Catholic University of America Press, 1993), p. 3.

40. Quoted from Lottin, *Le droit naturel chez Saint Thomas*, p. 20 n. 1. Cf. Bamberg, Staatliche Bibliothek, Can. 38 (D.II.20), p. 116.

41. Quoted from Lottin, *Le droit naturel chez Saint Thomas*, p. 108, Appendix 4. Cf. Universitätsbibliothek Leipzig, 986, fol. 3^{r}a-b. I have not as yet, however, been able to locate this comment among the extant works of Hilary.

42. William of Auxerre, *Summa aurea* (ed. Jean Ribaillier; Rome: Editiones Collegii S. Bonaventurae, 1986), Book 3, tr. 18, c. 3.

but by adopting an older set of categories, common among the decretists (although he attributes it to his teacher Gilbert Prevostin, known as 'Praepositinus', chancellor at the University of Paris between 1206 and 1209), distinguishing between 'precepts' (*precepta*), 'prohibitions' (*prohibitiones*) and 'demonstrations' (*demonstrationes*). The 'precepts', says William, are those commandments derived from the positive form of the Golden Rule: 'Whatsoever you would wish that men do to you, do also to them'; the 'prohibitions' are derived from the negative form: 'Do not do to others what you do not wish done to you'—'in this prohibition are contained (*continentur*)', according to William, 'the prohibitions of the decalogue'—and finally the 'demonstrations' are those further, more particular commandments derived from the 'precepts' and 'prohibitions'.[43]

So although the terms William uses differ from the ones Thomas employs, the basic thrust of their positions is similar: the Commandments of the Decalogue are 'derived from' or 'contained in' the more fundamental commandments to love God and love one's neighbor as oneself—or in the case of the latter, the alternative formulations to 'Do unto others what you would want them to do to you', or 'not do to another what you wouldn't want done to you'—while the rest of the moral precepts of the Old Law are 'derived from' or 'contained in' the basic Ten Commandments of the Decalogue.

Nor was this view to be found exclusively among the theologians. Among the secular masters who wrote on the subject of ethics, perhaps none is better known, albeit somewhat notoriously, than Peter Abelard (d. 1142). Abelard's concern, as is made clear in his *Ethics*, is primarily with the interior act of the will or the 'intention'; this is perhaps his most famous contribution to the history of ethics. Yet he too, confirms that the foundations of the natural law are expressed by the two great love commandments and the two forms of the Golden Rule. Commenting on the verse in Rom. 2.14 that says 'For it is not those who hear the law who are righteous', Abelard suggests that 'we do not please God by exterior works, but rather by the will', but goes on to add, tellingly, that 'not only those who hear the words of the natural law are just, but those who fulfill them in practice'. But the words of the natural law are those which commend the love of God and neighbor, such as these: 'What you do not wish, do not do to others', and 'What you wish that men do to you, you also do to them'.[44]

When we turn to the theologians working in and around Paris during the generation that directly preceded Thomas's (the early to mid 1200s), we find once again that these thinkers commonly define the natural law

---

43. William of Auxerre, *Summa aurea*, Book 3, tr. 18, c. 1.

44. Peter Abelard, *Commentary on the Epistle to the Romans* (Fathers of the Church: Mediaeval Continuation; trans. Steven R. Cartwright; Washington, DC: Catholic University, 2011), p. 133.

in terms of either the Golden Rule, or in terms of love of God and neighbor. Indeed, some of the most striking parallels to Thomas's discussion of the natural law in the *Summa of Theology* can be found in the work of the two Franciscan regent masters, Alexander of Hales (d. 1245) and his successor John of La Rochelle (d. 1245), who together authored what has become known to history as the *Summa fratris Alexandri*, or more simply, the *Summa halensis*.[45] We know that Thomas read the *Summa halensis* before composing the questions on the law in his own *Summa of Theology* because it is from the *Summa halensis*, for example, that Thomas adopted the useful and important category of the 'eternal law'.[46] Like Aquinas, John argues that the precepts of the written law are manifestations of the precepts of the natural law given to man because of his failure to understand the natural law. According to John, the innate 'law of nature' was inscribed upon the heart of man at his creation. Before the Fall, there was no need for a written law because 'man was provided with a spiritual mind' (*homo spirituali mente praeditus*) and he did not have need of a 'prohibition for restraining concupiscence, which was not inordinate' (*nec prohibitio ad coercendum concupiscentiam, quae inordinata non erat*). Thus, says John, quoting Augustine:

---

45. What seems to have happened is that John's treatise *De legibus* was woven into the *Summa theologiae* attributed to Alexander of Hales. On this, see for example, the judgment of Smalley in 'William of Auvergne', p. 47: '*De legibus* [of John of La Rochelle] was quoted, though not swallowed whole. Much of it is woven into the texture of the *Tractatus de praeceptis et legibus* which forms part of the *Summa* ascribed to Alexander of Hales, OFM. Modern research has established that John of La Rochelle, OFM, compiled the *Tractatus*. It is older than the *Summa*. John collaborated with Alexander in preparing some parts of the latter, 1236–45, but his teaching on natural law differs from Alexander's, as we have it in Alexander's *Sentences*, to such an extent that we must credit John with authorship of the *Tractatus*; it represented an original contribution to the *Summa*. John was master of theology at Paris in 1238 and died in February, 1245.' On this, see also O. Lottin, *Psychologie et morale aux XIIe et XIIIe siècles* (Louvain: Abbaye du Mont César, 1942–60), I, pp. 128, 135; II, pp. 19, 52; and W.H. Steinmüller, 'Die Naturrechtslehre des Joannes von Rupella und des Alexander von Hales', *Franziskanische Studien* 41 (1959), pp. 310-422.

46. On this, see for example the judgment of Michael Crowe, *The Changing Profile of the Natural Law* (The Hague: Martinus Nijhoff, 1977), p. 172: 'A close parallel shows that St Thomas must have been conversant with the Franciscan synthesis when he came to write the articles on the eternal law in the *Summa theologiae*. Before then he only refers to the eternal law in a passing way. Once in the *Commentary on the Sentences*... The eternal law is not mentioned in the *Summa contra Gentiles* although both "divine law" and providence are prominent there. Nor is it mentioned in the *prima pars* [of the *Summa theologiae*]... It seems, then, probably, that St Thomas became acquainted with the Franciscan account of the eternal law about the time of writing the *Prima-Secundae*.' See also Lottin, *Psychologie et morale*, II, pp. 52-63, 67.

As Augustine says in the *Questions on the New and Old Testament*: 'The first Law did not have to be given formatted in letters, because inserted in nature in a certain manner is the very knowledge of the Creator. For who does not know what is appropriate to the good life or is ignorant that, "what he does not wish done to himself, ought to be done to others"? Hence first it was necessary that man use the natural law, and when that failed him, as it did Adam...the [written] Law was added to him.'[47]

The written law was 'added' (*adderetur*), then, so that it might reveal the unwritten natural law, which had become obscured by sin. Once again quoting Augustine as his authority, John says of the Ten Commandments:

[The Law of the Decalogue] is compared to the law of nature as something to be manifested (*Lex Decalogi comparatur ad legem naturae manifestandum*), namely so that the things which were hidden through the shadows of sin might be made manifest. Whence Augustine, in the *Questions on the New and Old Testament*, says: 'the Law was given so that the things that might be known would have authority, and the things which began to be hidden would be made manifest'.[48]

The written law reveals or 'manifests' the natural law by making explicit what the natural law, implanted in the conscience, holds implicitly, in an unwritten way. John explains—once again claiming Augustine as his guiding authority:

For what the natural law, which is implanted in each person's conscience has implicitly (*Nam quod lex naturalis quae insita est conscientie cuiuslibet habet implicite, lex scripta decalogi habet explicite*)—for example, the natural law says, 'do not do to others what you would not want done to you'—the written Law makes this explicit: 'Do not kill', etc. according to what Augustine says.[49]

The use of Augustine here is quite fascinating, since Augustine is well known for the idea that what was hidden implicitly in the Old Testament was 'made manifest' in the New.[50] And yet, in this context, it is 'the written law', especially the Commandments of the Decalogue, that 'makes explicit' what is implicit in each person's conscience. Indeed, these basic principles

---

47. *Summa halensis*, Book 3, pt 2, inq. 3, tract. 1, q. 1, chap. 3, *solutio*; cf. Augustine, *Quaestionibus Novi et Veteri Testamenti*, q. 4 (*PL*, XXXV, col. 2219). Citations from John's *De legibus* are taken from the *Summa fratris Alexandri*, IV (Quaracchi: Collegii S. Bonaventurae, 1948).

48. *Summa halensis.*, Book 3, pr. 2, tr. 2, sec. 1, q. 1, tit. 2, c. 3 (283); cf. Augustine, *Quaestionibus Novi et Veteri Testamenti*, q. 4 (*PL*, XXXV, col. 2219).

49. *Summa halensis*, Book 3, pr. 2, inq. 3, tr. 2, sec. 1, q. 2, tit. 10, no. 2 (396); cf. Augustine, *Sermo* 9, c. 19, n. 14 (*PL*, XXXVIII, col. 86).

50. For this oft-quoted statement of St Augustine's, see his *Quaestiones in Heptateuchum*, 2.73.

of the natural law are not only 'implicit', they are, like the 'shadows' of the Old Testament, 'hidden through the shadows of sin', so much so that 'the Law of the Decalogue' was given so that 'the things which began to be hidden would be made manifest'. Thus just as the New Testament makes explicit what was hidden implicitly in the Old, so too, analogously, the Commandments of the Decalogue make explicit what was implicit in the consciences of humanity and which had begun to be hidden by the shadows of sin.

Thomas, as we now know, incorporated much of the material from the treatise *De legibus* in the *Summa halensis* into his own treatment of the various kinds of law in the *Summa*. But when we turn to the *Summa de bono* of Thomas's great teacher, Albert the Great, we see a treatment in many ways even closer to Thomas's, especially with regard to the 'universality' and relative certainty of the most fundamental precepts of the natural law, and also with regard to their being fundamentally in accord with right reason. So, for example, we read in the *Summa de bono* that

> The universal [principles] of the law are in the natural judgment, as in a similar vein the Apostle says to the Romans (2.15): 'They show that the work of the law is written in their hearts'. And the universal [principles] of the law are those things which direct us in our actions, in which there is neither error nor doubt, and in which the natural judgment of reason, or informed synderesis, grasps what ought to be done or not done. Thus, however much more universal the common rules of human law are [than the particular ones], so much the more substantially [universal] are the common rules of the natural law; such as those two which are given in comparison to each other; of which one is taken from the Gospel: namely: 'All things whatever you wish that men do to you, do also the same to them', and the other which is taken from Tobit, namely: 'What you do not wish done to you, do not do to others'…for all these things are universally accepted as belonging to the natural law and are written in man in that he accepts reason.[51]

And finally, if we turn to Thomas's own generation, and look at the work of Thomas's colleague at Paris, the Franciscan master Bonaventure, we will find all the same elements we have been reviewing above. We find him, like Thomas, and certainly in imitation of his Franciscan predecessors Alexander of Hales and John of La Rochelle, reducing the whole of the law to the Decalogue, and the Decalogue in turn to the two great commandments to love God and love your neighbor as yourself. In his *Collations on the Ten Commandments* for example, we find Bonaventure saying to his fellow Franciscans:

---

51. Albertus Magnus, *De bono*, in H. Kühle *et al.* (eds.), *Alberti Magni opera omnia* (Cologne: Institutum Alberti Magni, 1951), tr. 5, q. 1, a. 1 (504.27-34).

But, 'What is the first and greatest commandment of the Law?' The Lord replies in *Matthew*: 'You shall love the Lord your God with all your heart and with all your soul and with all your mind. This is the greatest and the first commandment. Moreover the second is like it; you shall love your neighbor as yourself. On these two depend the whole Law and the Prophets.'[52]

And then several sentences later, he adds, with respect to the Decalogue in particular that:

> The holy decalogue which was given to Moses on Mount Sinai shows how we should keep the commandments. And I wish to show you that just as there are eight parts of speech, which are the basis of all those things which can be expressed in language, and just as there are ten categories, which are the basis of all those things which can be determined by logic; so the ten commandments are the basis for all laws and divine precepts. And this was the reason why the Lord wished that they be given to Moses.[53]

And finally, after listing the Ten Commandments, he distinguishes them according to the famous 'two tablets':

> And it should be noted that the whole of the Law commands nothing but justice. For the Law is the rule of justice. Moreover justice is that which orders the human person to God and to his neighbor. And so there is a twofold justice; one by which we are ordered to God, and the other by which we are ordered to our neighbor. And so two tables were given to Moses: on the first are contained the commandments ordering us to God; on the second the commandments ordering us to our neighbor.[54]

With regard to the precepts on the second table—those ordering us with respect to our neighbor—Bonaventure reduces them, finally, as we have seen others before him do, to the two forms of the Golden Rule, which he equates with the natural law:

> On the second table are contained the seven commandments ordering us to our neighbor, which are expressed by two precepts of natural law; namely, do to others what you would wish done to yourself, and do not do to others what you do not wish done to yourself.[55]

The Franciscans and Dominicans of the thirteenth century may have been divided on any number of important issues in philosophy and theology, but on the question of the Decalogue and its fundamental relationship to the natural law, they were largely of one mind.

---

52. St Bonaventure, *Collations on the Ten Commandments* (trans. Paul Spaeth; St Bonaventure, NY: The Franciscan Institute, 1995), 1.19; cf. *Collatio de decem praeceptis*, 1.19 in *Sancti Bonaventurae opera omnia*, V (Quaracchi: Collegii S. Bonaventurae, 1891).
53. Bonaventure, *Collations*, 1.20.
54. Bonaventure, *Collations*, 1.21.
55. Bonaventure, *Collations*, 1.23.

Now it should go without saying with respect to the quick review we've made of Thomas's predecessors in this section that I've not developed in an adequate way the thought of any one of these remarkable twelfth- and thirteenth-century thinkers, nor, for example, have I really made clear the interesting and important differences that remained between them. My goal in reviewing these texts has been simply to give a general picture of the intellectual context within which Aquinas was operating and in response to which he had to craft his own contributions. I trust that by now the point has been made: once we become aware of the relevant historical context within which Thomas lived and worked, it becomes clear that it would not have been at all controversial or strange for Thomas to relate the Decalogue to the natural law. Indeed, given what we now know of that context, it would have been stranger if he hadn't.

The Old Law and the New Law

I should like to make a final point before closing, however, if I may, with regard to Aquinas and the Decalogue. As readers of Aquinas know, the 'divine law' has two parts: the Old Law *and* the New Law.[56] The Old Law is good, says Thomas, but it is incomplete. Along with 'instructing us by means of his law', says Thomas, it remains for God to 'assist us by means of his grace'.[57]

Indeed, Thomas and his contemporaries agree that human nature has been so corrupted by the effects of sin that what was characteristic or 'natural' for human beings in that time when their nature was healthy and uncorrupted is no longer so. On this view, the 'natural law' with which we were created has been effaced by sin—not completely, but in substantial and critical ways. Our *knowledge* of the natural law has not been completely eradicated, claims Thomas. We still know, for example, 'the first and common precepts of the natural law' such as 'love your neighbor as yourself' and 'Do unto others as you would have them do unto you'. These, he thinks, *cannot* be abolished from the heart of man.[58] As to the secondary precepts, such as 'Do not lie' or 'Do not steal', these can in some instances be abolished from men's hearts, claims Thomas, but generally only owing to 'vicious customs and corrupt habits'.[59] What *has* been effaced substantially since the Fall, however, is the ability of our will to do the good that we know.[60] Recall, in this regard, St Paul's famous complaint that 'the good

---

56. On this, see in particular Thomas's discussion in *Summa theol.* 1–2, q. 91, art. 5.
57. This is a comment Thomas makes in his prologue to the entire Treatise on the Law; cf. the *divisio textus* at the very beginning of *Summa theol.* 1–2, q. 90, art. 1.
58. On this, see in particular the discussion in *Summa theol.* 1–2, q. 94, art. 6.
59. *Summa theol.* 1–2, q. 94, art. 6.
60. On this, see in particular Thomas's discussion in *Summa theol.* 1–2, q. 109 on 'the

which I would do, I do not; but the evil which I would not, that I do' (Rom. 7.19). Even when we manage to have the law written on our minds, it is too often still not 'written on our hearts'.

Similarly, it is important to remember that, on Thomas's view, the first and common precepts that lie behind the Decalogue are the two commandments to 'love God' and 'love your neighbor as yourself'. What this means, according to Thomas, is that we are not meant merely to obey the commandments out of fear, but to heed them freely as an expression of the wisdom of a God of love.[61] We are called by a God who has revealed his selfless love to us in salvation history, a history culminating in the sacrifice of his own beloved Son on the cross, to see the commandments as an expression of the respect we owe the dignity of others and abide by them willingly out of love. The problem is that if we are not animated by this kind of selfless love, then the moral rules that are meant to be a divine guide to moral wisdom can become instead for me, sadly, a horrible 'burden', or perhaps even a goad to greater sin. As Thomas says:

> Now [fulfilling the law] is very difficult to a man without virtue: thus even the Philosopher states (*Eth.* v, 9) that it is easy to do what a righteous man does; but that to do it in the same way, viz. with pleasure and promptitude, is difficult to a man who is not righteous. Accordingly we read also (1 Jn 5.3) that 'His commandments are not heavy': which words Augustine expounds by saying that 'they are not heavy to the man who loves; whereas they are a burden to him that loves not'.[62]

I mention these last points merely as a way of gesturing meekly at the larger theological project of which Thomas's treatment of the natural law and the Decalogue is merely a part. For Thomas, even the divinely authorized teaching of the natural law such as is found in the Decalogue alone is not enough; it is merely the first part of a two-part remedy for sin. For after God 'instructs us by means of his Law', says Thomas, it remains for him to 'assist us by means of his grace': both are necessary to help restore in us the 'law written on our hearts' at our creation, a law effaced tragically by sin and that can only be restored fully, not by fear, but by God's love and our response in love.

Thus the divine law, according to Aquinas, has two parts: the Old Law and the New Law, which are related to one another as the imperfect is to the perfect. The Old Law is good, says Thomas, but it is incomplete. It requires the grace given with the New Law, by which 'charity is spread abroad in our

---

necessity of grace', esp. art. 1 (Whether without grace man can know anything), art. 2 (Whether without God's grace man can do or wish any good) and art. 4 (Whether without grace man can keep the commandments of the Law).

61. On this, see Thomas's discussion in *Summa theol.* 1–2, qq. 106 and 107.

62. *Summa theol.* 1–2, q. 107, art. 4.

hearts'. The second and truly essential step in restoring in us the 'law written on our hearts' at our creation, but effaced by our own sin, comes with the advent of the new covenant when, as the prophet Jeremiah says, God will 'give His laws into our minds and in our hearts will He write them' and when, as the prophet Ezekiel promised 'God will give us a new heart and a new spirit, spreading charity abroad in our hearts, so that we may walk in the Lord's commandments and keep them' (Ezek. 36.26-27). For we know that we are children of God, the Apostle John tells us, when we love God and keep his commandments, and when keeping his commandments is not burdensome (cf. 1 Jn 5.1-3).

Part III

WORLDWIDE DISSEMINATION IN
EARLY MODERN CATECHISMS AND CATECHESIS

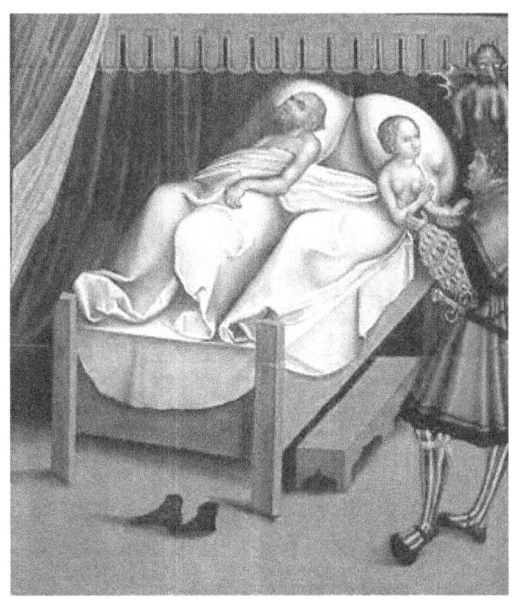

The Dissemination of the Decalogue in English and Lay Responses to its Promotion in Early Modern English Protestantism

Ian Green

This chapter explores how a standard version of the Ten Commandments in English evolved in the mid-sixteenth century, and how that version was disseminated among the population at large by a variety of techniques. It also indicates some of the ways in which different sections of the English laity may have responded to the Decalogue from the sixteenth to the eighteenth centuries.

The Decalogue in Medieval England

The status of the Ten Commandments had been acknowledged in England for many centuries before the Reformation. In the late ninth century, King Alfred 'the Great' tried to fuse native law with the ordinances of the Church by prefacing his summary of Saxon law codes with a 'Mosaic Prologue' which contained an English version of the Decalogue and other Mosaic codes.[1] The Ten Commandments of the Old Testament, together with the Two (Great) Commandments of the New, were also among the basic texts included in the schemes of instruction that the Western Church developed from the thirteenth to the fifteenth centuries to help parish clergy prepare their flocks for auricular confession. Thus, at the Council of Lambeth in 1281, Archbishop Peckham ordered the clergy to expound to their parishioners the Creed, the Decalogue and Two Commandments, and the seven works of mercy, virtues, vices and sacraments.[2] In the next centuries a number of texts were drafted to help less educated priests expound these and other basic formulae of the faith such as the *Paternoster* and *Ave Maria*. One such text was Archbishop Thoresby's *Catechism* of 1357, which promised the laity 40 days' indulgence if they could demonstrate adequate

---

1. Stefan Jurasinski, 'Violence, Penance, and Secular Law in Alfred's Mosaic Prologue', *Haskins Studies* 22 (2010), pp. 25-42.
2. Eamon Duffy, *The Stripping of the Altars: Traditional Religion in England 1400–1580* (New Haven: Yale University Press, 1992), p. 52.

knowledge and practice of what they had heard the clergy declaim. It survives in dozens of variant manuscript forms composed in different parts of the country, and some of these devoted several pages to expounding a form of the Commandments in English verse that comprised a loose paraphrase of the Latin Vulgate version of Deuteronomy 5.[3] Another aid was John Mirk's *Festial*, a collection of sermons in English, probably composed in the late 1380s by an Augustinian canon, which survives in many manuscript copies as well as in two dozen editions printed by Caxton and his successors between 1483 and 1532. A large section of Mirk's sermon for Quadragesima was devoted to expounding the Ten Commandments, presumably to help hearers prepare for their annual confession during Lent.[4]

Through these and other forms of indoctrination, the uneducated laity of late mediaeval England were encouraged to master the *gist* of the Decalogue rather than memorize a verbatim version. Indeed, during the period 1408–1536, when fear of the Lollard heresy was still strong and the reading of an English Bible was severely restricted, exact translations of the Commandments into English were viewed with some suspicion, especially in the case of full-length versions and unconventional expositions.[5] As a result of this ambiguity, the versions that we know *did* circulate in English in the century before the Reformation, and there were probably over two dozen of them, were either heavily abbreviated or turned into verse, or consisted of a paraphrase rather than a close translation.[6] There was some partial compensation in the expositions of the Decalogue becoming available: where earlier expositions had been designed to help confessors do their job, those issued after 1500 were targeted at other groups thought worthy of supervised help, such as nuns and devout lay householders, as we shall see shortly.

The late mediaeval *metrical* versions were often quite inventive, padding out the original with phrases that would catch an audience's attention,

---

3. *The Lay Folks' Catechism* (ed. T.F. Simmons and H.E. Nolloth; Early English Text Society, 119; London: Kegan Paul, Trench & Trubner, 1901), pp. 30-61; Anne Hudson, 'A New Look at the *Lay Folks' Catechism*', Viator 16 (1985), pp. 243-58.

4. Duffy, *Stripping of the Altars*, pp. 55, 57-59; Philippa Tudor, 'Religious Instruction for Children and Adolescents in the Early English Reformation', *Journal of Ecclesiastical History* 35 (1984), pp. 391-413 (398).

5. Tudor, 'Religious Instruction', p. 397; Margaret Aston, *Lollards and Reformers: Images and Literacy in Late Medieval Religion* (London: Hambledon, 1984), pp. 210-12; Richard Rex, *Henry VIII and the English Reformation* (Basingstoke: Palgrave Macmillan, 1993), Chapter 4.

6. Julia Boffey and A.S.G. Edwards (eds.), *A New Index of Middle English Verse* (London: British Library, 2005), pp. 340-41; Duffy, *Stripping of the Altars*, pp. 81-83; above, nn. 3-4 and below, nn. 7-12; and Ian Green, *Word, Image and Ritual in Early Modern English Protestantism* (Oxford: Oxford University Press, forthcoming).

or adding Christian elements to the Hebrew original. Metrical versions were often quite clumsy too, necessitating a comment such as 'learn this poor rhyme, and thou shalt soon ken them [know the Commandments], and keep them better in mind'. There are many examples of ear-catching (albeit non-scriptural) phrases in the unofficial Corpus Christi cycles of plays. In one the First Commandment read 'Thou shalt have, neither night nor day, / none other God but the king of bliss'; in another the precept against murder was 'thou shalt not be / man-slayer, for gold nor fee, / nor for love, nor for hate'; in yet another the Ninth Commandment read 'desire not thy neighbour's wife, / though she be fair and white as swan, / and thy wife brown'.[7] An example of clumsiness combined with Christianization occurs in the version of the Decalogue in *The Crafte to Lyve Well*—a little devotional work for the laity published in 1505. The Second and Third Commandments read: 'God in vain thou shalt not swear, *nor by his saints verily.* / The *Sundays* thou shalt keep *in serving God devoutly.*' The accompanying woodcut was also typical: on the left Moses is depicted (with horns, based on the common mistranslation of Exod. 34.35) holding up the Decalogue, while on the right stands Aaron with his rod (but wearing a bishop's mitre), and behind him the bearded, turbaned tribes of Israel.[8]

An example of the Decalogue in English *prose* is provided by *The Pilgrymage of Perfecyon*, published in 1532 as one of a series of guides prepared for the nuns living in the Brigittine community of Syon in Middlesex, who were literate but not Latinate. William Bonde presented the nuns with a woodcut showing a pair of round-topped, hinged tablets (reflecting the 'two tables of testimony' brought down from Mount Sinai in Exod. 32.15). On these were inscribed in English, in Gothic lettering, on the left the three Commandments of the 'first table' (have no God but me, take not his name in vain, sanctify the Sabbath), and on the right the seven precepts of the 'second', based on Deuteronomy 5 (honour parents; do not kill, commit lechery, steal, or give false witness; and do not covet neighbour's wife or goods). So condensed was this version that the whole Decalogue was rendered in fewer than fifty words. On the other hand, Bonde did provide an exposition of the Decalogue, though this was heavily slanted towards not

---

7. A.C. Cawley, 'Middle English Metrical Versions of the Decalogue with Reference to the English Corpus Christi Cycles', *Leeds Studies in English* 8 (1975), pp. 129-45 (135-36).

8. A.W. Pollard and G.R. Redgrave, *A Short-Title Catalogue of Books Printed in England... 1475–1640* (3 vols.; London: Bibliographical Society, 2nd edn, revised and enlarged by W.A. Jackson, F.S. Ferguson and K.F. Pantzer, 1976–91) (hereafter STC²), no. 792: Anon., *The Crafte to Lyve Well* (1505), fol. xxxvii^r [sig. Eiii^r] (my italics); J.T. Rhodes, 'Syon Abbey and its Publications in the Sixteenth Century', *Journal of Ecclesiastical History* 44 (1993), pp. 11-25.

174   *The Decalogue and its Cultural Influence*

the average lay reader but those who spent much of their time in collective worship and private meditation.[9]

A good example of a pre-Reformation *paraphrase* of the Ten Commandments is found in a work composed by another brother at Syon, Richard Whitford, but this time aimed at helping the lay paterfamilias prepare his children for confession by teaching them both the text and the application of the Decalogue. In *A Werke for Householders*, Whitford changed the wording of Deuteronomy 5, from the second-person singular 'thou shalt not' and the imperative (remember the Sabbath day, honour thy parents) to the much more inclusive first-person plural: 'we shall not'. He also added explanatory clauses which clarified the meaning and application, even if as a result it became unclear where the scriptural text ended and his expansion started. Thus, in the second, he wrote 'we may not take the name of God in vain, *and therefore we may not use to swear*'; and the fifth became 'we shall not [slay] …any persons *neither in deed, nor yet in will or mind, nor may we hate any persons in heart. For whosoever so doth is an homicide and man-slayer.*' That Whitford's *Werke* passed through seven editions between 1530 and 1537 suggests many householders in the London area were exposed to this version.[10]

The Decalogue in Transition, c. 1535–1563

By then, however, England was entering what proved to be a protracted period of change, starting with Henry VIII's break from Rome in the early 1530s, and proceeding through Edward VI's more radical reformation and Mary's counter-reformation, to Elizabeth's version of an ecclesiastical settlement in the late 1550s and early 1560s.[11] Various Bible-based translations of the Decalogue into English prose had already begun to emerge or re-surface in the early 1530s. Some were in works smuggled into England such as Tyndale's new translation of the *Pentateuch* and Joye's evangelical primer, *Ortulus anime*; others were in home-produced works such as Marshall's *Prymer in English* and Redman's *Prayers of the Byble*.[12] But the first officially sponsored moves date from 1535 to 1537: the licensing of a translation of the Bible into English to be placed in every parish church; the issuing of a set of royal injunctions ordering the clergy to teach the laity the

---

9. [W. Bonde], *The Pilgrymage of Perfecyon* (1532) (STC² 3278), fols. ccxxxiv^v-ccxxxix^v.

10. [R. Whitford], *A Werke for Householders* (1530) (STC² 25422), sig. Ci^{r-v} (my italics); for other editions, see STC² 25421.8 and 25422.3–25425.5.

11. Christopher Haigh, *English Reformations: Religion, Politics, and Society under the Tudors* (Oxford: Clarendon Press, 1993).

12. C.C. Butterworth, *The English Primers, 1529–1545* (Philadelphia: University of Pennsylvania Press, 1953), Chapters 2–8.

Lord's Prayer, Apostles' Creed and Ten Commandments 'in their mother tongue'; and the publication of an official exposition of these formulae in the so-called 'Bishops' Book' of 1537.[13]

Support for this campaign to increase Scripture knowledge came from various directions, if for rather different reasons. Erasmian humanists, both Catholic and Protestant, believed that vernacular, Bible-based instruction would renew individual spirituality and reform social mores within a predominantly traditional framework. Evangelicals, at this stage mainly inspired by Luther, shared his view that the Decalogue served both doctrinal and moral functions: it acted as a Pauline schoolmaster to bring fallen human beings to a sense of their sinfulness and need for Christ, and it showed them how God expected them to behave. The ex-Carmelite reformer John Bale represented both Erasmian and Lutheran tendencies when he urged on his Suffolk parishioners in 1537 'what godly understanding and remembrance they might have' in learning the Paternoster, Creed and Commandments 'in English, which they could never have by the Latin'. And 'where…no understanding was, nothing could be asked in faith', and what rose 'not of faith was sin after St Paul'.[14] Meanwhile, Henry VIII saw himself as a godly, reforming ruler, albeit one who at a time of danger at home and abroad appreciated the advantages of the laity being regularly reminded to honour their parents—a Commandment which had for centuries been interpreted as covering obedience to princes as well.[15] The campaign was also enthusiastically supported by members of the emerging English print trade and the much better-established trade in France, who wished to extend their profitable line in devotional works by adapting existing works to the new situation.[16]

What is immediately clear about the versions of the Decalogue that circulated during the transitional period from 1535 to 1563 is the increasing

---

13. W.H. Frere and W.M. Kennedy (eds.), *Visitation Articles and Injunctions of the Period of the Reformation* (Alcuin Club Collections, 14–16; London: Longmans, Green & Co., 1910), II, pp. 6-7; the next set of injunctions, in 1538 (pp. 36-37), ordered the Lord's Prayer and Creed to be taught first, then the Decalogue.

14. L.P. Fairfield, *John Bale: Mythmaker for the English Reformation* (West Lafayette, IN: Purdue University Press, 1976), p. 47.

15. Lucy Wooding, *Rethinking Catholicism in Reformation England* (Oxford: Clarendon Press, 2000), Chapters 2–3; eadem, *Henry VIII* (Abingdon: Routledge, 2009), Chapters 1–2 and 5; George Bernard, *The King's Reformation: Henry VIII and the Remaking of the English Church* (New Haven: Yale University Press, 2005), Chapter 3; and Green, *Word, Image and Ritual*.

16. STC² 15867–985; H.S. Bennett, *English Books and Readers 1475–1557* (Cambridge: Cambridge University Press, 1952), Chapter 3; Eamon Duffy, *Marking the Hours: English People and their Prayers, 1240–1570* (New Haven: Yale University Press, 2006), Chapter 8.

reliance on close translations of the Bible rather than the bald summaries, metrical versions and paraphrases of the previous period. This reliance did not immediately produce a single text that was used universally: for some time there remained differences over whether the Latin Vulgate or the Hebrew original should be the basis for translation, and whether Exod. 20.1-17 should be used rather than Deut. 5.6-21. There were also disagreements over how these blocks of text should be subdivided to make ten precepts, and whether the text should be taught in full or in a partly abbreviated version.

A good example of an early transitional version survives in a Sarum primer produced in Rouen in 1536 but licensed for the English market. It was conservative in stipulating that the Second Commandment was against taking the name of God in vain (which meant only three precepts in the first table), and in using Deuteronomy 5 (which first forbade coveting of a neighbour's wife, and then his goods); it also used red-letter for the heading. The most innovative feature of this version was the use of an abbreviated English translation in the inner column of each page; and even here the unknown editor has played safe by retaining the Vulgate text in the margin, also in black-letter type. And as still happened quite often at this stage, it was the Vulgate version that formed the basis for a literal translation into English. Thus the Second Commandment reads 'Thou shalt not *usurp* the name of thy God in vain', from *non usurpabis nomen Dei*, and the third 'Observe the Sabbath day' from *Observa diem sabbati*. Many similar examples can be found through to the 1550s.[17]

Other versions of the Decalogue appeared as a result of the royal injunctions of 1536, which insisted not only that Lord's Prayer, Creed and Commandments were taught orally in English in church, but also that copies of these formulae should be made available to the literate. This led printers to rush in to try to capture a new niche market with rival editions of *The Paternoster, the Creed and the Commandments of God*—cheaply produced works, with title-pages that either sported a royal coat of arms to reinforce their authority or used an eye-catching decorated border. These included not only English translations of all three formulae but also 'other godly lessons, right necessary for youth and all other persons to learn and know'; indeed, the 1539 edition also included that standby of late mediaeval Mariolatry, the *Ave Maria*, in English. It is intriguing, however, that the versions of the text of the Decalogue in different editions of the *Paternoster* from 1537 to 1539 were not the same as each other, and not even the same as in the licensed primers or in the 'Bishops' Book' to which Henry VIII

---

17. *Thys Prymer in Englyshe and in Latin* (Rouen, 1536) (STC² 15993), sig. Biiii^r; and see other primers in English and Latin, STC² 15997–16085.

had given provisional approval in 1537.[18] The senior churchmen and royal councillors who could, and perhaps should, have supervised the primers and *Paternosters* appear to have had more pressing matters on their minds than reaching consensus on the wording and numbering of the Commandments and imposing them nationwide. Indeed, while some changes had been made after the break with Rome to both the text and approved expositions of the Decalogue—a greater reliance on Hebrew sources, the removal of all references to the Pope and Catholic Church as spiritual parents of the faithful, the excision of supporting citations from glosses in the Vulgate and the Decretals, and the addition of an Augustinian doctrinal framework for the exposition of the Commandments—other features remained conservative, not least the use of the Decalogue in harness with the seven deadly sins as a tool of confession, and a continuing stress on the merit to be achieved through the works of mercy and the seven sacraments.[19]

By the mid-1540s, differences of opinion remained on the exact meaning and function of the Decalogue, but the variations between the vernacular texts in circulation had been much reduced. The 'King's Book' of 1543 and the 'King's Primer' of 1545 contained the most authoritative official statement so far;[20] a revised, abridged version appeared in the 'Catechism...to be learned of every child before he be brought to be confirmed of the bishop', the so-called 'Prayer Book catechism' of 1549; and the version that finally became the norm in early modern England appeared in a full-length version of the same in the Prayer Book of 1552, in both the catechism and the communion service. The text of the Ten Commandments used in 1549 and 1552 was derived from the Hebrew version of Exod. 20, and, unlike the transitional primers of the late 1530s, was presented in English only. The 1552 version, unlike Luther's catechisms but anticipating the *Heidelberg Catechism* of 1563, gave the full texts of Commandments Two, Three, Four and Five. This added over eight lines to numbers Two and Four (from 'For I the Lord thy God am a jealous God' to 'keep my commandments', and from 'Six days shalt thou labour' to 'hallowed it'), and an extra clause to three and five ('for the Lord will not hold him guiltless that taketh His name in vain', and 'that thy days may be long in the land which the Lord thy God giveth thee'). It also retained the division of Exodus 20 used in William Tyndale's translation of the Pentateuch in 1530 and in the evangelical primers of the 1530s, all of which listed a Second Commandment against idolatry

---

18. (STC² 16820), sigs. Biv^{r-v}; and equivalent passages of *Paternosters* in STC² 16821–21.5 and 16819.

19. As previous notes; Anon., *The Institution of a Christen Man* (1537) (STC² 5165), fols. 54^v-79^v; and Bernard, *King's Reformation*, pp. 475-88.

20. Bernard, *King's Reformation*, pp. 583-89; Butterworth, *English Primers*, Chapters 18–19; *A Necessary Doctrine* (1543) (STC² 5168.7), sigs. Oiv^v-Pi^r (and Pi^y-Xiv^v); and *[The Primer in English and Latin]* (1545) (STC² 16033.5), sigs. Bi^r-iv^v.

and a final Commandment against all forms of coveting. This resulted in tables of four and six precepts, which in the accompanying short exposition were immediately equated with the two 'Great' Commandments of Mk 12.29-31: from the Decalogue, said the Prayer Book catechumen, 'I learn my duty towards God, and my duty towards my neighbour'.[21]

When we look at the handbook which the conservative Bishop Bonner prepared for schoolteachers and clergy to use in London diocese in 1555 under the strongly Catholic Queen Mary, we might expect to find a major reaction. But his text of the Decalogue is substantially the same as that in the Protestant Prayer Book catechism of 1549. He followed Exodus 20, not Deuteronomy 5; the Second Commandment was against worshipping graven images (though he claimed this division came from Origen, not Tyndale, and broadened the definition of which images were acceptable); and his exposition of the Commandments was preceded by an Augustinian account of faith, and supported by scriptural rather than patristic or scholastic proofs. Bonner did occasionally look back to the late 1530s or early 1540s: he restored the Latin in the margin (though now in roman typeface); and the compositor, as well as restoring red-letter for headings, gave nearly equal space to the English and Latin versions. Bonner was more conservative elsewhere in his handbook: he paved the way for a restoration of the seven virtues and works of mercy as a prime basis for confession, and in the exposition that accompanied the Commandments he reinstated the Pope and clergy as spiritual fathers, and renewed the emphasis on the necessity and merit of good works.[22] But the Elizabethan settlement in turn restored the full-length, 1552 version of the Decalogue to solitary splendour, and the Protestant expositions, which we will soon encounter, again removed all references to papacy and merit.

How the Decalogue Was Disseminated

At this point we are moving from the evolution of a broadly accepted vernacular text of the Decalogue to a fuller consideration of the *mechanisms* by which that text was disseminated, and the functions it was supposed to serve. During the transitional period from 1535 to 1563, the techniques of dissemination consisted of modifications of old methods and experiments with new. As already indicated, modifications included the insertion of scripturally based English versions into modified primers for the literate minority; regular oral declamations of similar versions of the Commandments

21. The Prayer Book catechisms of 1549, 1552 and 1661 can be easily compared in F.E. Brightman, *The English Rite* (2 vols.; London: Rivingtons, 1915–22), II, pp. 778-91.

22. E. Bonner, *An Honest Godlye Instruction* (1555) (STC² 3281), sigs. Biv^v-v^v; Bonner, *A Profitable and Necessary Doctrine* (1555), sigs. Eeiii^v-Ttiii^v.

(and other formulae) in English in church by the clergy, until the laity had, in theory, memorized them word for word; and the introduction of question-and-answer catechizing for both literate and illiterate youngsters, through the Prayer Book and other catechisms.[23] Much more innovative was the *liturgical* deployment of the complete text of the Ten Commandments in the revised communion service in the 1552 Prayer Book. In that service, the priest was to 'rehearse distinctly' each Commandment in turn, and 'the people', kneeling, were to ask 'God's mercy for their transgression of the same' by responding 'Lord have mercy upon us, and incline our hearts to keep this law'.[24] Also new at this date was the painting of Scripture texts, including part or all of the Decalogue, on canvas or cloth stretched across the front of the old rood loft and the tympanum above it, or on the church walls which previously had contained painted depictions of men breaking individual precepts, such as blaspheming or working on the Sabbath. Bishop Hooper recalled that in London dioceses Commandments were 'graven almost everywhere in churches', and examples have since been traced in other southern dioceses.[25]

However, the dissemination of the Commandments in English was at this stage still haphazard. The pressure on the clergy to declaim the Decalogue in church in the late 1530s may have eased in the early 1540s as some of Henry's conservative bishops dragged their heels; and even when the pressure was renewed under Edward, there may have been confusion as to which was the approved text. The visitation of the clergy in Gloucester diocese by Bishop Hooper in 1551 is usually held to have revealed massive ignorance of the text of the Decalogue, though the results can also be interpreted as suggesting a lack of familiarity with the text approved as recently as 1549 which would have taken months to reach rural Gloucestershire.[26] As for the full-length version in the 1552 Prayer Book, that was in circulation for only a few months before Mary acceded to the throne, and a number of

---

23. Ian Green, *The Christian's ABC: Catechisms and Catechizing in England c. 1530–1740* (Oxford: Clarendon Press, 1996), index, under 'Prayer Book catechism'; Green, *Print and Protestantism in Early Modern England* (Oxford: Oxford University Press, 2000), pp. 182-85, 209-10.

24. Brightman, *English Rite*, II, pp. 638-45.

25. Duffy, *Stripping of the Altars*, p. 485; Roger Rosewell, *Medieval Wall Paintings in English and Welsh Churches* (Woodbridge: Boydell, 2008), pp. 30, 34, 87-90, 204-205, 216-17; Robert Whiting, *The Reformation of the English Parish Church* (Cambridge: Cambridge University Press, 2010), p. 131.

26. Frere and Kennedy, *Visitation Articles*, II, pp. 116, 119, 282-83; D.G. Newcombe, 'The Visitation of the Diocese of Gloucester and the State of the Clergy, 1551', *Transactions of the Bristol and Gloucestershire Archaeological Society* 114 (1996), pp. 87-96; and Green, *Word, Image and Ritual*. The clergy did not have the advantages of Hooper's daughter, who was taught it soon after she had teethed: Tudor, 'Religious Instruction', p. 396.

the visual aids recently 'graven' on church walls were defaced during the Catholic reaction that then began.[27]

In the next phase of development, from the first years of Elizabeth I to the mid-eighteenth century, the dissemination of the Decalogue became much more systematic. The late Elizabethan and Stuart parish clergy were better educated than their Edwardian predecessors, and much more familiar not only with the Bible as a whole, but also with the complete text of the Ten Commandments, which was now regularly deployed both in communion and ante-communion services and in catechizing.[28] The Elizabethan and early Stuart periods also witnessed a continued rise in the number of schools and a surge in lay literacy, a growth in the number of English printers and presses, and longer print runs for officially approved titles. As a result of these developments literally millions of copies of the Decalogue were published from the 1560s to the mid-eighteenth century in hundreds of editions of the Book of Common Prayer, *The ABC with the Catechisme*, and *The Primer and Catechisme*, for use with literate and illiterate adults and children in church, school and home.[29]

However, these developments did not transform techniques of instruction so much as consolidate and elaborate existing ones. From the 1560s there was partly greater *effort* in the use of these techniques—more frequent catechizing, greater numbers of sermons or catechetical homilies on the Decalogue, and more treatises on the Commandments and handbooks on 'godly living'—and partly a constant search for greater *sophistication* of techniques of instruction, to meet the learning needs of all types of children and adults, and to test not just memorization but also understanding at an elementary level. And in the intermediate and advanced catechisms, expositions and handbooks targeted at better informed believers, the clergy also showed a greater inclination to tackle the remaining doctrinal and didactic problems thrown up by the greater prominence being given to the Decalogue, not least the semi-Pelagianism of the laity who persisted with the view that doing good works would please God and merit some reward.[30]

27. Whiting, *Reformation*, pp. 131-33.
28. Rosemary O'Day, *The Professions in Early Modern England, 1450–1800* (Harlow: Longman, 2000), Chapter 3; Green, *Print and Protestantism*, pp. 27-31, 566-70; on ante-communion, see Ian Green, '"Hearing" and "Reading": Disseminating Bible Knowledge and Fostering Bible Understanding in Early Modern England', in Kevin Killeen et al. (eds.), *The Oxford Handbook of the Bible in Early Modern England, c. 1530–1700* (Oxford: Oxford University Press, 2015), pp. 272-86.
29. Ian Green, *Humanism and Protestantism in Early Modern English Education* (Farnham: Ashgate, 2009), Chapters 1–2 and 5; and above, n. 23.
30. Green, *Christian's ABC*, Chapters 2–5, and 10; Green, *Print and Protestantism*, chaps. 5-6; and on semi-Pelagianism, see below, pp. 185-86, 188-89.

Some of these problems were the legacy of debates between Catholic and Protestant theologians over the role of good works in salvation, and in another chapter of this volume Dr Willis explores the reconceptualization of the Decalogue by English reformers. Those conservatives who treated the law primarily as a moral guide, one of various formulae to help the faithful prepare for confession of sins to a priest prior to absolution and participation in the Mass, had a different view of its function from those reformers, such as Luther, who thought the law had been given primarily for spiritual ends, to convict human beings of their permanent sinfulness and their constant need to repent, and to persuade them that forgiveness (or justification) could not come from human effort to be good but through faith in Christ alone. For the latter, the Ten Commandments could be kept only through divine grace which fuelled a lively faith in and love of God. But there remained disagreements over the correct interpretation of Augustine's views on justification, and complications within the Protestant concept of the law, which some English authors felt had to be tackled. Did the law perform the same function for regular, reprobate evildoers as for the righteous elect? Was there any role at all left for the human will to play in trying to keep God's commandments? How could Protestant pastors strike the delicate balance needed between risking despair and fostering complacency: on the one hand stressing humanity's complete inability to keep the law and the dire penalties they faced for their sins, while on the other assuring them that once they had felt sincere repentance and started to show signs of leading a better life they were among God's elect and could not fall from grace?

However, while the position held by a high Calvinist such as Perkins was very different from that of a Catholic such as Bonner and on some matters from that of fellow Protestants such as Henry Hammond and Jeremy Taylor,[31] what all these clergy felt the need to make clear was the applicability of a code of moral teaching written down by an ancient desert-dwelling people to the population of early modern England. Thus, in practice, a wide range of theologians and catechists argued that the two tables of the Old Testament corresponded to the two 'Great' Commandments of the New, to love God and your neighbour as yourself; that each negative precept had a positive duty embedded in it and vice versa; that each outward duty had an inner, spiritual counterpart; and that the specific prohibitions of Moses, such as not killing or stealing, had a wider application in later ages: do not ruin someone's reputation by slandering them, and do not cheat them in business dealings. Much of the ingenuity shown by catechists, preachers and authors of treatises and other works of this period was directed at ensuring not just that the laity had grasped the text of the Decalogue, but also that

---

31. Green, *Christian's ABC*, Chapters 8–10.

they understood these principles of interpretation well enough to be able to apply them to problems of piety and morality in their daily lives.[32]

We can see some of these developments in the most popular unofficial work on the Decalogue—a long treatise composed by two 'godly' preachers called John Dod and Robert Cleaver, *A Plain and Familiar Exposition of the Ten Commandments*, which sold perhaps 20 editions in the first 60 years of the seventeenth century. Despite their frequent brushes with authority and occasional darts at Catholics, and fellow Protestants, Dod and Cleaver aimed above all at edification. That they were also high Calvinists is evident from their preoccupation with 'God's children' and the lists of 'marks' of those who, as part of the process of sanctification, obeyed his commandments. But the printed form of their work was targeted at all reasonably well-educated adults and students, as can be seen from the pruning of the rustic phrases used in the original sermons, the marginal references to Scripture proofs and the helpful index, and the deployment of the type of page layout then fashionable (and perhaps reminiscent of the scholastics) to show how far one original statement could be logically extended. In the case of the Third Commandment, the heading reads 'God's name is abused by unholy'…'works' at the top, and then unholy 'words' underneath, the latter being divided into 'without an oath' and 'with an oath', and then subdivided into further types of sin thereafter.[33]

Other examples of innovation in technique that built on older foundations included the growing number of visual aids which, after a brief interlude of iconophobia, were again tolerated by the English authorities. Thus among the images built into the title pages of various translations of the English Bible—at the outset the Coverdale and 'Matthew' Bibles, and later some editions of the 'Geneva', the 'King James' and Walton's Polyglot—was one of Moses holding the tablets of the law. In the first folio edition of the 'King James Bible', Moses and Aaron appear either side of the main title. Moses holds a jointed table with round tops, but has curls rather than horns over his forehead, and Aaron also looks less like a bishop. Local painters would copy these images of Moses and Aaron on to the walls of many churches in the seventeenth century alongside the Commandments.[34]

---

32. Green, *Christian's ABC*, pp. 426-30; and his *Word, Image and Ritual*.

33. [John Dod and Robert Cleaver], *A Plaine and Familiar Exposition of the Ten Commandements* (1625) (STC² 6976), p. 86, and *passim*; Arnold Hunt, *The Art of Hearing: English Preachers and their Audiences, 1590–1640* (Cambridge: Cambridge University Press, 2010), pp. 155-57.

34. T.H. Darlow and H.F. Moule (eds.), *Historical Catalogue of Printed Editions of the English Bible, 1525–1961* (revised by A.S. Herbert; London: British and Foreign Bible Society, 1968), pp. 10, 17, 125, 132; Margaret Aston, *England's Iconoclasts*. I. *Laws against Images* (Oxford: Oxford University Press, 1988), pp. 78, 363n.; Tara Hamling, *Decorating the 'Godly' Household: Religious Art in Post-Reformation Britain* (New Haven: Yale University Press, 2010), pp. 41, 43-44, 54, 106-109; and above, n. 25.

Another innovation based on older foundations resulted from the recognition of the value of congregational or family singing of psalms and other approved texts, which soon included the Ten Commandments. Probably the most widely circulated of the many new forms of the Decalogue in metre was the one printed at the start of the metrical psalter known as 'Sternhold and Hopkins', which passed through hundreds of editions from the 1560s to the mid-eighteenth century. Compared to metrical summaries of the Decalogue in the late middle ages, the version in 'Sternhold and Hopkins' was both much fuller and recognizably based on a translation of Exodus 20. It has the usual quirks of ballad-type verse in the form of clunking rhythms and words added to fill gaps in the scansion, as in 'Hark Israel, and what I say give heed to understand. / I am the Lord thy God that brought thee out of Egypt land. / E'en from the house wherein thou didst in thraldom live a slave. / None other Gods at all before my presence thou shalt have.' Sometimes the text stumbles: 'Yield honour to thy parents that prolonged thy days may be / Upon the land, the which the Lord thy God hath given unto thee'. But on other occasions it carries a punch: 'Thou shalt not murder. Thou shalt not commit adultery. / Thou shalt not steal, nor witness false against thy neighbour be.' And this version also came complete with music, and thus facilitated the extra dimension of collective performance which singing could add, as recent work by Chris Marsh and Jonathan Willis has convincingly shown.[35]

Another new technique, this time to aid understanding as well as memorization was to supply catechumens with scriptural 'proof texts' for the answers to each section, including the section on the Commandments. Such proof texts can be found as early as the 1570s and 1580s, but the best example of their use for different *levels* of catechumen can be found in two presbyterian catechisms issued in 1647. The *Shorter Catechism* was targeted at the young and less educated, and in the case of each Commandment offered a few proofs in full for what was 'required' by that precept, and a few more for what was 'forbidden' by it. While the question put by the catechist was set in black-letter type, and the answer was in roman type, these proofs were set in italic, and linked by superscript italic letters to the relevant part of the preceding answer. By contrast the *Westminster Larger Catechism* was designed for well-educated adults and ordinands, and here we find a huge number of supporting 'proof texts' for each word or phrase, completely swamping the answer they are meant to illuminate. And these are Scripture

---

35. [Thomas Sternhold and John Hopkins], *The Whole Booke of Psalms Collected into English Meter* (1565) (STC² 2434), fols. 21-22; Green, *Print and Protestantism*, Chapter 9; Christopher Marsh, *Music and Society in Early Modern England* (Cambridge: Cambridge University Press, 2010), Chapter 8; Jonathan Willis, *Church Music and Protestantism in Post-Reformation England* (Farnham: Ashgate, 2010). Other examples of verse forms of the Decalogue will be given in Green, *Word, Image and Ritual*.

proofs only, no reliance on the patristic or conciliar sources that were still being deployed in many Catholic catechisms.[36]

Another example of instruction for more advanced students took the form of special catechetical lectures given to undergraduates and ordinands at university. The best known and intellectually most demanding example of this genre was the lectures given to Cambridge undergraduates on Saturday and Sunday afternoons in the late 1570s by Lancelot Andrewes, then still a young fellow of Pembroke College Cambridge. Inaccurate notes soon circulated widely, and it was some time before a version corrected from Andrewes's own lecture notes was published; but this corrected version would still be in circulation a century later in 1675. The wide context in which Andrewes placed the Decalogue for the next generation of clergy, teachers, patrons and oligarchs can be seen in the headings of Chapters 8–11 of his long introduction on 'I am the Lord thy God', where he tackled the views on the deity held by 'the four religions in the world'—paganism, Judaism, Islam and Christianity. Then in Chapters 14–20 Andrewes discussed the nature of different forms of law in general, as well as the delivery and purpose of the Decalogue in particular. And all this before he came to each Commandment in turn, and produced a tour-de-force of scriptural, classical and patristic scholarship and of dialectic and rhetoric which clearly impressed many who heard it.[37]

Lay Responses to the Decalogue

Lay responses to the different stimuli we have just seen are much harder to document. It is quite possible that initially there was some reluctance among adults to learning texts such as the Decalogue in English alongside their children and servants. When John Bale encountered opposition in his Suffolk parish in the late 1530s, it was probably over a number of issues on which he had set out to challenge parishioners' assumptions. But one that stands out is the protest of 'John Page's wife' that 'neither for the King nor the Council would she ever learn the Paternoster, Creed, or Ten Commandments in English'.[38] At about the same time, better results appear to

---

36. Green, *Christian's ABC*, pp. 66-67, 80-81; for texts, see Donald Wing, *Short-Title Catalogue of Books Printed in England, Scotland, Ireland, Wales, and British America, and of English Books Printed in Other Countries, 1641–1700* (4 vols.; New York: Modern Language Association of America, 1972-98), nos. W1436–1454B; Ian Green, 'The Bible in Catechesis, c. 1500–c. 1750', in Euan Cameron (ed.), *The New Cambridge History of the Bible: Volume 3* (Cambridge: Cambridge University Press, 2016), pp. 546-62.

37. Green, *Christian's ABC*, pp. 147, 201-203; Lancelot Andrewes, *The Pattern of Catechistical Doctrine at Large* (1675), pp. 34-48, 58-82, and *passim*.

38. *Letters and Papers, Foreign and Domestic, Henry VIII*, IX (ed. J. Gairdner; London: HMSO, 1888), p. 446; Fairfield, *Bale*, pp. 41-47.

have been achieved—at least in the case of the young John Hooker, who later became a Protestant and the historian of Exeter—by Dr Moreman, the learned and traditionalist vicar and schoolmaster of Menheniot in Cornwall, who, Hooker remembered, 'was the first in those days that taught his parishioners and people to say the Lord's Prayer, their Belief and the Commandments in the English tongue, and did teach and catechize them therein'.[39]

Under Edward and Elizabeth, the task of learning the Ten Commandments actually became harder as the faithful were expected to master the full-length text of Exod. 20.1-17, and this (initially at least) without the help of mnemonics or verse, and without the reminders on church walls of individual breaches of the Decalogue, now covered in whitewash. However, as catechizing became increasingly common and regular for children and teenagers during the second half of the sixteenth century, mastery must have become more common; and strong motivation to learn both the formulae and the catechetical explanations of them was provided by the knowledge that mastery of the catechism could open a number of doors: to a grammar school, to confirmation and admission to Holy Communion, and to acting as a godparent and getting married.[40] Even later in life, pressure could be put on the laity: when William Lambarde erected an almshouse at Greenwich in 1575, he stipulated that candidates should be able to recite the Lord's Prayer, Creed and Commandments—all of which were said daily in the house.[41] In the 1590s William Perkins actually complained that 'ignorant people' were misusing the Decalogue and other formulae by imagining that bare repetition was in itself a pious act. 'God is served by the rehearsing of the Ten Commandments, the Lord's Prayer, and the Creed', they told him, and 'a man prayeth when he saith the Ten Commandments'. Rather than see the law as an indictment of their perpetual sinfulness, they believed they could 'keep the Commandments as well as God will give [them] leave'.[42]

That a number of the literate laity took a more intellectual and spiritual interest in the Decalogue is indicated in a variety of ways. There are the repeat editions of the *Holy Meditations upon the Lordes Prayer, the*

---

39. A.L. Rowse, *Tudor Cornwall: Portrait of a Society* (London: Jonathan Cape, 1941), pp. 151-52.

40. Green, *Christian's ABC*, Chapters 3–4; Christopher Haigh, *The Plain Man's Pathways to Heaven* (Oxford: Oxford University Press, 2007), pp. 26-30, 60-63; Brightman, *English Rite*, II, pp. 744-46, 758-60, 776-77, 790-91; Frere and Kennedy, *Visitation Articles*, I, Index (under 'Communion, admission to'), and III, pp. 98-100, 259-60, 275-76, 306. Conditional admission was the theory, but clergy were pragmatic when faced by those who wished to participate but had not mastered all three formulae: Aston, *England's Iconoclasts*, pp. 349-50.

41. Aston, *England's Iconoclasts*, p. 361.

42. W. Perkins, 'The Foundation of Christian Religion', in *Workes* (1616) (STC^2 19651), I, sig. A2^r.

Beleefe, and Ten Commaundements by the Marian martyr John Bradford, which was printed nine times between 1562 and 1633, and of Dod and Cleaver's *Exposition*, from 1603 to 1662.[43] There also survive, in manuscript as well as print, texts of maternal advice to children which stressed the importance of learning the Decalogue in order to know how to walk in God's ways. 'Whatsoever thou art about to do, examine it by God's commandments; if it be agreeable to them, go on cheerfully', wrote Elizabeth Josceline in her 'Mother's Legacy' (c. 1622); and about the same time, Lady Anne Southwell turned her meditations on the Commandments into carefully crafted and revised verses, incorporating long passages of advice to her children.[44] Such authors tended to draw a link between observing the Decalogue and receiving divine blessings: in *The Mother's Blessing* (1616) Dorothy Leigh told her children to learn how to keep God's Commandments, and 'He will show thee the figure of that everlasting rest, which he will bring thee to through Christ'.[45] In his verses and pamphlets, the 'Water-Poet' John Taylor gave prominence to the seven deadly sins as well as the Ten Commandments and, like mediaeval preachers, used cautionary tales to draw direct links between breach of Commandments and divine retribution. He described himself as 'a plain Protestant', but clearly believed that a faith without good works was not worth the name of faith at all.[46]

Other adults can be seen using the Commandments as a checklist to analyse their own sins, as in the one of the autobiographical notebooks of a 'godly' London turner, Nehemiah Wallington, and the diary of a classically educated gentleman-farmer and committed supporter of the Church of England from East Anglia, William Coe. About 1619 the young Wallington wrote:

> I was born in inquity and in sin did my mother conceive me (Ps. 51.5). And have lived in sin all my childhood hitherto. Likewise I knew that those my sins were against the express commandment of God in Exodus 20. For by the law cometh the knowledge of sin (Rom. 3.20). Nay I knew not sin but by the law.

Resolved to live by the law thereafter, in 1620 Wallington bought two standard expositions of the Decalogue (by Dod and Cleaver, and Edward Elton) to which he then often referred.[47] Where Wallington was tormented and

---

43. Green, *Print and Protestantism*, p. 602; above, p. 182.

44. Sylvia Brown (ed.), *Women's Writing in Stuart England* (Stroud: Sutton, 1999), pp. 120, 124-29; *The Southwell–Sibthorpe Commonplace Book* (ed. Jean Klene; Tempe, A2: Medieval and Renaissance Texts and Studies, 1997), pp. xxvi-xxviii, 17-20, 44-71.

45. Brown, *Women's Writing*, pp. 59, 65-66.

46. Bernard Capp, *The World of John Taylor the Water-Poet, 1578–1653* (Oxford: Clarendon Press, 1994), pp. 130-34.

47. *The Notebooks of Nehemiah Wallington, 1618–1654: A Selection* (ed. David Booy;

often overcome by his sense of sin, William Coe was often deeply ashamed and perplexed but pragmatic and hopeful of forgiveness. He too acquired useful handbooks, such as Jeremy Taylor's *Holy Living* and *The Great Exemplar*, and, when preparing himself for taking Communion by fasting and self-analysis for sin, showed a reasonable grasp of the Decalogue as a guide to pious conduct. His account of the kind of sins to which a layman of his background felt exposed is revealing. Under the First Commandment, he admitted fearing men more than God; under the Second and Fourth, he listed irreverent behaviour; and under the Third, rash vows; under the Sixth, he identified wishing harm to troublesome neighbours; under the Eighth, cheating them in business matters; the Ninth, being too ready to believe ill reports about them; and the Tenth, secret covetings.[48]

A very different example of lay familiarity with the Commandments, though preoccupied with moral lapses under the second table, is provided by a libel against an unpopular landlord in Dorset in 1616. The first four and last three lines accuse Andrew Abington of plain malevolence and dishonesty, but the intervening three are straight inversions of the original Bible text, and the penultimate charge echoes the Old Testament reference to an 'ox'.

> Here be Andrew Abington's Commandments
> Thou shalt do no right, nor shalt thou take no wrong.
> Thou shalt catch what thou canst.
> Thou shalt pay no man.
> Thou shalt commit adultery.
> Thou shalt bear false witness against thy neighbour.
> Thou shalt covet thy neighbour's wife.
> Thou shalt sell a 100 sheep to Henry Hopkins [and] after [with]draw the best of them.
> Thou shalt sell thy oxen twice.
> Thou shalt deny thy own hand.

Such satire was hardly new: 'The Ten Commandments of the Devil', which had included such lines as 'Be drunken upon the Sabbath day', had circulated in late mediaeval England. But as ever the power of satire depended on those who read or heard such examples having a working knowledge of what the real Decalogue said.[49]

Aldershot: Ashgate, 2003), p. 41; Folger Shakespeare Library, MS. V.a.436, p. 11; STC² 6967, 7615; Paul S. Seaver, *Wallington's World* (London: Methuen, 1985), p. 5 and *passim*.

48. *Two East Anglian Diaries, 1641–1729: Isaac Archer and William Coe* (ed. Matthew Storey; Suffolk Records Society, 36; Woodbridge: Boydell, 1994), pp. 208-11, but see also pp. 203-205, 241, 251, 253, 260.

49. Adam Fox, *Oral and Literate Culture in England, 1500–1700* (Oxford: Clarendon Press, 2000), p. 330; Duffy, *Stripping of the Altars*, p. 83.

There is also sufficient evidence in domestic houses of part or all of the Commandments being pasted or painted up on walls, and of carvings of Moses holding the tablets of the law, to suggest that this may have been not uncommon in the late sixteenth and early seventeenth centuries, though whether from piety or for prestige remains unclear.[50] In the early eighteenth century, many young girls who were improving their needlework at home or in school by preparing a 'sampler' were encouraged to include a religious text such as the Commandments. Some of these were shortened or in verse, but several surviving samplers have the text in full, set within round-topped tablets flanked by Moses and Aaron.[51] Evidence of lay interest can also be found on many church walls in England, where growing numbers of lay patrons and churchwardens went to the trouble of presenting the Commandments, not in the cheapest way possible—paint on board or wall—but in lavishly decorated or expensively carved and gilded frameworks. Thus when William, 5th Baron Digby, and the richer parishioners of the small parish of St Mary Madgalen, Castleton, in Dorset had the church rebuilt and refitted in the first quarter of the eighteenth century, gold leaf replaced black paint for the text of the Decalogue, which was framed not by a Moses and Aaron but by a reredos incorporating a classical pediment, enhanced by floral carving, scrollwork, and a dove hovering over a sunburst. By these means the status of the Decalogue as both text and icon was confirmed.[52]

Conclusion

The clergy of early modern England made sterling efforts to ensure that the laity mastered a scriptural version of the Ten Commandments in English, and the laity in turn, though not without some initial difficulty or resistance, seem to have been prepared to accept the Decalogue as the main standard for judging the rightness of outward actions and inner thoughts and feelings. However, this did not mean that all, or even a majority, of the English laity necessarily accepted the stern warnings given by Protestant clergy that, no matter how diligent or sincere were their efforts to keep the law, they could not earn merit or improve their prospects of salvation thereby. This is evident from sources we do not have space here to explore fully. There was the persistent semi-Pelagianism allegedly displayed by many of the poorer laity in their views on forgiveness and salvation. As Perkins warned them, 'it is not enough to say [the Commandments] without book, unless ye can

---

50. Hamling, *Decorating the 'Godly' Household*, pp. 106-109, 162, 285.
51. Rebecca Scott, *Samplers* (Oxford: Shire Publications, 2009), Chapter 2.
52. *An Inventory of the Historical Monuments in the County of Dorset*. I. *West Dorset* (London: Royal Commission on Historical Monuments, 1952), p. 211 and plate 66. This shift will be explored further in Green, *Word, Image and Ritual*.

understand the meaning of the words' and 'make a right use' of them by 'applying them inwardly to your hearts and consciences, and outwardly to your lives and conversations'. This, he stressed, 'is the very point in which you fail'.[53] Among the literate minority, there were those solicitous mothers, the popular poet Taylor and the Tory farmer Coe who apparently still regarded good thoughts and works, as deduced from the Decalogue, as prerequisites of salvation. Then there are the moralistic expressions of hope found in the wills and family memorials of many of the richer laity, that God would, indeed must, recognize and reward the efforts of the deceased to obey his commands.[54] Moreover, among that growing minority of English boys and youths who were exposed to a classical education, this moralistic tendency was reinforced by immersion in ancient pagan texts which equated the pursuit of virtue with the earning of honour and reward. The tensions between Christian and classical ethics *could* be resolved by teachers and theologians but, as I have tried to show elsewhere, the evidence for a concerted campaign to resolve them is patchy, and classical norms became increasingly influential.[55]

In short, while the Ten Commandments, along with the gospel, were seen by Protestant clergy as sturdy pillars for the doctrine of justification through grace by faith alone, the Decalogue was probably widely seen by many of the laity in early modern England, as to some extent it had been in pre-Reformation times, as an authorized source of moral teaching rather than doctrinal insight. And in the case of morality, from the Renaissance to the eighteenth century there would be a growing number of alternatives—pedagogical, philosophical, judicial, economic and social—by which public and private morality could be judged. These alternative criteria would eventually either subsume the Decalogue or render it superfluous.

---

53. Perkins, 'Foundation', sig. A2ᵛ.
54. To be explored in Green, *Word, Image and Ritual*.
55. Green, *Humanism and Protestantism*, Chapter 6 and *passim*; and see Keith Thomas, *The Ends of Life: Roads to Fulfilment in Early Modern England* (Oxford: Oxford University Press, 2009), Chapters 5–7.

Repurposing the Decalogue in Reformation England[1]

Jonathan Willis

1. Introduction

The Decalogue is both ubiquitous and invisible in historical accounts of the English Reformation. On the one hand, the Ten Commandments were everywhere in sixteenth-century England: in the new vernacular liturgy of the Books of Common Prayer; painted on the whitewashed walls of churches or written on wooden boards and hung up above Communion tables by archiepiscopal command; at the core of innumerable works of theology, catechesis, popular piety and practical divinity; and even given expression in artistic, musical and dramatic form.[2] On the other hand, the use of the Commandments in these sorts of ways often passes without much comment: it is simply accepted that this is something which Protestants 'did' after the Reformation.

There are some notable attempts to deal with the Decalogue in the period under discussion, for example John Bossy on the moral shift from seven sins to Ten Commandments, Ian Green on treatments of the Commandments in catechetical works and Margaret Aston on the Second Commandment and iconoclasm.[3] However, these and other works tend to take

---

1. This essay comes out of a larger project on 'The Ten Commandments and the English Reformation', funded by the Leverhulme Trust Early Career Fellowship scheme. It represents a series of initial findings which are developed further in *The Reformation of the Decalogue: Religious Identity and the Ten Commandments in England, c.1485–1625* (Cambridge: Cambridge University Press, 2017). The author would like to thank the Leverhulme Trust for their invaluable support, as well as the delegates of the conference from which this volume arises for their questions and comments regarding the original paper.

2. Archbishop Parker's *Aduertisements*, for example, required every minister to 'prouide a decent table standinge on a frame, for the Communion table…and to sett the tenne Commaundementes vppon the East wall ouer the said table' (Church of England, *Aduertisments Partly for Due Order in the Publique Administration of Common Prayers and Vsinge the Holy Sacramentes, and Partly for the Apparrell of All Persons Ecclesiasticall* [1565], sig. Aiiii^v).

3. John Bossy, 'Moral Arithmetic: Seven Sins into Ten Commandments', in Edmund Leites (ed.), *Conscience and Casuistry in Early Modern Europe* (Cambridge: Cambridge University Press, 1988), pp. 214-34; Ian Green, *The Christian's*

individual Commandments, or particular functions of the Decalogue, in isolation. Rather than just accepting the place of the Ten Commandments in post-Reformation English religious life, this essay aims to reveal why and how they came to assume such a central role, by considering the broader shift in interpretation and application that the Decalogue underwent during the period of the Reformation. Where historians do discuss the impact of the Reformation on the Ten Commandments, they often seize upon the issue of renumbering. Protestant iconoclasm and a reaction against what reformers perceived as the idolatrous worship of the late mediaeval Church have long been a fundamental part of the Reformation story, and the separation out of the prohibition against the making of graven images to form a 'new' Second Commandment among Reformed Protestant communities (in the manner of Jerome and the Jewish and Orthodox traditions) has been seen as 'symbolic of the Reformed tradition's profound suspicion towards any religious use of material objects'.[4] This essay will argue that it was something much more fundamental than their renumbering that underpinned the centrality of the Ten Commandments in the theology and religious life of post-Reformation England: it was their repurposing. In other words, the reformers took the Decalogue and stripped away many of its previous layers of meaning in order to render it suitable for a completely different set of theological functions. Not only was this repurposing the most fundamental change to affect the Ten Commandments during the Reformation, and perhaps throughout the whole of their history: but in turn the repurposed Decalogue profoundly shaped the character and development of the English Reformation itself.

2. The 'Traditional' Approach

If Reformed Protestants were allegedly guilty of 'repurposing' the Decalogue, then what was its original 'purpose'? This is a fair question, impossible to answer here in full, but let us begin by briefly considering the role of the Decalogue in traditional late mediaeval and Counter-Reformation

---

ABC: Catechisms and Catechizing in England, c. 1530–1740 (Oxford: Clarendon Press, 1996), pp. 422-478; Margaret Aston, *England's Iconoclasts*. I. *Laws against Images* (Oxford: Clarendon Press, 1988), pp. 220-42. Ian Green has since developed his arguments regarding the Decalogue in an essay written especially for the present volume.

4. Alec Ryrie, *The Gospel and Henry VIII* (Cambridge: Cambridge University Press, 2003), p. 231. See also Bossy, 'Moral Arithmetic', pp. 228-29; Diarmaid MacCulloch, 'The Latitude of the Church of England', in Kenneth Fincham and Peter Lake (eds.), *Religious Politics in Post-Reformation England* (Woodbridge: Boydell, 2006), p. 42. Cf. Margaret Aston, 'Puritans and Iconoclasm', in Christopher Durston and Jacqueline Eales (eds.), *The Culture of English Puritanism 1560–1700* (Basingstoke: Macmillan, 1996), pp. 92-121.

theology and pious practice. The Commandments were something of a minority interest for much of the Middle Ages, although a minority that included figures such as Augustine and Thomas Aquinas was clearly not one to be discounted.[5] Generally the seven sins were held to be a more appropriate guide to Christian morality, and were the dominant tool of instruction in confessors' manuals for much of the period under discussion.[6] John Bossy highlights the early fifteenth-century writings of Jean Gerson, theologian, conciliarist and Chancellor of the University of Paris, as launching

> A new departure in the teaching of Christianity...by treating the Commandments as the rock of Christian ethics, by establishing a tradition of effective vernacular exposition, and by integrating this into a larger theological position and into a general scheme of Catholic piety which included the practice of confession.[7]

This tradition can be clearly observed, matured but largely unchanged, in the early fifteenth-century dialogue *Dives and Pauper*, printed in England in 1493, in which the Commandments are used to trace in detail the vital line between sinful behaviours and the proper worship of God. The Decalogue was a reasonably handy and indisputably authoritative guide to the performance of meritorious works and a life of good behaviour on the one hand, and to the identification and confession of lapses into bad behaviour on the other. The compendious moral, social and theological commentary provided in *Dives and Pauper* boiled down neatly to the Ten Commandments, which in turn could be reduced to two, and to a single virtue. 'And so alle the ten commaundementes been comprehendyd', the author remarked, 'in the two preceptes of charitie'.[8]

Moving forward some two centuries from the first appearance of *Dives and Pauper*, these same themes can be detected in the writings of the Italian Jesuit who was also one of the defining figures in the formulation and promulgation of post-Tridentine Catholicism, Cardinal Roberto Bellarmine. Bellarmine's 1598 *Dichiarazione più copiosa della dottrina cristiana* was translated into English by the exiled Catholic priest Richard Haydock (or Haddock), and published at Douai in 1604 as *An Ample Declaration of the*

---

5. Bossy, 'Moral Arithmetic', pp. 215-21.

6. Often referred to as 'Deadly', more accurately as 'Capital', on the seven sins see Morton W. Bloomfield, *The Seven Deadly Sins* (East Lansing, MI: Michigan State College Press, 1952). Forthcoming work by Eric Carlson is likely to substantially modify Bossy and Bloomfield's account of the decline of the sins.

7. Bossy, 'Moral Arithmetic', pp. 222-23. On Gerson, see Daniel Hobbins, *Authorship and Publicity before Print: Jean Gerson and the Transformation of Late Medieval Learning* (Philadelphia: University of Pennsylvania Press, 2009).

8. Henry Parker [misattr.], *Here Endith a Compendiouse Treetise Dyalogue. Of Diues [and] Paup[er]* (1493), sig. Avii[r].

Christian Doctrine. This catechetical dialogue explained that there were four principal parts of the Christian doctrine, corresponding to the three theological virtues of faith, hope and charity, and to grace. The Creed was necessary for faith because it taught the people what to believe; the *pater noster* taught hope; the sacraments were instruments of grace; and the Ten Commandments were necessary 'for Charitie, because they teach vs what we haue to doe, to please God'.[9] The pursuit of charity, and its concomitant and obverse, the avoidance of sin, were a central and ongoing concern for the faithful. Sin, Bellarmine explained, was 'nothing else but a voluntary committing or omitting against the lawe of God', and consisted of three elements: the commission of an act forbidden or omission of a thing commanded; for the act concerned to be against the law of God; and for the act of commission or omission to be voluntary, that is, performed with the consent of the will.[10] An act performed without the consent of the will was therefore not a sin: Bellarmine gave the example of a man who accidentally uttered a blasphemy in his sleep, an act which clearly could not have been sanctioned by the will or have involved the conscious use of reason. Finally, Bellarmine defined the law as not only that which had been given by God himself, 'as the ten commandements are, but that also, which he giueth us by his vicar in earth, the Pope his holines, and other superiors, aswell spirituall as temporal: because al are the ministers of God, and haue authoritie from him'.[11]

Bellarmine also explained the relationship between the Decalogue, original sin and the classificatory system of moral and venial sins. The original sin committed by Adam and Eve, he explained, had robbed humanity of the seven gifts bestowed upon them at their creation, including their just status and their knowledge of how to shun evil. The grace won through Christ's sacrifice and applied through the sacrament of baptism restored the first and principal of these gifts: a person's justified status in the eyes of God. The other six gifts, including immortality and eventual translation into heaven to sit alongside the angels, were to be restored to the faithful in their afterlife in return for good behaviour during their earthly travails.[12]

He likewise explained the difference between mortal and venial sins. Mortal sins were distinguished because they observed two conditions. First, they were committed with the full and premeditated consent of the will.

---

9. Robert Bellarmine, *An Ample Declaration of the Christian Doctrine* (trans. Richard Hadock; 1604) (STC² 1834), p. 4. This was a common trope, both in Catholic and Protestant texts, but the two confessions employed fundamentally different theological conceptions of Charity, as will be explored later.

10. Bellarmine, *An Ample Declaration*, pp. 246-48.

11. Bellarmine, *An Ample Declaration*, p. 247.

12. The other three gifts were: obedience of the flesh to the spirit; promptness and facility to do well and fly evil; and freedom from all labour and fear: Bellarmine, *An Ample Declaration*, pp. 250-54.

This meant that 'a man must stand vpon his gard, and presently as he is aware of an euil thought, or desire, he must driue it away' before the consent of the will converts an involuntary urge into a voluntary and potentially mortal sin.[13] Secondly, sins were deemed to be mortal when they were so contrary to charity, to law and to love of God and neighbour that they were sufficient to break friendship. This was so because, by a rather circular reasoning, to break friendship was to be against charity, and (as charity was the fulfilling of the law) against the law of God as well. When either of these two criteria were absent, the sin in question was not mortal but venial. The example he gave was the theft of a great quantity of money versus the theft of a pin. Both were voluntary acts, and both sinful, but whereas the theft of money was 'a matter of weight, and in the judgement of most men sufficient to breake frendship, and so is against charitie', the theft of a pin 'although it be not according to charitie, yet it is not against charitie: because it is not a thing that in reason can breake frendship'.[14]

To aid them in their duty of identifying and enumerating sins, Bellarmine's readers were provided with a number of tools: there were the Ten Commandments; the seven capital sins; the six sins against the Holy Ghost; and the four sins so 'manifestly enormous' that they cried out to heaven for vengeance. These last four were an odd collection, comprising wilful murder, carnal sins against nature, oppression of widows and orphans, and defrauding workmen of their wages. They were so named 'because the iniustice of these sinnes is so maniefest, that it can not be couered or hidden by anie means'.[15] Similarly, the catechetical *A Profitable and Necessarye Doctrine* by the Marian bishop of London Edmund Bonner featured, alongside the traditional fare of the Lord's Prayer, the Creed, the sacraments and the Ten Commandments, additional expositions of the *Ave Maria*, the 'vii. deadlye synnes', the corresponding 'pryncypall vertues', and the 'eyghte Beatitudes', as well as a series of orations for the 'most holy father' the Pope, Cardinal Archbishop Reginald Pole, the king and queen, the prosperous voyage and safe return of Philip from Spain, and, last but not least, the bishop of London himself.[16] Bonner's programme of elementary religious education, *An Honest Godlye Instruction and Information for the Tradynge, and Bringinge vp of Children*, in addition required the learning of the *Confiteor*, the *de profundis*, graces for dinner and supper, the seven works of 'mercye bodely' and 'mercy gostly', and the seven gifts of the Holy Ghost.[17]

    13. Bellarmine, *An Ample Declaration*, p. 256.
    14. Bellarmine, *An Ample Declaration*, pp. 255-56.
    15. Bellarmine, *An Ample Declaration*, p. 257.
    16. Edmund Bonner, *A Profitable and Necessarye Doctrine with Certayne Homelyes Adioyned Therunto* (1555), sigs. Aaaiii^r-Ccciv^r.
    17. Edmund Bonner, *An Honest Godlye Instruction and Information for the Tradynge, and Bringinge vp of Children* (1555), sigs. Aii^v-Aiii^r.

This was a common topos.[18] While the Decalogue was therefore a key element in Catholic instructional texts dating from the late mediaeval period right through to the early part of the seventeenth century, their importance was primarily in identifying meritorious works to be carried out in order to live well and achieve salvation; in allowing the individual to recognize sinful behaviours, in order to avoid them if possible and otherwise seek to confess them to a priest; and to shore up a series of doctrines, including those concerning the nature of sin, the effects of original sin and the distinction between mortal and venial sins. What is also striking is the extent to which the Commandments were often presented as just one option on an extensive menu of moral classifications that also featured the seven sins, the corporal and spiritual works of mercy, the cardinal and theological virtues, alongside other more imaginative fare. Bellarmine's *Dichiarazione* received papal approbation and was translated from its original Italian into numerous languages as well as English and, in a sense, is therefore fairly representative of the broader attitude towards sin and the Decalogue in the post-Tridentine Roman Catholic Church.

In many ways, Bellarmine's treatment of the Commandments also fits into the paradigm suggested almost 25 years ago by John Bossy in his influential essay 'Moral Arithmetic: Seven Sins into Ten Commandments'. For Bossy, the Commandments were the most prominent part of what was essentially a new moral system in the Christian West, which had received isolated support in the eighth, thirteenth and fifteenth centuries, but did not achieve real prominence until the universal spread of the catechism during the sixteenth. Of course Catholics and Protestants differed on some aspects of the Commandments, most notably whether or not to enumerate the prohibition against idolatry as a separate dictum, but, generally speaking, both Catholic and Protestant authorities took comfort from the biblical provenance of their new ethical framework, and were grateful for the increased emphasis the first table placed on religious (by which Bossy predominantly meant ecclesiastical) obligations.[19]

---

18. *The Pater Noster, the Crede, and the Commaundementes of God in Englysh* (London, 1538), published in the middle of the Henrician religious reforms, is a complicated text but a striking example of this trend. Alongisde most of the elements already mentioned, it expounds the five ghostly and bodily wits, the four cardinal virtues, seven things to have always in our mind, sixteen conditions of charity taught by St Paul, four tokens of salvation, five wonders of St Augustine, and four things needful to each person. Edmund Chertsey, on the title page to *The Floure of the Commaundementes of God* (1510), listed 'the fyve commaundementes of the chyrche' immediately after 'the x commaundementes of the lawe'.

19. John Bossy, 'Moral Arithmetic', pp. 215-16, and *passim*.

3. *Repurposing Sin*

The reformed Protestant repurposing of this 'traditional' approach to the Decalogue was integral to their broader reconceptualization of great swathes of traditional Catholic theology. It follows, I would like to argue, that the fundamental significance of the Decalogue for the historical development of the English Reformation was theological. This significance stemmed from a complete reassessment of the role, purpose and function of God's law in the writings of English reformers, from the earliest evangelicals who came to prominence during the reign of Henry VIII to the mature English Protestantisms of the reigns of Elizabeth I and James I. For, as well as determining social relationships, political loyalties and moral obligations, the Decalogue also sat at the very heart of a whole range of central doctrinal issues, including repentance, justification, faith, sanctification and sacramental theology. As Protestant divines reshaped the Commandments, therefore, the Commandments in return conditioned foundational concepts of their own religious beliefs, practices and identities. The issues and concerns discussed by Bellarmine in the *Dichiarazione* were almost literally in another language from the complex web of significances and associations that occupied Protestant divines. To all intents and purposes, the respective laws of God discussed by Bellarmine and his English Protestant contemporaries had absolutely nothing in common with one another. They were a different Ten Commandments.

Let us begin with an issue of the utmost importance to the pastoral and theological concerns of the Reformation. Central to the reformers' theology and anthropology, from Luther onwards, was the notion of the total depravity (or sinfulness) of humanity. This lay at the heart of the Protestant rejection of the mediaeval economy of salvation and the development of a new soteriology centred around the notion of justification by faith alone, probably the single most defining doctrine of the Protestant Reformation. Original sin, argued the Protestant convert Thomas Bell in a 1608 treatise against the Jesuit Robert Parsons, was not amended by baptism. The tendency towards evil engendered in Adam after the fall, known as concupiscence, was ever-present in humanity and represented not only the potential to sin, or even an inclination toward sin, but a sin in and of itself. Bellarmine, let us remember, had made the active and voluntary connivance of the will one of the preconditions for recognizing a given action as sinful. However, in *The Iesuits Antepast*, Bell contested the interpretation of Augustine presented by Parsons and Bellarmine in order to conclude that the Church Father had named concupiscence as sin both materially and formally: concupiscence of the flesh was not only the cause of sin and the punishment of sin, but also sin itself.[20] Bell's proof of this lay not only in his criticism of his

---

20. Thomas Bell, *The Iesuits Antepast Conteining, a Repy against a Pretensed*

opponent's deployment of the Church Fathers, but also in the second table of the Decalogue. The last precept against covetousness, he claimed, 'prohibited not onely actually and voluntary concupiscence, but the very Originall and Fountaine of all concupiscences with all her involuntary branches'.[21]

Actual concupiscence, Bell reminded his readers, was already prohibited in the Sixth, Seventh and Eighth Commandments of the law. Christ's Sermon on the Mount had expanded the scope of these Commandments as originally delivered in Exodus 20 and Deuteronomy 5 beyond the mere actions of murder, theft and adultery. 'Ye have heard that it was said by them of old time, Thou shalt not commit adultery', stated Mt. 5.27-28, 'But I say unto you, That whosoever looketh on a woman to lust after her hath committed adultery with her already in his heart'. As Bell explained, if the Tenth Commandment only forbade actual concupiscence, then it was essentially redundant, for this was already to be understood from the New Testament gloss on the earlier Commandments. Therefore, the last Commandment forbade not only actual and voluntary concupiscence, that is concupiscence acted upon by consent of the will, but also the very existence and presence of formal, original and unconscious concupiscence. 'No scripture can be produced', Bell claimed, 'which denyeth that Originall concupiscence with the involuntary motions thereof, is properly sin'.[22] He cited both Paul and Augustine in support of view that 'that Originally Concupiscence is prohibited by this Precept (Thou shalt not Lust;) and not onely the habituall concupiscence it selfe, but also all the actual involuntary motions thereof'.[23] In other words, while consent to concupiscence was forbidden by the Sixth to Eighth precepts, concupiscence itself was forbidden by the Tenth. Even the logic of the scholastics dictated this conclusion, Bell noted, for it was a generally held axiom that the cause being taken away, the effect would also be taken away. As death was the effect of original sin, if baptism removed original sin then it would also take away death. 'Wherefore, seeing both olde and young after Baptisme still dye, as we daily see; it is an euident Argument, that the cause thereof (which is originall concupiscence) is not taken away'.[24]

At a stroke, Protestant authors therefore theologically repurposed the Catholic use of the Decalogue as a tool for identifying sinful behaviours to startling new effect. Whereas Catholic authors such as Bellarmine recommended that believers use the Commandments as a guide for avoiding sin,

---

Aunswere to the Downe-fall of Poperie, Lately Published by a Masked Iesuite Robert Parsons by Name, Though He Hide Himselfe Couertly Vnder the Letters of S. R. Which May Fitly Be Interpreted (a Sawcy Rebell) (1608) (STC² 1824), p. 80.

21. Bell, *The Iesuits Antepast*, p. 81.
22. Bell, *The Iesuits Antepast*, p. 82.
23. Bell, *The Iesuits Antepast*, p. 83.
24. Bell, *The Iesuits Antepast*, p. 85.

Protestant divines such as Bell presented the Commandments as proof that the avoidance of sin was a practical and theological impossibility. The Decalogue provided knowledge of sin for Catholics and Protestants alike, but while for the former it functioned as practical guidance for forestalling and making amends for sinful behaviour, for the latter it was deployed to engender in the believer a sense of overwhelming horror at the all-consuming extent of their own rank unworthiness and utter sinfulness.

While the Catholic Commandments existed to be obeyed, the point of the Protestant Commandments was that they could not be obeyed. The thrust of this was nothing new. 'In this precept is declared specially our infirmity and weakness', John Hooper had written in his 1548 work *A Declaration of the Ten Holy Commandments of Almighty God*: 'that we are all miserable sinners…for never was there, nor ever shall be, only Christ excepted, but offended in this precept, to what perfection or degree of holiness soever he came into'.[25] The Tenth Commandment required 'such a charity and sincere love towards God and man, that the mind should not have as much as any contrary motion, or any resistance at all, to stain the glory and beauty of this love, which comprehendeth all those commandments afore rehearsed'. While the mediaeval Commandments and the Decalogue expounded by Bellarmine were designed to form a roadmap for godly living, outlining works of charity and identifying the pitfalls of sin, the law of God explicated by Bell and Hooper was closer to a terrifying fairground mirror, designed to reflect and magnify the grotesque enormity of human depravity.[26] The Catholic Commandments taught humanity how to recognize their sin so that they could make amends for it: the Protestant Decalogue told them how irredeemably sinful they were, in order to make them realize that they possessed neither the inclination nor the capacity to make amends for it.

As William Tyndale explained in his *A Pathway into the Holy Scripture*, the law 'was given to bring us unto the knowledge of ourselves, that we might thereby feel and perceive what we are, of nature'.[27] Tyndale,

---

25. John Hooper, 'A Declaration of the Ten Holy Commandments of Almighty God' (1548), in *Early Writings of John Hooper* (ed. Samuel Carr; Cambridge: Cambridge University Press, 1843), p. 410.

26. The notion of the books of Scripture as a 'looking glass' or 'mirror' was a common one. Samuel Cottesford called upon sinners to examine themselves 'by the two looking-glasses of the Law, and the Gospel'. 'Doubtlesse in the one and first, which is the Law', he wrote, 'he shall find out in himselfe nothing but sin and iniquity, and thereby that he stands in the seuerity of Gods extreame iustice, in and vnder the danger of eternall death and condemnation' (*A Very Soueraigne Oyle to Restore Debtors* [1622], p. 20).

27. William Tyndale, 'A Pathway into the Holy Scripture', in *Doctrinal Treatises and Introductions to Different Portions of Holy Scriptures* (ed. Henry Walter; Cambridge: Cambridge University Press, 1848), p. 10.

and many others besides, picked up on the words of St Paul in 2 Cor. 3.7, the law 'written and engraven in stones' was the 'ministration of death'. By nature and through the fall, humans were 'the children of wrath, heirs of the vengeance of God', of 'fellowship with the damned devils, under the power of darkness and rule of Satan, while we are yet in our mothers' wombs' and 'full of the natural poison, whereof all sinful deeds spring'.[28] The first office of the Protestant law, then, was knowledge. The fall left neither the will nor the law of God written in human beings, their members or their hearts, 'neither is there any more power in us to follow the will of God, than in a stone to ascend upward of his own self'. People were 'as it were asleep, in so deep blindness, that we can neither see nor feel what misery, thraldom, and wretchedness we are in'. Not, that is, 'till Moses come and wake us, and publish the law'. It was not until humanity heard the law of God preached that they might come to realize their true nature and incapacity. The Ten Commandments were like a series of hurdles over which human beings was originally quite capable of jumping: however, by eating of the fruit of the forbidden tree Adam had eternally hobbled both himself and his progeny. The Commandments were not impossible to fulfil, for Christ had fulfilled them, but in their sickness human beings could not manage to make the least part of the least of them. If proof were needed of the impossibility of observing the Decalogue, it was confirmed by the judgment of Jas 2.10 and Mt. 5.19 that 'whosoever shall keep the whole law, and yet offend in one point, he is guilty of all'. In other words, the smallest breach of any part of one of God's law was the same as a breach of every precept in the Decalogue.

4. *Repurposing Salvation*

The Protestant repurposing of the law did not end there. The purpose of the knowledge of sin outlined above was to incline the individual towards repentance, and in this sense the Protestant Decalogue did begin to assume some of the attributes of a guide. For, in enumerating people's sins, it enabled them to begin to repent, not through a sacramental ritual of priestly confession but directly to God, a process expressed in language strikingly redolent of evangelical conversion. For Tyndale, baptism was the signal of the beginning of this process of repentance, which lasted the entirety of a person's life on earth. Repentance was a crucial step in the process of salvation, because without knowledge and repentance humans could not realize their inability to save themselves by means of works and the outward fulfilment of the law. Knowledge and repentance were the critical first steps in turning away from sin and embracing the promises of Christ as outlined in

---

28. Tyndale, 'A Pathway', p. 14.

the gospel. In other words, knowledge and repentance in the face of the Ten Commandments were a means to faith in Christ.

Protestant divines were therefore keen to publish aids in order to bring the people into the full knowledge of their sins, and thus to the very depths of repentance. It might be assumed that one of the easiest Commandments to obey was the Sixth, 'Thou shalt not kill'. But as William Perkins was happy to remind readers in his treatise 'Of the Nature and Practise of Repentance', actual sins 'shalbe founde by examination to be innumerable as the haires of a mans head, & as the sands by the sea shore: if any will but search themselves a litle by the ten commandements of the Decalogue, for all their sinful thoughts, words, and deeds against God and man'.[29] Perkins identified around 30 breaches of the Sixth Commandment, supported by reference to Scripture, included being 'given to hastinesse' (Mt. 5.22), 'chiding and crying out' (Eph. 4.31), forgiving but not forgetting, giving 'not almes to relieve the poore' (Lk. 16.19), moving 'contention and debate' (Rom. 1.29), and teaching erroneously, slackly, or not at all.

As Protestant divines were only too eager to point out, Scripture itself was full of examples of individuals who had been brought to faith and repentance through the office of the law. George Abbot explained in his *Exposition vpon the Prophet Ionah* of 1600 that it was only after 'the whip of God, and the rod of his iustice' had overtaken Jonah, 'so that he now seeth heauen and earth to be against him', that his proud heart was humbled and the sleeper within him awoke. 'Contrition and confession', wrote Abbot, 'came now tumbling vpon him, yea to make vp his full penance, there shalbe satisfaction, if his life can make amends'.[30] It was only the demolition of Jonah's pride through spiritual and temporal tribulations, and through the application of God's law and justice, that had enabled the Holy Spirit to awaken something good within him, leading to penance and a reformed life. Jonah could now 'confesse his sinnes against him selfe' openly to God. Once Jonah himself had experienced this repentance, his task was to enact the same among the sinful people of Nineveh. Abbot described the process in the familiar terms of Protestant conversion as follows:

> For first albeit the words of his Sermon, be most briefly set downe here, yet without question he inveighed aghainst their sinnes, the enormitie of their liues, the crookednesse of their wayes, their outragious impiety, their insolent intemperancie. And vppon this they were stricken with a biting remorse, and feare, that some diuine essence, or supreme Iusticer, would take vengeance vppon them.[31]

---

29. William Perkins, *Tvvo Treatises. I. Of the Nature and Practise of Repentance. II. Of the Combat of the Flesh and Spirit* (1593) (STC² 19758), p. 19.

30. George Abbot, *An Exposition vpon the Prophet Ionah* (1600) (STC² 34), p. 95.

31. Abbot, *An Exposition*, p. 404.

Abbot portrayed Jonah as the bringer of knowledge to the carnal and sinful inhabitants of Nineveh through the preaching of God's law. With Jonah himself, knowledge brought repentance, and repentance led to faith: he was the agent of the same realization in the citizens of Nineveh. Nineveh's repentance was a powerful precedent for the transformational power of preaching, and also for crucial role of God's word in enacting evangelical conversion. The people of Nineveh, Abbot noted, had many temporal comforts and false beliefs, 'yea all the things that might be, to deteyne them from these good motions', including 'prosperitie, securitie, satietie of bread, a wall of sinne about them, a sea of sinne within them, superstition and ignorance and contemning pride, which so loueth it selfe that it loueth not to be controlled'. But in the face of this, in God's law Jonah had no more nor no less than he needed, and so 'the breath of one mortall man… inspired indeede from an immortall God' was able 'to ouertumble all'.[32] True repentance reminded and confirmed to penitent sinners that salvation could not be achieved through corrupt works or flawed obedience to an impossible and condemnatory law, but only through the promises of salvation made in the Gospels and the grace achieved through Christ's sacrifice and perfect fulfilment of the law. The Decalogue, therefore, was the means to knowledge, to repentance, and thence to faith.

Neither was the acquisition of faith the end of the journey, or faith itself an uncomplicated matter. The Puritan divine William Attersoll described the proper office and function of justifying faith as being in 'apprehending, receiving, and laying hold vppon Christ and all his benefits'.[33] The property of a true faith, a faith against which 'the strongest fates of hell' would not prevail, was to say 'though the Lorde would kill me, yet still I wil trust in him'. This saving faith was a lively faith, and it was to be known by its relationship to the Decalogue. The great paradox of the Protestant Commandments was that the reprobate—who were under the law—were condemned by the law and therefore hated it. At the same time, the godly—who were freed from the condemnation of the law through Christ—evidenced their faith through a lust to fulfil the Commandments. This lust was born not from a misguided desire to earn salvation, but from a love of Christ, of God, and therefore of his law. As Ezekiel Culverwell put it in *A Treatise of Faith*, 'the gift of the sanctifying spirit' was 'the first and chiefest fruit of faith, and roote of other graces necessary to saluation' and 'most sure euidence, that we bee the children of God, and heires of saluation by Christ'. The principal effect of the spirit, which was 'most generall, and containes the rest', was 'the keeping of Gods commandments, which in sundry places is made

---

32. Abbot, *An Exposition*, p. 404.
33. William Attersoll, *The Badges of Christianity. Or, a Treatise of the Sacraments Fully Declared out of the Word of God* (1606) (STC² 889), p. 357.

a sure mark of sauing grace'. 'Hereby we know that we know him', Culverwell explained, 'if wee keepe his commandements: the meaning whereof, is, that the conscionable endeauour to frame our liues, according to Gods will reuealed in his word, is a most certen mark, that we be true beleeuers, and so the true children of God & heires of glory'.[34] Through justifying faith, Tyndale explained, the believer would know God 'as our Father most merciful, and consent to the law, and love it inwardly in our heart, and desire to fulfil it'.[35] The godly were consumed by a hunger and a thirst for more righteousness and for the fulfilment of the law.[36] The Ten Commandments therefore not only brought humanity to knowledge and repentance: they were also one of the means by which the elect could test the quality of their faith, and find it to be true and lively—'to know that we know him'—and not the dead, barren faith of hypocrites and the damned. Faith was in effect love: love of God and his mercy, but also love of his justice and his law.

It was therefore not simply an inner desire to fulfil the works of the law that Protestant divines looked for, but concrete evidence that, through the intervention of the Holy Spirit, those chosen individuals predestined for salvation would themselves aspire and begin to emulate Christ and perform the actions prescribed in (and refrain from those prohibited by) the Decalogue, albeit in a tainted and imperfect fashion. Lest they become complacent, the godly were reminded that, even after justification, their righteousness was 'as a stained or defiled cloath, such as Gods pure eyes cannot endure', but the 'satisfaction made by Christ for the pardon of their defects' enabled their obedience 'to be well liking in his sight'.[37] Tyndale had explained to readers of the *Pathway* that 'by the fruits shall ye know what the tree is. A man's deeds declare what he is within'. In fact, he went on to outline three ways in which good works, the fruits of justifying faith, offered service to the godly: they certified them as the heirs of everlasting life, helped to tame the flesh, enabling them to wax more perfect in the spirit, and also fulfilled their own comfort and duty to their neighbour through the office of charity.[38] As Thomas Bentley explained for the benefit of godly ladies in his 1582 treatise *The Monument of Matrones*, 'if we by faith be trulie graffed in Iesus Christ, and call vpon God to saluation, we will no more bring foorth the works of the flesh, but the fruits of the spirit'.[39] The grace imputed to the godly by

---

34. Ezekiel Culverwell, *A Treatise of Faith Wherein Is Declared How a Man May Liue by Faith and Finde Releefe in All his Necessities* (1623) (STC² 6113.5), pp. 224-25.

35. Tyndale, 'A Pathway', p. 14.

36. Tyndale, 'A Pathway', p. 20.

37. Culverwell, *A Treatise of Faith*, pp. 274-75.

38. Tyndale, 'A Pathway', pp. 23-24.

39. Thomas Bentley, *The Monument of Matrones Conteining Seuen Seuerall Lamps of Virginitie, or Distinct Treatises; Whereof the First Fiue Concerne Praier and*

Christ's perfect fulfilment of the law meant that their own imperfection was no longer counted against them, and the Holy Spirit 'engendreth in vs a continuall desire and mind, to doo all that the lawe commandeth us, as neere as we can'.[40] The fruits of faith, in other words, were charity: and the works of charity were the works of the law.

5. Conclusion

The English Catholic missionary priest Oliver Almond, in his 1623 work *The Vncasing of Heresie, or, The Anatomie of Protestancie*, noted that all the 'chiefe doctrines and principles' of Protestantism were but 'old condemned heresies', the most damned 'ever hatched in any age'.[41] Almond contended that prime among these heretical doctrines was the contention 'that the law appertained not vnto Christian men', and there was a widespread view among Catholics, frequently expressed certainly in works of polemic, that Protestants of all stripes were effectively antinomians, abrogating not only the Jewish ceremonial and judicial laws but also the moral law of the Ten Commandments. In contrast, Protestant authors such as Hugh Broughton decried their Papist opponents as 'contemners' of the law, and reviled the Pope for his wicked 'theft' of the prohibition against idolatry.[42] This genuine and mutual religious incomprehension was perfectly expressed in Cranmer Covbridge's 1618 treatise *The Ladder of Hell*. This short work set out to refute a popish list of Protestant 'heresies' by explaining to readers that, rather than causing them to descend into hell, the doctrines in question formed a ladder which ascended out of it, and pointed the way to salvation. Number two on the list was the proposition that 'the ten Commandements are impossible to be kept'.[43] Oliver Almond was therefore right to suggest that his native Protestants maintained 'that the Law of God, or the ten Commandments are impossible to be kept, no not though a man be neuer so much assisted or holpen by Gods grace'.[44]

But his charge of antinomianism was wide of the mark. Although only Christ had been able to fulfil the law, a love of the Decalogue and a continuous striving to obey the Commandments better was a central aspect of

Meditation: the Other Two Last, Precepts and Examples, as the Woorthie Works Partlie of Men, Partlie of Women (1582) (STC² 1892), p. 238.

40. Bentley, *The Monument of Matrones*, p. 239.

41. Oliver Almond, *The Vncasing of Heresie, or, The Anatomie of Protestancie* (1623) (STC² 12), p. 32.

42. Hugh Broughton, *A Reuelation of the Holy Apocalyps* (1610), p. 113.

43. Cranmer Covbridge, *The Ladder of Hell, or, The Protestants Libertine Doctrine Being the Broad Way Which Leadeth the Followers of It to their Eternall Ruine and Destruction in Hell / Set Foorth in Prose and Verse* (1618), sig. A6ʳ.

44. Almond, *The Vncasing of Heresie*, p. 40.

the godly life as stressed by a range of authors. Cardinal Bellarmine, in his catechetical *Dichiarazione*, had equated the Ten Commandments with the theological virtue of charity: faith was represented by the catechism, hope by the Lord's Prayer, and grace by the doctrine of the sacraments. These other elements also formed the core of Protestant catechesis, and yet it is possible to argue that by virtue of its theological repurposing, the Protestant Decalogue was the key not only to charity, but to faith, hope and grace as well. Through the preaching of the law sinners were brought first to knowledge of sin and the impossibility of exercising salvific agency: then repentance, faith, love of the law and a godly life as demonstrated by the fruits of charity. William Attersoll even made it clear that preparation for participation in the sacraments had to involve the same process of the hearing of the law, including further knowledge and self-examination, the strengthening of faith, ongoing repentance for sin, reconciliation with God and the eventual assurance of salvation.[45]

As Tyndale explained, the office of the baptized Christian was to 'give our consent unto the law' and to yield ourselves 'to be scholars thereof'.[46] The broad remit of the Decalogue remained unchanged during the Reformation: it prohibited certain behaviours, and prescribed others, in order to help Christians live a better and more godly life. But the theological underpinnings and religious implications of these basic functions were completely reconfigured by reformers such as Tyndale, Hooper, Perkins and Bell. Sin could still be identified, but no longer avoided or remitted. Justification was an entirely passive affair, with the performance of the works of the law now the consequence, not the cause, of salvation. And behind these indelible theological paradigm shifts stood the repurposing of the Decalogue.

---

45. Attersoll, *The Badges of Christianity*, p. 351.
46. Tyndale, 'A Pathway', p. 27.

The Reception of the Decalogue in Protestant Catechisms

Hans-Jürgen Fraas

According to their confessional development, Protestant catechisms can be separated into two main types. For the Lutheran Church there is Luther's *Small Catechism* of 1529, and for the Reformed Church there are Calvin's *Genevan Catechism* of 1542 and, in the German-speaking territories, the *Heidelberg Catechism* of 1563. In addition there are other catechisms with limited territorial acceptance.[1] Yet only Luther's and the *Heidelberg Catechism* are of lasting importance.

Reformation

Luther adopts the Deuteronomic version of the Decalogue (Deut. 5.6-21),[2] whereas the *Heidelberg Catechism* follows the Exodus version (Exod. 20.1-17).[3] Luther follows the medieval tradition[4] by not including the prologue (Exod. 20.2) in the text to be learnt. He also adopts the enumeration of the Commandments, the arrangement according to two tables and the conventional formulations, even if he does not accept them exactly. His intention is to make the Commandments approachable for his contemporaries. It should be made clear that his version represents unaltered medieval Christian doctrine.

Luther ignores the ban on images. The prohibition of alien gods thus appears as the first commandment, followed by that of taking the Lord's name in vain. He places the promise attached to the ban on images (Deut. 5.9b-10) at the end of the Commandments. But the Reformed Church

---

1. E.g. the three catechisms by Johannes Brenz (the most important from 1535), which are used exclusively in Württemberg, and the catechisms for Strasbourg by Martin Bucer and for the Palatinate by Zacharias Ursinus, a disciple of Melanchthon and Calvin, and others.
2. Together with the Catholics.
3. Like the Jews and the Anglicans.
4. Johannes Meyer, *Historischer Kommentar zu Luthers Kleinem Katechsimus* (Gütersloh: C. Bertelsmann, 1929), p. 85.

maintains the ban on images, given their own rejection of pictures, and separates it from the prohibition of alien gods. At the end of the Commandments, Luther differentiates coveting a neighbour's wife and coveting a neighbour's possessions. This places emphasis on monogamy and recalls the Sixth Commandment. The Reformed Churches and the Anglicans apply the Sixth Commandment to the 'house of the neighbour', which in biblical usage includes the entire household—all familial dependants and assets.

Two main themes can be identified in the reception of the Decalogue in Protestant catechisms: the relationship between the Decalogue and natural law and the relationship between law and gospel.

The first theme, the relationship between Decalogue and natural law, can be dealt with relatively quickly. The Decalogue is considered by Luther to be the positive law of the Jews, the 'Jews' version of the *Sachsenspiegel*'. This allows him to rearrange the Old Testament form of the Decalogue in so far as it was determined by the special situation of Israel. This liberty regarding the traditional text is expressed in Luther's call for 'new Decalogues': 'If we have Christ, we can make new Decalogues'.[5] However, where 'the Law of Moses and natural law are the same', the Decalogue's validity remains.[6] In that sense the Decalogue serves to maintain social order. However, Luther certainly does not mean natural law in the philosophical sense. As the standard for each updated interpretation of the Decalogue, for Luther natural law is not a timeless, abstract principle. It is a sign of the living willingness of God to love. The Decalogue, in this aspect identical with natural law, is for Luther the binding law of God, in the sense of the creation-preserving grace of God. Later, as the catechism turns more and more into a doctrine under the influence of Melanchthon, the term 'law' becomes more closely connected with the adoption of *lumen naturale* from ancient and medieval ethics.

For Calvin, the positive Israelite law is the basis of natural law and thereby of his Christian communal code. As opposed to Luther's liberal attitude towards tradition, Calvin represents a legalistic standpoint. He does not follow Luther's omission of the ban on images and the separation of the introductory phrase ('I am the Lord, your God') from the Commandments themselves. Like Luther, Calvin equates the Decalogue and natural law but, unlike Luther, he interprets natural law only through the Decalogue.

The second theme, the relationship between law and gospel, is more complicated. The Lutheran and the Reformed models already differ in where they locate the Decalogue within the catechism, according to their theologically differing approaches to justification and sanctification. Luther's *Brief Form of the Faith, the Ten Commandments and the Lord's Prayer*

5. WA XXXIX.1, 47, 25-30.
6. WA XVI, 378, 11; 18, 81, 14f.

from 1520 appears as a kind of programme, in which he seems to allocate the Decalogue its theological place, including it among the three things necessary for human blessedness. First, humans need to know what to do and what to avoid (Decalogue). Second, if this is impossible through their own efforts, they need to know where to find salvation (Credo) and, finally, how they can appropriate it for themselves (Lord's Prayer and sacraments).[7] The Decalogue is seen here, according to the common interpretation, in the Pauline sense of law, which humans fail to keep, but which guides them to Christ and prepares them for Christ's saving act.[8]

Nearly all subsequent authors are dependent on the *Brief Form*. In the later history of the *Small Catechism*, the question of whether the sequence of the three elements is obligatory becomes the subject of continuous dispute. This is understandable, because it is a central theological question that concerns the interpretation of law, the doctrine of justification and the question of good works. Until the nineteenth century, interpreters maintained the idea of an ongoing progress from chapter to chapter of the catechism. Calvin's *Genevan Catechism* of 1542 differs fundamentally from Luther's position on this point. Reformed thinking aims at the cooperation of governmental and ecclesiastical jurisdiction regarding observance of the Commandments. For Calvin, law is the rule of conduct for the life of the Christian community. The new obedience becomes the standard of the law. The *Heidelberg Catechism* is composed essentially of three large parts, dealing respectively with human misery, salvation and gratitude. Together with the Lord's Prayer, the Decalogue stands for gratitude. Good works, which emanate from the Decalogue, are, in a good Reformed sense, the grateful answer to the grace that humans receive through Christ.

However, the question remains as to whether the formulation of the *Brief Form* indeed represents Luther's basic theological programme. Luther's motivation in the *Brief Form* seems to be based more on a didactic or pedagogical interest than a theological one. The emphasis on promoting the law (*das Treiben des Gestezes*) has a purely pedagogical character in relation to certain raw, uneducated groups. But when he considers Christians in their full Christian being, Luther strikes different notes. Evidently in the *Brief Form* he only wants to put his material in a reasonable didactic arrangement. He leaves the order to parish priests. If the *Brief Form* represented the main thrust of the Reformation, Luther would not have left this question undecided. Yet, if it is not possible to understand the sequence of this text as a dogmatic system, then the question arises as to how its main elements are connected. Compared with other statements, and in parallel with the *Small*

---

7. WA VII, 204, 13.
8. Hans-Jürgen Fraas, *Katechismustradition: Luthers kleiner Katechismus in Kirche und Schule* (Göttingen: Vandenhoeck & Ruprecht, 1971), p. 11.

Catechism, it is noticeable that Luther postulates a relative independence for individual elements.

A recurring point of discussion in the interpretation history of the *Small Catechism* is whether, and to what extent, the Decalogue is for Luther not only instruction, but also promise. Luther clearly affirms the latter.[9] For him, law and gospel stand in a dialectical relationship; one does not suspend the other but both find unity in Christ. In Christ, not only do grace and forgiveness become visible, but also sin and rage. In the dialectics of law and gospel, humans can be affected by various nuances of the meaning of the law, depending on the situation of their faith.[10] Humanity can be both *peccator* and *justus* at the same time. For the first the Decalogue appears as accusation; for the second as a standard of Christian obedience, the order of a new life. In that sense the Decalogue becomes an instruction, which admonishes Christians and sketches for them the direction of their actions. For Christians the commandments become achievable, because they no longer appear as a 'so that' (so that one *becomes* just), but as a 'because' (because one *is* just). The works of the commandments arise not from what one ought to do, but from what one is. Here the scope of lived obedience widens towards the Sermon on the Mount and the New Testament parenesis. Therefore, Christians can be affected by the Decalogue once as law and once as gospel. 'Demand and grace are opposites for the troubled, but identical for the consoled.'[11] For Luther it is not a question of interpretation, but of face-to-face encounter. The content of the terms 'law' and 'gospel' cannot become subdivided schematically without damaging the character of the encounter between humans and God's Word.

This interpretation centres on the exegesis of the First Commandment. Luther separates the beginning of the Commandments, 'I am the Lord, your God', from the Commandments themselves, and describes it as *promissio*. That *promissio*, for him, is not only the foundation of the entire Decalogue, but also of the catechism itself. With it, the Commandments are preceded by God's love, which is itself based on the documented salvific history of the *gratia praeveniens*. The Decalogue itself, and within the Decalogue the First Commandment, for Luther includes the complete will of God.[12] Luther radicalizes the meaning of the Decalogue, by contrast with late antique and medieval moralism, by deducing all the Commandments from the first one

---

9. WA XXX.2, 358, 1ff.; XXX.2, 663; *Tischreden* II, 328.

10. G. Heintze, *Luthers Predigt von Gesetz und Evangelium* (Munich: Chr. Kaiser Verlag, 1958), p. 275.

11. O. Gühloff, *Gebieten und Schaffen Gottes in Luthers Auslegung des ersten Gebotes* (Göttingen: H. Eschenhagen, 1939), p. 9.

12. E. Schott, 'Luthers Verständnis des ersten Gebotes', *TLZ* 13 (1948), cols. 199-204 (199).

and turning them into the foundation of the relationship between humans and God. All sins are ascribed to selfishness and all virtues to charity and the love of God.

The *promissio* includes the invitation to faith and love, meaning that the gospel has to adopt the form of commandments in order to lead humans to salvation.[13] However, such commandments would be useless if Luther did not know at the same time about grace, which gives humans faith, fear and trust. The character of the commandment is expressed in a way which causes Luther, in his interpretation of the Commandments, to go beyond prohibition and to write in terms of positive instruction: 'We shall fear and love God, so that we...' The constant repetition of the words 'fear and love' once more accentuates the First Commandment as the central one and as the basis of the later concretization of God's will. The epilogue, after all, is a re-enactment of the First Commandment, which thus frames the others.[14] Luther sees in the law the gospel as well, while the Reformed tradition sees in the gospel the law as well.[15]

Orthodoxy

Immediately after the publication of Luther's *Small Catechism*, its history of explanation and application begins. Its theological meaning becomes adapted to the spirit of the times, and Luther's complex dialectical understanding of law and gospel is not maintained. The order of chapters, for Luther a methodical support, now becomes a theological principle. The theological tradition after Luther is influenced by Philipp Melanchthon and is characterized by the pursuit of the accurate formulation of doctrine. With the requirement of systematization the distinction between dogmatics and ethics is established. To the extent that the catechism becomes a 'doctrine', the term 'law' is associated with the takeover of the *lumen naturale* from antique and medieval ethics.

Now the standardized doctrine of the triple use of law becomes central to internal Protestant debates. The *triplex usus legis* distinguishes between the *usus politicus*, the *usus spiritualis* or *elenchthicus* and the *usus moralis*. In the case of *usus politicus*, law is the basis of all human interaction (in the

---

13. P. Althaus, *Die Theologie Martin Luthers* (Gütersloh: Gerd Mohn, 1962), p. 119.

14. A. Hardeland, 'Das Furchtproblem in Luthers Katechismen', *Luther: Mitteilungen der Luthergesellschaft* 11 (1929), p. 105, thinks the epilogue therefore gets to the end, because it is incompatible with the prologue understood as promise. Cf., on the other hand, J. Meyer, 'Das erste Gebot bei Luther', *Luther: Mitteilungen der Luthergesellschaft* 11 (1929), p. 24.

15. E. Weismann, 'Der Predigtgottesdienst und die verwandten Formen', in K.F. Müller and W. Blankenburg (eds.), *Leiturgia. Handbuch des evangelischen Gottesdienstes*, III (Kassel: J. Stauda-Verlag, 1956), p. 89.

sense of natural law); whereas in the case of *usus spiritualis* or *elenchthicus* it teaches, promises and threatens, but is unaccomplishable—it causes humans to fail and shows them their limitations in sin. Finally, in the doctrine of *usus moralis*, law returns to its original basis and becomes the norm for the new obedience of the believer, the religious and moral order of life. Abandoning Luther's dialectic between law and gospel, the relationship between them is now defined by the idea of development. In the common form, the *triplex usus legis* is taught almost universally (also by Calvin). The *usus politicus* is presupposed as the basis of social organization, with or without theological relevance. The *usus theologicus* or *spiritualis* is not completely denied, but differently weighted. Nevertheless the doctrine of *tertius usus legis* stands at the centre of debate within Protestantism. It remains in tension between justification and sanctification, and is discussed in relation to the question of good works. 'Sanctification' becomes an independent element of doctrine, the object of a special order, the 'order of sanctification'.

From this, the following differing positions arise. The 'Antinomians' (opponents of law) declare the Decalogue to be irrelevant for Christians. The so-called 'Gnesio-Lutherans' (the strong Lutherans) teach the *duplex usus legis*, that is, the political importance and the function of the penitential sermon as proof of sin. Melanchthon and his followers, the 'Philippists', teach the *tertius usus*, meaning the application of law for a Christian life. For Calvin and the *Heidelberg Catechism*, the Decalogue is the basis of a Christian communal code, so that *usus politicus* and *tertius usus* virtually coincide.[16]

In connection with both the political and the moral use of law, the Decalogue constitutes the principle of order for handling ethical questions. So, for example, *de magistratu politico* is discussed under the Fourth Commandment, the acceptance of the death penalty for thieves is dicussed under the Fifth Commandment and so on. In a content-related way, works pleasing to God correspond to the Decalogue, and to the domestic code in the New Testament, the instruction for members of the family (*Haustafel*). Here the connection of *lex naturalis* with the emerging *tertius usus legis* tends towards a moralizing interpretation of Christian status on the basis of the law, which is strange for Luther.

Pietism

During the period of Pietism the question of a 'merciful God' (the question of justification) shifts to the question of the right way of life in rebirth

---

16. John Calvin, *Unterricht in der christlichen Religion. Institutio christianae religionis* (ed. M. Freudenberg; Neukirchen–Vluyn: Neukirchener Verlag, 2008), II, 7, 13.

and sanctification. Rebirth means a realized participation in the divine nature; and sanctification signifies the consequences of that. It follows a specific 'order of salvation', understood in a rationalistic sense.[17] It is naturally and rationally transparent that faith comes before good works. The dialectic that corresponds to the Lutheran *simul* is thereby cancelled. Rebirth has to correspond to the moral conduct of the *justus*, the justified, and the character of that conduct is described in the Decalogue and the *Haustafel*. The Decalogue offers guidance for life in the world and at the same time for the realization of rebirth. Consequentially, the *triplex usus* of the understanding of the Decalogue takes precedence. Accordingly the dialectic of law, the Lutheran *simul*, is required once again. The *pietas* itself takes over the role of law. The gospel runs into the danger of itself becoming a law, the law of faith. As a consequence, the *tertius usus* attains a preferential status.

Enlightenment

So the ground is prepared for the Enlightenment, which leaves faith to be absorbed into an ethical attitude. The arrangement of the material in the catechisms of the Enlightenment is free. In the revised versions deontology plays an essential role, taking the place of the Decalogue. The Decalogue becomes the object of hard critique. As Jewish law, it is considered irrelevant for Christians. It is by no means qualified to be a compendium of Christian morality.[18] For Christians only the natural law is in force (which sometimes coincides with the Decalogue) and, on the other hand, the law of Christ. The instructions in the Decalogue are obligatory only as far as they are located in rationality and in the nature of things. Humans love the law, because it corresponds to their nature.[19] This disposition towards and love of the Commandments is given by the 'religion of Jesus Christ'. By its rejection of the subordination of human actions under the First Commandment, sin becomes pure immorality. Obligations are a proper way to attain grace, but the prohibitions of the Decalogue are not. Rather, the positive behaviour of humans has to be emphasized, and the imagination must be stimulated in that direction.

The moralizing concept of faith, together with the rejection of the *simul peccator et justus*, leads to a consistent, unbroken understanding of law.

---

17. J.J. Rambach, *Der wohl-informirte Catechet* (Jena: Johann Felic Beilcke, 1722), p. 66.

18. C.G. Salzmann, J.B. Basedow *et al.*

19. J.G. Herder, *Luthers Katechismus mit einer katechetischen Erklärung zum Gebrauch der Schulen. Neue Auflage für die protestantischen Schulen im Großherzogthum Würzburg* (Würzburg: Stahel, 1809), p. 41.

The *usus elenchthicus* does not play a role any longer. Law and gospel find the same level. The rationalist theologians turn the gospel itself into law: 'You have to believe'. The immediate parenetic reference leads to the concretization of the Commandments. The completion of duties is as typical for the Enlightenment as the completion of doctrine is for orthodoxy. It is proposed to look back on each day in the evening with regard to the Commandments. A miniature doctrine of education can be accommodated within the Fourth Commandment. The prohibition against killing is considered with regard to animals. With the Seventh Commandment, a catalogue of direct and indirect interventions on the property right is given.[20]

The Nineteenth Century

The nineteenth century is characterized by efforts towards restoration. Initially, there is the reclamation of the Decalogue. Besides Christology, it is one of the areas where the period of Enlightenment most affected the substance of catechisms. The total claim of the First Commandment wins out again. From the First Commandment onwards, the honour of God is seen as the leading idea of the Decalogue. Thereby pure moralism is brought to an end.

Against this background, Lutheranism begins a period of renewed self-reflection. The dialectic in Luther's thinking is recognized. However, the vast majority of authors continue to teach the triple use of law, explicitly under the emerging terms of *Spiegel, Riegel, Zügel*, that is, 'mirror, bolt, reins'.

With the return to the original sense of the Decalogue begins the criticism of Luther's free treatment of the wording of the Old Testament. Above all, it is assumed that the prohibition of images cannot be given up. As originally, the last two commandments coincide again. Occasionally someone argues against the address, because it is missing from Luther's original text, but commonly it is accepted as a meaningful amplification and understood in the sense of promise. The explanation of the Christian character of the commandments as opposed to the Jewish, and of their enlightened, reasonable character, are seen as the main task of the exposition of the Decalogue. The disciples of the educationalist Friedrich Johann Herbart subordinate the catechism totally to the biblical story. The Decalogue, then, has its legitimate location within the theophany at Mount Sinai.

Prussia's attempts to achieve a union between the Lutheran and Reformed Churches leads to a comparison between the *Small Catechism* and *Heidelberg*

---

20. J.L. Parisius, *Materialien zu Katechisation nach Anleitung des Katechismus Luthers* (Magdeburg: Keil, 1806), pp. 58, 122, 139, 161.

Catechism.²¹ This shows that the *Heidelberg Catechism* includes more theology, and the *Small Catechism* more private piety.²² Whereas the *Heidelberg Catechism* has a systematic character, the *Small Catechism* tends to be more personal. The aim is to combine both catechisms.²³ In general, the Reformed enumeration of the Commandments is adopted.²⁴ At the same time, the opinion prevails that the catechism has to remain in force confessionally, 'because the truths of the gospel cannot be taught otherwise than through denominations'.²⁵ The two versions are neither interchangeable nor transferable.

Neo-Lutheranism first comes to prominence in the shape of the 'Erlanger Theology' and emphasizes, as the Herbartians do, the historical place of the Decalogue within the salvific history of the Old Testament, but newly understood as part of Christian salvific history. A few authors assert that the address to the people of Israel must be transferred to Christianity, and that everything concerning historical circumstances has been rightly eliminated by Luther.

The Neo-Kantian Albrecht Ritschl combines the religious aspect with the ethical one in his central expression, 'kingdom of God'. The motto is 'ethics contra metaphysics'. With the shift of the main emphasis from dogmatics to ethics, retaining the early Christian symbols in the Protestant Church is ultimately considered unProtestant and insincere.²⁶ The accusatory function of the law is therefore no longer tenable. The understanding of law is pushed in a new direction. It is not the insight that God's will is impossible to fulfil, but the inner perception of Jesus that leads to the transformation of humans.²⁷ The Decalogue is renounced in favour of developing Protestant ethics solely from the life of Jesus, or by stressing the 'Christian' interpretation of the Decalogue in the Sermon on the Mount.

---

21. J.L. Ewald, *Entwurf eines christlichen Religionsunterrichts für die Jugend in gebildeten Ständen* (Hannover: Christian Ritscher, 1793).

22. J.L. Ewald, *Etwas über Catechismus überhaupt, über Ursins und Luthers Catechismen insbesondere, und über Vereinigung beider evangelischer Confessionen* (Heidelberg: Mohr, 1816), p. 47.

23. J.C. Augusti, *Versuch einer historisch-kritischen Einleitung in die beyden Haupt-Katechismen der evangelischen Kirche* (Elberfeld: Büschlersche, 1824).

24. R. Stier, 'Probe eines verbesserten Lutherischen Katechismus', *Evangelische Kirchenzeitung* 14 (1834).

25. H. Seebold, *Dr Martin Luthers Kleiner Katechismus, ausführlich erklärt in Fragen und Antworten und mit Zeugnissen der hl. Schrift und Liedversen versehen* (Einbeck, 1850), p. x.

26. J. Berndt, *Methodik des Unterrichts in der evangelischen Religion* (Leipzig: Teubner, 1909), p. 61.

27. G. von Roden, 'Ein Wort zur Katechismus-Frage', in G. Schöppa (ed.), *Pädagogische Blätter für Lehrerbildung und Lehrerbildungsanstalten*, XVIII (Gotha: Thienemann, 2nd edn, 1890), p. 142.

The Present

The anniversary year of 1929 brings forth a number of historical studies.[28] In research on Luther,[29] insights into the inner dialectic of Luther's thinking prevail, as demonstrated above. The differentiation between law and commandment attempts to do justice to the dual function, political and moral, of the Decalogue, the *usus politicus* and the *tertius usus*. Great importance is attributed to the all-encompassing significance of the First Commandment and the indicative character of the form of address.

These insights connected with Old Testament research lead to a consolidation by comparing the Israelite understanding of the Decalogue with the parenesis of the New Testament.[30] The old misunderstanding that, according to the Old Testament, observing the law is a precondition for relationship with God, is excluded by Luther's prior understanding that God makes his demands as one who has already proved himself as the God of liberation. In his self-revelation, 'I am Yahweh, your God', he shows his character from the beginning, according to which the liberation from Egypt is envisioned as the fundamental saving act of God for Israel, and which makes the Decalogue the 'primary confession of Israel'.[31] Through the Commandments, territory and order of life are guaranteed.[32] This comes closer to the ideas of Calvin, not least under the influence of Karl Barth, the most important Reformed theologian of the twentieth century for this theological discussion.

Since the sixties, the structure of society has changed. Religious education is no longer seen as founded on the Church alone, but also on its extra-ecclesial, social function. As a result, problem-orientated instruction becomes more important than the transfer of traditional ecclesiastical knowledge. Therefore the Decalogue in religious education is no longer the object of Christian doctrine, but is now connected in a narrative sense with the history of Israel (the Exodus tradition), or is seen as a example for an ethical motto ('Being free because there are rules'), as a guide for a Christian conduct of life, or as a selective impulse for certain ethical themes.

There is a considerable discrepancy between the importance of the Decalogue in history and the contemporary loss of historical consciousness. It

---

28. J. Meyer, F. Cohrs, J.M. Reu, A. Albrecht.

29. At first the Scandinavians (L. Haikola, A. Siirala, L. Pinomaa, O. Modalsli *et al.*), but also German authors such as W. Joest, A. Peters and G. Ebeling.

30. G. von Rad, H. Reventlow.

31. M. Noth.

32. E. Steinwand, *Der Heilsweg. Arbeitshilfen für die Darlegung der Heilsgeschichte in der christlichen Unterweisung* (Göttingen: Vandenhoeck & Ruprecht, 1949), pp. 35, 57; H. Girgensohn, *Katechismusauslegung 'Was zum Christsein zu wissen notwendig ist'* (Witten: Luther-Verlag, 1956), pp. 23f.

would be interesting to study to what extent the moral conceptions existing today are consciously or unconsciously influenced by the Decalogue, to what extent the former religious socialization still produces an after-effect, and to what extent, beyond moral common sense ('one doesn't act like that'), the transcendent foundation of morality still plays a role. In doing so, one would think, for example, about the ethical committees of governments, or certain institutions or movements (the 'peace movement'), and on the other hand about the attitudes of ordinary people.

If L. Kohlberg's research on the development of moral judgment in children and adults at its height inspires the question, 'Why be moral at all?', then this indicates the point at which moral and religious thinking are related. The obligatory character of moral principles relates to the question of human responsibility and the 'before whom' of that responsibility. How to mediate the Decalogue anew as a religious or transcendent basis for ethics under current social conditions is an important task for practical theology and religious education.

The Decalogue and the Moral Manual Tradition: From Trent to Vatican II

James F. Keenan

In the history of moral theology, the Decalogue becomes the central organizing principle for all moral teaching from the end of the sixteenth century until the middle of the twentieth century. This is the period that begins as textbooks were first developed for the training of priests. As an outgrowth of the mandates of the Council of Trent, these textbooks were first *summaries of cases of consciences* that later evolved into the *moral manuals*. In this essay I will examine two major works that effectively mark the beginning and the end of this period of more than three centuries. But, in order to appreciate this period, we should first consider a very brief look at the centuries prior to it.

Summa confessorum *and* Summa theologiae

From the twelfth to the fifteenth century, moral theology operated on two tracks. First there was the instruction for priests for the pastoral practice of absolving sins and giving penances. This track actually started much earlier, around the sixth century, with the *penitential manuals*, first used in Ireland and eventually appearing throughout Europe. They were called 'penitential' because they helped abbots and abbesses to assign fixed penances for sinful acts.

These manuals were fairly brief and very local, inasmuch as they dealt with sins committed for the most part by those few regional Christians who confessed: monks, nuns, clerics, bishops and occasionally devout nobility. They used the tradition of the seven vices or deadly sins to categorize the sins and penances.[1]

In 1215 Pope Innocent III imposed on Western Christendom the 'Easter Duty', that is, the obligation to receive Communion at least once a year during Easter. To fulfill this obligation, Christians had to be in the 'state of grace', and therefore each one had to confess their sins annually so as to fulfill their duty.

---

1. John T. McNeill and Helen M. Gamer (eds.), *Medieval Handbooks of Penance* (New York: Columbia University Press, 1990).

Not only did the laity now have to learn how to confess their sins, the clergy had to learn how to hear them. Moreover, since the sins of monks and nuns tended to focus on their vows and religious practices, and were generally less complex than those of people with families and businesses, the penitential manuals became very inadequate for this much larger and more diverse group of sinners. In the thirteenth century, the much more extensive *Summa confessorum* were published and, like the manuals before them, they were organized around the seven deadly sins.[2]

At the same time, for an elite group of religious and clerics there developed the intellectual track of theology known as scholasticism. These theologians (Albert the Great, Thomas Aquinas, Bonaventure, Duns Scotus and William of Ockham, to name a few) taught at the universities recently established (think here of Oxford, Bologna, Padua, Paris). Eventually, they gathered their teachings together in tomes known as the *Summae theologiae*.

In sum, from the twelfth to the end of the fifteenth century, there were two very different tracks in moral theology: the practical, pastoral and very specific *Summa confessorum* and the highly academic *Summa theologiae*. The genius of the later *moral manuals* is that they merged these two tracks together: the foundational first half of the manuals was developed out of the academic *summae* and the specific material for determining what belonged to sin and what did not came, in the second half, from the confessional *summae*.

In the sixteenth century, Europe was bent on enormous expansionism both in the Americas and in the East. Coupled with this was the religious upheaval throughout the continent. For reasons too many to explain here, a method known as 'high casuistry' developed. For nearly one hundred years, moralists reinvestigated nearly every moral question using inductive, analogical reasoning: every form of moneyed activity, questions of lying, property, dueling, governance, war, international law, temporal authority and even the killing of tyrants. Every type of case was reconsidered, from abortion to the end of life.[3]

---

2. John Mahoney, 'The Influence of Auricular Confession', in *The Making of Moral Theology* (Oxford: Clarendon Press, 1987), pp. 1-36. On this history, see James Dallen, *The Reconciling Community* (New York: Pueblo, 1986); Bernhard Poschmann, *Penance and the Anointing of the Sick* (trans. Francis Courtney; New York: Herder & Herder, 1964).

3. Albert Jonsen and Stephen Toulmin, *The Abuse of Casuistry* (Berkeley: University of California Press, 1988); James Keenan and Thomas Shannon (eds.), *The Context of Casuistry* (Washington, DC: Georgetown University Press, 1995); James Keenan, 'Casuistry', in Hans Hillerbrand (ed.), *Oxford Encyclopedia of the Reformation* (New York: Oxford University Press, 1996), pp. 272-74. For a review of the literature, see Keenan, 'The Return of Casuistry', *TS* 57 (1996), pp. 123-39. On the evolution of casuistry and the institution of confession, see Miriam Turrini, *La coscienza e le leggi.*

By the end of the sixteenth century, Europeans were exhausted with this high casuistry. Around 1590, moral theologians, instead of entertaining arguments for new cases, began assembling the resolved cases into summary statements: the latter became known as the *Summae casuum conscientiae*, the summaries of the cases of consciences. These *summae* eventually became the 'textbook' material for the seminaries that the Council of Trent had mandated (1545–63). They later developed into sophisticated textbooks, the *moral manuals*, which began appearing in the eighteenth century.[4]

A major shift happens in the organization of the summaries of cases of consciences. The cases were no longer organized according to the seven vices, but now according to the Decalogue. This transition first occurred in the fifteenth century in the newly minted catechisms that appeared as books of doctrinal and moral instruction for home and parish, whether Catholic or Protestant, whether produced by Erasmus, Luther, Calvin or even the Council of Trent.

The appeal of the Decalogue was strong. First, unlike the seven deadly sins, the Commandments claimed divine sanction: they and not the seven deadly sins appeared in revelation. Second, they were a solid pedagogical tool that resisted embellishment. The seven vices afforded the medieval mind the opportunity to expand and compound each vice into a multitude of sins and fellow vices. The Commandments, as a Scriptural text, needed no such expansion. They simply needed explanation. Third, unlike the vices, they offered not only negative prohibitions but also positive prescriptions. Finally, with the possible exception of pride, the vices were primarily offensive to human life; the Commandments specified prescriptions and prohibitions regarding our responsibilities toward God and humanity. By the time the *Catechism of the Council of Trent* appeared in 1566, the tradition of the Decalogue as the organizing framework for moral instruction in the Church was settled.[5]

Morale e diritto nei testi per la confessione della prima Età moderna (Bologna: Società editrice il Mulino, 1991).

4. James Keenan, 'Was William Perkins' *Whole Treatise of Cases of Consciences* Casuistry? Hermeneutics and British Practical Divinity', in Harald E. Braun and Edward Vallance (eds.), *Contexts of Conscience in Early Modern Europe: 1500–1700* (New York: Palgrave, 2004), pp. 17-31; Keenan, 'The Birth of Jesuit Casuistry: *Summa casuum conscientiae, sive de instructione sacerdotum, libri septem* by Francesco de Toledo (1532–1596)', in Thomas McCoog (ed.), *The Mercurian Project: Forming Jesuit Culture, 1573–1580* (Rome: Institutum Historicum Societatis Iesu, 2004), pp. 461-82.

5. See, for instance, Thomas Tentler, *Sin and Confession on the Eve of the Reformation* (Princeton, NJ: Princeton University Press, 1977); John Bossy, 'Seven Sins into Ten Commandments', in Edmund Leites (ed.), *Conscience and Casuistry in Early Modern Europe* (New York: Cambridge University Press, 1988), pp. 214-34.

The First Text: Francisco de Toledo's Summa casuum conscientiae

The *Summa casuum conscientiae sive de instructione sacerdotum, libri septem* by Francisco de Toledo (1532–1596) is one of the first Jesuit texts of casuistry and, arguably, one of the first textbooks of moral theology.[6]

In it we find a striking concern for the social conduct of Christians in the institutional world. Unlike the penitential and confessional manuals that focused more on the individual actions of persons who violated one of the seven deadly sins, by excessive drinking or eating, by lying to another, or by being envious of another's estate, Toledo's sins are much more concerned with behavior within institutional structures: moneylending, witnessing in a court of law, honoring one's bishop, etc.

Toledo's *Summa casuum conscientiae* developed while he was teaching theology at the Roman College from 1562 to 1569. In those years he lectured on God and the Trinity, grace, the sacraments, the Incarnation, the virtues and the beatitudes. He also developed the reputation of being one of the greatest exegetes of his time as well as a respected commentator on Aristotle.[7] During this same time, he lectured on the priesthood, the administration of sacraments, the Decalogue as it was used for the hearing of confession and, finally, the sacrament of marriage. These latter lectures were the material for the *Summa casuum*. Copies of these lectures, as well as students' notes, were in circulation years after his teaching. Eventually they were published posthumously in 1598,[8] among the first of a series of Jesuit works on cases of consciences that began to appear in the 1590s.[9]

After his teaching in 1569, Pope Pius V made Toledo preacher of the papal court and then theologian of the Sacred Penitentiary and the Roman Inquisition, and consultor to several Roman Congregations. In time, he served seven popes: Pius V, Gregory XIII, Sixtus V, Urban VII, Gregory XIV, Innocent IX and Clement VIII. He was made cardinal in 1593, the first

---

6. Francisco de Toledo, *Summa casuum conscientiae sive de instructione sacerdotum, libri septem* (Constance: Nicolaus Kalt, 1600).

7. Francisco J. Rodriguez Molero, 'Toledo, François de', in Marcel Viller (ed.), *Dictionnaire de spiritualité ascétique et mystique, doctrine et histoire* (Paris: G. Beauchesne et ses fils, 1932–), XV, pp. 1013-18; G. Van Ackeren, 'Toledo, Francisco de', in *New Catholic Encyclopedia* (New York: McGraw-Hill, 1967), pp. 187-88; Feliciano Cereceda, 'En el cuarto centenario del nacimiento del P. Francisco Toledo', *Estudios eclesiásticos* 13 (1934), pp. 90-108.

8. John O'Malley, *The First Jesuits* (Cambridge, MA: Harvard University Press, 1995), p. 147. Also Luis Gómez Hellín, 'Toledo, lector de filosofía y teología en el Colegio Romano', *Archivo teologico granadino* 3 (1940), pp. 7-18.

9. Giancarlo Angelozzi, 'L'insegnamento dei casi di coscienza nella practica educativa della Compagnia di Gesù', in Gian Carlo Brizzi (ed.), *La 'Ratio Studiorum': Modelli culturali e pratiche educative dei Gesuiti in Italia tra Cinque e Seicento* (Rome: Bulzoni Editore, 1981), pp. 121-62.

Jesuit to receive that honor. Not surprisingly, then, his work was a major success,[10] going through 72 editions and multitudinous translations, remaining in print until 1716.[11]

Toledo's *Summa casuum conscientiae* is divided into seven books: on priesthood; the administration of the sacraments; the practice of confession; the first three Commandments; the remaining seven; the six precepts of the Church; and matrimony.

The first book answered the question, 'What is a priest?' Toledo underlined the unique dignity of priests and highlighted the need for critical attention to the heavy responsibilities expected from those acting on God's commission. Toward this end, he began with a definition that he subsequently parsed throughout the first chapter: a priest is a man commissioned by divine authority, communicated through specific persons, for the true worship of God.[12] For this reason, the priest was the servant of no creature. Kings and princes had various attendants, but only God had priests and priests served only God.[13]

Toledo asked: who communicated the divine authority? He established a causal chain of commissions: the divine power was in Christ the Lord, from whom the apostles derived their authority; they in turn were the source of episcopal authority. Through this extension of power, priests were created.

Power was an overriding concern for Toledo: by power the priest is ordained; through power priests exercised their ministry. In Chapter 3 he discussed the twofold power of the priesthood: the power of orders and of jurisdiction. The former was the power to confect the body of Christ and to administer the other sacraments. The latter was the power of rendering judgment on the excommunicated, granting dispensations, conferring indulgences and applying the laws of the Church. The 35 chapters of this first book were an elaboration on these institutional, jurisdictional powers.

The second book was on the sacramental ministry of the priest. By this point, Toledo has established the seriousness of the priestly vocation. Priests reading this work would probably have been overwhelmed by the

---

10. Phillip Schmitz, 'Kasuistik: Ein wiederentdecktes Kapitel der Jesuitenmoral', *Theologie und Philosophie* 67 (1992), pp. 29-59.

11. Feliciano Cereceda, 'Tolet, François', in Bernard Loth and Albert Michel (eds.), *Dictionnaire de théologie catholique* (Paris: Letouzey & Ané, 1953–72) XV, pp. 1223-25.

12. Toledo, *Summa*, fol. 1: 'Est autem Sacerdos, Vir, Dei veri cultui, autoritate divina, determinatis personis concessa, firmiter deputatus'.

13. Toledo, *Summa*, fol. 1: 'Secunda pars est; *cultui Dei deputatus*... Unde sit quod nulla creatura Sacerdotes habeat sibi ministros. Habent quidem reges & principes, oeconomos, cubicularios, villicos, iudices, & alios huiusmodi: solus Deus Sacerdotes habet. Unde sibi Sacerdotes facere, ac sacrificium, precesque ab eis petere, est se Deum facere.'

onerous responsibility of their vocation and would want to read further so as to find the directions about how wisely and prudently to exercise the power that they have. In short, rather quickly Toledo established that he was a man of great authority who was willing wisely to mentor fellow priests who needed to be aware of the power that they were commissioned to exercise.

Book 2 basically treated the power of orders for the Mass, the divine office and the administration of the sacraments. Here, Toledo has developed a rather significant agenda: priesthood was effectively an institutional position to determine the law and administer the sacraments. Ministerial functions such as preaching, counseling and other services were not even mentioned.

In this context, the central focus became the administration of the sacrament of penance. Wisdom and prudence in exercising the power to absolve was the most urgent concern for sixteenth-century priests. No other sacrament or task scrutinized the complex personal matter of human conduct; no other sacrament or task so definitively relied on the particular skills and judgment of priests; and, no other sacrament or task so directly related to the salvation of an individual soul. In sum, no other divine action was so vulnerable to the fallibility of human judgment as absolution, and yet no other divine activity was as significant as that which absolved a person from eternal damnation. Yet, Toledo added a new feature to the confessional: by focusing the matter of sin on decidedly institutional concerns, he basically outlined what social structures were morally permitted and what were sinful. He brought the jurisdiction of the confessional into the world of commerce.

Book 3 opened with a definition of sin as any voluntary withdrawal from divine rule or law.[14] Sin was not some matter or body or positive entity but rather a separation, a defect.[15] The entire book, consisting of 21 chapters, concerned general issues related to the administration of the sacrament: the role of the confessor, the power to absolve, the terms of contrition, determining the matter that ought to be confessed, etc.

The fifteenth chapter was entitled 'The Wisdom of the Confessor', but its content was simply six issues that confessors had to know: the difference between mortal and venial sins; the significance of circumstances; those cases that one cannot absolve; the task of restitution; the liceity of contracts; and impediments.

---

14. Toledo, *Summa*, book III, fol. 140, 'peccatum est recessus a regula divina voluntarius'.

15. Toledo, *Summa*, book III, fol. 140, 'Prima est, Recessus, id est, quaedam deviatio, & separatio, ab aliquo stabili principio. Peccatum enim est, non aliqua substantia, aut corpus, aut entitas positiva, sed quaedam separatio, quidam defectus.'

Book 4 began with the theological virtues. In Chapter 12 the first precept of the Decalogue appeared. Here Toledo offered some preliminary explanations. First, he divided the ten precepts into two parts, the first three concerning the honor due to God. Second, he highlighted the difficulty in committing mortal sin by focusing on those three causes that diminish the seriousness of sin: lightness of matter, the lack of deliberation or a defect in the full use of reason. If any of these were present then, even if the sin was in its genus or object considered mortal, it became venial.

In Toledo's writings, mortal sin was a 'perfection'. It required not simply the doing of a gravely wrong action, but concomitantly the agent's full knowledge and full consent. The modern reader recognizes this in contemporary literature as well.[16] However, one could argue that Toledo and others have at this point changed the tradition considerably. For Aquinas, when people performed gravely wrong actions, for instance, those belonging to the genus of mortal sin, he presumed that to perform such an important act people would have needed consent and knowledge. Aquinas considered an act of such magnitude as, say, blasphemy, as already embodying consent and knowledge. By the sixteenth century that presumption was no longer held. While the thirteenth century placed the burden on the penitents to demonstrate how they could not have had knowledge and consent in doing such an action, the sixteenth century asked the penitent whether *in addition* to the grave act they had *full* knowledge and *full* consent.[17]

A similar 'moral minimalism' appeared in the third preliminary note to the Decalogue. Toledo wrote that the precepts of the Decalogue required, not their perfection, but rather a minimal adherence. People were required to fast; though its perfect end was for the taming of the flesh and the raising of the mind, they were not required to pursue that end. They needed only to perform the act of fasting. If they did not fast when they were required, they must acknowledge their sinfulness. Likewise, they were required not to kill; but though the perfection of that Commandment was to do so out of charity, they were not required to act out of charity. They were simply required not to kill.[18]

---

16. For instance, see Richard Gula, *Reason Informed by Faith: Foundations of Catholic Morality* (Mahwah: Paulist Press, 1989), pp. 108-14.

17. I emphasize the word 'full' because, when reading sixteenth-century texts such as Toledo's, it was precisely that word that helped confessors determine whether the sin was perfect, that is, mortal. For instance, Toledo specifically wrote that full deliberation was necessary for mortal sin; if the deliberation was half-full ('semiplena'), the action was a venial sin. Similarly, if there was a defect in the full use of reason then it was not the perfect use of reason and this too causes a mortal sin to become venial. Clearly, it was much more difficult to commit mortal sin according to the Spanish Jesuit Cardinal at the end of the sixteenth century than it was for the Italian Dominican in the middle of the thirteenth century.

18. Toledo was, however, consistent when he added that the observation of these

In Chapters 13 to 19 he examined actions that were considered as sins against the first Commandment, for example blasphemy and superstition, but here he alerted confessors to note excusing circumstances. For instance, blasphemy could well arise from an angry outburst. The second precept was treated rather briefly (Chapters 20 to 23), reflecting on the liceity of swearing and taking oaths. The third precept appeared in the twenty-fourth chapter and was followed by the book's closing chapter, on excuses concerning failure to heed dominical observance.

In the fifth book, we see Toledo's strong social and institutional concerns. The Fourth Commandment was not only about the honor due parents (Chapter 1), but also the honor due spouses (Chapter 2), bishops (Chapters 3 and 4) and even curates (Chapter 5). The Fifth Commandment, ostensibly about not killing, was predominantly about when one could kill: to defend the faith, the country, a friend, one's neighbor, etc. Similarly, the seventh chapter was about unintentional homicide or indirect killing. The eighth concerned legitimate or extenuating circumstances for killing; the ninth summarized the Commandment, admonishing against being prepared for killing, but then granting instances when such preparation was excusable.

With the Sixth Commandment he addressed simple fornication in the tenth chapter, adultery in the eleventh, and incest and rape in the twelfth (maintaining a strong stance against rape because of its violence). The thirteenth chapter focused on sins against nature. Though he discussed concubines, sodomy and bestiality, for the most part he reflected on masturbation, which according to St Paul (1 Cor. 6.9) caused the loss of heaven. Predictably, after making this assertion, he raised extenuating circumstances.

In terms of the simple number of folios dedicated to the individual Commandments, the Seventh (on stealing) was by far the most considered. While 19 folios were devoted to the Fifth Commandment (on killing) and its exceptions, 18 to the Fourth (on honoring parents), and a mere 12 to the Sixth Commandment (on adultery), 88 folios focused on the Seventh Commandment. Herein were the discussions on usury and related matters. Similarly, the Eighth Commandment (on false witness) consisted of 31 folios and the Ninth Commandment (coveting neighbor's property), a surprising 35 folios. Furthermore, his evident lack of interest in sexual matters is affirmed as he dismissed the matter of the Tenth Commandment (coveting the neighbor's wife) by simply stating that it was treated under the Sixth.

Toledo's treatment of the Seventh to the Ninth Commandments concerned social conduct. Rather than being about simple personal, or even private, acts of theft, lying or concupiscence, their subject matter was about the structures of relationships in civil and ecclesiastical societies. In particular

---

minimal requirements did not mean that these actions were meritorious. On the contrary, unless they were done out of charity, there was no merit to the actions.

they considered the relevance of financial and testimonial transactions in these societies.

With the Seventh Commandment, he examined the fundamental structures of financial institutions. Beginning with two chapters (15–16) on the meaning of the Seventh Commandment, he then spent eleven chapters (17–27) on restitution, that is, the social repair of an act of theft. Then he turned to usury and stipulated five conditions without which an action was not usury. After four chapters (28–31) on usury, he then discussed mutual compensation (*lucrum in mutuo*) for loans in three chapters (32–34), restitution of gains accrued from usury in three chapters (35–37) and the innovative public pawnshops turned commercial banks endorsed by the Franciscans (*de monte Pietatis*) in four chapters (38–41). His longest section (Chapters 42–49) was dedicated to annuities ('*census*'), and he concluded his comments on the Seventh Commandment with credit agencies (*cambium*) in Chapters 50–55.

After these chapters, the Eighth Commandment (on false witness) was basically about duties in a court of law. A chapter was dedicated to each of the different functionaries in the court: the accused, the state, witnesses, advocates, notaries and procurators. The final chapters were about what would constitute detraction.

Though Toledo described the Ninth Commandment as about the social impact of avarice, actually it was about the financial responsibilities of ecclesiastics. After extensive comments in three chapters (72–75) on stipends, he turned to six chapters (76–81) on benefices. Here, as elsewhere, we see him exploring what was specifically prohibited. He concluded the fifth book with two chapters (82–83) on pensions and ten (84–93) on simony.

An in-depth look at one of these concerns will help us to see how conscious Toledo was of the social nature of our licit and illicit activities. In Chapter 80 he asked whether it was licit to have several benefices at the same time. He gave six reasons why multiple benefices were in fact wrong. For instance, since it was better to have a specific minister for each location, multiple benefices deprived God of the worship due God; similarly, they deprived the Church of its ministers. After six arguments, he concluded that there was no doubt that, generally speaking, one ought not to possess several benefices. He turned in Chapter 81 to the exceptions. He noted multiple cases both before and after the Council of Trent in which it was ruled that, in certain instances, multiple benefices were permitted. He then explained that one must exercise great caution here. First, the person should act out of conscience and for the love of God. Second, the person must have a dispensation and this must be either for the good (*in utilitatem*) or the necessity of the Church. If the dispensation was not at least for the good of the Church, then it was neither a good dispensation, nor could the agent claim to be acting out of the love of God. Neither conscience nor law alone were sufficient for this dispensation. For Toledo, the social good was the necessary warrant for any exceptions to any practice that supports the common good.

In the sixth book, 51 folios in length, he explained the precepts of the Church. The seventh book was on matrimony. Of its 21 Chapters, 13 (Chapters 3–15) were on impediments and four (Chapters 18–21) were on the many sins that occur in the use of marital prerogatives. At the end of the work we find 60 folios of a sophisticated topical index.

When we see Toledo's concern for social matters in these closing commandments, we realize that the self-conscious power we saw at the beginning of this work was also social. The priest had a social function: to lead the people in giving God justice, which was the virtue of religion. He served no one but God. When read in this context, the previous Commandments also take on significant social meaning. The Fourth Commandment, for instance, was not about individual children's obedience to their parents, but rather about the disposition towards honor that ought to arise from children to parents, from spouses to one another, and from the laity to their pastors and bishops. The Fourth Commandment was not primarily, according to Toledo, about a private disposition, but rather about a social disposition of respect for familial and ecclesial authority. Similarly, the exceptions to the Fifth Commandment were not about private jealousies that lead to violent acts, but about acts of homicide that might be necessary for social defense.

When we move three hundred years forward we see that, though the institutional and relational issues of moral teaching are still very present in the application of the Decalogue, there is something terribly disappointing in the tradition. Noteworthy is the fact that when the Decalogue is brought into the moral manual tradition, it is only brought to bear for the use of the confessional, that is, it only concerns matters of sin. None of the positive ways that the Commandments have been used over the centuries in the catechetical tradition are present in this tradition. Moreover, the requirements of the Commandments are minimalistically interpreted. Inevitably little is asked of the Christian believer. Finally, the power of divine authority that Toledo invokes becomes, by the beginning of the twentieth century, little more than the power of ecclesial law. The result is that the judgments of the author tend, at best, to be rather mechanical and legal.

The Second Text: Thomas Slater's Manual for Moral Theology

The *Manual for Moral Theology* (1906) by Thomas Slater (1855–1928) was, for 20 years, the most consulted such manual in English, going through five editions, the last appearing in 1931. The *Manual* was later accompanied by his two-volume work, *Cases of Conscience for English-Speaking*

Countries (1911), and another large compendium, *Questions of Morality* (1915).[19]

At the beginning of the twentieth century, moral manuals appeared for the first time in the vernacular. Slater's *A Manual of Moral Theology* is the first manual in the English language. In the preface, he argued that moral manuals 'are necessary for the Catholic priest to enable him to administer the sacrament of penance and to fulfill his duties'.[20] This duty restricted him from writing on other matters, and so he pled that the manuals 'should not be censured not being what they were never intended to be'.

In the preface, in remarkably stark terms, he described the manuals of moral theology as books of 'moral pathology':

> They are the product of centuries of labor bestowed by able and holy men on the practical problems of Christian ethics. Here however, we must ask the reader to bear in mind that the manuals of moral theology are technical works intended to help the confessor and the parish priest in the discharge of their duties. They are as technical as the text-books of the lawyer and the doctor. They are not intended for edification, nor do they hold up a high ideal of Christian perfection for the imitation of the faithful. They deal with what is of obligation under the pain of sin, they are books of moral pathology.[21]

Slater acknowledged that if anyone was looking to learn how to become a better disciple of Christ, they should look elsewhere: to the manuals of ascetical, devotional or mystical theology, where they would find the 'high ideal of Christian perfection'. 'Moral theology', he added, 'proposes to itself the humbler but still necessary task of defining what is right and wrong in all the practical relations of the Christian life'. He concluded the stunning preface, basically bisecting the natural law's fundamental principle, 'do good and avoid evil'. 'The first step on the right road to conduct is to avoid evil'. By consigning the doing of the good, that is, Christian perfection, to other manuals, Slater held that for morality the natural law has only a singular task: to guide us in avoiding evil.[22]

Slater's *Manual* was classical in form and divided into two parts. The first was two hundred pages long and made up of five 'books': on human acts, conscience, law, sin and the theological virtues. The second part consisted in four books: on the Decalogue, contracts, the commandments of the Church and the specific duties of clergy, religious and 'certain laymen'

---

19. Thomas Slater, *Cases of Conscience for English-Speaking Countries* (New York: Benziger, 1911–12); Slater, *Questions of Morality* (New York: Benziger, 1915).

20. Thomas Slater, *A Manual of Moral Theology for English-Speaking Countries* (London: Benziger Brothers, 1906), p. 6.

21. Slater, *A Manual of Moral Theology*, pp. 5-6.

22. Slater, *A Manual of Moral Theology*, p. 6.

(physicians and those with different roles in the courts). These latter 460 pages focus on fairly institutional issues. Alone, the Decalogue covered 270 pages, with 112 dedicated to the combined Seventh and Tenth Commandments and another 90 to the book of contracts. While 30 pages each were dedicated to the First and Fourth Commandment, a mere 20 covered the Fifth, and 10 each to the Second and Third. Only 16 pages were dedicated to the combined Sixth and Ninth Commandments, with one topic, consummated sins against nature (masturbation, sodomy and bestiality), appearing in Latin, presumably so as not to lead a less educated reader into sin.

Let us consider Slater's exposition of three Commandments. He divided the Fourth Commandment into seven chapters, each basically framed around some issue of authority and subservience: the duties of children to parents, of parents to children and of guardians to children; and the duties between parents, masters and servants, masters and scholars, and rulers and subjects. In the first chapter, he briefly discussed the piety and obedience children owe their parents, stating that the obligation of obedience ceases with the child's emancipation (in England) at 21 years of age. To this he appended a note regarding the different state laws in the United States on the emancipation of a minor.

He began the second chapter with love, piety and emotional and material support. He then specifically mentioned the obligation to breast-feed: a mother 'is bound at least under venial sin to nourish it with her own milk, unless some good reason excuse her'.[23] He quickly turned to education:

> The Church condemns all non-Catholic schools, whether they be heretical and schismatical, or secularist, and she declares that as a general rule no Catholic parent can send his young children to such schools for educational purposes without exposing their faith and morals to serious risk, and therefore committing a grave sin.[24]

He added that only a bishop, and not a priest, could deny the sacraments to parents who act in this regard. Here he cited the Third Plenary Council of Baltimore (9 November–7 December 1884), and then argued that if a bishop (as happened in St Louis) expressly prohibited all parents in his diocese from sending their children to non-Catholic schools, then no priest might absolve such parents if they continued to send their children.[25]

Later, he turned to university education, noted that the Holy See allowed English Catholics to attend Oxford and Cambridge, but granted no analogous permission in the United States; the Third Plenary Council was not

---

23. Slater, *A Manual of Moral Theology*, p. 274.
24. Slater, *A Manual of Moral Theology*, pp. 275-76.
25. Slater, *A Manual of Moral Theology*, pp. 276-77.

at all in favor of such a policy.²⁶ Clearly, no other topic was as extensively parsed by Slater as this one, simply because on this matter the Holy See and the specific Episcopal offices made their decisions law.

In the third chapter he turned to matters of custody; for these, national policies from England and United States were invoked. The fourth chapter, only two pages, concerned duties between husband and wife. A wife is to be subject and obedient to, but not a slave or servant of, her husband; if she shows great contempt for him and neglects his commands, she sins grievously. Likewise, he is bound by justice and piety to support her and sins grievously if he treats her with harshness or neglect. Slater concluded: 'the wife would not be guilty of sin if she took from her husband without his knowledge what was necessary for decent support of family'.²⁷

Leo XIII's *Rerum novarum* (15 May 1891) was invoked five times in the fifth chapter, and in most instances at length, basically stipulating the duties of employers to employees on just working conditions, respectful treatment and fair wages.²⁸ The sixth chapter was a mere two hundred words and the seventh basically asserted the connection between a local authority and divine right.

On the Fifth Commandment, Slater treated six issues: suicide, capital punishment, justifiable homicide, killing the innocent, war and dueling. Throughout, he appealed to applications of the principle of double effect. In the first chapter, he established that since 'God is the Author of life and death, He has reserved the ownership of human life to Himself...we have not the free disposal of our lives'. Thus suicide, which has one's death as 'the direct and immediate object of the will', was prohibited,²⁹ but that did not mean that we cannot do something that could cause our own death. He applied the principle of double effect to the case of the captain of a ship who, during war, fears that his ship will be seized and become a danger to his own country and destroys it, knowing that he and his crew will lose their lives. The captain 'does not intend the destruction of human life; the immediate effect of his action is to prevent the ship from falling into the enemy's hands. The public advantage counterbalances the loss.'³⁰

With his usual economy, in one single paragraph Slater differentiated suicide from foregoing extraordinary means to preserve one's life. He gave two instances of such means: a painful and costly operation, and the situation of someone who would die if he were to spend the winter in England; in this case he concluded, he 'is not bound to expatriate himself and go and live in a milder climate'.³¹

26. Slater, *A Manual of Moral Theology*, pp. 277-81 (279).
27. Slater, *A Manual of Moral Theology*, p. 288.
28. Slater, *A Manual of Moral Theology*, pp. 289-95.
29. Slater, *A Manual of Moral Theology*, p. 302.
30. Slater, *A Manual of Moral Theology*, p. 303.
31. Slater, *A Manual of Moral Theology*, p. 304.

He justified capital punishment with arguments from Scripture, including Rom. 13.4, and from 'natural reason'. He began the chapter on justifiable homicide stating simply, 'In defense of my own life from unjust attack I may use whatever violence is necessary and even to the length of killing the aggressor'. He then added that no one should use greater force than necessary, nor act out of vengeance or anticipation of attack. Under these limitations, one may use such violence to defend limbs, property (as long as it is of considerable amount) and chastity. He noted that some theologians once held that one could commit justifiable homicide over an insult, but noted that Popes Alexander VII and Innocent XI condemned these positions.[32]

On killing the innocent, he noted that not even the good of the State makes it right to take an innocent life, though he invoked the principle of double effect to demonstrate the liceity of civilian deaths in an attack on a 'beleaguered town'. He declared the direct procuring of abortion as an intrinsic evil, but noted that a pregnant woman may appropriate a life-saving means even if that means were indirectly to cause the fetus's death. Finally he argued against the direct killing of a fetus to save the mother's life, 'even if otherwise both child and mother were certain to die'. His position is historically interesting inasmuch as it had been held until the end of the nineteenth century that a woman could defend herself against a fetus that was threatening her life.[33]

While in three pages he invoked several popes and the Council of Trent to demonstrate the unequivocal wrongness of dueling, in four pages he upheld the certain teaching of Catholic theology on just war.

Finally the Sixth and Ninth Commandments (on adultery and on coveting the neighbor's wife) were treated in four chapters: on the nature of impurity, consummated sins of impurity, consummated sins against nature and non-consummated acts of impurity. He began the first chapter: 'The means devised by God for the preservation and increase of the human race is the union of the sexes, which has as its primary object, the procreation of children'. He upheld the teaching that there was no parvity of moral matter concerning sins of impurity: 'all sins of impurity of whatever kind or species are of themselves mortal'.[34] He invoked 1 Cor. 6.9-10, Gal. 5.19 and Mt. 5.28.

Under the consummated sins of impurity he treated in six paragraphs the following sins: fornication, adultery, incest, criminal assault, rape and sacrilege. The last five violate other virtues as well. On the consummated

---

32. Slater, *A Manual of Moral Theology*, pp. 308-309.

33. John Connery, *Abortion: The Development of the Roman Catholic Perspective* (Chicago: Loyola University Press, 1977); John T. Noonan, Jr, 'An Almost Absolute Value in History', in his *The Morality of Abortion: Legal and Historical Perspectives* (Cambridge, MA: Harvard University Press, 1970).

34. Patrick Boyle, *Parvitas Materiae in Sexto in Contemporary Catholic Thought* (Lanham, MD: University Press of America, 1987); James Brundage, *Law, Sex and Christian Society in Medieval Europe* (Chicago: University of Chicago Press, 1987).

sins against nature, he treated, in Latin, masturbation, sodomy and bestiality. Clearly the parsing of the first sin evidenced widespread pastoral anxiety. Sadly, in the final chapter he treated touching, kissing and embracing as sins.

Conclusion

Though many commenting on the tradition of the moral manuals have often held that they were fixated on sexual sins and private peccadillos, our review shows that, on the contrary, the tradition used the Decalogue to shape the moral contours of social and institutional practices. Indeed, much as Moses used the Decalogue to shape the people, the moral theologians of the sixteenth to nineteenth centuries used it for the same social and institutional effect.

However, unlike those who wrote in the catechetical tradition (both Protestant and Catholic), the moralists incorporated the Decalogue into their own vocation which, until the twentieth century, was, as Slater states well, to teach the priest in the confessional what pertains to sin and what does not. That is, the moral theologians never really gave the Decalogue a chance to develop as a form of moral instruction on its own terms.

The entire Decalogue was interpreted by a hermeneutics of simply asking what belongs to mortal sin and what does not. The prescriptions of the Decalogue were only treated when the failure to fulfill the prescriptions pertained to sin. Then those prescriptions, together with the prohibitions, were interpreted almost universally by a pastorally paternalistic minimalism. Tragically, the only area where any rigor appeared was in the Sixth Commandment, admitting no 'parvity of matter' at all.

Catholics were able to live in a moral world which was only concerned about whether they sinned or not. To find out that answer they saw their benevolent confessors. Fortunately many of the laity wanted more than this and turned to the ascetical or devotional manuals that implored Catholics to grow in virtue and to perform corporal and spiritual works of mercy. But here they found no Decalogue.

By the middle of the twentieth century, when moral theologians themselves look to reform their own field, they turn away from the sin manuals and begin to cultivate the life of Christian discipleship through an ethics of virtue. By this time, however, moral theologians show little interest in the Decalogue.[35] Nonetheless, their turn to discipleship and virtue eventually led them back to the Scriptures and therein, in this very year, do we find one of them happily investigating the Decalogue. Now we have a

---

35. James F. Keenan, *A History of Catholic Moral Theology in the Twentieth Century* (New York: Continuum, 2010).

moral theologian giving the Decalogue a chance to be understood in its own terms.[36] It is to be hoped that, this time, we in moral theology will understand what it asks of us.

---

36. Yiu Sing Lúcás Chan, *The Ten Commandments and the Beatitudes: Biblical Studies and Ethics for Real Life* (New York: Rowman & Littlefield, 2012).

The Decalogue in American Catechisms of the Sixteenth Century

Luis Resines

With the discovery of the New World, religious orders, including the Franciscans, Dominicans, Augustinians and later Jesuits, sent their members to America in order to convert and Christianize the inhabitants of the newly discovered lands. As I shall show, the abundance of languages in the first places where the missionaries landed—the Caribbean islands and what is now Mexico—presented a major difficulty for them. As this problem was overcome, catechisms began to appear, some of which have been preserved.

It is very important to note that all the religious who went to America received their formation in Europe, most of them in territories ruled by Spain; and, therefore, when they tried to teach the Christian faith, they did so out of the European mentality in which they were located. It could not be otherwise. At that time, bridging the language gap was felt to be much more important than another factor which seems essential today: inculturation and the accommodation of the Christian message to the indigenous people's world-view.

The missionaries to America were well aware of the usefulness of the printing press, since they had already encountered printed books in Europe. But early written attempts at evangelization had to be in manuscript form, since the first printing press was not installed in Mexico until 1542 (at Juan Pablo's printers, a branch of Juan Cromberger's of Seville, thanks to the intervention of Bishop Juan de Zumárraga).[1] Handwritten catechisms were at risk from imperfections and mistakes in copying; in addition, the small number of copies produced made it uncertain that the person who wrote one (or other friars of his order) would be able to continue the missionary work that had

---

1. There is no certainty about the date when printing presses began to operate in America. The most probable year seems to be 1542. Some printed works were mentioned in 1535 and 1537, but there is no evidence of any surviving copies. The petition made in 1533 by Zumárraga to Charles V for financial resources to set up a printing press and paper mill doesn't mean that these were actually functioning, merely that they were an aspiration; the same can be said about Zumárraga's claim in 1538 that he had works ready to be printed.

been undertaken.² The arrival of the printing press guaranteed an abundance of cheap copies with many fewer mistakes; as there were more, not all of them would be lost, and indeed some have been preserved to this day.

I shall now turn to the Decalogue. It is important to remember that, to a greater or lesser extent, for all the orders involved in missionary work, the Decalogue was essential to the presentation of the Christian faith. It is not enough to speak only of what we must believe (dogma, the Creed), but of what we need to do, and that leads directly to the Decalogue. All catechisms talk about it and include it among their statements. There are no exceptions, except for fragmentary catechisms.

1. *Three Groups of Catechisms*

The catechisms written in America can be divided into three groups.

First group. These catechisms include only the formularies of faith (the Creed, Lord's Prayer, sacraments, prayers, virtues...) and the wording of the Commandments. They are usually brief works, presented as a simple list intended to be learned and repeated by heart. These texts are short, and have no explanations to clarify the meaning of what they say. Someone who learned such a catechism would be able to repeat the statements it contained, but not necessarily understand them. If there were any accompanying explanations, they do not appear in the catechisms of this group. Of the American catechisms I know, those in this group include, in chronological order:

1. Francisco Javier, *Doutrina cristâ*, 1542. Portuguese.
2. Alonso de Molina, *Doctrina christiana breve*, 1546. Spanish, Nahuatl.
3. Pedro de Gante, *Doctrina cristiana en lengua mexicana*, edition of 1553. Nahuatl (Tarascan).
4. Francisco Marroquín, *Catecismo y doctrina cristiana en idioma utlalteco*, 1556. Utlalteco.
5. Pedro de Feria, *Doctrina christiana en lengua castellana y çapoteca*, 1567. Spanish, Zapotec.
6. Juan de la Cruz, *Doctrina christiana en lengua guasteca*, 1571. Guasteco.
7. Luis Zapata de Cárdenas, *Catechismo*, 1576. Spanish.
8. Francisco de Pareja, *Doctrina christiana muy util...*, 1578. Spanish, Nahuatl.

2. It is known, for example, that when Pedro de Gante had achieved some command of the Nahuatl language in the Tarascan dialect, he wrote a *Doctrina cristiana en lengua mexicana* ('Christian Doctrine in the Mexican Language'). As there was no printing press, he sent the manuscript to Antwerp in 1528 so that it could be printed there; later, once a printing press was available, the 1547 second edition was printed in Mexico.

9. Melchor de Vargas, *Doctrina christiana muy útil...*, 1576. Spanish, Nahuatl and Otomí.
10. José de Acosta, *Doctrina christiana y catecismo...*, 1584. Spanish, Quechua and Aymara.
11. Juan de la Plaza, *Doctrina christiana mexicana*, 1585. Spanish, Latin (two versions).
12. Domingo de Nieva, Juan de San Pedro, *Doctrina christiana en lengua española y tagala*, 1593. Spanish, Tagalo.
13. Juan Cobo, *Doctrina christiana en letra y lengua china*, 1593. Chinese.
14. Jerónimo de Oré, *Symbolo catholico indiano*, 1598. Spanish, Quechua and Aymara.

Second group. The second group of catechisms include explanations of the Decalogue as a whole and of each Commandment. These catechisms are not limited to listing the Commandments, but comment on their meaning, on what needs to be done to obey them and on the sins that must be avoided. Some of the catechisms listed below are already included in the first group; this is because they give both the basic formulary and an explanation; some others only have an explanation. This can be very detailed or very brief, but it is why they belong to the second group.

1. Juan de Zumárraga, *Doctrina breve...*, 1543. Spanish.
2. Pedro de Córdoba, *Doctrina christiana para instrucción...*, 1544. Spanish.
3. Juan de Zumárraga, *Doctrina christiana más cierta...*, 1546. Spanish.
4. Pedro de Córdoba, *Doctrina christiana en lengua española y mexicana*, 1548. Spanish, Nahuatl.
5. Pedro de Gante, *Doctrina christiana en lengua mexicana*, 1553. Nahuatl.
6. Pedro de Feria, *Doctrina christiana en lengua castellana y çapoteca*, 1567. Spanish, Zapotec.
7. Juan de la Anunciación, *Doctrina christiana muy cumplida...*, 1575. Spanish, Nahuatl.
8. Dionisio de los Santos, *Breve y muy sumaria institución...*, 1576. Spanish.
9. Alonso de Molina, *Doctrina christiana en lengua mexicana*, 1578. Nahuatl.
10. José de Acosta, *Doctrina christiana y catecismo...*, 1584 (*Catecismo mayor*): Spanish, Quechua and Aymara. Also, in the same work, *Confessionario...*, also *Sermonario*, 1585. Spanish, Quechua and Aymara.
11. Juan de la Plaza, *Doctrina christiana mexicana*, 1585. Spanish, Latin (two versions).

I shall say more about these catechisms after a brief consideration of the third group.

Third group. This consists of a small number of very special pictographic catechisms that use drawing and painting, rather than words, to communicate the faith to the Native Americans. The indigenous people in Mexico had a pictographic system of writing, and the missionaries observed this fact and took advantage of it. Using drawings, they wrote catechisms that connected with the mentality of the people and presented the Christian faith to them. This is a very specific group consisting of about 20 catechisms that are particularly difficult to understand. I have almost completely deciphered eight of them.

2. *Explanations of the Decalogue*

The catechisms that provide explanations of individual Commandments are of particular interest to modern readers. They help us to understand how the missionaries who worked in America explained Christianity, and which aspects of the faith were emphasized in the sixteenth century.

Most of the explanations offered have much in common with those found in catechisms used in Spain and the rest of Europe, and there is no need to repeat them, since they do not add anything new to our reflection. What really matters is material unique to American catechisms, including adaptations to the lives and circumstances of the Native Americans. This gives us a measure of the efforts that the missionaries made.

In a first global consideration of the Decalogue it is possible to see that the Commandments express God's will, and that the fact of having accepted him through baptism means having to do his will. Most of the catechisms present the analysis of the Ten Commandments into two, according to the teaching of Jesus, by way of conclusion. All of them follow the traditional formulations used in the Roman Catholic Church, and do not render the text of Exodus 20. The use of biblical quotations is limited both in the Commandments and generally with respect to the whole teaching of the faith.

In the following examples of explanations of single Commandments, I will concentrate on clear references to the situation of Christianity in America.

2.1. *Other Gods*

Here we have the first and most important problem in the presentation of the Decalogue, as it is inevitable that it must talk about the acceptance of one God. All American peoples and ethnic groups were polytheists, and this situation would not easily be changed by the arrival of the Christian faith. The authors of catechisms could not deal with it passively.

In his *Doctrina breve muy provechosa* ('Brief and Very Helpful Doctrine'), Juan de Zumárraga, bishop of Mexico, speaks of idolatry, superstition and polytheism as being opposed to the First Commandment (fol. 16^{r-v}.). The way in which he presents this refers to classical religion (and not to the situation of America), although what he says would also be valid for America. In talking about sins against the First Commandment he first refers to necromancy (divination by invoking the dead), but without condemning it as rigorously as if he were speaking of idolatry. Moreover he notes that most peoples have sinned in this way, including those of Mexico, 'like all this land, or at least that which has so far been discovered' (fol. 24^r); both people in antiquity and Native Americans 'worshipped...the sun, and the moon, and stars or fire, animals...others...worshipped artificial creatures made of stone, wood, gold, silver'. It is easy to see that, although he uses a large catechism intended for Spain, Zumárraga does not close his eyes to what he sees in the common practice of many indigenous people.

In Santo Domingo, Pedro de Córdoba wrote a catechism in Spanish to organize Dominican teaching on the island itself and on the nearby islands. A version was printed in Mexico in 1544 with the same content as earlier manuscript copies. Although Pedro de Córdoba had died in 1521, he is seen as the main author of this work. The first printed impression of 1544 may be closer than later ones to his original text, but it is not known with certainty if it had already been modified to be used in Mexico. In it he says:

> The First Commandment is to honour and love one true God above all things. And notice that sinning is to say or do or think something against any of these ten Commandments of God. Thus, all you do in any ceremony to your gods, as well as to Vicilobos or Tezcatepuca, or any of the others that you had as gods before, sins against this Commandment. As well as those who sacrifice someone, or draw blood, or offer anything to these gods which you used to honour: you sin a great sin against this first Commandment, which commands you to love only one true God. And because those you honoured are not gods, but demons that seduce you, you sin a lot, because the honour and service that you had to give to only one true God, you give it to the demons (fol. 18^r).[3]

In 1548, a second edition of the work was published by the Dominicans, containing significant changes. They added and modified a number of important paragraphs, to adapt it more to the reality of the continent, which was different from that of the Caribbean islands. Moreover, the text appeared in two columns, in Spanish and Nahuatl, effectively creating a new work. This second version reads, with regard to the First Commandment:

---

3. 'Vicilobos' is a corrupt Spanish name for the god Huitzilopochtli, a deity in the Aztec pantheon who was widely worshipped on the Caribbean islands too. The Nahuatl name of the less important deity 'Tezcatepuca' is Tezcatlipoca, identical with the more ancient Xipe Totec (J.L. de Rojas, *México Tenochtitlán. Economía y sociedad en el siglo XVI* [Mexico City: Fondo de Cultura Económica, 1986], p. 158).

And be very careful, my beloved, because then it becomes sin when something is done or said, or when something is thought against these sweet and gentle Commandments of God. Therefore, if some men or women do something, or believe something from the devil, or offer him some offerings, or incense, or paper, *ocotl*, which is pine wood, or spill or give food to the fire for him, or for Tezcatlipoca or Tlalocatecutli or Vicilopuchtli, or believe in some other, which old men and women had as gods in the past; because if anyone is now doing these things, he offends much against this first Commandment of God. And if anyone worships a false god or a demon, sacrificing before him, or drawing straws through his ears to make them bloody and placing them before the devil, or does other things, or believes in them, as they were done in the past, he greatly offends our great Lord God against this Commandment that He commands us here now (fols. 80^v-81^r).[4]

Comparing this text with the previous edition, one observes that the account of the idolatrous practices is much more detailed. These were still taking place in 1548; deeply rooted in the mentality and customs of the Aztecs, they were not to be radically suppressed simply by the preaching of a new religion. It was undoubtedly a matter of time, and several generations would be needed to be able to talk about fundamental change.

The Dominican Pedro de Feria preached among the indigenous inhabitants of the Oaxaca region, particularly among the Zapotecs, and wrote his bilingual catechism in their language and in Spanish. With regard to the First Commandment, his exposition is very clear and direct regarding the practice of idolatry, which had not yet disappeared after almost half a century of Christian preaching:

…stone figures, which had been made by human craftsmen's hand, then by deception of the devil, the men came to worship them as their gods and to celebrate great feasts, and to make sacrifices to them, and to tear their own flesh, cutting open their tongues and their ears and other parts of their bodies, and to sacrifice men before them to appease them, and in that way they had their requests granted.

Along with this there was another thing by which this error grew a lot, and it was that the same devil went many times into those statues of stone and wood, and spoke in them, and said many things…

The second was in this way: that in the past some tyrant kings (being haughty, seeing themselves as great lords, and forgetting the true king and

---

4. On this occasion the two previous gods are mentioned, but also Tlalocatecutli, who is in fact the god Tlaloc. The 'ocotl' offered consisted of torches burning before the gods, which were made of pine wood (*ocotl*) known as 'ocotlapanque'. The paper (*amatl*) was also an offering to the gods. It is worth noting that the words 'ocotl', 'vicilobos' and 'chalchiuitl' are printed in Nahuatl in the column containing the Spanish text: this is not a misprint, but rather the precise terms are used so that they couldn't be misunderstood and some idolatry hence remain under the excuse that the teaching had not been presented precisely enough.

lord of heaven and earth, our Lord God) commanded that images of them were made in all their villages and people revered them...

Many of you (it being so long since you were baptized and since the true law of God was preached to you), continue in this error of worshipping idols and committing yourselves to them, and asking what you need; and in my opinion this is the reason why God sends you many punishments. The first, hunger, that it hasn't rained for many years and you haven't got hold of bread, and in this way you suffer great need. Second, you suffer serious diseases that kill many of you... The third thing that you suffer is very few of you are born, and of these few who are born, few escape... I have some suspicion that the sin of idolatry is the reason why God punishes you (fols. 62^r-64^v).

The teaching that Pedro de Feria transmits about idolatry is clear, vivid and direct. It accuses the Native Americans because, even if in the past they were not guilty since they were ignorant and living in error, their idolatry cannot be justified now: the Spanish have been teaching and preaching to them for 48 years. Their ancestors fell into the nets of idolatry laid by the devil, as well as by some kings and chiefs who demanded to be revered to the point of being considered gods. For this reason, these ancestors were responsible for their error and have been condemned to hell. For Feria ignorance of the Christian religion is in any case no excuse because, according to the prevailing mentality of the time, outside the Church there is no salvation at all (*extra ecclesiam nulla salus*).

The exposition that Pedro de Feria dedicates to idolatry and sins against the First Commandment does not end here. Once he has explained that the misfortunes of the Zapotecs are a consequence of sin (he makes himself the interpreter of the divine will when he suspects that idolatry is the cause of these misfortunes),[5] he adds, to clear away any possible doubts that the Native Americans might have, that the Spanish also sin, but if they do not suffer the same illnesses this is because they believe strongly in God and do not commit idolatry. For Feria, believing is an act of acceptance of God. God also punishes the Spanish for their sins, but they are not being wiped out as the indigenous people are. He condemns the Zapotecs for their infidelity:

---

5. The meeting of the two cultures, European and American, as well as the conquest, placed the Spanish in the ascendancy. This was reflected in religion with the supression of images, temples, social hierarchy and customs. Considering the Indians as barbarians enabled Europeans to treat their culture as a *tabula rasa* on which they could impose another model of society. Everything negative that happened was treated as divine punishment (defeat, hunger, disease, earthquakes). Of course, nowadays we see these events through different eyes, without assigning our misfortunes to God as punishment for sins. Today there is also a simplistic tendency to consider everything done by the Indians as good (*le bon sauvage*) and everything that the Spanish did to be bad; this is a widely held opinion, but unreliable.

> But you, who joined with God when you were baptized, and he received you as his children, and loved you more than the husband loves his wife; then you abandon God again and start living together with the devil, and turn back to your idolatries; that's why God gets angry with you and punishes you with hunger (fol. 65^{r-v}).

The guilty action of the Zapotec people is to have accepted God but then to have returned to their traditional religion. The preacher's words clearly resonate with expressions from the Old Testament, in which the prophets reproached the people of Israel for their unfaithfulness to the God whom they had promised to follow.[6] The only conclusion that Pedro de Feria can reach is: 'Believe in one single God, wholeheartedly love one single God and trust in one single God' (fol. 65^v).

There are further catechisms that stress the sin of idolatry. Dionisio de los Santos, the Bishop of Cartagena de Indias (Colombia), wrote a catechism shortly after entering his diocese in 1575. He sent it to the Council of the Indies in Seville to be approved. Never published, it was shelved there until today. On the First Commandment, he wrote:

> Q. How will you honour him with faith? A. Neither having or revering idols or false gods, or believing heresy, or dreams or omens, witchcraft or other superstitions, which is all vanity and deceit of the devil (fol. 139v).

This could seem relevant to any believer in Spain, especially if we focus on the word 'heresies', which could be understood in the context of the tense debate between Catholic and Reformed in the sixteenth century. But we must pay attention also to the mentions of 'idols' and 'witchcraft', which set the tone for his claims and refer directly to the pre-Hispanic religious practices that had not entirely disappeared from the thoughts and hearts of the Native Americans.

The Augustinian Juan de la Anunciación worked among the indigenous people of Mexico, either in the city itself or in Puebla de los Angeles. His bilingual catechism mentions the sin of idolatry as the most common among the people he taught. He writes:

> And he who bows to false and lying gods, or takes account of dreams, giving them full credence, or of any other abuse or superstition, believing it as if it were something true, or loves and esteems the things of the world, which are God's creatures, rather than God himself (fol. 248^{r-v}).

Most of his teaching, as with Dionisio de los Santos, could equally apply to the Spanish or to Europeans who had not moved to America; but it also refers to the false gods on which the Native Americans relied, according to their convictions, in matters of business and material things. Juan de la

---

6. See, e.g., Jer. 3.6-7; Hos. 1.3, Isa. 1.21; Jer. 2.2; Ezek. 16. Regarding the prohibition of incisions see Lev. 19.28; 21.5; 1 Kgs 18.28; Hos. 7.14.

Anunciación warns that these false gods try to communicate with their followers through dreams; this time the word 'sorcery' does not appear, but it is clearly implied. Undoubtedly, he is dealing with idolatry.

But it is worth drawing attention, in this as in previous testimonies, to the way in which preachers highlight dreams as a false way of looking back to traditional religions. In the world of the Old Testament, dreams were an important means for God to communicate with humans. The dreams that missionaries warned against, however, were not of this type, but were alleged to be communications from the non-Christian gods, against the will of the one God, who had already made that will known through revelation. The same word is used, but the context is very different.

For his part, José de Acosta, the main author of and inspiration for the catechetical documents of the Third Provincial Council of Lima, promulgated under the rule of St Toribio de Mogrovejo, proposed a corpus of various texts. Those that concern us here are a *Catecismo mayor* ('Main Catechism'), which is relatively broad and takes the form of questions and answers; a *Confesionario* ('Confessionary'), which is not a catechism, but helps explain some of the claims present in the *Catecismo mayor*; and the *Tercer catecismo (Sermonario)* ('Third Catechism' or 'Sermons'), which presents the previous doctrine more extensively through long expositions ready to be preached to adults. All the texts are composed in Spanish, Quechua and Aymara.

In the *Catecismo mayor* de Acosta has this to say in relation to idolatry:

> Q. Who breaks the commandment to honour God? A. He who worships any creature, or has idols or sacred places [*huacas*], or gives credence to false sects and heresies or dreams and omens [*agüeros*], which are vanity and a deceit of the Devil.
>
> Q. Therefore, are all the ceremonies that the old Indians and sorcerers teach against the law of the Christians vanity and deceit of the Devil? A. Yes, father, without any doubt, and those who take part in them will be condemned with the devil (fol. 58r).[7]

There are common elements with the catechisms written in Mexico, such as the outright rejection of idols, sorcery and any return to the religion of the ancestors ('the old'). There is also an individual element in the reference to *huacas* as equivalent to idols; they could be equivalent to the idol by substituting a generic name for that of each of the divinities, or even the place

---

7. In the *Catecismo breve* ('Brief Catechism'), which precedes the *Catecismo mayor*, a question which does not refer to the Commandments can be linked to this teaching: 'Q. So, are the sun, the moon, stars, morning star, lightning not God? A. None of them is God, but they were made by God, who made the heaven and the earth and everything that there is in them for man's welfare' (fol. 14r). There seems to be an error in the printed version, since the manuscript has: '…are the sun, the moon, stars, morning star, lightning, *huacas and hills* not God?'

where the image was. It was the inevitable adaptation to the situation shared by the Incas.[8]

The Jesuit Juan de la Plaza, who moved from Lima to Mexico after the Third Provincial Council of Lima, was the author of the catechism that was approved at the Third Mexican Provincial Council in 1585; the text he wrote is clearly indebted to the one enacted in Lima, with some differences.

The role attributed to the devil in the context of idolatry in several catechisms is striking. Instead of just saying that he is able to tempt humans, they assign him a prominence that seems to make him an antagonist of God. While God calls us to do good, the devil calls us to do evil. Humanity thus becomes a battlefield between two nearly equal powers. Although their relationship is not expressly formulated like this, people who had received the Christian faith only a short time ago could easily perceive it that way.

Even stranger is the assertion that appears in the catechism of Pedro de Feria, according to which the devil enters idols, appropriates them and makes them an instrument of his will. He speaks through them and, therefore, the Native Americans can hear his voice coming from the images. It seems that supernatural powers are attributed to the devil. Pedro de Feria's exaggerations are certainly the product of good will, but he does not provide the most perfect expression of the nature of idolatry.

2.2. *Images*

The exposition of the First Commandment does not end with the rejection of idolatry itself. There was another important issue to consider: that of the images. Both missionaries and other Spanish settlers took care to remove idols, most of which were destroyed.

However, new Christian images (paintings and sculptures) representing Christ, the Virgin or the saints, were put before the Native Americans' eyes. Having been told that idolatrous images should be removed, they showed their surprise at these new images, which, to their minds, were the objects of similar worship. While in Europe some proponents of the Reformation destroyed Christian images in the name of the Decalogue's prohibition,[9] in America pagan images were replaced by Christian ones. On both continents

---

8. The *Instrucción contra las ceremonias y ritos que usan los Indios conforme al tiempo de su infidelidad* ('Instruction against the Ceremonies and Rites that the Indians Practise according to the Time of their Infidelity'), incorporated to the corpus of instruments of the Catechism says in the first chapter: '1. It is common to almost all the Indians to worship *huacas*, idols, streams, rocks or large stones, hills, mountain tops, springs, fountains and, in the end anything in nature which seems outstanding and different from the others... 6. When they worship *huacas*, they frequently bow their heads and raise their hands and speak to them asking for what they want.'

9. On the interpretation of the prohibition of images by reformers see V. Thum's article in this volume, pp. 258-77.

the point was to avoid, at all costs, the risk of committing idolatry through the use of sculptures or paintings. That is why some of the texts already cited refer to images, and we can add some more below.

So, Juan de Zumárraga wrote in his *Breve doctrina*:

> Other gentiles in these parts worshipped artificial creatures, made of stone, wood, gold, silver, and other any materials or paints. They sacrificed to and worshipped these idols, and from there they received answers and commandments, some of the devil. These vanities of the blind gentiles stopped the evangelical preaching of Jesus Christ showing that only eternal God should be given such honour and service (fol. 24r).

And the same Zumárraga, in the *Doctrina cristiana más cierta* ('Truest Christian Doctrine'), puts especial emphasis on the question of images in the supplement that he added in the edition of 1546, where he teaches on this subject in general and also with particular reference to Mexico:

> They should know that the Christians have images of Jesus Christ, and of our Lord and of the cross and of the other saints; not for the board, paint or substance of which they are made, nor do we take them for gods, or living things, nor because they have divinity or grace (as the heathen did in this land), but we honour in them what they represent (fol. 82v).

In the *Doctrine* attributed to Pedro de Córdoba, and printed and published in Mexico in 1548, there is a serious warning against a hidden form of idolatry in relation to images, in which the Native Americans pretended a conversion to Christianity but practised their former religion in the family, hiding images in their homes:

> And if anyone has saved an image or figure of the devil, whether of stone, or of wood, or of *chalchiuitl*, or if anyone preserves for him the land that used to be his: or gives food to the dead, or offers them any sacrifice as used to be done, he greatly offends the true and one God in this (fol. 81r-v).[10]

He does not say that the images represent non-Christian gods, but calls them directly an 'image or figure of the devil'; in the mind of Pedro de Córdoba, or any of the missionaries who spread this teaching, they amounted to the same thing.

Pedro de Feria had already spoken about idolatry when he wrote about the first Commandment. He extends his teaching, and connects it with the understanding that the Zapotecs are to receive regarding images:

> I want to tell you only one more thing, children, concerning the images of God our Lord, of the cross, of our Lady, and of other saints, because it belongs to this Commandment. Do not think, children, that the images

---

10. *Chalchiuitl* was a green precious stone, like jade, from which some idols were made. In the astral sign of *ce atl*, sellers of fish, frogs and shrimps had a feast in honour of Chalchiuitlicue.

which are at the altar or in any other part are the same God, or are the same saints. Not so, children… Therefore, children, when you have an image of God our Lord, or the saints his servants, kneel on your knees before them, and give them very great reverence and, remembering the same God or the saints (whose images they are), entrust yourselves to them heartily. Some of you have images in your houses; if you are really Christians, and have completely left your ancient rites, congratulations, keep them (fols. 66ʳ-67ᵛ).

Dionisio de los Santos also deals with the question of images, trying not to make it a source of confusion for the Native Americans that the Spanish have in their worship images that they revere:

Q. So, how do Christians revere the images of painting and those made of wood or metal? A. Because we do not worship or revere the painting or the wood or metal, thinking they have in themselves some divinity, that we know that the image of our Lord Jesus Christ is not Christ himself, but it represents him; nor the image of our Lady is not our Lady, and so the images of saints.

Q. So, why do you revere and worship them? A. Because of what they represent, as the cross of Jesus Christ crucified, and so the other images (fol. 139ᵛ).

The Catechism of the Third Provincial Council of Lima deals with the same issue, in the context of the Incas rather than the more northerly peoples of the previous texts, in relation to the eradication of pagan idols and the reverence for Christian images:

Q. Then, why do the Christians worship images of wood and metal, if it is wrong to worship idols? A. Christians do not worship the images of wood and metal in themselves, like idolaters, and do not think that they have virtue and divinity in themselves, but looking at what they represent, they worship Jesus Christ on the cross in his image, and revere Our Lady the Virgin Mary, and the other saints who are in heaven, asking for their favour; and they revere the same images not because of what they are, but what they represent (fols. 59ʳ-60ʳ).[11]

The conclusion is clear: pre-Hispanic idolatry had a large pantheon of deities, whose images were worshipped on certain holidays and with special

---

11. Cf., very similarly, the catechism that Juan de la Plaza wrote for the Third Provincial Council of Mexico: 'Q. Then why do Christians worship images of wood and metal, if it is wrong to worship idols? A. Christians do not worship wood or metal, as idolaters, nor do they think there is any virtue or deity in them. // Q. So, why do they worship them? A. Because of that which they represent. And they worship that in them, as to our Lord Jesus Christ on the cross because they are his image. // Q. And why do they revere the images of our Lady and the saints? A. Because they are friends of God and enjoy him in heaven; and to be our advocates with God in our need for the remedy' (fol. 449ʳ).

rites for each. With the advent of the Christian religion, polytheism was replaced by a single God. However, the new temples were filled with images (carvings or paintings) which, in the eyes of the indigenous people, were merely substitutes for the old gods. Hence there was a risk of their deifying the images themselves. If the ceremonies in which the images were somehow the centre of attention (processions, the use of incense, bowing, kissing the cross) were added to this, images might well come to be perceived as 'minor' gods, who were going to receive the Native Americans' former worship, and to whom certain powers were attributed. Despite this risk, and perhaps stimulated by the tradition of revering images promoted by the Counter-Reformation (the Council of Trent), the missionaries chose to use images plentifully, although they had to explain to the Native Americans that these were not new gods to replace the old ones.

2.3. *Priests and Sorcerers*

One aspect of the First Commandment remains to be considered, beyond presenting the idea of one almighty God who displaced the old gods and erasing the images of idols. Although these things had to be done, there still remained, like an ember, the lively and active figures of the ancient priests of pagan cults. They did not easily accept the disappearance of a religion they had propagated and of which they were firmly convinced. These priests (sorcerers, clairvoyants, magicians) were the direct antagonists of the missionaries. Therefore the latter could not remain silent about the risks of a secret but living religion that hid itself under the appearance of Christian conversion, encouraged from the shadows by the priests of the past.

Thus we find sentences in the 1544 edition of the catechism attributed to Pedro de Córdoba that reflect the text used in some Caribbean islands, which deals with the question of the survival of priests of the old religion:

> And all of you who honour your priests who served in your temples, you sin, because you do all that honour for love of the devil, and take it away from the true God (fol. 18^r).

Virtually the same ideas appear in the version from 1548, distributed on the American continent, which says about this issue:

> And if now there are some servants of the devil or priests that used to be his, or who serve him, they offend much against our great God, and the reason is because they revere and respect what is unworthy and take away from God the reverence that he is due (fol. 81^r).

The difference between them is that in the 1544 version the catechism is directed against those Native Americans who still revere, protect, shelter and give credit to the priests of the ancient cult and therefore reject Catholic worship and its own priests. By contrast the 1548 version is aimed directly at the priests responsible for maintaining the ancient cult. Those priests and their secret cult were still finding an echo in the hearts and the behaviour of some of the indigenous people, who had not entirely given up the religious convictions in which they had grown up and lived.

Pedro de Feria gives us another example of the kind of confrontation with the priests of the cult that the missionaries were trying to eliminate. He writes:

> ...and do not worry about sorcerers and soothsayers, who are liars and scoffers, and servants of the devil; and do not believe either in dreams or omens, because God commands all of this in the First Commandment (fol. 65v).

José de Acosta does the same in the catechism that he offered to the Third Provincial Council of Lima when he refers to the 'old': obviously he does not simply mean the oldest people, the elderly; he means the people who, because of deep-rooted belief (having lived for a long time in their previous religion and inwardly adhering to it), oppose the settlement of Christianity. They cannot do it openly, because they would face the power of the conquerors; but they are able to do it in a hidden, covert way, that is no less effective:

> Q. Therefore, are all the ceremonies that the old Indians and sorcerers teach against the law of the Christians vanity and deceit of the Devil? A. Yes, father, without any doubt, and those who take part in them will be condemned with the devil (fols. 58^v-59^r).[12]

In the *Sermonario*, also called *Tercer catecismo*, José de Acosta dedicates the whole of Sermon 19 to this issue, along with that of images, as an example of the survival of indigenous cults long after the new religion had been preached and presented. The sermon is long, longer than would be normal for a single address, but its title is expressive, 'In Which the Sorcerers, and their Superstitions and Vain Rituals Are Reprimanded'. And it deals with the difference between Christians worshipping before the images of the saints and unbelievers worshipping their idols or *huacas*. He dedicates a long paragraph to sorcerers, attempting to discredit them in the eyes of the Native Americans who had hitherto trusted them as representatives of the pagan religion:

---

12. The wording of Juan de la Plaza's catechism is practically the same: 'Q. According to this, are all the things that the sorcerers teach men, which are not in accordance with those which the Christians use and practise, a deceit of the Devil? A. Yes. And those who believe them and do what they say commit sin against the faith, and are condemned in hell' (fol. 449^r). The Latin version is: 'Secundum [hoc], omnia quae docent malefici homines, quae non sunt conformia his quae Christiani exercent et operantur, sunt fraudes Demonis? R. Ita est, et qui illis credunt, et operantur quae dicunt, pecant contra fidem et obligantur Inferno' (fols. 260^v-61^r).

> In this sermon, brethren, I want to declare the deceits and lies that the old sorcerers teach you against the law of God, so that you flee from them as if from the devil. Know ye, brethren, that the devil, since he is the mortal enemy of humanity and regrets that they are saved, has sought and seeks to deceive you, so that you are condemned; and just as our Saviour Jesus Christ sent his apostles and disciples around the world to teach the truth, in the same way the devil sends his ministers who are these old sorcerers to deceive men.
>
> Do you not see that these sorcerers are foolish and stupid and wretched people, who know nothing but lying and deceiving? …
>
> In his Holy Scripture God commands that you do not ask these sorcerers what is to come, or ask them to provide for your needs. And he orders that the person who does so be stoned to death. God also commands that a person who knows of these evil sorcerers must reveal them to the Father, so that they cannot do evil, and the person who hides them is the son of the devil and will burn forever in hell (fols. 108v-10v).

In this last paragraph, the use of Scripture is striking. It applies Old Testament prohibitions against consulting soothsayers and necromancers to the sorcerers: 'Do not turn to mediums or wizards; do not seek them out, to be defiled by them: I am the LORD your God' (Lev. 19.31; 20.6). In Lev. 20.27 the penalty of stoning is decreed for sorcerers and necromancers, but nothing is said about the people who consult them, though it is assumed they are doing wrong.[13]

However, Acosta interprets Scripture freely and says, without hesitation, that those who consult sorcerers also have to be stoned. Moreover, claiming the authority of a Scripture that in reality says nothing about it, Acosta presents as the law of God that the Native Americans have to denounce those who go to sorcerers secretly as a sign of continuing to practise the ancient Inca religion.

The exposition of the First Commandment is long and extensive, precisely because the new Christian religion could not be introduced without difficulties and resistance. The greatest challenge, no doubt, was the establishment of another God who put aside all the gods in which the various peoples and ethnic groups had traditionally believed as useless.

2.4. *The Sabbath Commandment*

With regard to the Third Commandment, Zumárraga, bishop of Mexico, points out in his *Doctrina breve muy provechosa* (1543) what was an extensive failing in Europe, the toleration of fairs on Sundays, as distinct from necessary markets for strictly subsistence products. He says:

---

13. In 1 Sam. 28.3-25 Saul consults the witch of Endor, and a prediction of his death is issued by the dead prophet Samuel, precisely because Saul invoked the dead and did not rely on God. However no explicit punishment is designated for those who consult necromancers, despite its being directly prohibited.

Of the things that this right prohibits beyond menial work, one is markets; by which fairs are not understood, because the bishops see them and conceal them: but it is understood about weekly markets: they are forbidden on those days (fol. 33ʳ).

Having said this generally, with an eye to European markets, he then applies his teaching, with some tolerance, to the existing markets in America, particularly in Mexico City:

And because in this land the markets belong to the natives, with whom the Supreme Pontiff dispenses more generously in the keeping of feast days than with other nations because of their weakness and poverty; and because it has not been settled about what is appropriate to allow or to ban, according to their condition and manner in their *tianguez* or markets, it is not stated now (fol. 33ʳ).[14]

Zumárraga also speaks of the obligation to attend Mass as a way to define the fulfilment of the Third Commandment. After a long exhortation, which would be perfectly valid for Spain, in which he condemns common abuses of Sundays and holidays, he adds a sentence that has clear resonances for the reality he knew in Mexico:

They leave Mass, and do not heed its teaching; mostly these new Christians; it seems to be great infidelity (fol. 34ʳ).

There is another valuable text that applies the teaching of the Third Commandment to Sunday rest and makes specific reference to life in the Americas, to the extent that it would hardly be comprehensible in Europe. In addition to giving a general doctrine, it goes into detail about people's usual occupations. We find it in the 1544 edition of the catechism attributed to Pedro de Córdoba:

The Third Commandment is: keep and sanctify holidays. They sin against this Commandment who work on Sundays and on the holidays that the church commands them to keep, or who sow their land, or harvest maize [*mahyz*], or carry loads, or weave cloth, or do other significant work on these days (fol. 18v).

Most of these statements could be applied in Spain. But there was no way that 'harvest maize' could be understood in Europe.[15] Moreover the two

---

14. 'Tianguez' was the colloquial way for the Spaniards to refer to the markets, really named 'tianquiz' or 'tianquiztli'.

15. At the time of the discovery of America, this plant was a staple of the agriculture of the New World, from Rio de la Plata to what was to become the United States. The natives sowed it around their homes, if they did not live in large and fixed villages. Old graves in North America, the tombs of the Incas and burials in Peru contain ears and seeds of maize with the same frequency as those in Ancient Egypt contain wheat, barley or millet. In Mexico the people worshipped a deity, Ciuteutl, whose name came

expressions that follow, 'to carry loads or weave cloth', referred to the ordinary tasks of those who occupied the lowest positions in the social scale. Carrying loads of firewood or other products for upper class individuals was a form of obligatory personal tribute, and was referred to as 'coatequitl'. In Spain, although it was ordinarily done in every home, the trade of weaver was a specific profession, whereas in America it was customary for each family to weave according to their own needs. The weaver was known in Mexico by the name 'hiquitqui'. When the catechism makes these allusions, it is clear that the Native Americans could understand what the teaching meant concerning activities that had to be suppressed to comply properly with the Sunday rest.

2.5. *Honouring One's Parents*

The lesson presented by American catechisms about this Commandment is generally in line with what was taught in Spain. There are no big differences, except in one case. Because the general teaching indicated that people had to obey their parents unless they ordered something contrary to God's law, Pedro de Córdoba applies this specifically in the *Doctrina* of 1544 when he states that if parents (being older and perhaps more attached to the ancient traditions) order their children to return to idolatry, the children must not obey:

> As well as if they ordered you to lie or to steal, or to do harm to others, or not go to the sermons, or to make some sacrifice or to worship idols (fol. 18v).

Parental authority is not so great that children should obey their parents and therefore sin directly against God. This is a typical case in which 'we must obey God rather than humans' (Acts 4.19), which also has a practical application to what was going on in the New World.

2.6. *The Prohibition of Murder*

There seems to be an incomprehensible silence about the teaching that this Commandment demands, given that a considerable number of the ceremonies of the Aztec empire involved sacrificing many prisoners of war to the gods. These bloody ceremonies had horrified the first Spanish who arrived in Mexico. Along with the nakedness of the people's bodies and their apparent lack of writing, such rites contributed to the conclusion that the people were barbarians. It seemed preferable to 'wipe the slate clean' of their customs and traditions, to exchange these for alternatives provided by the Spanish. The inexplicable silence on human sacrifice hence seems as though it

---

from Nahuatl 'ciutli', meaning maize, and the first fruits of the crop were consecrated to this deity.

should have been broken, to show that the violent and arbitrary sacrifice of human prisoners was not God's will.

There are, however, some features of the catechisms that have already appeared and which, in a very discreet way, refer to the bloody customs of the subject people. They arise in the context of the First Commandment, condemning these customs as manifestations of the worship of false gods and therefore as opposed to the acceptance of the one Christian God. They could also have been taken up in the exposition of the Fifth Commandment, but in the three cases I cite below this does not happen.

In the 1544 version of the catechism of Pedro de Córdoba it is said that people 'who sacrifice any person, or draw blood, or offer anything to these gods' (fol. 18ʳ) are committing a sin. And the 1548 version of the same catechism states that people who go before their god 'sacrificing before him, or drawing straws through his ears to make them bloody and placing them before the devil' (fol. 80ᵛ) are sinning against the first Commandment. Thirdly, in the *Doctrina* written by Pedro de Feria it is mentioned as an idolatrous practice 'to celebrate great feasts, and to make sacrifices to them [demons], and to tear their own flesh, cutting open their tongues and their ears and other parts of their bodies, and to sacrifice men before them to appease them' (fol. 62ʳ).

Only twice, in the catechism of 1544 ('who sacrifice any person') and in the doctrine of Feria ('to sacrifice men before them to appease them') does the issue of human sacrifice appear. And human sacrifice is treated together with other idolatrous religious practices without any apparent distinction being made between them. Sacrificing other people to appease and to gain the favour of the gods is thereby rendered less important that it would have been on an objective consideration.

If such murderous actions are passed over, another objectionable practice does appear in the catechism of the Third Provincial Council of Lima, clearly linked to the Fifth Commandment. Acosta says in it:

> Q. According to that, does everyone who deprives himself of his senses by getting drunk sin gravely? A. Yes, they sin, because men make themselves into beasts, and put themselves in danger of doing great evil (fol. 62ʳ).[16]

At first glance this might seem to be a way of breaking the Commandment because excessive drinking entails a loss of reason and dignity, with the risk of committing actions which people then have to repent. At least that is what follows from a direct reading of the language used. But there is a

---

16. The Spanish words in the catechism of the Third Provincial Council of Mexico are virtually the same as those in the catechism from Lima; the Latin text is: 'P. Secundum hoc, qui se privant intellectu se inebriantes graviter peccant? R. Peccant quia homines faciunt se bestias et constituunt se ad periculum multorum et gravium malorum' (fol. 262ʳ).

subtext that goes much further since, in the culture of the Incas, drunkenness was a kind of act of worship of the gods, in which they went into a trance and partook in the divine spirit. This can be inferred from the *Instrucción contra las ceremonias y ritos que usan los Indios*, which is part of the corpus making up the catechism. In the chapter 'About Sacrifices' it is said that in the course of carrying out various agricultural tasks, the Incas 'offer [to Earth, Pachamama] burned fat, or coca, guinea pig, lambs and other things; and all this drinking and dancing'; and in the chapter on 'Special Holidays', it describes how, especially on the feast of Yten, they first fast, forgo intercourse and salt, and do not drink *chicha*, and then, wearing the special costumes of the festival, they make a procession that lasts a whole day and night 'and the next day they ate, drank and danced for two days and nights… They use the fasting that precedes and the drunkenness that follows for urgent needs.'

In the *Confessionario* that served to guide priests in the questions they should address to penitents, in relation to the Fifth Commandment the fourth question is, 'Have you been deprived of your sense getting drunk, or have you been the cause for others getting drunk, inducing or forcing them to it?' The issue of drunkenness is dealt with even more deeply in the *Tercer catecismo* or *Sermonario*. The Sermon 23 is dedicated exclusively to this question:

> Against drunkenness. In which it is taught how drunkenness in itself is a mortal sin, and the damage it does to the body, causing disease and death, and dulling the senses, and to the soul, bringing about the grave sins of incest and murder and sodomy, and above all that it is the principal means of destroying faith and promoting superstitions and idolatries (fols. 147^r-48^v).

2.7. The Prohibitions of Adultery and Concupiscence

Sometimes these Commandments were presented together to demonstrate Christian teaching about impure acts and desires. In the exposition from Pedro de Córdoba's catechism of 1544, the story of Sodom is presented in brief as a sign of God's punishment for the sins of impurity. Then, though they were not exclusive to what happened in America, the text records that, among the indigenous people, such sins were committed as routine:

> And in this way Justice will destroy and burn and kill you if you commit this sin. And all those who commit this sin, the devil will take you to hell, and will give you very great torment for it, and those who commit it against nature with women, or a woman with another woman, will have the same pain, and those who commit it will have the same pain as those who suffer it (fol. 18^r).

The *Confessionario* of José de Acosta notes a more subtle practice: the use of the sorcery of the former Inca religion to seduce women:

Have you used the *huacanqui* to get women? Have you gone to the sorcerer or *huaca* to ask for medicine or potions to make women love you? (fol. 12ʳ).

This forms a complement to the explanation that appears in the *Instrucción contra las ceremonias y ritos que usan los Indios*, where Chapter 4, 'About Witches and Witchcraft', says:

> Item: they go to sorcerers to give them medicines to get a woman or to move her, or to prevent a mistress from leaving, and women go to them for the same. And to this end they often give them clothes, blankets, coca and their own hair, or the hair and clothing of their associate, and sometimes the blood of the same, because they do their magic with these things (fol. 3ʳ).

2.8. *The Prohibition of Theft*

Some explanations of this Commandment refer to specific aspects of life in America. The 1548 catechism of Pedro de Córdoba refers, among various ways of sinning against this Seventh Commandment, to damage that may affect the corn crop:

> If anyone spoils something, or burns the house of another, or another's corn on the corncob, or someone else's cotton, or any other thing belonging to someone else. (fol. 86v)

Damage from an arson attack could happen anywhere, but the burning of corn or cotton is a clear reference to the New World, since these plants had not yet been brought to Europe.

Another exposition of the Seventh Commandment appears in the doctrine of Pedro de Feria. It refers to the widespread abuse whereby those in power made use of the work of their subordinates without paying them their due. Uniquely in this case, the teaching is directed specifically to the chiefs (*caciques*), mayors and *tequitlatos*. The word 'cacique' is of Caribbean, not Mexican, origin. It was later used across the continent, designating the master or head of any group, who was himself subject to some higher authority. The Mexican *tequitlatos* were the officials of a district or a tribe, in charge of land surveying and the inventory of all assets. The word 'mayor', brought to America by the Spanish, referred to the principal local authority. Such authorities frequently committed the abuses that Pedro de Feria denounces:

> You chiefs, mayors and *tequitlatos*, sin gravely in taking the work and sweat of the commoners, not paying them when they build your houses, work on your land and go with your messages; and if they hire themselves by the day to the Spanish, or sell the lime they make or the wood they collect, you do not give them their pay but take it, in which you commit a great theft. Moreover, you consume the assets of the community many times over and use them up to your own advantage. Also, for your whim, you seize

tomines,[17] cacao, chickens, blankets and other things from the ordinary people. In addition to this, what you take as a loan, you do not ever pay for it, or if you pay, it is too late (fol. 77$^{\text{r-v}}$).

The commoners, townspeople or unskilled workers—cheap labour—were easy victims for all kinds of abuse from those who had some authority and unfairly enriched themselves by the work of others. Though this is a nearly universal phenomenon, the catechism of Pedro de Feria situates it in a very clear and concrete way in the American reality.

From the data provided by the catechisms discussed above we can clearly conclude that the missionaries who undertook the evangelization of America were able to present the gospel using words and explanations that were not timeless and generic, but well suited to the reality before them. They presented the faith and tried to relate that reality as far as possible to the conduct that the Commandments require. In this way the indigenous people, from the Caribbean and Mexico to the Inca empire in Peru, could go about shaping their lives to the requirements stated in the Decalogue.

3. *The Pictographic Catechisms*

The small group of pictographic catechisms use images to transmit the faith. This can be said from the European perspective; however, from the Native Americans' point of view they were presented in typical and true writing, 'their' writing. Instead of having to learn the signs of the European alphabet, they passed directly to reading their own form of communication, to which they were accustomed.

This type of catechism comes only from the central and southern part of Mexico. Nevertheless, it is not even easy to localize the origin of each of the individual catechisms that are known, since there is often no evidence apart from the pictures or pictograms themselves to link them to a particular area. Likewise, we lack any evidence that would allow for precise dating. We may safely assume that they come from an early period; they may date from the early sixteenth century.

Further, we must bear in mind that the Nahua in Mexico wrote a series of pictographic works, of which some have been preserved, in which they narrated their chronicles and important events. But this kind of writing had nothing to do with Christianity and, in principle, it was not especially useful for conveying the Christian faith. As already noted, the conviction on the part of the Spanish that the Nahua people were backward and 'barbarians' established the policy of 'tabula rasa' in the early years, which made it possible to destroy many of these codices. Only the watchful eyes of men such

---

17. The *tomin*, from the Arabic *jumni*, was the name of a silver coin widely used in America.

as Pedro de Gante and Bernardino de Sahagun, who valued them, prevented them all from being completely lost.

Some missionaries, however, saw in the codices a model that the Native Americans understood; and the idea of doing something similar arose, with content that would help to make the new faith present in cultural forms to which the Nahuas were accustomed. The challenge was not easy. It was not just a question of making some drawings, simple pictograms, naive and beautiful. It was necessary for the person who drew them to intend to convey a particular and determined message, and for those who read them to understand that message exactly.

It was an essential condition that at least some missionaries should speak the Nahuas' language with reasonable confidence, to be able to acquaint themselves with those who had followed the profession of artists, the *tlacuiloque*. Only through such mutual understanding could the pictographic catechisms arise that now astonish us by their ingenuity and artistic beauty. Moreover, there had to be real communication, so that these catechisms would become a true work of collaboration. The task was difficult, because pictograms had to be created that included concepts and ideas absolutely unknown to the Native Americans: the Virgin, the Holy Spirit, grace, the Eucharist, etc. We can safely assume that, before the catechisms that we know were produced, many earlier attempts were abandoned because they either failed to express the Christian faith well, or were not sufficiently understood by the Native Americans.

Of the 39 pictographic catechisms of which we know anything, 8 have disappeared. There are 31 left, some of which are copies, and there are doubts about the whereabouts and contents of some of them, or I have not been able to locate and consult them. I managed to decipher—'read'— eight, almost in full:

1. One is *Anonymous*, though it bears the signature of Pedro de Gante; it is incomplete.
2. Another is called *Mucagua*, as it was intended for these people.
3. Another was named after *Pedro de Gante*, although he is not the author. It is complete, and has the same content as *Mucagua*.
4. There is the so-called *Mazahua*, whose name refers to some phrases in that language.
5. The so-called *Tolucano* was created for the valley of Toluc.
6. Another has pictograms accompanied by a parallel text in *Nahuatl*.
7. One is attributed to *Bernardino de Sahagun*, and has some annotations in Spanish.
8. Another has no conventional writing, is incomplete and located in *Berlin*.

These catechisms generally contain the most common formularies of the Christian faith. In their simplicity, they are similar to the first group of catechisms that do not contain any explanation. But not all share the same content or put it in the same order. It is clear that some authors knew of other, earlier pictographic catechisms, and employed pictograms that expressed the Christian faith and were well understood by the Native Americans.

All the examples above contain the Commandments except the first, which is incomplete. The variety among them is remarkable, because their form depended on the artistic ability of the artist, or *tlacuilo*, and also on the instructions given by the friar or friars who collaborated in their writing. Their contexts are also different: for example the eighth catechism (*Berlin*) is large, and it was possibly displayed on the wall of a church or a cloister, while others were drawn in small pocket books which could be carried by missionaries or catechists so that others could learn the faith.

The pictograms can fittingly be called hieroglyphs—sacred figures (from the Greek *hieros* and *glyphō* 'to carve')—since they are used to present the Christian faith. They have also been given the name *Testerian*, from the belief that the Franciscan Jacobo de Testera was their originator. This, however, is not true. He used images for preaching in Mexico, but he was not the inventor of the pictographic catechisms.[18] It is not easy to point out a particular name, as there was to be a work of intense collaboration between missionaries and draftsmen. The only known person who certainly used pictographic catechisms was Pedro de Gante.[19]

4. Conclusion

All this shows that one of the main problems that the friars who went to America to present the faith had to overcome was that of language, or languages. The great abundance of languages created a major problem. In addition, these languages were not written languages. They were first written down by the friars, once they had learned some indigenous

---

18. 'Having come to this land, as he [Testera] could not learn the language of the Indians as fast as he wanted to be able to preach in it, his spirit not suffering delay (as he was so fervent), he began to preach in another way through an interpreter, bringing with him on a painted canvas all the mysteries of our holy Catholic faith, and a skillful Indian who, in his own language, explained to the others what the servant of God said, and the consequence was that he made a great benefit among the Indians' (J. de Mendieta, *Historia eclesiástica indiana* [Mexico City: Porrúa, 1971], p. 665).

19. J. Cortés told me that among the people of his village, in the region of Puebla de los Angeles there were people who were able to understand the catechism without having seen it before. This is an example of how the missionaries were able to connect with the way of being and the culture of a people so as to convey the Christian faith to them.

languages. The mastery of Nahuatl, as a language that was widely understood, in part facilitated this work. But they did not stop at the knowledge of this one language, but made as much progress as they could in adapting to the languages used by each ethnic group. Presenting the faith in the people's own language was a giant step. Moreover, this was not simply a matter of using one language or another. Offering Christianity through pictograms like those in which the Nahua, and notably the Aztecs, composed their chronicles was another important, but difficult and laborious, step.

However, the greatest difficulty that the missionaries had to overcome, as we have seen, was that of inculcating principles different from those that had hitherto governed the life of the Native Americans, replacing former convictions so that Christian attitudes could be accepted over several generations—especially the belief in one God instead of their many ancient gods. The first missionaries who went to Mexico and then to Peru, Brazil, the Philippines, etc., put a lot of effort into this: we cannot ever say that they did not try.

to love   God   more than all   things

The First Commandment according to the pictographic catechism of Bernardino de Sahagun

Bibliography

Acker, G. van, *Dos alfabetos amerindios nacidos del diálogo entre dos mundos*, at http://celia.cnrs.fr/FichExt/Am/A_19-20_37.htm.

Acosta, J. de, *Historia natural y moral de las Indias* (Mexico City: Fondo de Cultura Económica, 1940).

Anders, F., 'Libro de oraciones. Ein mexikanischer Bildkatechismus des 16. Jahrhunderts', in M. Jansen, P. von der Loo and R. Manning (eds.), *Continuity and Identity in Native America: Essays in Honor of Benedikt Hartmann* (Leiden: E.J. Brill, 1988).

Arroyo, E. (ed.), *Los dominicos, forjadores de la civilización oaxaqueña. I. Los misioneros* (Oaxaca: Imprenta Camarena, 1958).

Basich de Canessi, Z., *México* (privately published, n.d.).

Bataillon, M., *Erasmo y España* (Mexico City: Fondo de Cultura Económica, 2nd edn, 1966).

Batalla Rosado, J.J., *El arte de escribir en Mesoamérica: El Códice Borbónico* (Madrid: Universidad Complutense, 1992).

Beristáin y Souza, J.M., *Biblioteca hispanoamericana septentrional* (3 vols.; Mexico City: Imprenta de Valdés, 1816–1821).
Burgoa, F. de, *Geográfica descripción* (2 vols.; Mexico City: La Nación, 1934).
Cortés, J., *El catecismo en pictogramas de Fray Pedro de Gante* (Madrid: Fundación Universitaria Española, 1987).
—*El catecismo en pictogramas de Fray Pedro de Gante* (Madrid: Testimonio, 2001).
Cuervo, J., *Historiadores del Convento de San Esteban de Salamanca* (3 vols.; Salamanca: San Esteban, 1914).
Dávila Padilla, A., *Historia de la fundación y discurso de la Provincia de Santiago de México de la Orden de Predicadores* (Madrid, 1590).
Durán, J.G., *Monumenta catechetica hispanoamericana*, I (Buenos Aires: Facultad de Teología de la Universidad Católica Argentina, 1984).
Egaña, A., *Historia de la Iglesia en la América Española. Desde el descubrimiento hasta comienzos del siglo XIX*, II, *Hemisferio Sur* (Madrid: BAC, 1966).
Etchegaray, A., *Historia de la catequesis* (Santiago de Chile: Paulinas, 1992).
Galarza, J., *Doctrina christiana. Méthode pour l'analyse d'un manuscrit pictographique mexicain du XVIIIeme siècle avec application à la première prière, le Pater Noster* (Paris: Société d'Ethnographie, 1980).
Gante, P. de, *Oraciones para enseñar a rezar a los indios* (Mexico City: Porrúa, 1975).
García Icazbalceta, J., *Bibliografía mexicana del siglo XVI* (Mexico City: Andrade y Morales, 1886).
García Icazbalceta, J., and A. Millares, *Bibliografía mexicana del siglo XVI* (Mexico City: Fondo de Cultura Económica, 2nd edn, 1981).
Gayo, J., *Doctrina christiana. Primer libro impreso en Filipinas* (Manila: Universidad de Sto. Tomás, 1951).
Glass, J.B., 'A Census of Middle American Testerian Manuscripts', *Handbook of Middle American Indians* 14 (1975), pp. 281-96.
Guerrero, J.R., 'Catecismos de autores españoles de la primera mitad del siglo XVI (1500–1559)', in *Repertorio de historia de las ciencias eclesiásticas en España*, II (Salamanca: Instituto de Historia de la Teología, 1971), pp. 225-60.
León, N., *Un catecismo mazahua* (*Un jeroglífico testeramerindiano*) (Mexico City: Biblioteca Enciclopédica del Estado, 1968).
León-Portilla, M., *Un catecismo náhuatl en imágenes. Introducción, paleografía y traducción al castellano* (Mexico: Cartón y Papel, 1979).
Medina, J.T., *La imprenta en Méjico (1539–1821)* (8 vols.; Santiago de Chile, 1911–1912).
Medina, M.A., *Doctrina cristiana para instrucción de los indios por Pedro de Córdoba* (Salamanca: San Esteban, 1987).
Navarro, F. (ed.), *El catecismo de Fray Pedro de Gante* (Madrid: Ministerio de Educación, 1970).
Normann, A.W., *Testerian Codices: Hieroglyphic Catechisms for Nativs Conversion in New Spain* (New Orleans: Tulane University, 1985).
Resines, L., *Catecismos pictográficos de Pedro de Gante, Incompleto y Mucagua* (Madrid: Fundación Universitaria Española, 2005).
—'Estudio sobre el catecismo pictográfico mazahua', *Estudio agustiniano* 29 (1994), pp. 243-306, 455-528.
—'Estudio sobre el catecismo pictográfico tolucano', *Estudio agustiniano* 31 (1996), pp. 245-98, 449-548.

—'Estudio sobre el catecismo pictográfico náhuatl', in *Estudio agustiniano* 40 (2005), pp. 449-529.
—'Estudio sobre el catecismo pictográfico de Alemania', *Estudio agustiniano* 45 (2010), pp. 449-89.
—*Catecismos americanos del siglo XVI* (Salamanca: Junta de Castilla y León, 1992).
—*Diccionario de los catecismos pictográficos* (Valladolid: Diputación de Valladolid, 2007).
Ricard, R., *La conquista espiritual de México* (Mexico City: Jus / Polis, 1947).
Streit, R., *Bibliotheca missionum* (2 vols.; Aachen: Xaverius, 1916, 1924).
Torre, E. de la, 'Estudio crítico en torno de los catecismos y cartillas como instrumentos de evangelización y civilización', in Fray Pedro de Gante, *Doctrina cristiana en lengua mexicana* (Mexico City: Centro de Estudios Históricos Fray Bernardino de Sahagún, 1981), pp. 13-104.
Valton, E., *Impresos mexicanos del siglo XVI. Estudio bibliográfico con una introducción sobre los orígenes de la imprenta en América* (Mexico City: Imprenta Universitaria, 1935).
Wolf, E., *Doctrina christiana: The First Book Printed in the Philippines, Manila, 1593* (Philadelphia: Library of Congress, 1947).

The Decalogue in Late Medieval and Early Modern Imagery: Catechetical Purpose and Theological Implications

Veronika Thum

In the late Middle Ages and the early modern period representations of the Ten Commandments were widespread in the Holy Roman Empire, particularly in German-speaking areas. Artistic representations of biblical subjects were the most effective didactic medium to inculcate faith and moral norms, since only a small proportion of the people could read. When Pope Gregory the Great affirmed that pictures were the books of the illiterate and that Christian truth could be transmitted by 'reading' pictures, he not only settled the early Christian aniconism controversy but also defined the didactic foundation of the use of images.

Almost every church in mediaeval times was adorned with representations of the Decalogue, as murals and panel paintings, reliefs and sculptures. In gothic churches some of the large stained-glass windows showed the Decalogue as well. Tablets bearing the Ten Commandments in the form of inscriptions or illustrations were not only displayed in churches, but also in courtrooms, schools, hospitals and private homes, and thus were always present. Knowledge and observance of the Commandments were required by both ecclesiastical and secular authorities. The Decalogue was the basis not only of Christian education, but also of common law. Thus it was a guide for the direction of moral, religious and public behaviour, as well as the standard of the Last Judgment.

Since Carolingian times, the Decalogue as God's eternal Law held an important place in catechesis and, above all, in sermons. Religious education was practised in the form of parish and family catechesis. Representations of the Decalogue in churches supported the sermons of clerics. They also facilitated and reinforced the indoctrination of illiterate people. Illustrations of the Commandments were a pictorial catechesis, a didactic medium for the religious and moral education of the people. Pictures were exempla of the moral doctrine of the Commandments.

With the introduction by the Fourth Lateran Council in 1215 of the obligation to confess and to go to communion in Easter week, the Decalogue gained importance as a moral norm and a basis for the examination of conscience, being a comprehensible and easily memorizable model for confession. With universal confession, a controlling instrument for the faith and morals of humanity had been created.

By the thirteenth century the Decalogue was well established not only in catechesis but also in art and literature. The pictorial language of Ten Commandments cycles needed to be universally comprehensible. Moses and the tablets of the Law are the most striking representation of the Decalogue as God's legislation. Before the Reformation, three types of illustrations of the individual Commandments prevailed: simple symbols; scenes of everyday life combined with the Egyptian plagues; and scenes of everyday life combined with angels and / or demons. Only a few cycles differ from these models. Genre scenes showing people wearing garments of the time in the setting of their local landscape and architecture linked the Commandments to contemporary life. They facilitated identification with the subject matter and a sense of emotional relevance, as well as underlining the validity of the Commandments for anyone at any time. Inscriptions in Decalogue cycles of the late Middle Ages stressed the relationship between everyday life and God's Law.

Only two woodcuts showing secular symbols are known. These representations were aids to memory as their 'language' was easily understandable for both literate and illiterate. The inscription of a woodcut from the Monastery of Tegernsee, dated c. 1480, names the recipients as the 'simple folk'.[1] It shows the Ten Commandments, the five senses and the seven capital sins in simple pictures, similar to the symbols in the fragment of another woodcut of the same time (Fig. 1).

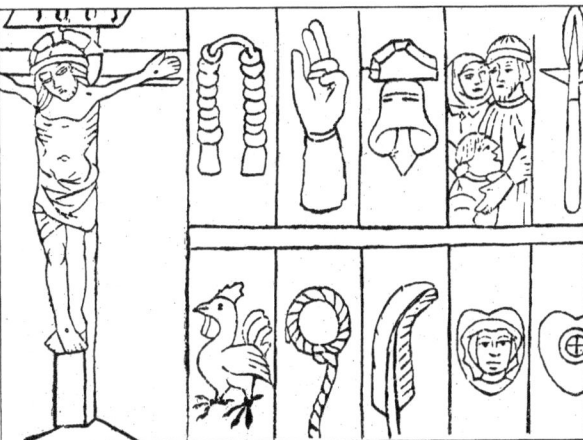

Fig. 1. Single leaf woodcut, fragment, 134×197 mm, lost. Formerly Fürstenbergische Sammlungen, Donaueschingen,

1. The original reads: 'das sein die zehen bott für die ungelerte leut'.

In about half of the known Decalogue cycles the Commandments were combined with the Egyptian plagues. This correlation created a pictorial argument. The earliest evidence of combination is the sermon *De decem plagis quibus percussa est Aegyptus* by Origen.[2] But most mediaeval authors referred to Augustine who, when bringing together the Ten Egyptian plagues and the Ten Commandments in his sermon VIII, *De decem plagis et decem praeceptis*,[3] explained the plagues as representing the condition of sinners who break the Commandments. The images, though, didn't interpret the plagues allegorically, as Augustine did. They referred to God's anger and justice, and how he could at any time make use of particular punishments for particular transgressions of the Commandments (Fig. 2).

Fig. 2. Anonymous. Woodcut, book illustration, 92×72 mm, in Johannes Schott, *Spiegel christlicher Walfart* (Strassburg: Knobloch 1509), Sixth Commandment.

Mediaeval people lived under constant threat from catastrophes. Anomalous celestial phenomena and inexplicable natural disasters such as earthquakes, floods and droughts, storms and fire, war, disease, plagues and vermin attacks were regarded as signs from heaven and as punishment from God, who reigns over all powers. As Psalm 148 says, 'Praise the Lord from

2. *PG*, XII, pp. 317-25.
3. *PL*, XXXVIII, pp. 67-74.

the earth, ye dragons, and all deeps, fire and hail, snow and vapour, stormy wind fullfilling his word'. Conscious of the fallenness of this world and of their own sinfulness, human beings felt exposed.

The oldest known illustrations of the Commandments in combination with the Egyptian plagues are in a manuscript from Picardy, dated about 1300, and in the Lilienfeld *Concordantiae* from the middle of the fourteenth century. The correlation between the Commandments and the relevant plagues is not graphic but only schematic in Robert de Lisle's *Psalter* from 1339, held by the British Library. A mural in the church of Zierenberg, dating from 1480, still shows a monumental representation of Moses with the tablets of the Law, surrounded by small pictures of the Ten Commandments and the Egyptian plagues. The same arrangement appears in a single-leaf woodcut held by the British Museum (Fig. 3). In cycles with scenes from everyday life, the figure of Moses with the tablets of the Law for the First Commandment expounds the relation between the Commandments and everyday life. In some pictures Moses is dominant.

There was another widespread interpretation, besides that of relating the Commandments to the plagues. In these Decalogue cycles, angels and demons represent humanity's choice between a godly and a sinful life. They symbolize the good and bad forces to which humans were believed to be constantly exposed. Using 'talking' figures—figures with inscriptions such as those in the Heidelberger block-book (Fig. 4)—the argument between an angel and his adversary represents the conflict between good and evil. It is an allegory of the human conscience, the contradictory dialogue of the soul, but it also indicates that people are free to decide. The accompanying figures—an angel in the role of protector of humankind, the devil as tempter to sin—characterize the righteous and devout, and the sinner. Sometimes these figures even interfere—the devil, for example, guiding the weapon of the murderer, reminding people of the omnipresence of temptation. These supernatural beings can be interpreted eschatologically as well, often referring not only to the sinfulness of an action, but also to its eternal punishment.

The prototypes for the scenes of everyday life were representations of the virtues and vices, also called capital sins or mortal sins. Until the thirteenth century these were widespread in western Christendom, even more so than depictions of the Ten Commandments. The oldest existing Decalogue cycle in a church, in the choir stalls of Cologne Cathedral, dating to around 1320, combines the Commandments and the vices. Several of the more elaborate mediaeval Decalogue treatises regard the vices as a distinctive disposition to sin and the root of disobedience of the Commandments. Some murals, paintings and graphic cycles refer indirectly to the vices, for example by depicting luxurious garments and idleness, dance and intemperance in eating and drinking, envy and avarice. Symbolic references to Adam and Eve and the *hortus conclusus* are also to be found (Fig. 5).

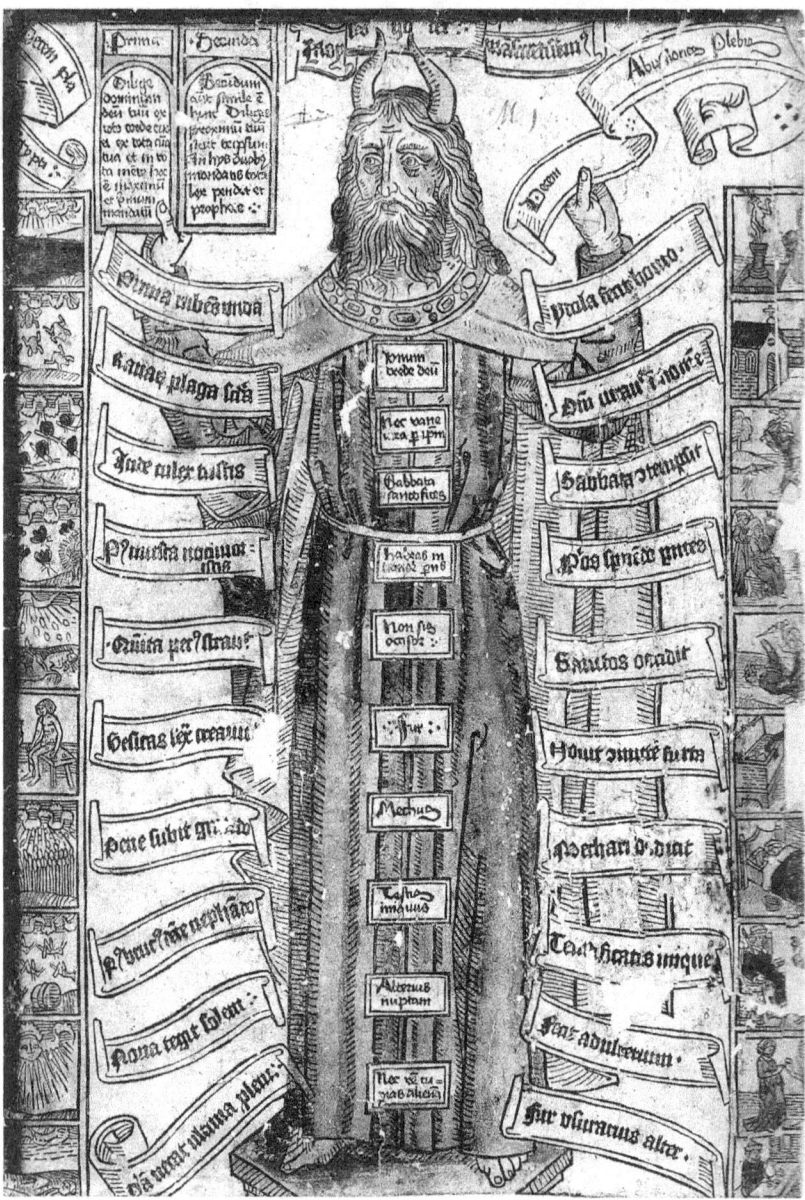

Fig. 3. Anonymous. Single leaf woodcut, 410×287 mm, 1465–1480.

THUM *The Decalogue in Late Medieval and Early Modern Imagery* 263

Fig. 4. Anonymous. Xylographic woodcut, 213×152 mm, *Heidelberger Blockbuch-Dekalog*, 1455–1458, Fifth Commandment.

Fig. 5. Sorg-Meister. Woodcut, book illustration, 183×118 mm, in Johann Moirs, *Der selen trost* (Augsburg: Anton Sorg, 1478 and 1483), Sixth Commandment.

Divine Law and Secular Justice

In 1516 Lucas Cranach the elder painted a large panel for the courtroom in the Wittenberg town hall with the Ten Commandments interpreted in genre scenes with angels and demons. From the Middle Ages onwards the Decalogue played a dominant role in legislation and jurisdiction, partly as building the human character and the sense of justice through religious indoctrination, partly because of the direct relation of law codes to the Decalogue as the oldest—and God-given—Law. The mandates of the second part of the *Admonitio generalis* of Charlemagne to a great extent reflect the Ten Commandments. The author of the *Schwabenspiegel*, a Franciscan from Augsburg, expressly refers to the Ten Commandments. This was in its time a leading book of law, incorporating parts of the *Sachsenspiegel* by Eike von Repgow, the first extant German law book, which dates from around 1230. The preface to the *Schwabenspiegel* reminds human judges to pronounce sentence according to God's will in order to avoid his anger on the day of the Last Judgment. At the close of the book there is another warning: 'Remember God's judgment with fear and judge equally the wealthy and the poor man'.[4]

According to Augustine, the Ten Commandments express natural law and contain the two Commandments of Love which, in turn, summarize them.[5] Thomas Aquinas and Martin Luther also regard the Decalogue as the summary of natural law that enables humans to live in community. The Commandments, which Luther once called the *Sachsenspiegel* of the Jews,[6] became the basis of commmon law in Germany. The compendium of laws by Johann von Schwarzenberg, the *Bambergische halssgericht und rechtlich Ordnung*, printed in 1510, is illustrated with woodcuts drawn by Lorenz Katzheimer and carved by Albrecht Roder and Fritz Hamer. In it the figure of Christ at the Last Judgment precedes the introduction, which also contains exhortations to judges. This introduction is followed by another woodcut depicting Moses and a high priest or judge. In yet another picture the people show the tablets of the Commandments to those destined to be judges. Accompanying biblical texts advocate equity and warn 'beware of false judgment'.

Graphic Cycles and Book Illustrations

Decalogue cycles were printed as single leaves and block-books as well as being included in incunabula and later books. In the form of woodcuts and engravings, Decalogue cycles were very popular in *Beichtspiegel*

---

4. 'Gottes gericht bedenck mit sorgen. unnd richt dem reichen als dem armen': *Schwabenspiegel* (Grossfoliodruck, Bibliotheca rerum historicarum, Corpus iuris europensis, 17/1; Göttingen: Musterschmidt, 1974), p. 229.
5. Augustine, *Contra Faustum*, *PL*, XLII, pp. 301-302.
6. *Wider die himmlischen Propheten*, WA, XVIII, p. 81.

and *Ablasszettel*, confession guides and indulgence certificates. Manuscripts and paintings in churches were the models for these and they, in turn, served as models for murals and panel paintings. Prints appeared up to and around 1400, the earliest examples being single leaves. The invention of paper—the first paper mill north of the Alps was set up in 1395 in Nuremberg—facilitated their production at a low price. Prints were produced and distributed in large numbers. More than 30,000 copies of an *Ablassbrief* (letter of indulgence) from 1480, sold to pay for the construction of St George's Church in Nördlingen, were printed within a few weeks. Still higher sales figures are given by a printer who in 1483 produced 50,000 *veronicas* (pictures showing the *vera icon*) for a Franciscan convent and in 1499 printed for the same convent 142,950 indulgences for the living and 46,500 for the dead.[7]

Single engravings were sold to the laity in churches, convents, cloisters and places of pilgrimage, but also at fairs and markets. The texts on these single engravings of Decalogue cycles described each Commandment, and include prayers and catalogues of sins, virtues and vices to facilitate the examination of conscience and prepare for confession. Indulgences also explained that the guilt of sin must first be absolved by confession and penance, and then the remission of temporal punishment for sins may be given. More simple prints, mostly woodcuts, interpreted the Commandments in the form of a pictorial argument only.

From the second half of the fifteenth century onwards, after Gutenberg's invention of printing from movable type, printed Christian instruction books provided another medium to represent the Commandments. But the possibilities of this new technology did not lead to new catechetical texts until the early sixteenth century. Before the Reformation older works had mainly been reproduced, such as *Die zehen Gebot* of the Franciscan Marquard von Lindau (d. 1392) or *Der selen trost*, an instructional manuscript by Johann Moirs from the Minorite convent in Bonn, written c. 1400. These texts had been intended to aid priests and monks in interpreting the principal Christian doctrines in sermons and educational work. They had been copied frequently from the start; and after Gutenberg's invention they were adapted for printing.

Above all treatises and catechisms in the German language were illustrated with woodcuts. These were not meant for educated theologians and members of religious orders but for lay people who were 'theologically unlearned' but literate. The 'theologically unlearned' were not just the non-clergy, but a heterogenous group of priests and preachers, monks and friars, nuns and

---

7. Falk Eisermann, 'Auflagenhöhen von Einblattdrucken im 15. und frühen 16. Jahrhundert', in Volker Honemann, Sabine Griese und Falk Eisermann (eds.), *Einblattdrucke des 15. und frühen 16. Jahrhunderts: Probleme, Perspektive, Fallstudien* (Tübingen: Max Niemeyer, 2000), pp. 152-55.

members of the Third Order, nobles and patricians, bourgeois and peasants, tradespeople and artisans, children and adolescents. These were the ones addressed. *Lehrbücher* (instruction books) had to be read and explained to the illiterate majority. Thus their interpreters themselves became mediators and, in the sixteenth century, also propagators of their particular 'true faith'.

In small catechisms destined for the simple laity, illustrations clarified the contents. Pictures address people directly and were also 'readable' by the illiterate. They facilitated access to books and the understanding of the printed text. They implanted their meaning much more deeply than the spoken or read word, and promoted efforts to teach and learn. Looking at pictures with Christian themata was a form of a 'pictorial catechesis'. Illustrations stimulated the sense of sight and aroused interest in the written text. They encouraged people to buy and use books. Short inscriptions accompanying pictures also encouraged people to learn to read; many of the catechisms included *abecedaria*.

Woodcuts, engravings and illustrated books were primarily intended for prayer and Christian education, and were used privately. This is demonstrated by both pictorial and written sources. High print-runs show that these imprints were bought by the laity. Lay people regarded *Wallfahrtsbilder* (pilgrimage cards) not only as confirmation of a pilgrimage, and *Ablasszettel* not only as receipts for indulgences, but also as media for contemplation, especially when they showed an image of grace. People trusted that the 'holy picture' could possess miraculous powers and transmit grace and blessings as well as remission from the temporal punishment for sins. These single sheets were pinned to walls and doors, placed in chests and boxes or slipped into books, and used as a private medium for prayer, a mediation, an aid to investigating one's conscience and to gaining indulgence. For simple people who could not afford paintings but were in need of a point of reference when praying privately or a model of confession when examining their consciences, a single engraving or an illustrated text provided a religious image for use at home. Prints or illustrations in books became *Volkskunst*, art for the people.

Catechesis and Catechisms

Manuscript catechisms are known from the time of Charlemagne. Alcuin, who is considered to be the author of the *Admonitio generalis*, attributed to Charlemagne, is said also to have written a catechism for the instruction of young people, the *Disputatio puerorum per interrogationes et responsiones*.[8] This systematic, didactic treatment of the main doctrines of Christianity became the prototype for later catechisms in its question-and-answer form. Alcuin is also believed to be the author of the *Brevis expositio*

---

8. Alfred Läpple, *Kleine Geschichte der Katechese* (Munich: Kösel, 1981), p. 77.

Decalogi.⁹ From the Middle Ages onwards these catechetic examples for instruction were integral to sermons, as is confirmed by an abundance of literature on the subject. The sermon was the most important didactic medium for the continuous transmission of the Christian faith to adults. A special chapter of the *Admonitio generalis* expressly obliges clerics to preach sermons on faith and morals in their mother tongue.¹⁰ The Decalogue was to be discussed in church at least once a year. Alongside other themata, the sections of the catechism were to be read after sermons. This, for instance, was affirmed at the Synod of Würzburg in 1453.¹¹ From 1516 on Luther explained the Decalogue and the other parts of the catechism repeatedly in a series of sermons. He wrote hymns based on the Ten Commandments as well.

The basic Christian tenets were taught to parents and godparents, who were responsible for the education of children. The catechesis in church intended for adults formed the basis for catechesis within the household. This included the extended family and servants, and, in tradespeople's families, craftsmen and apprentices as well. The head of the family was responsible for their Christian and moral education, a lifelong process in the course of which the learner became the teacher. In the age of confessionalization, religious education was also intended as a guide to confessionally correct behaviour as well as the establishment of a collective identity.

This pedagogical effect was strengthened by combining illustrations with interpretation. Illustrated cycles on single leaves and in books helped in explaining to children and servants at home what had been preached in church and to teach them the catechism. Pictures did not express what the Scriptures said literally, but supplemented them, and were interpreted more or less individually. Such representations helped people to internalize and remember what was said. Small editions of the catechism enabled simple people to afford a guide for domestic catechesis and the repetition of what they had been told in sermons. Illustrations were *Merkbilder*, memory aids. Illustrations of obedience to a Commandment would indicate God-fearing behaviour, those of disobedience the impending penance—its worldly side as enforced by secular jusrisdiction as well as its spiritual side at the Last Judgment.

Canonical catechisms containing the essential *Lehrstücke* (teaching materials) existed from the time of confessionalization. Luther wanted to formulate the 'pure' Christian faith and implant it as *gemein Gut*, the common property of the people. He intended to interpret the basics of faith in a way true to the

---

9. *PL*, XXXVIII, cols. 567-70.

10. *Capitularia regum Francorum* (ed. Alfred Boretius; Monumenta Germaniae historica, Legum, 2; Hanover: Hahn, 1883), I, pp. 52-62.

11. Paul Bahlmann, *Deutschlands katholische Katechismen bis zum Ende des sechzehnten Jahrhunderts* (Münster: Regensbergschen Buchhandlung, 1894), p. 38.

word and the sense, and to represent its important elements in a conprehensible form. Luther concentrated his catechism, by contrast with the mediaeval plurality of themata, on three *Hauptstücke* (main elements): the Ten Commandments, the Creed and the Lord's Prayer. He referred expressly to the tradition: 'However, for the common people we are satisfied with the three parts, which have remained in Christendom from of old'.[12] Luther established a trinitarian relation between the parts of the catechism: the Commandments show the will of the Father who issued them; the Creed, inspired by the Holy Spirit, allows the realization of God's will in the Commandments; and the Lord's Prayer, given by the Son, strengthens faith and confers the energy to fulfil them.[13] Later, Luther added the two sacraments of baptism and Eucharist to the catechism and, in 1531, the parts referring to confession, morning and evening prayers and prayers at table.

Number and Sequence of the Commandments

The number of commandments on the tablets is not mentioned in Exod. 20.2-17 and Deut. 5.6-21. Augustine thought they were written on two stone tablets corresponding to the dual Commandment of Love: to love God and neighbour,[14] the first three relating to God on one tablet, the other seven relating to humanity on the second tablet. This seemed to be confirmed by the fact that the second tablet begins with the Commandment to honour one's parents and is the introduction to the Commandments regarding one's neighbours: according to Paul 'thou shalt honour thy father and thy mother, this is the first Commandment' (Eph. 6.2). Parents are the first 'neighbours' children encounter and with whom they build up a relationship. Augustine, after considering several different ways of dividing them, established the figure of Ten Commandments as an absolute number. In the background, for Augustine, was the mystery of numbers, *Sapientcia studiosis sui inquisitoribus sese in via ostendit, numeris videlicet cuique rei impessis*. According to Augustine the divine wisdom is reflected in numbers, which are intrinsic to everything. His view is based on the Bible: 'Thou hast ordered all things in measure, and

---

12. Martin Luther, *Der Kleine Katechismus* (1531), WA, XXX.1, pp. 130, 348. Original: 'Wiewohl wirs fur den gemeinen hauffen bey den dreyen stücken bleiben lassen, so von alters her ynn der Christenheit blieben sind'.

13. Gerhard Bott (ed.), *Martin Luther und die Reformation in Deutschland: Ausstellung zum 500. Geburtstag Martin Luthers* (Frankfurt: Insel-Verlag, 1983), no. 541.

14. Augustine, *Quaestiones in Heptateuchum* 2.71, *PL*, XXXIV, col. 620: 'Quaeritur, decem praecepta legis quemadmodum dividenda sint: utrum quatuor sint usque ad praeceptum de sabbata, quae ad ipsum Deum pertinent: sex autem reliqua, quorum primus est Honora patrem et matrem, quae ad hominem pertinent: ad potius illa tria sind, et ista septem'.

numbers, and weight' (Wis. 11).[15] The number three is a symbol of the Trinity, and seven is the symbol of humanity. Augustine makes this is the basis for the division of the Decalogue: the first three Commandments refer to God the Father, the Son and the Holy Spirit, and the other seven to humankind. Moreover Augustine also affirmed that the Commandments were not only given to men but also to women, *Sed utique ista lex non solis viris in populo, verum etiam feminis data est.*[16]

Illustrations of the Commandments were not uniform as regards their sequence and distribution between the tablets. Divisions into three and seven, four and six or five and five can be found. In pre-Reformation Decalogue cycles the sequence makes it possible to assume the influence of specific authors. In Protestant catechisms the Vulgate sequence of three and seven was used. The aniconism controversy and the discussion of a prohibition on images led to changes in the wording and sequence in some of the catechisms.

Reformation and Confessionalization

With the Reformation the type of genre picture combining the Commandments with the Egyptian plagues or angels and devils was replaced by a historical programme of biblical scenes, chosen by Melanchthon and realized in woodcuts by Lucas Cranach. The basis for this was Luther's categorical demand: *sola scriptura*. He and other reformers accepted for the education of the faithful only exempla that were considered historically true and were confirmed by the Bible. Melanchthon took his exempla for sinful behaviour solely from the Old Testament (Fig. 6).

First Commandment: Thou shalt have no other gods before me
Moses receives the tablets from God at the peak of Mt. Sinai. God also appears in the burning bush and at the same time the Israelites dance around the golden calf (Exod. 3.2; 31.18; 32.1-6, 18).

Second Commandment: Thou shalt not take the name of the LORD thy God in vain
The son of Shelomith who cursed and blasphemed the name of God is being stoned by all the people according to God's judgment, as told to Moses (Lev. 24.10-16).

Third Commandment: Thou shalt remember the sabbath day
The Sabbath is dishonoured by a man collecting sticks (Num. 15.32-36). This biblical story is generally incorporated into a picture showing a church service, in which the preacher is very often a portrait of Luther.

---

15. Augustine, *De libero arbitrio* 2.16, *PL*, XXXII, col. 1263.
16. Augustine, *Quaestiones in Heptateuchum* 2.71, *PL*, XXXIV, col. 622.

Fig. 6. Lucas Cranach the Elder. Woodcuts, 183×118 mm, illustrations for Luther's publications since *Deudsch Catechismus* (Wittenberg: Georg Rhau, 1529, and several later editions), Ninth and Tenth Commandements.

Fourth Commandment: Thou shalt honour thy father and thy mother
The drunken Noah has exposed himself while sleeping, and is discovered by his three sons. While Shem and Japheth cover their father's nakedness with their faces turned away, Ham points spitefully to the nudity of his father (Gen. 9.18-24).

Fifth Commandment: Thou shalt not kill
Cain slays his brother Abel when his offering of grain is rejected by God while Abel's animal sacrifice is accepted (Gen. 4.3-8).

Sixth Commandment: Thou shalt not commit adultery
David watches and longs for Bathsheba, the wife of his commander Uriah, whom he then sends into a hopeless battle where Uriah dies (2 Sam. 11.2-3).

Seventh Commandment: Thou shalt not steal
Achan buries the booty he has taken from Jericho against God's prohibition on looting (Josh. 7.1).

Eighth Commandment: Thou shalt not bear false witness against thy neighbour
Susanna is accused of adultery by three old men and charged by two false witnesses before a judge (Dan. 13).

Ninth Commandment: Thou shalt not covet thy neighbour's house
Laban and Jacob water their herds at a well. Jacob had slyly obtained the right of the firstborn and the blessing of his father Isaac. Accepting advice from his mother Rebekah, he had fled to her brother Laban. After 20 years of service to Laban, Jacob asked for his reward. Laban agreed to give him all the speckled animals from his flocks—which, in fact, he already had put aside and hidden. At the watering place Jacob holds a wooden rod with the bark peeled in white streaks over the remaining animals in order to make them bear only speckled young ones (Gen. 30.25-43).

Tenth Commandment: Thou shalt not covet thy neighbour's wife, nor his manservant, nor his maidservant, nor his ox, nor his ass, nor any thing that is thy neighbour's
Joseph had been sold into slavery in Egypt by his brothers. There he was bought by an officer of the Pharaoh, Potiphar. Here he escapes from Potiphar's lustful wife who had caught him by his garment (Gen. 39.7-20).

In pre-Reformation cycles scenes from the Old Testament had only rarely been used for individual Commandments: in the choir stalls at Cologne Cathedral from around 1320, combined with vices; in the Lilienfeld *Concordantiae*, where the plagues of Egypt refer to individual Commandments; on the incompletely preserved altarpiece of a church in Hanover, c. 1400, with Old Testament scenes only; and on the retable at St Mary's Church, Gdańsk, dated 1480, where biblical and profane scenes as well as angels and demons are painted. In most cases the biblical examples shown were not identical with those later chosen by Melanchthon. All these early works were created by and for monks and clerics, not by secular artists for lay people.

Lucas Cranach transposed the biblical stories into his own German surroundings. His pictures show, with the exception of the scene with Cain and Abel, not Israelites in the desert but German citizens and peasants in present-day clothes, surrounded by local scenery and architecture. Thus Cranach's pictures referred to everyday life. The picture cycle Cranach designed for Melanchthon was taken over by the Lutheran catechisms; in the *Large Catechism* the pictures are accompanied by detailed examples from everyday life in the text; the small one briefly cites the Commandments and the biblical sources for the pictures, along with the command to love and fear God (Fig. 7). The biblical stories chosen for the Decalogue by Melanchthon became canonical, and Cranach's woodcuts were the prototype for Decalogue illustrations during the time of confessionalization.

The Aniconism Controversy

Reformation Decalogue cycles reveal a further consideration: the question of whether images are allowed or prohibited by God's Commandments. This

Fig. 7. Monogrammist H in A. Woodcuts, 88×66 mm, illustrations for Luther's *Enchiridion*, *Betbüchlein* and *Geistlich Lieder* (Leipzig: Valentin Babst, 1544), Fifth Commandment

goes back to the beginning of Christianity, but during the Reformation it turned political and became a question of faith, leading to stormy disputes between Protestants and representatives of the Roman Catholic Church, but also to controversy among the reformers themselves. Andreas Bodenstein of Karlstadt had initiated the debate by his strict rejection of pictures showing religious scenes and his demand for iconoclasm. The reformers were mainly opposed to images in churches and their veneration, which were rejected from several different points of view. The main argument was that religious images led to idolatry. They were also against representations of scenes not based directly on biblical events. But all the reformers, except Karlstadt and later Calvin, agreed as to the didactic value of pictures for educating the people.

Luther, who sharply criticized Karlstadt, regarded pictures in churches as being neutral, *adiaphora*. To him pictures were one of the bases for the faith, though he attacked their misuse in veneration and the *Werkgerechtigkeit* (justification by works) of donors—the expectation of special grace in return for commissioning images.[17] To Luther the destruction of paintings could not be based on the Bible.[18] The ban on religious images and sculp-

17. Luther, *Predigten des Jahres 1522*, WA, X.3, p. 35.
18. Luther, *Predigten über das 5. Buch Mose* (1529), WA, XXVIII, pp. 716-17.

tures was part of the First Commandment and therefore referred chiefly to the prohibition of idolatry rather than of the artistic creation of religious pictures.[19] Zwingli banned biblical representations in churches and had them collected and returned to their donors. But he tolerated pictorial representations for religious education in the private sphere. Leo Jud and Calvin categorically rejected pictures and even incorporated the prohibition of images into their catechism as a Second Commandment. In order to keep to the total of ten, they amalgamated the Ninth and Tenth Commandments. In some of the Strasbourg catechisms also, the *Bilderverbot* is a Commandment by itself and, ironically, is illustrated as such, generally by the worship of the golden calf.

Works by the reformers of Strasbourg display variations from convention, such as the illustration by Hans Baldung Grien for the Third Commandment in a catechism by Martin Bucer of 1537. The foreground shows a preacher, probably a portrait of Calvin, the background the Communion with bread and wine. Copies of Calvin's catechisms produced in Switzerland or the Netherlands were not illustrated at all, or only scarcely so compared to those of Strasbourg and Lutheran or Roman Catholic ones.

Catholic Catechisms

The Catholic Church reacted to the flood of Reformation treatises with their own catechisms, but these were seldom illustrated. Of the catechism of Peter Canisius, first printed in 1560, and the *Catechismus romanus*, printed in Latin in Italy (1566) and in Germany (1568), only some German-language editions were illustrated. Counter-Reformation catechism illustrations did not use the pictorial concepts of the fifteenth century, nor did they show new developments. The historic Protestant-Lutheran scenes from the Old Testament were used, but not conforming as strictly to Scripture as Melanchthon and Luther demanded. The picture for keeping the Sabbath, for example, was totally changed. It did not show a preacher and a man collecting wood, but illustrated the eucharistic liturgy.

The increasing production of books in the sixteenth century—Protestant and Catholic—led to a competition among printers over sales numbers. This in turn influenced the quality of illustrations. Decalogue cycles were mostly copied, resulting in a loss of quality in printed images, the more so as old woodblocks were reused and rearranged for new prints. So biblical and secular scenes got mixed up, and angels and devils were incorporated again. Moreover, in the very few retables that picture the Commandments in the age of confessionalization, scenes from everyday life were chosen, as in the time before the Reformation. This is the case with the *Rosary* retable, painted by Hans Ostendorfer in 1536 for Duke Wilhelm IV of Bavaria. The prototype may have been a woodcut by the Master MTR, printed in 1519 by Jobst

---

19. Luther, *Wider die himmlischen Propheten* (1525), WA, XVIII, p. 69.

Gutknecht in Nuremberg. The retable, which originally probably adorned Munich Cathedral, demonstrates thus the reuse of the pre-Reformation iconography, as well as the religious politics of the Bavarian duke, who did not permit the Reformation to take hold in Bavaria and maintained Catholicism.

During the second half of the sixteenth century Commandment cycles were produced in the Netherlands in the form of loose-leaf folders and in illustrated books. High-quality engravings printed in Catholic Antwerp by Maarten van Helmskerk from around 1566 and, after 1568, by Maarten de Vos, show only biblical scenes in the tradition of typological texts such as the *Bible moralisée*, the *Biblia pauperum* and the Lilienfeld *Concordantiae*. These display in places different stories from those chosen by Melanchthon, or are arranged differently. The catechisms of Peter Canisius, which are orientated around Cranach's illustrations for the Lutheran catechisms, were printed in Antwerp too.

At the beginning of the seventeenth century newly designed picture cycles combined stories from the Old and the New Testaments and the Apocrypha. A copper-plate by Martin Engelbrecht from the beginning of the eighteenth century, of which only two prints have survived, shows biblical scenes only in the background, while in front the classical gods are overwhelmed by Christ and the Virgin Mary (Fig. 8). Later on some of the very few known Decalogue cycles from this period show secular and/or biblical scenes.

Fig. 8. Martin Engelbrecht. Copperplates, 115×65 mm, first half of the eighteenth century, Second and Sixth Commandments, Augsburg, Stadt- und Staatsbibliothek.

Difference between Catholic and Protestant Catechisms

In illustrations of the Decalogue there is not only a difference between the pre-Reformation cycles, with scenes from everday life, and those of the age of confessionalization, showing examples taken from the Old Testament. Pictures referring to individual Commandments also differ, despite the fact that the reformers' programme of historical scenes had been taken over for Catholic prints. The First Commandment was often illustrated with the scene of Moses receiving the tablets combined with that of the idolatrous Israelites. Before the Reformation the Israelites adored an idol, but after the Reformation they worshipped the golden calf. In Catholic works since the twelfth century Moses often had horns, from a mistake in translating Exod. 34.29: *cornuta esset facies sua*. In Lutheran and other Reformation catechisms, by contrast, rays emanate from the head of Moses, as Luther had correctly translated the text and had also referred to it in sermons, *Non heissen horner sed stral*.[20]

In all German-speaking catechisms the Third Commandment is illustrated by a tableau of worship—in Catholic ones with the Eucharist and in Protestant ones with a preaching scene (Fig. 9). As printing plates were often sold or borrowed by printers, those made for Lutheran catechisms were also sometimes used for Catholic prints. Thus Luther, portrayed as the preacher in a Third Commandment scene, even appeared in the *Catechismus romanus*.[21]

Summary

Visual representations of the Ten Commandments have existed since at least the thirteenth century. Their language had to be understood by all, though it underwent changes during the period of confessionalization. Decalogue cycles adorned both churches and secular buildings, since the Decalogue was the measure for life on earth as well as for the Last Judgment. Single engravings and illustrated books were primarily used in prayer and Christian education, but also as a means of approach to art for the majority of the people.

In the sixteenth century the catechisms of Luther and other reformers formed a substantial literature. Small catechisms in the vernacular concentrating on the main issues and illustrated with woodcuts were widely

---

20. Luther, *Predigten des Jahres 1535*, WA, XLI, p. 432.

21. *Römischer Catechismus, welcher auß Bevelch Bäpstlicher Hayligkeit, Pii des Fünfften, nach hiervor gegebner Ordnung des zu Triendt gehaltenen Concilii gefertigt worden; und anjetzo in hochteutsche Sprach gebracht, und zum erstenmal im Truck außgangen ist. Dem allen nach ein Ermanung und Erinnerung an die Clerisey, von Othon Bischoffen undd Cardinal zu Alban und Augsburg vorgesetzt ist* (Dillingen: Sebald Mayer, 1568).

used in secular circles. The production of single-leaf engravings, by contrast, diminished. Most of all, indulgences fell out of use. The decoration of churches with images was reduced after the Reformation as well, under the influence of the reformers and, later on, of the Roman Catholic Church itself, and particularly of the Jesuits. As the number of illiterate people reduced there was less need for pictorial catechisms. Finally the Thirty Years' War represented an interruption, as all efforts related to art stopped and only slowly revived.

Fig. 9. Illustrations of the Third Commandment, left: Anonymous, woodcut, 75×62 mm, in Petrus Canisius, *Kurtzer underricht vom Catholischen Glauben* (Dillingen: Sebald Mayer, 1560); rigth: Lucas Cranach, woodcut, 113×74 mm, in Martin Luther, *Deudsch Catechismus* (Wittenberg: Georg Rhau, 1529).

Bibliography

Bartsch, Adam, *The Illustrated Bartsch* (ed. Walter L. Strauss; New York: Abaris Books, 1978–).
Christin, Olivier, *Les yeux pour le croire. Les Dix Commandements en images XVe–XVIIe siècle* (Paris: Editions du Seuil, 2003).
Geffcken, Johannes, *Der Bildercatechismus des fünfzehnten Jahrhunderts und die catechetischen Hauptstücke in dieser Zeit bis auf Luther* (Leipzig: T.O. Weigel, 1855).
Hollstein, Friedrich W.H., *Dutch and Flemish Etchings: Engravings and Woodcuts 1450–1700* (Amsterdam/Rosendaal/Rotterdam, 1949–).
Laun, Christiane, *Bildkatechese im Spätmittelalter. Allegorische und typologische Auslegungen des Dekalogs* (Dissertation, Munich University, 1979).

Markl, Dominik, *Der Dekalog als Verfassung des Gottesvolkes. Die Brennpunkte einer Rechtshermeneutik des Pentateuch in Ex 19–24 und Dtn 5* (Herders biblische Studien, 49; Freiburg: Verlag Herder, 2007).

Passavant, Johann David *et al.*, *Le peintre graveur* (Leipzig: R. Weigel, 1860–1864).

Schiller, Gertrud, *Ikonographie der christlichen Kunst*, IV/1 (Gütersloh: Gütersloher Verlagshaus, 1976).

Slenczka, Ruth, *Lehrhafte Bildtafeln in spätmittelalterlichen Kirchen* (Pictura et poesis, 10; Cologne: Böhlau, 1998).

Thum, Veronika, *Die Zehn Gebote für die ungelehrten Leut'. Der Dekalog in der Graphik des späten Mittelalters und der frühen Neuzeit* (Munich: Deutscher Kunstverlag, 2006).

Part IV

INTERPRETATIONS AND TRANSFORMATIONS
IN THE EIGHTEENTH TO TWENTY-FIRST CENTURIES

'THE LAW OF TEN COMMANDMENTS':
WILLIAM BLAKE AND THE DECALOGUE

Christopher Rowland

An invitation to participate in a celebration of William Blake's birthday at St James's Piccadilly, the church of Blake's baptism, prompted me to ask the rector whether, like other Wren churches in London, it too had ever had tables of Commandments behind the Communion table. I hadn't remembered seeing any when I was last there and discovered that they had been taken down and were in storage. We used them as visual aids for the Blake talk that evening! The little bit of reading I have done suggests that this practice of placing the tables of Commandments, along with the Apostles' Creed and Lord's Prayer, seems to go back at least to the late Middle Ages. Then, in the later part of the sixteenth century, tables of Commandments were to be set up as part of a concerted attempt 'to give some comely ornament and demonstration that the same was a place of religion and prayer' as well as assisting in pedagogy.[1]

The presence of the tables, either behind the Communion table or prominently positioned on walls of a church, reminded me of the importance of the tables for Blake, as is evident from the occasional appearance of the Decalogue in his texts and images. I would suggest that familiarity with churches in London probably inspired this creative printer, engraver, poet, artist and visionary. Their prominence ensured that, as Nicholas Ridley put it, 'they were learnt by everybody, young and old'. Reference to this ecclesiastical background is important, as Blake's criticism of the Decalogue was not a rejection of the Old Testament but of the *use* made of it by Christianity in England. Indeed, he includes both the Old and the New Testament as the 'Great Code of Art', though elsewhere Blake does call the Pentateuch 'The Five Books of the Decalogue', in what appears to be a truncated biblical canon outlined in *Jerusalem*, Plate 48:

---

1. See R. Whiting, *The Reformation of the English Parish Church* (Cambridge: Cambridge University Press, 2010), pp. 131-32; C.J. Cox, *English Church Fittings, Furniture and Accessories* (London: Batsford, 1923); I.M. Green, *The Christian's ABC: Catechizing and Catechizing in England, c.1530–1740* (Oxford: Clarendon Press, 1996).

> Then, surrounded with a Cloud: In silence the Divine Lord builded with immortal labour, Of gold & jewels a sublime Ornament, a Couch of repose, With Sixteen pillars: canopied with emblems & written verse. Spiritual Verse, order'd & measur'd, from whence, time shall reveal. The Five books of the Decalogue, the books of Joshua & Judges, Samuel, a double book & Kings, a double book, the Psalms & Prophets / The Four-fold Gospel, and the Revelations everlasting.

Interestingly, in his address to the Jews in *Jerusalem* Blake does not reproach them about their adherence to the Decalogue and law, but reminds them that they are inheritors of the belief in the Giant Man who contained in his mighty limbs all things in heaven and earth. This is probably a reference either to the giant Adam or the body of God (*shi'ur qomah*) of the Jewish mystical and kabbalistic traditions, such an important theme for Blake and indeed an inspiration for the title of this work, *Jerusalem: The Emanation of the Giant Albion*.

From his earliest illuminated book (*All Religions Are One*), the image of the tablets of stone plays its part. We see a contrast in the images between the static tablets of stone and the sense of a journey into obscurity on which the figure at the bottom determinedly sets himself. Such a journey of hermeneutical exploration, feeling one's way through the obscurities of received wisdom rather than receiving without question what has been handed down, is key for Blake, who famously wrote 'that which is not too explicit is the fittest for instruction... As it rouzes the faculties to act'.[2] For Blake, both the Old and New Testaments described as articulations in language of 'the Poetic genius, the Spirit of Prophecy':

> The Jewish & Christian Testaments are An original derivation from the Poetic Genius. this is necessary from the confined nature of bodily sensation.[3]

The frontispiece of *The First Book of Urizen* (1794), is seen in two of the variant versions of the book. *The First Book of Urizen* is Blake's retelling of the book of Genesis. It sets the emergence of a religion of obedience to the details of biblical prescription in the context of the genesis of a remote, divine scribe, seen busy copying and producing the material for sacred codes. The image in the frontispiece has the bearded deity, with eyes closed, transcribing, mechanically, from one book to another, following the contents of the book with his big toe. This image epitomizes Blake's challenge to an interpretation of a sacred book based solely, or mainly, on memory rather than inspiration, with no imaginative hermeneutical

---

2. William Blake to Rev. Dr Trusler, 1799, in *The Complete Poetry and Prose of William Blake* (ed. David V. Erdman; Berkeley: University of California Press, 1988), p. 702.

3. Blake, 'All Religions Are One', Principle 6 in *The Complete Poetry and Prose*, p. 1.

engagement. It is just passing on what has been written without any contextual application.

We see from a later plate in *The First Book of Urizen* that the contents of the divine book are brightly coloured smudges or, in some versions, quasi-hieroglyphs. These parallel the (at least to me!) indecipherable Hebrew on the tablets of stone in Plate 15 of *Milton: A Poem*. In the latter, the fracturing of the stone tablets signals the moment of redemption, with which, among other themes, this complex poem is concerned, signalled by the music and rejoicing at the top of the image. Returning to *The First Book of Urizen*; this divinely sanctioned code is indecipherable to any but the deity and the priests who are in thrall to him and his sacred text. We shall note a different approach in one of the later images we shall consider, but here the meaning of the signs and their application is dependent on a priestly caste, which claims to understand what the divinity expects—another feature of the religion of his day that Blake challenges.

Priests and monarchs are explicitly the focus of Blake's attack in this angry image from *Europe: A Prophecy* (1794), in which the King of England, crowned with a papal tiara and with the holy book open on his lap, is the one who endorses the hierarchical arrangement holding sway in the old order of Europe at the end of the eighteenth century. This sacred code, copied in heaven, is then imitated and applied by the priests and kings on earth.[4] The disastrous effect of that sacred code is summed up in 'The Garden of Love', where the chilling results of the religion of 'Thou shalt not' are evoked:

> I went to the Garden of Love,
> And saw what I never had seen:
> A Chapel was built in the midst,
> Where I used to play on the green.
>
> And the gates of this Chapel were shut,
> And Thou shalt not. writ over the door;
> So I turn'd to the Garden of Love,
> That so many sweet flowers bore.
>
> And I saw it was filled with graves,
> And tomb-stones where flowers should be:
> And Priests in black gowns, were walking their rounds,
> And binding with briars, my joys & desires.[5]

Blake's amusingly pungent work *The Marriage of Heaven and Hell* (1790) sets out to be a very deliberate attempt to challenge the errors of 'Bible or sacred codes'. It shows why Blake's texts and images constitute

---

4. Blake, 'Europe', 11 in *The Complete Poetry and Prose*, p. 64.
5. Blake, 'The Garden of Love', in *The Complete Poetry and Prose*, p. 26.

the high-water mark of two centuries of antinomian thought in England. *The Marriage of Heaven and Hell* does this first by challenging dualism in religion and persuading the reader of the need to undergo the cleansing of the doors of perception, which is key to the work. *The Marriage of Heaven and Hell* is a peculiar form of conversion literature, in which the angels are the narrow-minded purveyors of a strict religion, threatening hell to the disobedient and reckless narrator, whereas the devils are the advocates of the narrator's point of view. The climax comes when an angel is confounded by the demonstration by the Devil that the angel's hero, Jesus, is actually on their side, so that the angel is consumed in a flame of fire:

> This Angel who is now become a Devil, is my particular friend: we often read the Bible together in its infernal or diabolical sense which the world shall have if they behave well I have also: The Bible of Hell: which the world shall have whether they will or no.[6]

The 'Bible of Hell' here may be *The First Book of Urizen*, written four years after *The Marriage of Heaven and Hell*, in which the 'religion of commandments', divinely endorsed, and interpreted by priests and monarchs, is specifically challenged. The 'infernal or diabolical sense' is probably a reference to the deeper meaning that emerges after engagement by the imagination.

Crucial in the conversion of the angel to a devil is Jesus' challenge to the 'law of ten commandments' by acting from 'impulse not from rules'.[7]

> The Devil answer'd…did he not mock at the sabbath, and so mock the sabbaths God? murder those who were murderd because of him? turn away the law from the woman taken in adultery? steal the labor of others to support him? bear false witness when he omitted making a defence before Pilate? covet when he pray'd for his disciples, and when he bid them shake off the dust of their feet against such as refused to lodge them? I tell you, no virtue can exist without breaking these ten commandments: Jesus was all virtue, and acted from impulse not from rules.[8]

The biblical passages here cited by the Devil as indicative of Jesus' antinomianism come from all the Gospels.[9] Some are more convincing than others,

---

6. Blake, 'The Marriage of Heaven and Hell', 24 in *The Complete Poetry and Prose*, p. 44.

7. Blake, 'The Marriage of Heaven and Hell', 23-4 in *The Complete Poetry and Prose*, p. 43.

8. Blake, 'The Marriage of Heaven and Hell', 23 in *The Complete Poetry and Prose*, p. 43.

9. Passages include Mk 2.27 (cf. Mt. 12.1-8; Lk. 6.1-5), Jn 16.2 (cf. Mt. 24.9), Jn 8.1-11, Mt. 10.8-10, 14 (cf. Lk. 8.3), Mt. 27.13-14, and Jn 17.24 (it is not clear what 'murder those who were murder'd because of him' refers to, unless it concerns the

but this hardly matters in the context of this amusing challenge to strait-laced religion. Also, it should be noted that Blake did not want to suggest that Jesus' virtues are the moral virtues of the philosophers[10] but those 'virtues of delight' of one who lived by the Spirit not the letter.

In his approach to the 'law of ten commandments' in *The Marriage of Heaven and Hell*, Blake may seem to be doing what many commentators on the Bible have done down the centuries, pitting one part of the Bible against another. That would be a correct reading of the priority given to Jesus here, but this contrast should be seen in the context of *The Marriage of Heaven and Hell* as a whole. It is not about the rival claims of Jesus and the 'law of ten commandments' so much as a text which, by means of word and image, aphorism and fantastic narrative, is seeking to enable the reader to cleanse 'the doors of perception' so that 'every thing would appear to man as it is: infinite'.[11]

One of the biblical texts mentioned in the passage just quoted from *The Marriage of Heaven and Hell* is the story of the woman caught in adultery in Jn 8.1-11, which inspired Blake's watercolour and a remarkable series of lines that Blake wrote in his notebook, known as 'The Everlasting Gospel'. The image captures the moment when the accusers drift away (8.9), leaving Jesus alone with the woman (whom Blake identifies with Mary Magdalene). Jesus is depicted as stooping down, apparently to write, though his finger does not touch the ground. In effect he bows before the woman as he points to the ground (in a similar pointing action to the famous 'Ancient of Days' image from the Frontispiece of *Europe: A Prophecy*, whom we see measuring—thereby ordering—with hair ruffled by the wind of the creative Spirit; cf. Gen. 1.2). Jesus acknowledges the divine in the woman and points to the space between them that she can share with Jesus.

Here are the opening lines of this section of 'The Everlasting Gospel':

> The morning blushd fiery red:
> Mary was found in Adulterous bed;
> Earth groand beneath & Heaven above
> Trembled at discovery of Love
> Jesus was sitting in Moses Chair
> They brought the trembling Woman There
> Moses commands she be stond to Death.

---

deaths of the first Christians such as Stephen, Acts 7.58-60, and James the son of Zebedee, Acts 12.2). Indirectly, Jesus would have been responsible for their deaths because of calling them (particularly James, Mk 1.19) as disciples; see, further, C. Rowland, *Blake and the Bible* (London: Yale University Press, 2010), p. 191.

10. Blake, 'Annotations to Watson's Apology', in *The Complete Poetry and Prose*, p. 619.

11. Blake, 'The Marriage of Heaven and Hell', 14 in *The Complete Poetry and Prose*, p. 39.

> What was the sound of Jesus breath
> He laid his hand on Moses Law
> The Ancient Heavens in Silent Awe
> Writ with Curses from Pole to Pole
> All away began to roll.
> The Earth trembling & Naked lay
> In secret bed of Mortal Clay
> On Sinai felt the hand Divine
> Putting back the bloody shrine
> And she heard the breath of God
> As she heard by Edens flood
> Good & Evil are no more
> Sinais trumpets cease to roar (Exod. 19.16)
> Cease finger of God to Write (Exod. 31.18)
> The Heavens are not clean in thy Sight
> Thou art Good & thou Alone
> Nor may the sinner cast one stone…[12]

Though 'The Everlasting Gospel' was written nearly 30 years later, we find similar views enunciated to those in *The Marriage of Heaven and Hell*. Here Jesus rejects a religion of commandments, but as the end of this section of the poem shows, the space offered to the woman by Jesus enables her to reflect on her past life.

What is probably Blake's last image of the Decalogue comes in his *Illustrations of the Book of Job*, completed in 1825. In it the story of Job is retold by Blake in a centrally placed series of images with marginal textual references. There is a closely related watercolour of 20 years earlier which was the model for the engraving. This is just one of a remarkable collection of nearly 150 images of biblical texts that Blake painted for Thomas Butts. In it we see the way in which Blake interprets Job's nightmare vision as a terrible encounter with a divinity who demands that Job obey the Commandments of the Decalogue or face the fires of hell. The terrifying apparition has the characteristics of divinity seen in previous images in the series of engravings, but now intertwined with a serpent and with a cloven hoof. The figure points with his right hand towards the tablets of commandments, while below Job other figures stretch up, trying to pull him down into the fiery inferno below. In the main caption Blake paraphrases Job 7.14 which in the KJV reads 'Then thou scarest me with dreams, and terrifiest me through visions'. We are not told in the book of Job the content of Job's night visions, but Blake exploits to the full the space left by the text in his image. Below the image there is a long quotation from Job 19.22-27 which is pretty close to the KJV:

---

12. Blake, 'The Everlasting Gospel', in *The Complete Poetry and Prose*, p. 521.

Plate 11

KJV Job 19.21-27

Have pity upon me, have pity upon me,
O ye my friends;
for the hand of God hath touched me.
Why do ye persecute me as God,
and are not satisfied with my flesh?
Oh that my words were now written!
oh that they were printed in a book!
That they were graven with an iron pen
and lead in the rock forever!
For I know that my redeemer liveth,
and that he shall stand at the latter day
upon the earth:
And though after my skin worms
destroy this body, yet in my flesh
shall I see God:
Whom I shall see for myself,
and mine eyes shall behold,
and not another;
though my reins
be consumed within me.

Blake Job 19.22-27

Why do you persecute me as God
& are not satisfied with my flesh.
Oh that my words were
printed in a Book
that they were graven with an iron pen
& lead in the rock forever
For I know that my Redeemer liveth
& that he shall stand in the latter days
upon the Earth
& after my skin
destroy thou This body
yet in my flesh shall I see God
whom I shall see for Myself,
and mine eyes shall behold
& not Another

tho consumed be my wrought Image

The words 'Why do you persecute me as God', which in Job 19 are addressed to the friends, are here an address to the hybrid being of Job's nightmare, who 'as God' is persecuting Job. God *and* Satan together, who are *both* implicated in Job's persecution, are captured in Blake's image of the nightmare experience by a being which possesses both divine and diabolical characteristics.

Compared with the later engraving, in the watercolour Hebrew letters are clearly visible. They start with the words 'HEAVEN' from the Sabbath Commandment on the right-hand tablet and on the top left tablet the end of the Commandment to honour father and mother, 'which the Lord your God giveth', and then go on to the Commandments 'Thou shalt not kill', 'thou shalt not commit adultery', 'thou shalt not steal', just visible. The divinity gestures generally towards the tablets and the religion of commandments. What he actually points to, however, are the words 'which the Lord your God giveth' (אלהיך נותן). So, in the middle of the terrifying vision of judgment is an offer of the divine gift at the very moment when Job is made to face up to his failure to keep his obligations.

If this were an isolated piece of evidence one might not attach too much significance to it. But there are other indications in the Job series which support this point. In addition to the cleansing of Job's perception by vision, the change in Job also involves a change from a life dominated by obligation to one open to gifts, not least from his neighbours. For example Blake draws attention to Job 42.11, 'Every one also gave him a piece of money', in one of the later images.

Central to Blake's work is the attack on heteronomy, epitomized by the divinely sanctioned Decalogue, and on the Church's quenching of the Spirit in his, and indeed every, age (cf. 1 Thess. 5.19). His advocacy of human autonomy is rooted in his theology, and the divine in humanity and human difference are the basis of his politics and ethics. The 'poetic genius, the Spirit of Prophecy' is not an occasional charisma reserved for an elite or an elect but the property of being human. That awareness may lie dormant because of culture or ideology, or distorted by self-interest, but Blake saw his vocation to 'open the doors of perception',[13] to see God and the world differently, and in particular to see the indwelling presence of the divine as that which constitutes being human. While it is a golden thread running through his art and writing, it is especially present in the two works which have been the focus of this essay: *The Marriage of Heaven and Hell* and the *Illustrations of the Book of Job*. Though they are separated by over 30 years, there is an affinity about the way in which they prosecute these concerns. In *The Marriage of Heaven and Hell* what we find is a challenge to

---

13. Blake, 'The Marriage of Heaven and Hell' 14, in *The Complete Poetry and Prose*, p. 39.

orthodox theology which sees energy and desire linked with the fiery Spirit as diabolical and infernal, and a need for the messiah to recapture them so that his disciples can enjoy their fruits once more. In a diversion from the Job story there is a description of a fall from heaven followed by Jehovah appearing as Christ on earth to Job and his wife. The religion of heteronomy is seen by Job for what it is: in the words of *The Marriage of Heaven and Hell*, 'All that we saw was owing to your metaphysics', an 'imposition on one another', 'only Analytics',[14] and the theological edifice crumbles to be replaced by 'God with us' (cf. Mt. 1.23).

The Marriage of Heaven and Hell is a satirical work, whose profoundly serious theological, hermeneutical and political purpose the reader can easily miss because of its irreverence. There are several targets. First of all, there is dualism (Plate 4). But elsewhere the critique is more diffuse, of a form of religion which is about control, and the suppression of 'the Prolific' by the 'Devourer' (Blake's law-giving, restraining deity, Urizen, is so described in *The Four Zoas* 7a-80.49).[15] Blake also wants to show that Milton linked energy, desire, and the Spirit with the Devil in *Paradise Lost*, just as many of the orthodox down the centuries and thought that he was really 'of the Devil's party without really knowing it'.[16] So, Milton was a purveyor of a theology in which Christ is depicted as a stern restraining deity ('the Governor or Reason'),[17] like Michelangelo's famous image in the Sistine Chapel, rather than the giver of the fiery spirit. In *The Marriage of Heaven and Hell* the devils are the advocates of true religion— of the Spirit, of desire and energy—and it is the angels who are the stern, narrow-minded puritanical agents of restraint. Blake turns upside-down the religion of the angels, which he regards as a perversion of New Testament theology. That revolution is depicted pictorially at the top of Plate 5, with a rider tumbling head first from his horse. Blake's major theological point is expressed somewhat tongue-in-cheek by a clever satire on the doctrine of Christ's descent into hell. The messiah does indeed descend to hell, but on a rescue mission not to save souls but to steal the fiery religion of the Spirit which had been consigned to Hades by the exponents of the angelic, orthodox religion; and then after Christ's death he becomes Jehovah who dwells in flaming fire (Plate 6).

In *Illustrations of the Book of Job*, Plates 16 and 17 also involve a descent to Hades and a change of location from heaven to earth, as Jehovah appears

---

14. Blake, 'The Marriage of Heaven and Hell' 19-20, in *The Complete Poetry and Prose*, p. 42.

15. Blake, 'The Four Zoas', in *The Complete Poetry and Prose*, p. 356.

16. Blake, 'The Marriage of Heaven and Hell' 6, in *The Complete Poetry and Prose*, p. 35.

17. Blake, 'The Marriage of Heaven and Hell' 5, in *The Complete Poetry and Prose*, p. 34.

as Christ to Job and his wife. The God who in his night visions had appeared to be Satanic and had colluded with Job's torment now appears to him—and his wife—on earth. It is not Satan, but Jehovah and Jesus merged. God is no longer the tormentor but the divine in human, something that Job recognizes in himself too, as he and his wife share the divine glory. In Plate 16 the biblical texts printed around the plate include passages from John 12 and Revelation 12, which describe Satan's ejection from heaven and, in the case of Rev. 12, the statement about his appearance on earth. But in contrast to Rev. 12.12-17, it is not Satan who appears on earth but Jehovah as Christ.

Plate 16

ROWLAND *'The Law of Ten Commandments'* 291

In Plate 16 it is as if Blake is showing a reorientation of Job's theology. In earlier plates we learned that not only does Job come to see that the God who tormented him has Satanic features, but also that the universe as a whole tells him something about the divine (Plates 12–15). It is now time for him to have his theology 'disinfected' as he comes to see that Jehovah can only be discerned (to use Paul's language) 'in the face of Jesus Christ' (2 Cor. 4.6). If one looks closely at Plate 16, there is what appears to be a mark on the hand of the Almighty, possibly the mark of the nail beginning to appear on the hand of Jehovah as Christ becomes

Plate 17

Jehovah,[18] though it is impossible to be sure of this, because there is no indication of it on either the Butts watercolour or the Fitzwilliam sketch of 1823.

The mark of the nails was very important for Blake, possibly derived from his Moravian piety, and has been much discussed in recent Blake scholarship, contributing importantly to Elisabeth Jessen's[19] work on Blake's understanding of conversion. Thus, in one of the images that Blake engraved for Edward Young's 'Night Thoughts' (p. 73) we see Christ with nails piercing his hands and the distinctive mark of the wound that we also see, albeit faintly, in Plate 16 of *Illustrations of the Book of Job*. But the juxtaposition of this plate with the subsequent one seems to expand on the points made in *The Marriage of Heaven and Hell* and to link the 1790s understanding of Job with what appears in the iconography of 1825. In Plate 16, Job sees what precedes Jehovah becoming Christ as the transcendent falls to earth. In the very next image the divine *on earth* is seen by Job and his wife, who also share in the divine glory radiating from the divine apparition. Thus, Plate 17 represents Job seeing both that he shares in the divine and that the hitherto remote Jehovah, having descended to earth as Jesus Christ, is now with him and in him. Job, who is now aware of his part in the divine glory, can participate in normal life again. The following plates then depict Job's gradual reintegration into his former life, now recast and infused with the divine: as a religious man (Plate 18); a man whose vision of Christ has ethical implications (Plate 19); a narrator of true stories and an artist (Plate 20); and as fully integrated with his former world but with a different perspective on it (Plate 21).

Returning to where we started with the images of the Decalogue, what we have here is prescription, an uninterpreted and absolute demand. It is unqualified obligation without any sense of imaginative application or attention to context. What is more, as is indicated in the Temple Church reredos, commissioned in 1678 and made by one of Christopher Wren's craftsmen, the English understanding of the Christian religion is distilled into the Decalogue, the Apostles' Creed and the Lord's Prayer. The reredos is placed in a prominent position and was a crucial means of dissemination of what was taken to be the heart of Christianity. This Blake challenged, and replaced the official distillation of Christianity with his own: 'The Gospel is Forgiveness of Sins & has No Moral Precepts'.[20]

Ethical concerns are not negated by Blake—far from it. Blake is often described as an antinomian, and that is a correct designation—but only up to a point. There are stories about his activities in his youth, though what we

---

18. Blake, 'The Marriage of Heaven and Hell' 6, in *The Complete Poetry and Prose*, p. 35, and Jn 20.25; cf. 19.34.

19. E. Jessen, *William Blake and Conversion* (Oxford DPhil, 2013).

20. Blake, 'Annotations to Watson', in *The Complete Poetry and Prose*, p. 619.

are presented with in many of the reminiscences and in his correspondence is of a conventionally pious, though somewhat eccentric, man. His comments about theology and his outspoken remarks, not least in his marginalia, indicate an outsider and one who refused to be tied down by convention in law, politics or theology.

Two points need to be made. First of all, his advocacy of energy and desire is always complemented by the consistent ability to channel and to mediate the fruits of inspiration. The Poetic Genius, the Spirit of Prophecy, expresses itself in the often minute designs accompanying his handwritten texts. Blake may not have welcomed such a blunt statement, involved as he was in enabling freedom from the hegemony of Urizen. But the artistic genius is dependent on the dialectic between boundedness and inspiration or, to use the language of *The Marriage of Heaven and Hell*, 'The Devourer' and 'The Prolific'.[21] Secondly, at the heart of Blake's theology is participation in the Divine Body. This is not something one enters but recognizes an already existing participation. His task, therefore, is challenging false consciousness and 'cleansing the doors of perception'. This is not to re-inscribe the religion of commandments. It is about recognizing the divine image in the other, and recognizing difference.

The religion and the philosophy of 'contraries', which Blake may have in part inherited from Jacob Boehme, is crucial for understanding his theological anthropology. He may not have used the notion of the forgiveness of sins until the late 1790s, when in 1798 he wrote in the margins of Richard Watson's book attacking Tom Paine, 'The Gospel is Forgiveness of Sins & has No Moral Precepts these belong to Plato & Seneca & Nero'.[22] The forgiveness of sins, which he outlines brilliantly in his rereading of Joseph's discovery of Mary's pregnancy in *Jerusalem*, does not involve an appeal to what the law required. Indeed, according to Blake, the righteous Joseph moves from enacting what the law requires, via his acceptance of Mary and attention to the dream about God's rejection of a religion based on retribution, to an understanding of the heart of divinity as the forgiveness of sins:

> But Jehovahs Salvation Is without Money & without Price, in the Continual Forgiveness of Sins In the Perpetual Mutual Sacrifice in Great Eternity! for behold! There is none that liveth & Sinneth not! And this is the Covenant Of Jehovah: If you Forgive one-another, so shall Jehovah Forgive You: That He Himself may Dwell among You.[23]

---

21. R.D. Williams, '"The Human Form Divine": Radicalism and Orthodoxy in William Blake', in Zoë Bennett and David Gowler (eds.), *Radical Christian Voices and Practice* (Oxford: Oxford University Press, 2012), pp. 151-64.

22. Blake, 'Annotations to Watson', in *The Complete Poetry and Prose*, p. 619.

23. Blake, 'Jerusalem' 61, in *The Complete Poetry and Prose*, p. 212.

I have explored how Blake fitted into the history of antinomianism, and how antinomianism fitted into the theology of some Pauline passages.[24] Blake's is not the religion of Rom. 8.4, where the saving act of Christ enables 'the just requirement of the law [to] be fulfilled in us, who walk not according to the flesh but according to the Spirit'. Here there are echoes of Jer. 31.33, where the indwelling Spirit bypasses recourse to the external code to enable the life of holiness. Blake's take on the Pauline material is different.[25] His is the religion of life in Christ, in which there is no need for law and the Spirit allows one to know the deep things of God (1 Cor. 2.10-14). This crucially important passage, to which the history of Christianity has often appealed,[26] is one that is central to the first plate of Blake's *Illustrations of the Book of Job*. So, Blake differs from Paul in his refusal to countenance any concession to a religion of commandments. The ethical tone that Blake sounds emphasizes instead the task of forgiveness of sins, the rejection of violence—not least, as he pus it, 'religion hid in war', with its sacrifice of young men in the military to the modern god Moloch. Blake's appropriation of Paul is to link the emphasis of 1 Corinthians 2 with the theme of the Body of Christ, particularly in its cosmic dimension in Colossians and Ephesians. A divine space opens up in which 'Religion & Politics [are] the Same Thing? Brotherhood is Religion'[27] and 'As God is Love: every kindness to another is a little Death In the Divine Image nor can Man exist but by Brotherhood'.[28]

The terrifying image of *Job*, Plate 11, captures the forbidding and exclusive divinity who speaks in the opening words of the Decalogue. When Blake wrote of God in humans being 'mercy, pity, peace, and love' ('The Divine Image') and of 'every kindness to another', these were major biblical themes, but shorn of a biblical understanding of holiness and its related exclusiveness. Perhaps this counts as what Blake describes as 'the Laws of Eternity'—one of the few positive references to law in the Blake corpus. Also, with regard to the Decalogue, for Blake the prohibition of images was completely contrary to his interpretative method. What Blake saw was that 'The five books of the Decalogue' and 'the law of commandments' had become a form of Christianity which was quenching 'the Poetic Genius, the Spirit of Prophecy' (cf. 1 Thess. 5.19) and ignoring the gospel of the forgiveness of sins of which William Blake was such an ardent advocate.

---

24. Rowland, *Blake and the Bible*, pp. 200-16.
25. Rowland, *Blake and the Bible*, pp. 202-203.
26. A.C. Thiselton, *The First Epistle to the Corinthians* (Carlisle: Paternoster Press, 2000), pp. 276-85.
27. Blake, 'Jerusalem', 57:10 in *The Complete Poetry and Prose*, p. 207.
28. Blake, 'Jerusalem', 96:27-8 in *The Complete Poetry and Prose*, p. 256.

Select Bibliography

Blake, W., *The Complete Poetry and Prose of William Blake* (ed. David V. Erdman; Berkeley: University of California Press, 1988), also at http://www.english.uga.edu/~nhilton/Blake/blaketxt1/home.html.

Online versions of Blake's illuminated books, including all those mentioned in this article, as well as some of Blake's images of biblical stories at http://www.blakearchive.org/blake/indexworks.htm.

—*Illustrations of the Book of Job* are at http://www.blakearchive.org/exist/blake/archive/work.xq?workid=bb421&java=yes.

—*Illustrations of the Book of Job*, The Butts set, at http://www.blakearchive.org/exist/blake/archive/work.xq?workid=but550&java=yes

Bindman, D., *William Blake: The Complete Illuminated Books* (London: Thames & Hudson, 2000).

—*William Blake's* Illustrations of the Book of Job: *The Engravings with Related Material* (London: William Blake Trust, 1978).

Butlin, M., *The Paintings and Drawings of William Blake* (New Haven: Yale University Press, 1981).

Cox, C.J., *English Church Fittings, Furniture and Accessories* (London: Batsford, 1923).

Green, I.M., *The Christian's ABC: Catechism and Catechizing in England, c. 1530–1740* (Oxford: Clarendon Press, 1996).

Lindberg, B., *William Blake's Illustrations to the Book of Job* (Åbo: Åbo Akademi, 1981).

Rowland, C., *Blake and the Bible* (London: Yale University Press, 2010).

—*Radical Prophet: The Mystics, Subversives and Visionaries who Strove for Heaven on Earth* (London: I.B. Tauris, 2017).

Thiselton, A.C., *The First Epistle to the Corinthians* (Carlisle: Paternoster Press, 2000).

Whiting, R., *The Reformation of the English Parish Church* (Cambridge: Cambridge University Press, 2010).

Williams, R.D., '"The Human Form Divine": Radicalism and Orthodoxy in William Blake', in Zoë Bennett and David Gowler (eds.), *Radical Christian Voices and Practice* (Oxford: Oxford University Press, 2012), pp. 151-64.

Joseph Haydn's *Die heiligen zehn Gebote als Canons* and Sigismund Neukomm's *Das Gesetz des alten Bundes, oder die Gesetzgebung auf Sinaï*:

Exemplification of Changes in Musical Settings of the Ten Commandments during the Eighteenth and Nineteenth Centuries

Luciane Beduschi

The use of the Decalogue in music dates at least as far back as the sixteenth century. It was associated first with liturgical church music. Examples include compositions by John Hake, Barthélemy Le Bel, Michel Ferrier, John Brimley (sixteenth century), John Ferrabosco, Matthew Locke, Henry Purcell (seventeenth century) and Samuel Sebastian Wesley (nineteenth century). Their music consisted mostly of responses to the Commandments.[1] By the beginning of the eighteenth century, composers began to use the Decalogue as the argument for sacred pieces—pieces composed at this time were not exclusively for church use. From the eighteenth century, there are oratorios, cantatas and sacred dramas on the Decalogue composed by Francesco Conti (*Dio sul Sinai*, 1719, an oratorio); Johann Gottfried Schicht (*Die Gesetzgebung oder Moses auf Sinai*, 1790, a *geistliches Drama*); Félicien David (*Moïse au Sinaï*, an oratorio after a prose sketch by B.-P. Enfantin, 1846); Paul Gilson (*Sinaï*, 1889, a cantata); and Jules Massenet (*La terre promise*, after the Vulgate, 1897–99, an oratorio). An oratorio is:

> An extended musical setting of a sacred text made up of dramatic, narrative and contemplative elements. Except for a greater emphasis on the chorus throughout much of its history, the musical forms and styles of the oratorio tend to approximate those of opera in any given period, and the normal manner of performance is that of a concert (without scenery, costumes or action).[2]

---

1. For the musical reception of the Ten Commandments, as well as for the tradition of chorales on the Ten Commandments in the early period of its musical reception, see Paul G. Kuntz, 'Luther und Bach: Ihre Vertonung der Zehn Gebote', in Erich Donnert (ed.), *Europa in der frühen Neuzeit* (Festschrift Günter Mühlpfordt; Göttingen: Vandenhoeck & Ruprecht, Göttingen, 2005), pp. 99-106.
2. Howard E. Smither, 'Oratorio', *Oxford Music Online*, accessed March 2012.

From the seventeenth to the eighteenth centuries there were major changes in the use of the Decalogue in music: instead of being used for the Church (during services) it began to be used in concerts—thus frequently being performed outside the Church. During the twentieth century this change has become even more apparent. Composers have worked on music for films based on the Decalogue: Zbigniew Preisner (for Krzysztof Kieślowski's film *Dekalog*) and Elmer Bernstein (for Cecil B. DeMille's *The Ten Commandments*). Also during the twentieth century, Alfred Schnittke composed his opera *The Eleventh Commandment*; Elie Chouraqui and Pascal Obispo composed a musical, *Les dix commandements*, that was first performed at the Palais des Sports in Paris in October 2000.

In 1791, Joseph Haydn wrote a set of canons, first published in 1810:[3] *The Ten Commandments* (Hb. XXVIIa: 1-10) or *Die heiligen zehn Gebote als Canons*, one canon for each Commandment. It is about eighteen pages of printed music in the modern edition.[4] In 1828, his pupil Sigismund Neukomm (Salzburg, 1778–Paris, 1858) composed for the King of Prussia an oratorio in two parts for three soloists, chorus and orchestra: *Das Gesetz des alten Bundes, oder die Gesetzgebung auf Sinaï (10 Gebothe)*.[5] A version for voices and piano was published in London in 1832 by J.B. Cramer, Addison and Beale: *Mount Sinai, or, The Ten Commandments: An Oratorio, in Two Parts, Taken from the Holy Scriptures, Translated from the German*.[6] The oratorio was first performed at the Derby Festival (England) in

---

3. *Die heiligen zehn Gebote als Canons in Musik gesetzt und seinem Freunde Herrn G.A. Griesinger Königl. Sächsischem Legationsrathe zugeeignet von Joseph Haydn. Nach der Original-Handschrift des Componisten* (Leipzig: Breitkopf & Härtel, 1810); *Die X Gebothe Gottes. In Musik gesetzt als Canons von Joseph Haydn* (Vienna: Artaria und Comp., 1810).

4. *Joseph Haydn Werke*, XXXI, *Kanons* (Munich: G. Henle Verlag, 1959). 'Haydn sent the first of these canons to Oxford University in 1792 as a sign of appreciation of the doctorate of music conferred upon him. He changed, however, at this occasion the original text "Du sollst an einen Gott glauben" (Thou shalt have no other gods before me) to the more appropriate words "Thy voice, O Harmony". The Ten Commandments were printed frequently, the German and English versions appearing at approximately the same time [...]. In the seventh of the Ten Commandments, according to an unproved old story, he used a melody that he himself had taken from another composer, as if to poke fun at the seventh commandment, "Thou shalt not steal". The tale is based on an unconfirmed rumor, but it would be very much in keeping with Haydn's delightful sense of humor'; see Karl Geiringer and Irene Geiringer, *Haydn: A Creative Life in Music* (Berkeley: University of California Press, 1992), p. 341.

5. Autograph manuscripts, Bibliothèque nationale de France, Ms. 8239 and Ms. 7627. See also Sigismund Neukomm's manuscript catalogue, vol. 1, p. 69, nos. 316, 335, 338ff., 36ff., and 417ff., Bibliothèque nationale de France, Ms. 8328 and Ms. 8328 (*bis*).

6. This edition can be found online on the website of the Bayerische Staatsbibliothek: http://daten.digitale-sammlungen.de/~db/0005/bsb00053629/images/.

September 1831, then in Berlin in September 1832 by the Sing-Akademie and the Royal Chapel, employing more than four hundred musicians for two hours of music.

Sigismund Neukomm composed approximately 2,000 works, 50 masses, 5 oratorios, almost 150 canons, and 14 enigmatic canons.[7] Nowadays, Neukomm is known principally because in 1814 he composed an enigmatic canon for the first tombstone of his mentor, Joseph Haydn. For more than 30 years, several composers and musicians tried, without success, to find a solution to this enigma. Several papers were published about the enigma during Neukomm's life.[8] Neukomm thus succeeded in calling attention to his mentor, who had been too soon forgotten after his death. Almost 150 years later, when Neukomm himself was considered forgotten, his name reappeared in connection with his enigmatic canon.

We will see that the change in the use of the Decalogue in music is very well represented by these two composers, despite their being so close to one another in time and so closely connected personally: Neukomm used to call Haydn 'my father'. To examine these changes, we will look at the first canon in Haydn's collection and the sixth movement of the first part of Neukomm's oratorio, each of which treats the first commandment.[9]

The First Canon in Joseph Haydn's Collection

One of the manuscripts for this first canon of Haydn's set of the Ten Commandments is today in New York's Pierpont Morgan Library.[10] This manuscript gives the score as an *inventio*,[11] in which all the voices are written together and the different entries of each part in relation to the others are not self-evident for the modern reader (Fig. 1).

G. Henle Verlag published one of the modern editions of this first canon in 1959: *Joseph Haydn Werke*, XXXI, *Kanons* (Munich). The editor retraces the history of various sources (manuscripts and editions of the era) in order to explain how the modern edition was established. This canon is an enigmatic canon with multiple solutions—all the more numerous

---

7. Luciane Beduschi, *Sigismund Neukomm (Salzbourg, 1778–Paris, 1858). Sa vie, son œuvre, ses canons énigmatiques* (3 vols., PhD dissertation, Sorbonne University, Paris, 2008).

8. Gerhard Winkler, 'Non omnis moriar: Sigismund Neukomms Rätselkanon auf Haydns Grab', *Haydn Studien* 8.3 (September 2003), pp. 253-74.

9. The Commandments are not the same for the two composers. See p. 312.

10. Dept. of Music Manuscripts and Books (http://www.themorgan.org/music/manuscript/115073).

11. See Johann Georg Albrechtsberger, *Méthode élémentaire de composition, par J. Georg Albrechtsberger* (trans. M.A. Choron, Paris: Vve Courcier, 1814), pp. 144-54, and Luciane Beduschi, *Sigismund Neukomm*, III, pp. 95-111.

because the sources differ with respect to the use of clefs as well as the number of voices. Some sources propose a three-voice canon, others three or four. Some use soprano clefs for the three voices, others use treble clefs, others still use both clefs.

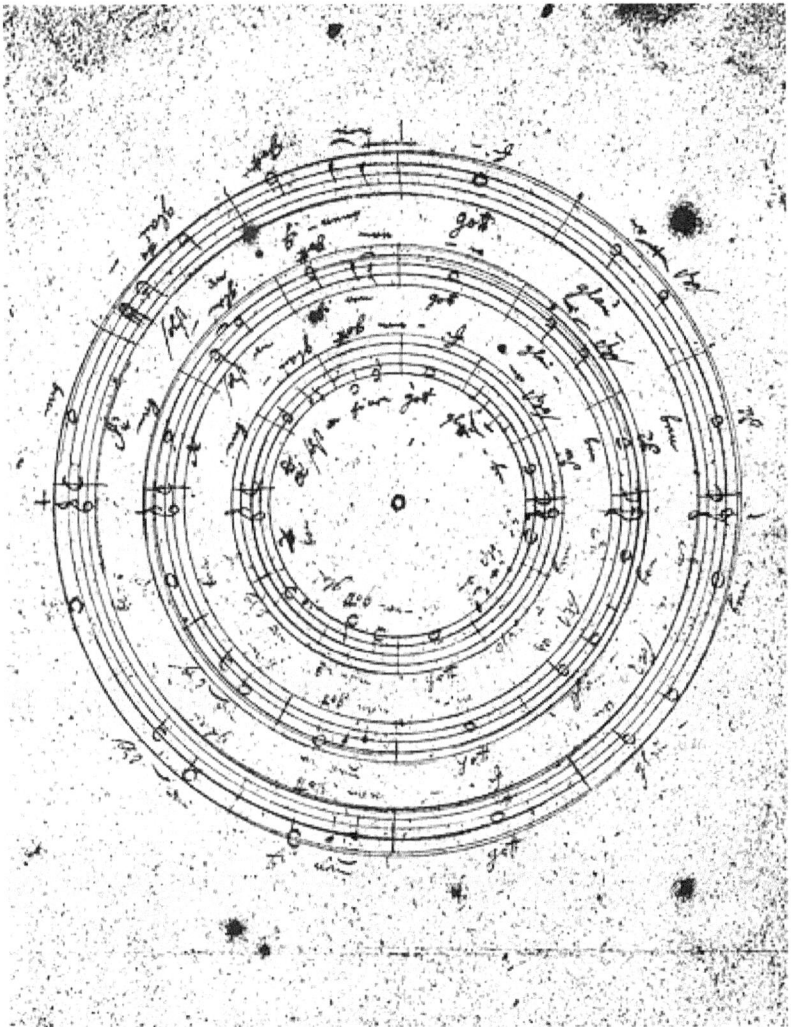

Fig. 1. J. Haydn, Heiligen zehn Gebote. 1. Du sollst an einen Gott glauben. Das erste Gebot, H. XXVIIa:1, autograph manuscript, 1791.
The Morgan Library and Museum.

G. Henle Verlag proposes a solution based on different sources using soprano clef (C-clef bottom line). At the time of this edition, the Morgan Library manuscript was only known by a photograph published in *Storia della musica* by F. Abbiati, Milan.[12] This source presents the canon in treble clef and gives a different solution from the one proposed by the Henle edition of 1959. The following explanation is based on a solution (Fig. 2) from the Morgan Library manuscript.

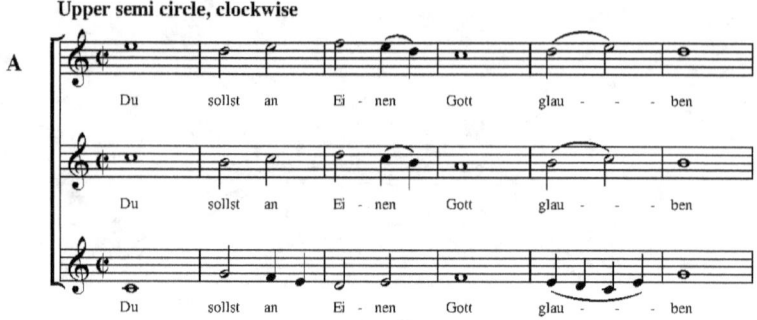

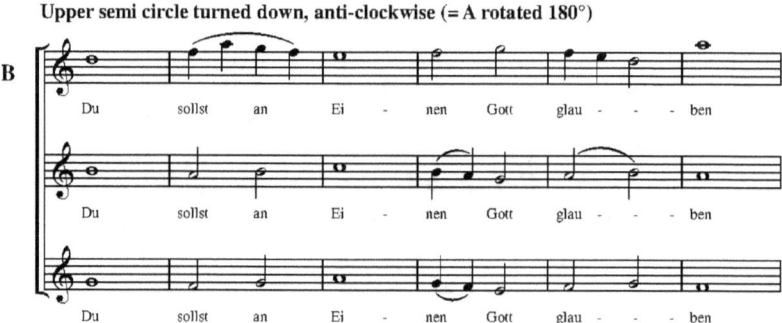

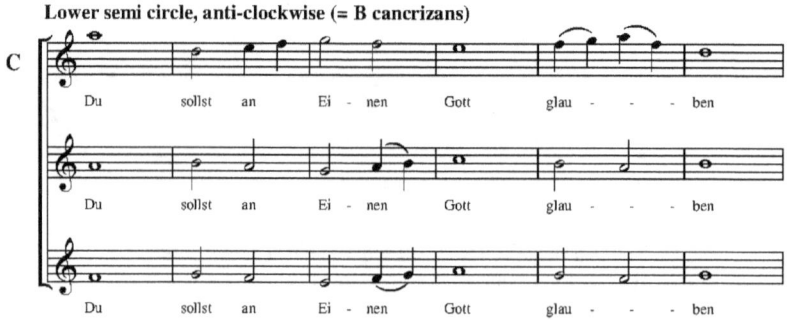

12. (1939–1946), III, p. 296. See *Kritischen Bericht* volume of the G. Henle collection with the complete works of Joseph Haydn, p. 11.

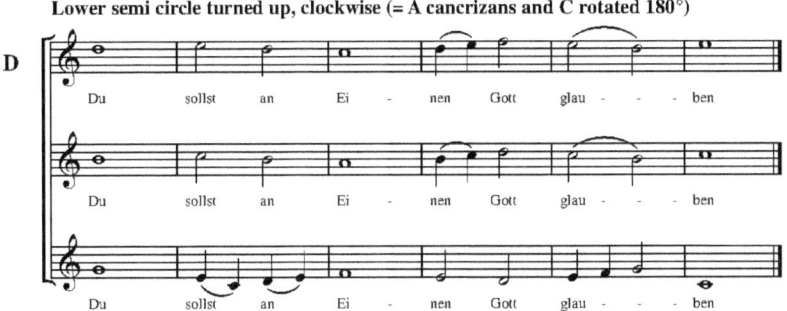

Fig. 2. J. Haydn, Heiligen zehn Gebote. 1. Du sollst an einen Gott glauben. Das erste Gebot, H. XXVIIa:1, autograph manuscript, 1791. The Morgan Library and Museum, transcription.[13]

From this autograph manuscript (Fig. 1), which appears in the form of a circle, we can easily deduce four realizations for the canon (Fig. 2). The circle is divided into two parts that form two semicircles, one above, one below. The two semicircles mirror each other. Each has three staves: outer, middle and inner. The complete canonic lines are obtained by reading the three semicircles one after another. Because the semicircles can be read forwards and backwards, clockwise and anticlockwise, there are four different canonic lines which lead to four different realizations for the canon.

The four realizations (A to D) of this transcription (Fig. 2) relate to the manuscript as follows. Realization A reads the upper semicircle from left to right (clockwise); the outer circle gives the upper voice, the inner one the lower voice. The page is then turned upside down by 180° and the same semicircle (now at the bottom) is again read from left to right (anticlockwise), producing Realization B, which is both an inversion of the voices—the inner circle becoming the upper voice and the outer one the lower voice—and a retrogradation of the reading (the technical term is cancrizans). The page is put back in its normal position and Realization C is read left to right from the lower semicircle, with the inner circle as upper voice. The page is turned upside down again and the same semicircle (now at the top) is read to produce Realization D, a cancrizans and inverted reading of C. The order of reading the four realizations is not clearly prescribed and could be undertaken otherwise, but the order presented here has the advantage that each successive realization starts on the chord on which the preceding one ended and that the final chord is the same as the first.

In order to obtain canonic entries of the voices in each of these four realizations, one voice must begin alone, say the top one. After having sung six

---

13. The slurs are reproduced as in the original: four quarter notes under one single slur in the upper part, the same under two slurs in the lower, mirror part.

bars, it turns to the middle staff while the second voice enters with the top one. And after twelve measures, the third voice enters with the top staff, the second sings the middle one and the first voice the bottom one. After these eighteen bars, they begin to the next version in the same manner.

First realization (A): upper semicircle, clockwise
The first voice begins by reading clockwise the outer staff of the upper semicircle. When the first voice arrives at the end of the staff, after half a circle, it continues at the beginning of the middle staff (still clockwise) and the second voice enters beginning at the outer semicircle. Upon concluding these two semicircles, each voice descends again: the first voice reads the inner semicircle, the second reads the middle, and the third enters at the beginning of the outer semicircle.

Second realization (B): upper semicircle inverted, anticlockwise
For the second realization of the canon, the manuscript must be turned upside down: the upper semicircle becomes the lower semicircle. This second realization is a retrograde canon and an inversion of the first realization. Now it is the lower (formerly upper) semicircle that will be read. The first note of the inner staff is now D on the fourth line of the treble clef. This note begins the second realization of the canon. This same note was the last note of the first realization. Read with the page right-side up, it was a G on the second line of the treble clef.

Thus the first voice begins the canonic line with the D of the inner semicircle by reading the staff anticlockwise. When the first voice arrives at the end of this inner semicircle, it continues at the beginning of the middle semicircle (still anticlockwise) and the second voice begins its canonic line with the inner semicircle. It continues with the same process as for the first realization.

The third (C) and fourth (D) realizations are obtained like the first two, but reading the lower semicircle: the third realization with the score right-side up and the fourth realization with the score upside down. In relation to the third realization, the fourth is retrograde and inverted—like the relationship between the second and first realizations.

This canon may sound as if it was a very simple piece of music but, if one thinks about the two semicircles mirroring each other and constituting four different canonic lines that can be arranged in four different realizations, one comes to see that this is in fact an extremely elaborate composition.

Neukomm's Oratorio

Neukomm wrote two versions of his oratorio on the Ten Commandments: one in German, the other in English. He had also foreseen a third translation into Swedish:

I believe that I spoke to you...about my Oratorio: *Les dix commandments*. I have my heart set on this work, which is dedicated to the King of Prussia, and seeing as I would like it to be well received in the musical world, I am thinking of directing a performance of it in Berlin... I will use you and Frigel to translate the 10 Commandments into Swedish:—this will not be too difficult because of the structure of your language in relation to German. Since I used Luther's *prose* translation, yours will probably not necessitate any changes to the music. I will bring you the printed parts and one can glue strips of paper with the translation.[14]

Neukomm prepared the English translation in Valençay between August and October 1829.[15] As we can see in Fig. 3,[16] it is not merely a matter of translating the text, but also of adapting it to the music.

Fig. 3. S. Neukomm, *Das Gesetz des alten Bundes, oder die Gesetzgebung auf Sinaï*, No. 6, Preparation for the bilingual edition, autograph manuscript, Bibliothèque nationale de France, L. 19037.

14. *Je crois vous avoir parler* [sic] *... de mon Oratorio: Les Dix commandements. Cet ouvrage qui est dédié au Roi de Prusse me tient à cœur et comme je voudrais qu'il fut un peu bien reçu dans le monde musical, je me propose de le faire exécuter à Berlin sous ma direction ... Vous et l'ami Frigel serez mis à contribution pour traduire en suédois les 10 Commandemens:—cela ne sera pas difficile à cause de l'anatologie* [sic] *de votre langue avec l'allemand. Comme je me suis servi de la traduction en prose de Luther, la vôtre se prêtera probablement sans rien changer à la musique, dont je vous apporterai les parties gravées sous lesquelles on pourra coller des petites bandes de papier avec la traduction* (Letter from Neukomm to Silverstolpe, Paris, 20 March 1830, Internationale Stiftung Mozarteum Salzburg).

15. Neukomm's manuscript catalogue, vol. 1, p. 75, no. 335, Bibliothèque nationale de France, Ms. 8328. See Beduschi, *Sigismund Neukomm*, II.

16. Manuscript autograph for the bilingual edition, Bibliothèque nationale de France, L. 19037.

In Neukomm's manuscript catalog, vol. 1, p. 90, after entry no. 417, we read:

> September 27th 1832… performance of my oratorio, Les 10 Commande-ments… as a benefit concert for blind people… The entire Sing-Akademie and the Royal Chapel, along with the necessary instrumentalists from the Regiment of Guards, all in all more than four hundred people.[17]

Besides three soloists and a large choir, Neukomm's Oratorio *Mount Sinai* employs a large orchestra: trumpets, trombones, horns, timpani, flute, oboe, clarinet, trombone, bassoon, ophicleide, trompa di basso, serpent, buccin, harp, violin, viola, cello, bass. It is divided into two parts, each about an hour long. The first part presents the first four Commandments: those relating to God. The second part contains the remaining six Commandments: those relating to our neighbors. The Commandments are systematically sung by the choir (Fig. 4).

First Part

1. Introduzione
2. Recitative, Basso (Deut. 33.2)
3. Quartetto, or Semi Chorus (Deut. 33.3)
4. Recitative, Basso Aria (Exod. 19.3, 4, 5, 6)
5. Recitative, Tenore (Exod. 19.11, 16, 19)
6. *Chorus I, The First Commandment* (Exod. 20.2-3)
7. Aria, Tenore (Neh. 9.6)
8. *Chorus II, The Second Commandment* (Exod. 20.4, 5)
9. Recitative, Soprano (Isa. 40.18, 26). Chorus (Ps. 89.8, 9)
10. *Chorus III, The Third Commandment* (Exod. 20.7)
11. Recitative, Soprano (Ps. 48.11). Aria, Soprano (Ps. 111.9; 86.11; 96.2, 8, 9)
12. *Chorus IV, The Fourth Commandment* (Exod. 20.8, 9, 10)
13. Finale, Basso Solo (Ps. 84.1, 2, 11; 92.5)
14. Solo, Tenore, Quartetto or Semi-Chorus (Ps. 26.8, 6, 7)
15. Solo, Soprano (Ps. 65.5)
16. Chorus (Ps. 100.1, 2, 4, 5)

Second Part

1. Chorus V, The Fifth Commandment (Exod. 20.12)
2. *Recitative ed Aria, Soprano* (Sir. 3.6, 9, 10; 3.15, 16)
3. *Chorus VI, The Sixth Commandment* (Exod. 20.13)
4. Recitative, Basso (Lev. 19.16, 18)
5. Chorus VII, The Seventh Commandment (Exod. 20.14)

17. *Le 27 Sept[embre] 1832 à 3hs, l'exécution de mon oratorio les 10 Com / mande-mens à l'église de la garnison au profit des invalides aveugles / Toute la Sing-Academie et toute la Chapelle du Roi avec le nombre / nécessaire d'instruments tirés des Regi-ments de la garde, en tout / plus de 400 personnes. J'ai conduit moi-même l'orchestre. / Il est bien probable, que je n'entendrai plus cet ouvrage exécuté / avec tant de perfec-tion. Les solos ont été chantés par / M[adam]e Milder, Mr Bader (Tenor) et Mr Devrient (Basse)* (Sigismund Neukomm, Manuscript Catalogue, vol. 1, p. 90).

6. *Duetto, Tenore and Basso* (Prov. 31.10, 12, 20, 26; Ps. 128.1, 3, 5. 6)
7. *Chorus VIII, The Eighth Commandment* (Exod. 20.15) Chorus (Mal. 3.5) Chorus (Ps. 34.17)
8. Duetto, Chorus (Ps. 37.18, 39; Ps. 64.11; 37.18)
9. *Chorus IX, The Ninth Commandment* (Exod. 20.16)
10. Recitative ed Aria, Tenore (Ps. 5.7, 10) Aria (Ps. 34.14; Jn 3.21)
11. *Chorus X, The Tenth Commandment* (Exod. 20.17)
12. Chorus (Lev. 19.2; Deut. 27.26)
13. Chorus (Ps. 143.2). Quartetto, Semi Chorus, or Solo (Ps. 143.10)
14. Recitative, Soprano (Isa. 25.7, 8)
15. Canon and Chorus (Deut. 33.26)
16. Chorus, Fugue (Ps. 97.12)

Fig. 4. S. Neukomm's oratorio, index

In 1831, a review of the oratorio's first performance was published in London by the *New Monthly Magazine*:[18]

> You ask me to give you an account of the Festival at Derby… The Festival of Derby was given for the benefit of 'The General Infirmary'; [the] Sacred Music being performed in All Saints' Church, and the Miscellaneous (or profane) at County Hall… It is a pleasant thing to find oneself in a place devoted to enjoyment of any sort; and this pleasure is not diminished when music of the loftiest character is to form a part of the recreation… The chorus singers (in number from one hundred and twenty to one hundred and fifty, I believe) were alone worth a journey thither; for there is never the same vast body of voice to be heard in London… The person, however, who mainly interested me (and who was in effect the solid prop of the Derby Festival) was the Chevalier Sigismond Neukomm.[19]

This review also states very clearly how Neukomm sought to contextualize the presentation of the Ten Commandments:

> The Oratorio of 'Mount Sinai' has been the subject of so much detailed criticism, that I shall touch merely upon a few of its prominent parts. You will understand that it, in fact, consists of 'The Ten Commandments', each of which is prefaced and followed by various portions of the Old Testament, selected with infinite taste, and adapted to recitatives and airs, duets, quartets, and solos, according to the judgment of the composer.

---

18. 'A Week at Derby, during "The Festival"', *New Monthly Magazine and Literary Journal* (1831, 2), pp. 481-86.

Further contemporary commentaries can be read in: 'On the Chevalier Neukomm's Oratorio, "The Ten Commandments", and Cantata, "Napoleon's Midnight Review"', *The London and Paris Observer or Weekly Chronicle of Literature, Science and The Fine Arts* 7 (1831), p. 334; and 'London Musical Letter, London, 5th October 1831', *The Edinburgh Literary Journal or Weekly Register or Criticism and Belles Lettres* (July–December, 1831), p. 228.

19. 'A Week at Derby', pp. 481-86.

Contrary to what we might assume, the Oratorio's text is not drawn exclusively from Exodus and Deuteronomy. Rather, it is assembled from several biblical passages and constitutes what Neukomm calls a poem. The composer includes other biblical texts with the Ten Commandments in order to depict the moment when the Law is given, and also to provide commentary on each Commandment (see pp. 313-17). In a letter written in Manchester, dated 14 June 1836 and addressed to Silverstolpe,[20] Neukomm explains how he conceived the argument for his oratorio:

> I have spent the better part of these last six years in England, and during that time I have composed almost entirely on English texts. Most of my works have been sacred music with biblical texts, the Bible being an endless source of sublime and touching thoughts. I became accustomed to creating (I dare to call it that) a poem by putting together passages which, if well chosen, are capable of forming a whole... Jeremiah, Isaiah and the Psalms are where I most often look for texts.[21]

From the London review published in 1831 we can also gain some insight into what effect such an assemblage of texts had on the public at that time:

> The Commandments themselves, which are invariably given in chorus, may, for high and imposing effect, stand almost by the side of Handel and Haydn. The Oratorio opened with a recitative, describing the giving forth of 'The fiery law'; and then followed a charming quartet, 'He loveth his flock', which, in its tenderness and a certain pastoral simplicity, can scarcely be excelled. Mr. Phillips's fine voice was then heard chanting a striking air, 'I carried you upon eagles' wings'. Then Braham gave out, in his great style, the descent of God upon Mount Sinai, among thunders and lightnings, and 'The voice of the trumpet exceeding loud'. And then all the grandeur of music broke loose, and the words of the first Commandment, 'I Am The Lord Thy God' came down, in vast oracular tones, that left no room in the mind for any thing but admiration and surprise. I do not remember ever to have been so awe-struck by music as by this first chorus, proclaiming the 'I Am' of the Deity, and his eternal law. I positively trembled before it. The great effect here produced seemed to me not to arise from any sudden startling transitions of sound, nor from any mysterious combinations, but to be the result of feeling and of extreme simplicity. In the recitative, which introduces the

---

20. Typewritten copy at the Internationale Stiftung Mozarteum Salzburg.

21. *Pendant les 6 dernières années que je viens de passer pour la plupart en Angleterre, j'ai composé presqu'exclusivement, sur des paroles anglaises; le plus grand nombre de mes derniers ouvrages consiste en morceaux de musique sacrée, dont les paroles sont tirées de la Bible, cette source inépuisable de pensées sublimes et touchantes. Je pris l'habitude de me construire (si j'ose m'exprimer ainsi) un poëme* [sic] *en mettant ensemble de passages qui, habilement choisis, peuvent former un tout... Jérémie, Isaïe e les pseaumes* [sic] *sont les sources où je puise le plus souvent.*

Commandment, there is, indeed, a very solemn effect of trumpets; but the Commandment itself does not depend on any one particular instrument. It is borne upon a vast even body of sound, and is given upon exceedingly few notes.

Indeed, the difference between the musical setting of the Commandments and the setting of what precedes and follows the Commandments is striking. The Commandments are set with surprising simplicity. The grandiose effect that Neukomm achieves for the text of each Commandment is conveyed by the music that heralds their pronouncement.

The First Commandment (No. 6) (Fig. 6) is preceded by a tenor recitative (No. 5) (Fig. 5). The manuscript of the orchestral accompaniment for the recitative and the first page of the first Commandment can be seen in Fig. 5.[22] In this figure I have added the texts sung by the tenor and chorus:

Recitative
And on the third day the Lord will descend before all the people up on Mt. Sinai.
And it came to pass on the third day in the morning, that there were thunders and lightnings,
and a thick cloud upon the mount,
and the voice of the trumpet exceeding loud:
so that all the people, that was in the camp, trembled.
And the voice of the trumpet sounded long, and waxed louder and louder.
Moses spake and God answered him by a voice,
and spake all these words saying:

Chorus
I am the Lord, thy God, which have brought thee out of the land of Egypt, out of the house, of the house of bondage. Thou shalt have none other gods but me.

Neukomm holds nothing back when musically illustrating the text of Moses: *andante maestoso* in the introduction with double-dotted rhythms typical of a French overture, a change in tempo to *vivace* after the introduction (mes. 7), tremolos in the timpani and strings (mes. 7–21), 'thunders and lightnings' in the flute (mes. 26–28), etc. The transformation between this and the Commandment that follows is stark: all voices now become completely homophonic and homorhythmic. The melody is extremely simple (Fig. 6).

22. Bibliothèque nationale de France, Ms. 8239.

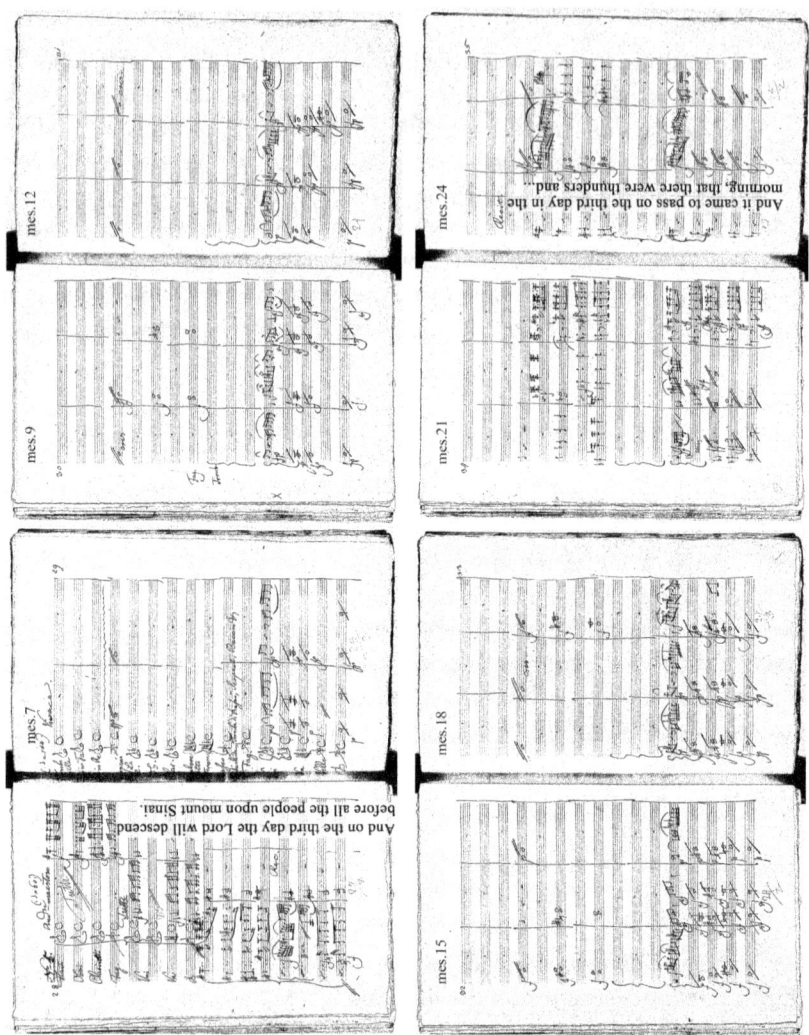

Fig. 5a. S. Neukomm, *Das Gesetz des alten Bundes, oder die Gesetzgebung auf Sinaï*, No. 5, Recitative, Tenore (Exod. 19.11, 16, 19), autograph manuscript, Bibliothèque nationale de France, Ms. 8239.
Orchestral accompaniment with tenor text added.

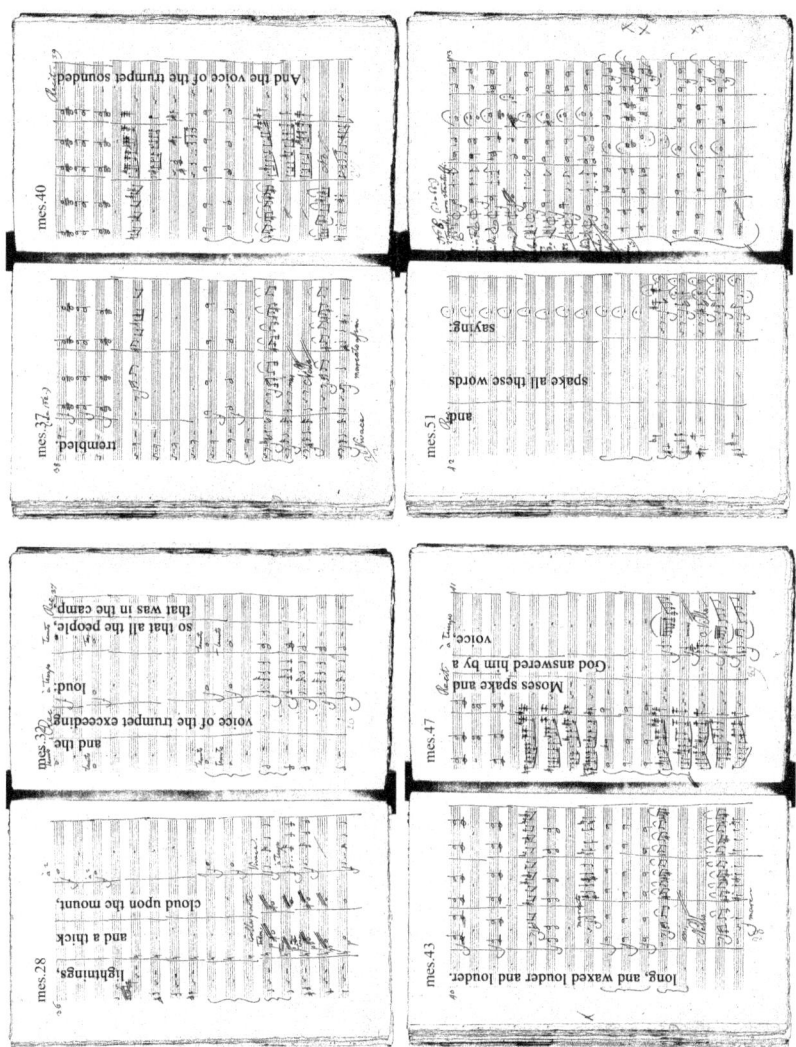

Fig. 5b. S. Neukomm, *Das Gesetz des alten Bundes, oder die Gesetzgebung auf Sinaï*, No. 5, Recitative, Tenore (Exod. 19.11, 16, 19), autograph manuscript,
Bibliothèque nationale de France, Ms. 8239.
Orchestral accompaniment with tenor text added.

Fig. 6. S. Neukomm, *Das Gesetz des alten Bundes, oder die Gesetzgebung auf Sinaï*, No. 6, Chorus I, The First Commandment (Exod. 20.2-3);
Mount Sinai, or, The Ten Commandments: An Oratorio, in Two Parts, Taken from the Holy Scriptures, Translated from the German (London: J.B. Cramer, 1832), pp. 20-21.

In the letter addressed to Silverstolpe in June 1836, Neukomm refers to the musical setting of the Commandments. He compares music meant for large churches to painting done for theatre decor. Neukomm wishes the music composed for these occasions to be 'gigantic and colossal'. Referring to Haydn's *Creation* (and not to the canons in the Ten Commandments collection), the composer affirms that in his old mentor's oratorio the notes 'seem to shrink and only shine from time to time instead of glowing like a sun':

> I have recently written six large choruses meant for the *Music Festivals* which take place in England every three years in multiple cities and in which three to six hundred musicians participate. Almost all the concerts take place in large churches where delicate details are lost in the Gothic vaults. It took me a while to realize that a completely different kind of composition is necessary for these spaces. It is necessary to paint with a broad paintbrush, as for theatre scenery. Handel was the only composer (after the old masters such as Palestrina and his contemporaries) to have known this secret. Handel's music (he being the greatest of the greats) becomes colossal and gigantic under these huge holy vaults, whereas the immortal masterpieces such as Haydn's *Creation* and Mozart's *Requiem* seem to shrink and only shine from time to time instead of glowing like a sun. I wish you were able to hear in England one of Handel's works, such as *Israel in Egypt* (which I consider foremost amongst this composer's works and which I find even better than *Messiah*). After a performance, one is exhausted and

feels like saying 'nunc dimitte Domine'. Anyone insolent enough to leave saying 'anch'io son pittore' should be sent straight to the hospital.[23]

In Neukomm's oratorio, the impression of grandeur comes from the context, from the pieces that precede and follow each Commandment. It is also achieved through the use of a romantic orchestra and more than four hundred performers. Haydn's elaborate counterpoint for the canons could hardly be sung by four hundred singers. It is not theatre music. Neukomm's intention was very clear: 'It took me a while to realize that a completely different kind of composition is necessary for these spaces. It is necessary to paint with a broad paintbrush, as for theatre scenery.' Neukomm is using a very broad brush. Haydn is using very small (and delicate) ones. Haydn is dealing with the old tradition: music for Baroque churches—perhaps even just for contemplation. Neukomm is using old procedures (figured bass, homophony, pieces that sound like a Lutheran chorale), but he is using these old procedures in a new context: his music is made for the stage—or for Gothic cathedrals.

---

23. *J'ai composé récemment 6 grands chœurs, calculés pour les* Music Festivals *qui ont eu lieu en Angleterre de 3 en 3 ans dans plusieurs villes et auxquels il y a un concours de 300 à 600 musiciens. Ces concerts sont presque tous exécutés dans de grandes églises, où tous les détails délicats meurent dans ces voûtes gothiques. Une longue expérience m'a appris qu'il faut écrire pour ces vaisseaux d'une manière tout à fait différente : c'est de la peinture à grosses brosses, comme pour les décorations de théâtre, qu'il faut. Händel était le seul compositeur (après les anciens maîtres, tels que Palestrina et ses contemporains) qui ait su ce secret. Aussi la musique de Händel (le plus grand des plus grands) devient-elle colossale, gigantesque sous ces voûtes sacrées, tandis que les chefs d'œuvres immortels, tels que la création de Haydn et le Réquiem de Mozart se rapétissent, n'y brillent que par intervalles et comme des éclairs, au lieu de luire comme un soleil. Je voudrais que vous puissiez entendre en Angleterre un de ces ouvrages de Händel, par exemple Israël en Égypte, (que je mets à la tête de tous les chefs d'œuvre de ce compositeur, et que je trouve supérieur à son Messie). Après une telle exécution on est anéanti et on a envie de dire: « nunc dimitte Domine ». L'homme qui en sortant de là serait assez insolent pour dire: « anch'io son pittore », devrait être envoyé tout droit aux petites maisons* (Typewritten copy at the Internationale Stiftung Mozarteum Salzburg).

Commandments in Joseph Haydn's Canons Collection

1. Thou in one God alone shalt believe.
2. Thou shalt the name of God never vainly utter.
3. Thou shalt keep the Sabbath a holyday.
4. Thou thy father and mother shalt honor that so a long life on earth to thee shall come, welfare in Zion.
5. Thou shalt not murder.
6. Thou shalt not yield thee to lewdness.
7. Thou shalt not pilfer.
8. Thou shalt not false witness utter.
9. Thou shalt not go lusting for thy neighbor's wife.
10. Thou shalt not go lusting for thy neighbor's goods.

Commandments in Sigismund Neukomm's Oratorio

1. Thou shalt have none other gods but me.
2. Thou shalt not make to thy self any graven image, nor the likeness of anything that is in heav'n above, or in the earth beneath, or that is in the water under the earth. Thou shalt not bow down to them nor worship them.
3. Thou shalt not take the name of the Lord thy God in vain, for the Lord will not hold him guiltless, that taketh his name in vain.
4. Remember that thou keep holy the Sabbath day. Six days shalt thou labor and do all that thou hast to do, but the seventh day is the Sabbath of the Lord thy God. In it thou shalt do no manner of work; thou and thy Son, and thy Daughter, thy servant, and thy maid servant, thy cattle, and the stranger that is within thy gates.
5. Honor thy Father and thy Mother, that thy days may be long in the land which the Lord thy God giveth thee.
6. Thou shalt do no Murder.
7. Thou shalt not commit Adultery.
8. Thou shalt not steal.
9. Thou shalt not bear false witness against thy neighbor.
10. Thou shalt not covet thy neighbor's house, thou shalt not covet thy neighbor's wife, nor his servant, nor his maid, nor his ox, nor his ass, nor anything that is his.

Sigismund Neukomm's Oratorio Text

First Part
1. Introduzione

2. Recitative, Basso (Deut. 33.2)
And Moses spake and said: The Lord came from Sinai, and rose up from Seir unto his people. He shined forth from mount Paran, and came with ten thousands of saints: from his right hand went a fiery law for them.

3. Quartetto, or Semi Chorus (Deut. 33.3)
He loveth his flock! All his righteous Saints are in thy hand and they shall sit down at thy feet and every one shall receive his Commandments, he leadeth them, he loveth his flock.

4. Recitative, Basso. Aria (Exod. 19.3, 4, 5, 6)
And the Lord call'd unto Moses out of the mountain, saying: Thus shalt thou say to the house of Jacob, and tell the children of Israel:
I carried you upon eagles' wings, and I have brought you unto myself. Therefore if ye will obey my Commandments, and if ye will keep my covenant, then shall ye be my children above all people, for all the earth is mine. Ye shall be to me a kingdom of priests and a holy nation, ye shall be a holy nation above all people.

5. Recitative, Tenore (Exod. 19.11, 16, 19)
And on the third day the Lord will descend before all the people upon Mt. Sinai. And it came to pass on the third day in the morning that there were thunders and lightnings and a thick cloud upon the mount and the voice of the trumpet exceeding loud so that all the people, that was in the camp, trembled. And the voice of the trumpet sounded long, and waxed louder and louder. Moses spake, and God answered him by a voice, and spake all these words, saying:

6. CHORUS I, THE FIRST COMMANDMENT (Exod. 20.2-3)
I am the Lord, thy God, which have brought thee out of the land of Egypt, out of the house of bondage. Thou shalt have none other gods but me.

7. Aria, Tenore (Neh. 9.6)
Thou, ev'n Thou, Thou art Lord alone: Thou hast made the heav'ns, Thou hast made the heav'n of heavens, the heavens with all their host, Thou hast made the earth and all things, all that are therein, the waters and all things that are therein, the heaven, the earth, the waters, and all things, all that are therein Thou, Lord! Thou, O Jehovah! Thou art Lord alone. Thou guardest all thy creatures, and the host of heaven adoreth thy name, O Lord! The heavens

with all their host, the earth and all things that thou hast formed, the seas and all things thou hast created, They ev'n they are the work of thy hands! They all shall wait upon thee, all shall praise thy name, for thou art God alone.

8. CHORUS II, THE SECOND COMMANDMENT (Exod. 20.4, 5)
Thou shalt not make to thy self any graven image, nor the likeness of anything that is in heav'n above, or in the earth beneath, or that is in the water under the earth. Thou shalt not bow down to them nor worship them.

9. Recitative, Soprano (Isa. 40.18, 26). Chorus (Ps. 89.8, 9)
To whom then will you liken God? or what likeness will you compare unto him?
Lift up your eyes on high, and behold! Who hath created these things, who bringeth out their host by number, and calleth them all by names?
Great is Jehovah in the assembly of the Saints in the assembly of the righteous, Lord! God of Sabaoth, who is a strong Lord like unto thee, who is like to thee? Lord! God! Great is thy justice round about thee, Lord God of hosts!

10. CHORUS III, THE THIRD COMMANDMENT (Exod. 20.7)
Thou shalt not take the name of the Lord thy God in vain, for the Lord will not hold him guiltless, that taketh his name in vain.

11. Recitative, Soprano (Ps. 48.11). Aria, Soprano (Ps. 111.9; Ps. 86.11; Ps. 96.2, 8, 9)
According to thy name, O God! So is thy praise unto the ends of the earth. Holy and great is thy name, O Lord.
Teach me thy way, O Lord! I will walk in thy Commandments, instruct my heart to fear thee! Teach me thy way, O Lord! I will walk in thy Commandments. Sing to the Lord, O praise the God of Jacob, bless his salvation from day to day! Give unto the Lord the glory due unto his name. Glorify his name, his holy name from day to day. Worship the Lord in the beauty of holiness. Bow ye down before him all the earth!

12. CHORUS IV, THE FOURTH COMMANDMENT (Exod. 20.8, 9, 10)
Remember that thou keep holy the Sabbath day. Six days shalt thou labor and do all that thou hast to do, but the seventh day is the Sabbath of the Lord thy God. In it thou shalt do no manner of work; thou and thy Son, and thy Daughter, thy servant, and thy maid servant, thy cattle, and the stranger that is within thy gates.

13. Finale, Basso Solo (Ps. 84.1, 2, 11; Ps. 92.5)
How lovely are thy dwellings, Lord of Sabaoth! My soul longeth, yea even fainteth for the courts of the Lord, my heart and my flesh crieth out for the

living God. One day in thy courts is better than a thousand: for thou, O Lord! lettest me sing of all thy mercies and I shew forth thy salvation, yea, I shew forth thy salvation.

14. Solo, Tenore, Quartetto or Semi-Chorus (Ps. 26.8, 6, 7)
Lord, I love thy house, I love thy habitation and the place, where thine honour dwelleth.
So I will compass thine altar, O Lord! That I may publish with the voice of thanksgiving and tell of all thy wondrous works.

15. Solo, Soprano (Ps. 65.5)
How bless'd is the man, whom thou choosest and permittest to approach thee, that he may dwell in thy courts, in thy sacred habitation. He hath consolation in thy house, ev'n in thy holy temple.

16. Chorus (Ps. 100.1, 2, 4, 5)
Make a joyful noise to the Lord, serve ye the Lord, with gladness, sing to the Lord, come to his presence with thanksgiving and know ye that the Lord he is God. Sing to the Lord all ye lands! Enter into his dwellings, be thankful, enter into his dwellings with praise and serve the Lord with gladness. Praise him, shew forth his salvation from day to day. For the Lord is gracious and ever lasting is his mercy.

Second Part
1. CHORUS V, THE FIFTH COMMANDMENT (Exod. 20.12)
Honor thy Father and thy Mother, that thy days maybe long in the land which the Lord thy God giveth thee.

2. Recitative and Aria, Soprano (Sir. 3.6, 9, 10; 3.15-16)
Who so honoureth his Father shall have joy of his children, and when he prayeth, he shall be heard. Honor thy Father, honor thy mother both in word and in deed, yea honor them both in word and in deed that a blessing may descend on thee. For the father's blessing buildeth the houses of the children, but the curse of the Mother rooteth out their foundations. Help thy father in his age and grieve him not as long as he liveth; for the relieving of thy father shall not be forgotten, and in the day of thine affliction it shall be remember'd. And all thy sins shall melt away as the ice before the Sun.

3. CHORUS VI, THE SIXTH COMMANDMENT (Exod. 20.13)
Thou shalt do no Murder.

4. Recitative, Basso (Lev. 19.16, 18)
Thou shalt not stand against the blood of thy neighbor, for I am the Lord.

Thou shalt not hate thy brother in thine heart. Thou shalt not avenge, nor bear any grudge against the children of thy people. But thou shalt love thy neighbor as thyself: for I am the Lord.

5. CHORUS VII, THE SEVENTH COMMANDMENT (Exod. 20.14)
Thou shalt not commit Adultery.

6. Duetto, Tenore and Basso (Prov. 31.10, 12, 20, 26; Ps. 128.1, 3, 5, 6)
Happy the man who hath found a virtuous woman, for she is nobler than the precious rubies: she is his glory, she is his blessing. Happy the man who hath found a virtuous woman. She comforteth the needy to those who suffer, her hand is ever ready to those who suffer. She op'neth her mouth her tongue speaketh wisdom and on her lips is the law of kindness.
Blessed is everyone that feareth Jehovah, walking in his statutes and keeping his Commandments. His Wife shall be as a fruitful Vine by the sides of his dwelling. His Children shall be like the olive plants around his table. The Lord shall bless him, the Lord of Zion, and he shall see the good of Jerusalem all his life time. Yea, he shall see his children, Jehovah shall bless him! Blessed be Israel.

7. CHORUS VIII, THE EIGHTH COMMANDMENT (Exod. 20.15)
Chorus (Mal. 3.5). Chorus (Ps. 34.17)
Thou shalt not steal.
I will be a swift witness against those that oppress the hireling in his wages; the widow and the fatherless, and that turn aside the stranger from his right, and fear not me said the Lord of Hosts.
The face of the Lord is against the unrighteous, to cut off the remembrance of them from the face of the earth.

8. Duetto, Chorus (Ps. 37.18, 39; 64.11; 37.18)
He knoweth the days of the godly, he leadeth the righteous for He is their strength in time of need, he leadeth the righteous, and they shall be glad in the Lord, and all the upright in heart shall be glad, all the upright in heart shall glory, all shall glory. He knoweth the days of the godly. Their inheritance shall be for ever and ever, and all shall trust in him; the Lord knoweth the days of the godly.

9. CHORUS IX, THE NINTH COMMANDMENT (Exod. 20.16)
Thou shalt not bear false witness against thy neighbor.

10. Recitative and Aria, Tenor (Ps. 5.7, 10). Aria (Ps. 34.14; Jn 3.21)
He will destroy the lying tongue, the Lord will abhor the bloody and deceitful man; who hath forsaken thy righteous statues and speaketh only

wickedness; his throat is an open sepulchre, there is no fear of God before his eyes.
Preserve thy tongue from evil, and keep thy lips from speaking falsehood. He that loveth truth cometh to the light, that his deeds may appear, that they are wrought in God.

11. CHORUS X, THE TENTH COMMANDMENT (Exod. 20.17)
Thou shalt not covet thy neighbor's house, thou shalt not covet thy neighbor's wife, nor his servant, nor his maid, nor his ox, nor his ass, nor anything that is his.

12. Chorus (Lev. 19.2; Deut. 27.26)
Be ye holy, for I am holy, I, the Lord, I am your God, thus saith the Lord. For whoso shall not obey and do the words of my Commandments, on him shall fall my Judgments.

13. Chorus (Ps. 143.2). Quartetto, Semi Chorus, or Solo (Ps. 143.10)
Lord! Enter not into judgment with thy servant: in thy sight shall no man be justified.
Teach me, O Lord, the way of thy Commandments, for thou art my God! Lead me, O Lord! Lead me into the paths of truth.

14. Recitative, Soprano (Isa. 25.7, 8)
The Lord will scatter the darkness that is cast over the nations, and the vail that is spread over all the people; and he will swallow up death in victory, and the Lord our God will wipe away the tears from off all faces.

15. Canon and Chorus (Deut. 33.26)
There is none like to Jehovah, the God of the righteous, he, O Israel! He will be thy savior, he, O Israel! There is none like thee, O Lord Jehovah! He shall be thy Savior, He, O Israel.
Holy, holy, holy is the Lord, the Lord, the God of hosts.
Holy, holy is the Lord, the Lord of Sabaoth. Praise ye Jehovah!

16. Chorus, Fugue (Ps. 97.12)
Glorify the Lord, give thanks to him, rejoicing in his holiness.

THE LAW AND THE ARTIST IN THE AGE OF EXTREMES: ON THOMAS MANN'S *DAS GESETZ*[1]

Gerhard Lauer

In 2007, at the end of the trial of the Holocaust denier Ernst Zündel, the judge, Ulrich Meinerzhagen, read out a passage from a novel.[2] It was Thomas Mann's *The Tables of the Law* (*Das Gesetz*). The judge quoted from the last paragraph of Mann's short novel—the great curse with which Mann concludes his story. There, Moses addresses the people with these words:

> In the stone of the mountain I carved the ABC of human behavior, but it shall also be carved into your flesh and blood, Israel, so that anyone who breaks one word of the Ten Commandments shall secretly shrink back from himself and from God, and his heart shall turn cold, because he has stepped outside the limits set by God. I know well and God knows beforehand that His commandments will not be kept and that there will be transgressions against His words always and everywhere. But if any man breaks one of them, his heart shall turn ice-cold, because they are written into his flesh and blood, and he knows well that the words are binding.[3]

It is obvious how much the judge believed in the Decalogue as a moral charter, even for modern modes of social existence. To go on lying and to

---

1. Many thanks to my colleague Ian Cooper, University of Kent, whose sense of language transformed my words into readable English. All errors are, however, mine.
2. Cf. *Süddeutsche Zeitung* 63 (16 February 2007), p. 7.
3. Thomas Mann, *The Tables of the Law* (trans. Marion Faber and Stephen Lehman; Philadelphia: Paul Dry Books, 2010), pp. 110-11. Original: 'In den Stein des Berges metzte ich das ABC des Menschenbenehmens, aber auch in dein Fleisch und Blut soll es gemetzt sein, Israel, so daß jeder, der ein Wort bricht von den zehn Geboten, heimlich erschrecken soll vor sich selbst und vor Gott, und soll ihm kalt werden um's Herz, weil er aus Gottes Schranken trat. Ich weiß wohl, und Gott weiß es im Voraus, daß seine Gebote nicht werden gehalten werden; und wird verstoßen werden gegen die Worte immer und überall. Doch eiskalt um's Herz soll es wenigstens jedem werden, der eines bricht, weil sie doch auch in sein Fleisch und Blut geschrieben sind und er wohl weiß, die Worte gelten' (Thomas Mann, 'Das Gesetz', in *Gesammelte Werke in Einzelbänden*, VI [ed. P. de Mendelssohn; Frankfurt: Fischer, 2nd edn, 1996], pp. 339-408 [407]).

deny the suffering of others is not only an offence committed out of an idiosyncratic and retrograde *Weltanschauung*. It violates the very fundamentals of morality. This was the conviction shared by the judge and many in the world who followed the trial. Nevertheless, Judge Meinerzhagen quoted the Ten Commandments, not directly from the Bible but from a novel, a fictional text which seems to have only weak ties to reality. He might have had good reasons for his choice: the accused would never listen to a 'Jewish book' such as the book of Exodus or the book of Deuteronomy. But, even then, a novella does not seem to be the best means of delivering a fundamental truth, and of saying unambiguously that to deny the Holocaust is to step outside the limits set by God. However, I would like to show why the alliance of the Decalogue and this novella is a good one: why the judge made a wise choice in reading the Ten Commandments through a story, written by Thomas Mann in the age of extremes.[4]

1

The background story to the novella *Das Gesetz* is quickly told. In the summer of 1942, the Austrian-American publisher and Hollywood producer Armin L. Robinson sought out Thomas Mann, in his new home in Pacific Palisades near Los Angeles, to win him over to write a film script about the Ten Commandments. According to Robinson, not only Mann but also a couple of other well-known authors were going to join his initiative. Robinson had been familiar with the film industry since his script *Zwei glückliche Herzen* ('Two Lucky Hearts') was filmed in 1931–32 under the title *Ein bißchen Liebe für Dich* ('A Bit of Love for You'). He brought Thomas Mann along to a meeting in September 1942 with the Hollywood studio head Louis B. Mayer. However, the negotiations with Metro-Goldwyn-Mayer came to nothing, and the group around Robinson decided to publish a book. Thomas Mann was to write the opening part of this proposed book.

Robinson felt directly obliged to pursue his project after hearing about Hitler's fanatical notes on the Decalogue. On the basis of a common pseudo-Nietzschean *Weltanschauung*, Hitler and Goebbels attacked Christianity and Judaism as Asiatic slave moralities. Hitler declared that the Nazi movement would fight against God and his commandments: 'The day will come when I shall hold up against these commandments the tables of a new law. And history will recognize our movement as the great battle for humanity's liberation, a liberation from the curse of Mount Sinai.'[5] Robinson heard about

---

4. Eric J. Hobsbawm, *The Age of Extremes: The Short Twentieth Century* (London: Michael Joseph, 1994).

5. Quoted in Hermann Rauschning, 'Preface', in A.L. Robinson (ed.), *The Ten Commandments: Ten Short Novels of Hitler's War against the Moral Code* (New York: Simon & Schuster, 1943), p. xiii.

this attack by reading Hermann Rauschning's *Gespräche mit Hitler* ('Hitler Speaks'), a record of Rauschning's supposed conversations with Hitler, which appeared in the US in 1940 under the title *The Voice of Destruction*. At the time Rauschning's conversations were thought to be genuine, although it is now known that he invented the dialogues. Under these circumstances the novel was written as a direct answer to Hitler's fanatical repudiation of the Decalogue, or, as Robinson wrote later, in his preface to the published book: 'to open the eyes of those who still do not recognize what Nazism really is'.[6] Like Robinson, Thomas Mann must have believed that his novel was not an aesthetic end in itself but a public defence of the Ten Commandments in the age of extremes.

Because Thomas Mann had given more than one radio speech since 1940—including his famous BBC broadcasts—and because his condemnation of anti-Semitism in 1942 had made his name highly visible throughout the world, he was the best choice Robinson could make for his project. At this time Mann was primarily a political writer, not an artist. He accepted the invitation, not because of the $1,000 fee, although later he made fun of this fee and spoke of *Das Gesetz* as his '$1,000 novel'.[7] Rather, what drove him was the prospect of counterattacking on the same footing as his enemies and doing so in a way that would be highly visible throughout the world. For the first and only time in his career, with *Das Gesetz* Thomas Mann wrote a commissioned work. Thus his novella was born.

Robinson admired Thomas Mann's novella at first reading and published it under the rather misleading title *Thou Shalt Have No Other God before Me*, as the opening work in the volume *The Ten Commandments: Ten Short Novels of Hitler's War against the Moral Code*, translated by Helen T. Lowe-Porter.[8] The volume came out in 1943, just in time for the Christmas market. Hermann Rauschning himself wrote the preface; the other authors each contributed a short novel on one of the Ten Commandments: *Thou Shalt Not Make Any Graven Image*, by Rebecca West; *Thou Shalt Not Take the Name of the Lord thy God in Vain*, by Franz Werfel; *Remember the Sabbath Day, to Keep It Holy*, by John Erskine; *Honor thy Father and thy Mother*, by Bruno Frank; *Thou Shalt Not Kill*, by Jules Romains; *Thou Shalt Not Commit Adultery*, by André Maurois; *Thou Shalt Not Steal*, by Sigrid Undset; *Thou Shalt Not Bear False Witness against thy Neighbor*, by Hendrik Van Loon; and *Thou Shalt Not Covet*, by Louis Broomfield. After the volume was published, Thomas Mann was not amused to find his novella

6. Hans R. Vaget, *Thomas Mann. Kommentar zu sämtlichen Erzählungen* (Munich: Winkler, 1984), p. 275.

7. Hans Wysling (ed.), *Dichter über ihre Dichtungen*, XIV/2 (Munich: Heimeran; Frankfurt: Fischer, 1975), p. 644.

8. Rauschning, 'Preface', in Robinson (ed.), *The Ten Commandments*.

situated by a more or less crude direct defence of religion and tried, successfully, to place his story on its own. Today only Mann's contribution can be seen as a work of art rather than simply a text written for propaganda purposes, and is now known under its correct title, *The Tables of the Law*.

In contrast to his usual approach, Thomas Mann wrote the novel after only a week of study. This was untypical for a writer who normally took years of careful preparation before writing the first page. But this time Mann wrote his hundred-page novel in nearly eight weeks in 1943 and called it afterwards 'a quick improvisation', the process of writing which had been 'fast, easy, and airy but not carefree'.[9] This was possible because he could make heavy use of his extended studies for the Joseph tetralogy, on which he had worked since 1926 and which he finished in the same year, 1943. In a letter he characterizes the aim of his quick improvisation: 'It was my artistic intention in the Joseph books as well as in the Moses story, to bring these far and legendary figures close to the modern reader in an intimate, natural and convincing manner. This required much phantasy and a certain affectionate brand of humor.'[10] And that is exactly what he did in his novella: he entangled fantasy with historical legends, severe commandments with light speculations, critical explanations with categorical verdicts, anachronistic projections with historical events, all with the unambiguous goal of convincing his readers.

But of what was he trying to convince them: that Moses was a killer, that the Ten Commandments were written somehow by cheating the people of Israel? Thomas Mann's story isn't as simple as Armin L. Robinson thought, and his intention is not as clear as the text's place of first publication suggests. Therefore, today literary critics think that the novella was simply published in the wrong place. They also conclude that Thomas Mann's 'Moses fantasy'—as he called his novel—seriously impeaches the credibility of what he is trying to defend, the Decalogue. The moral outrage of the great curse does not suit his disorderly narrative story, Mann tells us.[11] The curse seems just to be a compromise concocted by Mann for Robinson. There is, critics argue, too much propaganda for us to call it a work of art.[12] Moreover, they add, law and narrative do not fit together as well as Mann himself seems to have declared. Laws should not be too ambiguous, nor can

---

9. Original: 'rasch, leicht und sorgenlos, wenn auch nicht sorglos' (Wysling [ed.], *Dichter über ihre Dichtungen*, XIV/2, p. 644).

10. Quoted by Michael Wood, 'Afterword', in Mann, *The Tables of the Law*, pp. vii-viii.

11. Helmut Koopmann (ed.), *Thomas Mann Handbuch* (Stuttgart: Kröner, 3rd edn, 2001), p. 606.

12. Cf. Wolfgang Frühwald, 'Thomas Manns "Moses-Phantasie". Zu der Erzählung *Das Gesetz*', in W. Frühwald, *Das Talent, Deutsch zu schreiben. Goethe—Schiller—Thomas Mann* (Cologne: DuMont, 2005), pp. 315-33 (318).

law be described in aesthetic categories. And problematic characters are not the best figures to use for the purposes of giving force to law. In short, law and narrative are not elective affinities. How could they become so for the greater good?

2

Whoever tells a story needs a minimum of two components: characters and events. The author must find an interesting way of relating them. As E.M. Forster puts it: '"The king died and the queen died" is a story. "The king died, and then the queen died of grief" is a plot,'[13] which is to say a good story. It is obvious that, in this sense, characters and events mean different things in literature and in law. In law characters are abstract entities, without a face, with just a pure individual psychology and very general characteristics, too few for a good story. And in legal texts events are cases, and could only seldom be integrated into a plot or a storyline. As Tolstoy writes so well in the opening lines of *Anna Karenina*: 'All happy families are alike; each unhappy family is unhappy in its own way'. A good story spins out hundreds of pages around the unhappy disorder into which individual characters each enter in their own way. While law is based on general cases, literature deals with singular moments, each in its peculiar way, and tells their stories. And so does Thomas Mann.

His novella begins with a very special disorder, the disorder of Moses: 'His birth was irregular, and so he passionately loved regularity, the inviolable, commandment and taboo'.[14] This is the particular unhappiness of Mann's main character; with it everything begins. And to emphasize this simplistic psychological deduction, the novel continues by making a very direct connection, when the narrator tells us that the fundamental commandments and taboos are nothing other than an immediate consequence of Moses' irregularities: 'As a young man, he had killed in a fiery outburst, and so he knew better than those with no experience that to kill may be sweet, but to have killed is ghastly in the extreme, and that you should not kill'.[15] The purity of the commandments is, according to Mann's novella, nothing but the reverse side of his ambiguous irregularities. Mann, and with him

---

13. E.M. Forster, *Aspects of the Novel* (London: Edward Arnold, 1927), Chapter 5, p. 82.

14. Mann, *The Tables of the Law*, p. 3. 'Seine Geburt war unordentlich, darum liebte er leidenschaftlich Ordnung, das Unverbrüchliche, Gebot und Verbot' ('Das Gesetz', in *Gesammelte Werke in Einzelbänden*, VI, p. 339).

15. Mann, *The Tables of the Law*, p. 3. 'Er tötete früh im Auflodern, darum wußte er besser, als jeder Unerfahrene, daß Töten zwar köstlich, aber getötet zu haben höchst gräßlich ist, und daß du nicht töten sollst' ('Das Gesetz', in *Gesammelte Werke in Einzelbänden*, VI, p. 339).

Robinson's collection, opts for this provocative exposition. At first glance the Decalogue is the outcome of a very special experience and could hardly claim any universal significance.

The novel plays with the books of Exodus and Deuteronomy, and gives the order of events and the evaluation of the characters and their deeds a good shaking. We mention here only the most prominent modifications, if not anomalies, that Mann's Moses fantasy has introduced into the biblical order. There is, first, the parentage of Moses. Instead of being the son of Amram and Jochebed, Moses is portrayed as the result of a dalliance between Pharaoh Rameses' second daughter and a passing Hebrew slave. This is important for the internal structure of the story in so far as the exodus from Egypt only becomes possible because the pharaoh knows too well the truth of Moses' parentage. And not only the pharaoh: God elects Moses because of his half-Egyptian, half-Hebrew origins. Moreover these origins are relevant for the meaning of the novella as a whole. From its very beginning the author repeatedly underscores the 'racial' impurity of Moses, a direct challenge to the racial fanaticism and belief in purity prevalent in Nazi Germany. Here in Thomas Mann's short novel, the purest and most holy things emerge out of impurity and sin.

A second modification relative to the book of Exodus is Moses' relationship with language and writing. '[Moses] wasn't really at home in any language', the novel tells us, 'and when speaking would cast about in three: Aramaic Syro-Chaldean, which his father's blood kin spoke and which he had learned from his parents, had been overlaid by Egyptian, which he had had to acquire at school, and in addition Midianite Arabic, which he had spoken for many years in the desert'.[16] Not only is Moses' lack of speaking ability portrayed as deriving from his nomadic wandering, but his choice of a new and holy alphabet is directly linked with his 'impure' language and inability to speak persuasively. In Mann's novel Moses invents a new system of writing, and again Mann does not even mention the Hebrew alphabet by name. Instead he re-emphasizes universality:

> To write the words of every language of every people, and since Yahweh was the God of the whole world, then the pithy code that Moses intended to write down was the sort that could serve as a basic directive and a rock of human decency among all the peoples of the earth—across the whole world.[17]

16. Mann, *The Tables of the Law*, p. 18. Original: 'war aber außerdem in keiner Sprache zu Hause und suchte in dreien herum beim Reden: Das aramäische Syro-Chaldäisch, das sein Vaterblut sprach, und das er von seinen Eltern gelernt, war überdeckt worden vom Ägyptischen, das er sich in dem Schulhause hatte aneignen müssen, und dazu kam das midianitische Arabisch, das er solange in der Wüste gesprochen' (Mann, 'Das Gesetz', in *Gesammelte Werke in Einzelbänden*, VI, p. 348).

17. Mann, *The Tables of the Law*, p. 96. Original: 'wie aber mit der Handvoll

Again an irregularity leads directly to the universal clarity of the Commandments, and long before the end of the novel every reader understands this recurring pattern of impurity leading to purity, particularity to universality. The story of the Ten Commandments is a universal one, and the people of Israel, Moses and Moses' writings all carry universal significance. Nevertheless, here everything seems to be just the outcome of a highly individual case. In Mann's novella, particularity and universality are closely interlinked.

This is most obvious in a third modification Mann has made. The tablets containing the Ten Commandments are not given by God directly. God speaks to Moses and tells him the laws. But it is Moses who inscribes them in stone, not God, as the Bible tells us. Moreover, the novel doesn't distinguish explicitly between God and Moses, and so Mann's readers never get a clear clue as to whether there is a holy authority speaking to Moses behind the commandments. Maybe everything is, in the end, just Moses' imagination. Once again, impurity could be at the origin of the universal commandments. They might all be 'from within Moses' breast',[18] as the novel stresses. This secular and persistent subtext is present throughout the novel, as when, for example, Aaron wants to impress the pharaoh with a miraculous rod that turns into a snake. Even the Egyptian priests could easily perform similar magic, we are told. And it is Joshua who comes at night to visit and to provide for Moses when he is on Mt Sinai. Even there, Moses is not the holy man of the Bible but a very mundane character who argues with God. At no point in the novel is the existence of any supernatural power explicitly affirmed. Everything stays in the realm of secular explanation and often impure motivations. The reader has to understand that the establishment of the Ten Commandments could be explained in terms of very earthly and profane reasons. And the novella is more than explicit in constantly emphasizing this interpretation.

Fourthly, Mann creates profane and unheroic characters. His Moses killed another man by indulging his 'sweet anger', and more than once flies into a rage over the narrow-mindedness of his people. Aaron and Miriam are not much better. Joshua, in Mann's novella Moses' most loyal follower, is the mundane explanation for the angel of death who does Moses' bloody work more than once, especially when the story describes Israel's conquest of the

---

Zeichen notfalls die Worte aller Sprachen der Völker geschrieben werden konnten, und wie Jahwe der Gott der Welt war allenthalben, so war auch, was Mose zu schreiben gedachte, das Kurzgefaßte, von solcher Art, daß es als Grundweisung und Fels des Menschenanstandes dienen mochte unter den Völkern der Erde—allenthalben' (Mann, 'Das Gesetz', in *Gesammelte Werke in Einzelbänden*, VI, pp. 397-98).

18. Mann, *The Tables of the Law*, p. 92. 'Gott befahl ihm laut aus seiner Brust' (Mann, 'Das Gesetz', in *Gesammelte Werke in Einzelbänden*, VI, p. 395).

oasis of Kadesh. Mann also makes use of the episode concerning Moses' Kushite wife and his depiction of her is exaggerated in more than one way to play up Moses' worldly need for 'recreational pleasure'.[19] Doubtless much exaggerated typification, not to say stereotyping, is involved.

In sum, the difference between Thomas Mann's novel and Exodus 1–20, 32–34, Deuteronomy 5 and some passages out of the book of Numbers couldn't be more obvious. Mann's novella is a Moses fantasy that retells the founding history as a profane story and nods to the reader as well as to the holy books. Mundane explanations that derive the universality of the Ten Commandments from unholy causes are central to the novella. Although Thomas Mann had to use some biblical events, he could have transformed any of them into a story; and picking up any biblical name he could have unfolded it into a fully realized character. The way he did this changes a holy tradition into a profane one. The history of the Ten Commandments that Mann has written is obviously dominated by a simplistic, if not grotesque, psychological mechanism that jumps from irregularity and impurity directly to order and purity. For a founding history of the Decalogue this is not enough: too much propaganda rather than art. One might conclude that Judge Meinerzhagen did not, perhaps, make the best choice.

Literary critics explain Mann's lack of purity with reference to the sources that he more or less openly quotes.[20] When he calls Moses, more than once, 'Mann Moses', this is an undisguised citation of Sigmund Freud's last book, *Moses and Monotheism* (*Der Mann Moses und die monotheistische Religion*) of 1939, published three years before Thomas Mann's own Moses fantasy. Furthermore, Freud invented the Moses-the-Egyptian thesis, and Mann partly follows him here. Mann's Moses is half-Egyptian but, much more than that, he is a mixture of Hebrew and Egyptian. Above all, Mann is not only committed to Freud but also to the nineteenth-century critique of religion. As Ludwig Feuerbach puts it briefly in *The Essence of Christianity* (*Das Wesen des Christentums*) of 1841, 'the secret of theology is anthropology'[21]—this could serve as a rule for the way Thomas Mann chooses to tell the founding history of the Ten Commandments. Certainly Mann has written an ironic anthropology of the Decalogue, but it is anthropology and not theology. The history of human behaviour explains everything.

---

19. Mann, *The Tables of the Law*, pp. 80-81. 'Mose hing gewaltig an ihr um seiner Entspannung willen' (Mann, 'Das Gesetz', in *Gesammelte Werke in Einzelbänden*, VI, p. 388).

20. Cf. Klaus Makoschey, *Quellenkritische Untersuchungen zum Spätwerk Thomas Manns 'Joseph', der Ernährer', 'Das Gesetz', 'Der Erwählte'* (Frankfurt: Fischer, 1998).

21. 'Das Geheimnis der Theologie ist die Anthropologie' (Ludwig Feuerbach, *Gesammelte Werke*. V. *Das Wesen des Christentums* [ed. W. Harich and W. Schuffenhauer; Munich: Oldenbourg, 2006], p. 13).

To foster his anthropological view of the origins of the Ten Commandments, Mann also read exegetical literature.[22] Above all he adopted the thesis of Elias Auerbach, an early Zionist and physician, founder of the first modern hospital in Haifa, who argues that Moses formed the people into his people of Israel at the oasis of Kadesh. In his book *Wilderness and Promised Land* (*Wüste und gelobtes Land*), printed by the avant-garde publishing house of Kurt Wolff in 1932 and 1936, Auerbach claims that it took Moses a whole generation to transform a slavish crowd into the people of God. Auerbach did not invent this assumption, but rather promoted the ideas of the highly influential historian Eduard Meyer and the prominent Old Testament scholar Hugo Gressmann. From Auerbach, Thomas Mann also borrowed the bold thesis that Moses was the inventor of script. This tells us a lot about Thomas Mann's way of writing and his particular preference for adopting such audacious propositions. Mann drew on yet another authority, the pan-Babylonist Alfred Jeremias,[23] an orthodox Lutheran pastor from Leipzig and the first German translator of the *Epic of Gilgamesh*. In his book *Das Alte Testament im Lichte des alten Orients* ('The Old Testament in the Light of the Ancient Orient') from 1906 he expresses similar views to those of Elias Auerbach. The title of his book already emphasizes Jeremias's pan-Babylonist thesis, which explains the origins of the Bible in terms of Babylonian mythology. Neither Auerbach nor Jeremias was an established scholar. Both were amateurs, in the best sense of the word, and Mann admired their views because of this. He makes use of theories that offer storylines; this was also the significance for him of the assumptions that Moses was the inventor of script, and that it was not until the years at the oasis in Kadesh that the crowd of slaves became the people of God. To summarize, the novel makes use of any source that offers a good secular story, and from these stories a mundane explanation emerges of how the Ten Commandments came from Mt Sinai to the world. The narrative overcomes the law.

In addition to criticism of religion and biblical scholarship, a last influence that should be mentioned is the airy and light style of the writing of Voltaire. The severity of law is counterbalanced by an easiness in writing about it that is exemplified by Voltaire in his *Essai sur les moeurs* (1756), *Candide* (1759) and other writings. This style was also adopted by Goethe in pieces such as *Israel in der Wüste* ('Israel in the Desert'). Voltaire is not an

---

22. Cf. Friedeman W. Golka, *Mose: Biblische Gestalt und literarische Figur. Thomas Manns Novelle* Das Gesetz *und die biblische Überlieferung* (Stuttgart: Calwer, 2007).

23. Käte Hamburger, *Thomas Mann: Das Gesetz* (Frankfurt: Fischer, 1964); Rudolf Smend, 'Thomas Mann: *Das Gesetz*', in W. Barner (ed.), *Querlektüren: Weltliteratur zwischen den Disziplinen* (Göttingen: Wallstein, 1997).

unproblematic influence, owing to the historical misuse of this way of writing on Moses by anti-Semites such as Adolf Bartels and others.[24] And the irony of Voltaire's biblical writings does not seem helpful in defending the universal claims of the Decalogue. But there is no doubt about how much Thomas Mann owes to Voltaire's treatment of the biblical books. Again the pivotal question arises as to whether such a text as Thomas Mann's Moses fantasy is appropriate to confront Nazism. Is it an adequate way of presenting the 'edict' (*Erlassung*)[25] of the Ten Commandments, as Thomas Mann puts it? These are legitimate doubts.

3

Given the way in which Thomas Mann retells the founding history of the Decalogue, the question is inevitable as to whether a novel whose writing was 'fast, easy, and airy but not carefree'[26] makes any sense in the age of extremes. Part of the answer is given in the distinction just quoted: 'airy but not carefree'. The novel is written very carefully, even if it is nothing more than a fantasy. As Käte Hamburger notes in her ingenious early interpretation of Thomas Mann's biblical work, at the heart of the novel there is a grave topic: the ethical constitution of Israel as the people of God. This is at the same time the constitution of the human moral law.[27] The allusions in Mann's narrative may not be suitable to such a topic: the obvious ones being to Freud, the less obvious to Richard Wagner, Friedrich Nietzsche, Goethe and Voltaire, with academic references to Old Testament scholars and so on. But the joy of these variations and the airiness of the style are not an end in itself. They are part of the implicit anthropology of telling. And that is my thesis.

To get this point it is once more necessary to return to the novella. The Decalogue is given to the people twice—so say the books of Exodus and of Deuteronomy, and so says Thomas Mann. When Moses comes down from Mt Sinai the first time and finds the crowd jumping around the golden calf he smashes the two tablets against the stone pedestal. 'You rabble, you godforsaken people!', he shouts, 'Here lies what I brought down to you from God and what He wrote for you with His own finger, to be your talisman against the misery of ignorance! Here it lies in pieces by the wreckage of

---

24. Jacques Darmaun, *Thomas Mann, Deutschland und die Juden* (Tübingen: Niemeyer, 2003), pp. 212-26.

25. Thomas Mann, 'Reden und Aufsätze 3', in Thomas Mann, *Gesammelte Werke in dreizehn Bänden*, XI (Frankfurt: Fischer, 1974), p. 154.

26. Cf. n. 8.

27. Käte Hamburger, *Thomas Manns biblisches Werk. Der Josephs-Roman/Die Moses-Erzählung* Das Gesetz (Munich: Nymphenburger, 1981), p. 181.

your idol. What can I tell the Lord about you now, to keep Him from consuming you?'[28] At that point the reader knows very well that it was Moses who wrote the two tablets with his own finger (and not God, as in the book of Exodus). The question is therefore: what does this idolatry mean for Moses? First it leads him to violence: Moses condemns the sinners to death and Joshua takes care of the execution of Moses' orders. Meanwhile Moses is to 'go up again to God's mountain and'—as he says—'see what I can still manage to do for you',[29] that is, for the people, since they are still superstitious. Moses does not write the Ten Commandments again in the original version, as it says in the biblical text (Deut. 10.4). He renews the tablets 'even better than the first time';[30] and the narrator, with Moses, proudly underlines the fact. Moses rewrites the Ten Commandments following Deuteronomy very closely in the revised Lutheran Bible of 1912, but shortening it to very clear sentences, which are more law-like than they are in the biblical text, and more Luther-like than the text of Luther itself: 'Du sollst deinem Nächsten nicht Unglimpf tun als ein Lügenzeuge' ('You shall not bear false witness against your neighbour'); 'Du sollst kein begehrliches Auge werfen auf deines Nächsten Habe' ('You shall not covet your neighbour's house').[31]

This overemphatic, if concise, rewriting of the Ten Commandments is important: Moses makes the Commandments better than before—which is indicated here by the more biblical and more Lutheran style—although he accepts that this second time is only the beginning of an endless retelling of the Ten Commandments. There is no such thing, then, as a mythical first version. This is much more than the Decalogue retold by Moses with significant changes to the wording in the wilderness of Moab given by Deut. 5.6-21. The novel first discusses, in an imaginary dialogue between Moses and God, the possibility of not rewriting the Decalogue at all. Moses would live as the only survivor in the covenant with the Lord. But Thomas Mann's novel rejects exactly this kind of purity, and tells the story of how, out of sin,

---

28. Mann, *The Tables of the Law*, p. 103. 'Du Pöbelvolk, du gottverlassenes! Da liegt, was ich dir herniedergetragen von Gott, und was Er für dich geschrieben mit eigenem Finger, daß es dir ein Talisman sei gegen die Misere der Unbildung! Da liegt's in Scherben bei deines Abgottes Trümmern! Was fang' ich nun an mit dir vor dem Herrn, daß er dich nicht fresse?' (Mann, 'Das Gesetz', in *Gesammelte Werke in Einzelbänden*, VI, p. 402).

29. Mann, *The Tables of the Law*, p. 106. Original: 'denn ich will wieder hinaufgehen auf Gottes Berg und sehen, was ich allenfalls noch für dich ausrichten kann, halsstarrig Volk!' (Mann, 'Das Gesetz', in *Gesammelte Werke in Einzelbänden*, VI, p. 404).

30. Mann, *The Tables of the Law*, p. 109. Original: 'die wurden besser sogar, als das erste Mal' (Mann, 'Das Gesetz', in *Gesammelte Werke in Einzelbänden*, VI, p. 406).

31. Mann, 'Das Gesetz', in *Gesammelte Werke in Einzelbänden*, p. 399.

the Decalogue was written again. Because the reader already knows that Moses is the author of the Ten Commandments, the second writing is only part of a series of retellings of the truth, each one a bit different. And the novella itself is only part of this series. In this perspective the Decalogue is no longer a myth. What we can say about it is a genealogy of morals.[32] As a genealogy it is just a narrative; it is unmythical and impure; but it has to be retold again and again to be meaningful for us. This is the duty of culture.

Moses argues with God and pushes God to forgive his people: not till God has done so can the Ten Commandments be rewritten. The acceptance of human impurity and of the retelling are once again two sides of the same coin:

> And Moses appealed to God's honor and spoke: 'Just imagine, Holy One: if You now kill these people as You would a man, then the heathen, on hearing their cry, would say: "Bah! There was no way the Lord could bring these people into the land promised to them; He wasn't up to it. That's why He slaughtered them in the desert." Is that what You want the peoples of the world to say about You? Therefore let the strength of the Lord grow great and by Your grace show mercy for the people's transgression!' And it was this argument in particular that prevailed with God and persuaded Him to forgive them.[33]

The retelling is the first step in God's forgiveness, and therefore the Decalogue tells not only the story of the Commandments but also the true story of God's mercy. The starting point for this story is the rewriting of the Decalogue. And that is what Moses does after his arguments with the Lord. The novel explicitly emphasizes how much this retelling will be necessary again and again. 'I know well and God knows beforehand that His commandments will not be kept, that there will be transgressions against His words always

---

32. Brunhild Neuland, '*Das Gesetz*. Zu Thomas Manns poetischer Fassung der Mose-Mythe', in H. Brand and H. Kaufmann (eds.), *Werk und Wirkung Thomas Manns in unserer Epoche. Ein internationaler Dialog* (Berlin: Aufbau, 1978), pp. 249-72; Peter J. Brenner, 'Die Befreiung vom Mythos. Recht und Ordnung in Thomas Manns *Das Gesetz*', in M. Braun and B. Lermen (eds.), '*Man erzählt Geschichten, formt die Wahrheit'. Thomas Mann: Deutscher, Europäer, Weltbürger* (Frankfurt: Peter Lang 2003), pp. 187-201.

33. Mann, *The Tables of the Law*, pp. 108-109. 'Und er nahm Gott bei der Ehre und sprach: "Stelle dir, Heiliger, das doch vor: Wenn du dies Volk nun tötest wie einen Mann, so würden die Heiden sagen, die das Geschrei vernähmen: 'Pah! Der Herr konnte mitnichten dies Volk ins Land bringen, das er ihnen geschworen hatte, er war's nicht imstande; darum hat er sie geschlachtet in der Wüste.' Willst du dir das nachsagen lassen von den Völkern der Welt? Darum laß nun die Kraft des Herrn groß werden und sei gnädig der Missetat dieses Volkes nach deiner Barmherzigkeit!" Namentlich dies Argument war es, womit er Gott überwand und ihn zur Vergebung bestimmte' (Mann, 'Das Gesetz', in *Gesammelte Werke in Einzelbänden*, VI, pp. 405-406).

and everywhere'.[34] It is not enough to know the Ten Commandments, it is more important to rewrite them, maybe rewrite them better.[35] And that is exactly what Judge Meinerzhagen did, when he quoted from Mann's story: he told the story again. Through such retelling the Decalogue stays alive.

The novella steadily and emphatically suggests that Thomas Mann's worldly story is itself a retelling, a better retelling for today's people. 'Better' means that the old story has been adapted for those who worship the golden calf in the twentieth century. For Thomas Mann the golden calf was the idol of Nazism. If one takes a closer look at Mann's diaries for the year 1943 it is intriguing how strongly Mann believed not only in the coming end of Nazism after the battle of Stalingrad but also, even more, in the need to re-educate the German people.[36] More than once the novella talks about Moses' 'Bildungswerk' (educational work), which is to be done in the next years, and more than once it speaks of Moses' 'Gotteslust' (lust for God),[37] which is necessary to do this work. To be a teacher of his felonious and foul people becomes a major, but nevertheless doubtful, task for Thomas Mann, as it was for Moses thousands of years before. His *Gotteslust* is also the lust of the artist to rebuild his people. *The Tables of the Law* is part of this artistic re-education, but Mann more than once doubted the possibility of wholly achieving it. Mann first flirted with the idea of assuming a leading position in the new Germany, as Wolfgang Frühwald has shown. But as Mann's diaries confirm, this idea soon lost its power for him, and melancholy thoughts about Germany dominated his entries.[38]

For Mann his task as an artist in the age of extremes is to retell the Decalogue. It is not by accident that his main character, Moses, is depicted in the last chapter of the novella as an artist—not as a writer, an orator or a composer. The artist with whom Mann compares him in his work of re-education is Michelangelo:[39]

---

34. Mann, *The Tables of the Law*, p. 110. 'Ich weiß wohl, und Gott weiß es im Voraus, daß seine Gebote nicht werden gehalten werden; und wird verstoßen werden gegen die Worte immer und überall' (Mann, 'Das Gesetz', in *Gesammelte Werke in Einzelbänden*, VI, p. 407).

35. Cf. Peter Mennicken, *Für ein ABC des Menschenbenehmens. Menschenbild und Universalethos bei Thomas Mann* (Ostfildern: Matthias Grünewald, 2002).

36. Thomas Mann, *Tagebücher 1940–1943* (ed. P. de Mendelsohn; Frankfurt: Fischer, 1982), pp. 505ff.

37. Mann, 'Das Gesetz', in *Gesammelte Werke in Einzelbänden*, VI, pp. 351, 355.

38. Cf. Frühwald, 'Thomas Manns "Moses-Phantasie"', in Frühwald, *Das Talent, Deutsch zu schreiben*, pp. 328-29.

39. Claus-Michael Ort, 'Körper, Stimme Schrift. Semiotischer Betrug und "heilige" Wahrheit in der literarischen Selbstreflexion Thomas Manns', in M. Ansel, H.-E. Friedrich and G. Lauer, *Die Erfindung des Schriftstellers Thomas Mann* (Berlin: W. de Gruyter, 2009), pp. 237-71 (256-61).

> One has to imagine how he sat up there, with a bare torso, his chest covered with hair and with very strong arms that he probably got from his ill-used father—with his wide-set eyes, his flattened nose, the parted, graying beard, chewing on a piece of flatbread, also coughing occasionally from the metallic fumes of the mountain; how he hewed the tablets by the sweat of his brow, chiseled them, planed them; how he crouched before them as they leaned against the rocky wall and, toiling painstakingly over each detail, notched into their surfaces his chicken scratches, these runes that could do everything, after first sketching them in with his graver.[40]

This description is based on Michelangelo's monumental *Moses* of San Pietro in Vincoli, but is at the same time a portrait of Michelangelo and a self-portrait of Thomas Mann.[41] The task for the artist is huge, and one might expect that Mann would have envisioned an outstanding artist with no human impurity. But as his novella points out, Moses is a problematic character until the end, until he rewrites the Decalogue a second time. And so Mann chooses, not the pure Raphael but the untamed and impure (homosexual) Michelangelo. Thomas Mann's Moses is not an *Übermensch*. There had been too many of those in the dark years, and too many vain artists. Not moral severity, but a humanization which reckons with human evil, is the way to re-educate the crowd. This is the reason why the novella is so airily written and deals so lightly with its serious topic, and is so simplistic in its psychological genealogy of morals. Thomas Mann believes not in prophets but in the problematic characters produced by artists. And maybe the most problematic part of this kind of belief is the self-styling of the writer Thomas Mann.

Only then, only if one accepts and believes in this understanding of art and artist, and only if one thinks that retelling is better than the purity of the first text, is the decision of the judge in the trial a wise decision—or, more precisely, another retelling of the Ten Commandments. As in Thomas

---

40. Mann, *The Tables of the Law*, p. 97. 'Man muß ihn sich vorstellen, wie er dort oben saß, mit bloßem Oberleib, die Brust mit Haaren bewachsen und von sehr starken Armen, die er wohl von seinem missbrauchten Vater hatte,—mit seinen weit stehenden Augen, der eingeschlagenen Nase, dem geteilten, ergrauten Bart, und, an einem Fladen kauend, zuweilen auch hustend von Metalldämpfen des Berges, im Schweiße seines Angesichts die Tafeln behaute, abmeißelte, glatt scheuerte, wie er vor den an die Felswand gelehnten kauerte und sorglich im Kleinen schuftend seine Krähenfüße, diese alles vermögenden Runen in die Flächen einsenkte, nachdem er sie mit dem Stichel vorgezeichnet' (Mann, 'Das Gesetz', in *Gesammelte Werke in Einzelbänden*, VI, p. 398).

41. The parallel between Moses and Michelangelo is introduced by Mann himself: see Thomas Mann, *Die Entstehung des Doktor* Faustus, *Roman eines Romans*, in Thomas Mann, *Gesammelte Werke in Einzelbänden*, XVI (ed. P. de Mendelssohn; Frankfurt: Fischer, 2nd edn, 1984), pp. 130-288 (139-40); cf. also Golka, *Mose: Biblische Gestalt und literarische Figur*.

Mann's novella it is not enough to know the Decalogue. It is important to make the Ten Commandments public and to say the words, not only as they appear on the page but in our own voice, so that the Decalogue is still a guide, but a guide with a story which has to be retold again and again: '"Thus the earth shall be the earth once more, a vale of misery, but not a field of depravity. Everyone say Amen to that!" And they all said Amen.'[42]

---

42. Mann, *The Tables of the Law*, p. 112. '"Dass die Erde wieder die Erde sei, ein Tal der Notdurft, aber keine Luderwiese. Sagt alle Amen dazu!" Und alles Volk sagte Amen' (Mann, 'Das Gesetz', in *Gesammelte Werke in Einzelbänden*, VI, p. 408).

THE DECALOGUE:
THE SCHOLARLY TRADITION CRITIQUED

David J.A. Clines

Reception criticism—and this book is devoted to the reception criticism of an iconic biblical text—is most worthy of the name when it is critical. For reception criticism to be critical, the object of criticism may be the reception itself, that is, the way the text has been interpreted, misinterpreted, understood or misunderstood. Alternatively, the object of criticism may be, with the help of the reception (that is, the character or the history of the text's reception), the text that gave rise to the reception. Both of these objects of criticism concern me in this paper.

The scholarly reception of the Decalogue, down to the present day, has in my estimation been essentially uncritical, accepting at face value the claims of the text. In the field of Old Testament criticism, where it seems that almost every ancient verity has been challenged, from the priority of the law over the prophets to the historicity of the patriarchs, it is astonishing that the Decalogue has been immune to criticism. To view its reception invites one to review the text from which the reception took its rise.

Biblical scholarship on the Decalogue in many cases amounts to little more than propaganda on behalf of the claimed authority and the supposed divine origins of the Decalogue. Here is one example:

> [The Ten Commandments] function as the essence of divine standards and expectations against which every conceivable human attitude and conduct is to be measured. They are, in fact, expressive of the very character of God Himself and for that reason alone timeless and universally applicable. They may be couched in the framework of a covenant between God and a particular people at a particular time, but they cannot be limited by those or any other circumstances.[1]

And here is another:

> At the dawn of Israelite history the Ten Commandments were received in their original short form as the basic constitution, so to speak, of the

---

1. Eugene H. Merrill, *Deuteronomy* (The New American Commentary, 4; Nashville, TN: Broadman & Holman, 1994), p. 145.

> Community of Israel. The words were chiselled[2] or written on two stone tablets... These commands are 'categorical imperatives' universally applicable, timeless, not dependent on any circumstances whatsoever.[3]

And another:

> In function the Ten Commandments can be compared to ten posts supporting the fence separating the viable community of Israel from the marauding beasts of disorder, confusion, and bloodshed howling outside the pale... Should any one of these ten fenceposts collapse, chaos could break out and wreak havoc in the community. For Israel, survival itself was at stake with every one of these ten categorical imperatives.[4]

In England today, young people of sixteen preparing for their GCSE exams in Religious Studies have to learn how to write essays from at least two points of view, a religious and a secular. The scholarly tradition on the Decalogue, however, seems never to have considered more than one approach to the text. In this scholarly tradition, it is simply not acceptable to critique a commandment, to evaluate the function of such a decalogue for law and ethics, or to resist the claim that this set of laws has timeless and universal applicability.

To test such allegations, you have only to ask as you read a commentary or essay on the Decalogue: does the author remark that the Decalogue prohibits freedom of religious opinion? If you think, as I do, that it is wrong to compel people to subscribe to one set of religious views, that it is wrong now and that it has always been wrong, then you will be pulled up short by the first and second commandments, which impose the worship of Yahweh. Even if the first commandment does not explicitly deny the existence of other deities beside Yahweh, it prohibits the worship of them. And it does not allow you to believe in no god either. Non-religious people existed in ancient Israel, apparently, if we may take at face value the admission in the Psalms (10.4; 14.1; 53.2 [EVV 1]) that 'the fool has said in his heart, There is no God'. By the standard of the Decalogue, an atheist is worse than a fool; such a person is in breach of divine law. And if the implied penalty for breach of any of the commandments of the Decalogue is death (as many argue), the situation is even worse.

---

2. The term is strange, since it implies a tool, and nothing in the biblical narrative suggests that the deity was envisaged as using anything other than his finger to 'write' the Decalogue.

3. Moshe Weinfeld, 'The Uniqueness of the Decalogue', in *The Ten Commandments in History and Tradition* (ed. Ben-Zion Segal; Jerusalem: The Magnes Press, 1990), pp. 1-44 (27-28, 8).

4. W. Sibley Towner, 'Ten Commandments, the', in *Harper's Bible Dictionary* (ed. Paul J. Achtemeier; New York: Harper & Row, 1985), pp. 1033-35 (1034).

I am not here adopting a non-religious approach to the study of the Decalogue. I am drawing attention rather to what I see as an uncritical importation of certain religious values into what should properly be a scholarly endeavour. In the matter of scholarly objectivity religious people should be united with non-religious people especially when the subject matter is religion.

In this paper, I will look at two aspects of the Decalogue where I think the scholarly tradition needs to be critiqued, and conclude with some more general critical observations about the Decalogue itself.

1. The Divine Origin of the Decalogue

The Decalogue, in both its Exodus and Deuteronomy forms, professes to be the words of God. The Decalogue is presented in Deuteronomy 5 as spoken by Yahweh to Moses and then reported by Moses to Israel. It consists of words spoken by Yahweh with a loud voice from Sinai to the whole assembly of Israel; but Israel is afraid of the voice of Yahweh, and implores Moses to go and hear what Yahweh is saying (5.25-27). It is also said that Yahweh 'wrote' the words on two stone tablets (5.22). In Exodus, the people stand at the foot of the mountain (19.17), and Yahweh gives Moses on the top of the mountain twelve chapters' worth of laws (20.2–31.17, including the Covenant Code of 21.2–23.33). Before Moses goes down, God gives him the two tables of the covenant, 'tables of stone, written with the finger of God' (31.18), written on both sides,[5] the tablets being the work of God and the writing the writing of God (32.15). On descending from the mountain, Moses sees the Hebrews dancing around the Golden Calf and smashes the tablets (32.19). Subsequently, Moses is told by Yahweh to cut two tablets like the first ones (though those ones were cut by God himself), on which Yahweh says he will write the same words as before (34.1). In the event, however, it seems that it is Moses who writes on the tablets 'the words of the covenant, the ten words' (34.28).[6]

---

5. This element in the description is little remarked on, and certainly not in artistic representations of the scene. The idea that each tablet contains all ten commandments and that, in accord with ancient Near Eastern custom, there is one copy for each of the parties to the covenant, is an attractive one (Meredith G. Kline, 'The Two Tables of the Covenant', *Westminster Theological Journal* 22 [1960], pp. 133-46). On this view, it is not at all surprising that both copies of the Decalogue should end up in the Ark of the Covenant, for the Ark is regarded as having a dual function, both as the dwelling of Yahweh and as the centre of the people of Israel.

6. That it is Moses who writes the second set of tablets is acknowledged by, for example, J. Philip Hyatt, *Commentary on Exodus* (New Century Bible Commentary; London: Oliphants, 1971), p. 326. Thomas B. Dozeman, *Commentary on Exodus* (Grand Rapids: Eerdmans, 2009), p. 749, even thinks that the 'ambiguity of

No matter; the Decalogue, in whichever version we read it, is presented as the words of God. Leaving aside the questions whether Yahweh could speak and write Palaeo-Hebrew and whether his finger could be used as an engraving tool, the important fact is that the scholarly tradition both affirms and denies the divine origin of the Decalogue. On the one hand, it wants to maximize the authority of the Decalogue,[7] and on the other, it is uncomfortable with the supernaturalism of the narratives, and is looking for an origin of the Decalogue in some historical circumstances, like clan wisdom or the father's instruction.

A critical historian or commentator would be bound to say that the claim that 'God spoke all these words' cannot be historically true. Yet not a single commentator I have read says any such thing, not one confronts the claim of the text with their own personal refusal to accept its ideology, not one draws any conclusion about the status of the text once they have decided they do not believe some significant part of it.[8] Not one commentator remarks that, if God did not in fact say all these words and the text says that he did, the text is trying to deceive us, and that is a strange state of affairs in a text that is in the business of laying down ethical principles.

So-called critical scholars have been reading this unquestionably important text as if it contained divine words when what it really contains (and they know it) are human words, social and religious laws that their authors want to ascribe to God because they want other people to obey them. From the point of view of critical biblical scholarship, what stands written in Exodus 20 and Deuteronomy 5 is there not because of some supernatural event on Sinai but because it was in the interests of the framers of the Decalogue, whoever they were, to promulgate its contents.[9]

---

authorship' may be the point of emphasis: it 'blurs the distinction between divine and Mosaic authorship', he says. I don't think so; even if Moses is chiselling the commandments himself, there is no question but that that their content is created by Yahweh.

7. It is curious that the verb רצח, commonly translated 'murder' in Exod. 20.13, is often understood as 'illegal killing inimical to the community' (so notably by J.J. Stamm, 'Sprachliche Erwägungen zum Gebot "Du sollst nicht töten"', *Theologische Zeitschrift* 1 [1945], pp. 81-90). If that were so, in that case the divine law would be secondary to the human law, since it is the community that decides what is legal or illegal.

8. The great majority of commentaries do not make even a single comment on the verse 'And God spoke all these words, saying' (Exod. 20.1). Not even the 659-page commentary of Brevard S. Childs on Exodus (*Exodus: A Commentary* [Old Testament Library; London: SCM Press], 1974) finds room for a single remark, though on p. 397 Childs does observe that the first-person formula 'points to direct, unmediated communication of Yahweh himself' (he presumably means: to a literary fiction of direct communication by Yahweh).

9. I interpolate here a quotation from Michel de Montaigne: 'Now laws remain in credit not because they are just, but because they are laws. That is the mystic foundation

2. The Place of Women

Nowadays, now that we are coming to recognize, belatedly, that the Bible is a male text through and through, it is incumbent on us to undertake a gender analysis of whatever biblical passage we are studying in order to see how deeply masculinity is embedded in the text, and to what extent the roles and rights of women are marginalized. This is a subject never treated in the scholarly tradition on the Decalogue, which remains steadfastly gender-blind.[10]

There are four elements in the Decalogue relevant to gender that I will mention.

1. The first is the matter of who is addressed. In the setting of the Decalogue in Exodus the 'people' (עם) to whom Moses brings the Ten Commandments are males exclusively. As they wait for the promulgation they are under strict instructions 'not to touch a woman' (Exod. 19.15), which shows they must be males. Moreover any living creature that so much as touches the sacred mountain is to be killed, 'whether animal or man (איש)' (19.13); evidently, no females are present.

As for the Decalogue itself, it can hardly be a secret that it is addressed to a male individual, for the 'you' of every commandment is a masculine singular form of a verb. There is no merit in the argument that the masculine gender 'includes' the female.[11] If the framers of the Decalogue had been alert to issues of gender, it would have been easy to couch all the commandments in the plural, so including both men and women. As it is, women are systematically excluded as addressees, just as are aliens, children, and others. This

---

of their authority; they have no other... They are often made by fools, more often by people who, in their hatred of equality, are wanting in equity; but always by men, vain and irresolute authors' (quoted from James Mille, *The Philosophical Life* [Oxford: Oneworld Publications, 2012], p. 169).

10. Drorah O'Donnell Setel forms an honourable exception when she remarks of the legal codes of the Hebrew Bible that '[f]or the most part, there is no consideration of female subjects. The text is written from the perspective of male experience, and is addressed to a male audience. Women enter this framework as exceptions to the [male] norm or as special cases' ('Exodus', in *The Women's Bible Commentary* [ed. Carol A. Newsom and Sharon H. Ringe; London: SPCK, 1992], pp. 26-35 [34]).

11. Tikva Frymer-Kensky argues from the omission of the wife from the Sabbath commandment that 'the "you" that the law addresses includes both women and men, each treated as a separate moral agent' ('Deuteronomy', in *The Women's Bible Commentary*, pp. 52-66 [54]). But at the same time she affirms that the Tenth Commandment addresses men only ('It is only when the text considers sexual lust that it stops being inclusive and looks at the wife as the object rather than the subject of the law'). Though I do not agree with her, and think it very improbable that the Decalogue should at one place address women and at another neglect to do so, she is one of the first commentators even to raise the issue of whether women are addressed.

state of affairs may not be always noticed among speakers of languages like English that do not have gendered pronouns of the second person or gendered verbal forms, but the Israeli biblical scholar Athalya Brenner reminds us how those distinctions, which persist in Modern Hebrew, affect her, for example, as a woman driver every day of her life. Road commands, Stop!, Wait!, Go!, are all addressed to males, and as a responsible road-user she must be constantly constructing herself as a male.[12] The Decalogue, in short, systematically fails to address women.

2. The Tenth Commandment (Coveting) is a clear example of the exclusion of women: the male addressee of the Decalogue is enjoined not to 'covet' or 'desire'[13] his neighbour's wife. Since women are not addressed, they are not required to abstain from coveting their neighbour's husband. It is not that they are permitted to do so, but rather that not only their sexuality but their very presence in the community is ignored.

3. The Fourth/Third Commandment (Sabbath) notably forbids the male addressee of the Decalogue to do any work on the sabbath, along with his son, daughter, male servant, female servant, ox, ass or cattle—but not his wife. Why she is not mentioned is not easy to understand, since female daughters and female servants are referred to. I suspect that the reason for the omission is that the domestic work of women was not recognized as work (though it has been estimated that the Israelite housewife spent more than ten hours a day in work).[14] By the standards of traditional masculinity, cooking, cleaning and childcare are not real work.[15] Daughters may be mentioned just because sons are, and female servants just because male servants are. Or it may be that their work was more like male work if they were occupied in agricultural labour or semi-industrial processes like weaving or dyeing. The absence of the wife is, perhaps not surprisingly, rarely remarked on in the scholarly tradition.

---

12. Athalya Brenner, 'The Decalogue: Am I an Addressee?', in *Exodus and Deuteronomy* (ed. Athalya Brenner and Gale A. Yee; Texts @ Contexts; Minneapolis: Fortress Press, 2012), pp. 197-204 (198), expanding her article of the same title in *A Feminist Companion to Exodus to Deuteronomy* (The Feminist Companion to the Bible, 6; Sheffield: Sheffield Academic Press, 1994), pp. 255-58.

13. The verb is חמד; KJV has 'desire' in Deut. 5.21, but 'covet' for the same word in Exod. 20.17. Deut. 5.21 actually has חמד with the neighbour's wife as the object, and אוה hithp. 'desire' with the other items as objects.

14. Carol L. Meyers, 'Everyday Life: Women in the Period of the Hebrew Bible', in *The Women's Bible Commentary*, p. 247.

15. Peter C. Craigie, *Deuteronomy* (NICOT; Grand Rapids: Eerdmans, 1976), p. 157, suggested that wives are omitted 'in order to avoid any suggestion that the law also applied to domestic activities'. A.C.J. Phillips, *Ancient Israel's Criminal Law* (Oxford: Basil Blackwell, 1970), p. 69, likewise remarks that 'Wives are omitted to avoid any ambiguity that the law applied to domestic activity as well'. Neither male commentator notices, I suppose, that he saying that women's work is not real work.

4. The Fifth/Fourth Commandment (Honouring parents) is different from the general tendency in the Decalogue to ignore or marginalize women, for here the mother, along with the father, is to be the object of 'honour'. This is an exceptional use of the term 'honour', since normally speaking a woman cannot be honoured and honour is an exclusively male possession, being attributed and recognized in public, a sphere in which women do not move.[16] A woman can be shamed, she can have a minus quantity of honour, but her normal state is one of zero honour, which cannot be augmented. Perhaps our text means that one should honour one's father and *not dishonour* one's mother.[17] In any case, it is significant that women are being honoured for their motherhood, not for any other quality;[18] clearly the honour that fathers acquire rests on a much broader foundation than their fatherhood.

---

16. Lev. 19.3 is sometimes mentioned as a parallel (though the issue there is respect rather than honour): 'Each man should fear (ירא) his mother and his father'. It is noteworthy that the mother precedes the father, a fact that inspires some very fanciful explanations, such that (1) (improbably) respect for parents and especially for the mother had been disrupted by the Babylonian exile (J.R. Porter, *Leviticus* [Cambridge Bible Commentaries; Cambridge: Cambridge University Press, 1976], p. 153); or (2) that (a stab in the dark) 'some loosening of the kinship and family arrangements in connection with the end of the old pre-exilic Israel brought into special prominence respect for parents, and especially for the mother' (M. Noth, *Leviticus: A Commentary* [OTL; Philadelphia: Westminster Press, rev. translation 1977], p. 141); or (3) that (another guess, without foundation in the text) it reflects the husband's concern for his wife if he should predecease her (Rainer Albertz, 'Hintergrund und Bedeutung des Elterngebots im Dekalog', *ZAW* 90 [1978], pp. 348-74 [372-73]); or (4) that (though honour is not the issue in the texts cited) in 'familial contexts' (Lev. 21.2; Gen. 35.18) respect is paid first to the mother (Baruch A. Levine, *Leviticus: The Traditional Hebrew Text with the New JPS Translation* [Philadelphia: Jewish Publication Society, 1989], p. 125); or (5) that (irrelevantly, since we are reading here about the responsibilities of adults to their parents) the mother plays a decisive role in the socialization of the child (E.S. Gerstenberger, *Leviticus: A Commentary* [OTL; Louisville, KY: Westminster/John Knox Press], p. 265). Jacob Milgrom (*Leviticus 17–22: A New Translation with Introduction and Commentary* [AB, 3A; New York: Doubleday, 2000], p. 1608) takes a much less fanciful line when he remarks how this text, while alluding to the Decalogue, seems deliberately to reverse or alter its wording ('fear' rather than 'honour'; object before subject; mother before father; and, he might have added, plural rather than singular verb), though the reason for these changes remains obscure.

17. In the most immediate context of the Decalogue, viz. the Book of the Covenant in Exod. 21.2–23.33, at least part of the 'honour' due to a mother seems to be the right not to be struck and not to be cursed (21.15, 17).

18. The one other place where honour (כבוד) is attributed to women is Isa. 66.11, where Jerusalem as a mother is said to have glory. Those who mourn for her are to suck and be satisfied with her breasts of consolation; they should drain them out and delight themselves 'in the nipple(s) of her glory' (מזיז כבודה). The honour or glory of women in this context is full breasts. That is so far from the kind of meaning 'honour' has in reference to a man that we might ponder whether we should use the word 'honour' for it at all.

I conclude that a text that so systematically fails to recognize the interests of women and does not address them as moral agents but regards them as chattels along with cattle does not deserve to be hailed as universal and timeless.

3. *The Decalogue Critiqued*

If, as I am suggesting, the Decalogue is not to be regarded as timeless and universal, how is it to be regarded? I see no reason to regard it differently from the material in Exodus that immediately follows, in the Book of the Covenant and the other laws, or the Deuteronomic laws that follow Deuteronomy 5. They all have a historical and a social context, and they are the laws of ancient Israel. As with any body of law, there will be some items in them, perhaps many, that people of a different place and era can gladly assent to, but that will not be because the laws have a prior claim on their adherence.

No one wants to claim that the laws of the Book of the Covenant are timeless laws of universal applicability. On what grounds, then, are such claims made for the Decalogue, when it is so plainly time-conditioned, with its manifestations of patriarchy, its casual sexism, its class discriminations, and its illiberal dragooning of all members of its society into a uniform set of religious beliefs and practices?[19]

If we can dispense with the aura of universality and timelessness that has attached itself to the Decalogue, we may be in a position to make some new critiques of the Decalogue as a collection.

1. We will be free, for example, to ask what the consequences may be of regarding ten such sentences as the quintessence of law or morality. If there

---

19. A tendency toward universalization may even have taken place before the present form of the Decalogue. The commandment against stealing, for example, is often thought to have been originally against a specific form of stealing, viz. kidnapping, i.e. stealing a person (so A. Alt, 'Das Verbot des Diebstahls im Dekalog', in his *Kleine Schriften zur Geschichte des Volkes Israel*, I [ed. M. Noth; Munich: Beck, 1953], pp. 330-40), while the commandment against murder was perhaps earlier a commandment against a specific kind of killing, viz. revenge killing (as Henning Graf Reventlow, *Gebot und Predigt im Dekalog* [Gütersloh: Gerd Mohn, 1962], pp. 71-73). More common has been a process of universalization subsequent to the Decalogue itself. The commandment against bearing false witness, for example, was later understood as prohibiting lying in general, though the wording in the Decalogue is plain that it is a matter of false testimony in court (so, for example, Dozeman, *Exodus*, p. 495). The commandment about keeping the sabbath has been re-applied in Christian interpretation to a day that is not the sabbath. The commandment against adultery has become understood almost universally as concerned with all extramarital relations, though in its biblical context it refers only to a man having sex with a woman married to another man.

is anything that is true about both law and morality, speaking generally, it is that they are very complex and never straightforward. To suggest that all of morality and law is in principle reducible to ten short clauses is misleading and simplistic in the extreme, and actually not very interesting. It is not hard, for instance, to gain assent to the belief that theft is wrong; the hard work for lawyers and ethicists alike (as well as for ordinary citizens) is in figuring out what exactly will count as theft.[20] There is little merit, and little profundity, in establishing that theft is wrong if a society does not reach agreement on what, in detail, constitutes theft.

2. Secondly, I ask, as Hebrew Bible scholars never do: what is the effect of a moral or legal code that is framed entirely in the imperative?[21] Such a lawcode affirms that right behaviour is right because God says so, not because of any rational grounding. Most parents have had recourse, at the end of their tether with an argumentative child, to blurting out 'Because I say so!', but most do not find that a very productive approach for daily life. If every element in the foundational lawcode stands as the simple command of the deity, all moral decisions are reduced to a single issue of obedience, and no one under its authority is called on to function as a rational moral agent.

3. What is the effect of the sequence of negative commands found in the Decalogue? Some modern parents abstain from ever using the word 'Don't' with their children on the ground that negative criticism decreases motivation and that being positive about the child's strengths and potential is more effective in shaping the child's behaviour. Even if you don't agree with this approach, it is worth discussing the impact of the negativity of the second half of the Decalogue. What values are these commandments promoting? Or is their chief intention actually to proscribe certain acts rather than to inculcate positive behaviour?

4. What is the effect of all the address to the listener or the reader being in the second-person singular? It maintains the fiction that in the Decalogue

20. Is plagiarism theft, for example? See Hagith Sivan, *Between Woman, Man, and God: A New Interpretation of the Ten Commandments* (JSOTSup, 401; London: T. & T. Clark International, 2004), p. 188.

21. A distinction between such 'apodeictic' laws and casuistic laws (case law) was apparently first made by the early twentieth-century critic Albrecht Alt, who regarded the apodeictic as characteristically Israelite and the casuistic as 'Canaanite', a classic binary opposition in which one term was the privileged one (see 'The Origins of Israelite Law', in his *Essays on Old Testament History and Religion* (trans. R.A. Wilson; Oxford: Basil Blackwell, 1966), pp. 79-132 [original, *Die Ursprünge des israelitischen Rechts* (Berichte über die Verhandlungen der Sächsischen Akademie der Wissenschaften zu Leipzig; Philologisch-historische Klasse, 86/1; Leipzig: S. Hirzel, 1934]); we still have not found any 'Canaanite' laws, but we do know that both forms co-existed all over the ancient Near East (cf. G.W. Mendenhall, 'Covenant', *IDB*, I, p. 720a). And the prejudicial binary opposition is clearly due for a deconstruction.

the male householder is personally addressed by the deity, heightening the force of the Commandments and the gravity of any breach of them. But if ever the Decalogue were addressed to Israel at Sinai by Yahweh, it was not so addressed to any other generation of Israelites, and much less to non-Israelites of any time. Deuteronomy itself is aware how self-limiting the narrative setting of the Decalogue has been when it has Moses asserting, some forty years after Sinai, that 'not with our fathers did Yahweh make this covenant, but with us, who are all of us here alive today' (Deut. 5.3), which is patently false. Moses, we realize, is working hard to extend the time range of applicability of the Decalogue, but that means, we should not misunderstand, that we have only Moses' word for the continuing validity of the Decalogue, not Yahweh's. Or rather, since these are not likely to be the words of the historical Moses (granting his existence), we have only the assurance of some anonymous Hebrew author that the Decalogue remains valid for later generations.

A study of the reception of the Decalogue shows, I conclude, that critical questions of this kind are rarely if ever asked in the realm of biblical scholarship. Experts in biblical scholarship, who, you would have thought, would be among the first to resist the claims of ancient texts, have aided and abetted the general public and religious believers alike in their belief that the Decalogue carries unique divine authority and deserves to remain a bastion of Western civilization.

The Reception of the Decalogue in Film: Krzysztof Kieślowski's *Decalogue*

Lloyd Baugh

In 1989, Krzysztof Kieślowski's ten *Decalogue* films were released in Poland; each less than an hour in length, they were first seen on Polish television. The original longer version (85 minutes) of *Decalogue Five* had been screened at the Cannes Film Festival the previous year. The film had received a surprisingly enthusiastically response and the prestigious *Prix du Jury*, and Kieślowski, until then relatively unknown outside Eastern Europe, was launched on to the Western European and world scene. The *Decalogue* films were very soon subtitled and released in cinemas in France and Italy, and later elsewhere.[1]

Kieślowski on God and the Commandments

Soon after the triumph at Cannes, in an interview with an Italian journalist, and in answer to the 'God question', Kieślowski, with playful irony and tongue-in-cheek ambiguity, declared: 'I don't believe in God, but I have a good relationship with him'.[2] An attentive screening and consideration of the *Decalogue* films belies the first part of that statement, or at least cautions against concluding that the director is a hard-line, dogmatic atheist, and it allows for wholehearted assent to the second part of his statement.

After 23 years of working with the *Decalogue* and Kieślowski's four later films—screening and teaching them, using them in prayer and spiritual retreat experiences, and writing about them—I am convinced that Kieślowski, in a sincere, sometimes troubled, sometimes settled way, not

---

1. Kieślowski adopts the Catholic–Lutheran tradition for the division/organization of the Ten Commandments. The original version of the films, in Polish, are titled by number only, e.g.: *Dekalog, jeden*. The Italian version adds the word-titles of the Commandments. E.g.: *Decalogo 1 (Dekalog, jeden)—Io sono il Signore tuo Dio. Non avrai altro dio all'infuori di me*; *Decalogo 6 (Dekalog, sześć)—Non commettere atti impuri*; *Decalogo 9 (Dekalog, dziewięć)—Non desiderare la donna d'altri*.

2. Kieślowski, interviewed by A. Crespi, 'La mia Bibbia senza certezze', *L'unità* (Rome) (19 September 1989), p. 78.

only was searching for God, but, in fact, found and experienced God, not in a once-and-for-all, smug, self-satisfied way, but rather as a willingness to enter hesitantly, questioningly, into the darkness of the human mystery and behind that, the darkness/light of Holy Mystery.

Later in that same interview, Kieślowski made another revealing statement, this time about the Decalogue—not his ten films, but the Ten Commandments of the Mosaic law. He said: 'What fascinates me about the Commandments is that we all agree that they are just and appropriate, but at the same time, we violate them every day. They interest me because they allow me to examine the moral ambivalence of human beings.'[3]

It is in the context of these two statements of Kieślowski that I write this essay, for it is in the dynamic tension among Kieślowski's faith/non-faith/ searching faith in God, his conviction of the universal human experience of the commandments of the Mosaic moral law and of the ambivalence of the human response to the commandments, that he 'receives' that law and that he actualizes this reception in the ten—really, they are twelve[4]—films of his *Decalogue*.

Radically different from Cecil B. DeMille's epic treatment of the Mosaic Decalogue in his colossal film, *The Ten Commandments* (1956),[5] these are ten very human and very convincing stories of life in the contemporary world. Each film is independent of the others in terms of its narrative, but all of them are interrelated both morally and in terms of the repeated appearances of the protagonists of one film in others of the series. The films are set in a high-rise condominium complex in Stowki/Warsaw in 1988, and most of the protagonists seem to live in one of the buildings. For Kieślowski, Warsaw is emblematic of any major urban environment and the specific struggles of the characters of the ten films clearly have a universal scope. The protagonists of the films are a cross section of society at large. They include: doctors, taxi drivers, professors, an artist, musicians, a lawyer, a writer, businessmen; women and men, old, middle-aged, young

---

3. Crespi, 'La mia Bibbia senza certezze', p. 78.

4. In the series called *The Decalogue*, released in 1989, there are ten films, each 55–58 minutes in length. The year before, the longer, original versions of two of the *Decalogue* films, each approximately 85 minutes in length, were released: *A Short Film About Killing* (*Krótki film o zabijaniu*), the longer version of *Decalogue Five*, and *A Short Film About Love* (*Krotki film o miłósci*), the longer version of *Decalogue Six*. The shorter versions of the films are not simply edited-down reductions of the original ones, but they include considerable new material. Consequently, significant differences between the shorter and longer versions warrant their being treated as different films.

5. For a treatment of that film's reception of the Mosaic Decalogue, see M.J. Wright, *Moses in America: The Cultural Uses of Biblical Narrative* (Oxford: Oxford University Press, 2003), pp. 89-127.

and children; public figures and private; a troubled delinquent and responsible citizens.

The Ten Commandments and The Decalogue

Kieślowski's films are anything but simple illustrations of each of the Commandments, whatever that might be, or a simple illustration of the violation of the Commandments or of obedience to them. Though each of the *Decalogue* films focuses nominally on some dimension of the moral imperative of the Commandment to which it refers, in fact, the films range widely in their interpretation of the Commandments, investigating an impressive variety of critical moral issues: faith and non-faith in God, maturity and fidelity in marriage; responsible parenting; respect for life, abortion, capital punishment; honesty and care in relationships; sin and forgiveness; and the morally just use of authority, of property and of human sexuality.

In some of the films, *One* and *Five*, for instance, the thrust of the narrative remains close to the traditional sense of the Mosaic Commandment. In the former a man has replaced God and trust in God with the false god of human intelligence and rationality; in the latter, two killings take place, a murder and a legal execution, and both are represented as morally reprehensible.

In others, the film offers a new and original moral twist to the traditional understanding of the Commandment: in *Four*, in an intense relationship between a father and his precocious daughter, moral chaos is finally avoided not by the daughter's respecting her father but by the father's respecting his daughter; in *Seven*, what is savagely stolen is not a concrete, material object, but rather the soul, the life of a little girl.

In still other of the films, the precise connection to the Commandment in question is tenuous, while another Commandment, in fact, is honored: in *Two*, the name of God is honored by renewed fidelity in marriage and by respect for the life of an unborn child; in *Three*, the Holy Day of Christmas is sanctified not so much by the protagonist's *pro forma* presence at Mass, but by his decision to remain faithful to his wife; though *Six* does consider impure acts as immoral, its primary focus is a story of the redemptive power of love.

The protagonists of the *Decalogue* live out their struggle with good and evil and for human integrity in a fragmented, postmodern environment, an often dark world characterized by moral confusion and ambiguity, by the inevitable clash between traditional values and contemporary disvalues, between faith and non-faith, and by the frightening complexity of personal moral integration and of interpersonal relationships. In Kieślowski's films, life is complex and good moral choices are difficult, fraught by ambiguity, by fear, by selfishness.

God in The Decalogue

The biblical Decalogue came to Moses from God; it is an expression of God, the law of God meant for the people of God. Kieślowski's *Decalogue* comes from Kieślowski, an expression of what he believes. Where is God in Kieślowski's ten films? What role does God play in the lives and actions, in the moral life of the various protagonists? This is a very complex issue and one deserving of a wider and more nuanced treatment than I can give it here. However, and to put it most simply, God is everywhere in the *Decalogue* films.

On a first level, Kieślowski references God indirectly and many times, in most of the films of the *Decalogue*. At critical moments in their moral struggle and decision making, characters use the name of God as exclamations that much of the time seem more like prayers, like invocations of the Deity.[6] Repeatedly, the films offer visual references to churches, crosses, priests, religious rituals, at times and in ways that give them greater valence than that of mere Polish-Catholic cultural references.

On a second level, Kieślowski makes the God question explicit in several of the films. In *Two*, the desperate woman, in a life-and-death moral struggle and angry with the old doctor because he seems unwilling to help her, demands to know if he believes in God. The doctor, who has been living in isolation since a personal tragedy 40 years before, answers, almost ashamedly, 'I have a private God'. By the end of the film, he has come out of his isolation and rediscovered the authentic God of love. In *One*, Kieślowski situates the God question in the forefront of the narrative: the facade of a modern church, its doors wide open, dominates several crucial shots of the film; a little boy questions his father about God; the father can offer him only the 'bland explanations'[7] of the atheist/agnostic he has become; the boy's aunt, a believing, practicing Catholic, offers a concrete and eloquent demonstration of affection and love as her evocation of God.

On a third level, and most significantly, the moral philosophy professor in *Eight*, when she explains her pedagogical method, makes a precise identification between God and the moral life, explaining that her approach is to place her students in situations in which the Good (the God) 'in them' moves them to morally correct reflection, decision and action. The moral law, she is saying, is God's, is an expression of God, and that moral law dwells in the human heart and so it is God who moves women and men to just moral decisions and actions.

---

6. The Polish word for God is 'Bóg', the vocative form is 'Boże'. Annoyingly, the English subtitles do not always translate these expressions that are clearly audible on the soundtrack of the films.

7. S. Murri, *Krzysztof Kieślowski* (Milan: Il Castoro, 1996), p. 85.

Divine Grace in The Decalogue

Kieślowski goes even further than this by embodying in two of his characters a direct presence of God or of salvific divine Grace. The first is the mysterious young man, Tomek, in *Decalogue Six*. The narrative of the film is a transparent parable of the redemptive encounter between Mary Magdalene the sinner[8] and, by extension, every sinner, and Jesus Christ.[9] Magda is so deeply caught in a web of sinful sexual behavior that she has given up on love, she is convinced it does not exist, neither for her nor at all; she is fully aware of her sinfulness and she is certainly convinced that she is not loveable. Tomek, innocent, non-judgmental, generous, wants only to love her and, by shedding his blood and, at least symbolically, dying for her, he touches her heart and—to use the logic of Zofia, the professor in *Eight*—releases the Good that dwells there. She changes; her life changes; she is redeemed; the Sixth Commandment is respected.

In another highly symbolic character, Kieślowski represents God's providential presence or Grace. Appearing in nine of the ten films, always played by the same actor but in a different guise and function each time, always silent—I call him the 'Silent Witness'[10]—always seen by the viewer but not always by the protagonist, this enigmatic character appears at crisis moments in the moral *iter* of the protagonists, often moments when the characters are about to do something morally wrong or dangerous, and in eight of the nine films, his presence and his gaze of care and compassion—one critic qualifies it as a look 'of pure goodness and care, a point of view that we might call 'divine''[11] and another critic says he is 'christlike'[12]—have a positive, salvific impact on the protagonists who, after he has passed by, shift their attitudes and moral behavior in directions that are grace filled and morally liberating: one character recovers his faith in God; another decides not to have an abortion; one is saved from a tragic act of dishonor to her father; and yet another is saved from suicide.

---

8. Kieślowski is caught in the error of Pope Gregory the Great that makes Mary of Magdala a prostitute.

9. I analyzed this central theme of *Decalogue Six* comprehensively in a two-part essay: L. Baugh, 'Cinematographic Variations on the Christ-Event: Three Film Texts by Krzysztof Kieślowski–Part One: *A Short Film about Love*', *Gregorianum* 84 (2003), pp. 551-83, and L. Baugh, 'Cinematographic Variations on the Christ-Event: Three Film Texts by Krzysztof Kieślowski–Part Two: *Decalogue Six* and the Script', *Gregorianum* 84 (2003), pp. 919-46.

10. L. Baugh, 'The Grace of Divine Providence: The Identity and Function of the Silent Witness in the *Decalogue* Films of Kieślowski', *Gregorianum* 86 (2005), p. 523.

11. T. Sobolewski, 'La solidarietà dei peccatori', in M. Furdal and R. Turigliatto (eds.), *Kieślowski* (Torino: Museo nazionale del cinema, 1989), p. 64.

12. S. Žižek, *The Fright of Real Tears: Krzysztof Kieślowski between Theory and Post-Theory* (London: British Film Institute, 2001), p. 122.

In his Silent Witness, Kieślowski goes even further in connecting God with the moral life by insisting on the crucial element of human freedom. The Witness never imposes his will on those he visits, but rather invites them to higher levels of moral integrity, respecting their freedom to accept his challenge or to refuse it. And he does not withdraw from the moral fray when his challenge is refused; the young man about to commit murder in *Five* sees the Silent Witness, but hides from his gaze and brutally kills the taxi driver. Yet when later the young man, condemned to death by the courts, is about to be executed, the Witness is present twice in his favor, 'as if preparing to meet Jacek in death',[13] and, in fact, provides him with a morally redemptive experience.

Kieślowski's Fundamental Moral Principles: From Ten to Four

In a very synthetic overview, the fundamental moral principles that prevail in Kieślowski's filmic reception of the Mosaic Decalogue are four. The first principle, the one Kieślowski most often deals with, the one providing the most complex dynamics in the series, is that of the primacy of love. All the films of the *Decalogue*, sooner or later, have as a central or as a very important theme the essential and constitutive and salvific human experience of love.

A second moral principle is that of the primacy of the physical and moral life of the child, the right of the child to be born, to live, to be protected, to be free. A repeated theme in many of the films, it is addressed directly as a moral principle in *Decalogue Eight* and it is the focus of the most grave moral violation of the series in *Decalogue Seven*, a film in which two women claim to love a child, loudly and perversely protesting their love, and yet neither is capable of loving, creating a moral hell in which, and to which, the child is condemned.

Related to the absolute primacy of the life of the child is the sacrality of human life in general, a point Kieślowski makes repeatedly. Announced appropriately and most dramatically in *Five*, in the parallel representations of a murder and then of the execution of the murderer, Kieślowski clearly is announcing that both actions are equally unacceptable and immoral. In two of the films (*Three* and *Nine*), the spectre of suicide is raised, a gesture here represented as a cowardly and desperate desire to escape from moral responsibility. Kieślowski not only prevents the suicides, but renews the hope of the individuals concerned. For most of *Two*, Kieślowski represents

---

13. L. Baugh, 'The Christian Moral Vision of a Believing Atheist: Krzysztof Kieślowski's *Decalogue* Films', in Peter Malone (ed.), *Through a Catholic Lens: Religious Perspectives of Nineteen Film Directors from around the World* (Lanham, MD: Rowman & Littlefield, 2007), p. 165.

one of the protagonists in a hospital bed in his death agony but then in a surprise ending, he saves the man, a moment of great satisfaction for the viewer.

A fourth principle is that of the moral commitment of husband and wife, of the sacrality of marriage; it is the central theme of three of the films, *Two*, *Three* and *Nine*, and functions as a secondary theme in *One* and *Seven*.

Not only does Kieślowski have his characters act in morally unacceptable or acceptable ways, but he also gives them awareness of their violation of a moral norm: he has them consciously reflect on their behavior. In eight of the films (*Two*, *Three*, *Four*, *Five*, *Six*, *Eight*, *Nine*, *Ten*), he represents powerful confessional scenes in which the offending protagonists confess their moral violations either to the offended person or, in one of the films, *Five*, to a third party, whom Kieślowski represents, at least symbolically, as a priestly/sacramental confessor.[14] This confession leads to a moral resolution and redemption.

In two of the films, Kieślowski amplifies this theme of reflection on the law by developing within the diegesis quite explicit moral discussions/debates. Kieślowski begins *Five* with a debate on capital punishment between the young and idealistic lawyer protagonist and an older lawyer on the panel of his bar exam; he then inserts this debate in background voiceover during the whole first part of the film, a kind of ongoing moral commentary on the actions of the three main characters.

In *Eight*, a film that can be considered a theoretical foundation for the series and its moral issues, Kieślowski represents the moral debate explicitly first in an extended scene in a university classroom where one of the protagonists, the professor of moral philosophy, moderates a public case study debate of burning moral issues. Kieślowski then continues this debate in a private, confessional conversation between an offender and the offended, a hard-hitting discussion that, however, leads to forgiveness and reconciliation.

Kieślowski represents sinfulness as a near-univeral existential situation. Most of the protagonists of the *Decalogue* films, at least the adults, are sinners and are guilty of violating at least one of the Commandments, most often in very serious ways. And yet, as I have already suggested, in the conclusion of all but one of the films, *Decalogue Seven*, the protagonist-sinners overcome their sinfulness, make good and courageous moral choices and restore order in their lives.

In *One*, the atheist / agnostic, after the tragic death of his son, reclaims his lost faith as he goes into a church and prays; and the husbands and

---

14. Paul Coates calls Piotr, the condemned man's lawyer, a 'secular priest' (*The Gorgon's Gaze: German Cinema, Expressionism, and the Image of Horror* [Cambridge: Cambridge University Press, 1991], p. 191).

wives of *Two* and *Nine*, and perhaps of *Three*, are reconciled and recommitted to one another. In *Six*, the Magdalene character—her name is actually Maria Magdalena—joyfully recognizes that she has been redeemed by the sacrificial love of the man who has chastely pursued her, and in *Four*, the father and daughter are saved from the moral chaos of an incestuous sexual encounter. In *Eight*, the two women, some 40 years after the sin that has divided them, are reconciled, and in *Ten*, two brothers who have sinned gravely against one other meet, confess, forgive and are reconciled.

Kieślowski does not represent these moral shifts or conversions in his characters as easy, unambiguous experiences, made without struggle or personal cost. Nor does he have his characters experience their conversions as taking place in a moral vacuum, the result of pure chance or blind fate. In this, and very significantly, he is reversing a position he takes in his 1982 film, *Blind Chance*—the literal translation of the original title, *Przypadek*, is 'accident'—in which the protagonist is tossed to and fro by events over which he has no possibility of making free and determining moral choices.

Grace as a Challenge

For Kieślowski, grace is not magic, a panacea; it takes away neither the pain that marks human existence, nor the need to struggle against the human tendency to sin. The moral resolutions in the conclusions of the films offer anything but fairy-tale, 'they-lived-happily-ever-after' endings. For Kieślowski, the grace-supported resolution of one moral crisis does not give the characters involved a definitive grasp on righteous living and does not offer any clear guarantees against the need for future moral struggle.

In fact, in several of the films, Kieślowski quite brilliantly shifts the direction of the narrative just slightly, proposing brief, cryptic images of the ambiguity that will continue to be a challenge for the protagonists. The father of the dead boy in the conclusion of *One* enters and prays in a church and seems to have recovered his faith, but then he reappears at the beginning of *Three*, apparently in a situation of despair. At the end of *Two*, the doctor's moral decision has brought life and hope to the couple and their unborn child, but he must continue to live with the horror of the tragic death of his family, years before. The protagonist of *Three* clearly renews his commitment to his wife and family, but in a very subtle gesture, the wife indicates her reluctance to trust him. In the conclusion of *Eight*, having offered the viewer the reassuring experience of the reconciliation between the two women, Kieślowski inserts a powerful note of ambiguity: a third party, also 'victim of the broken commandment',[15] refuses the offer of reconciliation.

---

15. A. Insdorf, *Double Lives, Second Chances: The Cinema of Krzysztof Kieślowski* (New York: Hyperion, 1999), p. 111.

Grace Refused: The Unrepentant Sinner

Kieślowski also allows for the possibility of the unrepentant sinner, the refusal of grace. Though in nine of the films he represents the successful experience of repentance, forgiveness, hope and love, in *Seven*, he radically shifts register and creates a moral and spiritual wasteland. The most bleak of the films, *Seven* represents two women, mother and daughter, as aggressive opponents, violent rivals for the affection of the latter's little daughter, legally adopted at birth by her grandmother. The women, both unbalanced emotionally and locked in an 'unrelenting clash of two egotisms',[16] insist repeatedly that they 'love' little Anka, but neither woman is capable of loving. The gravity of the sin against the child—we recall the first of Kieślowski's fundamental principles—and the obstinacy of the two women in their non-loving reduces the Silent Witness to one brief and very ambiguous appearance, hobbling on crutches, distant from the protagonists, unable to help. Where there is no love, divine Providence, the power of grace, represented by this mysterious figure, is unable to function.

An Autobiographical Note

It is a truism to say that all authors, and so all film directors, put something of themselves into their works, and Kieślowski is no exception. In two of his *Decalogue* films he creates a character who most clearly embodies the two poles of the moral-spiritual dynamic he seems to live in his own life, the atheist/agnostic professor in *One* who struggles with the faith/non-faith/renewed faith cycle, and the old professor of moral philosophy in *Eight*, who not only admits her faith in God, but considers that faith in God, that presence of God, as the foundation of all moral awareness, sensitivity, discernment, decision and action.

Both of these quite magnificent characters have clear autobiographical connections to Kieślowski. To the first, the protagonist of *Decalogue One*, Kieślowski assigns his own name, Krzysztof, and makes him a Catholic by upbringing and an atheist/agnostic by choice, rather like himself. To the second, the protagonist of *Decalogue Eight*, he gives the name Zofia, 'Wisdom', he confers on her the wisdom that comes from a long moral struggle, and he makes her the professor of a seminar in moral philosophy using the case study method, in which one of the cases raised is the moral dilemma represented by Kieślowski in *Decalogue Two*. It is as if Zofia not only represents Kieślowski, but in her course she is doing exactly what Kieślowski is doing in his ten films, receiving and appropriating the Mosaic Decalogue, the moral law, and guiding others to do the same.

16. A. Helman, 'Women in Kieślowski's Later Films', in Paul Coates (ed.), *Lucid Dreams: The Films of Krzysztof Kieślowski* (Trowbridge: Flicks Books, 1999), p. 123.

Ultimately, in these two films and in the experiences of their protagonists, what is most significant is their ability to love, their being loving persons, Krzysztof in his relationship with his son, and Zofia in her experience of reconciliation with her co-protagonist. This, of course, reflects the pattern of moral progress in all the films. In his reception-appropriation of the moral law, in his reflection on it, Kieślowski is saying that the most important moral disposition a person can assume, the most important decision or action they can take, is that of loving, of responding to others with love, regardless of the difficulty or effort that entails.

Referring to Kieślowski's statement mentioned at the beginning of this essay, about the moral ambiguity or ambivalence of human beings, the characters of the *Decalogue* films deal with a variety of moral imperatives, covering the range of the entire Mosaic Decalogue. Often they violate this law: they adore false gods, they violate the Holy Day, they do not respect the name of God, they show disrespect to parents, they kill, they commit impure acts, they steal, they lie, they covet both people and material things.

But to go beyond Kieślowski's pessimistic suggestion that human beings act only in morally ambiguous ways, it is clear that the director gives each of his commandment-violating protagonists a moral journey at the end of which, in nine of the ten films, variously, they recognize the Judeo-Christian God, they respect the Holy Day, they reverence the name of God, they respect parents, they overcome killing, they cease committing impure acts, they tell the truth, they stop coveting both people and material things. In short, they accept and fulfill the Mosaic Decalogue.

But in the end Kieślowski reaches beyond the letter of the ten precepts of the Mosaic law, to find the Spirit of that Law, a Spirit already announced in the Old Testament, and then proclaimed by Jesus and later St Paul in the New Testament. In all ten of the films (and, indeed, in the four films that follow the *Decalogue*) Kieślowski places at the center of the moral dynamic lived by the protagonists the imperative to love, the decision and action of loving. In nine of the *Decalogue* films, the moral resolution of the moral conflicts that fuel the narrative is ultimately the capacity, the decision and the experience of love.

Not only do these decisions and experiences of love allow the protagonists to escape the moral chaos they are in or that threatens them, but it is love that allows them to go on with their lives in new, personally and socially integrating and satisfying ways. It seems to me that finally, for Kieślowski, what most marks his full reception of the Mosaic Decalogue is his conviction of the absolute centrality of the law of love. In this, he is in very good company. Paul, in his Letter to the Romans, enunciates a position very close to that of Kieślowski:

Owe no one anything, except to love each other, for the one who loves another has fulfilled the law. For the commandments, 'You shall not commit adultery, You shall not murder, You shall not steal, You shall not covet', and any other commandment, are summed up in this word: 'You shall love your neighbor as yourself'. Love does no wrong to a neighbor; therefore love is the fulfilling of the law.[17]

---

17. Rom. 13.8-10.

The Ten Commandments and the Problem of Legal Transplants in Contemporary America

Steven Wilf

On the steps of the Dixie Country Courthouse, Florida, a monument to the Decalogue was built out of granite. Over five feet tall and weighing six tons, the monument, constructed with private funds, included both a version of the Ten Commandments and, inscribed along its base, a quotation from Exodus, 'love God and keep His commandments'. The Decalogue monument was set in place in November 2006. Less than three months later, the American Civil Liberties Union of Florida brought an action under the Establishment Clause of the First Amendment, challenging its display as a violation of the separation of Church and state. Dixie County was enjoined from the continuing display on the courthouse steps since it appears to advance a particular religion. Nearly 1,500 demonstrators responded by taking to the streets as part of the protest against removing the Ten Commandments.[1]

The *pas de deux* between conservative promoters of the public display of the Ten Commandments and civil libertarian challengers has been much discussed. Courts and constitutional scholars have debated whether the Decalogue is indeed a religious text within the ambit of the Establishment Clause. According to the current interpretation of the Establishment Clause, 'the government's use of religious symbolism is unconstitutional if it has the effect of endorsing religious beliefs, and the effect of the government's use of religious symbolism depends upon its context'.[2] The United States Supreme Court's recent decisions in *Van Orden v. Perry* and *McCreary County v. ACLU*, underscores the reading of text within context by focusing on the ways the text of the Ten Commandments must be read as embedded

---

1. *American Civil Liberties Union of Florida, Inc. v. Dixie County Florida*, 797 F. Supp. 2d 1280, 1282 (2011). CF. Rob Boston, 'Decalogue Defiance in Dixie: Florida County Defends Fundamentalist Christian Activist's Commandments Display at Local Courthouse', *Church and State* 65 (January 2012), 4-6. My essay does not discuss the textual forms of the Decalogue, which varies in its presentation, and is based upon Exod. 20.2-14 and Deut. 5.6-18.

2. *County of Alleghany v. American Civil Liberties Greater Pittsburgh Chapter*, 492 U.S. 573, 109 S. Ct. 3086 (1989).

in culture and the historical past as well as within its immediate physical setting. With their ambiguous legacy, however, these cases have only added to the controversy.[3]

What interests me here is not the Ten Commandments as a religious text, but a very different issue—the significance of the Decalogue as a *legal* text. What is the purpose of such public exhibition for the communicating of legal norms? Why has this display become the cause of a social movement launched by legal conservatives? And what does it mean to consider this particular set of laws which, after all, is the legal code of an obscure ancient Near Eastern tribe, so salient for modern US law?

This essay argues that Decalogue monuments erected in US public spaces must be understood as embodying legal meaning. It looks at the ways legal conservatives envision the Commandments as *constituting* a legal code which poses a counterpoint to contemporary United States law. As opposed to a contingent legalism imbricated with liberal values, conservatives appropriate the Ten Commandments as a form of natural law. Its moral roots, they maintain, should be contrasted with a merely instrumental American legalism concerned solely with the physical or material well-being of the citizen. Seemingly contradicting the assertion that the Ten Commandments embody truths about universal natural law, legal conservatives also claim that the Decalogue represents a culturally specific law—one that recognizes the United States' Christian heritage rather than a legalism that denies fealty to any particular cultural tradition.[4] In short, the Decalogue is a parallel system of law.

While it was customary in the ancient world to erect a monumental stele inscribed with a code of laws there is no corresponding custom in the Anglo-American legal tradition. Dating from approximately 1750 BCE, the diorite stele of Hammurabi's Code, for example, stands over seven feet tall. Now on display in the Louvre Museum, it lists some 282 laws, dealing with issues ranging from contract to family relations. Rome's Twelve Tables, written on ivory—Livy says bronze—were placed in the Forum in order for Roman citizens to be aware of basic legal norms. In essence, these were boundary markers, setting in place the demarcation between legal and illegal acts. Early North American courthouses, on the other hand, followed the aniconic aesthetic of Protestant places of worship and there were few

---

3. *Van Orden v. Perry*, 545 U.S. 677 (2005) and *McCreary County v. ACLU*, 545 U.S. 844 (2005).

4. There is little to justify the claim that the Decalogue has influenced the making of American law during much of its history. As Scott Langston has shown, the reception of the Ten Commandments in American legal thinking was an innovation of the Progressive era in the end of the nineteenth and beginning of the twentieth century. See Scott M. Langston, 'The Americanization of the Ten Commandments: 1880s–1920s', *Perspectives in Religious Studies* 35 (2008), pp. 393-410.

symbols. True, courthouses erected in the late nineteenth century and early twentieth century represented a more ebullient aesthetic, including images such as blind justice or portraits of notable judges.[5] But these were often in the form of frescos or murals. The display of a singular, massive Decalogue monument is a particular feature of our own times, and a repudiation of an aniconic Protestant tradition. Such a new-found insistence upon the exhibition of a legal text requires explanation.

Operating in the field of visual representation, the Decalogue monument encompasses multiple meanings. It identifies a once-and-future legal tradition. On one side, it is the tradition that has been lost, exiled and driven from the public legal sphere. An archaeology of United States legal knowledge, conservative activists claim, would uncover the past significance of the Ten Commandments. Monuments create what historian Pierre Nora calls *lieux de mémoire*, sites of memory.[6] On the other side, it sets forth the idea that United States law *should* be more in the tradition of biblical law. But, in either case, the surfacing of ancient Hebrew legalism signifies a fundamental irony. Legal conservatives, who generally reject the importation of foreign law, have embraced the idea of the Decalogue as a legal transplant.

The Coming of the Contested Public Sphere

From the outset, I want to emphasize that taking Decalogue monuments as a parallel system of law is not the only way to interpret the pervasive litigation over their display. Since the middle of the twentieth century, there has been significant jostling over the place of religion in the public forum in the United States. Struggles over crèches, prayer, Hanukkah menorahs and Christmas decorations in municipal parks, schools and public buildings are commonplace. Accordingly, many religious Christians have felt excluded from the public sphere, and both silenced and disenfranchised. Those secularists arguing for the separation of Church and state as an insurmountable barrier often claim that public religious expression is an attempt by threatened religious groups to reassert power in an increasing secular and, certainly, increasingly religiously diverse United States.

Employing the three-pronged Lemon Test—which permits such displays only if the government has a secular purpose, the government's action does not have the primary effect of advancing or inhibiting religion, and if there is no excessive entanglement of the government with religion—courts have enforced the often difficult to police border between Church and state.[7] The

---

5. For a broad discussion of legal iconography see Judith Resnik and Dennis Curtis, *Representing Justice: Invention, Controversy, and Rights in City-States and Democratic Courtrooms* (New Haven: Yale University Press, 2011).

6. Pierre Nora, *Les lieux de mémoire* (Paris: Editions Gallimard, 1984).

7. *Lemon v. Kurtzman*, 403 U.S. 602 (1971); *Edwards v. Aguillard*, 482 U.S. 578,

Ten Commandments provide a useful mechanism for challenging this separation. The Commandments are Judeo-Christian; not merely belonging to one sect of Christianity, even if their ordering varies according to different denominations. And, perhaps, if courts do require the dismantling of Decalogue displays, then this, too, provides an opportunity for mobilization. Since the Decalogue is considered such a universal historical document, contemporary United States constitutional law appears unreasonable, even a form of persecution. Sometimes conservative and religious discussions of the Ten Commandments cases have a whiff of bloodless martyrdom about them.

Yet the Decalogue is not simply an artifact from the modern United States *Kulturkampf.* It is not simply the fault line for confrontations over the symbolic terms of public space or the influence of the religious conscience on civil society. The Ten Commandments embody an alternative legal system to contemporary United States law. Part of the attraction of this parallel, counterpunctual legalism is its brevity. A mere ten apodictic prescriptions exemplify all of biblical legalism. By contrast, the United States Code consists of over 60,000 pages of statutes printed in 45 bulging volumes. Equally importantly, the Decalogue gestures to a form of covenantal natural law—a sense that even when the United States' higher law, the Constitution, seems to be variable, subject to unsettled and conflicting interpretations, there is a code that can be as immutable as a stone monument.[8]

The Decalogue became part of the United States' iconographic landscape owing to a campaign launched in the mid 1950s by the Fraternal Order of Eagles, a civic association founded in Seattle by theater owners. Following the proposal of T.J. Ruegemer, a Minnesota state court judge who was distressed by the rise of juvenile offending, it began a crusade in 1951 to distribute paper copies of the Ten Commandments, which included a version of the commandments approved by Catholic, Protestant and Jewish clergy. These copies were to be displayed in juvenile courts and were festooned with such symbols as a Star of David, an eagle and the Masonic image of a pyramid with an all-seeing eye.

During the filming of *The Ten Commandments* in the Sinai, its director, Cecil B. DeMille, conceived of the idea of subsidizing the distribution of brass copies of the Decalogue—which would simultaneously promote the

---

583, 96 L. Ed. 2d 510, 107 S. Ct. 2573 (1987) (state action violates the Establishment Clause if it fails to satisfy any of these prongs); *County of Allegheny v. American Civil Liberties Union Greater Pittsburgh Chapter*, 492 U.S. 573, 109 S. Ct. 3086, 106 L. Ed. 2d 472 (1989) (placing special focus upon the endorsement prong whereby the government prefers one religious denomination to another or religion to non-religion).

8. Jack Balkin, *Living Originalism* (Cambridge, MA: Harvard University Press, 2011), pp. 3-6 (underscores the need for constitutional legitimacy as a constructed document which expands beyond its original meaning).

ideal of the United States as a god-fearing country (unlike the Soviet Union) and his forthcoming epic film. Aware of the Fraternal Order of Eagles' project, DeMille approached Ruegemer. Ruegemer prodded DeMille to carve the Ten Commandments in stone—just like the original. Paramount Pictures organized film screenings of *The Ten Commandments*, released in 1956, in order to raise funds for purchasing stone copies of the Decalogue. Some monuments were also funded by the Fraternal Order of Eagles. Between two hundred and two thousand of these stone Decalogue monuments were erected in towns and cities across the United States.[9] They should be seen as an expression of what might be called mid-century covenantism. In 1954, for example, the phrase 'one nation under God' was added to the pledge of allegiance.[10]

The Supreme Court's first brush with the Ten Commandments was remarkably unproblematic. Decided in 1980, *Stone v. Graham* was a mere seven paragraphs long. The Court invalidated a Kentucky statute that required the posting of the Decalogue on the wall of every public school classroom in the state, even though these posters would be paid for through voluntary private contributions. The Court stated that the presentation lacked a secular purpose.[11] It was unimpressed with the statutory requirement to add to each copy the notation: 'the secular application of the Ten Commandments is clearly seen in its adoption as the fundamental legal code of Western Civilization and the Common Law of the United States'.[12] The Court determined that the 'avowed secular purpose' of the Ten Commandments was something of a sham since the Decalogue is, at its core, a sacred text. 'No legislative recitation of a supposed secular purpose can blind us to that fact'. This decision was so straightforward that it was delivered as an unsigned *per curiam* opinion reached without the benefit of oral argument.[13]

If it was not for the ensuing cultural conflicts of the late 1990s and early twenty-first century, the Decalogue might not have emerged as a deeply contested legal issue. United States parks and government buildings are littered with detritus of earlier eras, and Ten Commandment monuments would simply have rubbed shoulders in public forums with Civil War monuments, water fountains dedicated by the temperance movement and

---

9. Alan Nadel, 'God's Law and the Wide Screen: The Ten Commandments as a Cold War Epic', *Proceedings of the Modern Language Association* 108 (May 1993), pp. 415-30; T. Jeremy Gunn, *Spiritual Weapons: The Cold War and the Forging of an American National Religion* (New York: Praeger, 2008), pp. 69-71.

10. Pub. L. 83-396, Chap. 297, 68 Stat. 249, H.J. Res. 243, enacted 14 June 1954; *Newdow v. United States Congress, Elk Grove Unified School District et al.* 542 U.S. 1 (2004).

11. *Stone v. Graham*, 449 U.S. 39, 101 S.Ct. 192, 66 L.Ed.2d 199 (1980).

12. Kentucky Revised Statutes, KRS §158.178.

13. *Stone v. Graham*, 449 U.S. 39 (1980).

other civic statuary. However, a number of high-profile controversies kept the Decalogue in the public eye.

The most famous of these involved Justice Roy Moore. Elected Chief Justice of Alabama in 2001, Moore had previously garnered attention while he was still a circuit judge by hanging on a courtroom wall, behind the bench, a wooden plaque on which the Decalogue was inscribed. During the election he was already known as 'the Ten Commandments judge'.[14] A month after taking office as Chief Justice, Moore commissioned a larger, more impressive monument. Known as 'Roy's rock', it is a privately funded 5,280-pound granite structure with quotations on the pedestal from the Declaration of Independence and the Framers, and crowned by tablets inscribed with the Decalogue. He installed the monument in the state Supreme Court building's rotunda in order to restore 'the moral foundation of the law' to the people.[15]

In response to a lawsuit launched by the American Civil Liberties Union, the district court decided against Moore. On 5 August 2003, this court, after being upheld by the 11th Circuit Federal Court of Appeals, ordered the monument removed. Moore announced that he would refuse to comply with the district court's order. Large rallies were held facing the courthouse in support of Moore. Faced with a fine of $5,000 per day, however, the other Justices on the Alabama Supreme Court overruled Moore, and had the monument placed in a side room of the building. The Alabama Court of the Judiciary, an ethics panel composed of leading judges, lawyers and elected officials, determined that Moore should be removed from office.[16] After being ousted, Moore travelled through the country with the monument gathering support. He founded the Foundation for Moral Law, where a plaque with the Decalogue can be purchased, to provide legal support for the display of the Ten Commandments.[17]

The story of Moore's quest seems extraordinary. But this case was simply a particularly dramatic episode in a broader brushfire war over the Ten Commandments. Throughout the 1990s and the first decade of the twenty-first century, numerous cases were litigated concerning the public display of the Decalogue. 'From about 1997 on', according to one observer, 'hardly a month went by without a decision being issued by either a district court or court of

---

14. *Glassroth v. Moore* (M.D. Ala. 2002) 4.
15. *Glassroth v. Moore* (M.D. Ala. 2002) 4.
16. The Supreme Court of Alabama noted that the case did not involve the Chief Justice's right to acknowledge God but, rather, was a case involving a public official's refusal to obey a valid court order; see *Moore v. Judicial Inquiry Comm'n*, 891 So. 2d 848, 2004 Ala. LEXIS 312 (Ala. 2004), cert. denied, 543 U.S. 875, 125 S. Ct. 103, 160 L. Ed. 2d 126, 2004.
17. See http://morallaw.org/ and Joshua Green, 'Roy and his Rock', *Atlantic Magazine* (October 2005).

appeals on the constitutionality of some Ten Commandments display somewhere in the nation'.[18] Take, for example, a California case involving a public school's rejection of a commercial advertisement with the text of the Decalogue to be posted on the school's baseball field, where impressionable students might be given the sense that the state had placed its imprimatur on a particular religious creed. There exists, the court decided, a compelling state interest in upholding the strictures of the Establishment Clause which might even trump freedom of expression.[19]

Trial and appellate courts seemed unable to take a consistent approach in the Ten Commandments cases. The United States Court of Appeals for the Tenth Circuit determined that a Ten Commandments monument in Salt Lake City which had been erected by the Fraternal Order of Eagles simply reflected 'the religious nature of an ancient era' and need not be removed.[20] As the cases percolated upwards to federal appellate courts, the disparities

---

18. Jay A. Sekulow and Francis J. Manion, 'The Supreme Court and the Ten Commandments: Compounding the Establishment Clause Confusion', *William and Mary Bill of Rights Journal* 33, 35 (2005–2006); *Books v. Elkhart County*, 401 F.3d 857 (7th Cir. 2005); *ACLU of Ohio Found., Inc. v. Ashbrook*, 375F.3d 484 (6th Cir. 2004), cert. denied, 125 S. Ct. 2990 (2005); *ACLU Neb. Found. v. City of Plattsmouth*, 358F.3d 1020 (8th Cir. 2004), vacated and reh'g granted by No. 02-2444, 2004 U.S. App. LEXIS 6636 (8th Cir. Apr. 6, 2004); *ACLU of Ky. v. McCreary County*, 354 F.3d 438 (6th Cir. 2003), aff'd, 125 S. Ct. 2722 (2005); *Glassroth v. Moore*, 335 F.3d 1282 (11th Cir. 2003), cert. denied, 540 U.S. 1000 (2003); *Freethought Soc'y of Greater Phila. v. Chester County*, 334 F.3d 247 (3d Cir. 2003); *King v. Richmond County*, 331 F.3d 1271 (11th Cir. 2003); *Adland v. Russ*, 307 F.3d 471 (6th Cir. 2002); *Summum v. City of Ogden*, 297 F.3d 995 (10th Cir. 2002); *Books v. City of Elkhart*, 239 F.3d 826 (7th Cir. 2001); *Summum v. Callaghan*, 130 F.3d 906 (10th Cir. 1997); *Turner v. Habersham County*, 290 F. Supp. 2d 1362 (N.D. Ga. 2003); *Mercier v. City of La Crosse*, 276F. Supp. 2d 961 (W.D. Wis. 2003), rev'd and remanded sub nom., *Mercier v. Fraternal Order of Eagles*, 395F.3d 693 (7th Cir. 2005); *ACLU of Tenn. v. Rutherford County*, 209 F. Supp. 2d 799 (M.D. Tenn. 2002); *Baker v. Adams County/Ohio Valley Sch. Bd.*, No. C-1-99-94, 2002 U.S. Dist. LEXIS 26226 (S.D. Ohio June 11, 2002), aff'd, 86 F. App'x 104 (6th Cir. 2004); *ACLU of Tenn. v. Hamilton County*, 202 F. Supp. 2d 757 (E.D. Tenn. 2002); *Kimbley v. Lawrence County*, 119 F. Supp. 2d 856 (S.D. Ind. 2000); *Ind. Civ. Liberties Union v. O'Bannon*, 110 F. Supp. 2d 842 (S.D. Ind. 2000), aff'd, 259 F.3d 766 (7th Cir. 2001).

19. *DiLoreto v. Board of Education* (1999, Cal App 2d Dist) 74 Cal App 4th 267, 87 Cal Rptr 2d 791, review denied *Diloreto v. Board of Educ. of Downey Unified Sch. Dist.* (1999, Cal).

20. *Alma F. Anderson, Diana Barclay, Betty Jean B. Neilsen, and Parker M. Neilsen v. Salt Lake City Corporation and Salt Lake County*, 475 F.2d 29 (10th Cir. 1973); *The State of Colorado, Roy Romer, Governor of the State of Colorado, Forrest Cason, Executive Director, Department of Administration v. The Freedom From Religion Foundation, Jeff Baysinger, Howard Huguley, Glenn v. Smith, and Lee Whitfield*, 898 P.2d 103 (1995).

became even clearer. The Supreme Court of Colorado, on the other hand, decided that a quite similar Fraternal Order of Eagles Ten Commandments monument 'constitutes a permanent government display of symbols associated with the Jewish and Christian faiths'.[21] The two cases that the Supreme Court took on a writ of certiorari, which are described below, reflected split circuits with one court upholding the public display of the Decalogue while another found it unconstitutional.[22]

In two separate 5–4 decisions delivered on the same day, *Van Orden v. Perry* and *McCreary County v. ACLU*, the United States Supreme Court handed down a pair of opinions on the display of the Ten Commandments.[23] These cases were intended to settle the uncertainty surrounding this issue, but instead they have left in their wake still more confusion. In *Van Orden,* the Court affirmed the right to display the Ten Commandments near the Texas State Capitol, concluding that the state was recognizing 'the role the Decalogue plays in America's heritage', and therefore that the government did not run afoul of the Establishment Clause.[24] The Texas depiction of the Ten Commandments was a 'passive monument'.[25] However, in the case of the Ten Commandments posted on the wall of a Kentucky courthouse, as decided in *McCreary County*, the Court found probative the historical and social context of the state's religious purpose.[26] The Court affirmed that this particular display violated the separation of Church and state.[27] For the Court, context, history, iconography, political maelstroms, the geography and architecture of the placement, and even grassroots political activism, all contribute to a robust understanding of the underlying purpose behind the Decalogue's display.

Quite remarkably, Justice Stephen Breyer is the only member of the Court in the majority for both the *Van Orden* and *McCreary County* decisions. It therefore behooves us to pay special attention to Justice Breyer's

---

21. *The State of Colorado, Roy Romer, Governor of the State of Colorado, Forrest Cason, Executive Director, Department of Administration v. The Freedom From Religion Foundation, Jeff Baysinger, Howard Huguley, Glenn V. Smith, and Lee Whitfield*, 898 P.2d 103 (1995), cert. denied, 516 U.S. 1111, 116 S. Ct. 909, 133 L.Ed.2d 841 (1996).

22. *ACLU of Ky. v. McCreary County*, 354 F.3d 438, 440, 462 (6th Cir. 2003), aff'd, 545 U.S. 844 (2005) (finding unconstitutional the hanging of the Decalogue on a Kentucky courthouse wall); *Van Orden v. Perry*, 351 F.3d 173, 182 (5th Cir. 2003) (permitting the Texas Ten Commandments monument to remain in a park near the capitol). The Court refused to hear the much more politically charged case concerning Justice Moore: 335 F.3d 1282 (11th Cir. 2003), cert. denied 540 U.S. 1000.

23. *Van Orden v. Perry*, 545 U.S. 677 (2005) and *McCreary County v. ACLU*, 545 U.S. 844 (2005).

24. *Van Orden v. Perry*, at 681, 688-90.

25. *Van Orden v. Perry*, at 682.

26. *McCreary County v. ACLU*, at 850-851.

27. *McCreary County v. ACLU*, at 881.

concurrence in *Van Orden*, in which he cast the deciding vote to permit a six-foot tall granite monument displaying the Ten Commandments to remain on the state capitol's grounds. Erected in 1961 with funds provided by a private civic organization, the Fraternal Order of Eagles, the monument included not simply the text of the Decalogue, but also a carving of an eagle grasping the United States flag, the image of an eye inside a pyramid, the superimposed Greek letters of Chi and Ro representing Christ, and an acknowledgment to its donors. In addition to the Ten Commandments monument, 17 monuments and 21 historical markers, commemorating 'the people, ideals and events that compose Texas identity', were also erected in the capitol's park.

Breyer called *Van Orden* a 'borderline case'. By this he meant that a Decalogue monument conveys a variety of different messages—a religious message, a secular moral message and a historical message about the influences shaping contemporary United States society. He argues that the particular circumstances of the Texas monument distance it from religious motives. The monument was donated by a civic organization intent upon combating juvenile delinquency; the text of the Decalogue is based on a compromise wording from different denominations; and the placement in a park is near other monuments promoting civic ideals. However, Breyer found most convincing the fact that for over 40 years no one had challenged the monument. 'The context suggests that the State intended the display's moral message…and historical "ideals" of Texans—to predominate'.[28] Context, as conceived by Breyer, means the physical site of the display *and* the political context of the demand for the display.

Breyer distinguished *Van Orden* from *Stone v. Graham, McCreary County* and other cases where the display of the Ten Commandments was impermissible. Unlike *Stone v. Graham,* the Texas Commandments were not placed in a public school, among the impressionable young. The Supreme Court elsewhere has been concerned about an element of coercion in schools, where particular care must be taken in separating Church and state. While the decision in *Stone v. Graham* does not ascribe particular importance to the situating of the display in schools, as opposed to public spaces such as parks, Breyer introduced this principle to distinguish the two cases. In *McCreary County*, the display was disallowed because of the 'short (and stormy) history of the courthouse Commandments' displays' which 'demonstrates the substantially religious objectives of those who mounted them, and the effect of this readily apparent objective upon those who view them'. 'The history there indicates a governmental effort substantially to promote religion, not simply an effort to reflect, historically, the secular impact of a religiously inspired document.'

28. *Van Orden v. Perry*, at 627.

Is this a reasonable distinction? As we have seen, the Texas monument was erected as part of mid-century covenantism, when Americans sought to stress their fealty to God in the midst of the Cold War. What could be more of a religious expression? It was originally intended to address impressionable juveniles—the impact on youth seems to raise the same issues as school displays—with a moral religious message. True, the Decalogue text is constructed from an amalgam of Jewish, Catholic and Protestant versions. But this simply reflects the hegemony of a post-World War II consensus around Judeo-Christian belief systems as opposed to others. And is not it troubling that clerical figures were convened to agree upon a text? It certainly excludes a more diverse patchwork of non-Western religious which have no particular connection to a Judeo-Christian canonical text. The symbol of Christ at the base, the considerable size of the monument, and the placement before the very place where secular laws are debated suggests that even if this is, as Breyer suggests, a mixed message, it is difficult to tease out the moral and historical from the religious.

Breyer's decision only makes sense if you place it within the framework of his understanding of the goals of the Establishment Clause. In addition to the usual reasons of promoting religious liberty and tolerance, Breyer places special emphasis upon the purpose of preventing divisiveness. In other words, Breyer's reasonable observer of the display must take into account the context of contention. Judge Moore and Christian Decalogue movements have created such a controversy that, ironically, their call for placing the Commandments in courtrooms must be denied. The silent presence of the Texas monument is grandfathered into the system of American public iconography. Without explicitly pointing to this reference, Breyer seems to be resurrecting Justice Brennan's notion of ceremonial deism.[29] Mentioning God in the Pledge of Allegiance or printing currency with the phrase 'in God we trust' is simply ceremonial deism—a nominal gesture in which ordinary citizens are no longer expected to find any religious import.

But this focus on divisiveness has all sorts of odd implications. Past religious hegemony from the period of the Cold War is ignored. Breyer's reasonable observer is ever so presentist. He pays attention only to contemporary controversies and only to the dangers of present-day divisiveness. Consider all the sources for divisive debates: if an organization with religious overtones agitates for displaying the Decalogue; if the site is one where controversies are taking place—such as the courtroom; if legislatures made any reference

---

29. *Lynch v. Donnelly*, 455 U.S. 668 (1984); *Elk Grove Unified School District v. Newdow*, 542 U.S. 1 (2004), where Justice O'Conner claims that forms of ceremonial deism are 'protected from Establishment Clause scrutiny chiefly because they have lost through rote repetition any significant religious content'. The phrase 'ceremonial deism' was coined by the Dean of Yale Law School, Eugene Rostow.

to God in legislative debates when passing bills allowing what courts might otherwise disallow; if the American Civil Liberties Union decides to litigate these displays as a matter of policy; if the issue matters enough to be a matter of journalistic interest rather than simply an unremarkable part of our political landscape. There is a catch-22 aspect to this approach: if individuals do not push for the Decalogue's display, then it is possible to display the Commandments; but if they do vigorously promote its place in the public sphere, they will be barred from erecting new displays. The Decalogue may be displayed in the public domain—but only if it does not matter.

And why is the reasonable citizen observer so limited in the ambit of his or her observation? For example, Breyer's observer sees the scattered monuments across the park as if the observer hovered high above the landscape, but a real observer situated on the ground before the Ten Commandments monument would see a straight site line from the monument to the legislature, with the other memorials outside his or her view.[30] The observer envisioned by Breyer might have some knowledge of the immediate controversies and conflicts surrounding the display cases, but he or she has no deeper sense of how ceremonial deism has rendered these disagreements less significant over time. Most importantly, while Breyer's observer looks at the monument and the religious intent of those promoting its erection, the observer fails to notice that the desire to display the Decalogue is often infused with other motives, not simply with a religious mission.

If the speech of political movements (including those urging the Decalogue's display) is, in the words of the *Dixie County Courthouse* decision, transitory while monuments endure, then should there not be some mechanism for creating a reasonable observer who can evaluate the shifting significance of a Ten Commandments display over time?

Diversity and Discontent

McCreary and Van Orden drew a dividing line between new and old displays of the Decalogue, between the demand for expression of the Decalogue by religious or political organizations and those older statuary, placard and fresco depictions that might be said to be permitted owing to some sort of grandfather provision under the Establishment Clause.[31] However, the

30. There are a number of possible ways to construct the visibility of the observer. Those arguing for Van Orden placed their fixed point at the Decalogue statuary itself, and claimed 'no other monument is visible from the Ten Commandment monument'. *Van Orden v. Perry*, Pet'r. Br., at 1-5. The brief for Texas takes the reader on a long walking tour from one monument to another on the capitol grounds until one reaches the Ten Commandments monument (*Van Orden v. Perry*, Respondent's Brief, at 1-5).

31. A number of commentators have seen the two opinions as inconsistent: Tyson Radley O'Connell, 'How Did the Ten Commandments End up on Both Sides of the

Supreme Court's decision hardly quelled the divisiveness that Breyer so feared. Only a year later the Ten Commandments were back in the Supreme Court again. In *Pleasant Grove City v. Summum* (2006), the Court confronted the question of whether a city which has a Decalogue monument erected in its park must permit a church to put up its own monument of similar size.[32]

The Church of Summum, which claims to incorporate Gnostic elements, believes that the Ten Commandments were a lower form of knowledge suitable for the untutored Israelites, and that Moses also received a second set of stone tablets upon which were inscribed a higher law embodied in seven aphorisms.[33] Summum argued that a park is a traditional public forum for speech and therefore under the Free Speech clause it should be permitted to erect a monument funded through donations with a carved set of aphorisms. Justice Samuel Alito, writing for the Court, rejected this argument. The Supreme Court stated that city governments have a right to determine which statuary will be displayed in their own parks, and, especially, which monuments best reflect the government's own expression of its ideals.[34]

Precisely because the Ten Commandments seemed to embody a culturally specific set of ideals, polls have shown overwhelming support for the public display of the Decalogue in the United States. A poll taken in 2003, for example, identifies 70 per cent of United States citizens supporting the display of the Ten Commandments in schools or public buildings.[35] The issue percolated down to state legislatures which sought to overturn the limitations placed by the Court. Georgia, for example, enacted in 2011 a Public Displays of the Foundations of American Law and Government bill. This statute, passed unanimously, authorizes the posting in a 'visible, public location in judicial facilities' copies of a variety of documents, including the Magna Carta, the Mayflower Compact of 1620, the Bill of Rights, the Declaration of Independence and, not surprisingly, the Decalogue.[36] In 2012,

---

Wall of Separation between Church and State? The Contradicting Opinions of *Van Orden v. Perry* and *McCreary County v. ACLU*', *Montana Law Review* 69 (2008), p. 263.

32. *Pleasant Grove City v. Summum*, 555 U.S. 460 (2009).

33. *Pleasant Grove City v. Summum*, at 465. http://www.summum.us/philosophy/tencommandments.shtml (accessed 1 April 2012).

34. *Pleasant Grove City v. Summum,* at 460, 478-481 (2009).

35. http://www.gallup.com/poll/9391/americans-approve-public-displays-religious-symbols.aspx (accessed 1 April 2012).

36. O.C.G.A., §34-13-51 (2011). In addition, another statute outlines the purposes and objectives of the Georgia State Archives, including: 'Encourage the study of historical documents including but not limited to those which reflect our National Motto, the Declaration of Independence, the Ten Commandments, the Constitution of the United States, and such other nationally recognized documents which contributed to the history of the State of Georgia' (O.C.G.A. §45-13-41).

Indiana legislated that the Decalogue may be exhibited on state property if the Commandments have the 'same manner and appearance generally as other documents displayed'.[37]

In June 2011, Louisiana approved the erecting of a monument inscribed with the Decalogue on the grounds of the capitol which would include a plaque entitled 'Context for acknowledging America's religious history'. It would underscore the secular importance of the Ten Commandments for fundamental United States legal texts.[38] Montana also passed a statute listing the Ten Commandments as one of the monuments to be placed on its capitol's grounds.[39] Mississippi law allows for the Ten Commandments and 'In God We Trust' to be affixed to any public building at the discretion of the governing authorities.[40] Indeed, dozens and dozens of legislative proposals, some adopted and some rejected, circulated through state legislatures during the last decade.[41]

---

37. Burns Ind. Code Ann. §4-20.5-21-12 (2012).

38. La. R.S. 25:1282. According to the statute, the full text of the contextual acknowledgment must read: '(1) Some documents stand out as pivotal in the religious history of America and Louisiana's legal system, among which are the Mayflower Compact, The Declaration of Independence as a legal foundation for the United States Constitution, the Ten Commandments as one of the foundations of our legal system, and the Northwest Ordinance, which was a primary document affirming faith and the first congressional act legally prohibiting slavery. It is hoped that their study and relation to each other and the history of our state and nation will foster an appreciation for the role that religion has played in the legal history of America and the state of Louisiana and prompt further public study. (2) American law, constitutionalism, and political theory have deep roots in religion. American ideals about liberty, freedom, equality, legal responsibility and codes of law, to mention a few, have roots and underpinnings in religion and biblical literacy. The Ten Commandments, which are found in the Book of Exodus in the Old Testament of the Bible, was one of the earliest written expressions of law to be incorporated in American legal systems. The Ten Commandments, or the law of nature, also impacted the Declaration of Independence which refers to the "laws of nature and of Nature's God".'

39. Mont. Code Anno., §2-17-808 (including Ten Commandments among a list of monuments to be placed on the capitol grounds).

40. Miss. Code Ann. §29-5-105.

41. Alabama: S.B. 117, 2005 Reg. Sess. (Ala. 2005) and H.B. 170, 2011 Reg. Sess. (Ala. 2011) (finding public schools should have the Ten Commandments and other historical documents readily available for students and that public schools may display the Ten Commandments); Kentucky: H.B. 16, 2006 Reg. Sess. (Ky. 2006) (providing for posting of Ten Commandments in public buildings and property), H.B. 36, 2006 Reg. Sess. (Ky. 2006) (providing for a Ten Commandments monument on the grounds of the state capitol), H.B. 277, 2006 Reg. Sess. (Ky. 2006) (authorizing receiving of Ten Commandments from Fraternal Order of Eagles and creating a companion monument describing judicial history), S.B. 3, 2010 Reg. Sess. (Ky. 2010) and S.B. 3, 2010 Reg. Sess. Ky. 2010 (providing that no law shall prohibit government or its employees from posting Ten Commandments as part of a display of historic

Intervention at the state level reflects both a legacy of dissatisfaction with the Supreme Court's Decalogue decisions and their legacy of confusion. Such confusion, of course, elicits precisely the sort of divisiveness that Breyer sought to avoid. Take the example of Boise, Idaho. The Fraternal Order of Eagles donated a Decalogue monument to the city in the 1960s. Responding to concerns about the separation of Church and state, the city moved the monument to St Michael's Church in March 2004. A petition movement arose to construct a new Ten Commandments monument that would be 'substantially similar in size, composition, and content' and placed within 20 feet of the site of the original monument. This new monument would contain an excerpt from Jefferson's Virginia Statute for Religious Freedom. In the front of the monuments, and plainly visible to passers-by, shall be a plaque stating the city's commitment to religious freedom and acknowledgment of the secular influence of the texts displayed on the monuments.[42]

State legislation and court decisions, of course, are subject to scrutiny by federal courts under the incorporated Establishment Clause. Leading up to the Supreme Court decisions, the Ten Commandments Defense Act in 2003 was submitted to Congress.[43] It provides, in Section 3, 'the power to display the Ten Commandments on or within property owned or administered by the several states...is declared to be among the powers reserved to the states'. Although the bill was not passed, the very name of this act is striking. It is a defense act, much like the Defense of Marriage Act, which allowed states to deny recognition to same-sex marriages performed in another state.[44] It speaks to a deep-rooted federalism. Although Justice Clarence Thomas has continued to insist that the Establishment Clause does not apply to state and local governments, the Supreme Court has consistently held that the Establishment Clause cannot be severed from other provisions in the Bill of Rights that apply to the states.[45] It is dubious whether short

---

documents); Louisiana: H.B. 277, 37th Reg. Sess. (La. 2011) (providing for erecting Ten Commandments monument on state capitol grounds); Michigan: H.B. 4433, 93rd Leg. Sess. (Mich. 2005) (providing that the Ten Commandments may be displayed on public property if they are displayed with other documents of historical significance); Mississippi: H.B. 460, 120th Leg. Sess. (Miss. 2005) (authorizing government entities to display Ten Commandments in any public building).

42. *City of Boisie v. Keep the Commandments Coalition*, 143 Idaho 254; 141 P.3d 1123 (2006).

43. Ten Commandments Defense Act of 2003, 108th Congress (2003-2004), HR 2045.IH.

44. Pub.L. 104-199, 110 Stat. 2419, enacted 21 September 1996, 1 U.S.C. §7 and 28 U.S.C. §1738C.

45. *Everson v. Bd of Educ.*, 542 U.S. 1 (1947). Justice Thomas has repeatedly urged the Supreme Court to overrule Everson; *Elk Grove Unified Sch. Dist. V. Newdow*, 542

of a Constitutional Amendment such a federal statute would pass Constitutional muster.

Congress has shown its dissatisfaction with judicial decisions concerning the Decalogue. At the time of the Moore controversy, Congress passed a non-binding resolution stating that the Commandments 'are a declaration of fundamental principles that are the cornerstones of a fair and just society; and the public display of the Ten Commandments, including in government offices and courthouses, should be permitted'.[46] A movement is currently afoot for Congress to issue a resolution to declare the first week in May as Ten Commandments Week to recognize 'the significant contributions the Ten Commandments have made to shaping the principles, institutions, and national character of the United States'.[47]

Pat Robertson, a well-known evangelist, wrote *The Ten Offenses*, which urges Americans to rise up and change the Supreme Court before it destroys the fundamental values of the United States. According to Robertson, the American Civil Liberties Union 'will hunt down every display of the Ten Commandments for the purposes of eradicating them' by judicial fiat, much as Elijah destroyed the images of Baal.[48] Even Roy Moore, who certainly launched the most contentious of the Ten Commandments debates, seems to be having a second coming. In November 2012, he won re-election to his former seat on the Alabama Supreme Court.

The Decalogue as Legal Transplant

What does Justice Breyer's reasonable observer see? As I argued earlier, Breyer envisions the observer as a keen reader of the religious dimension of recent displays, as unaware of the historical background of earlier uses of the Commandments, and—above all—as someone who sees those agitating for Decalogue displays as one-dimensional religious actors. United States courts have insisted that it is 'the duty of the courts to distinguish a sham secular purpose from a sincere one'.[49] These courts have found to be disingenuous claims, whether historically true or not, that the Decalogue has

---

U.S. 1 (2004) (Thomas J., concurring in the judgment); *Zelman v. Simmons-Harris*, 536 U.S. 639 (2002) (Thomas, J. concurring). The Free Exercise of Religion clause came to be applied to the states through the incorporation into the Fourteenth Amendment with *Cantwell v. Connecticut* 310 U.S. 296 (1940) (striking down a state law requiring state license for the distribution of religious literature and in practice applied solely to the Jehovah's Witnesses).

46. H. R. Con. Res. 31, 105th Cong. (1997); S. Con. Res. 13, 105th Cong. (1997).
47. H. Res. 211, 112th Congress, 2011-2012.
48. Pat Robertson, *The Ten Offenses: Reclaim the Blessings of God's Eternal Truth* (Nashville: Thomas Nelson, 2004), p. 51.
49. *McCreary County v. ACLU*, at 848-51.

had a significant legal impact on the fundamental legal principles of Western civilization. They have ignored the accent on secular purpose in legislative texts, the surrounding of the Commandments with non-religious legal canonical texts, like so many bodyguards, and the chiselling into monuments of non-religious symbolism. All this, courts have pointed out in a large number of cases, is simply a charade. The existence of religious movements calling for the display of the Decalogue has made them identify the Decalogue displays largely as a matter of faith.

Yet purposes are as mixed as the text itself. As the Court wrote in *Pleasant Grove,* 'even when a monument features the written word, the monument may be intended to be interpreted, and may in fact be interpreted by different observers, in a variety of ways'.[50] We can treat the Decalogue as a biblical text much as we might treat any writing from a sacred canon— purely as a form of religious expression that should be barred from government buildings and parks under the Establishment Clause. In some ways, however, this has always been a mixed text—or, as Augustine might say, a double text. The beginning identifies the divine imperative that demands obedience in the first table. With seven of the Ten Commandments describing general moral prohibitions ('thou shall not murder'), on the other hand, the Decalogue indeed might be said to lean towards having a predominately secular purpose. Perhaps the most striking feature of the Decalogue monument is not the content of its text, but the very fact that it suddenly, strikingly transplants a set of ancient laws into America's legal landscape. The particular word-text has been effaced and the iconic text—the tablets as symbol—has taken its place with its message of a stolid, unchanging compass for moral law in a time of declining public and private moral values.[51] In other words, the primary expression of a monument may very well be the legal, rather than the religious, meaning of the Decalogue.

The idea of privileging the *legal* significance of the Ten Commandments nevertheless still might be seen as controversial. It reflects the deeply held notion that American law is a Christian and Western construct with its roots in biblical traditions. But relying on foreign ancient law—for that is how we must conceive of the Decalogue—to prove American legal exceptionalism is certainly ironic. American conservatives have introduced into thirty-three states legislative prohibitions on courts using foreign law. Oklahoma's law, which was adopted through a ballot initiative as a constitutional amendment, states that 'courts shall not look to the legal precepts of other nations or cultures'.[52] But what is the Decalogue? Its archaic provisions are surely

---

50. *Pleasant Grove City v. Summum,* at 474.
51. Rousas John Rushdoony, *The Institutes of Biblical Law* (Phillipsburg, NJ: The Presbyterian and Reformed Publishing Company, 1973), pp. 792-93.
52. Oklahoma State Question 755 §1©, amending OKLA. CONST. art 7 §1 (2010).

Middle East law as much as Sharia law—even though reliance on Sharia is specifically mentioned in the Oklahoma blocking measure.

Courts have become accustomed to the commonplace of seeing the Ten Commandments through Establishment Clause lenses. But so much of the purpose of agitating for their display is to prod the United States towards a less mutable, less instrumental, legalism. The Commandments were said to embody universal natural law principles—albeit divine natural law, and to reflect American legal exceptionalism—albeit an exceptionalism forged under a Protestant hegemony. In every sense, then, the Decalogue is currently undergoing another repurposing, another reception in contemporary America. There has been a conservative backlash against the importation of foreign law into American jurisprudence. But, it seems, the Decalogue is an exception in the midst of these claims for exceptionalism. Ancient Hebrew law not only has a second set of tablets—but also a second act.

Indexes

Index of References

Old Testament

Genesis				304, 310,	24.3, 7	16
1.1–2.3	22-23, 67			313	24.12	18, 145
1.2	285	20.2		15, 17, 19,	25–31	15
1.26	64			24, 34, 36,	25.16, 21	18
2.4	64			38, 114	25.22	19
4.3-8	270	20.3		36, 38, 114	30.6, 36	19
9.18-24	270	20.4		37	31.16-17	99
30.25-43	271	20.4-6		64	31.18	18, 269,
39.7-20	271	20.4-5		304, 314		286, 335
		20.5-6		17, 31	32–34	15, 325
Exodus		20.7		35, 119-20,	32.1-20	105
1–20	325			304, 314	32.1-6	269
1–15	23	20.8-10		304, 314	32.4	17
3.2	269	20.8		121	32.15	335
3.8	31	20.10		32	32.18	269
12	93	20.11		22-23, 33,	32.19	18, 335
15	90			66	32.28	61
19–24	15-16	20.12		30-31, 53,	34.1	18, 335
19–20	92, 97			115, 123-	34.4	18
19.3-6	16, 304,			27, 304,	34.6-7	17
	313			315	34.22	91
19.8	16	20.13-16		127	34.28	18, 95,
19.11, 16, 19	304, 308-	20.13-15		68		145, 335
	309, 313	20.13		304, 315,	34.29	275
19.13	337			336	34.35	173
19.15	337	20.14		304, 316	35–40	15
19.16	286	20.15		305, 316	40.20	18
19.17	335	20.16		305, 316		
20–23	105	20.17		29, 32, 38,	Leviticus	
20	7			114, 132-	18	55
20.1-17	16, 176-77,			33, 305,	18.22	56
	183, 185,			317, 338	19	55
	205	20.19		16, 20	19.2	305, 317
20.2–31.17	335	20.22–23.33		16, 23	19.3	56, 339
20.2-17	26, 140,	21.2–23.33		335, 339	19.12	36
	335	21.15		339	19.16	304, 315
20.2-3	65, 117,	21.17		126, 339		

Leviticus (cont.)		5.28-31	20	33.2	6		
19.18	115, 125, 304, 315	5.31	20	34.14	305, 316		
		6.1	20	34.17	305, 316		
19.31	246	6.4-9	85-86	37.18, 39	305, 316		
20	55	6.4-5	70	48.11	304, 314		
20.6	246	6.4	87, 115-17, 119, 133	51.5	186		
20.9	56			53.2	334		
20.13	56	6.5	115, 125	64.11	305, 316		
20.27	246	6–26	20, 23	65.5	304, 315		
23.15ff.	91	6–11	21	81.11	24		
24.10-16	269	10.4	18, 61, 95, 328	84.1, 2, 11	304, 314		
				86.11	304, 314		
Numbers		11.13-21	86	89.8, 9	304, 314		
15.32-36	269	12–25	21	92.4	6		
15.37-41	86	12.5	24	92.5	304, 314		
28.26-31	92	16.9-12	91	96.2, 8, 9	304, 314		
		19.14	69	97.12	305, 317		
Deuteronomy		27.17	69	100.1-2, 4-5	304, 315		
4.1-40	21	27.26	305, 317	111.9	304, 314		
4.12f.	18	30.11-15	90	128.1, 3, 5, 6	305, 316		
4.13	61, 95	31.9-13	7	143.2, 10	305, 317		
4.44	90	33.2-3	304, 313	144.9	6		
5	7, 23, 90, 173, 325	33.4	90				
		33.26	305, 317	*Proverbs*			
5.3	342			8	96		
5.6-21	27, 140, 176, 205, 328	*Joshua*		8.30	64		
		7.1	270	31.10, 12, 20, 26	305, 316		
5.6-7	65						
5.6	24, 34, 36, 38	*2 Samuel*		*Isaiah*			
		6	24	25.7-8	305, 317		
5.7	36, 38	6.6-7	142	40.18, 26	304, 314		
5.8-10	64	11.2-3	270	43.10-11	65		
5.8	37						
5.11	35, 119	*1 Kings*		*Jeremiah*			
5.12-15	32-33	5.9	19	7.9	24		
5.12	22, 121	*Nehemiah*		31.33	294		
5.14	22, 32	9.6	304, 313				
5.15	22			*Ezekiel*			
5.16	22, 30-31, 53, 123	*Job*		3.18	130		
		7.14	286	36.26-27	168		
5.17-20	127	19.22-27	286-88				
5.17-19	68	24.2	69	*Hosea*			
5.21	22, 29, 31-32, 34, 38, 132-34, 338	42.11	288	4.2	24		
				12.10	24		
		Psalms		13.4	24		
		5.7, 10	305, 316				
5.22	18, 61, 335	10.4	334	*Malachi*			
5.24-27	20	14.1	334	3.5	305, 316		
5.25-27	335	26.6-8	304, 315				

Index of References

DEUTERO-CANONICAL WRITINGS

Additions to Daniel		*Tobit*		*Sirach*	
13	270	4.16	159-60, 164	3.6, 9-10, 15-16	304, 315

NEW TESTAMENT

Matthew		18.20	25, 68, 123, 125, 127	13.4	229
1.23	289			13.8-10	353
5.19	199			13.9	68
5.21f.	25	18.22	126		
5.21	130			*1 Corinthians*	
5.22	200	*John*		2.10-14	294
5.27-28	25, 197	3.21	316	6.9	223, 229
5.28	229	6.1-14	106		
7.12	159	8.1-11	284-85	*2 Corinthians*	
10.8-11	284	8.34	123	3.7	199
19.16-22	102, 125-26	12	290	4.6	291
		16.2	284		
19.18	25, 68, 127	17.24	284	*Galatians*	
19.19	123			5.19	229
19.21	126	*Acts*			
22.37	70	2	86, 92	*Ephesians*	
22.37-40	125	7.58-60	285	4.31	200
27.13-14	284	12.2	285	6.2-3	125
		14.15	70	6.2	268
Mark		15.20, 29	68		
1.19	285	15.23-29	105	*1 Thessalonians*	
2.27	284			5.19	288, 294
10.17	126	*Romans*			
10.19	25, 68, 123, 125, 127	1.29	200	*James*	
		2.14	151, 161	2.10	199
		2.15	164	2.11	68
12.30-31	115, 178	2.17	151		
12.30	70	3.20	154, 186	*1 John*	
		3.31	152	5.3	167-68
Luke		7.19	155, 167		
10.27	70	7.23	155	*Revelation*	
16.19	200	8.4	294	12.12-17	290
16.19-25	130	8.20	120		

ANCIENT JEWISH TEXTS

Dead Sea Scrolls		*4QD*[e]		*4QPhyl G*	
1QS		7ii.11	86		29, 30
I.16	86				
		4QDeut[n]		*4QPhyl J*	
4QD[a]			29, 30		29
1.17	86				

4QMez A		*Spec. Leg.*		159	54
	29	III 7-82	55	211–12	54
				240–47	54
XQPhyl		Flavius Josephus		248–49	54
3	30	*Ant.*		263–64	53
		3.90-92	37	295–96	54
Mishnah				347–51	54
Ber.		*Apion*		359	54
2.2	88	2.199, 215	48	361	54
				364–67	54
Meg.		Pseudo-Phocylides		365	51
3.5	91	2	44		
		3	56	*Babylonian Talmud*	
Tam.		3–8	45-50, 55	*Ber.*	
5.1	100	8	53	12.a	88
Nash Papyrus		Syriac Menander		*Meg.*	
	30, 68, 87	2–8	53	31a	92
		11–14	53		
Philo of Alexandria		15	53	*Jerusalem Talmud*	
Dec.		15–19	54	*Ber.*	
1	56	20–24	54	1.5	88
29	68	45–46	54		
51	37	51	54	*Meg.*	
106-107	65	82–98	54	3.5, 74b	92
121-31	55	123	54		
168-69	55	145–47	54	*Tosefta*	
		154–56	54	*Meg.*	
		158	54	3.5	91

EARLY CHRISTIAN TEXTS

Acts of Andrew		*Ascensio Isaiae*		*Quest. in Hept.*	
and Matthew		4.2-6	65	2.71.2	115
8–10	66	10.7-13	66	2.73	163
29.4	61			61.1	124
		Augustine			
Acts of Paul		*Brev. in Ps.*		*Quest. Vet. et NT*	
3.17	67	32	115	1.7	125
Acts of Peter and Andrew		*Contr. Faust.*		*Serm.*	
5.3	70	15.5	115	8	40
		15.7	125	8.4	115
Ambrose				8.6	122
Expos. de Ps. 118		*Enarr. in Ps.*		9.7	115, 125
7.8	131	32.6	115	12.10.10	109
				33.4	125
Apocalypse of Peter		*Epist.*		250	40
11	70	55.11.20	115		

Index of References

Cassiodorus
Expos. Ps.
1.32.2   122
32.2   120

Gnostic Gospel of the Egyptians
IV 58.23-26   67

Isidore of Seville
Quest. in Pent., In Ex.
29,4-6   122

Letter of Jesus Christ concerning Sunday
2.16   67

Origen
Hom. on Exod.
VIII   75-76
VIII, 2   40, 114

Pseudo-Clement
Hom.
V 26.3   67
VII 4.4   68-69
IX 13.1   67
IX 23.1s.   67-68
X 6.2-4   68
XI 5.1-3   69
XII 14.1   67
XVI 12.1-2 64

Rec.
I 27-71   63
35.1-2   63

Second Treatise of the Great Seth
VII 51.30   67
VII 52.35   67
VII 53.30   67
VII 64.18-25 67

Visio Esdrae
           69

CLASSICAL AUTHORS

Aristotle
Eth.
v, 9   167

Rhet.
1.10.1368b3
1.13.1373b2   41, 43
1.13.1374a11-14 42

Pliny the Younger
           88

Index of Personal Names

Abbot, G. 200-201
Abelard, P. 77, 161
Acker, G. van 255
Acosta, J. de 234, 240, 245-46, 249-50, 255
Adret, Salomon ben 100
Ælfric of Eynsham 102-40
Albertus Magnus 164
Albertz, R. 339
Albrecht, A. 214
Albrechtsberger, J.G. 298
Alcuin of York 76, 116, 120, 122, 125, 128-29, 134, 140, 266
Alexander of Hales 79, 162, 164
Alfred the Great 3, 104-105, 111-12, 134, 171
Aliprantis, T.C. 3
Almond, O. 203
Alt, A. 340-41
Althaus, P. 209
Amir, Y. 25, 48, 114
Amsler, F. 62
Anders, F. 255
Andrewes, L. 2, 184
Angelozzi, G. 219
Anselm of Laon 77, 154, 159-60
Anunciación, J. de la 234, 239-40
Appleyard, D. 142
Aquinas, T. 2, 79, 148-68, 192, 217, 222, 264
Archer, I. 187
Armstrong, R.J. 156-57
Arroyo, E. 255
Arzhanov, Y. 52
Aston, M. 5, 172, 182, 185, 191
Attersoll, W. 201, 204
Attridge, H. 51
Audet, J.-P. 51-52
Augsburger, D. 7
Augustine of Hippo 40, 75-77, 106, 109, 114-16, 118, 120, 122, 124-25, 128-29, 133-34, 140, 162-63, 167, 181, 192, 196-97, 260, 264, 268-69, 369
Augusti, J.C. 213
Avis, J. 8

Baarda, T. 51-53
Backus, I. 67
Bahlmann, P. 267
Baldung Grien, H. 273
Bale, J. 175, 184
Balkin, J. 357
Barth, K. 2, 214
Barton, J. ix
Bartsch, A. 276
Basedow, J.B. 211
Basich de Canessi, Z. 255
Bast, R. 5, 7, 8
Bataillon, M. 255
Batalla Rosado, J.J. 255
Bately, J. 104
Baugh, L. 343
Bede 76, 106-107, 109, 116-17, 120, 122, 125-26, 128-29, 134, 140
Beduschi, L. 296
Bell, T. 196-98, 204
Bellarmine, R. 192-98, 204
Bennett, H.S. 175
Bentley, T. 202-203
Berger, K. 42, 45, 50, 54, 59, 68
Beristáin y Souza, J.M. 256
Bernard, G. 175, 177
Berndt, J. 213
Bernstein, E. 297
Bethurum, D. 108-109, 113, 130, 137-38
Bezold, C. 143-44
Bindman, D. 295
Bliemitzrieder, F. 159
Bloomfield, M.W. 192
Blum, E. 14
Bodenstein, A. 272
Bodin, J. 6

Index of Personal Names

Böhlig, A. 6, 67
Boffey, J. 172
Bonaventure 79, 164-65, 217
Bonde, W. 173-74
Bonner, E. 178, 181, 194
Bonnet, M. 70
Booy, D. 186
Boretius, A. 267
Bossy, J. 190-92, 195, 218
Boston, R. 354
Bott, G. 268
Bourgeault, G. 58, 75
Bovon, F. 61
Boyle, P. 229
Bradford, J. 186
Braido, P. 5
Braude, W.G. 93
Braulik, G. 21, 22
Brenner, A. 338
Brenner, P.J. 329
Brenz, J. 205
Brett, M. 111
Breuer, M. 37, 114
Bright, J.W. 103
Brightman, F.E. 178-79, 185
Brimley, J. 296
Brooke, C.N.L. 111
Broomfield, L. 320
Broughton, H. 203
Brown, S. 186
Brundage, J. 229
Bucer, M. 205, 273
Budge, E.A.W. 143-44
Budny, M. 108
Burchard, C. 57
Burgoa, F. de 256
Burkitt, F.C. 68, 87
Butler, A.J. 142
Butlin, M. 295
Butterworth, C.C. 174, 177

Caesarius of Arles 76
Calvet, M.-A. 64
Calvin, J. 2, 205-207, 210, 214, 218, 272-73
Camargo, M. 153
Canisius, P. 273-74, 276
Capp, B. 186
Carlson, E. 192

Carr, S. 198
Cartwright, S.R. 161
Cathrein, V. 156
Cawley, A.C. 173
Cereceda, F. 219-20
Chan, Y.S.L. 231
Charlesworth, J.H. 65-66, 69
Chenu, M.-D. 149
Chertsey, E. 195
Childs, B.S. 336
Chouraqui, É. 297
Christin, O. 4, 276
Clarke, E.G. 37
Cleaver, R. 182, 186
Clemoes, P. 103-107, 109-12, 118, 130, 137
Clines, D.J.A. 333
Coates, P. 349
Cobo, J. 234
Coe, W. 186-87, 189
Cohrs, F. 214
Cole, P. 89
Colson, F.H. 37, 65, 114
Connery, J. 229
Conti, F. 296
Córdoba, P. de 234, 236, 242, 244, 247-51, 256
Cortés, J. 254, 256
Cottesford, S. 198
Covbridge, C. 203
Cowley, R.W. 143, 145
Cox, C.J. 281
Craigie, P.C. 338
Cranach, L., the Elder 264, 269-71, 274, 276
Crawford, S.J. 103
Crespi, A. 343-44
Cross, J.E. 105, 113, 130-31, 137
Crowe, M. 162
Crüsemann, F. 15
Cruz, J. de la 233
Cubitt, C. 107
Cuervo, J. 256
Culverwell, E. 201-202
Curtis, D. 356
Czachesz, I. 62

Dallen, J. 217
Darlow, T.H. 182

Darmaun, J. 327
David, F. 296
Dávila Padilla, A. 256
Deferrari, R.J. 152, 159
DeMille, C.B. x, 9, 297, 344, 357-58
Derron, P. 45
Dihle, A. 159
Dod, B. 150
Dod, J. 182, 186
Dohmen, C. 15
Donner, C. 9
Dozeman, T.B. 335, 340
Duffy, E. 171-72, 175, 179, 187
Duns Scotus, J. 80, 217
Durán, J.G. 256

Ebeling, G. 214
Edward VI 174
Edwards, A.S.G. 172
Egaña, A. 256
Eisermann, F. 265
Elizabeth I 180, 196
Elizur, S. 96
Elton, E. 186
Enfantin, B.-P. 296
Engelbrecht, M. 274
Erasmus, D. 218
Erbetta, M. 61
Erskine, J. 320
Etchegaray, A. 256
Evetts, B.T.A. 142
Ewald, J.L. 213

Fairfield, L.P. 175, 184
Fehr, B. 107, 109, 111, 113, 117, 123-24, 126, 130-32, 135, 137, 139
Feria, P. de 233-34, 237-39, 241-42, 245, 249, 251-52
Ferrabosco, J. 296
Ferrier, M. 296
Feuerbach, L. 325
Finsterbusch, K. 21
Fischer, G. 15
Fishman, T. 98
Fleischer, E. 88-91, 96
Flusser, D. 57
Forster, E.M. 322
Fox, A. 187
Fraas, H.-J. 205

Fraenkel, J. 94-97
Frank, B. 320
Franz, M. 17
Freddoso, A.J. 148
Frere, W.H. 175, 179, 185
Fretheim, T.A. 19
Frühwald, W. 321, 330
Frymer-Kensky, T. 337
Fuller, R.H. 57

Gadamer, H.-G. x
Gairdner, J. 184
Galarza, J. 256
Gamer, H.M. 216
Gante, P. de 233-34, 253-54, 256-57
García Icazbalceta, J. 256
Gayo, J. 256
Geffcken, J. 276
Geiringer, K and I. 297
Geoltrain, P. 61-62
Gerson, J. 192
Gerstenberger, E.S. 339
Giesel, H. 6
Gilbert the Universal 77
Gillihan, Y.M. 86
Gilson, P. 296
Girgensohn, H. 214
Glass, J.B. 256
Glorieux, P. 79
Gneuss, H. 102, 116-17, 122, 137
Godden, M.R. 104-106, 109, 111-12, 117-20, 122-24, 126, 129-32, 135, 137-39
Gold, A. 94
Goldschmidt, D. 97
Golka, F.W. 326, 331
Gómez Hellín, L. 219
Goodspeed, E.J. 60
Gordley, J. 160
Gounelle, R. 58
Grant, R.M. 58
Gratian of Chiusi 160
Graupner, A. 13
Green, I. 171, 190-91, 281
Green, J. 359
Greenberg, M. 29, 87, 114
Greenman, J.P. 2
Grillmeier, A. 141
Grosseteste, R. 78
Grossfeld, B. 36

Grossman, A. 96-97
Gühloff, O. 208
Guerrero, J.R. 256
Gula, R. 222
Gunn, T.J. 358

Habteselassie, S. 143
Hadock, R. 193
Haigh, C. 174, 185
Haikola, L. 214
Hake, J. 296
Ha-Kohen, I.M. 100
Halbwachs, M. 60
Hamburger, K. 326-27
Hamer, F. 264
Hamling, T. 182, 188
Hammond, H. 181
Hardeland, A. 209
Harnack, A. von 5
Harrelson, W. 114
Hauptman, J. 92
Haydn, J. 297-301, 306, 310-12
Haymo of Auxerre 126, 129
Hays, R.B. 43-44, 46, 50, 54
Heidenheim, W. 96
Heintze, G. 208
Helman, A. 351
Hengel, M. 59
Henle, R.J. 148
Henry VIII 174-76, 196
Herbert, A.S. 182
Herder, J.G. 211
Hilary of Poitiers 160
Hill, E. 40
Hill, J. 105, 107
Hill, T.D. 105, 113, 131, 137
Himbaza, I. 28
Hobbins, D. 192
Hobsbawm, E.J. 319
Hoffman, A. 89
Hoffman, Y. 2
Hollstein, F.W.H. 276
Holter, K. 21
Hooker, J. 185
Hooper, J. 179, 198, 204
Horst, P.W. van der 45, 49
Hossfeld, F.-L. 13, 42
Houtman, C. 36
Hubbard, D.A. 143-44

Hudson, A. 172
Hugh of St Victor 77, 159-60
Hunt, A. 182
Hyatt, J.P. 335

Ibn Ezra, A. 6, 38
Innocent III 216
Insdorf, A. 350
Isaac, Simon bar 95-96
Isidore of Seville 76-77, 116-18, 120, 122, 125, 128-31, 134-35, 140
Isserles, Moses 100

Jacob ben Asher 100
Jacob, B. 36
Jastrow, M. 88
Javier, F. 233
Jessen, E. 292
Joest, W. 214
John of La Rochelle 149, 162-64
Jones, C. 108
Jones, F.S. 62-63
Jonsen, A. 217
Josceline, E. 186
Joseph Tov Elem 96-97
Josephus, F. 37-38, 42, 48, 50, 60, 114, 117, 124, 133, 140
Jost, K. 108-10
Joye, G. 174
Jud, L. 273
Jungbauer, H. 25, 49, 50, 53
Jurasinski, S. 171

Kaestli, J.-D. 61
Kanagaraj, J.J. 57
Kaplan, A. 6
Kapstein, I.J. 93
Karo, J. 100
Katzheimer, L. 264
Keel, O. 4
Keenan, J.F. 216
Kellermann, U. 24, 41-42
Kennedy, W.M. 175, 179, 185
Ker, N.R. 137
Keyes, S. 105
Kidane, H. 143
Kieślowski, K. x, 9, 297, 343-53
Kifle, K. 146
Killir, Elazar ben 93

Kimelman, R. 87
Klauck, H.-J. 62
Klein, M.L. 36
Kleist, A.J 102
Klene, J. 186
Kline, M.G. 335
Klingbeil, G.A. 23
Knibb, M.A. 65-66
Knowles, D. 150
Koch, D.-A. 43-44
Kohlberg, L. 215
Koopmann, H. 321
Kraemer, C.J., Jr 88
Kratz, R.G. 16
Küchler, M. 45, 47, 50-52, 54
Kuntz, P.G. 1, 4, 296

Läpple, A. 266
Lamsa, G.M. 34
Land, J.P.N. 51
Lange, N.R.M. de 114
Langer, R. 85
Langston, S.M. 355
Lapidge, M. 105
Larsen, T. 2
Lauer, G. 318
Laun, C. 276
Layton, B. 5
Le Bel, B. 296
Le Fur, L. 156
Lechner, M. 4
Lee, R. 141
Leigh, D. 186
Leinbaugh, T.H. 107
Leo XIII 228
León, N. 256
León-Portilla, M. 256
Leslau, W. 141
Levine, B.A. 339
Levinson, B.M. 20, 21
Liebermann, F. 112, 137-38
Lindberg, B. 295
Lioy, D. 57
Liuzza, R.M. 123, 137-38
Lluch Baixauli, M. 58, 75
Locke, M. 296
Löhr, H. 25, 41, 57
Lohr, C.H. 150
Lohfink, N. 20, 21, 24

Lombard, P. 77-80, 160
Longo, A. 9
Lottin, O. 154, 160, 162
Luria, I. 98
Luther, M. 2, 4, 175, 177, 181, 196, 205-14, 218, 264, 267-76, 303, 328

MacCulloch, D. 191
Mahoney, J. 217
Maimonides 2, 89, 98, 100, 150
Makoschey, K. 325
Manion, F.J. 360
Mann, J. 89-90
Mann, T. xi, 9, 318-32
Marcus, R. 114
Margulies, C.M. 100
Mark, M. 17
Markl, D. 1, 13
Markschies, C. 59
Marquard von Lindau 265
Marrassini, P. 143
Marroquín, F. 233
Marsden, R. 102-5, 112, 137-38
Marsh, C. 183
Massenet, J. 296
Matna, R. 88
Matt, D.C. 6
Maurois, A. 320
McCarthy, C. 31
McInerny, R. 148
McNeill, J.T. 216
Medina, J.T. 256
Medina, M.A. 256
Melanchthon, P. 7, 205-206, 209-10, 269, 271, 273-74
Mendenhall, G.W. 341
Mennicken, P. 330
Merrill, E.H. 333
Meyer, J. 205, 209, 214
Meyers, C.L. 338
Meynet, R. 17
Michelangelo 331
Mielke, J. 3
Miletto, G. 6
Milgrom, J. 339
Mille, J. 337
Miller, P.D. 14, 15
Mirk, J. 172
Mirsky, A. 94-95

Mochizuki, M.M. 4
Modalsli, O. 214
Moirs, J. 263, 265
Molina, A. de 233-34
Monaco, D.G. 46, 51-52
Montaigne, M. de 336
Moos, M.F. 80
Moule, H.F. 182
Mouselimas, S. 4
MTR, Master 273
Müller, C.D.G. 70
Müller, G. 57
Murphy, J.J. 153
Murri, S. 346

Nadel, A. 358
Naḥman, Samuel bar 88
Navarro, F. 256
Neukomm, S. 297-98, 302-17
Neuland, B. 329
Newcombe, D.G. 179
Niebuhr, K.-W. 55
Nieva, D. de 234
Nikiprowetzky, V. 75
Nolloth, H.E. 172
Noonan, J.T., Jr 229
Nora, P. 356
Norelli, E. 65
Normann, A.W. 256
Noth, M. 339
Novakovic, L. 57

Obispo, P. 297
O'Brien O'Keefe, K. 104
O'Connell, T.R. 364
O'Day, R. 180
O'Donnell Setel, D. 337
O'Malley, J. 219
O'Neill, P.P. 105
Orchard, A. 109-10
Oré, J. de 234
Origen 40, 58, 75-77, 114, 117, 124, 140, 178, 260
Ort, C.-M. 330
Ostendorfer, H. 273
Ostwald, M. 42-43
Otto, E. 13, 14, 20, 24
Otto of Lucca 77
Owen, J. 2

Pankhurst, R. 142
Pareja, F. de 233
Parisius, J.L. 212
Parry, S. 148
Parsons, R. 196-97
Passavant, J.D. 277
Patrick, D. 17
Paul the Deacon 106, 118
Pearce, S. 2, 25
Perkins, W. 181, 185, 188-89, 200, 204, 218
Pernigotti, C. 51
Peter of Poitiers 77
Peters, A. 214
Phan, P.C. 5
Philip the Chancellor 78
Phillips, A.C.J. 338
Philo of Alexandria 2, 24-25, 33, 37-38, 48-50, 55-56, 64-65, 68, 75, 114, 117, 124, 133, 140
Pinomaa, L. 214
Pius V 219
Plaza, J. de la 234, 241, 243, 245
Pollard, A.W. 173
Pollard, J. 104
Pope, J.C. 107
Porter, J.R. 339
Poschmann, B. 217
Pratscher, W. 57
Pratt, D. 104
Preisner, Z. 297
Prieur, J.-M. 61, 70
Purcell, H. 296

Quispel, G. 5

Raes, A. 142
Rambach, J.J. 211
Ramsay, R.L. 103
Rasmussen, M.B. 59
Rauschning, H. 319-20
Raynes, E. 109
Redgrave, G.R. 173
Regan, R. 148
Rehm, B. 63-64, 68-69
Reif, S.C. 87
Reinsma, L. 153
Resines, L. 232
Resnik, J. 356

Reu, J.M. 214
Reuter, T. 104
Reventlow, H.G. 2, 340
Rex, R. 172
Rhodes, A. de 5
Rhodes, J.T. 173
Ribera-Florit, J. 28
Ribner, J. 4, 7
Ricard, R. 257
Robertson, P. 368
Robinson, A.L. 319-21, 323
Roden, G. von 213
Roder, A. 264
Rodov, I. 6
Rodríguez Molero, F.J. 219
Rofé, A. 29
Rojas, J.L. de 236
Roland of Cremona 78
Romains, J. 320
Rordorf, W. 58
Rosales, A.-M. 5
Rosewell, R. 179
Rossetti, C. 2
Rottzoll, D.U. 6
Rowland, C. 281
Rowse, A.L. 185
Rushdoony, R.J. 369
Russ-Fishbane, E. 89
Ryrie, A. 191

Sachs, C. 6
Saeki, Y. 5
Sänger, D. 25, 57, 61
Sahagun, B. de 253, 255, 257
Salzmann, C.G. 211
San Pedro, J. de 234
Santos, D. de los 234, 239, 243
Sarfatti, G.B. 101
Sauer, H. 108
Schaik, M. van 6
Schenker, A. 28, 29
Scherman, N. 94
Schicht, J.G. 296
Schiller, G. 277
Schmitz, P. 220
Schneemelcher, W. 59
Schnittke, A. 297
Schott, E. 208
Schulthess, F. 53

Schumacher, W.N. 59
Schwarzenberg, J. von 264
Schwienhorst-Schönberger, L. 16
Scoralick, R. 17
Scott, R. 188
Seaver, P.S. 187
Seebold, H. 213
Segal, B.-Z. 1
Sekulow, J.A. 360
Shannon, T. 217
Shapcote, L. 155
Sicard of Cremona 160
Siirala, A. 214
Simmons, T.F. 172
Sivan, H. 341
Slater, T. 225-30
Slenczka, R. 277
Smalley, B. 149-50, 162
Smaragdus 129
Smend, R. 326
Smetana, C.L. 106
Smith, J.P. 53
Smith, R. 148
Smith, T. 63-64, 68-69
Smither, H.E. 296
Sobolewski, T. 347
Sonnet, J.-P. 19
Southwell, A. 186
Spaeth, P. 165
Spiegel, S. 96
Sprinkle, J.M. 15
Stamm, J.J. 336
Steinmüller, W.H. 162
Steinwand, E. 214
Stemberger, G. 24
Stier, R. 213
Stone, M.E. 69
Storey, M. 187
Strand, K.A. 5
Streit, R. 257

Tajadod, N. 5
Tang, L. 5
Tardieu, M. 5
Taylor, J. 181, 186-87, 189
Tentler, T. 218
Thackeray, H.StJ. 37, 114
Thiselton, A.C. 294
Thomas, J. 45, 55
Thomas, K. 189

Index of Personal Names

Thomas of Chobham 79
Thoresby, J. 171
Thum, V. 3, 258
Tigay, J.H. 36
Toledo, F. de 218-25
Torre, E. de la 257
Torrell, J.-P. 80
Toswell, M.J. 102
Toulmin, S. 217
Tov, E. 29, 39
Towner, W.S. 334
Tristram, H.L.C. 113, 119
Tudor, P. 172, 179
Turrini, M. 217
Tyndale, W. 174, 177-78, 198-99, 202, 204

Ullendorff, E. 141-43
Ulrich, E. 33
Undset, S. 320
Upchurch, R.K. 106
Urbach, E.E. 87-89, 99
Ursinus, Z. 205

Vaget, H.R. 320
Valton, E. 257
Van Ackeren, G. 219
Van Loon, H. 320
Vargas, M. de 234
Vokes, F.E. 57
Vos, J.C. de 41

Waldenberg, E.Y. 99
Wallington, N. 186-87
Walter, H. 198
Walter, N. 45
Watt, J.G. van der 57
Weber, R. 123, 125
Wehnert, J. 62, 68
Weinfeld, M. 35-36, 85-86, 334
Weismann, E. 209
Werfel, F. 320

Wesley, J. 2
Wesley, S.S. 296
West, R. 320
Whitaker, G.H. 114
Whitelock, D. 111
Whitford, R. 174
Whiting, R. 179-80, 281, 295
Wieder, N. 99
Wieland, G. 150
Wilcox, J. 109
Wilf, S. 354
William of Auvergne 78, 149
William of Auxerre 78, 160-61
Williams, R.D. 293
Willis, J. 181, 183, 190
Wilson, W.T. 45, 47-50
Wing, D. 184
Winkler, G. 298
Wippel, J.F. 150
Wisse, F. 67
Witakowski, W. 142
Wohl, O. 69
Wolf, E. 257
Wood, M. 321
Wooding, L. 175
Woodward, M.S. 151
Wormald, P. 108, 110
Wren, C. 8, 281, 292
Wright, M.J. 344
Wright, W. 51
Wulfstan 108-11, 113, 117, 127, 130-31, 134, 140
Wysling, H. 320-21

Yadin, Y. 87
Yuval, I.J. 92

Zapata de Cárdenas, L. 233
Žižek, S. 347
Zlotowitz, M. 94
Zumárraga, J. de 232, 234-36, 242, 246-47
Zwingli, H. 273

www.ingramcontent.com/pod-product-compliance
Lightning Source LLC
Chambersburg PA
CBHW071224230426
43668CB00011B/1296